ARISTOTLE
and His PHILOSOPHY

ABRAHAM EDEL

WITH A NEW INTRODUCTION BY THE AUTHOR

ARISTOTLE and His PHILOSOPHY

TRANSACTION PUBLISHERS
NEW BRUNSWICK (U.S.A.) AND LONDON (U.K.)

Library of Congress Catalog Number: 95-23377
ISBN: 1-56000-836-9
Printed in the United States of America

Library of Congress Cataloging-in-Publication Data

Edel, Abraham, 1908–
    Aristotle and his philosophy / Abraham Edel.
        p. cm.
    Originally published: Chapel Hill, N.C. : University of North Carolina Press, 1982.
    Includes bibliographical references and index.
    ISBN 1-56000-836-9 (pbk. : alk. paper)
    1. Aristotle.
B485.E33   1995
185—dc20   95-23377
                                                                                  CIP

CONTENTS

INTRODUCTION TO THE
TRANSACTION EDITION

Philosophies are organized in a variety of ways—for example, by their basic theses (e.g., materialism or idealism), by their social values (e.g., liberal, conservative, radical), by the period in which they were developed (e.g., ancient, medieval, early modern), or even by whether they are interesting or uninteresting. Now Aristotle's work is definitely of a type—we might even call it Aristotelian! It is characterized by systematic fullness, by attempting to cover all aspects of a field, by systematically related concepts as instruments of analysis. No elaboration is needed here, for it is the content of our study. For example, only skimming the *Nicomachean Ethics* will show how it covers nearly all the concepts found in what we regard as an ethical theory, and discusses nearly all the problems that such a theory raises. Plato's *Republic* has comparable depth and might seem to have greater scope, for he discusses different kinds of governmental and social organization in relation to the part of the psyche that is dominant in each—reason in monarchy, spirit in oligarchy, and passion in democracy. Aristotle discusses governmental forms in his *Politics* in relation to available abilities as well as geographical and economic features of habitation: monarchy is fitting where one man is far superior to everybody else, democracy where there is a high level of excellence in many people. But the unavoidable scarcity of resources provokes social unrest, and in extreme cases revolution. Hence in actual life the best is middle-class rule, since the rich are too arrogant and the poor too desperate. The difference in treatment between Plato and Aristotle is simply that Plato treats the two topics together, while Aristotle does it in two successive works. But in fact Aristotle may regard the *Politics* as a continuation of the *Ethics*; they might almost be published as a single work.

Plato and Aristotle represented one doctrinal side in Greek life. The sophists and atomists represented two other approaches. Unfortunately, the sophists are reported by Plato who is adversarial in his treatment of them. Democritus' atomic theory survives only in fragments and in the brief sketch given by Diogenes Laertius in his *Lives of the Philosophers*. It is, however, represented in Roman times by the fuller account of a disciple—Lucretius, in his *On the Nature of Things*. Lucretius traces the development of humankind from its pre-agricultural period to its situation once agriculture emerged, then to the growth of the crafts, and finally to the appearance of towns, cities, states, war, and empire.

Most historians of philosophy deal with types in discussing individual figures and movements. A few writers have, however, paid special attention to the theory of typology. For example, Edward Spranger, in his *Types of Men*, distinguishes the economic type, the theoretic, the aesthetic, the social, the self-affirming. On the other hand, Oswald Spengler focuses on a typology of periods, identified by the character of the people who dominate them. In his *Decline of the West* he offers the hypothesis that types of people at different times have fundamentally different modes of thought. Indeed each people goes through a progression in its thinking: the stages are comparable to seasons. In its spring a people is young and untried, experimenting to find its capacities. In its summer it blooms, reaching a height in late summer before the decline of autumn sets in. By winter it is near its end, ready to be conquered by some fresh barbarian group in its own spring. For the classical world summer came in the age of Pericles, while Aristotle belongs to the fall.

On Spengler's account, the barbarians who brought an end to the ancient world were the Germanic tribes. The Greeks were Apollinian, the Germans Faustian. The difference is best reflected in their constructions, particularly their cathedrals. Classical Greek he characterized as Romanesque—rounded, open, luminous, rational. The German spirit, on the other hand, is evidenced in the Gothic cathedral with its spire dark and lofty, giving a sense of the indefinite, the hidden, the mystic, aspiring upward into the unknown. It is the spirit of Nietzsche, whose madness breaks into the midst of speech with strong and sometimes vituperative language, exalting the will.

On this scheme, Aristotle's thought is definitely Romanesque. It is rounded, filled out theory, not a blind plunge into the unknown. Its breadth and scope are exceeded by no other figure in the history of the subject. Nietzsche may give us fire, Aquinas may draw us over heaven and earth, adding a concept of moral law quite alien to Aristotle's search for the fitting on each occasion of action. Augustine may point us to what is going on in our hearts. Kant may explore the repertoire of our sentiments and structures that organize experience, and fix on remorse as the guide to duty. Bentham may investigate the possibilities of pleasure as the measure of good conduct. Mill may have a more pointed unity directed to a specific set of sociocultural problems in his nineteenth-century society. But no philosopher furnishes an ethical theory that touches all keys and puts all aspects into systematic order as Aristotle does. Even philosophers who have a sense of change that Aristotle lacks—notably Marx and Dewey in the nineteenth and early twentieth century—and who tap the question of the causal and sociocultural bases of ethics, rarely give so expansive a view of the contents of an ethical theory. But of course Aristotle's is only one kind of ethical theory, however rich of its kind.

A philosophy is well understood by its solution to the problems it deals with, but equally—sometimes more—by the problems it is able to avoid. Think of the troubles early modern philosophy had with the relation of body and mind. Descartes, who, by the way, ridiculed Aristotle's theory of motion with its concept of potentiality, offered a clear conception of mind, and of knowledge as its ideas, but at the cost of matter becoming a mystery. Yet it was this very conception of potentiality that enabled Aristotle to avoid Descartes' difficulties. For he interpreted mind as the potentiality for thought, and so its relation to body was simply like that of the ability to cut to the knife. As the section on the *psyche* in his psychological works makes clear, Aristotle takes a functional view in which the *psyche* is an activity, not a substance: human beings think, they do not have a mind. This avoids the dualism that troubled later philosophy.

Furthermore, potentiality is essentially *relational* in character. A potentiality is for something—for thinking or feeling or doing or making. In any case it involves relations to the surrounding environment, which enters into the action and belongs to its fuller description. The road from Athens to Thebes may be the same as the road from Thebes to Athens, but one is uphill and the other downhill, and the people going one way or the other may be in a different state of weariness at the end. Actualizing the potential thus has multiple effects. Aristotle was well aware of this. He refers often to potentiality as the power people have to do things and bring about changes—for example, the doctor curing or the craftsman constructing. The doctor does not just cure, he cures a patient, and the scene of his activity extends from him to the patient; the locus of his activity is the patient, not himself. Aristotle is often concerned with the question *where* an activity takes place. If the activity is a process over time, as it is for the craftsman, it can be readily noted: the statue is finished or the table is built. Some actions may be complete at any moment. Seeing is complete each instant, but scanning something takes time. Even though building a house takes time the builder at any moment of his work is wholly building, not half building because the house is half done.

Aristotle's functional theory of mind both arose from and was continuous with his biological thought. There is a rising scale from motion and smell (which in animals guides the search for food) to human sensation and linguistic behavior or discourse. Sensation is a cooperative transaction with the environment and adjusts to change. The knowledge it brings is precarious. For example, I see a color, but I cannot be sure it will not undergo momentary change. (Such a question is far different from Descartes and Locke considering whether the color patch corresponds to a hidden reality.) The transaction with the environment varies with the sensation. Sound requires air, vision light, and thought a still finer intellectual analogue of light. The crux of the argument is that each sense has its proper medium, to which the sense organ is attuned. But thought is peculiar, because we can think of anything. Here Aristotle looks for a universal permeating medium, not related to a single organ, which will light up the mind. There is also speculation on when the capacity for reasoning enters the embryo. Augustine and Aquinas later amplified such questions. Augustine thought desire appeared at the outset—a consequence of the concupiscence of Adam and Eve in eating the forbidden fruit;

Aquinas calculates when, after the embryo acquires the ability to move, reason enters. In general, Aristotle provided the philosophical background for the Christian philosophers and also for Muslim philosophers such as Averroes, though they had to reject his view of the uncreated world.

In the medieval world generally, questions were raised about things that Aristotle had said or seemed to imply. For example, would a heavier body fall faster than a light one? If you tied together two bodies of equal weight would they fall faster than if not tied? If you bored a hole through the earth from pole to pole and then dropped a ball of earth, would it stop at the center when it reached its natural place? Or would it go falling forever, as the atomists claimed? If the earth as a whole got somehow dislodged, would it come back to its original place?

By the sixteenth century Aristotle was given an official status by the Catholic church, and thus became an orthodoxy. To question him was dangerous; Giordano Bruno was burned at the stake for heretical cosmological anti-Aristotelian beliefs, particularly the infinite universe. The set of famous prosecutions culminated in Galileo's imprisonment. The antagonism of science and Aristotelianism was intensified when philosophers of science in the eighteenth century developed the concept of mechanism and the idea of the world as a machine whose every movement of the whole and of its contents was in principle predictable. This was an ideology congenial to the commercial and industrial revolution, used against the restrictions of the older orders, and especially promulgated against the dominant religions. Interestingly, it was more common in eighteenth-century France whose rulers still preserved the old order than in Britain which was already under first commercial, then industrial leadership. In the nineteenth century, Darwinism, insofar as it emphasized chance variations and their consequences, undermined teleology. For example, as Thomas Huxley interpreted evolution, there was no fixed human nature of a social sort: man was a beast of the jungle, yielding only to force, and likely to burst out if not kept under control. Civilization is a constant control.

Yet Aristotle persisted in attracting attention to his thought. If one part of his corpus was disregarded as out of date, another part continued to raise problems for thinkers of the later period. Of course not all of his works were known in Europe at any one time. When they were discovered they usually created a stir. His *Poetics*, for example, took eighteenth-century France and Germany by storm. In France particularly, his analysis of Greek tragedy was made into fixed rules for the construction of a tragedy and the character of the tragic hero. Literary criticism became, in effect, the judgment of works by the criteria of the ancient Greek theater. Comedies would doubtless have suffered the same fate if Aristotle's work on comedy (which is mentioned in medieval times) had been discovered.

It must be remembered that Aristotle's works did not come into Europe at one time. They kept dribbling in from different sources in the East. For example, his *Constitution of Athens* is an early twentieth-century find in Egypt—a papyrus, the back of which had been used by a merchant to keep his accounts. The systematic building up of the Aristotelian corpus took a long time, until by the late nineteenth and early twentieth centuries a more or less comprehensive edition of his work was ready, prepared by Becker in Berlin. This became the standard Greek text, subject only to disputes about specific readings which older manuscripts found unclear. In the early twentieth century, Aristotle's texts were translated into English and published at Oxford. Then came the Loeb Classical Library edition giving both the Greek text and the English translation. Aristotle was now, so to speak, in the open, and any philosopher could study and write and teach whatever parts appealed to him or her. Research particularly, went in many directions, from biology to ethics and politics. Different interpretations were offered of the many works in different university philosophy departments.

In the 1920s and 1930s interest in Aristotle at Oxford focused largely on the *Nicomachean Ethics* and the logical works. In America, particularly at Columbia University in New York, a school of intensive Aristotelian study grew up under the influence of Dean F.J.E. Woodbridge. He encouraged students to work on the physical writings, resulting in theses on Aristotle's theory of movement, of the infinite, of the heavens, and so forth. In the 1960s and 1970s, in New York City, for many years an Aristotelian circle used to meet one Saturday a month, spending the whole day discussing first the *Physics*, then later the logical works. Scholars used to come for that day's study from universities all over the country. The works were read in the Greek, and discussion was related to particular passages. After several years the discussion shifted to Platonic writings. Similar group meetings were going on at Oxford at the same time. Thus, classical scholarship proliferated. Aristotelian thought was alive and pervasive, as it had not been for ages. Indeed, the study of Aristotle became a widespread concern, not as a figure in history of philosophy textbooks, but as a living philosopher inviting commentary—like Russell or Whitehead or William James— making a contemporary contribution.

At the heart of this inquiry lies an overarching question—whether the history of philosophy plays a major part in doing philosophy, in philosophical research and production. In many fields—in physical science, for example—the history of the field may be just a separate interest, not involved in original scientific experiment and theory. On the other hand, some philosophers have seen not only philosophy but all knowledge as a historical process, drawing on its past to make changes and new constructions in the light of what has been learned.

Such considerations suggest that contemporary work on Aristotle should not be directed only to determining his ideas; it should sift and evaluate them. As we saw, his teleology grew out of use of a medical model and a craft model for interpreting the order in the world, together with the assumption that order is primary. An evolutionary theory in giving a great role to chance variation sees order as a contingent consequence of "disorder." To what extent should we regard the exaltation of the orderly as imposing on the world the human characteristics of forethought and planning? In fact, however, the world does not, as history shows, follow the planned intentions of planners. We can neither predict nor adequately determine what the outcome of our plans may be. The standard example is, of course, the changes that were brought into our social life by the invention of the automobile. The best we can do is try to control outcomes as we go along, though this may be rather like warding off one threat to open the door to another. Hope of success, with no advance guarantee, supports continued effort.

ABRAHAM EDEL
July 1995

PREFACE

Interpretation of Aristotle is getting to be a thriving industry. Philosophical interpretations are, however, as different as artistic representations of the man himself—quite as different as the traditional Aristotle of the Vienna bust, the Chartres Aristotle, or Rembrandt's portrayal of Aristotle looking at the bust of Homer. And the complications grow when comparisons with Plato are brought into the picture, just as Raphael hardens the contrast in his *School of Athens* when he shows Plato pointing upwards and Aristotle gesturing towards the earth. It is therefore more than courtesy to the reader to explain an undertaking that seeks to present a view of Aristotle's philosophy as a whole. A statement of some of my aims will be found in the discussion of problems of interpretation in chapter 1.

Expositions of Aristotle's philosophy have been organized in widely different ways. Some follow the order of the works and discuss them topically. Some are guided by Aristotle's ideal of system and try to reconstruct his own thought along those lines. Some by reaction give up any attempt to find a system and discuss what they are interested in. Some quite clearly trace themes through Aristotle along the lines of a later philosophy that they take to be its natural outcome. And there are many more experiments. I say "experiments" advisedly, because ways of organizing the exposition of a rich historical philosophy are in effect experiments in working out fruitful ways of understanding the unity of a philosophical outlook, and perhaps beyond that, the nature of the philosophical enterprise. The method I am experimenting with here is to analyze Aristotle's fundamental ideas by eliciting a conceptual network or conceptual framework and then testing it by tracing its impact in the various domains of Aristotle's inquiry, scientific and humanistic. What a conceptual network is like, how we find it, and how it functions in a given domain will best be seen in exposition and application, and further reflections are best left until the reader has had a chance to see what is being done. I have added an epilogue on Aristotelian research.

I hope the book can serve as an introduction to Aristotle insofar as it takes little for granted. On the other hand, it goes into many advanced philosophical problems and problems of Aristotelian study and takes a stand on controversial and sometimes frontier issues. But it does not and could not cover the full range of topics and issues in the philosophy of Aristotle nor even look at every busy corner of Aristotelian scholarship.

In some areas the book barely sketches an exposition of Aristotle's views —just enough to indicate where he was heading. In others, it goes quite far because philosophical issues particularly relevant to interpretation are involved. Some particular controversies, as well as some issues about the text, have been pursued in depth to illustrate the kinds of problems that arise in Aristotelian interpretation, especially the difficulties that stem from the impact of philosophical approach. I could not hope to be exhaustive, but I have made a reasonable attempt to let the reader appreciate how the results of interpretation are reached.

For the most part, the more technical questions have been put into notes. While many of the notes simply give references, Greek terms, or bibliographical material, many others are continuous with the treatment in the text. They may carry a discussion further and into more complex issues, consider controversies among Aristotelian scholars and how they are to be dealt with, connect the issue at hand with different philosophical movements, or even engage in broad reflection or digression. The reader might find it useful to glance at such notes to see what each offers of interest.

A comment on transliteration is required. It should be remembered that Aristotle was fashioning a philosophical vocabulary and that reference to Greek terms may therefore be essential at some points. These will be found for the most part in notes, except for a few very central terms in which the Greek is relevant to the exposition. In transliterating the Greek I have followed a growing tendency to stay as close to the original letters as possible, and have, for example, used *phusis* rather than *physis*. The long vowels omega and eta, for which we have no counterparts, are written as ō and ē; iota subscript is written alongside the letter to which it belongs.

In quoting from Aristotle I have of course been greatly aided by the Oxford translations and the Loeb editions, to whose many translators I am very grateful. My own translation has been guided for the most part by interests of precision and uniformity, and at times by the importance of literalness rather than elegance.

One special point of policy in the book requires advance comment. In order not to force Aristotle's treatment of the relation of language and being into any particular contemporary mold, I have used italics for concepts and terms generally, and quotation marks only where a narrow focus on the word is intended.

In writing the book I have built on a previous study that experimented with the method used here. This appeared in my *Aristotle*, a biography and selections from the works, published in the Laurel Great Lives and Thought series by Dell Publishing Company, New York, 1967. That book is now out of print. I would like to express my gratitude for the many comments and suggestions I received in the interval, as well as my general debt to the scholars of the two-stage Aristotelian renaissance, particularly in Britain, in our century—first in the earlier decades and then after World War II. As for my own half-century of association with Aristotle, who has it that primary principles are of the essence, let me mention only H. W. B. Joseph of New College, Oxford, with whom I began the study of Aristotle, and F. J. E. Woodbridge of Columbia, under whom I wrote a doctoral thesis on Aristotle's theory of the infinite. Finally, I do want to give my special thanks to those who went through the manuscript in its last stage and were generous with detailed and fruitful suggestions: Professor A. A. Long, Professor H. S. Thayer, and my wife, Professor Elizabeth Flower, as well as one anonymous reader; and Laura Oaks, whose editorial work on behalf of The University of North Carolina Press combined a fine classical and literary scholarship.

ARISTOTLE'S WORKS:

TITLES, ABBREVIATIONS,

AND TRANSLATIONS

Wherever possible, the English titles have been used rather than the Latin versions, except for *Historia Animalium*, *Parva Naturalia*, and *Magna Moralia*, whose Latin titles seem firmly entrenched. In the case of Aristotle's chief psychological work (Latin, *De Anima*), the current English translation, *On the Soul*, seems likely to mislead; I have resorted to *On the Psyche*, staying close to the original Greek term, which has become an established English word. The individual works—almost a cast of characters in the story—are described in appendix A. Where abbreviation is desirable the following are used:

Categ.	*Categories*
Interp.	*On Interpretation*
Pr. An.	*Prior Analytics*
Post. An.	*Posterior Analytics*
Top.	*Topics*
Soph. Ref.	*On Sophistical Refutations*
Phys.	*Physics*
Heav.	*On the Heavens*
Gen. Corr.	*On Generation and Corruption*
Meteor.	*Meteorology*
Psych.	*On the Psyche*
Sens.	*On Sense and Sensible Objects*
Hist. An.	*Historia Animalium*
Part. An.	*Parts of Animals*
Mov. An.	*Movement of Animals*
Gen. An.	*Generation of Animals*
Meta.	*Metaphysics*
Prob.	*Problems*
Nic. Eth.	*Nicomachean Ethics*
Eud. Eth.	*Eudemian Ethics*
Mag. Mor.	*Magna Moralia*
Pol.	*Politics*
Rhet.	*Rhetoric*
Poet.	*Poetics*

Other works (for example, *On Sleep and Waking*) are referred to by full title.

For passages within the works the standard procedure, here employed, is to refer to the Bekker edition (Berlin, 1831–1870). Most modern editions and translations are keyed with Bekker's pagination; for example, 1037a7 means Bekker's page 1037, column a, line 7. When more general reference is sufficient, book and chapter of a work will do; for example, *Nic. Eth.* 2.5 means book 2, chapter 5 of the *Nicomachean Ethics*. (The books of Aristotle's works are in size more like our chapters and the chapters are more like our sections.)

The major translations of the Aristotelian corpus into English are the Oxford Translations, edited by J. A. Smith and W. D. Ross, 12 vols. (New York: Oxford University Press, 1908–52), and the Loeb Classical Library editions (Cambridge: Harvard University Press; London: Macmillan, in progress). Both contain translations by many different scholars, and the Loeb volumes provide parallel Greek texts. There have been numerous other translations of individual works and, in materials intended for college use, parts of works. Sometimes special clarity is achieved, sometimes felicity of style. Perhaps among these translations special mention should be made of J. L. Ackrill's *Categories and De Interpretatione* (New York: Oxford University Press, 1963), Martin Ostwald's *Nicomachean Ethics* (Indianapolis: Bobbs-Merrill, 1962), Ernest Barker's *The Politics of Aristotle* (New York: Oxford University Press, 1958), and S. H. Butcher's *Aristotle's Theory of Poetry and Fine Art* (New York: Dover Publications, 1951).

Other texts and translations, as well as individual ones from the Oxford and Loeb editions, that have been specially referred to in this book are listed in the Bibliography.

Part 1

THE WORKS, THE MAN, THE THOUGHT

INTRODUCTION

Why is it that in the contemporary as in the ancient world, writing about Aristotle and commenting on him, and claiming him or attacking him, have assumed the proportions of a sizable intellectual industry? Why are there struggles over the interpretation of his philosophy? What do we know of the man? What patterns of thought are found in his works, what kind of a scientist and philosopher is he, and what are the broad attitudes embedded in his philosophical method?

I

ARISTOTLE'S WORKS AND THE

PROBLEM OF INTERPRETATION

Aristotle was the systematic philosopher of ancient times. In the Middle Ages he was raised again to authoritative prominence. Dante's famous characterization of him is often cited: he is the central "master of those who know," with Socrates and Plato at his side. The break of the modern sciences with "arid scholasticism" from the seventeenth century on resulted in a long eclipse of Aristotelian philosophy. The revolt against authority in favor of appeal to experience, coupled with a genuine devotion to the novel elements in the growth of science, pushed Aristotle into what seemed at times merely a backwater in the history of philosophy. And the history of philosophy itself seemed to many an advanced thinker simply the history of human error before men got on the proper path. The more Aristotle's writings on questions of physics remained unread, the more items that were cited tended to be curious scraps. Why should one take seriously a philosopher who believed that the sublunar elements are earth, air, fire, and water, when Democritus already had advanced an atomic theory; who reported that when a menstruating woman looks at a mirror, the mirror is tinged red; who attacked Empedocles because he offered an evolutionary-sounding idea; and who, when he approached something like a principle of inertia, declared it absurd?

Yet Aristotle's eclipse was only partial. His social and humanistic side —his ethical, political, and aesthetic writings—continued to be influential. Was that because these were backward areas, or because they present perennial problems—the same for ancient and modern times—or because he had fashioned adequate solutions? Aristotle's logic, his clearest claim to originality, remained the staple throughout the nineteenth century, though encased in later oversimplifications, and permeated college texts as late as the 1930s.

In the twentieth century a very surprising thing happened. Instead of remaining in "appropriate" relegation in the history of philosophy, Aristotle became once more a living philosopher. The more our contemporaries developed logic, the more they found Aristotle interesting to look at afresh. The more the philosophy of science advanced in its probing of contemporary problems, the more it asked itself what could have been the structure of a system that held men's minds for two millennia, and what held it together conceptually. The more ethical and political theory diverged, the greater became the interest in a philosophy that had unified ethics and politics within a single comprehensive outlook. The more metaphysics was indicted in a positivist onslaught as "bad grammar," the more attractive it found a philosophy that had attempted to combine linguistic and functional analysis. Contemporary philosophy itself, now more than ever questioning its own nature, discovered it could learn much from seeing how a systematic philosophy was built under different conditions of human knowledge, and how it held together. Of course, there are still some who look back with regressive longing for dogmatic philosophical truth—a strange status to assign to Aristotle, who in the thirteenth century represented science against mysticism. But on the whole it is fast becoming clear that what attracts in Aristotle is a great philosopher at work, and the way in which ideas are being forged, organized, and used. Our age is one in which there is a critical need in all fields for ideas—ideas that will make sense of rapidly accumulating data and break through older frameworks of thought. Thus the modern fascination with Aristotle is the fascination of mind with mind at work, sharply, profoundly, and systematically. Aristotle may yet come to be understood as he never was understood before. In the fashionable language of the moment, modern consciousness is involved in a philosophical dialogue with Aristotle.

In this dialogue, Aristotle is represented by his works, now long a traditional corpus with a life and career of its own. There are five volumes in the massive Berlin edition (the Bekker edition) of Aristotle's works, and there are twenty-three volumes of the Greek commentators on Aristotle (also published in Berlin, between 1882 and 1909), not counting supplementary volumes. Both numbers are deceptive, but in opposite directions. Of the five volumes of Aristotle's own works, only the first two contain the Greek texts; then come Latin versions, and then notes, fragmentary quotations, and index. On their side, the twenty-three volumes of ancient commentary give only a small picture of the vast historical enterprise of commenting on Aristotle.

The corpus of Aristotle's own works covers almost every major area of human inquiry. The list of general topics dealt with is itself impressive: logic, philosophy of science, physics, astronomy, meteorology, biology, psychology, metaphysics, ethics, politics, rhetoric, theory of poetry. (A fuller outline of the works and their contents is given in appendix A.)

What are the works like? They are clearly technical products in science and philosophy, laying the foundations of field after field. They may have been texts for teaching or guidelines for research or both. Yet for all their systematic and encyclopedic character, they do not appear to be treatises that flowed continuously from the master's pen. They have a put-together quality; in many cases treatments of separate topics are joined in a larger work with connecting threads. The parts of some of the works are even named separately in some of the ancient lists. The putting together may have been Aristotle's own doing, or that of his disciples or editors. It has sometimes been suggested that we have here lecture notes taken by students; but without going into comparative reflection on the character of studentship in various eras, we may note the hypothesis that they are lecture notes prepared by the professor himself either for delivery or as topical treatments to be read for discussion. Different versions of the same subject, such as we find in the Eudemian and Nicomachean ethics, would thus represent such outline discussions as edited by Eudemus, Aristotle's friend and colleague, and Nicomachus, his son. On the other hand, some scholars impressed by the fullness and subtlety of treatment do not rest content with any mere lecture-note or outline-discussion theory, and believe that Aristotle compiled many of the works, at least, rewriting and perhaps expanding them. But it has even been suggested that the works are the product of a whole school over several generations rather than one man's massive accomplishment.[1]

Whatever determined their form, the writings had an exciting history, both in ancient and in modern times. They were used as a basis for teaching, and were handed on; they were put into a definitive edition by Andronicus in the first century B.C. and were destined for endless commentary. One account has it that the works were left by Theophrastus, Aristotle's successor, to a disciple who took them away to Asia Minor, where they were hidden in a cellar for protection and recovered in a dilapidated condition only shortly before the time of Andronicus, when they were returned to Athens and later carried off to Rome. Controversy has centered on whether Aristotle's successors did have his technical works for the centuries that followed his and Theophrastus' death. The preponderant view now seems to be that there was some access through other copies; the school did branch out to other centers in the Hellenistic world.[2] It does, however, appear as if the public at first received Aristotle in terms of his earlier dialogues; his technical works became the subject of commentary and gained a wider influence only after being taken up by the Neoplatonists in the third century A.D. By the early sixth century, when it is usually said—though apparently incorrectly[3]—that the Emperor Justinian closed the philosophical schools of Athens (529 A.D.), the works had already engaged the energies of important commentators of such different philosophical schools and religions as the Aristotelian (Alexander of Aphrodisias, 200 A.D.), the Neoplatonist (Porphyry, ca. 232–304 A.D., and Simplicius, early sixth century A.D.), and the Christian (Philoponus, ca. 490–530). It was Simplicius who carried the works to Persia shortly after 529. Constantinople already had an Aristotelian school, and from this source the works went into Syriac versions. In the ninth century they went from Syriac into Arabic, and so through the Arab world into Spain. The great Arabic commentators were Avicenna (980–1037) and Averroës (1126–98). In Hebraic philosophy during this period, Maimonides (1135–1204) is the outstanding Aristotelian.

The Christian world of the early Middle Ages knew very little of Aristotle's works. Boethius (ca. 480–524) in the late Roman world had translated two of the introductory logical works (*Categories* and *On Interpretation*) together with Porphyry's introduction to them. This was practically all that was directly known for a long while; even Abelard in the twelfth century knew only the *Prior Analytics* in addition.

From roughly the mid–twelfth century to the mid–thirteenth century the works came into the Christian world, translated from the Arabic along with Arabic commentaries. They rapidly became the basis of philosophical education in the universities as well as the inspiration for philosophical development in Christian thought. But troubles arose with conservative religious authorities, who feared the impact of the scientific elements in Aristotelian thought. For that matter, Arabic religious influence had led to the condemnation of Averroës in the Arab world, and some material that the Arabic commentators had stressed came most into conflict with Christian dogmas. This situation was gradually ameliorated when the Greek texts became available after the capture of Constantinople by the Crusaders in 1204; then fresh commentary on the text, taking issue with the Arabic versions, became possible. Even those who knew little or no Greek, like Thomas Aquinas, could have Latin translations made for themselves from the Greek. In any case, Aristotle triumphed and his works remained the basis for university education into the sixteenth century, in spite of critical attacks by Renaissance thinkers. This was not, however, a dogmatic Aristotelianism, as recent researches have shown, but a use of the works for setting problems and engaging in alternative interpretations.[4] A school of careful commentary existed in Padua, whose outstanding representative was Zabarella (d. 1589). It is ironic that just when the intellectual world was probably best prepared for appreciating the Aristotelian works critically, it lost interest in them.

Classical scholars, however, never stopped burrowing. The nineteenth-century Berlin edition became in turn the basis for further advance. Textual emendations eventually filled the gaps left by slips of the pen in transcriptions over the ages, by uncertain Latin, by Syriac and Arabic translations, and even—if we give momentary romantic credence to the cellar story—by the nibbles of mice. The twentieth-century texts are a collective scholarly achievement of insight, patience, and devotion. For example, Joachim, in the preface to his revised text and commentary on *On Coming-to-be and Passing-away*, tells us of the patient line-by-line discussions in the meetings of the Oxford Aristotelian Society that Bywater had founded: "The study of Aristotle (we could not but feel) demanded our utmost efforts: no labor could be spared, no detail neglected, no difficulty slurred. We were engaged upon an enterprise arduous indeed and infinitely laborious, but emphatically and supremely worthwhile. It was as if we were privileged to spend those Monday evenings in close and intimate communion with the very spirit of original work."[5] He points out that when he worked on his book in the second decade of the twentieth century, there existed no modern English editions of the *Physics*, *On the Heavens*, or *Meteorology*. And, of course, there was a gap between textual edition and English translation. It was not, however, to remain so for long. Out of the same group came the Oxford translations of Aristotle's works in twelve volumes. Later, in the United States, the Loeb Classical Library editions appeared, so that anyone in the English-speaking world today, with only a smattering of Greek, can correlate the original on the left-hand page with the English on the right. Even more, the last few decades have witnessed the novel phenomenon of a diversity of translations of some of the works. In the contemporary revival of Greek literature and philosophy in translation, Aristotle is not yet running second to Homer, but he is coming on apace.

Moreover, just as the ancient and medieval world heaped commentary on commentary, so the contemporary classical and philosophical scene is the setting for an almost exponential outpouring of articles and books. The diversity, often the conflict, of interpretation is striking. From small-scale disagreements over a passage or middle-sized variations in interpreting a chapter or even a whole work, to large-scale conflicts over the philosophy in its total pattern, it is as if the corpus were functioning as a Rorschach test to focus and bring out the beliefs and intellectual aspirations of the writers.

The reader may be tempted to ask whether all this expenditure of energy is worthwhile. Indeed, if the scene is so crowded and so variegated, why are we interposing another book between the reader and the corpus? For that matter, why does not philosophy simply tackle its problems afresh, using the latest available techniques, as science seems to do, rather than try to develop itself by studying its history? The answer involves two more questions. One is why there exists such an intense interest in the history of philosophy and in the analysis of individual, particularly central, figures. The second is how we are to explain the diversity of interpretation and assess the effects of different philosophical approaches on our current understanding of Aristotle.

The intense interest centers of course not only on Aristotle, but on Plato, Descartes, Kant, Hegel, Marx, and Wittgenstein, among others. No doubt there are different grounds for interest in the different figures. Plato was the first philosopher in the western tradition to articulate the full range of philosophic problems, and he did it with passion. (One can sympathize with Alfred North Whitehead's remark that all the rest of western philosophy is a footnote to Plato.) Aristotle gives us the first explicitly systematic philosophy and fashions the shape of traditional problems. Descartes is a turning point of vast significance. Kant is a colossus standing at the crossroads: nearly all the fields of previous philosophy converge in him, and he refashions the directions that they all take thereafter. Hegel unifies philosophical thought in a historical synthesis. Marx overturns a world. Wittgenstein bewitches a generation. And so on. The phenomenon we are considering is not the property of philosophy alone. Giants of literature, music, and art invite the same interest and stimulate the same attention—witness the obvious cases of Shakespeare, Beethoven, and Michelangelo. Scientists are no exception, as the increasing work on Newton, Galileo, Darwin, and others makes clear.

So pervasive an interest must have a profound basis. Is it itself a historical phenomenon? The founders of our country read the ancients as if they were contemporaries to argue or agree with, and the Bible, especially the Old Testament, as history from which current lessons or solutions to current problems were easily gleaned. After Hegel it is more likely that the ancients were read to learn how problems originated than to find possible answers. A decade or two ago there was a strong tendency to look on the past as gone and transcended and the present as utterly new with its own utterly novel problems; it became almost a defiant commonplace of the young that we cannot learn from the past. But the very fact of rapid change has turned attention to the understanding of change itself and added a historical dimension to the traditional search for the perennial in human life and thought. Accordingly, today we see a resurgence of historical consciousness. We are beginning to accept the lesson that to neglect the past is to rob ourselves of the knowledge and the sense of growth, of the development, the dynamics of change, the alternatives that are posed in events and ideas particularly at critical and turning points, and to leave ourselves provincially bound to the presuppositions that for historical reasons happen to be the ones in our current patterns. Science itself is the most recent field to learn this lesson, and the scientific study of the history of science is its latest product. Whatever the explanation, in the case of philosophy at least, the revival of the history of philosophy as a way of philosophizing, rather than as an archaic interest, has been striking in its scope and its results.

As to the second question, the problem of explaining the diversity of interpretation is part of the general question of the possibilities of historical truth. On the one hand there are the sheer objectivists, who believe that the historian simply tells us what happened and that the Aristotelian scholar as a master of the corpus simply tells us what Aristotle thought. From their perspective, diversity of interpretation results from either ignorance or perversity, or else stems from the sheer difficulty of sources. At the other extreme are the subjectivists—we might even call them romantics—for whom interpretation is an art, not a science. They think that the real historical event, or the real Aristotle, is unattainable, indeed a myth, a will-o'-the-wisp: interpretation is portraiture in which interest and perspective and selection lie at the heart; the character and purposes of the artist as well as current styles are evident in the result.

In philosophy, why should we have to choose between the objectivists and the subjective romantics? By itself the diversity of interpretation is hardly a bad thing. A school of philosophy gets going by calling attention to some fresh aspect or technique or approach that has not been sufficiently appreciated; making the technique into a school ensures that much of human life and thought in the whole range of human disciplines will be reassessed in this fresh light. The new school usually has a contribution to make and sometimes asks questions in a novel way that opens new channels for inquiry. If the different schools communicate with one another, it becomes possible to build a fuller and deeper picture of the subject not only by adding their perspectives but by tackling the new questions their conflict may raise.[6] It is therefore not by disregarding diversities of interpretation, but by working through them—and in the case of Aristotle, going back afresh to the corpus as a constraint—that we can maintain the ideal of a more comprehensive as well as a deeper and more accurate understanding. This does not preclude a frank discussion of modern philosophy in an ancient setting, any more than it does the explicit romanticism of a historical novel. But discussions of this nature should be explicitly such and not pose as history of philosophy.

Unfortunately, what has so often happened (sadly more often in our century) is that each school dwells in splendid partisan isolation, talks to itself and in its writings refers to itself, and so becomes thoroughly inbred. Progress becomes possible then only when the school has at last run its course, its basic techniques have been integrated, and what was once revolutionary pride has become obvious commonplace.

In Aristotle's case, the conflict of schools of philosophy is an old story. Platonizing Aristotle is not only a modern occupation, but goes back almost to the beginning; it grew into the Neoplatonic versions of Aristotle, and so joined battle in the struggle between the mystical and the rational in late ancient and in medieval philosophy. In Aquinas's time Aristotle represented the scientific pole of thought, and Aquinas's interpretations of Aristotle sought the reconciliation of science and Christianity. (At the same time Aquinas did battle with Arabic interpretations of Aristotle that were incompatible with Christian doctrines.) Catholic interpretations, which traditionally have assimilated Aristotle to Thomistic doctrines, have focused strongly on those tendencies in Aristotle's theories of motion, thought, and substance that culminate in a conception of the divine, but also on the problems of teleology and a natural moral order.

In the late nineteenth and early twentieth centuries, work on Aristotle was carried on in an atmosphere saturated with Kantian and Hegelian thought. The Kantian and neo-Kantian components contributed a stress on the constructional character of mind, so that Aristotle's categories, for example, could be seen as modes of shaping the world. Hegelian philosophy itself had a strong Aristotelian element in its metaphysics, for in building its concept of a monistic world development it tools many a stone out of the Aristotelian foundations. It therefore tended to see Aristotle as a precursor of its own idealism. In the United States the St. Louis Hegelians, who relied on Hegelian philosophy as a base from which to reshape institutions, appreciated the part that Aristotle had played in the development of Hegelianism itself and attempted a reassessment of his role and in some cases a fusion of the two philosophies. In Britain, much detailed Aristotelian research did reflect a neo-Hegelian outlook. But others in England and in Europe used Aristotle as a kind of commonsense or realistic counterweight to Hegel.

In the twentieth century, phenomenological interpretations of Aristotle emerged. Much in Aristotle, especially his careful delineation of the qualitative in experience, and his theories of change and motion, can be given a phenomenological turn. But the phenomenological animus against the methods of physical science contrasts with Aristotle's ready acceptance of a unity of scientific endeavor in all fields. (Interestingly, Aristotle did have a serious influence on the European precursors of phenomenology, particularly Brentano.)

A study of the influence of different philosophical schools on the interpretation of Aristotle would be a vast and fascinating contribution to the theory of criticism. It would require an encyclopedic knowledge that combines erudition in the history of philosophy and an active philosophical imagination, as well as encyclopedic familiarity with the Aristotelian corpus. Certainly it would advance the self-consciousness of Aristotelian study.[7] No such effort is intended in the present volume, which seeks only to promote an awareness sufficient to provide insights for tackling a number of the specific questions of interpretation we shall meet in the course of our exposition. For this purpose, too, it is well to add a few comments on the analytic approaches of our century and their specific influence.

What was widely regarded in analytic circles as the "revolution in philosophy" spanned roughly the middle third of our century. It saw its work as carrying out a logical–linguistic analysis that was neutral, as contrasted with the hitherto theory-laden philosophies of the past. It had two phases, each quite different in its impact on Aristotelian studies. The earlier was logical positivism; the later was the ordinary language analysis of the Oxford schools.

Under the influence of the new logic and the new science, positivists felt that philosophy could now get on the right track and that the history of philosophy was therefore at best the story of early fumbling efforts from which we could learn chiefly the mistakes to be avoided. The central tenets of positivism—particularly the sharp separation of logic, fact (empirical, experiential), and value—made Aristotle almost the natural object of attack. He could be cast as the archenemy in a kind of positivistic anti-Aristotelian society, or for that matter be seen by an occasional existentialist as the philosopher of essence as against existence. Aristotle is heedless of all the positivists' central tenets. He talks of necessary truths about the physical world (a violation of the separation of logic and empirical fact), he appeals to nature and the natural to ground his ethics (a violation of the separation of fact and value), and he holds to a teleological view of science (in effect a violation of the separation of logic or method and value). At best, Aristotle remained for the positivists the founder of formal logic in its early narrowly syllogistic scope, now long left behind. It is understandable that such a philosophic approach did not stimulate intensive Aristotelian research.

The case was different for ordinary language analysis. Ordinary language and its nonformal analysis in the contexts of its use was pitted against the large construction of formal systems and the technical language that positivism encouraged. Aristotle now emerged as a kindred spirit, for in almost every field in which he works he takes pains to gather what people *say* and to analyze its complexities. The formalists at most looked to the *Posterior Analytics*, in which Aristotle outlined the structure of a science with its first principles and its deduction of theorems, and so saw Aristotle as the grandfather of Rationalism. The informalists were impressed with the more dispersed burrowings of the *Topics* and the analysis in the *Physics* of how people talk about movement and change. They made of Aristotle an early ancestor of Oxford analysis. In any case, it looks as if respect for ordinary language and its analysis, in the traditionally classical Oxford atmosphere, generated another great twentieth-century revival of Aristotelian studies in Britain, a revival that involved a thorough study of the linguistic aspects of Aristotle's work. It remained, however, saddled at crucial points with some of the dogmas of the older positivism. For example, as we shall suggest later, the conception of a pure analysis that would separate the linguistic and the empirical, and the concentration on the former, robbed it of a fuller appreciation of the intimate interrelation of language and science that Aristotle's works so often exhibit.

In the naturalistic and pragmatic philosophies that have flourished in the United States, the centrality of science moved Aristotelian studies to a different starting point. American naturalism sought to incorporate man into nature, to see the works of the spirit as natural products and science as the single reliable mode of study. It therefore embraced a broader conception of science than the older physical materialism and coupled its opposition to reductionism with this broader sense rather than with the antiscientific attitude that phenomenology tended to foster. Hence in many respects Aristotle proved a congenial ancestor. In the Aristotelian studies that naturalism stimulated, his scientific works served as a starting point, and metaphysical concepts were analyzed in terms of the way they functioned in the scientific work. The naturalistic attitude often found itself in accord with Aristotelian realism, in which the results of analysis are assigned the status of structures of the world. Pragmatism shared a great deal of this unified view of the world and the functional view of concepts, but its Kantian inheritance of the active work of the mind led it to dwell more on the way Aristotle fashions a system of concepts as intellectual instruments for ordering human experience, and hence on the constructional character of his analysis.

Such differences in philosophical approaches concern not only how general Aristotelian ideas and their place in contemporary philosophy have been assessed but also how specific topics and many significant textual passages have been understood. There are, for example, differences in modern attitudes to formal systems and informal analysis, the relation of linguistic analysis and scientific work, the meaning of reduction, and the character of science; or again, there remain the traditional metaphysical differences on the relation between body and mind, or epistemological differences on representational or constructional theories of knowledge. All such issues have to be faced if we are not to fall into the trap of interpreting Aristotle as answering questions he did not ask and in terms of presuppositions he did not make. It is to be noted also that such traps are not avoided by thrusting aside philosophical differences to play the role of a pure classicist concerned simply with the Aristotelian corpus. The question is not only what Aristotle said (though occasionally there are also involved problems of certifying the text and proposing emendations), but what he meant. And what he meant is understood, as is evident from the work of the classicists, in terms of ideas and meanings that reflect the current philosophical background of their times. For example, talk of body and mind is likely to reflect the traditional Cartesian dualisms, and talk of free action, the traditional ideas of freedom of the will. Thus, much as philosophical neutrality may be desired, actual interpretation is carried on with contemporary presuppositions. Neutrality is much more likely to be achieved by comparing different standpoints and by a greater self-consciousness that may release us from our separate philosophical cells. To achieve this broader relation of interpretation to the present state of philosophical discussion and philosophical problems and conflicts is one of the central aims of this book.

A second aim concerns method in the history of philosophy, which has long grappled with the problem of determining wherein lies the unity of a philosopher's thought, and how the various parts of his outlook fit together. Because Aristotle is the earliest western systematic philosopher and because he worked in so many different fields and because he (together with Plato) furnished the structural outline of the problems of philosophy, to see the unity of his thought could offer a paradigm for understanding what holds a philosophy together. This interest turns out to provide an approach to Aristotle quite different from either of the familiar answers to the question whether he has a philosophical "system." This approach will be outlined in the introductory remarks to part 2.

A third aim is, of course, to see what relevance Aristotle has for the present. This includes the lessons we may learn at points where he followed different paths and asked questions in a way far different from ours. It also concerns those of his analyses that offer clearer approaches to areas of inquiry than the (sometimes blind) alleys we have pursued. And of course we may also learn from his mistakes.

Finally, throughout there remains the paramount aim of understanding and expounding what Aristotle wrote. We must stay close to the text, and no matter how far afield a question takes us, we must come back to the corpus. Even more, we must keep our eye on the corpus as a whole, rather than invest our interpretations in only selected areas. Only in this way, when we see how Aristotle's ideas work out in his own varied explorations, can we hope for a comprehensive understanding. This explains (and I hope it will excuse) the fact that at many points examples are piled on examples. They are advanced not to overweigh an argument, but to see where they strengthen an interpretation or where they weaken it.

So much for the story of the works and the problems of interpretation. But there was behind the works a man, with his attitudes in a given life and time, and his ideas. Can we separate them? How are they woven together? How much in his ideas is a reaction to challenges of his day, to master events? How much is an abiding human response for all men at all times? How much of his life in turn is guided by his ideas? Clearly, we must try to see what can be discerned of his life in his times from what sparse sources are available, and couple that with attitudes garnered from his works. Then we can go on to consider the character of the mind at work, as it forges and uses basic ideas.

2

THE MAN BEHIND THE WORKS AND

THE MAN WITHIN THE WORKS

Our knowledge of Aristotle's life is limited. There are some known facts, some stable inferences, and many speculations based on what is known about the age rather than the man. There are stories found in the literature of later generations and centuries, in which it is almost impossible to sift fact from legend.

Aristotle was born in 384 B.C. in Stagira, a Greek colony in Chalcidice, a peninsula in the northern Aegean, bordering on Macedonia. His father, Nicomachus, was physician to King Amyntas II of Macedonia. His interest in biology may have stemmed from his father's profession; he may have had some medical training early, or at least enough stimulation to sharpen his later research in biology. Certainly the biological segment of the corpus is sizable and reveals an intensive research interest. His mother, Phaestis, was connected with Chalcis, the mother city of Stagira, on the island of Euboea. These facts had an important bearing on Aristotle's life. He had Macedonian connections, and the rise of Macedonia to dominance in Greece, and Greek resistance to it, were to be persistent features in his life. Although his career was to be largely tied to Athens, his home affiliations were Stagira and Chalcis; he remained always an outsider to Athenian life, a noncitizen hampered by legal restrictions. Being an outsider may have given Aristotle an impartial view of Athenian institutions, or instead it may have robbed him of a rooted sense of participation. The historian Bury thinks that Aristotle was prevented from ever judging Athenian institutions impartially, on account of possible influence from his boyhood surroundings; there was a general bias against Athens in the Chalcidian area because Athens was constantly seeking to dominate the region.[1] Bury also posits a Chalcidian prejudice against Macedonia as being a lower civilization and thinks Aristotle's early Macedonian experience engendered a later lack of sympathy with Alexander's enterprises. For all we know, however, Athens may have been the city of Aristotle's youthful dreams—he did go there at the age of seventeen. His attitudes toward Macedonia are better understood from his later works and his relations to its leaders.

While we know next to nothing of his childhood and early youth, we do know his philosophic reflections on childhood, youth, and sport. He waxes enthusiastic about the rattle as a device for directing and releasing childhood energies.[2] He criticizes Plato, who would stop children from straining their lungs and sobbing; Aristotle sees this as exercise. He warns against excesses in sports: since in the lists of victors at the Olympic games only two or three who won in the men's events had previously won in the boys', he suggests that early rigorous exercise results in loss of energy.[3] The Spartans turn their youth into savages by overtraining. Training is necessary, but it should aim at character development and cultivation of the mind. Play is important, too, but its aim should be relaxation.

As for their character, the youth are guided by sensual pleasure and unable to control their desires.[4] They desire with ardor, but tire rapidly. They are hot-tempered and impulsive. They want honor and victory; they act for the noble rather than the useful. They are full of passion and hope. They live in hope, not yet in memory. They are fond of friends and they go astray through excess. They are fond of laughter and have an optimistic view of man.

In his biological theory, Aristotle came to look on children as dwarfs.[5] This is tied into his general view that the proportion of the body shifts in the more perfect animal form from a heavier upper and a lighter lower part to the reverse, a heavy lower and a lighter upper part. Children growing up change in these proportions. In the ethical writings, he sees children as undeveloped in their rationality. Children are coupled with the sick and the insane as having many opinions no sensible man would discuss; a child really is not engaging in action any more than a wild animal, for there is no rational consideration; no sensible person could endure going back to the kind of life children live.[6] Aristotle could have agreed with Bernard Shaw's apothegm that youth is wasted on the young. Perhaps a more basic philosophical perspective is involved. He sees childhood and youth as a transition, a development toward something beyond, not as living in its own right and in its own time and in its own way.

Aristotle's works do not contain much about the sheer love of the child. Parents love their children as coming from themselves, whereas children love their parents as their origin; or again, the love of children for parents is compared to that of men for the gods, an affection for what is good and superior to oneself.[7] We know that Aristotle's own parents died in his boyhood and he was brought up by a relative named Proxenus. There is mention, but barely more, of a brother and a sister. Then we hear of him as the youth who at the age of seventeen came to Athens and entered Plato's school in 367 B.C., staying on for twenty years, till about the time of Plato's death. Both Athens and Plato became his teachers. In the long run he was both to accept and to reject much from each.

The Athens of Aristotle had recovered from the havoc and defeat of the Peloponnesian War. The restored democracy had already lasted for about thirty-five years when Aristotle arrived. Athens had embarked, for the most part, on a policy of cautious moderation; she avoided internal revolution and was wary in her relations with other cities. Her democracy was intensified, she continued to be a great cultural center, her renewed confederacy in the Aegean was less exploitative than its fifth-century predecessor, her commerce was thriving. All this made for a felt continuity with fifth-century Periclean Athens. Modern historians writing of the fourth century as a whole are prone, however, to see it as an age of transition. The city-state was increasingly threatened as a political unit in the face of rising empire, and an abiding insecurity became a primary feature of fourth-century life. The individual was insecure before the threat of starvation, war, and social conflict; impoverishment rose with population growth, and large numbers of mercenaries in effect severed their ties with the mother state. Whole cities were likewise insecure, for they might be wiped out. What Athens had done to Melos in the fifth century, any great Greek city might suffer in the fourth; indeed, Thebes was destroyed by Alexander, its population killed or enslaved. Fate hung in the balance—on a mistake in policy, on a single turn in battle, on luck. It is not surprising that Luck soon became a goddess to be worshipped.

Historical judgments of the transitional character of the fourth century tend to reflect the long view, sharpening contrasts in the light of what was to come. They compare the city-states—now overcome by Macedonia, now struggling against it—with the sprawling Alexandrian empire, broken in the last quarter of the century into three large masses. In philosophy, they contrast the Platonic and Aristotelian conception of the social individual oriented to the city-state with the later isolated individual of the Stoic and Epicurean ethics. The Stoic saw himself achieving serenity by carrying out his duties as a member of the cosmos, not of the city-state. The Epicurean sought serenity in the pursuit of his own pleasure. Both attitudes reveal a common search for tranquillity, for peace of mind and security. Yet the participants of the fourth century can scarcely have seen all this in the light of the outcomes that later historians trace.[8] How much of what the latter take for granted as the trend of the times was discernible to the intellectuals of the fourth century when the young Aristotle came to the heart of the Greek world?

There must have been some consciousness that large changes were taking place and basic problems were emerging. For example, there was the question of slavery. The Theban Epaminondas had broken the power of Sparta and liberated Messenia, freeing its people, whom the Spartans had long held as helots. The Athenians helped Sparta in hope of restoring some balance of power, and in the period that followed found themselves debating the Spartan demand for the restitution of Messenia. Though political considerations were doubtless primary, and helots were not exactly considered slaves, there were voices raised to declare that no man is a slave by nature.[9] The first book of Aristotle's *Politics*, years later, was to take stock of this problem.

Again, there was the entry of other parts of Greece onto the political stage. No longer was it merely a question of cold or hot war between Athens and Sparta. Thebes, Thessaly, Arcadia, Phocis, and many another lesser candidate for expansive power had to be reckoned with. On a small scale, the Athenians must have had to rethink their external politics, as modern powers did with the rise of the countries of Asia and Africa. Within the twenty years that Aristotle now spent in Athens (to 348–47), there was a continual seesaw until the dominant power fell to Macedonia under Philip.

There was also the contention between the rich and the poor, reflected in the rivalry between oligarchs and democrats. Thucydides in his *History of the Peloponnesian War* had portrayed class struggle as the unrestrained destructive force of fifth-century Greek history. In Athens, precisely because of its successful avoidance of constant revolution, Aristotle could see the struggle translated into political form.

Conflicts of ideals were correlated with this social unrest. In the late fifth century, Pericles had impressed his Athenian hearers with the contrast between the Athenian and the Spartan ways of life: democratic versus authoritarian government; social and intellectual and political freedom versus coercive discipline; rational criticism, uniting speech and action, versus taciturn passivity; pursuit of the beautiful versus impoverished culture; preference for peace but courageous readiness to defend versus the adulation of war. Yet Plato's *Republic* in the early fourth century had mentioned Sparta as the nearest approximation to the ideal state, though definitely not to be equated with it. Where would Aristotle stand on these issues? What a milieu it must have been for a keen young mind to move into! Like the era of the French Revolution, or the world of today, it called for basic decision.

The social issues were part of a wider set of problems. These were cosmic problems and problems of human destiny, which were also subjects of controversy on the Athenian scene. This was no longer simply a confrontation of traditional religious beliefs and Ionian science, or again, of Homeric religion and the later Orphic religion with its beliefs in immortality, transmigration of souls, and personal salvation. (Not that conflicts of that sort were absent: impiety could readily be employed as a charge against an intellectual opponent, just as in the previous century, when Anaxagoras had been attacked for saying that the sun was not a god but an incandescent rock no bigger than the Peloponnesus.) It was rather that opposing paths had found full philosophical articulation by this time. A highly intellectual young man drawn to philosophy needed no longer to construe his choice as one between philosophical reflection and traditional belief; it was rather which philosophy to choose. On one side were the materialistic philosophies such as the atomism of Democritus, who explained all phenomena in terms of the motion of the constituent particles, or the empiricism of the sophist Protagoras who thought that all knowledge comes from the individual's sense experience and who proclaimed man the measure of all things. On the other was Plato, who believed in absolute standards both for knowledge and for human ways and made a firm distinction between the changing sensory material world and the eternal domain of Ideas or absolute Forms or Patterns, and who believed fervently in the immortality of the soul and in human life as a quest for the eternal truth. To be in Plato's school did not necessarily entail a total commitment to his philosophy, but it was a powerful influence. Later, Aristotle was to give his own explanation for the belief in Forms. The believers, he said, were convinced by the Heraclitean view that the sensible world is in constant flux; since there could be no knowledge of what is in flux, they posited permanent entities to be the objects of knowledge.[10] Aristotle, less convinced by Heraclitus, could look for order in the processes of nature, not merely in the ideal.

But Plato's Academy was not an indoctrination center.[11] It was heir to the Socratic dialectic, extended into the intensive study of all knowledge. Aristotle had both a keen mind and a devouring appetite for knowledge. Plato is said to have called him "The Mind" and to have remarked, comparing Xenocrates to Aristotle, "The one needed a spur, the other a bridle."[12] Aristotle was also called "The Reader." There was a jest in this term, for it designated the servant who read aloud to a group. This was a common way of reading a book in those days. Aristotle, however, apparently did his own reading. Was it that he could cover more? Read more constantly? Stop and think? Go over and over passages to summarize facts and analyze concepts? We would have to know him much better than we do to say which prompted his break with custom. Perhaps too, it represented a turn toward the accumulation of knowledge as against simply clarification of the mind in action.

After the maturing process of his student days, Aristotle continued in the fellowship of the Academy, lecturing, writing, and pursuing his research. We are told that at one point he lectured on rhetoric, in a kind of critical rivalry with Isocrates, the great teacher of rhetoric in Athens. Competition of educational approaches was strong, and the demand for rhetorical and political training was great. Its institutional bases lay in the assembly, in which all citizens could participate, and in the law courts, where a citizen had to present his own defense (or prosecution) before large juries selected by lot. Rhetoric thus served as access to power. Isocrates was opposed to the mere speech-writers who trained directly for cases before the court, but he also attacked the Platonic diversion of training toward the pursuit of higher knowledge through dialectic. His own program called for long practice in eloquence for those of ability, and for conveying ideals as the poets and artists did. For Aristotle, who was associated with the Academy, to lecture on rhetoric might have seemed to be abandoning the Platonic educational approach. But—if we may judge from Aristotle's own *Rhetoric* (see our ch. 19)—it could equally be an application of the philosophic program, for he insisted on the importance of broad knowledge in the study of rhetoric. Rhetoric thus became an applied productive science. Followers of Isocrates seemed to resent Aristotle's teaching, and some of the stories derogatory to Aristotle that got into later biographies are thought to have started here.[13]

Aristotle also wrote dialogues in this period, and it was for these that he was best known for a long time. "What shall I say of Aristotle?" asked Quintilian, the Roman teacher of rhetoric in later days. "I doubt whether I admire him more for his knowledge, for the copiousness of his writings, for the charm of his language, for his keenness of invention, or for the wide range of his works."[14] Indeed, the extant fragments of the dialogues are largely extracted from quotations in later writers; their authentication has required intensive scholarly investigation and interpretation. And there is always the problem in any fragment of a dialogue whether the view it presents is Aristotle's or belongs to one of the participants with whom he does not identify.

It is believed that during these years Aristotle did considerable research in the natural sciences. This emphasis was in line with Plato's concern in his own later work *Timaeus*, in which there are conjectures about the physics of heaven and earth and man. The one area in which Aristotle contributed nothing, though that field was highly prized in the Academy, was mathematics. Here he could keep abreast, but he had no creative bent for it and came to have serious theoretical differences with the Platonists about the nature and philosophical import of mathematics.

The Academy was a community of friends. In the *Nicomachean Ethics* Aristotle regards the highest type of friendship as that whose bond is not utility or even pleasure, but a common pursuit of the good. This is possible, he says, only for men who are good. Since the highest good is taken by Aristotle to be contemplation, the common pursuit of the intellectual life by men devoted to it and to one another stands out clearly as his paradigm. But exactly what did Plato mean to Aristotle? In part, Plato transmitted the Socratic influence (Socrates had died fifteen years before Aristotle was born). But Plato's thought was more than an external influence; it furnished the very groundwork of Aristotle's outlook.

In our own century, Werner Jaeger revolutionized Aristotelian studies by adopting a developmental approach to Aristotle.[15] Insisting that Aristotle was first a convinced Platonist who then moved away step by step, Jaeger reconstructed the doctrines of the earlier dialogues and sought to assign portions of the standard corpus to different periods and different strata of Aristotle's thought according to their nearness to Platonic views. The earlier dialogues, the *Eudemus* and *Protrepticus*, stand out as undiluted, even intensified Platonism. The soul is seen as imprisoned in the body. The sharpness of this dualism is indicated in an extreme analogy reported in a fragment: "For as the Etruscans are said often to torture captives by chaining dead bodies face to face with the living, fitting part to part, so the soul seems to be extended throughout and affixed to all the sensitive members of the body."[16] The dialogue *On Philosophy*, in which Aristotle opposes Plato's theory of Ideas, is taken by Jaeger to date after Plato's death. From then on, he holds, Aristotle moved toward a naturalistic empiricism and ended as a compiler and interpreter of factual data.

What Aristotle's own philosophy became we shall have to judge later on from his works. His relation to Plato may have been much more complex and much less linear. Aristotle's most mature views contain a substantial Platonic element. The indebtedness of his ethics to Plato is considerable, as is the relation of his *Politics* to the later Plato of the *Laws*, and his physical and cosmological theory is linked to Plato's *Timaeus* and *Parmemides*, though it offers different answers.[17] The aphorism that even a dwarf standing on the shoulders of a giant sees farther should not obscure what happens when a giant stands on the shoulders of a giant. The search for either-or contrasts that sees every man—not merely every philosopher—as inherently a Platonist or an Aristotelian is like W. S. Gilbert's line that every boy and every gal that's born into this world alive is either a little Liberal or else a little Conservative. No slogan of rationalism versus empiricism or dualism versus naturalism is rich enough to encompass the full range and complexity of either philosopher.

Jaeger's work opened up an era of rich scholarship, and if his method of interpreting the strata in the corpus had yielded definitive results, it might have prevailed. Available evidence, however, is so slender that the outcome seems arbitrary. As a consequence we have adverse theses—for example, that the young Aristotle opposed Plato and only much later came nearer the master's doctrine![18] One salutary consequence of the contemporary controversy is that the focus shifts once more to the corpus itself. Aristotle is after all what the corpus says. As to how Aristotle felt about Plato, there is his own near-apology when, in the *Nicomachean Ethics*, he is about to criticize the Platonic theory of the good: faced with a choice between friendship and truth, the philosopher's duty is to follow the truth.[19]

After twenty years in the Academy, Aristotle seemed well established. But some time in 348–47, about the time of Plato's death, he left Athens and moved to Assos in Asia Minor at the invitation of its ruler, Hermias. Some ascribe his action to pique at his failure to succeed Plato as head of the Academy. Speusippus, Plato's nephew, got the job. But can we read modern academic politics into ancient intellectual life? Since Aristotle disapproved of Speusippus' overmathematical stress in philosophizing, some scholars regard his departure as a secession from the Academy; Jaeger points out that Xenocrates accompanied Aristotle. It is possible, on the other hand, to interpret the move as the spread overseas of the Academy itself. Yet the most pressing grounds for Aristotle's departure are to be found in the trend of Athenian politics and the relations of Athens and Macedonia. In the latter part of the 350s, Philip II passed from consolidating Macedonia against northern neighbors to expanding in the Greek sphere of influence. By 348 he had taken the cities of Chalcidice, destroying Olynthus, which Athens had tried to help. Within Athens the anti-Macedonian party had come into power under the single-minded leadership of the orator Demosthenes. It is likely that Aristotle, with his Macedonian connections, felt endangered in Athens. Düring, however, in his reassessment of the ancient biographical evidence, believes that Aristotle left Athens in the spring of 347, even before the death of Plato.[20]

In the realm of Hermias, at Assos, Aristotle continued his philosophical inquiries. Sometime during this period he married Pythias, the niece of Hermias. Aristotle was already in his late thirties, but the marriage fitted his theory, or possibly his theory was fitted to it, for he specified as the optimal nuptial ages thirty-seven for the man and eighteen for the woman. His reasoning combines sociological, biological, and ethical premises.[21] He takes a whole-life perspective and decides it desirable that cessation of the procreative period should coincide for husband and wife; he sets this at the ages seventy and fifty respectively. For the sake of the children, the man should not be too old, yet the gap between husband and wife should not be too little. He seems to want men to procreate after they have reached their physical prime, which he believes is attained by age thirty-five. Behind his calculations lies a theory of procreation, which we shall touch on later. Its net effect is to regard the female as an incomplete male. Psychologically, too, he sees woman as somewhat incomplete in the possession of deliberative reason; she is not wholly without it, as Aristotle says the slave is, but her reason is not firm and lacks authority.[22] Her husband provides this guiding authority, and virtue is therefore different in husband and wife; his courage is shown in command, hers in subordination. As for the friendship of husband and wife, in the *Eudemian Ethics* it is called one of utility, or of benefactor and beneficiary.[23] The *Nicomachean Ethics* achieves a clearer perspective: the friendship of husband and wife is one of utility and pleasure combined; they may even rejoice in one another's virtues, different though these be.[24] In general Aristotle does not trust women to do even what is good for themselves. For instance, he believes exercise to be good for pregnant women, and so he would have the lawgiver order them to make a daily journey to worship deities concerned with childbirth.[25] Apparently it never occurred to him simply to explain the desirability of exercise to the women themselves.

Of Aristotle's relationship with Pythias, of their married life, we know nothing. She died sometime during his later stay in Athens. They had a daughter, also named Pythias. In a tradition that has often been repeated, Aristotle is said after his wife's death to have formed a regular relationship with Herpyllis, also a native of Stagira, and had with her a son, Nicomachus. Düring, who questions this account, traces it to a single hostile source.[26] He points out that Aristotle's will, which is given in Diogenes Laertius' life of Aristotle, would not alone support the account, that what is said there is quite consistent with Herpyllis' simply managing Aristotle's household. Nicomachus is not given any special legacy; this is precisely what one would expect if, as legitimate son by Pythias, he inherited everything not otherwise assigned. (Of course the same consequences would follow if Aristotle and Herpyllis were legally united and Nicomachus were their son.) It is difficult, too, to make inferences about Aristotle's feelings from the will, except about his general kindliness to servants and slaves and his sense of duty in carrying out obligations and undertakings. For example, A. E. Taylor says of the will, "The warmth of the writer's feelings for Pythias is shown by the direction that her remains are to be placed in the same tomb with his own."[27] In fact the will says, "And wherever they bury me, there the bones of Pythias shall be laid, in accordance with her own instructions."[28] It was Pythias who was loving, or else had a well-cultivated sense of her wifely station.

Hermias did have a stable place in Aristotle's affections. Either he had been a student at the Academy or he had visited there. He appears to have won his way to power in Assos and Atarneus from a lowly start. Jaeger accepts the stories that associate him with the Academics in his neighborhood. He was eventually captured and killed by the Persians. From the fragmentary and gossipy material that remains, scholars have been left wondering how far he was bargaining with Philip to provide an entrance for a planned Macedonian invasion of Persia, and whether Aristotle could in any way have fitted into the negotiations. In any case, Aristotle wrote a memorial hymn of a most laudatory sort for Hermias; it was later charged against him as impiety by his Athenian enemies.

Probably in 345–44 Aristotle moved to Mitylene on the nearby island of Lesbos. It is generally agreed that he did a great deal of his biological observation there; the supporting evidence is the prevalence of place names from this area in the biological writings. It is believed that Theophrastus, who was a native of Lesbos, was with him at that time. Theophrastus is a central figure in Aristotelian philosophy. He remained a member of Aristotle's school, became its head after Aristotle's death, and was an eminent scientific philosopher in his own right (some of his own works survive). He is a favorite candidate of modern scholars as the compiler of some Aristotelian works out of notes or separate pieces, after Aristotle's death.

Aristotle apparently went back to his native Stagira after a while, but in 343–42 he accepted the invitation of Philip of Macedon to tutor his son Alexander, then thirteen. This he did for three years; Alexander became very busy after that, governing Macedonia while Philip was away, fighting along with Philip, and eventually, in 336, succeeding to full power upon his father's assassination. The relationship of the philosopher and the ambitious prince, both still to rise to the highest eminence in such different fields (Aristotle, it is usually thought, got the job through his Macedonian connections rather than through a fame not as yet fully achieved), early caught the imagination of historians, philosophers, moralizers, and rumor-mongers. The result is that one cannot separate gossip and fabrication from reality. Some things are plausible whether true or not; some are interesting stories. The solid comparison is to be found in the later ideas of the two men. We must ask here how far the broader orientation of Alexander, manifest at least in his attempted fusion of the Greek and Persian worlds, conflicts in principle with the city-state ideal of Aristotle's *Politics*. Or was there rather a Greek chauvinism in the philosopher that the Macedonian did not share? Plutarch tells us that "Alexander did not do as Aristotle advised—play the part of a leader to the Greeks and of a master to the barbarians, care for the former as friends and kinsmen, and treat the latter as beasts or plants, and so fill his reign with war, banishments, and factions; he behaved alike to all."[29] Whatever the truth of this alleged advice, Aristotle had the opportunity Plato had longed for—to educate a philosopher-king.

To judge from most of the accounts, Aristotle got on well with the young prince. It is even said that Alexander wanted him to come on the Persian campaign. Aristotle's nephew, Callisthenes, did go along and eventually got into trouble, being suspected of conspiracy against Alexander; he was executed or died in captivity.

Aristotle was probably back in Stagira after his work with Alexander was done. It is worth noting that in 339–38 Speusippus died and Xenocrates became head of the Academy. Some scholars accept accounts that portray Aristotle as the defeated candidate, and connect this with his founding a separate establishment a few years later. Whatever is the case, Aristotle did come back to Athens in 335–34. By that time Alexander had crushed Greek rebellion after Philip's death. The destruction of Thebes was the stern warning. Friends of Macedonia could be quite safe in Athens now. Aristotle was a friend of Antipater, who was in supreme command of Macedonia as Alexander's deputy when the latter went off to invade the Persian empire.

At this point, it is generally assumed, Aristotle founded his own school, the Lyceum, near a grove sacred to Apollo Lyceus. Here he discussed philosophy in the mornings, walking about with his students. The Greek term for "walking about," or more likely for the walkway in which they met, gave the name "Peripatetic" to the philosophy. The school became a research center, with the first large library. Here for about a dozen years Aristotle carried on his work, writing and organizing what later became large parts of the corpus.[30] The Lyceum differed from Plato's Academy in its concern for the systematic collection of material. Aristotle provided its initial scientific impulse by stressing the importance of the accumulation of knowledge. A different style of writing was developed, an expository analysis as contrasted with the Platonic dialectic. The school consequently engaged in more instruction.

When Aristotle came back to Athens, he was about forty-nine years old. In the picture of different times of life given in the *Rhetoric*, we are told that the mind is most fully developed at about forty-nine. Aristotle pictures the prime of life as a mean between youth and old age. Such men are neither overfearful nor rash; they are sober judges. They follow neither the noble nor the useful alone, but both together. Similarly, they are neither parsimonious nor prodigal. They have courage and self-control. They combine the advantages of youth and old age with moderation and fitness.[31] Perhaps this is Aristotle's portrait of himself at the age when he first came within grasp of his major ambition.

Alexander died in 323. Athens, among other cities, revolted. It was no longer a safe place for Aristotle. He was charged with impiety, as Socrates had been; the hymn he had written for Hermias years before was cited against him. He withdrew to Chalcis, on Euboea, his mother's old home. In a letter to Antipater—if we may trust a later quotation—he explains that he would not let the Athenians sin twice against philosophy.

Aristotle died in the following year, 322, from a stomach illness, it is said. Shortly thereafter, in October, Demosthenes poisoned himself to avoid capture by Antipater. Antipater crushed the revolts and in his strict settlement with Athens insisted on a limitation of the democracy by a property qualification for citizenship. The list of citizens was cut by more than half, and the form of government became in effect what Aristotle in his *Politics* had described as a "polity," a rule by the substantial middle class.

What were Aristotle's activities in his last months, and what was his state of mind? One later story, in the Arabic tradition, has him studying the tides in the gulf of Euripus near Euboea.[32] In writing to Antipater, however, he says, "The more solitary and isolated I am, the more I have come to love myths."[33] Jaeger sees this as evidence of the mystical and inner life of Aristotle, as contrasted with the usual view that his scientific spirit predominated. Perhaps the Arabic story is closer to the spirit of the corpus.

Aristotle escaped the ills of crabbed age that he describes—the lack of confidence and lack of energy born of a realization that most human affairs turn out badly, a mistrust and indecisiveness in feeling, living not for the noble but the useful, being cowardly, without shame, living in memory rather than hope, incessantly talking of the past, substituting calculation for morality.[34] He was in his sixty-third year when he died. Even at that time this was not an advanced old age.

And death itself? In one context he quotes Sappho: "Death is an evil; the gods have so decided, for otherwise they would die."[35] But there he was concerned with modes of argument. His standard view is that men seek the good life, not just life itself, that life should not be lived on simply any terms. And immortality? We shall see that his psychology leaves no place for personal immortality. He asks whether the happiness of the dead is not influenced by the fortunes of their descendants, and decides that maybe it is, but not enough to change the verdict of their lives.[36] He seems to be dismissing customary beliefs—though gently— rather than reinforcing them, and locating the good worth scrutinizing within the pages of the life that is lived. As for his own children, Nico- machus died young. The daughter, Pythias, married Nicanor, as specified hopefully in Aristotle's will. Nicanor and then a second husband died, and she married the physician Metrodorus. Their son, Aristotle, is men- tioned in Theophrastus' will; he is assigned the right to join the school if he wishes, presumably when he is older. But there was no second philosophical Aristotle.[37]

Insofar as Aristotle's personal appearance is concerned, writers about him have little choice. They can report, following Diogenes Laertius' account from earlier sources, that he was thin-legged, had small eyes, was conspicuous in his attire, and spoke with a lisp. Or they can gaze on the bust that has come down to us. There is no known reason—but of course that is far from proof—for questioning that it is a copy that goes back eventually to an original. (In his will, also recorded by Diogenes, Theophrastus specifies where a bust of Aristotle is to be placed.) The danger is that in gazing, one will read one's beliefs about the qualities of the corpus into the features of the man. A. E. Taylor finds that Aristotle's features "are handsome, but indicate refinement and acuteness rather than originality."[38] His kindness is also sometimes stressed, because of his careful treatment of servants and slaves in his will. He also seems to have had a sharp and ready wit. Diogenes cites a number of his remarks.[39] When told that someone had abused him, he said, "He may even scourge me, so be it in my absence." Or again, there is his observation that men were divided into those who were as thrifty as if they would live forever, and those as extravagant as if they would die tomorrow. Or his reply to an inquiry why one should spend so much time with the beautiful, "That is a blind man's question." Or to a chatterbox who asked whether he had bored him, "Not at all, I wasn't attending to you." His very definition of wit as "cultured insolence"[40] shows a consciousness of the aggressive component in humor. In a lost chapter of the *Poetics*, which he mentions in the *Rhetoric*, he analyzed kinds of jests, distinguishing which are becoming to a gentleman, which not (e.g., irony is more gentlemanly than buffoonery).[41]

Whether he was able to enter into warm relations with others, or whether the relationship was predominantly intellectual, is a psychological question about which we have insufficient basis for conjecture. He was thoroughly aware of the need for friends and the part friendship can play in human life, but whether this was yearning or achievement we cannot say. There is a constant touch of aloofness, the ideal of self-sufficiency, the emotional independence of the proud man who gives lavishly but does not receive. Of course, Aristotle moved effectively in dealing with others. No less practical a man than Antipater testifies to his persuasive power.[42]

In his philosophical work, aloofness becomes objectivity. He is able to stand aside and look at alternative views—his own among the rest. Such objectivity does not mean abandoning his own convictions, but being explicit about them. Thus he is able to study in a neutral spirit the qualities and procedures that will ensure a tyrant of a lasting rule. This is not "Machiavellianism," and he is not abandoning a critical judgment of tyranny. He concludes that a tyrant who follows his recommendations will be half-wicked rather than fully wicked,[43] but he does not scorn the half-gain. Similarly, discussing formulae of justice in the *Nicomachean Ethics*, he is able to state neutrally the distributive principles of different types of societies, but at the same time make perfectly clear where his preference lies.[44] Again, when in the *Rhetoric* he gives a long list of the kind of people men like, and the sort of things people are ashamed of,[45] we cannot always tell how he feels about them.

This neutrality is sometimes misunderstood when taken out of context. It involves no abatement of a very stern integrity. When he teaches opposing tricks of the trade to would-be lawyers in the *Rhetoric*, it is in the same spirit as a contemporary law school might exercise its students on opposing sides of the same case, one after the other—as, for example, in a tax case, first on government enforcement, then on finding wider loopholes for the defense. This is not to cultivate an amoral outlook. We shall see how strongly Aristotle insists on the maintenance of standards, whether in law or politics or personal morality. "Tyrants enjoy being flattered," he tells us, and goes on immediately to declare that no free spirit would behave that way, carefully distinguishing between being friendly to a ruler and flattering him.[46] In general, his works make it clear that his overriding loyalty is to truth.

Was he modest about his own work? There are occasional self-conscious remarks, such as "it has been determined in the *Ethics* (if those accounts are of any value)."[47] He tells us where he has pioneered in a field and where he is drawing on the work of the past. In general, he has a realistic appraisal of his own contribution. He tends to see himself at the end of a philosophical tradition in which, by systematizing previous contributions, he is able to add his own and solve many previous problems. This brings us to the character of his thought and his philosophic method.

3

THE CHARACTER OF ARISTOTLE'S THOUGHT

AND HIS PHILOSOPHIC METHOD

The analytic character of Aristotle's thought is inherent in his method. He does not first get an idea, work out its implications, and then go looking for evidence. Instead, he first assembles a wide array of opinion and information in the form of common beliefs (*endoxa*), including previous theories, common linguistic usage, and reported observations. He then takes the greatest pains with the formulation of a problem and with a systematic breakdown of its issues. Here especially he develops the difficulties and puzzles and apparent contradictions that have emerged in traditional beliefs. Then he sifts thoroughly for what can hold up and what cannot and makes distinctions, offering solutions that will reconcile or harmonize the divergent elements in the theories, usages, and observations that have not been rejected or wholly reinterpreted.

Aristotle is not, however, merely analytical. His thought is also structural and systematic. There is always a systematic concern operative in his thinking, in two senses. First, he constantly employs a whole framework or network of concepts, in terms of which he formulates the problems of a given field. (The analysis of these concepts is, of course, a great part of his philosophical work.) And second, in working in any one domain he seems to carry with him a web of specific theory developed in other domains, so that the ramifications of one part of knowledge on other parts of knowledge are always near the surface. For example, he considers the suggestion that the world is elliptical in shape and revolves around one central point within itself; this, he notes, means we will have to allow some empty space for it to revolve through, whereas if it is spherical we will not need such an assumption—and he has earlier already rejected the possibility of empty space. In general, he is sensitive to the biological presuppositions of ethics and politics, the physical assumptions of metaphysics, and the psychological assumptions of the theory of knowledge. The cross-references in the corpus are not merely an editor's delight, but integral to his structural way of thinking. Whether the result is an Aristotelian "system" need not concern us now. This stress on structure sharply differentiates Aristotle from Socrates, who will plunge in anywhere and seems content with digging up any contradiction that will stimulate the mind of the interlocutor and shed light on a particular interest.

Besides the ability to analyze and to deal in structures, two other qualities usually found in outstanding philosophers are speculative capacity and originality. If "speculative" indicates ranging insightfully over wide problems, then of course Aristotle is a speculative thinker. If, however, it be taken in the sense of a soaring mind that leaps to imagine possible worlds, that constantly asks for alternatives to the principles it has settled on and speculates what the world would be like if that rather than this were so, then Aristotle either does not have this capacity in high degree or else he mutes it. He often seems too earthbound and too ready to accept as final the principles of order that have emerged from his inquiry, too ready to dismiss possibilities for which there are no existent specimens to examine. On the other hand, his creative originality should not go unrecognized simply because he seems to be extracting his conclusions from the examination of his predecessors and adding on to their work. In fact he is the great master in original concept formation, and he plays with traditions as a great musician works up older themes into a novel pattern. The concepts Aristotle fashioned, and the way of looking at the world they embodied, provided a framework for sophisticated thought in which men could for a time make advances in understanding their world and themselves.

Whether the works bear the stamp of a great scientist as well as a great philosopher is more debatable. The biological writings have won admiration not only for their scope and foundational character but also for their detail of observation. In comparative studies Aristotle shows tremendous insight in ordering descriptive materials and in sensing useful analogies. Again, he is quick to theorize and ready to offer explanations. Indeed, sometimes he jumps for explanations too quickly, without waiting to check the fact he is setting out to explain. Thus he gives the example, cited above, that the surface of a mirror becomes clouded red when a menstruating woman looks into it (and he adds, "If the mirror is a new one the stain is not easy to remove"), and he goes on right away to offer complex explanations in terms of his theory of vision why this should happen.[1] On many occasions there is an element of credulity in his acceptance of alleged facts, even where, as in this case, he could have arranged for tests. But there is no gainsaying his ingenuity in fashioning alternative explanations on the basis of his own hypotheses, even in relatively unsuccessful domains such as meteorology, as well as in his treatments of psychological and political phenomena (he was a political scientist, not merely a political philosopher). Take, for example, his complex reckoning with prophecy in dreams.[2] He notes first that small stimuli in waking life may go unnoticed because competing greater impulses crowd them out, but that in sleeping, with the competition cut off, a faint echo may be heard, like distant thunder and lightning. The problem of explaining successful prophecies is then posed as showing the relation of small stimuli to large events. Aristotle suggests three relations: signal, cause, and coincidence. A person might prophesy his coming illness because its first beginnings reverberated loudly in sleep and so signaled its coming. Or he might foresee doing something because the small beginnings of intention had come in a dream, and so begotten the action. Where the dreamer does not initiate an event, what happens is best understood as coincidence; most dreams do not coincide with what happens, so it is not surprising that an occasional one does.

In general, then, Aristotle's strength lay on the observational side in gathering and systematizing data. It was perhaps too early for controlled experiment. On the theoretical side it lay in ingenuity of explanation, but he sometimes pressed general theories into particular explanations without sufficient precision to test them against alternative possibilities.

It is not easy to decide which of the shortcomings of Aristotelian science are to be attributed to lack of specific qualities of scientific intellect. Some may follow either from immature development of specific sciences in his day, or from a lack of precision in instruments, or simply a lack of instruments (he did complain that insects were too small for observation), or an insufficient development of mathematical tools. The growing field of the philosophical history of science has not yet sufficiently explored these questions.

There are further specific attitudes that stand out in Aristotle's mode of inquiry: a stubborn commonsense attitude, a sensitivity to contextual differences, and a special kind of one-world outlook. These also require our preliminary attention.

Aristotle is often extraordinarily commonsensical. He has an essentially realistic orientation to the phenomena of a field and a stubborn how-is-it-used attitude to the meaning of terms. He has little patience with those who raise dialectical difficulties about the reality of initial phenomena. If a man denies motion (says Aristotle in the *Physics*), no physicist will have anything to do with him. More precisely, his point is that such disputes do not fall within the work of the physicist, but concern another scientist—the metaphysician. We shall see later how he deals with Zeno's paradoxes that seem to impugn the reality of motion. Again, if a philosopher wants to elevate Being into an ultimate One which is the reality of all that is, Aristotle sometimes invokes minute logical objections stemming from his logical views. More often he simply says that there are many senses of *being* (*is*) as well as many senses of *one*; in fact, things can be one by being of the same material, or by being instances of the same form, or by being continuous—as when they are stuck together by glue! Such calculated commonsensicality has the same sobering effect as Socrates' talk of carpenters and doctors and things of the marketplace, and of course like Socrates' method it goes through the commonplace to deal with difficult and complex problems.[3]

Sometimes, however, Aristotle's realism leads him into dogmatism. Thus, maintaining that not every doubt deserves inquiry, he says, "Those in doubt whether one ought to honor the gods and love one's parents or not, are in need of punishment, while those who doubt whether snow is white or not, lack perception."[4] Again, in the *Physics* he takes it to be obvious that things have natures. Yet this, far from being an obvious phenomenon, is a very sophisticated thesis. There is thus the danger that his sense of realism, while salutary in many contexts, may in others be blind to possible differences of interpretation when one interpretation is already built into the alleged phenomenon.

A commonsensical attitude may, even more, be a way in which significant philosophical views are introduced and taken for granted. It is one thing to attack as near madness the doctrine that all is one and immovable ("no madman is so out of his senses as to think that fire and ice are one; but in dealing with things that are fine and things that through habit appear fine, some people on account of madness seem to find no difference");[5] it is quite another to let such a passionate devotion to common sense establish the epistemological principle that whatever contradicts sense-perception is erroneous, or the ontological principle that whatever physical account may be given of sense-qualities, their observational properties are not to be denied or their reality impugned by "reduction." Indeed, we shall see that at a number of critical points—in analyzing the infinite, continuity, and the properties of motion, as well as the relation of potentiality to determinism—the commonsensical attitude becomes almost a technical philosophical instrument. In the light of the range of the commonsensical we shall therefore have to pay close attention to the occasions of its use in different contexts and see both its strengths and its weaknesses.

The second important attitude in Aristotle's mode of inquiry may be described as a kind of pluralistic contextualism: the meaning of an idea has to be understood in a specific context of inquiry; there is no universal context, and hence no possibility of dispensing with contextual reference. This attitude emerges clearly in his treatment of philosophical ideas, in the so-called philosophical lexicon of *Metaphysics* 5. Take, for instance, the term *principle* (*archē*). This has a sonorous sound; it conveys the idea of what is basic or fundamental in the area under investigation. Philosophy generally takes the notion for granted. Yet what, after all, is a principle? It is refreshing to see Aristotle dip down to the ordinary meaning of the Greek term, which is simply "beginning" or "starting point." He illustrates with the examples that the starting point of a journey is the beginning of travel and that the keel of a ship is the beginning of its construction, carefully pointing out that the latter is an internal part of what is constructed. Once we recognize the basic contextualism we find it hard thereafter to make philosophical sense of the use of a concept or a principle without specifying the kind of activity or inquiry involved. Principles or judgments of priority or primacy unavoidably pinpoint relations in some ordering. They are context-bound. (Even the sense "governing principle" comes from an ordinary usage—*archai* could also mean the rulers of government.) Of course some contexts become standardized for philosophical inquiry. Aristotle distinguishes repeatedly between the order of learning and the order of logical demonstration; in the one, perceived particulars will provide the starting point, in the other, primary premises. The contextual reference is usually not far below the surface. It may involve terms that are needed to enter into a basic definition in the field, or initial phenomena for investigation that are not to be denied, or regular starting points for understanding development, and so on. For example, a house is logically prior to the process of building because the account or statement (*logos*) of the process refers to the house, but the account of the house does not include the process of building.[6] (Of course, the particular process is temporally prior to the particular house.)

Such contextualism does not necessarily guarantee that the outcomes will be different. The contexts may be different, but the principles or starting points specified may turn out on investigation to be related or to converge in various ways on a single outcome. Any discovered unity would thus be subsequent to the inquiry, not laid down in advance.

There is a sense—and this is the third fundamental attitude in Aristotle's inquiries—in which he does approach the world as one world. He treats it as a single order of nature with no impassable barriers, with none of the cleavages that have characterized modern thought at least since the seventeenth century, and modern philosophy since Descartes: the partition of man from nature, spirit from matter, mind from its objects, in one or another explicit or subtle form. Aristotle asks questions we would not dream of asking, which at first seem odd and then shock us out of our presuppositions. Thus he wants to know whether, if a house grew up by nature, it would grow up in the same way as we would build it. He decides it would—for is not man in his crafts only imitating natural processes? Does not the doctor cure by trying to reproduce nature's operations? Aristotle's favorite paradigm of nature's operations is the doctor curing himself as patient—that is, nature raised to a conscious level. Now we moderns may find Aristotle's doctrinal view of the architecture of house-building archaically limited; we may suspect that he is having nature imitate man rather than the reverse. Yet there may be much to learn from his easy passage from one to the other. Think how much effort we spend today on the similar question whether the brain is a machine, some of us ingeniously multiplying the powers of the machine to approximate the variegated powers of man, and others, fearful of the continuity of man and machine, insisting on the uniqueness of consciousness. Whatever Aristotle's specific scientific errors and naïvetés, we cannot dismiss his one-world attitude as an immature pre-Cartesianism. It is a genuine, sophisticated philosophical alternative that he can help us understand and that we may today be better able to evaluate. After all, how can one simply settle by postulation whether spirit is or is not a separate stuff out of which thoughts and feelings are constituted? The answer has to be the cumulative outcome of investigation into one field after another, of psychological investigation added to physical and biological investigation.

In considering Aristotle's one-world attitude as a characteristic mode of thought we have passed from qualities of thought to principles of philosophical outlook. There are accordingly other matters that would clamor at this point for a place in our inventory—e.g., his attitude toward change, toward evolution and history, as contrasted with the search for a rational eternal order. Such questions can best be considered in relation to his philosophical concepts, to which we turn shortly. There is, however, one general matter in his method that has wide ramifications and ought to be considered before we go on, namely his attitude toward language and the place of language analysis in philosophizing. Precisely because linguistic analysis looms large in contemporary philosophy and because there has been some tendency to look back to Aristotle as having been engaged in a comparable practice, it is important to see both what he says on the question and what he does in his actual philosophizing.

There is, of course, a close relation in Aristotelian writing between logic, reason, and speech. The term *logos* (plural *logoi*) is kin to *legein* (to speak) and refers to a proposition, an account or formula, and becomes extended to mean a rational explanation or theory. On occasions Aristotle contrasts the adverb *logikōs* with *phusikōs*, or sometimes *logoi* with *pragmata*. The first may set off a logical or dialectical argument against a scientific one, but the scientific one could be of the order of theoretical results as well as an appeal to observational fact. Sometimes when Aristotle contrasts *logikōs* and *phusikōs* it is almost as if he were contrasting theoretical considerations with factual ones. The distinction between *logoi* and *pragmata* is more often one between the conclusion of an argument based on assumptions, and the obvious reality (how things stand).[7] The exact shade of contrast in both formulations doubtless varies with the context. We shall have occasion to examine specific contexts later.

We have already seen that Aristotle includes what people say and think or believe among the data or received opinions (*endoxa*) he records at the outset of an inquiry and that he follows this up by exploring shades of usage. It is perfectly clear that he expects to learn a great deal from the analysis of linguistic usages. Now this is a trap for modern interpreters, for modern linguistic thought has been intensely concerned with specifying a *general* relation between the structure of language and the structure of reality. It has been easy (much too easy) to say that for Aristotle speech embodies reason and reason grasps the structure of things, so that the structure of speech is the structure of the real—that, for example, because speech takes a subject-predicate form, therefore reality consists of substances and their properties. Such a generalization, we shall see, is misleading. It is not even to be assumed that for Aristotle the logical–linguistic is a separate order from the real or that its correspondence with the real poses a general problem. They may just be two modes of investigation or inquiry, one logical or dialectical, the other physical or scientific. Talking about things is itself a natural phenomenon; things get talked about just as they get played upon in other ways in this world, and so how we think about them and how we embody that thought in speech may give us clues to what they are like. Both our thoughts and our speech are therefore part of the evidence in any inquiry.[8] There will be all sorts of occasions on which linguistic formulations may be misleading. While there are appropriate names to distinguish some processes, such as "drizzle" when drops are small and "rain" when they are large, there are other cases in which the physical analysis clarifies the linguistic: Aristotle analyzes the process of boiling and then points out that the (apparently) common use of the term *boiling* to mean heating gold or wood is only metaphorical since the process is physically different.[9] Similarly, linguistic form may mislead us on appropriate category: "to flourish" has the same verbal form as "to cut" or "to build," but the first denotes a quality, while the others denote actions.[10] Again, there are cases in which Aristotle seems to be giving a linguistic analysis but is really drawing on linguistic corroboration for a physical analysis. In discussing growth and the addition of one thing to another, he wonders why when mixing water and wine we say we have more wine as a result rather than more water. It is clear that we do so because the function (*ergon*) of the mixture is to serve as wine; later on he points out that when we put in too much water the result is water.[11]

On critical occasions, when a conflict arises, Aristotle is quite explicit. In *Metaphysics* 7, when he is failing to solve the problem of substance in purely logical terms, he says, "We should certainly inquire how we should speak on each point, but not more than how the facts actually stand."[12] Further on in the same inquiry he says, "It is clear that if people go on in their customary way of defining and speaking it is not possible to answer and resolve the difficulty."[13]

If we look not for a correspondence of structures but to the simple fact that he spends much time analyzing what we ordinarily say and showing complex patterns of usage with a high degree of sensitivity, we have again to note that he does this to offer *partial* evidence for one or another thesis. For example, presenting the view that body has three dimensions, he points out that we say "both" of two things or two people, but not "all," whereas of three we say "all"; thus we are following nature, since three dimensions give us a complete body, and "complete" and "all" do not differ in form.[14] Linguistic usages are thus part of phenomena and so can serve evidentially for a thesis. Linguistic analysis, then, although it does play a large part in his inquiry when he wants greater precision or feels it necessary to fashion a technical term, is not for Aristotle a separate mode of analysis. But he does end with a set of highly refined terms that he uses in carrying out analyses in special fields from physics to politics. What, then, is the relation of his refined technical language to the ordinary language he uses?

We can distinguish three different levels of concepts conveyed by his terminology. At the top are the highly general concepts—*matter, form, nature, potentiality, actuality, substance,* and so on. These are very technical, and Aristotle is obliging enough occasionally to show how he has fashioned them. In the middle are concepts with only a moderate amount of fashioning, often expressed by ordinary words standardized for the purpose—for example, most of what he calls the "categories" (*quality, quantity, place, time, action,* etc.), and change and its species. At the bottom are concepts conveyed by the little words. These are not necessarily the imposing little words such as *the what-is* or *the one,* for these, in the guise of Being and Unity, already had an exalted metaphysical place in Platonic construction, and we have suggested that Aristotle in a commonsensical way tried to prick the Platonic balloon of inflated concepts. They have their place in Aristotle too, but chiefly as problems at the top. The heavy work at the bottom is done by the little words of ordinary discourse, such as *from, out of, in, having, prior, now,* and the like. Of course, there are also the little words that are used as a source for middle-rank terms like some of the category terms and the four causes: *how big, what sort, when, where, out of, what, whence, for the sake of,* and so on. Actually, we find an even wider range of little words in specific analyses throughout the corpus. They are especially resorted to at critical points in the analysis of more complex conceptions. Not only are *in* and *now* used in analyzing *place* and *time,* but subtle problems of mathematical continuity rest on a basic consideration of *together, apart, touching, next,* and so on. Problems of the motion of physical elements involve *up, down, right, left, front,* and *back.* Biological questions such as the order of development of parts of the body and functional relations therein prompt an aside on the meanings of *prior,* just as the relation of offspring to seed leads Aristotle to reflect on the meaning of one thing's *coming from* another. The question as to what constitutes a single physical movement necessitates an account of the different senses of *one*.

Of course, such a distinction between levels does not mean that some terms may not operate in different ways on different levels. *Matter* and *form* in the sense of material and shape are certainly ordinary terms. As a relative distinction on the middle level, Aristotle turns them into two of the four causes. *Matter* in a basic sense and especially *form* as *essence* become high-level. Similarly, *place* is an ordinary word, but as a category it is elevated to at least middle rank.

There is no simple uniform relation in Aristotle between ordinary language and technical language. The latter is not built up in a formal way out of the former, as complex definitions may be constructed out of simple elements. Nor is it one-directional; that is, no technical term on every occasion of its use is analyzable as a combination of elements in ordinary (bottom-level) language, with (of course) contextual differentiation. In fact, Aristotle is occasionally ready to refine the smaller, ordinary word by the more technical ones. In discussing the order of development of bodily parts, he distinguishes the meanings of *prior* first by applying his technical distinction between final cause and efficient or generative cause and then by breaking the latter into agent and instrument.[15] Similarly, in *Metaphysics* 5, *prior* seems to be explicated by reference to already established technical terms. Again, in discussing the relation of body and psyche, two senses of *for the sake of* are distinguished—one the end or purpose for which, and the other the person for whom.[16]

We cannot classify Aristotle in the modern sense as either a formalist or an informalist; he does not fashion his philosophical terms by precise combinations, logically explicit, out of simpler elements, nor does he use them merely as pointers to variegated contexts of ordinary language. He seems to have achieved something different, a kind of conceptual network, generated out of ordinary uses to be sure, but presupposing always some factual picture, some governing purposes, and sometimes a specific model of construction. The resulting network is different from either the formalist's system or the informalist's studied pluralism. Each concept reaches over to the others and only gradually becomes intelligible as its relations to the others and their grounding in existent phenomena are revealed.

Building such a network of philosophical concepts is a complicated business, and it is especially important to see how it is done. Because he employs his concepts in a variety of specific fields of knowledge and practice, Aristotle furnishes one of our best case histories in which to explore the nature of the task. We turn, therefore, to examine his concepts at some length in the context of the problems and conflicts that were already well developed as basic questions in Greek philosophy by his time.

Part 2

THE METAPHYSICAL NETWORK

INTRODUCTION

It was suggested earlier that the idea of a conceptual network would help us understand in what way Aristotle is a systematic philosopher. At the end of part 1, our discussion of his language suggested that he fashioned and used his technical terms differently than either the formalist or the informalist. We have now to ask what a conceptual network is and how it works.

The notion is a fairly simple one. The network consists of a group of basic concepts associated in such a way that starting with any one (attempting to understand or explicate it) leads to others, thus establishing interconnections within the group as a whole. The connections themselves may be of various sorts, sometimes tight, sometimes loose; thus mathematical systems may impose deductive bonds, sciences may at points impose empirical and probability relations, and ethical networks may sometimes emphasize instrumental relations. Some of the concepts have ties to (refer to) particular experiential fields, and their predicates thus reflect the properties of those fields. The concepts and principles of a network may therefore be used to structure or shape particular areas of inquiry.

Since some (though not necessarily all) of the concepts have experiential reference, one part of a network is affected by what happens to another part. The lessons of experience that affect one part may thus be transmitted in various directions along the network to some other areas of application. For example, when we examine how Aristotle's inquiry into sensation and thought is structured by means of his concepts of substance, potentiality, and actuality, we shall see that he does not have any difficulty relating the phenomenal and the physiological, precisely because the network already has a broad concept of qualitative change. This concept itself was stabilized by its interactions with common experiences of motion and change and growth and the way we see and interpret them. In principle such a process could continue and a network undergo refinement and alteration in part after part as knowledge grows in one or another corner of human experience.

Within the network itself, no concept has ultimate general primacy; primacy is relative to context, though some concept may win a greater role by its richness or its importance in many contexts. (We shall see that substance derives its ultimacy largely from the fact that all roads lead to it.) Again, since a network is a system of related ideas, when we study a network as a whole—as against the separate study of individual concepts —we are more likely to see the division of tasks among the concepts, their interlocking roles, how they reinforce one another, and redundancies that overguarantee a result. Isolated inspection might miss such properties of pattern or function. Moreover, since the result of a network analysis is a total pattern rather than a partial fragment, network analysis offers a better vantage point for studying philosophically the history of ideas and their growth, change, and interrelation with various areas of human culture and development.

Finally, the looseness of the notion of a network lets us see just what tightness and unity there is in the material to which the method of network analysis is applied; it does not define *system* in such a way as to limit it to one type. For example, anyone taking *system* to mean a deductive system and Aristotle's *Posterior Analytics* to offer this rationalistic ideal for all knowledge could only be disappointed that Aristotle did not achieve a Spinozistic deductive system in the style of geometric proofs. (Indeed the field seems almost at times to be divided between those who argue that Aristotle is a systematic philosopher though he did not achieve his ideal and those who argue that he is not a systematic philosopher at all, but simply an analytic one.) A careful study of the corpus as a whole shows that that is not the kind of unity to be found in Aristotle's philosophizing. We suggest that he is a systematic philosopher not in the sense of one who pursues a deductive system, nor in the attenuated sense of one who enunciates principles or dogmas on the basis of metaphysical analysis, but in the sense of one who has a well-constructed and fairly clearly analyzed conceptual network that he uses with considerable power in field after field of human inquiry. And this carries the further hypothesis that the unity of a philosopher's work is generally to be sought in some such direction.

It is important here to avoid a misunderstanding. We would search Aristotle's works in vain for an account of a conceptual network. It is not there in the sense in which we find an explicit analysis of the syllogism or of demonstration. But insofar as he has a definite set of concepts that plays a basic role in the way he structures inquiry in field after field, whether scientific or humanistic, and he analyzes these concepts and explicates them in ways that relate them to others in the set, we can speak of the network that he has constructed and examine the way he uses it. And we can with due caution compare and contrast the treatments of similar problems in subsequent developments. In much the same way, in the history of geometry, Euclid and his fellow geometers were not giving us our contemporary and hard-won philosophical analyses of geometry. But if we go back to them in the light of these analyses we may get a clearer understanding of their work, how they conceived it, what options they had, and what paths they selected—provided of course that we do not think of these things as simply early stages of development toward us. So too in looking for a conceptual network, we are dealing with a modern notion. But if, with appropriate cautions, we analyze Aristotle's work by looking for the conceptual network, we expect to gain a fuller understanding of the operations that are going on in his system as a whole. This book has been organized with that in mind: in part 2 we shall study the general conceptual network; in the remaining parts we shall see its use in psychology, in the theory of knowledge, in ethics and politics, and in rhetoric and poetics, and try to assess the kind of results that the network we find in Aristotle makes possible.

The general conceptual network as analyzed in part 2 has been titled the *metaphysical* network. Although none of its concepts are epistemological, it might be objected that matter and change belong to physics. But there is some discussion of them in the book to which the name *Metaphysics* was later given, and we shall argue (in chapter 7) that their discussion falls appropriately within metaphysics as it is to be construed in that book.

The idea of the conceptual network as a system of mutually supportive ideas and principles has grown in importance in modern philosophy both in the theory of analysis and in the theory of truth, or methodology. In either case it is directed against extremes that invoke ultimately simple elements: basic terms intuitively grasped, unitary data directly sensed and incorrigible, initial principles self-evidently true, axiomatic assumptions intellectually certified. The idea of a coherent body of concepts and truths not one of which was wholly true by itself was at first a revolt, often using an organic analogy, against one-directional elementaristic analysis that ended in certainty in the intellect or in sensation. It was not limited to one philosophical school,[1] nor to one philosophical field. Developments in mathematical logic (model theory) and philosophy of science have made the notion of a conceptual network both useful and broad, if not at times too loose—though perhaps not yet as loose as that of a conceptual framework.

In going at Aristotle's basic ideas in the way indicated in these remarks about networks, I have had, of course, to select the ideas at the outset. In a sense, then, although there is likely to be little disagreement about most of the list, their presentation for analysis of meaning, use, and principles of relation constitutes a large-scale hypothesis about how we can best approach Aristotle's work. Conceivably, we could have started in the opposite direction, by first examining Aristotle's account in various fields and having the concepts repeatedly forced upon our attention. This procedure would have been onerous in that we would have had to go to the fields a second time to reconsider them in the light of the intervening conceptual analysis. Why take so roundabout a route when Aristotle's *Physics* and *Metaphysics* in effect make us an intellectual present of the concepts?

Finally, let us note that we make no initial assumptions about the status of the concepts that make up the network. In examining them we look for their roots, their genesis and development, and their functions. Only in their initial bow do they stand out in analytic isolation and perhaps seem to be analytic givens. No assumption is made that Aristotle's concepts were unchanging, even in his own hands. We shall see that they grew and took different shape as he worked with them in the light of both the way in which he formulated problems and the results he got by their use.

4

MATTER AND CHANGE:

A PRELIMINARY SKETCH

Aristotle's concepts did not spring from his mind fully developed, as Athena is said to have sprung full-grown from the brow of Zeus. They were taken from common use in accounts of the world, from current use in specific fields of scientific inquiry, and from his philosophical predecessors; only a few were invented by him. They were stretched, extended, and refined, in connection with specific inquiries, sometimes physical, sometimes logical. The concepts tended to come in clusters, and clusters fused with one another in conceptual experiments that yielded fresh ways of looking at things and processes. When Aristotle came occasionally to sum up, as he did in parts of the metaphysical writings, he traced their interconnections—at least those that were useful for the highly general problems he there set himself.

What we have called his pluralistic contextualism is clear from the way he operates throughout. Take a particularly transparent example in the *Rhetoric*.[1] Persuasion may be directed to an observer, or to one who is to make a decision. In the latter case, it is a decision either about the past (as in judicial decision) or about the future (as in legislation). Hence three basic types of persuasion are labeled (in reverse order) *deliberative*, exhorting or dissuading with respect to future action; *forensic*, accusing or defending something in the past; and *epideictic*, praising or blaming something, usually the present. Different concepts are appropriated to each: the first is concerned with the expedient (advantageous) or harmful; the second with the just or unjust; the third with the honorable or disgraceful. It is as if different contexts involve different tasks, different tasks require different processes, and different processes beget their appropriate concepts. To unravel the concepts and their relations we have to work backwards to the processes and tasks and concepts and *their* actual relations.[2]

The situation is even more complex where the same concept has been used in different contexts of inquiry; for example, *matter* or *substance* may turn up in quite different investigations, say physical and logical. Critics sometimes rush to accuse Aristotle of ambiguity. But the similarity of the concept in different contexts is itself a contextual question. As we shall see (in chapter 14), Aristotle inquires whether a concept itself is being used in an analogical way or has a specifically common meaning or is a generic abstraction; and if it is ambiguous, he labels the type of ambiguity. Of course it does not follow that he is always successful in his conceptual experiments. Whether the concept that results from steering different contexts to a converging effect will be philosophically useful—especially in metaphysical experiments—has sometimes taken centuries to decide.

The best entry to the metaphysical outlook is to consider the central concepts used. In this chapter we shall start off with matter and change. In explicating a network we cannot expect to complete the account of a concept in a preliminary sketch, because as the further concepts in the network unfold, their analysis often adds to the analysis that has come before. This is the case for both matter and change. For example, each is enriched by the concept of potentiality; matter is almost equated with it later in the development of Aristotle's ideas, and the final definition of change incorporates the notion of the potential being actualized. Merely to point this out is not enough, for it is not the mention of potentiality but its analysis that adds the light. This warning for matter and change holds for the initial discussion of all the central concepts discussed in this part.

Matter

The assumption that there is one basic stuff—or perhaps a few more—out of which the world is made had been accepted early in Greek philosophy. Speculation had centered rather on their character. Was everything constituted of water (Thales), or air (Anaximenes), or fire (Heraclitus), or an indeterminate capable of generating opposite qualities (Anaximander)? Empedocles had settled on four unchanging elements—earth, air, fire, and water—whose mixture and separation produced the diversity of things. Democritus had elaborated the notion of atoms congregating in the void. There were, of course, others who went in different directions. Aristotle did two distinct things: he developed a generalized conceptual apparatus for dealing with matter that could be used in different fields without foreclosing empirical possibilities, and he adopted a specific type of physical doctrine. This contrast of method and specific content is one we shall have to make constantly, to ensure that the inadequacy of specific results does not obscure our view of the philosophic way in which they were pursued.

The conceptual apparatus consists in analyzing any object or happening into the correlative aspects of its *matter* and its *form*—words used chiefly in the relative sense of materials and organization. Matter (the Greek word *hulē* designated initially the timber for building) is the material of a process or product: "Matter is a relative term, for there is a distinct matter for a distinct form."[3] Thus bronze is the matter of the statue, earth is the matter of the bronze; but in the other direction the statue may be part of the matter of a whole temple, and the temple part of the matter of the city. How generalized the concept may become can be seen from its use for an abstract subject matter; thus in a logical argument, the premises employed are the matter, while the form determines validity. Aristotle does, however, draw a sharp line when he wants to be technical: even in the case of a natural event like an eclipse, "things that exist by nature but are not substance have no matter; their substratum is their substance. For example, what is the cause of an eclipse, what is its matter? It has none; it is the moon that is affected."[4] For its part, form (*eidos*) had been generalized from such a notion as shape (*morphē*); it had long been a technical term in Plato, as the central concept of the universal Idea. We shall later examine Aristotle's use of the term in some detail; meanwhile we are concerned with its use as the organization or shape of some raw materials in a given process or product.

This concept of matter in a matter–form analysis of things and processes is found in a number of distinct inquiries. One inquiry is into the *constituents* of existent things; here matter is one of the two constituents. A second is into the *process by which an object comes into being or is made*; here matter is the antecedent raw material. The second is the more significant, for the physicist is concerned with change, its description, analysis, and explanation. A third inquiry that Aristotle pursues on occasion is *what a thing would break down into or degenerate into*. All three lines of inquiry sometimes yield the same result: a bed consists of wood, is made out of antecedently existing wood, and breaks down into wood. But wine does not consist of grapes, though it is made out of grapes, and it degenerates into vinegar.

The concept of matter has an important place in Aristotle's metaphysical reflections. Several other ideas cooperated in its construction, and speculations about an ultimate stuff and interest in how change takes place provided the matrix in which it grew. One of the originating concepts, which we shall meet in the next chapter in considering cause, is the *out-of-which*. It is the *material cause* and covers sometimes the raw material (the bronze in the statue) and sometimes the material source (the seed from which the plant or the organism grows and the food on which it feeds). Most influential, however, in orchestrating the emergence of the concept of matter is the idea of *substratum* or *subject* in the analysis of change. (The Greek term is *hupokeimenon*, literally "what underlies.")[5] This is consolidated through a demand for a persistent element in change. In the simpler kinds of changes, such as quantitative growth or qualitative alteration or motion, ordinary experience identifies a subject under-going the change and ordinary language formulates it correspondingly. Thus the child is first small and then big, a cheek is now white and then red, a ball is now here and then there. In short, we think of the subject or substratum undergoing the change from one state to another. The sub-stratum is what becomes identified as that matter which in the change acquires the end-state as the form.

Now in what Aristotle calls substantival change, where one substance goes out of existence and another comes into existence, the situation is more complicated. For example, the seed is destroyed and the plant arises, the plant is destroyed and becomes food, the food is destroyed and becomes flesh. What persists that is first the one thing and then the other? Why not see it as disappearance and replacement? (Would we see it that way if it happened quickly instead of slowly—if, for example, changes in nature were as swift as we can now make them appear by speeding up our films of them?) Aristotle's solution is a kind of conservation prin-ciple: the generation of one substance involves the destruction of another. Thus what is persisting is not a particular subject of a given form, as with the child that was growing or the ball that was moving, but the matter that was elsewhere—before in the plant and now in the flesh. (It may have carried a property along with it, but that is not the issue.)

It is in terms of this outcome that Aristotle defines matter in its primary sense: "Matter (hulē) in the chief and strictest sense is the substratum that admits of generation and corruption [or coming-to-be and passing-away]; but in some sense the substratum of the other kind of change is also matter."[6] From the point of view of the history of science, this notion of matter was a genuine advance, whether regarded as a construc-tion or as a discovery. For one thing, as just indicated, it carried with it the idea of conservation, that the generation of one thing meant the taking of matter from other things and that the destruction of one thing did not mean the disappearance of matter. Again, Aristotle insists that the matter of perceptible bodies is not separable but is always endowed with some specific qualities or properties.[7] What those qualities are we are told by the theory of physics, that is, of physical change. In short, this matter is the basic matter that physics discovers. If, however, we ask what it is like by itself—though it never exists by itself—the only answer can be one by analogy: as bronze is to statue, as bricks are to house, as premises are to the syllogism, so this basic matter in the abstract is to form in the abstract. This is an abstraction resting on analogy. But when we say concretely that anything is ultimately made out of matter, it is a physical, specific idea of matter that is involved.

Aristotle thus escapes the chief trap for a philosophical concept of matter, the danger of lapsing into a sheer indeterminate stuff that cannot be known. Locke describes matter (he speaks of substance, whether body or spirit) as a something-I-know-not-what that must be presumed to lie behind all qualities because they cannot stand by themselves—in short, a bare *hupokeimenon*. Kant takes all reality, not merely material, to be an unknowable X behind phenomena, while Mill defines matter as the permanent possibility of sensation. Aristotle does speak of "first matter," or "prime matter," but in most passages this is relative to a special context. (We have, of course, to distinguish "first" as proximate or nearest to the form being discussed, from "first" as ultimate or last in the material analysis; it is the second sense that is here involved.) For example, if we are concerned with bronze articles, the first matter is bronze, and if all things are made out of water, it is water.[8] In *Generation of Animals* he calls menstrual blood prime matter, since he regards it as the seminal material of generation. Actually, prime matter, unless it is just matter talked about abstractly, is simply the basic physical matter that underlies substantival change and has the properties the physical science discovers. "Prime" matter is not thus a different kind of matter; it is just matter in its primary or strict sense.[9] In any case, Aristotle uses the term very seldom, chiefly in explaining the reciprocal changes of basic elements like water into air or earth into water.

We have looked at the main lines of development of the concept of matter, but there were many ancillary themes, and there were some ideas that we might have expected to play a part that do not. To note the latter first, neither the idea of nature (*phusis*) nor that of body (*sōma*) play any special part in the analysis of matter. Aristotle does speak occasionally of matter as the underlying nature, but this means simply that when we ask for the nature of something, one answer will carry us into the materials involved; another leads to the form. Thus its relation to nature does not carry the explication of matter very far. In the case of body, we are likely to think of post-Cartesian contrasts of body and mind (spirit, soul) and so to equate body and matter. While Aristotle speaks of *body* frequently in reference to perceptible bodies or natural bodies, it is not made the object of special analysis except where questions arise about the elements that make up perceptible bodies or about the definition of *body* itself— whether it is to be defined in terms of mathematical ideas of limits, or whether limits (planes, lines, points) are to be defined instead as dimensions of body.[10] It does not become a technical term and remains on the level of ordinary language and ordinary experience.

Among the ancillary themes, another facet of *subject* (*hupokeimenon*) plays an important part. We saw this term used for the constant element in change, that is, the subject answering to what is changing, or the substratum in which the transformation actually occurs. But what is more, in the logical works it also refers to the subject of which something is predicated or in which some feature is present. Indeed the study of predication joins the study of change in determining the character of matter. Let us take a brief, though explosive, example. There is a passage in the *Metaphysics* that speaks of other things being predicated of substance but substance being predicated of matter;[11] for example, "brown" could be predicated of "this table" but "this table" could be predicated of matter. In that case matter would be inherently indeterminate, for it would be neither a particular thing nor a quantity nor anything else. This treatment of predication would certainly be in flagrant contradiction with the earlier account of substance in the *Categories*, where we were told that in its strictest and primary sense substance cannot be predicated of nor present in anything else as subject.[12] Of course Aristotle may have changed his mind by the time of the metaphysical writings, but it does not appear likely on so fundamental an issue without his telling us. However, he is probably spared the contradiction because it looks as if the *Metaphysics* passage is part of a *reductio ad absurdum* argument against a view he is opposing. Indeed, he says shortly afterwards that if we argue in such a manner, matter would turn out to be substance, which is impossible.[13] It is well to warn the reader early in our book that this kind of problem has to be faced at many points in dealing with interpretation. Those scholars who take Aristotle to be speaking for himself in this critical passage of the *Metaphysics* have had to work out subtle reconciling theories or theories of successive development in Aristotle's views.[14] (Now that this warning has been conveyed, most further examples will be put into the footnotes.)

Matter as a technical concept, when thus unpacked, is very complex. It becomes established along different lines of inquiry, some logical and linguistic, some physical and experiential that deal with change. Principles developed along the way are turned into methods of analysis and extrapolated to preserve continuity. Certain functions are assigned to the concept initially and others are added after it is developed or are found to have been assumed in various parts of the corpus. The initial ones—that matter serves as material for construction and is the identical element in change and serves in limited contexts as subject in predication—have been considered already. Others to be discussed at later points are matter as a means of explaining the differences between individuals of the same form or species (matter as an alleged "principle of individuation"), matter as the source of *accidental* features (why one person has blue eyes, another brown), and matter as the home of potentialities for alternative lines of action. Matter becomes aligned in general with potentiality and provides the continuity in change that prevents change from collapsing into a bare succession of phenomena. Yet matter is never a catch-all. Its various functions are quite definite, and there are some functions that it takes on in later thought that it does not have in Aristotle. Thus the notion of matter as *mass* is not developed, although Aristotle does say it is the same matter when a body expands.[15]

On the whole, it looks as if Aristotle has a coherent philosophical concept of matter. Nevertheless, because it emerges out of a convergence of different lines of inquiry, its value cannot be judged until the convergence is shown to be legitimate, not a bare analogy or a confusion of linguistic with physical analysis. Since in Aristotle's view linguistic usage may serve as partial evidence about what our world is like, that talk about changes requires a subject of which a change is predicated is partial evidence that people find an element of persistence in changes they perceive in the world. Again, the convergence of different inquiries must not be a random association. The matter of different contexts is shown to be the same matter when, for example, the same physical theory is used to show both the generation of one particular from other particulars and the emergence of accidents (such as differences in eye color). In short, part of the unity of a general concept of matter is carried by the outcome of scientific developments. A great part also depends on showing that the unified concept of matter, when related to other concepts in the network (such as potentiality), helps solve serious philosophical puzzles. This will be considered below, as the underlying problems unfold. All these issues have been raised in this first discussion of a central concept to serve as a paradigm of Aristotle's process of concept-formation.

It is important also to note our method of analysis. We try to understand the concept not only by seeing how Aristotle generates or constructs it, but also how he uses it or how it functions, that is, what relations it has to other concepts and what tasks it carries out in different fields of inquiry. This carries us to different parts of the corpus. For example, the analysis of matter does not rest only on the early books of the *Physics*, in which the concept of an underlying *subject* is developed. It rests also on the parts of *On Generation and Corruption* that struggle with the problem of continuity in coming-into-being, the parts of the logical works in which the idea of predication emerges most clearly, and the parts of the *Metaphysics* in which the relation of matter and form is explored. To assign the parentage of the concept of matter to any one mode of inquiry—linguistic or empirical or metaphysical—by concentrating on a limited portion of text is to miss its richness. As is clear from the first book of the *Metaphysics*, Aristotle was dealing with theoretical ideas that had emerged from the history of physics up to his time, and he was refining, developing, and expanding them. There was a great deal of empirical investigation already built into the theories, as well as many dialectical puzzles (such as that about continuity and discontinuity), conceptual problems (such as that about the "reduction" of qualities to the arrangement and position of atoms), and linguistic questions (such as the difference between the *is* of predication and that of identity). In fashioning a concept like that of matter, Aristotle was still experimenting. The scope he was to give it would determine whether it would be a physical concept or have an unrestricted metaphysical range (in fact, it was limited to the world of the changing and did not extend to the eternal), and his theory of meaning would determine whether it was a unified concept or only an analogical one. But in answering such questions it is Aristotle's theory of the empirical (experience), Aristotle's theory of metaphysics, and Aristotle's theory of logic and language, that we have to deal with—not our contemporary theories of empiricism, metaphysics, and linguistic analysis.[16]

We turn now to Aristotle's specific physical doctrine. This followed what proved eventually to be the blind alley of a qualitative physics. Thus, it is customary in the exposition of Aristotle to pass lightly by this phase of his work. Yet it is worth dwelling on it long enough to see the character of his thinking in this field. Like Empedocles, he takes earth, water, air, and fire to be the elements of the ordinary world. Unlike Empedocles, he accepts at face value the qualitative transformations we see about us. Hence he works out what we might call a chemical theory of the constitution of the elements. The starting points are qualitative differences in the domain of the tangible: hot–cold, moist–dry, bitter–sweet, hard–soft, rough–smooth, viscous–brittle, and so on. *On Generation and Corruption* lines these up and systematizes them, using the hot–cold and moist–dry as basic opposites; the remainder are derived from these, the viscous and the brittle, for example, being special forms of the moist and the dry.[17] His theoretical manipulations then concern these basic opposites. Since opposites cannot be joined, there are four possibilities: hot–dry, hot–moist, cold–moist, and cold–dry. These are identified respectively with fire, air, water, and earth. A shift in a constitutive quality can produce transformation in the element: water heated becomes steam (a form of air). An interaction of fire (hot–dry) and water (cold–moist) can yield earth (cold–dry) and air (hot–moist). He takes flame to be burning smoke, which is, in his view, air and earth producing fire.[18]

Aristotle does not stop here. Each of the four elements is believed to have a distinctive natural movement. Earth and fire go respectively down and up, whether in minute or large quantities; hence they are respectively the heavy and the light. Water and air fall relatively in between. Aristotle uses the results both for large-scale construction of cosmic theory and for the explanation of specific phenomena. When we see him grappling with buoyancy by figuring out how much more fire there must be in one material than another because the former floats while the latter sinks, it is sobering to reflect that Archimedes' principle is just around the historical corner. Aristotle similarly puzzles over the nature of olive oil: "If its nature is water, cold should solidify it; if more of earth, fire should do so. In fact, however, it is solidified by neither but thickened by both. The reason is that it is full of air. Hence it floats on water, since air naturally moves upwards. Cold therefore thickens it by making water out of the air in it."[19]

More momentous in its historical influence is his conclusion about the constitution of the heavens. Since the heavenly bodies engage in circular motions, not movement up or down, he concludes that we have here a different kind of element, a fifth element that expresses itself in circular movement. This is restricted to the heavens from the moon up, while the four elements in the sublunar domain follow their own laws. Aristotle's philosophical one-world outlook has thus in his physical doctrine become a two-matter outlook. In the interplay of his philosophical outlook and his specific doctrine, Aristotle—caught up in his exaltation of the heavenly over the sublunar—betrayed his own sense of the one world by propounding a divided cosmos. When Newton finally formulated the theory of universal gravitation, it broke through the partition to restore the uniformity of nature. Such is the dialectic of ideas.

Actually, there is more flexibility in Aristotle's manipulation of physical concepts than appears on the surface. His theory of basic elements shifts a bit here and there. The hot—cold distinction assumes a more dynamic character, whereas the moist—dry is passive. At times the latter appears as the liquid—solid distinction: the moist is easily given shape but cannot be confined within its limits, whereas the dry stays by itself but is not easily given shape from outside.[20] By virtue of its quality of heat, fire plays the central role in most of the dynamic transformations in our world, both in the sublunar heavens and on earth. Yet the elements denoted as fire and water and so on are not pure or uniform, for the two qualities in each may combine in different proportions. Hence finer qualitative gradations are implicit in different transformations, and the picture of the stratification of elements in the upper heavens is considerably complicated. For example, the region from the heavens down to the moon is occupied by a stuff differing from fire and air; it varies in purity when bordering on the air and the earthy regions, and thus has an unstable internal balance and may be precipitated in different ways.[21] Other notions also come on the scene, like *pneuma* in some of the biological and psychological contexts, which is an ether-like, all-pervading material.[22] *Pneuma* is akin to the fifth element but operates widely in the sublunar domain. It figures in the way psyche brings about movement, and it carries out its mysterious role when some special subtle energy is required to burst into action, as, for example, when it appears as a special form of fire in the semen of animals or as a medium in vision. In general, then, Aristotle's concept of matter leaves its physical kinds empirically open.

Unlike his qualitative physics of matter, which fell by the wayside in the history of science, Aristotle's treatment of the matter of biological phenomena is still recognized as the starting point of biological science. It was of *Parts of Animals* that Darwin wrote admiringly to William Ogle, the translator, in 1882, "Linnaeus and Cuvier have been my two gods, though in very different ways, but they were mere schoolboys to old Aristotle." Here Aristotle systematically and comparatively maps the materials that enter into biologic processes, and the way they are constituted and function. Blood, fiber, bone, marrow, flesh, and the rest are examined, as are the organs throughout the body. Aristotle constantly keeps his eye on the relation of materials in this special field to the basic materials of physics and their processes. Book 2 of *Parts of Animals* contains a lengthy treatment of hot and cold and their effects, and then of solid and fluid (dry and moist). Book 4 of *Meteorology* studies familiar processes engendered by different relations of these basic qualitative changes, from ripening, boiling, and roasting to solidifying, drying, compression, combustion, and so forth.

Change

Previous Greek thought had already given a decisive place to the battle between change and the eternal. One the one side there had been Heraclitus with his sharp dicta—everything is in flux; you cannot dip your toes twice into the same stream. At least some among his disciples concluded that all discourse falsifies, for words give a misleading fixity to their apparent objects; Aristotle tells us that Cratylus went so far as to disparage all speech and simply wiggled his little finger as a symbolic representation of total flux.[23] Heraclitus' view was more than a general slogan; it embraced a way of looking at everything: strife is the father of all things, and everything is an unstable equilibrium of opposing forces, like the tense bow about to shoot. Here we find the starting point of later dynamic conceptions of reality, such as the Hegelian-Marxian notion of the unity of opposites in things. Interestingly enough, we also find in Heraclitus, though in the background, a conception of an underlying order, or *logos*, that permeates the flux and sets limits to its movement.

On the other side were a number of outstanding philosophical schools. The Pythagoreans believed that a mathematical structure underlay all phenomena. Parmenides offered a logical–dialectical proof of the utter Unity of all Being, and Zeno strengthened it with paradoxes intended to show that assertions about motion were really self-contradictory: to cover a given distance you have to cover half of it, then half the remainder, then half of that, and so on; and since half of something is always something, there will always be a half-interval still to travel. The great partisan of the eternal order, however, had been Plato. We noted above that Aristotle believed Plato had been convinced by Heraclitus that the physical world was in such indeterminate flux that no knowledge of it was possible, and that hence knowledge must be directed at a nonchanging or eternal order. Plato's Forms or Ideas are the generalized heirs of Pythagoras' numbers and possess the logical quality of Parmenides' One. They are universal patterns, grasped by the mind, eternal and unchanging, and constituting reality. Particular things are sensible shadows cast by the light of the Ideas; matter is reduced to a spatial receptacle for these shadows.

Though Plato was the most thoroughgoing partisan of the eternal as against the changing, even the physicists felt the impact of the eternalist tradition. They reacted in a different way, however: they looked for eternal unchanging elements out of whose mixture or arrangement things might be composed. Thus Empedocles took genesis, or coming-to-be, to be just a mixture, in different proportions, of unchanging earth, air, fire, and water, while Democritus even reduced qualitative change to a rearrangement of the atoms in varied congregations.

Aristotle's conception of change contends with all these fronts; he is fighting Heraclitus, Plato, Empedocles, and the atomists. Against Heraclitus, he believes in a thoroughly stable order that limits change: the world is full of all sorts of clearly demarcated—almost "well-behaved"— changes. Against Plato, he holds to the basic character of particular processes. Against the reductive physicists, he sometimes points out that their reductivism comes from clinging to a specific physical theory that can be challenged on physical grounds. (Change, for Aristotle, is a much broader idea than motion.) Other times, he works from a more general philosophical attitude, a kind of calculated unsophistication that says that what is found in ordinary experience has to be explained and should not be denied. If food becomes flesh, or parents have a child, what sense is there in denying that something new has come into being? If a green leaf turns yellow, there has been an undeniable qualitative change, however it is to be explained.

Aristotle's concept of change is therefore one of particular changes discernible by experience. Book 1 of the *Physics* works out the general principles of change, that is, the terms that enter into its definition. (The actual definition itself cannot be considered until later, when we examine the concept of potentiality.) Every change when fully analyzed involves three terms: a *privation*, a *form*, and a *substratum*. The substratum, as we have seen, is the subject that is changing. The form is the end toward which the change is headed—a boy is growing to adulthood, or a ball is falling to the ground position, or bronze is being fashioned into a statue of Apollo. The concept of privation indicates as a minimum that the form was not present at the beginning of the change. If it had been, there would have been no changing. A change, then, involves a replacement in a substratum of one property by another. But Aristotle seems to intend more than a minimal logical analysis. He takes the terminal points in a change—its beginning and end—to be contraries or opposites within a given track; hence changes in the world are determinate. Contraries in each class of properties control changes apparently not only by establishing the extreme termini, but in a causal sense. His standard instance is that colors are composed of a mixture of white and black, so that any change from white has to be either to black or to an intermediate compound.

One of the logical consequences of Aristotle's analysis is that there can be no open-ended changes. If there is a change, it is particular change to a given form; otherwise it is not *a* change. This allows no meaning to a single endless change, but there can be endless repetitions of a single change, such as the repeated generations of men, or an endless succession of different changes. If the change is of a particularly continuous sort, so that the end point of one change serves as the starting point for the next, there can be perfect endless changes in this derivative sense. The circular locomotion of a sphere can go on in this way, and he attributes this "eternal" movement to the heavens.

In Aristotle's specific theory of what is changing and what is unchanging in the totality of things, the eternalist strain is very strong. He believes not merely that the world has always existed, but that it has always had the same character—that the movement of the heavens has always been what it is now, and the generations of animal forms have always gone on as they do now. Paradoxically enough, Aristotle is here further along the eternalist limb than those philosophers whom he had accused of disparaging change: Plato wrote of something similar to a Creation, in the *Timaeus*; Empedocles had a vision of some evolutionary mechanisms and believed in periodic cycles of cosmic process in which the present world was destroyed and reformed; the atomists believed in many worlds forming by chance. It is, of course, quite possible to believe that there has always been a world, but that the form of things has undergone constant change. Later Christian doctrine, with its account that Creation occurred by divine fiat out of nothing, found this belief in the eternity of the universe a stumbling block to the reconciliation of Aristotle with the Bible.

The particular fusion of the changing and the eternal that Aristotle worked out will become clearer later one, when we have examined his interpretation of the inner nature of motion, and his grounds for rejecting evolutionist suggestions. For the most part, it must be recalled, the ancient world—whether in the Hebraic conception of an original paradise or in dominant Greek historical ideas—thought of decline from perfection, or of cycles, rather than of forward movement or of progress. Progress in the sense of an indefinite movement toward a fixed ideal is an eighteenth-century notion.[24] The full enthronement of change—the idea of an open changing of types and ends and ideals, the emergence of novel forms, the abandonment of belief in a fixed order—was achieved only in the evolutionary concepts that arose in the nineteenth century. It is important to keep in mind that Aristotle's vindication of the concept of change is effective in the sphere of ordinary experience, but it is itself trapped within a concept of an eternal order.

Thus far we have been dealing generally with Aristotle's outlook on change in contrast to other philosophical and cultural options. Let us now turn to his more specific, even technical, consideration of the types of change, their inner texture, and the conceptual formulations that set the problems for which he is to attempt a solution in terms of other parts of his network.

As for the terminology of change, the central concept is *motion* (*kinēsis*). This is sometimes used in a general sense, as our terms *movement* and *process* are used for many kinds of changes over a temporal span—for instance, the "movement of history" or "qualitative processes"—while our term *motion* tends to be restricted to change of position in space. His dependably wider term, like ours, is *change* or *transformation* (*metabolē*). This generic notion is parceled into four types. Change in quantity is *growth* or *diminution*. Change in quality is *alteration*. Change in place is *locomotion*. Change in substance, or substantival change, is *generation* or *corruption* (often translated as coming-to-be, or passing-away).[25] Aristotle thinks that every change can be classified under one or another of these four types, or under several in different respects; he thinks there are theoretical reasons for this, which are founded in his system of categories (to be examined in chapter 7 below).

Quantitative change is understood most simply when we think of mere increase of size in a body of water or a heap of sand. Such examples raise questions of contact and mixture. Contact is of course basic, involving fundamental issues of continuity and discontinuity. Mixture raises questions of evenness of distribution and of maintenance of form; for example, as noted earlier, when water is added to wine we think of the wine as increased rather than the water—up to a point. Greater complications in quantitative change arise when we move on to biological phenomena of growth and diminution. Here there are the further problems of how the material that enables growth to take place is absorbed, what the subject is that grows, and how it is preserved in the process. This requires an analysis of interaction or, in Aristotle's language, of action and passion. Book 1 of *On Generation and Corruption* is a fascinating exploration of such problems; it seeks to differentiate quantitative change especially from alteration and generation. It is philosophically intriguing because it draws our attention to the richness of ideas that is needed to analyze even the surface phenomena of our ordinary world, a task we are likely to forget in modern times with a sophisticated chemistry in our intellectual background. Perhaps we can recapture some of these issues in dealing with more complex modern concepts. In the controversies over the meaning of evolution, for example, critics have sometimes asked, "What precisely is it that evolves?" While the search for a subject to encompass the whole process may not be exactly the best way to analyze the concept, still such pressures help force clarification and alternative formulations.

Qualitative change is best exemplified in the alteration of sensory qualities, though it is by no means limited to them. What strikes the modern reader is the way Aristotle integrates the sensory qualities into the order of nature instead of relegating them to subjectivity—that is, how often he furnishes a metaphysical answer to a Cartesian-dualism (or at least shows it is possible to ignore the problems of dualism). For Aristotle, insofar as his opposition to Democritean atomism resembles later attacks against reducing mind to matter, it is more a question of physical theory. As we have seen in our discussion of matter, Aristotle's actual physical theory operates with qualitative opposites. Its derivation is largely from the medical tradition and from the analysis of qualitative processes in the biological domain. His chief paradigm of qualitative alteration is fire heating something or water cooling something. For the rest, there is the task of sorting the sensory contraries and explaining their appearance in a given context in terms of underlying mixtures and interactions. He takes on the further task of developing his model of analysis to cover psychological and social properties—for example, the cultivation of virtues and habits.

Substantival change differs markedly from all the other types. It barely seems to satisfy the minimal conditions for change, because it is difficult to locate a subject that is changing and yet maintaining its own identity. (In locomotion the full object is now here, later there. In qualitative change the same grass is first green, then yellow. In quantitative change, the same leg is now smaller, then larger. It was substantival change, we have seen, that prompted Aristotle's analysis of matter in its basic sense.) We may be tempted to say that the bronze is the subject that first was not a statue of Apollo and then became one. This may be misleading. If we consider that the shift is purely from one geometric shape to another, it would seem more properly to be alteration than generation (unless the latter is extended to cover loosely any kind of change, so that a white object's becoming red is a generation of red). Yet the bronze is the underlying material in which the statue comes to be. In the case of natural generation—for example, of a plant or an animal from seed—a persisting subject is even less identifiable. The seed is destroyed, as is the mass of material that comes in from the environment and serves as food. When the seed as a whole is transformed into blood, or water into air, or air as a whole into water, says Aristotle, nothing perceptible persists as identical substratum.[26] Nevertheless, as he recognizes, there remains an underlying material continuity, and in this matrix alteration and growth and change of position take place until *suddenly* there is a new form of being, a new substance. And in that process other substances have passed away in the same startling manner as the new substance is born.

Aristotle is emphatic that generation and corruption are instantaneous. Moving from here to there is temporal, growth is incremental, alteration can be bit by bit; but substantival change does not occupy time. If the attendant changes have not matured into an Apollo, what we have in the bronze is not yet Apollo, but just bronze; and when it is Apollo, lo! there it is. In *Metaphysics* 5, which analyzes all sorts of important philosophical concepts, we are surprised to find a brief discussion of the mutilated.[27] What conditions must a thing satisfy to be regarded as mutilated rather than destroyed? If the handle of a cup is broken, it is mutilated; but if a big hole is made in the bottom, then presumably the cup could not hold water, and so would cease to be a cup. We are tempted to amplify. What if several holes were gradually bored in the cup? It would go from an unmutilated cup to a leaky cup, then perhaps to a sieve, then to bits of pottery. Yet at any moment it is either a cup or not a cup, either a sieve or not a sieve. Therefore its generation or its corruption does not stretch over an interval; only the attendant changes take time, bringing it nearer to the instant of a new substance present or an old substance absent. That Aristotle emphasizes this feature of substantival change (though similar comments could be made about the presence or absence of a quality) suggests that some privileged status is being assigned to substance. Also involved are the problems of the nature of the instant, which he explores in his analysis of time and in his critique of Zeno's arguments. And for that matter, the instantaneous character of something just being there also holds for touching or moving: it is not possible to *become* touching or moving, for the thing either touches or moves or does not.[28] Consequently we should not expect the problem of the distinctive nature of substantival change to be settled in the theory of change alone; we have to wait for the basic analysis of substance itself.

Locomotion is regarded by Aristotle as fundamental to change, not reductively, but in the sense that whenever any other change takes place some locomotion is involved as a concomitant or a necessary condition. "Fundamental" is used here somewhat as it is when we say that energy transformations are fundamental because they underlie all macroscopic changes. Aristotle pays close attention to the different ways that change of place occurs in different kinds of change; for example, that which is moving changes its place as a whole, but in growth it is like a metal that is being beaten out.[29] A great part of Aristotle's physics is concerned with the analysis of locomotion. In what follows we shall deal in more detail with conceptual problems that arise in that analysis: the continuity of locomotion and the identification of *a* movement; the infinite divisibility of locomotion; the relation of locomotion to place and time, as well as some of Zeno's paradoxes; self-motion and natural movement; potentiality as it affects the definition of motion (and change in general); the role of contact forces in ensuring motion. Many of these are associated with explaining how movement takes place, so we must also study Aristotle's conceptual apparatus for explaining. Aristotle's answer to the problems involved in the concept of motion—as is the case for matter—will thus emerge bit by bit as the related parts of the network are traced.

5

EXPLANATION AND THE

TELEOLOGICAL MODEL

One sure key to understanding a philosophical outlook is the way it explains process or change, how it goes about analyzing the principles or causes of things and happenings. In this chapter we shall begin by giving Aristotle's theory of explanation as he presents it and then examine its scope in its operations. Its special character, and the problems it raises, lie in an emphasis on what later philosophers called (and attacked as) "final causes." In short, his view of explanation follows a teleological model. It is important to see as clearly as possible what went into the Aristotelian explanatory model, because the problem has been complicated by subsequent developments. The long tradition of religious teleology in the Western world has involved a divine plan that assigns a role to things and creatures and so explains both their creation and their operation, while the conflict between science and religion has produced a marked antagonism in the mechanistic stages of science toward any teleological explanation. We have therefore to be careful that the sins of the children are not visited upon the father. Finally, and perhaps most importantly, we shall explore Aristotle's concept of *nature* and the *natural*, which does the heavy work of explanation in his science.

The Theory of Causes

Aristotle's theory of causes (*aitia*), elaborated in several major contexts and quite self-consciously employed in specific investigations, embodies the kinds of questions to be asked in carrying out an analysis. The answers give us the "responsible" factors in the situation. Like so much of his technical terminology, the concepts in this theory crystallize out of ordinary modes of speech and ordinary experience.

1. The *material cause* is the out-of-which the thing is composed, as the statue is made of bronze. This is the relative concept of matter that we explored earlier.
2. The *formal cause* is the what-it-is, the way the material is organized, an account of which would tell us its *essence*.
3. The *efficient cause*, or *moving cause*, is the whence-the-change-

begins—the advisor for the action, the father for the child, and in general, the maker.

4. The *final cause* is the for-the-sake-of-which; health, for example, is the final cause of surgery. It is the end or goal (*telos*) toward which the thing is working or moving.[1]

This fourfold analysis of causes is united with his twofold analysis of matter and form. Form combines the efficient and final causes with the formal cause, leaving only the material cause, matter. But this is not a simple equation of meanings between three of the four causes; it rather reflects *a very special set of assumptions about their operations*. In human affairs, the end or final cause may appear as projected beyond the form: the statue may be intended to honor the god, and the house to be the center of familial life. In natural processes the final cause is the mature development of the form itself in the particular materials: the acorn grows into an oak tree whose end is simply to express in its career what it is to be an oak tree. Thus in nature the final and formal causes are one. Further, in an argument whose scope and significance is to be examined later, Aristotle insists that the efficient cause is always some activity of the same type that the developed form exhibits. Thus children, who are to grow into adults and procreate, are generated by similar adult parents; and something becomes hot only by the action of something else that is hot.[2] Therefore a prior actuality *of the same form* that is being developed is required as the efficient cause. Hence *in these specific senses*, presupposing a special philosophical outlook on how nature operates, the final and efficient causes become merged in the formal, and the technical reduction of the four causes to matter and form is accomplished. But in achieving it, Aristotle has given *form* a much more complex meaning than it had before. It ceases to be merely shape, organization, law, or formula. He has now built into it a central feature of the teleological model: form becomes *culminating design, achieved or maintained*.

Aristotle's basic explanatory model is a method of inquiry. Nature, he says over and over again, works like the artist or craftsman whose movement toward an end is evident in his actions. The beginning of *Parts of Animals* compares biological method to that of house-building and medicine.[3] The end determines the plan, the plan sets forth the steps of construction. Of course, such a methodology will operate in many different ways. What may strike the reader first are the amusing instances in which the wisdom of nature is exhibited. Bulls have horns in the proper place; they wouldn't work as well on the shoulders. The diaphragm keeps the exhalation and heat from the food consumed from affecting the heart region, which is the source of the sensory soul. (This is a more sober version of Plato's statement that the diaphragm keeps the baser desires from affecting the nobler emotions around the heart.)[4] Even a serious blunder shows Aristotle hard at work trying to combine limited observation with functional explanation: he finds the brain to be the coldest of all parts of the body and decides that the spinal marrow is continuous with the brain in order that the latter can serve as a cooling system.[5] In general the amusing instances and even the howlers are set in a persistent effort whose insights and groundbreaking character have earned Aristotle a rightful place in the history of biological science. What the teleological model does is to focus his inquiry on the exploration of functions and serviceable interlockings in the operation of organisms.

In addition to providing this orientation, the model plays a role in furnishing more specific concepts and guiding principles. Since nature works like a craftsman, some of the organism's constituents will function as tools; for example, the male sperm in generation is taken to be a tool imparting a distinctive movement rather than a component of the resultant embryo. There will also be an appropriate simplicity of design: nature disposes things in the fashion of an economical housekeeper, doing nothing in vain,[6] not usually assigning many functions to one instrument nor multiplying instruments for the same purpose. Nature is like a painter too, sketching the broad outline first, then adding the colors. Thus the embryo develops by marking off the upper part of the body first; Aristotle's ontogenetic picture is that generic features come first, then specific, then individual. The purposive element is not carried beyond the features of the species; thereafter chance may operate, as in determining the color of the individual's eyes, but not of course the plan-determined fact that he has eyes.

While some of these guiding principles may seem ancillary or even metaphorical afterflourishes, some have a decisive effect. Thus Aristotle's model prepares him to take in his stride that nature misses the mark, on occasions, for example, where the kind of offspring that results does not correspond to plan. Empedocles had spoken of strange mixed forms in earlier epochs, like man-headed progeny of cattle. Aristotle is somewhat sceptical and asks if there were also, in plants, olive-headed progeny of vines.[7] He recognizes the existence of what he calls "monstrosities"—he even describes numerous ones—and attempts a diversity of explanations for specific types. But his general explanation is provided by his model. Just as grammarians make slips and doctors give the wrong dosage, so nature makes occasional mistakes. Nature's purpose is not always achieved, and a mechanical explanation is appropriate for the failures. But it should not be generalized. Empedocles had tried to do so, using incidental occurrences to explain developed form, saying, for instance, that the backbone is divided into vertebrae because it is twisted in the womb. Anaxagoras had declared that man is the most intelligent of animals because he has hands. Aristotle, to the contrary, says he has hands because he is the most intelligent. He explains: "The hands are an instrument, and nature, just as a sensible man, always assigns each organ to one who can use it."[8]

That the teleological model can be used even further and can be built into the basic ideas of a particular field is seen most clearly in Aristotle's concept of locomotion. Such motion is more than merely change of position, although we have seen that the minimal description of locomotion involved a subject going from one place to another. Just as the acorn contains the plan of development into an oak, so different elements contain the plan of different kinds of locomotion. Earth is naturally heavy, tending downward, fire naturally light, tending upward. As every plan sets the end for its object, so every element has its natural place, the region toward which it moves. One medieval physics textbook presents this conception in full clarity: Suppose a hole were bored through the earth in a line passing through the center, and a ball of earth let fall at the opening. It would go straight to the center and stop there, for that is how it expresses its love of God. Here a transcendental religious teleology has taken over the Aristotelian picture, and modified it by having God stamp things with their nature. Aristotle's answer is simply that the natural movement of earth is an inherent tendency within it, a kind of striving to reach its natural place just as the embryo carries through programmed changes toward adulthood and the acorn moves toward being an oak. Aristotle even speculates that if the whole earth were moved to where the moon now is, a bit of earth separated and let fall would not move toward that new location but would seek the earth's original place.[9] The natural movements in Aristotle's physics are up and down for sublunar elements and circular for the fifth element that constitutes the heavenly bodies. The up-and-down natural movements would terminate when the specific natural places are reached. (The reason why the four sublunar elements do not eventually settle into their natural places is that the sun's heat, whose effect varies on account of the sun's motion, constantly changes the composition below.) The circular is, as we have seen, endlessly repeated. Other than natural locomotions are explained by contact forces; even an object thrown through the air is continually pushed by parts of the air to which the motion has been transmitted.

Aristotle's underlying principle of locomotion thus contrasts with the later law of inertia in Galilean-Newtonian physics whereby a body not subject to any unbalanced force will remain at rest or continue its motion in a straight line, the idea of force being linked to acceleration or change of motion, not to motion itself. In the one passage in which Aristotle considers something like a law of inertia, in an argument against the view that empty space is possible, he says, "No one would be able to say why a thing once moved should stop anywhere; for why rather there than there? So that either it will be at rest or must be moved *ad infinitum*, if something stronger will not get in its way."[10] And this he takes to be absurd, since it conflicts with what he regards as established theory.

It is clear from this extended use of the teleological model in physics and biology and the incorporation of teleology into the very concept of motion, that Aristotle's teleology is not simply a philosophical superstructure but a working tool. When he looks back on the history of method (in *Metaphysics* 1), he finds that emphasis on the final cause is his own special contribution to the theory of explanation. His predecessors had extricated first the material cause, by looking for the nature of things in such substances as water or air; then the efficient cause, by considering initiating processes such as condensation and rarefaction, or forces such as love (attraction) and hate (repulsion); and then the formal cause, by inquiry into the formal elements of number, reason, and order. But, Aristotle complains, reason was not employed in a sufficiently final or purposive way. (Indeed Socrates, in the *Phaedo*, had already complained that Anaxagoras treated Mind only as an efficient cause.) Aristotle insists that the final cause be the central methodological focus in all inquiry, and in his scientific treatises he tries to show how it works in nature.[11] However, before we look at this analysis of nature and the natural, some important questions remain. Beyond the advocacy of a kind of functional analysis, does his teleological model carry any wider picture of purposiveness in the world? How seriously are we to take his view that nature works like the craftsman? Did he intend by it anything more than functional description of processes? Can we think of a "plan" in things in an Aristotelian sense as a purposiveness without purpose?

Aristotelian Teleology: Readings and Misreadings

The history of philosophy sometimes divides teleologies into *transcendent* and *immanent*. In the former, some purpose is imposed from outside upon the operations of the natural world; in the latter there is a plan or design in some sense within it. Western religious teleology is generally transcendent: God, preexisting the world, creates it and designs the ways of things and creatures. Aristotle's teleology is not, of course, like that; moreover, his account includes no Creation, but offers a world eternal in its forms. It would thus be classified as an immanent teleology. The plans or designs (in a special meaning of these terms to be considered shortly) are to be found in examining the way things happen in the world; they are operative in the natures of things.

Another way of dividing teleologies would be between the *monistic* and the *pluralistic*. The former conceive whole-world plans, as Hegel traces the unfolding of reason in the marches of history, or some Christian theologies see God not only as creating and designing but also as superintending every corner of existence.[12] Pluralistic teleologies on the other hand postulate separate systems in the world, each with its own plan; what each system strives to do depends on its nature, but how systems intersect is largely a matter of accident that expresses no single comprehensive plan or nature. For the most part, Aristotle's teleology appears to be pluralistic. His science analyzes the natures of specific kinds of things—the natural elements or the plants and animals or the stars. Any wisdom of nature found in the structure of things or the way they fit their environment is evidence of an inner perfection of construction. Aristotle does, however, perceive an order of perfection in the kinds of existence, with man highest among the biological existents, and the heavens in their unchanging movement at the pinnacle of the order of substances, short of the Unmoved Mover.[13] Yet there is extraordinarily little in the corpus that speaks of one species being what it is (or one natural process going on) in order to service another.[14] Hence it is not a total-world teleology with a comprehensive plan for man at the center, nothing like the familiar religious conception of a God that creates plants and animals to serve mankind. Aristotle explicitly rejects the view that the earth is the primary part of the universe and that the rest is formed for its sake.[15]

It is time to consider more closely the use of such English terms as *plan* or *design* in discussing Aristotelian teleology. They are heavily loaded with the connotation of conscious purpose, and it is doubtful whether this freight can be sufficiently unloaded for the terms to be true to Aristotle's meaning. Can we successfully arrive at a kind of teleology that allows, to use an expression that Kant later employed, a purposiveness without purpose? One might, of course, try to save *plan* and *design* by citing occasional usages that do not involve purpose; for example, we do speak of the design that the wind or the waves have made on the sand, and we do admire the basic plan of an organism. It is better perhaps to look for a fresh term that will express more accurately the way Aristotle is now understood. The closest to Aristotle's sense is the contemporary use of *program* in genetic discussions, where a program is coded or prearranged information that is present in the cells and controls their behavior. The strong similarity of such ideas of what Aristotle is trying to express in his biological works has led some contemporary philosophers of science and biologists to reinterpret his works along these lines.[16] There has even been a tongue-in-cheek suggestion that Aristotle be awarded a Nobel Prize for ideas that reached a climax in the cracking of the genetic code! Such recognition should at least, for Aristotelian scholarship, underscore the importance of the work that is being done on reinterpreting his metaphysical ideas in terms of his actual biological researches.

The best path is to free ourselves from reliance on any one term by recognizing that the issue at stake is less a terminological one than one of the underlying metaphor, analogy, or model that the term carries and dealing with this issue directly as a problem in the philosophy of science. It leads us to ask how seriously we are to take Aristotle's reiterated statement that nature works like the artist or craftsman. This is a more difficult issue than it seems. The role and value of metaphors in science has long been a matter of controversy. At the extremes are the views that such devices belong only to the early stages of science and should be dispensed with in mature science and, on the other hand, that unavoidably some root metaphor underlies all scientific and philosophical work.[17] In between stands the view that metaphors and models are among the useful intellectual devices, though like all instruments they may sometimes lead astray; to ensure their responsible use requires close attention to how they function. This is particularly the case with models worked out of a metaphor or analogy in the career of philosophy, for they tend to have wide scope and considerable power. For example, the machine in the mechanistic materialisms of the eighteenth century and later, and the organism in the nineteenth and twentieth centuries, are as central as metaphor of the artist or craftsman in the teleological philosophies of ancient times.

There seem to be only three important analogies that could underlie the Aristotelian teleological model: conscious purpose, craft production, and organic growth or functioning. The first is too limited and leads too far astray; it is clearest as the root metaphor of the religious teleologies in which a transcendent being creates and expresses purpose in the things of the world that are brought into existence. Aristotle tends to give a subordinate place to such antecedent external direction. Even when he tells us that nature works like the artist or craftsman, he will formally say that the craftsman imitates nature, as the doctor tries to reproduce the curative processes of nature.[18] Still, to understand what nature does blindly, he often looks to what the craftsman does consciously. What contribution the idea of conscious purpose does make to his philosophical concepts is filtered through the analogy of craft production. The use of the craft metaphor in its implication of conscious purposive action had been frequent enough in Socrates and in Plato—for example in the picture given in the *Timaeus* of how and why the things of this world were fashioned—but in Aristotle the natural processes are clearly given priority. A familiar Aristotelian distinction might help out here. Aristotle frequently distinguishes between the order of being and the order of learning, that is, the logical or structural order and the way we come to know it. So we might say here that the purposive picture is first in our learning, but the unconscious operations of nature are first in being.

If Aristotle has a guiding analogy or a root metaphor, our choice would then seem to lie between craft production and organic operation. Because of his frequent use of biological modes of thought it is sometimes felt that the organic is his fundamental orientation. Yet when we look into the biology itself, the use of the analogy to craftsmanship in the detail of biological explanation is most striking. Not only is the general method of biology analyzed in such terms,[19] but detailed processes such as procreation are explored through distinctions between tools or instruments and raw materials and between these and form or blueprint. The question of priority between the two analogies in the teleological model is not itself as simple as it seems. One could ask which features of craft or organism appear in the development of philosophical concepts of Aristotle's network, that is, what relative place the respective ideas of construction and growth have in the formation of his concepts. Or one could look for the frequency and the relative importance of contexts in which he invokes each. In varying degrees both ideas turn out to play a serious part; the interesting question may be not which outdoes the other but how they interact and even coalesce. In any case we shall not undertake here to resolve any claims of priority but merely complete the comparison by noting the scope of the craft analogy.[20]

Of course we cannot appeal to the idea of craft as such. It is rather a question of what craftsmanship was like in Aristotle's time and what he had in mind. He refers constantly to the builder, the sculptor, occasionally to the painter, frequently to the doctor. We have here the small-scale production of individual objects or end-states by individual craftsmen working alone or with assistants, using materials of their own selection. It is not production by collective groups with miscellaneous materials put into a predesigned large-scale machine to issue in a stream of like products, as in the modern factory system. It is not even the case of a many-generational project with a distant goal, such as the medieval cathedral.

Some of the conceptual consequences of the craft analogy are clear enough. The four causes determine the raw materials that take part in the process, the form or shape that is assumed in the process, the initiating activity of the craftsman, and the guiding activity or plan. Aristotle uses this kind of analysis in all fields, throughout the physical world as well as in human areas. Substance (see chapter 8) has much the character of an end-product that embodies a plan, and matter and form are the obvious concepts for analyzing the product as product. Many of the details, such as the refinement of efficient cause into agent and instrument or the one-step-at-a-time character of potentiality (which will be brought out in the next chapter), can be referred directly to the analogy of the craftsman. The potential, in general, has the appearance of a situation all set for the action of the artist or craftsman to precipitate movement toward the planned result.

Such elaborations are sometimes employed in areas where we would not expect to find them—for example, in the treatment of motion as the realization of potentiality (see chapter 6). On the other hand we are not surprised to find standards of craftsmanship used in describing how nature works—her economy, her simplicity, her occasional multiple use of a single instrument, her care in ensuring that there are tools available for tasks assigned. And doubtless nature is well equipped with structured purposive processes, for it would be folly to work without a definite plan. (We almost expect Aristotle to say "Nature does no puttering.") In addition, a *constructional* character enters many contexts in which he deals with human enterprises—the ethical and political writings as well as, naturally, the productive or *poiētic*. His very concern, in *Metaphysics* 5, with notions such as *complete*, *part*, and *whole*, to some extent reflects this constructional character. For example, a *whole* is explained as that from which no part is lacking, and *complete*, or *perfect*, as that outside of which it is impossible to find even a single one of its parts.[21]

To find that an analogy of this scope guides inquiry does not disparage the concepts it helps create. (Aristotle himself appreciates metaphors as giving us insight into similarities we might otherwise overlook.) The worth of a conceptual scheme must surely be judged by what it can do, not from what area of human experience it took its rise. The root metaphor of craft production has human significance, because it was one of the earliest in which the idea of human control took shape. Agriculture was the other, but there were possibly too many elements of chance involved, and too many steps not understood between planting and harvest, to give it the same power. Craftsmanship dealt with smaller steps and intelligible and manageable relations, at least with the builder, potter, weaver, or sculptor—less so with the doctor.

It is ironic that the craft model that comes from production should provide the concepts for theory, for of the triad theory, practice, and production, production was lowest in Aristotle's scale of value.

Nature and the Natural

An analysis of nature (*phusis*) and the natural is central to Aristotle's teleology, as it is to the whole Greek philosophical tradition, and to subsequent thought as well. The concept of nature has been employed in scientific notions of laws of nature and in normative ideas of natural law and natural right, and both are somehow fused in notions of what is natural and unnatural, normal and abnormal. We do not even now simply discard such notions, for they are felt to impart something of importance, but we cannot get at the root of what is important without uncovering their several layers. Attention to what Aristotle did with this concept is extremely instructive.

Greek philosophy had begun in a search for the nature of things, but the meaning of the concept and the quest is disputed in modern literature. There were some mystical-religious components in the quest, so that to look for the *phusis* of things was almost equivalent to looking for a kind of hidden power; there were also metaphysical components, so that to dispute about *phusis* was to argue in some sense about what was real.[22] But if we focus on these aspects, we are likely to overlook the central conflict at that time in the scientific quest: the need to determine the direction that inquiry in physics (that is, natural science) should take. To appreciate the problem in early Greece we could draw a comparison with a modern science that is faced with a diversity of possible directions. Take the case of psychiatry. Is it to stress development along physiological lines, in hopes of finding that organic problems are the source of mental illness? Is mental illness to be understood rather as functional maladjustment in life situations? Or can we leap directly to the chemistry of the body and seek therapy through novel drugs? Or is there a realm of psychological entities, such as that envisaged in some psychoanalytic theories, whose inner laws would provide the clues for therapy? Each proposes a different path for the systematization of the science, a different mode of explaining phenomena, a different way of applying and dealing with problems. There are as yet no assured procedures for deciding the correctness of any one viewpoint, or for synthesizing opposites, or for pinpointing decisive phenomena that would play the critical role in verifying theoretical claims. Hence there is a crystallization of separate schools, each internally reinforced by a kind of self-assurance of consistency in elaboration, and by mutual disparagement.

Physics in Aristotle's day was like that. Competing schools of thought proposed different answers to the search for the *phusis* of things and developed competing schemes for understanding physical phenomena. Was the nature of things to be found in macroscopic material elements such as fire or air, or in qualities such as hot or cold, or in microscopic entities such as Democritean atoms, or in mathematical entities such as numbers or geometric shapes? At issue were the terms to be used in describing the states of a physical system, the terms that would enter into the laws to be used for explaining phenomena. What was to be the form that the laws would take in physical explanation? Were they to join a prior to a subsequent state by some relation of causal necessity (as we might say that if heat is applied to a metal, the metal must expand)? Or could they instead relate means-states to end-states that are emerging or aimed at (as we might say that if there is to be a house, certain materials must be furnished)? Aristotle makes a great deal of such contrasts.

A theory about *phusis* thus contains or packs away answers to the whole method of physical inquiry. It is no wonder that once it is done and Aristotle has established his account, his rebuke to some proposals will be an outraged "But to do this is to do away with nature (*phusis*)!" Or again, that he will feel it necessary to say it is obvious that there is nature or that nature exists.

Aristotle's formal account of nature is that it is a principle of motion and rest within a thing—that within a thing which determines basically what the thing does when it is being itself. Thus not every act or motion is natural to a thing. To unpack the idea we must therefore look for the actual criteria of the natural that Aristotle employs in different fields.

The primary way Aristotle identifies nature in her works is by finding out *what happens universally or for the most part*. In short, he looks for the exhibition of law, regularity, or order. In the perfect heavenly array he expects strict universal order, in the sublunar domain only for-the-most-part or probable order. Thus exceptions as such need not disprove the allegedly natural. A second criterion sometimes used is the *inherent*, in the sense native or instinctive or unlearned. This is the way a thing would behave if there were no systematic counterpressure or it had no special training. A third criterion is *conformity to essence*: the natural action expresses the essence in the sense that in doing it, the thing conforms to its formula (*logos*) or definition. (To grow into an oak is part of the definition of an acorn, but to be eaten by pigs is not.) Finally, in some cases the natural can be detected as being for *the good of the species involved*: "If it is better to do a thing in a particular way, it is also according to nature."[23] (This conception is akin to the one that Plato expressed, for instance, in the *Republic*: that the function of a thing is what it can do best—a knife to cut, a pruning-hook to prune, and so on.)[24]

The concept of the natural is attended by a few satellite concepts that deal with happenings that are not in accord with the nature of the thing under consideration. After all, it is not merely the imperfections of the sublunar but also the plurality of natures that leads to happenings contrary to nature. When a pig eats an acorn, it expresses the nature of the pig, but the same event is an accident to the acorn. From the recipient's perspective such happenings can be attributed to force (*bia*): the ball of earth thrown upward is subject to a special "external" force and does not exhibit its natural movement or development. Aristotle does not go into —but he readily could have—the way in which these forces express the natures of other forms. The term *bia* is not to be equated with our scientific concept of force; in Aristotle's usage it is much more like our idea of violence as a distortion of the order of things. A more neutral term that he uses in other contexts, as when he speculates on what force would be required to move the earth, is strength (*ischus*).[25]

Aristotle gives a more extended analysis of *chance*, or luck, and the *spontaneous*, or what happens of its own accord. He sets out to defend these concepts against those who would deny them, and against those who make a mystery of chance. In fact he reduces both concepts to special cases in which purposive or possibly purposive acts result from incidental causes. The really important notion here is the logical one of the incidental or coincidental, that is, what happens by virtue of some concomitant attribute: Polyclitus made a statue, but he did not do so in his capacity as a musical person or as the son of so-and-so, but as a sculptor. The incidental causes of a thing are endless, as are its incidental or accidental or contingent attributes. Aristotle tells us emphatically that there is no science of the accidental properties of things. It is not, then, in such notions as chance or spontaneity, a matter of something happening without causes; it is simply that the lines of connection lead back to properties that are not part of the essence.[26]

How comfortably does Aristotle manage with his analysis of the natural? Certainly, the little network of the natural and its satellite concepts is loose enough to give him considerable leeway. Any hypothesis about the nature of a thing is not easily refuted once it is accepted. If a thing does not behave according to the natural, it is possible to look for the distorting force, or assume there is one. If the unnatural becomes the statistically usual, it can still be regarded as unnatural if one denies that it is inherent. In one startling passage in the *Nicomachean Ethics* where Aristotle is showing that some laws of justice are natural, he mentions the complaints of those who say that the natural should be universal, as fire burns here and in Persia, while the laws of justice are different. But, says Aristotle, "it is not hard to see among the things that admit of being otherwise, which ones are by nature [i.e., natural] and which ones not by nature but by convention or agreement, although both kinds are equally changeable. The same distinction will fit other matters as well: by nature, the right hand is the stronger, and yet it is possible for any man to become ambidextrous."[27] Nevertheless he offers no precise way of testing for the natural in this sense. In the *Politics* his criterion for the natural is often what is best for men, rather than what is universal or inherent. Thus Aristotle proffers his ideal of an aristocratic state that would express men's nature fully, even though he recognizes that the existent or usual forms are chiefly oligarchy and democracy.

Yet even in the biological domain, the regular sequences may not be for

the good; the course of illness exhibits considerable regularity, and growing old is natural. Aristotle considers whether judgments that something
is according to nature or contrary to nature should be limited to cases of
locomotion, because in the other types of change either the terms may
not apply (there is nothing natural or unnatural about getting sick or
getting well) or else opposing changes may be equally natural (for instance, growing old and dying, and coming into being).[28] He concludes
that specific changes in such cases may be called natural or unnatural if
the latter means enforced—for example, by agriculture or medicine, or
even by luxury (which might promote the overrapid maturation of a
youth). (Even in the case of rest, Aristotle recognized enforced rest as
well as natural rest.) Similar complications arise from Aristotle's theory
of the female as a kind of deformity or lapse from the generic type; and
yet the female is a necessity of nature.[29] Obviously then, second-bests can
be fitted into the natural. In discussing monstrosities or deformities he
allows that what is contrary to nature may somehow be according to
nature "when the nature according to the form has not controlled the
nature according to the matter," though the departure must not be too
great.[30] It looks as though when a process is natural but is not carried
through to a successful completion, the outcome is still to be reckoned as
natural by comparison with some wholly outside interference.

These reflections do not really help to keep the criteria of regularity
and goodness together. Of course, in Aristotle's procedure, appeal to the
essence of the thing concerned is always possible. But this is simply
passing on a point of controversy to another field. The issue would then
be how the essence is to be determined; but the determination of essence
will not prove to be an independent process of a purely logical kind. We
shall see how value judgments of a pervasive sort come into Aristotle's
ethics and politics through the concept of nature.

There is one point at which the strain on the concept as a whole
becomes very direct and threatening. Natural bodies are defined by Aristotle as those that have a source of movement or rest within themselves.
The natural movement of the elements is explained in this way, while
animal motion, he takes for granted, is self-motion when it is not a
constrained or compelled moving[31] (compare a man jumping down from
a tree with one knocked down by a falling branch). Now the idea of self-
motion had been central to Plato's theory of the heavens, self-motion
being the mark of soul (*psuchē*). Aristotle, however, began to question
completely the idea of self-motion and concluded that in so-called self-
motion it is really one part of the thing that is responsible for moving the
other part.[32] This could readily have led him to take to pieces the idea of
nature and see what makes it tick. He does ask where the natural motion
of natural bodies such as earth and fire comes from, since if it were self-

motion fire should be able of its own to stop its action as an animal does; but he comes to rest on the view that the motion is still natural when it brings to actuality the structured potentialities of the object.[33] Thus concepts of potentiality and actuality are what support the concept of nature. The rejection of the concept of self-movement does have serious consequences in directing Aristotle toward the search for an ultimate unmoved mover, and it has reverberations in his theology and psychology. Yet the theory of natural motion survives.

It is important here to understand why the looseness of the concept and the conflict of the verdict by different criteria did not trouble Aristotle. The answer seems to lie in his basic teleological assumption. Consider the paradigm of a stable homeostatic system, that is, any system that automatically controls itself by using part of its energy to regulate its own operations—for example, a heating system equipped with a thermostat that operates to maintain a set temperature. There is a basic plan in the system; it works with a regularity that reflects the way its basic components are put together. Its well-being or its good is easily read from its condition when it is in "good working order." In a more complicated homeostatic system, such as the human body, if there are occasional hitches or disorders, subsystems are set into motion whose outcome is to restore the original order. Thus the criteria of regularity, inherent constitution, essential formula, and good of the system all lead to the same basic result, as long as the system operates according to the plan. Aristotle's teleology looks on the world as consisting of such systems, and it explains failures of operation or real breakdowns in terms of outside interference or accidental consequences that stem from the workings of other systems. It is not surprising that this concept of nature worked well for Aristotle, and that explanatory inconveniences could always be held in check by the satellite concepts.

Aristotle's view of the unfolding of nature in an individual thus presents a clear and well-articulated idea of development. But normal development is to be distinguished from evolution. When the underlying teleological model gave way eventually to an evolutionary-causal conception, the criteria flew apart. The index of regularity has become simply the mark of scientific law, without moral connotations. The component of inherent or native constitution has become simply the shape that things happen to have taken at given stages. (To Darwin, an instinct is just a mechanism that happens to have been developed, which may even in its operation be a hindrance to the species.) The essence has become simply man's attempt to formulate rationally a systematic picture in his knowledge; it is arbitrary and pragmatic. The good has become what the individual or species aims at, which may be variable or even frustrated by its makeup. In brief, there is no guarantee that the different criteria yield the same result; they may point in utterly different directions.

There are two passages where Aristotle seems to have broken through the neat conceptual structure in which he had enmeshed phenomena, and to have faced the genuine possibility of total alternatives—the primacy of disorder, with order only a secondary phenomenon; and the permanent seedbed of mutations, with constant transformation of species. Both are worth quoting for the depth of Aristotle's teleological commitment. The first is in *On the Heavens*:

> Further, the disorderly is nothing other than the unnatural, for the order proper to sensible things is nature. But also, to have an infinite disorderly motion is absurd and impossible. For the nature of things is that which most of them have for most of the time. These men turn out therefore to hold the opposite, that disorder is according to nature and order and system contrary to nature. Yet nothing that is according to nature arises as a matter of chance.[34]

The second passage occurs in the *Generation of Animals*.[35] Aristotle speculates on what would happen if offspring were dissimilar to their parents and able to copulate:

> There would again arise from them some other nature, and again some other from these, and this would go on *ad infinitum*. But nature shuns the infinite, for the infinite is incomplete, but nature always seeks an end.

To have followed the paths he so explicitly rejected might have led Aristotle to substitute something like a statistical concept of scientific law for a teleological concept, and a temporal evolutionary order for an eternalist order. Aristotle was not ready to abandon the basic commitments that guided his observation and stimulated his conceptual construction at every level of inquiry.[36]

We now turn to two more themes: continuity and discontinuity, and potentiality and actuality.

6

CONTINUITY AND POTENTIALITY

The previous exploration of matter, change, and nature, invites some consideration of continuity and potentiality. Matter as substratum was a concept developed to provide continuity in change, and change itself, as Aristotle eventually conceived it, is an actualizing of the potential. Since the nature of a thing is the source of the change inherent in it, its explication and the teleological conception of change eventually lead us to an analysis of potentiality itself. In that analysis we shall see how the concept of potentiality is itself a major instrument for ensuring continuity. Thus these several ideas hold together in a tight net whose connections are next on our agenda for discussion.

Continuity and Discontinuity

Earlier Greek philosophy had posed the problems of continuity and discontinuity in different contexts. Most sharply on the physical side, the atomists had asserted the discontinuity of matter in discrete particles in space. The fact that there was empty space seemed also to some to be a break in the continuity of the cosmos. On the other hand, Anaxagoras had speculated about a continuous material matrix in which everything, no matter how small a sample, contained everything else (there is dispute about the precise interpretation) and the qualitative differences found in perception represented a predominance rather than uniform quality in the particular sample. (In more modern times, theories of force centers were to struggle with theories of particles, and still later wave concepts with quantum concepts in the understanding of energy.)

On the mathematical and logical side, discontinuity found its home initially in the arithmetic of discrete numbers, and continuity in the geometric analysis of the line. The situation became confused for a time by certain Pythagorean tendencies to think of numbers in physical terms as well as by the general tendency not to separate conceptual schemes from physical reality. Zeno's paradoxes exhibit the resultant quandaries. For example, to cover a distance you have to cover half of it, then half the remainder, and so on. Since half of something is always something, you have an infinite number of intervals to cover. How can you do so in a finite time? This is Aristotle's formulation of the point of the paradox. Similarly, if Achilles gives the tortoise a head start in a race, how can he (logically) ever catch up? The ratio of their speeds is finite (say ten to one), so that for any given time interval of running, when Achilles gets to where the tortoise was at the beginning of the interval, the tortoise will be one-tenth of that distance ahead. The tortoise's lead thus is constantly diminishing but endlessly remaining. Another puzzle: the arrow is said to be in flight, but at any moment it is somewhere—that is, at a given point. Now if time consists of moments, and at every moment the arrow is at a given place, when is the arrow doing its moving? Is it not constantly at rest?

Problems of continuity and discontinuity have the widest scope in metaphysics. We have already touched the issue in considering Aristotle's principles of change—privation, form, substratum. His inclination toward continuity is apparent in the inclusion of substratum. For Aristotle, change is not simply the replacement of one quality or property by another, as if each were a scene flashed on a screen; there is always a *subject* (which has the one property) moving toward the situation in which it will have some opposite property. To envisage the opposing metaphysical position, one has to get rid of the subject, and see each state as separate or discrete (a scene on a screen) related to the subsequent state by nothing but sheer temporal precedence. State follows state, but each is wholly and actually what it is. Each is independent of the other. You may want to think of the screen on which the sequence appears, as the continuing reality, or of the projecting apparatus or of the perceiving eye or of the receiving mind. But each of these is capable of the same disintegrating analysis. Hume's empiricism later on carried through such a program, using sensory impressions as the units. Aristotle's philosophical concepts are fashioned to preclude such a theory, to manifest clear lines of continuity.

First let us ask how disputes about continuity and discontinuity are settled. Where it is a specific problem, it may of course yield to specific evidence. Whether matter has an atomic structure did not forever remain a secret. Similarly, whether or in what ways man is an animal continuous with the rest of the animal world yields to biological–historical inquiry. That the continuity of perception is possible in spite of a physical discontinuity because the gaps are smaller than what is needed to yield a perceptual effect has also become a matter of knowledge.

Where the issue is logical or mathematical, resolution is possible sometimes through further clarification of the concepts involved. Take, for example, Aristotle's rejoinder to the two of Zeno's paradoxes mentioned above. On the paradox that traversing a line means, because the line is capable of endless bisection, that an infinite number of intervals must be covered in a finite time, Aristotle turns attention to the divisibility of time.[1] Suppose the line is ten yards long and normal travel time is ten seconds. If the ten yards can be asserted to contain an infinity of space intervals by taking half, and half the remainder indefinitely, so too the ten seconds contain an infinity of time intervals by similar division. Thus we have an infinity of time (by division) to cover an infinity of space (by division). We must not confuse the two ways of looking at the process: the finite ten-yard line is coverable in the finite ten-second period; the infinite space intervals (by division) packed away in the ten-yard line are coverable in the corresponding infinite time intervals (by division) packed away in the ten-second time period. There is a precise correlation of space interval and time interval, no matter how far division proceeds. The paradox of covering infinite space intervals in a finite time arises only by fallacious miscorrelation of the one way of looking at space with the *other* way of looking at time.

As for the second paradox, the arrow is indeed at a given point at any moment, but the paradox arises only if being at a given point is identified with being at rest there.[2] Aristotle is presenting, in effect, two different pictures of being at a point for a given time span: one has the arrow at the *same* point for the whole time span; the other has the arrow at a *different* point for every moment of the time span, *no matter how close the moments may be.* The first is part of the picture of rest; the second, part of the picture of motion. Aristotle thus shows that the expression "to be at a point in a given moment" covers the possibilities of both motion and rest, or in other words, that "to be moving" and "to be at rest" are meaningful only with reference to time intervals, not to point-like moments. (Later physical usage does permit us to speak of velocity at a given moment, but it analyzes this in a way wholly compatible with Aristotle's point. This is not meant in Zeno's sense where the moving or resting takes place in what is apparently a nonextended moment. Rather, we have a linguistic device that enables us to say that a set of velocities in decreasing temporal intervals approaches a limiting value; this limit is the assigned "velocity at the given moment.") What Aristotle's analysis illustrates is that an interpretation that preserves continuity yields no paradox when clarified. It does not by itself settle the question of the character of physical space and physical matter.

Now how can metaphysics resolve the issue of continuity or discontinuity in states of the world? Is there evidence, or is it ultimately a matter of choice between conceptual structures on arbitrary esthetic or emotional grounds? There is a strange dialectic to this metaphysical problem. To choose continuity in one aspect is to find discontinuity coming up in some other aspect. For example, Aristotle's concept of matter maintains continuity at bottom by never running out of a subject substratum; but he has then to allow for discontinuity of different forms and to permit substantival change as a genuine discontinuity in substance. (Of course the latter could be accepted even without matter.) But if you follow Hume's path of discontinuous independent impressions, you will find in psychological tendencies of custom or association a continuity that ties them into bundles as things. Or discontinuous states of the world will find their continuity in laws or formulae that state the way they cluster or the regularity with which they occur. It is almost as if, while there is some choice in our metaphysical concepts, what is really going on in our world keeps a firm grip on our thought, so that what we leave out at one point we have to put back elsewhere in a different way.

In modern thought the idea of continuity has a very central place, not merely because a choice between continuity and discontinuity has become a serious option in specific scientific issues, but because the general formulation of philosophical problems is epistemological rather than metaphysical. Thus many questions are posed in terms of constructing a continuous world out of a flux of discrete or elementary experiences, and a continuous self over the passage of time. Continuity is sought in the basic notion of things themselves, in discerning identity (whether of individual existents or of meanings), in abstract notions of order (for example, a series lacks continuity if a member is missing); mathematical notions of a continuum are elaborated with refined logical equipment; community is a kind of continuity among individual lives, and tradition a continuity of generations. Whether by extension of meaning or by analogy, the notion of continuity, in its simple etymological sense "holding together," itself provides a continuity to these varied contexts.

It is surprising how many of these bases Aristotle touches with the same notion and analyzes with a fair degree of rigor. Just as the problems involving continuity range over the metaphysical and the mathematical and the physical, so his analysis of continuity itself has ties to the metaphysics of the One, the geometry of the line, and the psychology of touch. It is carried out in different contexts, but is a fine example of the way in which Aristotle's conceptual network, as we see it, not only derives its concepts from different contexts but is returned, when they are fashioned, for application to the several fields. We shall look briefly, with respect to continuity, at (1) the treatment of the One, which is the generic notion of the continuous, (2) the interpretations of the continuous, chiefly geometric, (3) the definitional relations of the continuous with other terms, and (4) its relation to contact.

(1) Unity and differences rate a whole book in the *Metaphysics*.[3] As noted earlier, Aristotle's analysis contrasts with the elevation of the One in the Parmenidean-Platonic tradition; there is no danger here that the One will emerge as the Reality of the world or the ultimate mark of Being. (Indeed, Aristotle's treatment of the One is strictly parallel to the

deflation that Being itself receives.) In effect, Aristotle's concern is to specify the criteria for regarding a thing or group of things as one; continuity emerges as one type of unity, and itself involves very complex criteria. The senses in which things are one embrace the naturally continuous, the whole, the individual, and the universal.[4] These are one because they are indivisible, some in the context of motion, some in that of thought or formula. Indivisibility of one kind or another is the essential mark of oneness; this is most evident in the uses of a unit in one field or another—whether the one in number or the measure employed for length or weight or speed. Theory, observation, and conceptual detail are all woven together in his treatment. Thus behind his treatment of astronomical units there lies the theoretical assumption that the motion of the heavens is uniform and most rapid; in music and language the absolutely indivisible is distinguished from the perceptually indivisible. In general he notes that divisibility is perceptibly more obvious than indivisibility; and in considering the concept *unity* itself he reckons with the kindred concepts *identity, similarity,* and *equality,* and their opposites—*plurality, otherness, difference,* and *inequality.*[5]

In these discussions continuity appears at the outset as one of the senses of "one" or more properly as part of its extension. In the very widest sense of continuity there might seem almost to be a reciprocity between continuity and the one, for whatever establishes its unity or identity in a given subject seems to establish at the same time its inner continuity. The very contrast between the one and the many, the latter as number being discrete and not continuous (compared to geometric quantity), suggests that there is a sense in which the one is continuous. The outcome may depend on the kind of indivisibility involved. Though indivisibility of one kind or another is the essential mark of the one,[6] continuity is not incompatible with potential divisibility (as the continuous line is capable of division), whereas the numerical unit would be absolutely indivisible, and the physical operation serving as a measurable unit would be relatively indivisible. Aristotle's approach is therefore basically sound in treating the one as the more general idea.

(2) Physical interpretations of the continuous are brought out more fully in the lists of philosophical concepts in *Metaphysics* 5, which give a variety of continuous forms—for example, a bundle held together with string, pieces of wood joined by glue, lines (even if bent), or a leg (whether outstretched or bent).[7] Since things are rated as artificially or naturally continuous, a conception of degree is introduced, the natural being more continuous than the artificial; so too something that has no joint and can be moved only with a single motion has a greater continuity than some-

thing that has a joint so that each part can be moved with a different motion. The case is parallel for the straight line and the bent line.

The discussion of continuity for one motion (i.e., what constitutes a single motion) is most revealing in that it shows the almost paradigmatic character of the geometry of the line in Aristotle's thinking about continuity: "Since anything that is moved is moved from somewhere to somewhere, and every magnitude is continuous, the movement goes with the magnitude. Because the magnitude is continuous, the movement too is continuous, and because of the movement, the time is continuous."[8] In all his arguments with Zeno, in his proofs that there can be no point *next to* another point,[9] and in general in his analysis of infinity and time, significant geometric properties of the line are applied to physical properties of movement.

(3) The notion of continuity in these contexts is not an undefined one. It is the culminating concept in a set that begins with *together* and goes on through *touching, between, succession, contiguous,* and finally the *continuous* itself.[10] *Together* is explicated in terms of being in the one *place*—place has been analyzed in the preceding book (4) of the *Physics.* Things *touch* when their extremities are *together. Between* is analyzed as what would have to be reached by a continuous change in going from the first to the second. One thing is next in *succession* to another if in moving from the first to the second nothing of the same form as the second lies *between.* A thing that is next in *succession* and *touching* is *contiguous.* And the *continuous* is a type of the *contiguous* in which the *touching* limits of the things involved become one and are held *together*; they are thus one and the same.

It is with such a conception of continuity that Aristotle approaches the consideration of movement, what constitutes a single movement, what kind of movement can be continuous, and so on. The full picture of continuity and the full solution to puzzles about motion rest on his treatment of potentiality, for it enables the line to be conceived as the potentially divisible while not actually divided, and it produces a notion of the point as a cut or an act of division.

(4) How contact makes action and passion (being acted upon) possible and how continuities arise in biological and psychological phenomena are problems to which Aristotle constantly calls attention. Contact is necessary for mixture and for the kind of action that occurs in growth.[11] The psychology of touch is relevant to the understanding of perceptual continuities; in explaining sensation generally, continuities in the underlying medium are necessary to produce unities in observational qualities.

The great role that contact plays in engendering or transmitting change leads Aristotle in effect to deny action at a distance, a step that reverberates in the history of thought, for it imparts a character of continuity to his picture of the world as a whole. It is involved in all forms of change, not merely locomotion. For example, fire heating at a distance does not really act at a distance; it heats the air that heats the body.[12] Contact or continuity in the efficient cause of locomotion is a premise in many of Aristotle's proofs. In the case of self-motion, analyzed as one part of the thing moving another part, continuity is already present in that the two parts belong to one thing. The case of external efficient cause of motion is discussed by an inductive consideration of all possible ways of moving something.[13] These Aristotle takes to be pulling, pushing, carrying, and turning. All other ways can be reduced to these: for example, throwing is a push that makes the motion in what is pushed stronger than its natural movement; breathing in is a pulling. Phenomena generally therefore seem to Aristotle to support a contact thesis. The difficult case of projectiles is analyzed as a succession of transmissions, with the air as an instrument, whereby the object continues its motion because parts of the medium have been moved and in turn move adjacent parts.[14] Aristotle distinguishes between moving something else and giving something else the power to move other things; it is the latter that peters out so that the last mover in the projectile's career merely causes motion without imparting the further power to move—hence that motion is the last.[15] He also mentions here the magnet's power to make what is moved move something else. Presumably it is this power of imparting magnetism to something else, and the conditions under which that imparted power ceases, that interest him, not the mere power of drawing at a distance, which might seem to us to be the striking counterinstance to the contact thesis. Obviously Aristotle assumes the power to pull is imparted all along the medium to the object attracted.

Aristotle's view of action through contact is an essential component in his view of a "full" world. As we shall see, he does not admit the existence of a vacuum either within the world or for that matter outside it, since the world is the totality.

Potentiality and Actuality

Aristotle's basic metaphysical concept that ensures continuity is potentiality (*dunamis*). This broad term had roots in the logical notion of the possible, in the general idea of power, and in previous technical medical usage, where it referred to distinctive qualitative substances such as the hot, the moist, the sharp, and the sweet. Aristotle is here concerned with potentiality especially as the ability to act or be acted upon in a specific way. It signifies that materials are so organized at a given stage that only some precipitating or moving cause is required for the activity or actuality to be realized in a given determinate shape or form. It is, as it were, the shape of what is to come, all set and ready to go in the constitution of the present. The present is not cut off from ensuing outcomes.

Aristotle was aware that even this minimal role he had assigned his concept of potentiality had been challenged. The Megarian school argued that a thing has the potentiality of acting only when it is engaging in action, and that that potentiality is absent when the actuality is absent.[16] Aristotle's attack on the Megarian theory is not wholly fair. He claims that if we abandon the language of potentiality, we must do away with many distinctions we make; for example, we would have to say we are blind or deaf many times a day, when we are not seeing or hearing. Obviously, the Megarians might well have pointed out actual differences between the structure of a blind man and that of a man who sees nothing in the dark but will see when it is light. Aristotle accuses them of abolishing motion and generation. Of this too they need not be guilty; they could simply have reanalyzed such phenomena in a language of discontinuous states.

What is significant about Aristotle's charge that to deny potentiality is to deny motion and generation, is the realization that Aristotle has built into his conception of motion the very idea of a potentiality's being actualized. We have seen that he construed motion and change as starting with the privation or absence of a specific form and terminating with the achievement of the form. The character of this process is indicated in Aristotle's formal definition of *motion*: the fulfillment (*entelecheia*) of what is potential as potential.[17] Here, for example, are building materials; building is a movement in which the potentialities of the materials are actualized or fulfilled. The end product is the house, but of course, when it is there, the building as movement is over. The same holds for all other types of change or motion. If nature works like the artist, and the artist's work is the embodiment of form in materials containing the potentiality of having such form, then motion and change are precisely this process of fulfillment.

This analysis of change in terms of the fulfillment of potentiality completes the picture of change by adding the internal character of the process to the initial principles of privation, form, and underlying substratum. Change can now be seen as a dynamic teleological unfolding of the potentialities or "readinesses" in a situation. Even locomotion comes under this description. It is interesting to reflect on how differently in the course of history the simple phenomenon of a body moving through space has been conceived—an expression no doubt of the different phenomenologies of ordinary experience in different times and cultures. We tend to see it in the reduced terms to which Hume's phenomenalism brought it, as a correlation of different positions in space with different moments in time. Before Hume, Descartes believed motion was "the action by which a body passes from one place to another."[18] (What was already built into this "action" is not an easy matter to uncover.) For Aristotle, locomotion is a transaction between the mover and the moved in which the potentialities of both are brought to joint fulfillment—the one as able to act, the other to be acted on.

Aristotle sees no theoretical difference between the natural movements of the elements and the progress of the body toward health. To ask why fire moves upward and earth downward is to ask the same kind of question as why that which has the capacity to be cured, when it is exercising that capacity, moves toward health and not toward pallor; to reach the proper place is to move from potentiality to actuality.[19] The miscarriage of a potential development is not actualizing an alternative potentiality of equal status: the body is potentially healthy but not potentially diseased, for disease is presumably a failure in the movement to health.[20] Nor is a living man potentially dead, nor wine potentially vinegar; they have the same accidental relations as the night following the day. The underlying relations are more complicated, involving first a reduction to the matter of each thing; for example, Aristotle holds that the wine becomes water, and then the water, vinegar.

What about actuality? Aristotle extends this term (*energeia*) from motion (to which it belongs especially) to other things.[21] He has, in effect, made a technical term out of it, giving it a wider coverage. Primarily it means the acting or being acted on of the subject whose potentiality is being realized; the subject is, so to speak, at work. The builder is functioning or at work; the materials are being given shape. A man is seeing; a colored object is being seen. A teacher is teaching; the student is learning. Aristotle often recognizes that the actuality or activity of the agent and the actuality of the patient (the person or thing being acted upon) are one and the same. In a striking phrase, he says that they differ as the road from Athens to Thebes differs from the road from Thebes to Athens.[22] His concept of actuality thus involves a situational or transactional character as the determinate form of activity; several subjects may participate in that activity and be expressing their potentialities.

This is the general picture. Within it there is a sharp distinction between actuality (*energeia*) and movement (*kinēsis*). While both are fulfillments, or realizations (*entelecheia*), actuality is wholly complete, the form entirely embodied at every point, whereas movement occupies a stretch of time. Aristotle's favorite illustrations of *energeia* are seeing, knowing, being pleased; when a man is seeing, he is fully seeing at every moment, not quarter-seeing because he has looked over a quarter of a page. The favorite illustrations of *kinēsis* in these discussions are building, curing, working at sculpture; these are not complete until the building materials are turned into the house, the patient healthy, the statue finished. We might be tempted to suggest a distinction between the *energeia* of the builder who is building, not half-building, and the *kinēsis* of the building materials, which have not at any point short of the end finished their destined career. But Aristotle's description of building seems to be definitely from the point of view of the buildable, not the builder.[23] The reason why a separation of the two aspects would not be congenial to Aristotle is that it would make two conjoint realizations of what is a unified happening. When he expounds the unity, he considers the possibility that the doing or making (*poiēsis*) is one thing and the suffering it, or passion (*pathēsis*), another. This possibility yields unacceptable consequences when we begin to ask where the two events are located. Aristotle concludes that the location of the unified interactive process is in the patient—the materials are becoming a house with the builder working on them, the sick man is becoming healthy with the doctor working on or in him. The same applies similarly to the student with respect to the teacher and to the marble with respect to the sculptor. After all, the builder is not just building; he is building a particular house. We shall see in a later examination of sensation how this is applied and what problems it raises.[24]

What about the building itself, or the statue once it is complete? Their continued existence is now seen as an actuality. The concept of actuality has been stretched to cover the case of existence. That something of a definite form exists now is seen as a continual embodiment of its form. We might interpret Aristotle as saying that if a statue became conscious and we asked it what it was doing, it would answer, "I am at work being a statue." The extension of the concept of actuality is thus at the same time a new way of looking at existence. It has built a teleological structure into the very heart of being, and it no longer refers only to things that have come into existence. Even the heavenly bodies, which in Aristotle's view have always existed in unchanging circular movement, are seen to have this constant actuality in their rotation.

The concept of fulfillment (*entelecheia*) is also a technical term. It is probably wholly of Aristotelian coinage and suggests perfection or completion; it is used by Aristotle as a highly general term to express the teleological character of his treatment of change or process. Both actuality (*energeia*) and change or motion are thus describable as fulfillment (*entelecheia*).

Let us return to the way that potentiality is characterized. Sometimes its properties emerge in a logical characterization, sometimes in a physical one. For instance, Aristotle distinguishes nonrational from rational potentialities; the former are capable of only one outcome, as fire only heats, while the latter allow of alternative outcomes, as medical science can produce health or disease. Again, this fact that opposites can potentially exist in a subject is used by Aristotle to limit necessary propositions about the future: it is necessarily true now that either a sea battle will take place tomorrow or it will not take place; it is not necessarily true now that it will take place, nor is it necessarily true now that it will not take place.[25] The logic of possibility and necessity is explored in the *Prior Analytics* at length, and propositions drawn from it play a role at key places in Aristotle's physical theory—for example, when he attempts to prove the indestructibility of the cosmos.[26] It is generally agreed that Aristotle leaves the area in an unsettled and unsatisfactory state. (Modal logic is still controversial today.)

Nonformal properties of potentiality are more clearly brought out. For instance, Aristotle uses it as a concept applicable to only one step at a time. Thus bronze is potentially a statue, and earth is potentially bronze, but it is wrong to say earth is potentially a statue. This suggests that Aristotle requires the full materials to be envisaged so that only a single unified activity will be involved in the actualization of the potentiality. This seems to reflect the craft process inherent in preindustrial modes of production. Modern machine production, where the raw materials pour into one end of the machine and a remote finished product comes out the other, would extend the range of potentiality.

One far-reaching principle about potentiality is that actuality is prior to potentiality. This is logically so because, by definition, a potentiality is for some given activity or state of affairs. Aristotle also intends this as a causal priority and often lists illustrations: actual fire converts flammable material into fire; the source of growth that turns food into flesh lies in the actual flesh of the body; the production of an individual of the species requires a prior individual of the species. In cases where information of such prior actuality is lacking or unclear, as in spontaneous generation, which might seem to violate the rule of the priority of actual form in genesis, he postulates that the actual movement takes place within the material, exactly as it does in a seed.[27] Similarly, he takes productions of art in his stride because the actual form of what is to be produced is present in the mind of the artist. Even learning takes place by actually practicing the activity that is being learned. The priority of the actual thus becomes one of those imposing metaphysical slogans that sometimes encourage discovery but sometimes take the place of inquiry.

Aristotle uses the principle to demand a certain kind of explanation for development. For example, he argues that whatever is formed either naturally or through art is formed by what is actually that kind of thing, out of what is potentially that kind of thing.[28] We should not say that an ax is formed by fire, though fire is used in the process; similarly, the organs are formed not by hot and cold, though these are instrumental, but by the movement derived from the generating parent that regulates their development. A similar account is given for the way in which growth takes place and is shaped.[29]

The philosophical power of the principle is far greater than these physical details may indicate. Since it entails the prior existence of an actuality of the form that is coming to be, it means that there is nothing new in the world and every kind of thing that is has always been. The principle thus expresses the presupposition of a world that always was, and always was what it is. Aristotle acknowledges this explicitly in the *Metaphysics*: "The same things have always existed, either passing through a cycle or in some other way—that is, if actuality is prior to potentiality"; and he adds, in a side remark a bit later, "Every art and philosophy has probably been repeatedly developed to the utmost and has perished again."[30]

To appreciate the character of this principle more fully, it may be contrasted with conceptions of emergence in twentieth-century philosophy that see a development over time, in which fresh and hitherto unknown qualitative levels appear in the world, often unpredictable even in principle. These reflect the open world of the post-Darwinian era; they go far beyond the eighteenth-century beliefs in indefinite progress, which are quite compatible with the idea of a fixed form constantly advancing toward a fixed ideal. This new evolutionary viewpoint was prompted by the realization that the earth, once molten, nevertheless produced in due course life and mind and culture and rationality. Its attitude to the future also changes from expecting the continuance of old forms to a preparedness to receive and to control the new.

In specific inquiries and specific fields the concept of potentiality serves Aristotle faithfully. He uses it against the atomists, arguing that matter is potentially divisible even where not actually divided. He is able to rebut Zeno's paradoxes with the view that the kinds of line divisions Zeno talks about are potential, not actual, so that the problem of covering a line by hopping over an actual infinity of actual points does not exist. We shall see shortly that he interprets the infinite as a special case of potentiality. Threshold phenomena in perception (that is, critical points which make just-perceptible differences) are no source of wonder to him, since their discovery shows only what the specific potentialities of the unobserved materials in fact are. Contraries in different fields—such as male and female in generation, or white and black in the range of colors, or hot and cold in the interaction of elements—are not seen as purely descriptive states but as dynamic sources of change or process, operating in different ways that can be discovered by specific inquiry. (Thus male and female operate as efficient and material cause respectively, and black and white are the elements out of which, by varying degree, Aristotle takes all colors to be compounded.) We shall also see how Aristotle uses the potentiality–actuality analysis in the ultimate structuring of every field, and how it furnishes him with the key to his solution of the problem of substance.

Let us pause here to take stock of the conceptual network. It has become clear by this time in what sense we have a network, that is, a set of loosely related concepts whose explication carries us from one to another until we end up discovering the connecting threads that hold them together and make it possible for them to be applied in a more or less systematic way. First we explored the "earthy" concepts (matter and change) and then the methodological concepts that serve in explanation (the causes, and the subnetwork of the natural). Then we examined continuity and potentiality, which, while themselves connected, play a large part in the interconnection of the others. In exploring all these ideas we saw what their roots were in different phases of experience, on what assumptions about the operations of our world they were hammered out, how they became generalized and how their scope was extended, and what jobs they became capable of doing and within what limitations.

The network is not yet complete. We have still to discuss the structural or formal side. The notion of form has been introduced but not yet analyzed—not because it plays a small part, but because it is so complex that many preliminaries are required. In the next chapter we go the long way round by taking a leap to the highest level of metaphysics and considering what Aristotle does with *being*.

In studying the general metaphysical network we also became used to the idea of a network and its ways of operating. We began to discern smaller subnetworks that exhibit the same features of connectedness and application in a more limited domain. They are subnetworks because the metaphysical ideas play a constitutive part in their own concepts. We first noted this in the cluster of ideas around nature and the natural. We shall meet marked instances when we come to explore Aristotle's methodology, and again—the clearest illustration—in a well-defined subnetwork of the ethical concepts.

7

BEING AND ITS PARTITIONS

We deal in this chapter with *being* and the questions Aristotle raises about it, how he confronts the dilemmas and puzzles that his predecessors had raised, the different ways of partitioning being that he considers—the true and the false, essence and accident, the categories, the potential and the actual (already discussed in chapter 6)—and his fundamental orientation toward determinate being, together with his efforts to tame the indeterminate in his analyses of the infinite and the principle of noncontradiction. This motley array of topics has a unifying thread not only in its concern with *being* but in the suggestions it produces about what experiments were going on in the laboratory of the *Metaphysics*.

The Concept of Being and Its Puzzles

Aristotle's common term for the real things of the world is *ta onta*, the plural participial form from the verb "to be." It designates the beings or things that *are*—that is, the entities of the world. In the opening sentence of *Metaphysics* 6 he tells us that his objective is to discover the principles and causes of—that is, to understand and explain—things that are, or more precisely, things that are *insofar as* they are. In short, he is studying the general character of being, not the existence of specific things or specific classes of things; this is primary, or first, philosophy, in contrast to the special sciences.

Aristotle had many doubts and internal struggles before he endorsed a general science of Being. Our analysis of these struggles has to be postponed until we have examined Aristotle's theory of meaning in part 4, for the arguments and counters in the struggle center largely on logical matters. But there will be glimpses of the problem all along, and it cannot be ignored even at this earlier stage. The reason is that Plato, with whom Aristotle had continually to reckon on these issues, had focused upon Being and related problems a veritable budget of paradoxes that was the heritage of previous Greek philosophy. Such brief headings as the One and the Many, Being and Nonbeing, the Universal and the Particular, the Eternal and the Changing, barely indicate the way in which the main lines of Plato's thought were channeled through these paradoxes. The Platonic Forms, or Ideas, as expounded in the *Republic*, provide unity in experience, lead us to the real, are in themselves universals, and focus on the unchanging.

What had happened, briefly, was this. Parmenides had concentrated on the logical method of analyzing ideas for their implications, and contrasted it sharply with the empirical method, which relied on sensory perceptions of a changing world. Plato in the *Phaedo* has Socrates tell how in his youth he too pursued natural science, but lost faith in its method and turned to the domain of ideas. The paradoxes in effect marked the development of logical problems in different areas and at the same time raised metaphysical questions of what was real, epistemological questions of truth and falsity, and logical questions of predication and identity. For example, if only Being is, and Nonbeing is not, what can we say of change or becoming? (Zeno's arguments against change have been indicated earlier.) Or, epistemologically, what is an erroneous belief about, if what it says is not the case? Is a false statement really just a meaningless sounding, if it is about what is not—that is, about nothing? Again, when we recognize that a subject has different properties and we express this as "A is B" and "A is C," how can the same A be many different things? The problem of the meaning of sameness and difference or of likeness and dissimilarity was thus posed by adducing logical quandaries.[1] Plato could joke about such issues, as he does in the *Euthydemus*, where participants engage in dialectic as a new kind of show instead of exhibiting the arts of combat (though at the same time very serious issues are developed). In the *Parmenides*, he could portray the old master in a dialectical performance in which he refutes opposite statements about Being and Unity; and the stage is thus set for Plato's own restructuring of logical problems. And he could, in the *Theaetetus*, probe theories about error, if it is not simply a substitution of what is not for what is, or in the *Sophist* suggest that perhaps Otherness could furnish an analysis of assertions of Nonbeing. Nevertheless, throughout all this he was building a coherent scheme in which Being and One and Good converge toward an apex, so that unity of knowledge increases the further the remove from individual particularity, and the material world becomes almost unreal.[2]

More important even than Plato's results is the fact that he came to rely, as did Parmenides, upon logical analysis against the systematic empirical study in which he had lost faith. This involved, of course, the tremendous and salutary installation of the mathematical ideal in science, but at a definite cost to the claims of experience. It is this cost that Aristotle eventually was unwilling to pay. When we witness him summarizing the approach of the Parmenideans and then of the natural philosophers in a given field,[3] we soon realize that he is trying to find an interpretation that will explain both how the former get off the track and how the latter narrow the scope of their inquiry. In short, Aristotle is insisting on a methodological cooperation of logical analysis and empirical study. His treatment of continuity is a good illustration not only of how he carried the problem of the one and the many into the analysis of a whole family of concepts, but also of how he invoked different sets of phenomena and hypotheses from physics and psychology as well as metaphysics and geometry.

Aristotle throughout rejects the Platonic use of the concept of Being for a single ultimate reality. He sticks to a sober pluralism and denies that Being is a single genus. Usually he offers a technical ground, based on the logic of *genus* and *differentia*.[4] If we say, "Man is a rational animal," the genus (animal) is not predicable of the differentia (rational); that is, it is not the case that rational is a kind of animal (it belongs rather in the genus of kinds of thinking). To treat Being as a genus is to violate this rule. If we say, "Animal is a living being," the differentia (living) would also have being predicable of it, for everything *is*. Being would thus be a queer kind of genus. Instead, Aristotle treats Being as a concept (like the one) whose unity is one of analogy. His pluralism with respect to Being is installed in his system through the theory of the categories.

For a long while, Aristotle apparently insisted that there was no science of being in general, since it did not even constitute a genus.[5] However, the first chapter of *Metaphysics* 4 announces a science of being-as-such, and the second chapter justifies it, and the third chapter is already launched upon it with a study of fundamental logical principles and an attack on the indeterminate. Controversies have inevitably arisen in Aristotelian scholarship about whether Aristotle is returning to Plato's ideas, what "being-as-being" really means and what sort of a science it is, and whether the *Metaphysics* as a whole, though probably put together by an editor, fits the bill for such a science. I shall argue in part 4 that Aristotle's shift marks rather a relaxation of the requirements for a science than a return toward Platonism. This is postponed here because the argument involves some questions about Aristotle's theory of meaning and about what constitutes a science. The meaning of "being-as-being" and the sort of science its study yields, together with the implications for our view of the *Metaphysics*, will be considered early in chapter 8; for whatever answers we may give, it is clear enough that Aristotle's primary emphasis in the outcome of the science centers about the theory of substance.

How Being is Partitioned

Being may be divided in many ways, along any of the traditional dichotomies we have encountered: one–many, changing–unchanging, continuous–discrete, actual–potential. (Nor need it always be a di-

chotomy, as we shall soon see in our discussion of the ten categories.)
Aristotle presents the most significant of these divisions in the second
chapter of *Metaphysics* 6. In the first chapter he stated that we were
looking for the principles and causes of things that are *qua* things that
are—in short, of being-as-being. He now lists the kinds of sciences there
are, ends up with the three theoretical disciplines of mathematics, physics, and theology, and raises the question whether primary (or "first")
philosophy will be universal or concerned with some one genus or nature.
He comments that if there is an immutable substance, the science studying it will be primary philosophy, but if there is no immutable substance,
physics itself will be the primary science. Aristotle does not appear to be
surrendering his belief in the universal character of the science of being-
as-being in either case; he seems to assume that an immutable substance
would impart its character to all things and that if physics were primary,
the principles of movement would hold for everything.[6]

At the beginning of the second chapter Aristotle takes *what is* in its
unqualified usage and lists four forms of being: (1) the accidental (or
more strictly, the incidental), (2) the true and the false (*to be* and *not to
be*), (3) the categories, and (4) the potential and the actual. Comparing
other contexts with slightly variant formulations suggests that the accidental is being contrasted with the essential, and that the essential—accidental is being grouped together with the categories.[7] This would give us
three ways of partitioning: accidental—essential, true—false, potential—
actual. In the context of book 6 Aristotle's interest is to see what comes
within the scope of a science of being-as-being, and he takes up accident
only to reject it since there is no science of the accidental at all. He goes
on to reject the study of truth and falsity as part of that science because
they are derivative, not ultimate; truth and falsity refer to thoughts about
what is the case, and these thoughts are true when we have accurately
grasped what is the case. In later terms we could say that Aristotle is here
asserting the primacy of ontology over epistemology; reality determines
truth, not truth reality. It remained for Cartesian and post-Cartesian
philosophy to experiment with giving primacy to epistemology and defining the real in terms of the concepts derived from the quest for truth—for
example, the flux of our impressions (in phenomenalism) or the belief
that wins out (in pragmatism). Relating these philosophical provinces
without a clear realization of the problem still causes many confusions
today. It is not yet decisively settled which approach is more fruitful in
resolving scientific and philosophical issues.

If we go on to the books that follow book 6, we see that Aristotle's
positive treatment of his science of being-as-being—not the rejection of
accident, and truth and falsity—actually deals with the remainder of
these ways of partitioning. In book 7 the essential and its logical discus-

sion plays an almost dominant part; in book 8 the potential–actual distinction contributes to solving the problem of the character of substance; in book 9 there is a full-scale analysis of potentiality and actuality. Thus there is a clear sense in which books 6–9 have as their subject matter the analysis of the major ways of partitioning being.

Now that truth and falsity have been counted out of the reckoning, what can we say about the two remaining ways of partitioning being, the essence–accident distinction and the potential–actual? From a historical perspective we can look at these as successive experiments, somewhat like the more protracted shift toward the primacy of epistemology that we just described. Aristotle did not, of course, see the process in this way, but it is suggestive of what is going on in his work. Indeed it fits well with what looks like the development of his work in his own grappling with the problems. If the essence–accident distinction with its categorial development comes earlier in Aristotle's work than the systematic development of the potential–actual partition, we should watch for possible confrontations between them, and for attempts on Aristotle's part to determine which will help him solve the philosophical problems with which he is struggling. The temporal relation of the two ways of partitioning does seem to fit the accepted order of Aristotle's works. The theory of definition in book 2 of the *Posterior Analytics* is in effect a study of how to reach the essence in any inquiry. The structure of the *Topics*, after the first book distinguishes the concepts that enter into differentiating essential and accidental, involves problems organized for the most part in the terms that derive from the essential–accidental distinction. The treatment of being in terms of the potential–actual seems to have gathered strength from Aristotle's physical (including biological) inquiries. It looks as if Aristotle's network of ideas were first developed in terms of the essential and the accidental, that these ideas were used in the organization of physical inquiry, that a relatively separate set of ideas was raised into the network by the latter inquiry, and that they moved in to help solve problems that the earlier ideas had failed to cope with adequately. The final confrontation, ending in an assimilation of the two subsets of ideas, comes in the analysis of substance.

If this way of approaching these materials helps make sense of Aristotle's arguments and the outcome of his inquiry, then the idea of looking at metaphysical ideas as intellectual experiments will itself have some support. We could then look back to the philosophical episode mentioned earlier—Parmenides' inauguration of the logical method, with Socrates' turning from physical investigation to the analysis of ideas, and Plato's exaltation of mathematics in science—as itself a large-scale experiment in philosophical and scientific method whose result Aristotle came seriously to oppose.[8]

Essence and Accident

The accidental, or the incidental, designates the indefinite set of properties that are true of an individual which cannot be deduced from the essence of its species or an account of individual identity. That Socrates is musical or that he is now seated are not facts that can be caught up and firmly embedded within a tight logical system such that they follow by necessity from the basic properties of his being human, or even—in a looser than logical relation—from his being Socrates. Perception, not thought working from knowledge, is required to grasp that the accidental has occurred. We might try to explain some cases by the crossing of systems, what is accidental with respect to one system being essential with respect to another. Thus it is an accident for an acorn to be eaten by a hog, but it is part of the essence of the hog to eat acorns—yet not that particular acorn. There are always, so to speak, masses of accidents hanging around, and if Aristotle did not so disparage the category we might see it (with modern eyes) as furnishing a seed-bed of continuous novelty. Aristotle tends to think of it as the indeterminate, as stemming from the matter of the situation rather than the form. Even here it should not be forgotten that the matter of a situation has its own nature. When Aristotle says in the last chapter of the *Meteorology* that the final cause is least obvious where matter predominates and it is easier to discern teleology in a living hand than in water or fire, it still remains true that on his analysis the movement of fire and water itself expresses the nature of these elements. The difference lies in the *degree* of finality; it is not a sharp distinction between final and mechanical causation.

To worry whether the accidental is itself determined is to risk modernizing the argument. That viewpoint on the issue has in its background a developed conception of determinism according to which all the elements of a field are embraced in a single system, a complete description of the state of the system is possible at one time, and there are laws of the system that relate earlier to later stages. The question may be raised whether even the early atomists thought in such terms about an all-encompassing determinism. Their antiteleological "determinism" lies rather in the type of cause they appeal to and its nature (the atoms, shape, order, etc.); they are opposing any appeal to a programmed plan or conscious purpose (of the gods). Aristotle is working with yet a different basic model, more like a time-process in which all sorts of novel features are occurring, some possibilities being continually foreclosed but others left open until the event we are concerned with actually happens. Given his conception of potentiality as allowing opposites, events need not be necessary until they happen. He can raise the question at what point beforehand some events may become necessary under given hypothetical conditions, stressing the continual contingency involved (he does this in *Metaphysics* 6. 3); or he can ask the general question whether of two opposing statements about a sea battle tomorrow—that it will take place or that it will not take place —one or the other must now be true. (This is the famous sea battle of *On Interpretation* 9, about which many analytic battles, more ferocious than the sea battle itself, have been fought.) Can we, out of all this, tease an answer to *our* question about a determinism that covers every detail, within the framework of our conceptions, and show that Aristotle is simply raising our question in a rudimentary way?

A more precise scientific idea of determinism than a general idea of causality is required. Sambursky outlines some of its specific demands: to analyze the cause-effect relation and move it toward the idea of natural law; to connect causal law and induction; to investigate the relation of the possible to the necessary; and to make a transition to functional thought.[9] We realize today, Sambursky adds, that causal law applies only to systems that can be more or less *isolated* from the rest of the world and that allow for recurrence. Attention to this has arisen largely from systematic experimentation and involves the idea of prediction. Mathematical tools enable a complex handling of these ideas. Apart from the general absence of the experimental and mathematical approaches, Sambursky thinks that the Stoics, who thought of a dynamic continuum of process or action in a single medium, first achieved a scientific idea of determinism, whereas Aristotle took a different turn in his notion of the final cause. But Aristotle may have possessed more of the conceptual ingredients of determinism than Sambursky recognizes. He did hold to the idea of a continuum of process in the physical analysis of any situation. He exhibits an embryonic idea of law in the concept of the natural as what happens universally or for the most part, although perhaps he used it for unanalyzed events rather than for systematically abstracted phases. And he had a conception of the world as a total system. But it is true that his focus on final causality—geared to biology rather than mechanics—was accompanied by a contextualism that always kept open the possibility of intrusion by the accidental and so did not make isolation a central qualification. What is required to answer the question of possible determinism in Aristotle is a more systematic analysis of his concept of necessity in order to elicit its underlying framework. This task is attempted in the appendix C, which supplements chapter 15.

Turning from accident to essence, the terminological considerations become particularly important. Let us work our way gradually. We begin with the question What is it? (*ti esti*), asked of anything; *esti* is the third person singular of the verb "to be" (*einai*), whose participial plural (*ta onta*) we met as the things in the world, the beings or things or entities that *are*. Now, to ask What is it? is to request an answer that states the what-it-is (*to ti esti*), and that is its essence. This gives us the formal aspect of the thing under consideration. This formal aspect is expressed logically when we make a definition (*horismos*), or more generally, an account or formula (*logos*), of the thing. Essence in this broad sense and an account in a similarly broad sense can be stated for almost anything; we can give an account of a quality as well as a substance. In the categories, however, substance has a special place, and so Aristotle has a much more specialized technical term for the account of a substance, the explication of its form. This term, thus reserved for essence in its strictest sense, is *to ti ēn einai*. Literally translated it is the what-it-was-to-be. It parallels the more general what-it-is, but it is more important because it is used for a substance. This, then, is the term we most need to analyze, particularly since interpretations vary. Scholars have suggested meanings that range from the continued-identity-of-the-thing, to the what-it-turned-out-to-be, to the what-it-meant-to-be-such-and-such. The implied such-and-such would actually be expressed in the dative—the what-it-meant-for-a-man-to-be, or for a lion or for a statue or for a house.

Let us rebuild this last phrase, taking it first without the initial definite article. In *Parts of Animals*, where Aristotle is advocating a teleological mode of inquiry in biology—that we explain man's having certain parts and features by the fact that they are required by the essence of man—he says, "Since this was (*ēn*) the to-be (*to einai*) for man (*anthrōpōi*). . . ."[10] This is an answering statement. Let us, put it in the form of a question: What (*ti*) is the to-be for man? We can now approximate the technical term for essence by putting the definite article before this question to indicate the form of the answer: The (*to*) what (*ti*) is the to-be (*to einai*) for man. Now part of the source of the controversy is that instead of "is" the technical term always uses the imperfect "was" (*ēn*) or "it was." The correct form, then, dropping the internal article, is the what-it-was-to-be-for-man and finally, as the generalized term for essence, the what-it-was-to-be. The use of the imperfect tense is what has led some interpreters to stress the idea of continued identity. More likely it conveys the notion of the end product of inquiry, as when Socrates would ask, "What is such-and-such?" and the participants in the ensuing discussion would at least realize that that's what it was. Thus the essence of something is the thing recognized as the object of the definition that ends the inquiry. Whatever the shades of interpretation, there is agreement that this is Aristotle's standard notion for the formulable essence (in the strict sense) that indicates substance.

Plato had raised a variety of questions that pointed toward a theory of essence. Initially, of course, his attention had been focused on the distinction between the universal and the particular, the unchanging character of the former and the changing character of the latter, the singleness of the former and the plurality of the latter. A universal in this sense could cover qualities as well as substances—*white* as well as *man*—and so universals give us the components of essence in the broad sense of the term noted earlier. Plato raised questions about the precise relation of the universal and the particular—for example (in the *Parmenides*), whether the universal "covers" the particular or the particular "participates" in the universal. In the *Timaeus*, however, the particular was almost dissolved to become in effect an intersection of universals reflected in a receptacle that resembles basic matter. This could invite a shift from the earlier concern with the relation of a set of universals to a particular, to an investigation of the kinds of relations between the universals that compose a form (or essence). Thus the issue of definition for a general term could become critical, as well as the way in which the definition captures the essence. Plato also raised the question whether everything had forms (essences)—for example, whether there was a form of an artifact, or a form of mud. Plato thus left a whole batch of problems for Aristotle to tackle in attempting to work out the theory of essence and to use the essence–accident partitioning of being in the various sciences and in philosophy.

The notion of essence as developed fits readily into the conceptual network. If we want to know the nature of a thing, we ask for an account (*logos*) of it, and this account will give us the essence. Indeed, the form of a thing, as distinguished from its matter, points to its essence; essence becomes almost identified with form.

The Categories

In the little work *Categories*, which was placed by editors at the beginning of the corpus, Aristotle presents ten concepts that have occasioned great controversy among interpreters. They obviously constitute a partitioning of being into ten parts, but precisely what is partitioned depends on the different approaches to being itself. It is best therefore to have the list before us, and to separate if possible the different kinds of questions about it.

The ten categories, given in full only twice, in *Categories* 4 and *Topics* 1.9, are as follows: substance (*ousia*), quantity (*poson*), quality (*poion*), relation (*pros ti*), place (*pou*), time (*pote*), situation (*keisthai*), state or condition (*echein*), action (*poiein*), and passion (*paschein*). In *Categories* 4 Aristotle gives examples: man, horse; two cubits; white, grammatical; double, larger; in the marketplace; yesterday; lying, sitting; armed, shod;

cutting, burning; being cut, being burned. Eight of the ten are amply referred to throughout the corpus, but situation and state are usually left out, so much so that it has been thought that Aristotle dropped them.[11]

We are faced with at least four interesting questions: how Aristotle got to the categories; what status he gives them; how he uses them; and what status contemporary philosophers might be likely to give such concepts.

There have been many suggestions in the history of Aristotelian studies as to the source of the categorial ideas. Some think he got them through grammatical distinctions: substance expresses the substantive; quantity and quality, the adjective; relation, the genitive and dative cases as well as comparative constructions and the like; place and time, the adverbs; action and passion, the active and passive verbs; situation and state, the intransitive verb.[12] Others believe he is classifying terms, as distinct from analyzing their use in statements, and is thus developing a classification of the main types of entities to be found in the world.[13] Although nineteenth and twentieth-century discussions of the categories have in various ways reflected different theories of logic and being,[14] these two general possibilities, that the categories represent a linguistic analysis or that they represent an ontological theory, have perhaps been the main focus of controversy in interpretation. Certainly Aristotle does deal fairly constantly with the categories as predicates and he does frequently call them the highest genera of what is, suggesting a classification of existents. In the light of what has been said about the relation of language and things in Aristotle, the attempt to compel a choice between these two interpretations is not very fruitful; it invokes later philosophical dichotomies.

Recent discussion of the categories has gotten away from this schematic conflict and suggested other specific ways Aristotle could have been led to the enterprise of listing categories. For example, Ackrill thinks that the categorial classification could have been reached by noting different types of answers appropriate to different questions or, alternately, by pursuing the particular question What is it? that could be asked about anything whatsoever; and there could even have been a convergence of the two.[15] In a different direction, Moravcsik proposes that the category list can be related to what is given in sense experience, so that any sensible particular (any entity or event) has to be related to each of them.[16]

A more general path would be to take the categories as a set of concepts developed out of the different philosophical and scientific interests Aristotle was pursuing.[17] For example, arithmetic and geometry (which Aristotle sees as the study of the discrete and the continuous), along with the problems of their relation and differences, would readily inspire a generic idea of quantity. Sensory experiences would suggest the idea of quality, which definitely was expanded by Aristotle to cover attitudinal qualities and dispositions. Certainly relation had become sufficiently prominent in Plato's puzzles that questioned how the same thing could be both large and small (in comparison to different things), to require a systematic study. Action and passion would come from the scientific domain of what we call chemical interaction, long theorized about among the pre-Socratic philosophers. And so on. This hypothesis need not oppose the other suggestions. Grammatical and other linguistic clues, and logical puzzles, could have led to the same result, an attempt to delineate broad generic fields for the more systematic organization of philosophy; thus substance would represent the convergence of logical interest in predication and natural-scientific interest in the basic "things" of biology and astronomy. The categories would not therefore be different in type from the other philosophical concepts, such as cause, nature, or the others given in *Metaphysics* 5. By the time they became a select list of ten they were already functioning to organize inquiry, although their special use was still continuous with ordinary use, as well as with other philosophical concepts that did not get on the list but played an equally productive role.

Whatever be the way in which Aristotle arrived at his categories, there is little doubt about their status. They are the highest genera of both predicates and existents, and he passes lightly from one to the other without (in his view of the relation of language and existence) worrying about any theory of "correspondence."

How Aristotle uses the categories in the corpus is a question that deserves more systematic study, particularly in view of the hypothesis that would relate them to his varied scientific and philosophical interests. Their use is widespread. In the logical works they occasionally help clarify terms, furnish definitions, and reveal ambiguities. For example, *white* cannot be the genus of *snow* and *swan* because they are substances and it is a quality.[18] Some of the categories help identify different sciences or disciplines of inquiry. Some are used in the *Physics* to determine the kinds of change; Aristotle tries to prove that the four types established are the only ones possible by checking the chief remaining categories and suggesting reasons why they are unsuitable for such a purpose.[19] And of course some of the categories, particularly substance, provide the channel for raising central metaphysical problems.

It would be worthwhile—independently of the question whether Aristotle came to his categories by such a route—to study the role that each individual category plays in diverse parts of the corpus. Substance, in addition to its function in the *Metaphysics*, applies to all natural bodies in the physical, astronomical, and biological studies. Quantity, as noted earlier, acts as the generic field for arithmetic and geometry. Place and time are constitutive properties of movements. Quality has a varied role. In logical contexts it is the differentiating mark of essence.[20] In physical contexts—as the sensory qualities—it furnishes the distinguishing character of elements in qualitative chemistry. Relation is not systematized, but appears in widely different contexts, clarifying, for example, the logical confusion of relational terms with simple unqualified terms, the interaction of agent and patient, the mean in ethics and politics, and the treatment of social relations in ethics and politics and functional relations in biology. Action and passion have an extremely wide application, and it seems one-sided to model an interpretation of the categories on the first few, overlooking this pervasive couple. They function in a fundamental way in Aristotle's analyses of chemical action, of interaction in physiological bases of psychological phenomena, of the emotions in the *Rhetoric*, and of the audience's reaction in the *Poetics*. Seen in this light, the categories are not merely a classification of terms or things, but embody the concepts that have come to play a central role in the way questions are formulated and that set directions for the way the questions will be answered. They become, in short, key members of the conceptual network. No vital distinction should be made between them and other significant concepts of the network. The categories cannot thus be taken as a separate inquiry but are part of the whole development of philosophical concepts in the corpus.[21]

Along these lines, a case might even be made that the two remaining categories—situation, and state or condition—are not abandoned. State could be seen as having been taken over in part by quality, which as described in the *Categories*, covers habits and dispositions, natural capacities and incapacities, sensible and affective qualities, and the form or figure of things.[22] In discussing qualitative change, Aristotle is concerned chiefly with the sensible qualities of the observational field, which of course occupy a central place in the category of quality. If habits or states of character (*hexeis*) are akin to the category of state (*echein*; the terms are linguistically related), the whole field of virtues and vices in ethics would be brought within its scope. Similarly, *keisthai* can be shown in some usages to convey the idea of actual situation in a much broader sense than mere position or posture. It would thus function much as *energeia* does in later contexts. On such an interpretation, situation and state may be seen as conceptual precursors of the family of concepts that eventually centered around actuality (*energeia*) and fulfillment (*entelecheia*).[23] They would belong to the earlier essence–accident metaphysical approach and merge into the central concepts of the later potentiality–actuality approach.

What status would contemporary philosophers be likely to give such concepts? Significantly, when philosophies began to move away from Aristotelian metaphysics and to criticize the categories, they offered substitute lists that reflected (as might be expected on our hypothesis) the new philosophy as a whole and particularly its scientific content. Thus concepts such as force, matter, measure, and mind began to appear.[24] Even in contemporary metaphysics, the struggle over the primacy of one categorial selection over another—whether everything is to be analyzed in terms of sense data or experience or events or matter and its qualities —would seem to be a successor of the initial positing of basic categories like substance and its properties. Further, there have been attempts, like Whitehead's, to invent fresh categorial concepts to do the job. Occasionally Aristotle's categories are interpreted as having a more limited function consonant with their foundational status. For example, in a work on Aristotle and information theory, Rosenfield takes the categories to be "analogous to coordinate axes in geometric space, which orient the referential aspects of a particular";[25] the rules of the classification system make it possible to locate every particular with reference to every other particular in the universe. In general, however, reinterpretations of what Aristotle is up to in the categories have tended to follow the philosophical proclivities of the interpreters.[26]

The Determinate and the Taming of the Indeterminate

There is a commitment to the definite in style and the determinate in content in all that Aristotle does. The indeterminate, in one form or another, is tamed, enclosed, and even repressed. Spengler's *Decline of the West* contrasts the Apollonian and the Faustian spirits. The one stresses order and measure; it develops a mathematics of the finite and builds rounded classical structures that are well lit; its ideals are moderate and within reach. The other grasps for the infinite; its space is infinite, its structures are Gothic in their dark, upward movement; its ideals are remote and productive of endless, dissatisfied striving for the unknown. The world of Aristotle is clearly Apollonian. It is wholly luminous, operating on intelligible principles that the mind can grasp. There are no inherently dark corners, no demonic forces that break out with unintelligible as well as unpredictable violence. Plato had made a metaphysical principle of intelligibility: the completely real is the completely intelligible. The mind was thus given full permission to delineate the structure of things and to feel assured of its results. Aristotle continues this rationalistic temper, but unlike Plato he does not offer a mystical end in which Being and One and Good converge at the summit, and individual particularity becomes almost unreal. For one thing, the categories ensure a sober pluralism throughout.

Throughout his physics and metaphysics Aristotle confronts two major threats to his belief in the determinate character of all that is. One is the view that the world is actually infinite and so cannot be grasped in its totality. The other is the idea that there is an actual indeterminateness in things (as Heraclitus proposed in his theory of constant change), which if pressed to an extreme would upset the reference of language and render things indescribable in principle—if one could even think of things. The infinite and this special form of the indeterminate are thus concepts that have to be tamed, and some of Aristotle's most acute analyses are directed at their rejection. Let us consider the infinite first and the associated problems of place, time, and the nature of mathematics; then the indeterminate.

THE ANALYSIS OF THE INFINITE

Aristotle's treatment of the infinite is found in book 3 of the *Physics*, immediately after the definition of motion. It is followed, in book 4, by the analysis of place and time, both being relevant to the theory of motion. They are also relevant to the problem of infinity, especially since the idea of an actual infinite absolute space is, in the atomists' outlook, a central feature of the universe. We may accordingly consider space and time together with the infinite.[27]

Aristotle brings the full weight of his conceptual structure to bear on the notion of the infinite (*apeiron*; literally, "without a limit"). He begins with the recognition that there are features of endlessness in time, division of magnitudes, and so on, that suggest that there is an actual infinite. But they can be more adequately understood in other ways. What is this notion, after all? Does the term designate a substance, a quantity, a quality, or what? Aristotle plays with the idea that *infinite* designates a substance: the parts of an infinite would then have to be infinites, just as the parts of earth are earth. (Would it not be odd to say, "Pass me a chunk of infinite," as I might say, "Pass me a chunk of cheese"?) He decides that infinity cannot characterize substance; it is taken instead to be a property of quantities.

His solution is to allow a *potential* infinite (in the category of quantity) in the following sense: a given object is potentially infinite if there exists some process that, when applied to the object, can be carried on in such a way that every step guarantees the possibility of the next. The paradigm case is the infinitely divisible finite line. (His favorite case is one where a constant ratio is used—for example, bisecting the remainder of a line at each step.) The potentiality is for endless process, but it is not a potentiality that can be fully actualized. Aristotle uses this analysis to give a meaning to *infinite* in varied contexts. It refines his definition of the continuous, which can now be stated as what is divisible into parts that are themselves divisible to infinity. It rounds off his answer to Zeno's paradox of motion (that each step covers an infinity in a finite time) beyond the argument already considered (that that finite time is also infinitely divisible) by showing that the infinity of the line is a potential one but the actual motion concerns the actual finite line. He also seems to derive the infinity of numbers by correlating them with the activity of dividing the line.[28]

Aristotle rejects the idea that a line can be infinitely produced, even potentially, in the same way that a designated whole line can be infinitely divided. Possibly this is because the parallelism does not strictly hold: in division there is a subject whole to begin with *within* which the process occurs, so that that line can be called potentially infinite with respect to division; but in the process of extending the line, where is the subject that is a comparable whole? Geometers never need to produce a line to infinity, only to have a finite line as long as they may require for a specific purpose.[29] Physically, the world is finite; anything else would render observable properties of the heavens impossible, or else it would upset the doctrine of natural motions.[30]

PLACE AND TIME

Aristotle's theory of space makes it possible for him to maintain his notion of the finite universe without worrying too much about the idea of endless emptiness. Actually, he does not use our familiar Euclidean concept of space. We do not always realize how complicated that conception really is, that it is a construction developed in a special way, rather than a matter of direct intuitive experience. There was nothing exactly corresponding to it in Aristotle's time. There were only different conceptual starting points in various aspects of experience: room, interval, empty, the atomists' paradoxical what-is-not—paradoxical because they went on to say that what-is-not is real (which was probably the closest approximation)—and place.[31] There were also directional concepts: up, down, etc. Aristotle focuses on place and direction, and the formulations he produces stay close to ordinary experience in that he is concerned with the operations used in locating things; but he manages to extract some surprising theses from the results.

Our usual aim in asking for the place of anything is to determine how to find it by relating to other things around it. We do not start with a ready-made coordinate system or a preassigned grid. For most purposes an indication is sufficient: a particular book is on a particular shelf in a particular room. If pressed for a more precise account of its place we might say that it is lying on a shelf between two named books standing upright on its left and right, with another book lying on top of it. But this has given us only four of its six faces. We may add that it is pressed against the wall at the back and has nothing in front of it. So far, so good; we have given the place of the book by specifying its immediate (very immediate, indeed touching) surroundings on all sides. But suppose the room is on a boat floating downstream. To know the exact place of the book we would have to know where the boat is; if it is changing place from moment to moment, we have only a partial location of the book. These seem to be the kinds of considerations that determine Aristotle's analysis of place; he examines the various senses in which one thing can be "in" another, and produces the formidable definition that the place of a thing is the innermost motionless boundary of what contains it.[32] Whether in specifically locating anything we would have to relate it eventually to the whole world to find something motionless, or whether we can judge parts of the world to be motionless, is another question. But for practical purposes we may get along with much less even than sailors did when they gauged their position by the stars.

Aristotle has thus produced an account that is very different from the depiction of space in Euclidean geometry. He was of course aware of the materials that Euclid later systematized, but he regarded them as pertinent to abstracted properties of things (lines, planes, etc.); he did not attempt to construct a concept of physical space out of them. Indeed, as we know, the question of the relation of a particular geometry to physical space became acute only after the problem of alternative geometries was explicitly formulated.

Omitting detailed dialectical issues such as whether one place can be in another place, we may note two very broad and startling Aristotelian theses about place. One is that the whole world, not being *in* anything or contained by anything, can have no place. The notion of place is simply not applicable to the totality. This did not, of course, satisfy the believers in an infinite extension. The atomists raised the question What if you step up to the end of the finite world and shoot an arrow straight out? If something stops it, there is matter beyond; if nothing stops it, there is space beyond through which it goes. Is not the idea of a finite whole that is not itself in place caught in a dilemma? We can almost imagine Aristotle answering, (1) What's the arrow doing up there? An arrow is made of earth while the stuff up there is the fifth substance. (2) If it got there it should behave according to the structure of the region, that is, bend into circular motion, neither being stopped nor going beyond. (This modernized version does not seem unfaithful to the spirit of Aristotle's analysis.)

The second important thesis can be elicited from our initial example. We said that the book on the shelf had nothing in front of it. Does this mean we approach it through a vacuum? Of course not, we hasten to add; there is air in front of it. Does the notion of place allow that there could be *empty* place? Aristotle presents a variety of arguments suggesting difficulties and inconsistencies (with other established conclusions) that would result if we assumed empty places were possible. Accordingly he reinterprets the idea of a vacuum along the same lines as he reinterpreted the idea of indivisible infinitesimal intervals in discussing Zeno's paradoxes. A medium in a place may be rarified indefinitely—imagine air being pumped out of a closed box—and to talk about a vacuum is to conjecture what the place would be like if we rarified it *ad infinitum*, that is, if we completed a potentially endless process. And this of course does not make sense. All we could properly say is that the rarifying could go on endlessly.

In dealing with time, Aristotle takes a similar relational approach. He focuses on the way we make the temporal judgments *earlier* and *later*, or *before* and *after*, among happenings, and how we determine lapse of time by comparing the changes we are interested in with other changes we use as measuring devices. He thus avoids the attitude that time is an absolute, separate, and initial framework in which all events can be pinned down. On the contrary, he ties the idea of time so closely to change that it becomes almost meaningless without reference to specific changes. Time is defined as the *number* of motion with respect to before and after; that is, time is one movement measuring other movements by parceling out the number of times the one takes place while the others take place. Aristotle does not intend to make time subjective in this account. The temporal relations of various changes hold true independently of our counting processes, as seasons change according to changing relative positions of the sun and the earth. That we have a dependable view of time-processes reflects ultimately the regularity of the movement of the heavenly bodies that we use as a basic mode of reckoning time.

Aristotle also makes an analysis of *now* as an interval stretching over the receding past and the incipient future, not as a kind of moment which is like a point. From a subjective point of view, we hold the now constant and events flow through it. Seen in terms of the flow of events, the now is constantly shifting; it characterizes moving reality, with the past an unchangeable record and the future not yet existent.

Aristotle's analysis has sometimes been criticized as circular because he uses the notions *before* and *after* in his definition of time although they already seem to presuppose time. He could have taken change to be prior to time in the order of learning and time to be prior to change in the order of reality. But that is precisely the view he is rejecting. Time is a dimension of change; change—or rather things changing—is the primary feature of the world. Absolute notions of time and space are not antecedent elements in our idea of reality; we build up relational notions of time and space as we discover or construct the relations themselves. In

Aristotle's view of time, the world is clearly not *in* time any more than it is *in* place; instead, the endlessness of time reflects the continuous endless revolving of the heavens. It is this belief in a constant endless movement that turns Aristotle's clearly relational concept of time into an absolute framework. But time in any case is within the world and cannot be an independent matrix in which worlds come and go.

ARISTOTLE'S VIEW OF MATHEMATICS

Before considering the concept of indeterminateness, it is necessary to look briefly at Aristotle's view of mathematics in general.[33] The key to a particular type of rationalism lies in the way it relates the order of mathematical entities to existent (usually sensory) entities. Plato's position is clear. He wants to formalize as much as possible and to forget the sensory, thereby getting closer to what he regards as eternal reality. The empiricist might take the opposite stand: to concretize and see mathematical propositions as convenient summaries of existent sensory patterns. Modern mathematics need be neither rationalistic in the Platonic sense, nor empiricist in the opposing sense. Yet instead of making some synthesis, it demands both a maximum of formalization in its pure development (this is often construed simply as dealing with linguistic expressions), and a large measure of concretization in empirical operations when a mathematical structure is to be applied. This mathematical structure need not be regarded as an independent reality, but can be used as a kind of model to be articulated fully and systematically and applied wherever the model features are empirically found to be applicable. (Of course mathematicians differ; and there is still an ample supply of Platonists.)

Aristotle's conception of mathematics seems to fall between the Platonic and the modern as described above, but in such a way as to leave us in doubt whether he is multiplying the virtues or the vices. Mathematics in his view deals with the features of things that can be separated in thought (that is, abstracted) and held separate; in this lies its difference from physics. Aristotle's favorite simple analogy is the difference between *snub* and *curved*. The former is physics because it embodies a reference to the nose; the latter can be separated in thought from any specific embodiment, and geometry can go on its happy, independent way. So far, Aristotle has piled up the advantages. Mathematics has no Platonic self-subsistent realm for itself; it stems from the one world and has an existential reference. Yet it can be independently developed; the mathematician need not stop to make measurements in the midst of his intellectual proofs. But from here on the central difficulty descends upon us; for Aristotle adds about the mathematical attributes, "They are separable from motion in thought, and it makes no difference, nor does any falsity result if they are separated."[34] Now a modern for whom the relation of pure and applied mathematics is the crucial issue will ask how Aristotle knows that no falsity results. For example, if the abstracted line is continuously divisible, can we argue that matter is continuously divisible physically, not merely in geometric thought? Aristotle does, and accordingly rejects the atomist view of discrete ultimate particles. Similar problems arise in his treatment of sensory discrimination in *On Sense and Sensible Objects*; he saves himself only by arguing that what is below the sensory threshold is *potentially* sensible. At many critically important points throughout the works, his analysis of mathematics pulls a veil over the legitimacy of passing from the logical or mathematical to the physical.

And yet he is conscious of something like our modern view of the issue when he attacks the Platonists immediately after the passage quoted above. For he says that they separate physical objects like flesh, bone, and man in the same way; and these are like *snub*. Yet if so, and if motion is the differentiating feature between physics and mathematics, then the domain where mathematics cannot go astray should be severely limited: even the geometry of the sphere would not guarantee the precise properties of the actually revolving sphere, but only tell us what it would be like if it continued to satisfy the geometrical conditions. Aristotle could have gone in this direction, but did not. He does not, therefore, face the central problem in the relation of mathematics and physics in our contemporary sense, though we shall have to ask whether he does not meet it partway, on his own quite different terms. It is not that he was unaware of the problem. It is rather that somehow he would not formulate it in a way that makes our modern sharp distinction of pure and applied mathematics central. But we must not leave the matter here. Aristotle is too keen to have simply overlooked or ignored an issue. It must be that some other elements in his perspective barred him from concern with our formulation. One of these is clear enough: mathematical entities are abstracted in thought; we may thus expect to find some explanation of the problem in his specific theory of thought. Another is that his epistemology required no *general* idea of existence. We shall examine these issues and how far he goes to meet our modern concerns when we consider his psychology and his theory of knowledge.

CONFRONTATION WITH THE INDETERMINATE

Aristotle's major confrontation with the indeterminate takes place in *Metaphysics* 4, where he enunciates as the most certain principle of all, and as a prototype of philosophical truth, what has come to be called the law of noncontradiction: "The same attribute cannot at the same time

belong and not belong to the same subject and in the same respect."
Moreover, he says, we must add any further qualifications required to
meet logical difficulties.[35] We have here the beginnings of a long and important chapter in the history of philosophical controversy. Logic books
have traditionally cited three principles as the basic laws of classical
logic: (1) identity: A is A; (2) noncontradiction: A cannot be both B and
not B at the same time and in the same respect; and (3) excluded middle:
A is either B or not B. Sometimes they raise the general question whether
these are proposed as laws of things or laws of thought, that is, as general
features of existence or conditions for the possibility of thinking something. With the modern formalization of logic, the laws are sometimes
translated into (1) p implies p: if a proposition is true, it is true; (2) not
both p and not p: a proposition is not both true and false; and (3) p or
not p: a proposition is either true or false. In this form it is clear that
these laws express what we mean when we call something a proposition. Since a proposition is commonly defined as an expression to which
one and only one of the values *true* or *false* may be significantly assigned, these laws are analytically necessary or follow by definition. But
of course, this formalization is unconcerned with the material truth of
the laws, in the sense that Aristotle claimed them to be laws of all that is.
In what sense then did he make this claim? Or did he make several
different claims?

Although very compact, book 4 is extremely rich, and deals with many
more topics than contemporary summaries recognize. It shows Aristotle
fighting the indeterminate on several fronts. Immediately after stating the
principle of noncontradiction, he directs it against Heraclitus, and in the
course of the arguments the principle comes to play a multitude of roles.
Let us distinguish these. It is a *principle of demonstration or proof*; since
it is presupposed in all proofs, those who want to prove it show their
ignorance of the nature of proof in demanding proof for everything. It is
a *principle of significance*, as can be shown if a man will only say something; if he won't he's no better than a vegetable! Here Aristotle is careful
to state that he is not asking for a proposition that is true or false, but for
any term meaningful to the utterer or to another, that is, simply a basic
unit of communication. It is a *principle of limitation of meanings*, for a
term cannot have infinite meanings. If it has several distinguishable ones,
each can be assigned a different word; not to have one meaning is to have
no meaning. (And presumably if a word meant something different every
time it was used, then communication would be impossible, or else a
mystery.)

So far the principle has led us to recognize that if *man* means "two-
footed animal" and if it is true of one and the same thing that it is a man,
it will be true of it that it is two-footed. It cannot be a man and not a

man. But we have not yet been assured that there is any one and the same thing that we can truly say is a man. This is yet to be considered. Even with respect to discourse, however, Aristotle goes on to treat his principle as a *principle of essence*. That is, those who deny the principle would annihilate the distinction between essence and accident and treat all attributes as accidents. They would be implying that particulars are only congregations of accidents rather than possessed of an essential nature. But Socrates is essentially human, only accidentally white. In short, Aristotle sees his principle as carrying the burden of his doctrine of essence.

Aristotle moves on from the indeterminate in meaning to face the question of the indeterminate in existence and the possibility of true assertion about existence. To assert contradictory predicates about an existent is to imply that nothing can truly inhere in that existent; this could end up in Anaxagoras' view that all things are mixed together. And Aristotle adds: "They [Anaxagoras and Protagoras] seem then to be speaking of the indeterminate, and though they think they are speaking of what is, they are speaking of what is not; for what is potentially but not actually is the indeterminate."[36] At this point, the principle seems to operate as a *principle of fixity in existence*: to be something is to be determinate and so maintain some character for a while.

Again, if existence does not have such determinateness, and a man can say both yes and no at the same time, why does he go on doing determinate things, like taking a walk to Megara, or not walking over a precipice? Here we have an appeal to a *principle of pragmatic utility*. We require noncontradiction in our behavior, however much we deny it polemically.

The end has not been reached in even these varied interpretations. Aristotle goes on to treat the principle in epistemological and ontological dimensions. He probes Protagoras' view that all sensible appearances and opinions are true, and the Heraclitean insistence on permeating flux. Against these he sets up a reality to which sensation refers and by which it is tested; to the domain of movement he adds an unchanging reality. The discussion is complex, and careful analysis is required to distinguish where he is appealing to his own doctrinal belief in a realm of fixity, where applying his conceptual structure (as when he argues that change cannot prove Heraclitus' view because the idea of change implies a constant subject during change), and where he is showing that knowledge such as we have would not exist if these extremist views were correct. This at least is clear throughout, that he regards his principle as a *principle of determinate order in existence*, as well as in thought and discourse and utility.

If this multiplicity of roles for the principle of noncontradiction is recognized, then historical controversy about the matter cannot be dismissed offhand, whether it be the original conflict between the Heracliteans and the Aristotelians or the later Hegelian and Marxian claims for a dialectical logic of contradiction against the classical Aristotelian logic. It is possible to take issue with Aristotle's principle in many if not all of its meanings. The theoretical possibility of many-valued logics undermines its primacy as a law of demonstration. With respect to essence and accident, there are other modes of specifying meaning, of a looser sort than his formal theory of definition allows. With respect to fixity in existence, the Heraclitean perspective may have greater weight than the partisans of fixed order have believed; in any case, this is a problem of physical evidence. Aristotle's principle is perhaps most impregnable when it is applied to the structure of system and communication. Even three-valued logics may require a two-valued metalogic somewhere up the scale: if a proposition allows of three possible values, then it either has a given one of them or it has not. Communication requires some degree of determinateness in symbols. Action requires determinateness too, although perhaps less than some of our cultural systems have embodied in their peremptory demands (for instance, that a deed is either right or wrong, in morality). All these are different issues, each of which would require its own formulation and mode of solution.

8

SUBSTANCE AND THE SUBSTANCES

We saw in the previous chapter that Aristotle staked out and legitimized (at the beginning of *Metaphysics* 4) a science of being-as-such, and then launched directly into a discussion of the laws of logic as the first topic of the new science. In the history of Aristotelian interpretation the relation of that science to the treatment of substance has been a matter of controversy. Aristotle seems to recognize a close connection between the science of being-as-such and his effort to identify substance. In his introduction to the science, he says, "In every case knowledge is chiefly of what is primary, that is, of that upon which other things depend and from which they get their names. If then this is substance, the principles and causes of substance are what the philosopher needs to have."[1] In *Metaphysics* 7, where he gets down to the business of analyzing substance, he remarks at the end of the introductory chapter that "indeed, the question that was raised long ago and is raised now and always, and is always a problem, *what being is*, this is what substance is."[2] He adds that it is our chief and practically sole concern. Obviously, then, this close relation between being and substance must be a serious consideration in any interpretation of the nature of the new science.[3] Aristotle also calls the science of being-as-such "first philosophy," and of course after Andronicus' ancient edition it came to be known as metaphysics, and later as ontology.

Our attention here is to only two of the three related concepts, being, being-as-being, and substance. Being was analyzed in the previous chapter. Being-as-being is the subject of the science, and substance, whatever it prove to be, is central to that science. In English translation, substance seems to stand farther away from the other two than it does in the Greek, where its original term, *ousia*, is simply a noun derived from a participial form of the verb "to be." Of the three, being-as-being was the last to be made into a technical notion. Being and substance were already included in the early analysis of concepts in *Metaphysics* 5, in chapters 7 and 8 respectively. There Aristotle assigned two meanings to the term *substance*: ultimate subject (as in the *Categories*), and separate existence.

Behind Aristotle there lay a formative period of metaphysical language, in which there was considerable play with the concept of being. When the atomists called space *the-what-is-not*, they also asserted that it *is*, in the familiar sense *being real*. Plato (in the *Republic*) used such expressions as *what-altogether-is* (*to pantelōs on*) in the sense *the completely real*; this he equated with the eternal. The changing (in contrast with the unchanging) he described as what is and is not, an intermediate between being and nonbeing. Aristotle too fashioned a technical vocabulary for his own inquiry into reality, that is, for his inventory of the kind of entities there are in the world and his deliberations as to which one of these deserves the ultimate label Substance: whatever candidate, from Platonic form to concrete individual, from universal to lines and points and numbers, from matter to genus or species, or any unexpected starter in the lineup, wins this "contest" and is decorated with the crown of Substance will hold the key to what the real is. That is why there is so fierce a struggle for the "office" of substance.

The textual sources for this story are *Metaphysics* 7 and 8, which we may call by their familiar Greek titles, Zēta and Ēta. Zēta is long and involved, and raises all sorts of problems and explores them. Ēta is short and offers a solution. Together they are Aristotle's richest treatment of substance since the early *Categories*, where substance was identified as simply the individual things of the world, the natural bodies of biology and physics and astronomy. There are so many issues raised in Zēta, so many discussions of the different candidates and why they are to be rejected, and so many digressions, that some chapters have been thought to be spurious additions or else interpolations drawn from other works in the different strata of Aristotle's development. These explanations do not seem to be enough. We may suspect that just as in the case of the categories, there is some more basic philosophical tangle involved.

Our present task in this chapter is not to offer a commentary on Zēta and Ēta. It is in part to outline the story of the contest for the office of substance and to identify the winner. More important even than that is to promote an understanding of what the whole contest is about. We find in Zēta a variety of explicit and implicit criteria for rejecting candidates, and these give some clues to what the winner should be. But we must not expect an easy answer, for Aristotle is asking the question that goes down through the history of philosophy as What is metaphysics—what is the nature of reality? Different metaphysical theorists naturally have decided that he has pointed the answer in their direction. My interpretation shares this difficulty. But it hopes, by continuing the themes of previous chapters and by taking advantage of the insights of interpretations already in the field from different philosophical standpoints, to throw additional light on what Aristotle is doing here.

In this chapter I accordingly look first at the kinds of interpretations that have been offered of what Aristotle is doing in his science of being-as-being, and then attempt to make some sense of the contest for substance and the choice of its winner—no secret is revealed by stating in advance that it is essence, or essential form. After this I examine form and its relation to the individual, the title-holder from the *Categories*, and ask whether Aristotle has really changed his mind in running the new contest. Finally, I review Aristotle's actual inventory of substances in the world, which raises the important issue of the existence and character of the Unmoved Mover. I conclude this over-burdened chapter with a brief reflection on the historical eclipse of some of Aristotle's concepts.

Interpretations of Being-as-Being

The conflict of interpretations of being-as-being has been extreme and takes place in several arenas. One is the grammatical interpretation of the term itself. A second is the interests that are brought to bear on the analysis of what Aristotle is doing in moving from being-as-being to substance. A third is the battle over the body of the book, the *Metaphysics*—somewhat reminiscent, at times, of the battle that raged over the fallen Patroclus in Homer's *Iliad*. This struggle to determine an accurate text is relevant to us because presumably the book is the original example of the new science in action, so that what is ruled authentic or spurious, what is judged an editor's or a later philosopher's interpolation, or an earlier stratum in Aristotle himself, cannot but affect our perception of what metaphysics is about. Each of these three main interpretive issues may be approached from a number of angles. In each stage of the discussion that follows, I have contented myself with touching on the principal approaches—theological, naturalistic, linguistic-analytic, and Kantian—as necessary. I conclude with my own hypotheses.

On the grammatical level there are various readings of the term *being-as-being* itself. For example, one takes *as-being* to qualify the initial being or pure being or being without qualification, unconditioned being. A second takes the qualification to be more abstractive and generic, designating simply the general traits that a thing has to have in order to be. A third takes it adverbially, as indicating rather how we study being than what being is.[4] These interpretations lead in different philosophical directions. The first heads toward the ultimate contemplation of unchanging or divine being. The second aims for a science of the fundamental characteristics that anything that exists must have if it is to be and to be known. The third steers in a Kantian direction, in hopes of discovering the necessary universal ways in which we organize experience and our world as a whole.[5]

These different attitudes extend into attempts to explicate Aristotle's account of the science of being-as-being and to describe what it covers. Aristotle speaks simply of being-as-being and its forms.[6] The religious or theological interpretation would move on rapidly from the science of being-as-being to concentrate on the science of substance, encouraged by Aristotle's insistence, early on, that indeed substance is the key to finding unity in the different forms or senses of being: "For some things are said to be because they are substances; others, because they are conditions of substance; others, because they are a path to substance, or destructions or privations of substance, or productive or generative of substance or of what is said in relation to substance, or negations of any of these or of substance."[7] As Aristotle's thought developed, his speculations progressed from the natural world to the categories, and from the several categories to substance as the basic one, and from this idea of the primacy of substance to an investigation of the kinds of substances. The theological interpretation assumes that in this last refinement he continued his search for primacy and that the eternal or unchangeable substance was to his mind more fundamental than the other kinds. (The sections of the corpus that speak of the Unmoved Mover obviously support this view.) Ultimately, then, from this standpoint metaphysics would be an attempt to discover the special kind of substance that is the divine, and the Aristotelian search for substance would be a religious one, whether it takes the form of a reversion to Platonic metaphysics or is carried beyond in Aquinas.

Naturalistic approaches tend to see Aristotle's metaphysical science as an effort to do on a more general level what other sciences do in special provinces. Many of Aristotle's remarks in the *Metaphysics* fall into this pattern of scientific inquiry. In addition his initial exploration in the new science is into the laws of logic; the logical principle of noncontradiction is shown to be also a fundamental law of being. The categories, and potentiality and actuality, and matter and form, are similarly pervasive features of things that are. In this sense, the search for substance can be interpreted as an attempt to exhibit the structures in the world that serve as starting points for any inquiry, whether it is logical or physical.

Linguistic interpretations generally see Aristotle's work in his metaphysics as primarily linguistic-conceptual analysis, first of the senses of *is* and then of the many special problems of logic and linguistic usage that emerge when he gets down to analyzing substance. Indeed, in a great part of Zēta, though not all, questions are approached via the theory of definition and the differences between essential and accidental predication. This carries us into the logical problems of what is later called essentialism (how we determine the essence of anything) and whether—in later Kantian language—essentialist statements are synthetic or analytic, and similarly into contemporary controversies over modal logic. Linguistic interpretations do not necessarily beget Kantian interpretations, but often the language of conceptual analysis (rather than simply linguistic analysis) inclines in that direction.

These several kinds of approach each explain from different contexts and in different measure what Aristotle is doing as he works his way. through the new science, and so they have been offered as interpretations of what his metaphysics is actually about. Kantian interpretations are less satisfactory in this respect, since Aristotle so clearly intends to be a realist (whether he succeeds or not) insofar as he thinks he is telling us what the world is like, not what conceptual apparatus we bring to the ordering of experience by virtue of our inherent makeup. But of course it is possible to discern in Aristotle's discussions such vital features as universal scope and necessity, which can then be interpreted as governing Aristotle's contribution to the science.[8]

It is beyond our present investigation to consider problems of the constitution and the origin of the *Metaphysics* as part of the Aristotelian corpus. But it should be remarked here that technical issues of textual scholarship must often be brought into our interpretation of Aristotle's science of being-as-being, for the book provides the primary initial material we have to work with in deciding what his science is like. For example, book 11 includes extracts from Aristotle's *Physics*. It is widely believed to be a later editor's addition. Now since some of these extracts deal with motion, does this mean that the analysis of motion was intended to be a part of the science of being-as-being, or not? The issue is whether a sharp line should be drawn between physics and metaphysics. Again, book 5, often referred to as the philosophical lexicon, is taken to be an earlier separate work, perhaps put in by an editor. If it is simply concerned with linguistic usage (and this is a separate issue), should we allow its character and contents to influence our conception of Aristotle's metaphysical science? In general, the various attempts to find a unified structure in the *Metaphysics* as it appears in the corpus have been as complex as the inquiries on which they rest—the scholar's criticism of the text and the philosopher's hypothesis about the science—and these cannot always be kept apart.[9]

The lines that my own interpretation follows may be summed up briefly:

(1) Basically, Aristotle's science of being-as-being is fairly inclusive. It contains the concepts that in their interrelations make up what we have called his conceptual network. There is no sharp distinction between the concepts that appear in the *Metaphysics* and those that are found in the *Physics*. Laws of logic, general concepts of being and the one, different ways in which the world is partitioned, even concepts more abstract than those that do the chief analytic and scientific work—for example, part and whole, and principle (*archē*)—all have a place. Substance gains its prominence because different lines of inquiry or analysis all converge on it.

(2) There is no need to assume that Aristotle had only one motive in dealing with substance; different interests may well have operated at different points. It was suggested (in chapter 7) that the heavy work of explicating substance was done in the logical mode of Aristotle's earlier thought, in which the essence–accident dichotomy was a dominant feature, though religious and scientific interests lay in the background; that his interests in the foundations of science were pervasive in the physical (including biological) works; and that the analysis of substance (in Zēta and Ēta) is the scene of a shift in which modes of thought characteristic of the scientific inquiries are found capable of solving the problems generated in the logical analysis. Here the religious interest has a more tangential role in the actual solution.

(3) The interpretations we have examined—even the naturalistic one, which takes metaphysics as a general science—seem to agree in treating metaphysics as an autonomous discipline. It may legislate for the special fields, scientific and humanistic, but they generally provide little feedback to illuminate the character of metaphysics itself and its findings. To bridge this gap, it was suggested that Aristotle's ways of partitioning being might be viewed as metaphysical experiments that not only proved more or less successful in resolving abstract philosophical problems but were helped to do so by the very ways in which they refined and advanced inquiry in the special fields from which they had originated and to which they were applied. This approach gives us a clue to what Aristotle is doing in Zēta and Ēta. It can best be stated by looking back to our discussion of nature and the natural. This we explored in terms of the fundamental issues of the structure of scientific inquiry in Aristotle's time. We saw how the concept of nature was tied to controversies over the direction that physical science should take, and compared the state of physics at that time with the state of psychiatry today. The theory of substance can be seen as arising from the theory of nature, just as substance itself has natural substances for its prime example. Whatever has a nature is a substance; it has a source of motion within itself, which lies in its form, or *eidos*. If we ask what the thing is, we get an account of it, a *logos*, and if we grasp that account we have got the essence. A natural substance is a thing that has a nature and can be observed to operate according to its own *logos*—that is, a thing that is essentially active.

The inquiry into substance is thus a generalization of the inquiry into nature, ranging over a possibly wider field of entities and judging among a wider set of candidates for primacy or ultimacy. The candidates come not only from the older rivals of Aristotle's methodological approach— the matter of the atomists and the universals and mathematical concepts of the Platonists—but also from the advances Aristotle has himself made in his logical and scientific work. The inquiry is thus also a reckoning that Aristotle is making with himself. The logical character of a great part of the inquiry in Zēta is a utilization of his ideas along the lines of the earlier experiment with essence and accident; the physical turn in Ēta, in which he invokes potentiality and actuality, draws upon his scientific labors. His conclusion, we shall see, sets his own conceptual system in order in a strikingly new way.

The Candidates and the Winner

Our attention is now on the candidates for substance and the criteria Aristotle used for rejecting most of them. These criteria in turn indicate what the problems are that the inquiry into substance addresses. Some of them at the outset seem to be the old set of logical problems that arose from his original disagreement with Plato about whether reality lies with the individual or with the Forms; this included all the logical questions about the ultimate subject in predication. But by the time he wrote Zēta, at the climax of the *Metaphysics*, Aristotle did not need to run a fresh contest to resolve that issue. He had long ago given his answer and he kept to it all the way. Nevertheless, residues of these old issues emerge in Zēta and suggest occasional criteria for substance as if they were reminding us not to forget that whatever substance turns out to be, it must involve the separateness of the individual; a substance should be an individual. What comes full strength from Aristotle's older interests, however, is something different, and of great significance: a reliance on the logical tools he had developed during his effort to distinguish essence and accident. Will they furnish the kind of concept Aristotle is looking for? The kind he wants is not one that enables him to identify an individual—that is by now long taken for granted—but one that provides the deepest understanding of that individual. It would enable us to see the individual in the light of what it is, not just that it has a singular existence. To ask what substance is, is therefore to ask where to go for this understanding. It is not surprising, then, that the different candidates come from different philosophies and sciences that each recommends its own distinctive concepts.

In the first two chapters of *Metaphysics* 1, Aristotle had projected his own ideal of the wise man. His account characterized in broad strokes the growth of knowledge and the marks of wisdom. Wisdom has scope: the wise man knows all things, in a general way, not in a detailed way. Wisdom grasps complexity, it has precision, it is instructive—for the wise man is more capable of teaching. And finally, it is authoritative.[10] Hence wisdom yields a science of principles. To ask what substance is, is to ask for the object of the understanding that a wise man has. Some of the criteria for substance simply embody the features of a wise man; for instance, Aristotle favors species rather than genus as a candidate, because species is the more instructive.

To search for substance, however, requires more than a recognition of the general character of wisdom. One must also identify the structure of inquiry that will lead to ultimate understanding. Should one pursue knowledge in the terms of the mathematicians, with their abstract entities of number and point, line and plane, as limits of things? Or of the Platonists, who had generalized the notion of Ideas as universal patterns and reduced the individual or particular to a meeting-place or crossing-point of a host of universals? Or of the physicists, who offered matter and substratum as ultimates? Or of the biologists, who found understanding of living specimens in a delineation of genus and species? Or of the logicians, who most attractively—like Aristotle himself—had developed a notion of essence to answer the question What is it? and furnished all sorts of ingenious linguistic tests to identify what was essential and what was accidental? Clearly, the attempt to characterize a science of substance was, in effect, an attempt to determine what shape the sciences in general should take, how far they were to be organized in a mathematical or other rational way, what their basic units were to be, what form of resultant system was to emerge, and so on.

To many moderns, the ancient treatment of these matters seems a hodgepodge of logical and linguistic considerations, physical and empirical considerations, specific results of specific sciences, programs of reconstruction, and intimations of mystical reality. And so no doubt it is. The question is whether all these elements can really be neatly separated and treated independently. If some of them cannot, then a great deal can be learned by seeing how they have been related and how those relations change. Modern treatments have not been wholly dissimilar; philosophy has witnessed programs for reducing physical objects to collections of sense data, for behavioristic reduction of all meaning as linguistic behavior, for mathematization by axiomatization of field after field on a grand scale. The ancient controversialists might feel quite at home, once they learned the contemporary modes of speech. Nor would they find the picture very different among the growing sciences of the last century. They would hear such questions as: Is the cell a natural unit for the study of the body, or is the whole organism the natural unit? Does *species* designate an existent entity that maps discontinuities in nature, or is it a notion of convenience in an inherently arbitrary classification? Is the subject matter of psychology our acts of consciousness or observable behavior or interpersonal relations? Is there a real unconscious? Is a trait or is a whole-culture pattern the primary unit of anthropological description? Is society a reality for sociological study, or should research begin with roles? And so on. Even physics, with its grander systematization, has had its chapter of worry about the "reality" of atoms, or whether microparticles were convenient fictions for describing macro-objects and the latter alone entitled to the designation "reality."

At any rate, whatever its ramifications, the nature of Aristotle's inquiry into substance is continuous with his earlier works. In the *Categories* he had identified primary substance with the individual, and secondary substance with the genus and species to which the individual belongs. Several motifs entered into this analysis. One seems to be the desire to designate an ultimate subject. To assert a proposition is to say something about something. The "something" that is referred to has a quality or a quantity or enters into relations. The term that designates this individual (Socrates, for instance) always figures as the subject in the assertion. Once you have tagged the individual you want an answer to the question What is it? You want an instructive account of it. Thus, when Aristotle distinguishes genus and species, he says that species is more substance than genus, since it tells us more. But this kind of comparison can take place only within secondary substances. In primary substance there is no such distinction: this man is no more substance than this horse. Here a third motif seems to enter, a search for what we may call a *natural unit*. If we ask whether this arm is no less substance than this man, Aristotle replies that to understand an arm we have to see it as part of a man; otherwise the substance is not arm but flesh.

It is sometimes suggested that the logical idea of substance simply reflects the grammatical distinction of subject and predicate in Indo-European languages. If, for example, the search for substance had begun in a language in which everything was built around a verb center, with an array of tense, location, and participant indicators, a philosopher might have wanted to assert the ultimacy not of substances but of events. Perhaps so. But Aristotle's subject–predicate logical analysis did not prevent him from working out a dynamic conception of actuality whereby different participants in an activity could find a common fulfillment; nor did it keep him from distinguishing predicates that were secondary substances involved in answering the question What is it? from those that were qualities present in an already identified subject. In any case, the notion of substance clearly embodied more than logical elements. For example, the idea that substratum endures over time, but attributes succeed one another, emerged in the analysis of change.

During the discussion in Zēta and Ēta, which reaches a resolution in a climactic passage in the last chapter of Ēta, we see Aristotle working through a mass of problems, but he already senses where he is going. It is a veritable Olympic race as the candidates—bodies, points, Platonic Ideas, and all the rest we have suggested—muster to compete for the office of substance. Aristotle spots the favorites: the essence, the genus, the universal, the substratum. The last of these covers three possibilities, which he lists as matter, shape or organization, and the combination of the two, which he here calls the *composite*.

In the lineup and preliminary consideration of candidates, the criteria of selection emerge more fully. They are more exacting than playing the roles of *ultimate subject*, *instructiveness*, and *natural unit* that we elicited from the *Categories*, although at least the first two of these are retained. Substance now will also have to be *separably existent*, possessed of *individual singularity*, and *prior*. Thus, for example, matter is early dropped from the race because it is not a particular or an individual; the composite falls out because it is not prior, being composed of matter and form. As noted, the genus, being less instructive than the species (articulated in the definition that answers the question What is it?), is lost by the wayside. It is essential form that will emerge as the winner, not the individual, which was the primary substance according to the *Categories*. But there is many an obstacle to pass before we really understand what form ends up as, and why it is awarded the prize.

Your form, says Aristotle, is what characterizes you as you. It is your essence, not your accidents. It is obvious that the essence—accident distinction is central to Aristotle's claim that form be regarded as substance. Form fuses a number of features. The question Aristotle faces is the source of its unity. Unless it can be explained why some selected features are tied together in the defining formula, what is to prevent our decomposing form into a meeting-place of universals, or again, our arbitrarily creating forms by bundling together a group of accidents? A modern might simply ask whether the whole notion of essence does not mask the bundling of attributes for special arbitrary purposes.

For a while Aristotle tries to meet this problem in purely logical terms through the theory of definition: the essence is what the definition of a term fixes, and in a strict sense only an essence is definable. This is merely moving the problem to another area rather than solving it, for the notion of definition can now have the same charge of arbitrariness leveled against it. Accordingly, he reminds us to face the facts: "We should certainly inquire how we should speak on each point, but not more than how the facts actually stand."[11] This is in effect to rely on what he has long established: that though we are permitted to give a definition of what is not substance, it is simply assumed that this is not definition in a primary sense. This is because the primacy of substance is a more basic assumption and governs the theory of definition. Is Aristotle then being purely dogmatic when he says, "Hence there will be a formula or definition even of white man, but in a different sense from that of white or of a substance"?[12]

This question, the joining of predicates, had beset Aristotle quite early in the corpus. In *On Interpretation* he already notes it: "Why is a two-footed animal one thing and not many? They [*two-footed* and *animal*] will not be one by being said together. But to discuss this belongs to another inquiry."[13] A little later he says, "Man is perhaps an animal and two-footed and tame, but these do make up some one thing; yet from *white* and *man* and *walking* we don't have one thing."[14] He is here pursuing the problem on the logical-linguistic line, for it is obviously the way in which he hopes to clarify the differentiation of essence and accident. Some predicates admit of combination, others not.[15] If we say that someone is an animal and that he is two-footed, he is a two-footed animal, and if white and a man, then a white man. But if he is a cobbler and good, it does not follow that he is a good cobbler. Some combinations that are allowable are nevertheless accidental; for example, a man may be white and musical, but *white* and *musical* do not make a unity.

Comparable problems arise with biological inquiry. For example, Aristotle asks why though male and female are opposites, men and women are not different species, and adds that this problem is nearly the same as why some opposites, like footed and winged, govern differences in species but others, like white and black, do not.[16] He suggests the answer here that contraries in the defining formula (the *logos*) yield different species but those in the concrete whole (that includes the matter) do not. Hence between white man and black man there is not a difference of species, and individual men are not different species though their flesh and bones are different. Nor do a bronze and a wooden circle differ in species; but a bronze triangle and a wooden circle do, because circle and triangle are different species. (Aristotle regarded the circle and the line as different species.) We may compare this with his remark elsewhere that a stone figure of a man is not a man but a representation of one and that a wooden saw is similarly not a saw.[17] The point there is obviously that such objects cannot do the appropriate work (*ergon*). An iron saw and a bronze saw would still presumably both be saws. In *Metaphysics* 10.9 Aristotle also points out that in the case of male and female the same semen with some modification becomes male or female. It is clear from these instances that Aristotle is looking to final and efficient causes to support formal distinctions. Obviously an appeal to a definition to settle whether a particular distinction determines separate species can only come when investigation is complete and the definition achieved. The full answer calls for the considerations or evidence that established the definition in the first place. To gain an understanding, then, it is not enough simply to offer a definition or report of essence. We must have the scientific understanding that resulted in the affirmation of essence. Or else we must find special meaning for essence that will connect it with the scientific inquiry.

When Aristotle resorted with fair frequency to the illustration that white is an accident and white-man does not constitute an essence, he could not have foreseen the devastating impact of racism two millenia later. It is worthwhile, however, to pursue the illustration, not by asking whether the black-white difference determines a difference in species or in essence, but by asking what the meaning of *essence* must be that enables us to say that such a species distinction does not designate a real entity, that we have not stated the essence of the people designated when we have described them by the terms *white man* and *black man*. We know that the achievement of this recognition has involved a whole chapter in the scientific study of man, which showed that color is not the key to a host of properties—biological, psychological, social, etc.—that give a systematic picture of a designated group over a wide field of its operations in many areas. It might have been, and one would not know a priori that it would not be—just as one would not know a priori that the hot and the cold would not be the unifying key to types of motion. (Aristotle was more fortunate in his chance illustration of white and black than in his elaborate physics.)

A statement of the essence of a designated subject thus constitutes a satisfactory unified theoretical understanding of the organization and pattern of its functioning. This seems to be the implication of the kind of inquiry Aristotle is pursuing in his investigation of substance. His solution in the last part of Ēta moves rapidly to a conclusion. He recognizes that he is dealing with a general problem of the unity in a definition of the features that make it up, not merely the lack of unity in an incorrect account. He looks for the unity in the factual, not in the linguistic connection: "A definition is one formula [*logos*] not by being joined together, like the *Iliad*, but by being of one object. What, then, is it that makes man one; why one and not many, such as animal and biped, especially if there are, as some say, an animal-itself and a biped-itself?"[18] In short, why regard man as one thing rather than a joining of the two? Aristotle is now sure that the usual manner of speech and definition cannot settle the question. What can? "But if, as we say, the one is matter and the other is form, and the one is potentially and the other is actually, the point we are considering will no longer be thought a difficulty."[19]

This seems a mild conclusion for what has been the drama of Zēta and Ēta. But its significance and its own dramatic character should not be overlooked. Aristotle has spent a great deal of time in Zēta trying to solve the problem of substance, of what individuals in the world "really" are and how they are to be understood, through the logical-definitional route. In the end he recognizes that this would not do the job. Still, it would be misunderstanding his solution to say that he turned away from the logical to the scientific. He does not abandon the notion that essence is substance. He concludes rather that the search for substance is not merely a logical, but also a scientific, endeavor. It is the notion of essence—as the form that answers the question What is it?—that is transformed in the process. The dramatic character of this climax is that it takes place through the fusing of two families of concepts, matter and form (essence) on the one hand, and potentiality and actuality on the other. Matter is now identified with potentiality, and form with actuality. This is a fresh mode of conceptualization, to be sure, but it is also a fresh experiment in metaphysics and so also a fresh way of looking at the world. Its consequences will be seen in Aristotle's treatments of psychology and ethics as well as in his methodology of investigation.

This is also the end of a long conceptual journey for form, which has traveled far from its earlier place in pre-Aristotelian philosophy as an abstract entity. Let us reconstruct the steps of its transformation. First, Aristotle joined it with matter, as a relative conception in matter–form analysis. There it conveyed the sense of shape or organization. Then, in the telescoping of the formal, efficient, and final causes, it emerged as a kind of culminating design, achieved or maintained. This cast it in a teleological model. Meanwhile, in his scientific studies, Aristotle had fashioned the concepts of potentiality and actuality, which in their own ways joined an active outlook with the teleological model. He must have felt that the fusing of the two families of concepts—matter with potentiality, form with actuality—was his crowning conceptual achievement. The world contains a plurality of material systems that achieve an equilibrium (a modern would call them homeostatic systems) and have a characteristic development and history. To know their form is to be able to classify them and understand their components and their dynamic organization, the direction of their movement and growth and striving, and their typical interrelations. A thing is not a mere *this*, nor a form an abstract *such*. A thing is a *this-such*. Substance can thus be identified with form because form contains within it all the actuality that matter is revealing.

A form (*eidos*) in this sense must be a very concrete kind of being. It is not an abstraction in the sense of a *sort* of thing. It is more like an individual or a part (the governing part?) of an individual. Although the various features that characterize the form are used for classifying individuals and the term *eidos* is frequently used to mean species, form has not thus turned into a universal.[20] On the contrary, it is much more like the individual seen in terms of the features within it that operate to carry it on its career. But what then are the relations between form and the individual?

Form and the Individual

There has always been some disagreement about the status of the individual in Aristotelian theory.[21] If, as is commonly thought, it loses the status of primary substance that it had in the *Categories*, then what remains of it? Is it simply mere existence endowed with a form of a general kind and garnished with a mass of accidents? Or does it in some sense recover its status as a primary substance, once form is identified with actuality? Perhaps the question should be put generally: In Aristotle's mature theory—granted that we have the initial terms for pointing to an individual (*this* or *this-something*) or referring to individuals in a class (*each*) or mentioning what is peculiar to or distinctively characteristic of one (*private*)—what is an individual and where does individuality lie? This question involves a nest of subsidiary problems: What differentiates individuals of the same species? What is the enduring identity of an individual over time? What makes a unity of an individual, though it has many parts?

In expositions of Aristotelian metaphysics, individuation is generally regarded as a function of matter, along with several other related functions—ensuring continuity, instantiating universals, and accounting for accidents—that to some extent already involve individuation. An account of continuity, which as we saw enmeshes movement and time, and of movement, which in turn entails a subject, already provides for a unified individual over time. And though we shall later have to consider the concept of existence and the shape it takes in Aristotle's work, it must at least be apparent here that to grant that universals can have instances is also to have affirmed the individual. To take matter in its relative sense, as the materials operative in a specific context, and to explain accidents by matter (for example, the color of someone's eyes, in contrast to his having eyes at all), for matter contains the potentiality of opposites, already takes care of many of the properties that differentiate one man from another, or more generally, one member of a species from another.

Again, Aristotle provides many of the necessary supplementary ideas for talking about similarities and differences in his analyses of such notions as *same, other, contrary, similar*, and so on. (He leads off book 7 of the *Topics* with a chapter devoted to the *same*, and starts by identifying its strictest sense, the one in number.) And he draws more detailed distinctions between things that are identical in number, in species, and in genus. These, added to the account of the differences in accidents, would seem to cover comparison of individuals under all the categories.

If we turn to inner constitution of the individual, Aristotle furnishes us with fairly detailed concepts of *whole, part, element, complete*, and *limit*. In terms of these, using the idea of limit and the dimensions length, breadth, and depth, he gives us the concept of a body. Since place can be analyzed in terms of the relation of bodies, we now have the apparatus for speaking about occupancy of the same place for a given period of time, and we can use difference of place to establish the absence of numerical identity in things.

Again, when we move from general concepts to those of a particular area—say biology—we find the organizational groundwork for the individual laid out in analyses in specific terms of structured wholes: the uniform continuous parts that are flesh and bone, the liquid parts that have the unity of a flow, the organs that have a unity of composition and find a unity of specific function, and so on. Among psychological phenomena, Aristotle treats individuality as a scientific question: Are the faculties of nutrition, sensation, thought, and movement separate psyches, or parts of the psyche? Are they separable only in thought, or also in space? This, he says, is easy to settle in some cases (the plants, for instance), hard in others.[23]

Still further, there are areas in which theoretical considerations are involved in a judgment about individuality. Thus Aristotle devotes great effort to proving that there is only one world and invokes arguments about the contradictions that will follow on assuming a plurality, presupposing of course the underlying theses of his physics. Again, when he develops the notion of Unmoved Movers, he has to face the question whether there are one or many. Whichever possibility he is considering—that the motions of the planets require fifty-five (or perhaps forty-seven) Unmoved Movers or, as he at last decides, that there is only one first Unmoved Mover[24]—the answer depends on underlying theory.

Taken all together, then, Aristotle's various treatments of related subjects provide us with a fairly rich set of concepts for discussing problems of the individual and individual differences. There is no single main concept to do the job by itself, to mark off and differentiate the individual; we have therefore used our network approach as a matter of course, to discover how these several concepts work together. We expect the marks by which we identify the individual to be contextual, and the results to cohere. As we explore each of the different modes of reference abstractly we find the familiar circular pattern in which each concept can be explicated and analyzed by use of the rest. For example, when we individuate a thing by its place, this on Aristotle's definition of place makes reference to the borders of other things whose individuation is assumed. But he never tries to reduce all these concepts to a predetermined set of initial terms, as some moderns attempt to translate mathematical statements into statements that use only logical terms. So too he makes no effort to translate identifying terms of, say, an individual man into the special language of physical bodies or collections of particles.

This man might be individuated by the distinctive sound of his voice or by its wave patterns. In spite of the circularity, or rather because of it, the whole set of concepts is systematically enriched when any one is refined under the stimulus of the kinds of problems and data that arise and are available in its specific area. The gains in analytic power are, so to speak, transmitted throughout. This is a basic feature of the whole metaphysical network we have been examining, and we shall again see it at work with tremendous effect in Aristotle's ethical theory. In the present context we have not even gathered the terms for individuation in a systematic way before going on to organize a subnetwork to cover the special area.

Nevertheless, there are a few questions—and passages—that trouble contemporary commentators, bearing largely on the relation between matter and essence in the constitution of the individual. Does Socrates have his own Socratic essence? In one sense, no: the essence of Socrates is the form—*human*—that he has in common with all human beings and that can then be talked about in universal terms in defining "human." There is no definition of the individual.

Is it then his matter that makes Socrates an individual? It looks as if Aristotle is saying Kallias and Socrates differ because each has different matter; each is *logos* with matter; things are one in number whose matter is one;[25] if all the available matter were used up in one object—if, for example, all the flesh and bones were made into one huge man—there could not be another individual of the same sort.[26] Aristotle's point here is that even then we could distinguish between what it is to be a man and the particular individual man. Yet in all these, and clearly in the last example, though matter is a source of individuality, it is not matter as such but matter taking a given form. He even speaks in a similar way of the essential nature of the circle and the essential nature of *this* circle (what it is for a circle to be and for this particular circle to be).[27] And we find the fuller term for essence (*to ti ēn einai*) applied to Kallias himself.[28] Again we are told that in the process of generation of the individual, "the causes of things that are in the same species are different, not in species but because the causes of individuals are different—your matter and form and moving cause, from mine—although in their universal formula they are the same."[29] In short, it is not matter that gives me my differences from you, but the individuals—my parents. Apparently, then, the real cause of individual differences is not the mere separateness of different bits of undifferentiated matter, but rather the potentialities latent in each separate bit by virtue of its generation from different individuals, themselves analyzable into matter and form. It may help here to look back to the process of generation itself. In *Generation of Animals* Aristotle tells us that both individuality and genus are at work in generation, but mostly the individual, because it is the substance (*ousia*).[30]

If it were simply matter as such that was responsible for individuation, and not form, then we could draw a sharp distinction between the form in Socrates—his general humanity—and all the idiosyncratic features of Socrates, and assign the latter to matter. We would have to accept that the really interesting part of Socrates is purely a set of accidents, matter being the source of the accidental. But this is not what Aristotle has said; matter as such is held responsible only for the *arithmetic* difference. If Socrates is ironical, with a fine sense of humor, and Kallias is practical and lacking in humor, these are not mere accidents in matter; they are different shapes that rationality has taken, and rationality is part of the essence of man. The fusion of the species-derived and the materially derived features and powers in an individual is thus not so simple as a neat partition of general form and individual matter would make it seem.

The relation between the essence and the individual seems even more complicated when we read Aristotle's chapter devoted to the question whether the essence of the individual and the individual itself are one and the same.[31] This is a corner Aristotle has maneuvered himself into because, as he says, "a particular thing [*hekaston*] is thought to be nothing other than its own substance, and the essence is said to be the substance of each thing."[32] He also recognizes here that to have knowledge of the individual is to have knowledge of its essence. Aristotle's answer to this problem is that in some cases the individual is identical with its essence, in some cases not. If we talk of an entity that can be separated from the individual, even though only in thought, the essence and that entity are one and the same; if it cannot, then the essence is not identical with the individual. His most striking illustration of this point compares man with psyche: psyche and the the essence of psyche are the same, but man and the essence of man (which is his psyche) are not.[33]

The interpretation of such passages is complicated because they are usually tied in with criticism of some other view. A more serious difficulty is that many of them occur in contexts where Aristotle is working his way through his earlier formulations in terms of essence and accident, form and matter—before he has arrived at his solution to the problem of substance by identifying matter and form with the potential and the actual. If we look back to the question of the relation of essence, matter, and individuality in the light of his solution, these questions become much clearer.

For one thing, it becomes evident that Aristotle did not abandon his view of the individual as primary substance, but rather refined it. Substance is not species conceived as a general type, but individuals talked about in a general way—much as we loosely say "governing law" when we explain why a particular thing reacted in a given way. What makes a thing react the way it does is the particular object that impinges on it in a particular way, not the law that tells us how things react universally under such conditions. The law helps us pick out what particular features in the particular situation had what effect; it does not do the causing. So too form (the victorious candidate for interpreting substance), though it has a universal character and conveys understanding in virtue of its universal scope, helps us pick out features that are essential. Hence the form is a complex of the individual's features that are effective in what the individual does. Now if the matter–form distinction is equated with the potentiality–actuality distinction, then when the actuality is happening—or the potentiality is being realized—there is no sharp distinction to be drawn between the matter and the form. This is precisely the lesson of Aristotle's remarks at the end of *Metaphysics* 8.

Let us try out an analogy. Take, for example, a burning candle. The flame is the actualization, for which the wax and wick in their organization constitute the matter or potentiality. The form, equated with the actuality, is thus the flame. Since the candle is not all aflame we can fairly easily distinguish the matter from the form. It is likewise with man and the psyche: in Aristotle's view, as we shall see, the psyche is the actuality, the form, of the man; put simply, it is his life being lived. The flame is the form of the candle, but if we ask in turn what the essence of the flame is, we can only say that since essence (the form itself, not its generalized statement) is actuality, the essence of the flame is identical with the flame itself. We cannot say that for the candle; its essence is the flame, but it has matter that is not yet burning, not yet actualized. So too, if we ask for the essence of a person's life, we can only say that it is identical with the living itself—and perhaps call it the "patterned life" to remind ourselves of the possibility of generalization. And if we ask for the essence of the person as a living whole, we have to say it is not identical with the person, but with his life. The clearest division of matter and form in the individual is between the still potential part, where the matter is separate, and the actual part, in which the matter is taken up into actuality. (Aristotle speaks this way of a building that is already finished.) The dilemmas and ambiguities about matter and essence in the individual can thus be resolved by recognizing the context in which we talk of matter and form, in the light of Aristotle's distinctive solution to the problem of what substance is. Aristotle's own comment at the very end of *Metaphysics* 8, in which his solution has been expounded, is a fitting analysis of why there have been puzzles on our question: "People seek a unifying formula for potentiality and fulfillment, and a difference. But as has been said, the proximate matter and the form are one and the same, the one potentially, the other actually. Thus to seek the cause of their being one is like seeking the cause of unity; for each individual thing is one and the potential and the actual are in a sense one. Hence there is no cause other than what initiates the movement from potentiality to actuality."

In the light of Aristotle's analysis of substance and form, we may conclude, there is no *general* problem of individuation. He has all the conceptual equipment that is needed for identifying individuals, for distinguishing them, for discourse about them, for explaining how they come into being and pass away or continue to exist, and for discovering what is essential and what is accidental, what is common and what is unique. To seek a general principle of individuation is as misguided in the Aristotelian conceptual scheme of things as to seek a general cause for the actualization of potentialities.

The Inventory of Substances

Let us look now at Aristotle's inventory of the substances contained in the world. This carries us from his concepts and his methods to his specific doctrine, the outcome of his inquiries and his occasionally tortured arguments. We may start from his center of the world, the earth. There are the natural elements that physics discovers. From these are constituted more highly organized materials, from basic organic substances to differentiated plant and animal and human forms. Among these substances man is ranked highest. He alone stands truly upright in the sense that Aristotle defined as absolute: his *up* coincides with the true *up* of the cosmos. (The test for this coincidence is a bit complicated: the *up* of any living thing is where its food enters the body, which in man is in the head; in the case of plants the root corresponds to the head in man; in the case of animals, since they stand on all fours, their *up* is in between man and plants. The *up* of the cosmos is of course toward the heavens.) More important, of course, is man's rational power, which changes the quality of all that he does, even the functions he shares with the animals. All these substances are in the sublunar domain, and their behaviors are studied in the various terrestrial and meteorological and biological sciences. Beyond this lie the heavenly bodies, themselves alive,[35] composed of the fifth substance and actualized in unending circular movement. These are studied by astronomy. Aristotle's treatment of these substances is a combination of star worship and the latest astronomical hypotheses of his day, explaining away with mathematical ingenuity the apparent irregular movement of the planets. So far, then, we have matter–form composites: the sublunar elements, which are of grosser material and undergo constant changes of various types, and the heavenly element, which is a purer matter and is limited to a uniform motion. Beyond this, there is the Unmoved Mover.

Aristotle's doctrine of the Unmoved Mover, which was to become a center of major controversy in subsequent Western philosophical theology, did not develop in an overall, systematic way. It emerged rather at the limit of several different inquiries. The most intensive of these is in the *Physics*, whose latter part works into a proof of the endlessness of movement and the necessity for a first, unmoved cause of motion. *On the Psyche* contains a brief section on pure thought and active reason. *Nicomachean Ethics* 10 gives a brief depiction of pure contemplation and the divine mind. What suggests—although we cannot be completely certain —that these several contexts relate to the same question, apart from Aristotle's occasional references to the divine, is his general inventory of substances in book 12 of the *Metaphysics*.

A number of lines of thought in the *Physics* lead Aristotle toward an Unmoved Mover. In the first place, he is not satisfied with purely contingent movement; to say that things just happen to be moving is unsatisfactory, for the continuation of movement seems to be unreliable. Is it mere chance that movement happens to continue? He regards it as necessary that there has always been motion and always will be. If it were not necessary, then everything might stop, and in endless time it would stop. Back of this lies a logical notion that it is somehow meaningless to say that something can happen but never in fact in all endless time will happen.[36] It looks as if he is saying that never-to-be-actualized potentiality for all time entails impossibility. This is a difficult position; its relation to his conception of possibility requires fuller systematization, and will be considered in appendix C. Occasionally there is a religious touch in Aristotle's explanation of the necessity of movement: generation was made continual by God because that is the nearest approach to eternal or everlasting being.[37]

In the second place, Aristotle does not accept a principle of inertia. He insists that (apart from natural motions) some exertion of force is required to keep something moving, and it has to be a contact force, not just an initiating force. The atomists stood alone in believing that motion is inherent in matter and so requires no explanation. This attitude cannot be compared even with Aristotle's doctrine of natural motions in the elements, for in those natural motions, after all, an element only moves towards its natural place (earth, in fact, is already in place and does not exercise its natural "homing" motion unless it is forcibly lifted up). Nor again can Aristotle accept any concept of self-movement. He simply tries to isolate the part of the entity that does the moving from the part that is moved, and applies his search for a cause of motion to that narrower field of inquiry.

In the third place, along with the logical presuppositions about impossibility and the factual assumption about contact forces, is the metaphysical assumption of the priority of the actual over the potential. The efficient cause is always, as we have seen, some actual specimen of the thing or event that is being brought into being—fire of catching fire, parents of children, ideas (actual in thought) of craft production. Hence the cause of motion will be some actual motion operating on what is capable of motion. This leads Aristotle to think that the endless motion of the heavens is the source of sublunar motions, but it leaves that endless motion itself without a satisfactory causal account.

Finally, there is Aristotle's decisive rejection of the infinite regress. The search for causes, whether outside the moving object or in the analysis of its inner precipitating parts, cannot go on endlessly.

The combined result of these four lines of thought reveals a dilemma. The basic cause of motion has to be necessary, operate through contact, and be a prior actuality, and it must not generate an infinite regress. How is that possible? If this cause is a necessary motion, it will satisfy the criteria of contact and prior actuality but will itself require explanation unless it is self-moving; but this Aristotle does not allow, for he analyzes it as one internal part moving another, and there to pursue the cause of a cause would provoke an infinite regress. Again, if the cause is a succession of local motions each actual and causing another, the endless succession through endless time may not be logically objectionable, but the necessity is omitted. And so on.

Aristotle's solution is the Unmoved Mover. It is eternal and necessary, it is pure actuality (*energeia*) without an element of potentiality and therefore not admitting of change. It is the ultimate first principle and unmoved, and so halts the regress. How can it satisfy the contact requirement? Aristotle's answer is to allow a kind of contact that is one-way in its influence. The Unmoved Mover moves things not by physical contact but by a different kind of encounter, the way that an object of desire and an object of thought move us without being moved.[38] It thus serves as a final cause, as the good toward which all is drawn, rather than as an efficient agent.

It is interesting to note that Aristotle also consciously uses the idea of a mover being unmoved but setting something else in motion, in his explanation of animal motion. In the first chapter of the little work *On the Movement of Animals*, he introduces this subject as if it were partial confirmation for his general argument in *Physics* 8. When one part of an animal moves, another part must be at rest; that is why animals have joints. Again, for an animal to move, there must be something at rest in the environment; for example, firm ground enables an animal to walk. He even argues that the myth of Atlas, who moves the heavens while his feet are planted on the earth, presupposes a motionless earth.[39] The second half of the notion of an unmoved mover—that something else is moved by what is itself unmoved—comes into play when he turns to the internal initiation of motion in animals. Here the phenomena of appetite and desire tie in with the intellect to attract the animal into motion. He accordingly compares the animal moved by desire with what is eternally moved by the eternal mover.[40] The respect in which they differ is, of course, that the one is eternal.

What is the nature of this prime actuality? In short, what is God doing? What kinds of actions, says Aristotle in the *Nicomachean Ethics*, must we assign to the gods? "Acts of justice? Wouldn't it be ridiculous to have them making contracts and returning deposits, and so on?"[41] So too for acts of bravery or temperance or liberality. Still, he says, they must live, we cannot suppose them to sleep. "Now if action be taken away from a living being, and—still more—production, what is left except contemplation? So that the activity of God, which surpasses in blessedness, would be contemplative."[42] When we couple this with the characterization of God as the Unmoved Mover, it follows that thought is the highest actuality that moves the world.

But what is that highest thought about? Thought in human life has an object, the intelligible structure of things. (Precisely how thought is related to its object is a problem for *On the Psyche*; see our discussion in chapter 10.) But perhaps God is free to think anything; Aristotle considers this problem in *Metaphysics* 12. God has been described as "a living being, eternal, most good."[43] Now the divine mind thinks "either itself or something else; and if something else, then either the same thing always, or different things. Then does it make any difference or not whether it thinks what is fine or something at random? Surely it would be absurd for it to think about some things. Clearly, then, it thinks what is most divine and worthy, and does not change." Moreover, thought by itself cannot be the supreme good, because one can think the worst thoughts. "Therefore the divine thought thinks itself, if it is what is best; and its thinking is a thinking of thinking."[44]

Pure, necessary, fully actual, eternal, unchanging, living, self-conscious thought, embracing within itself the vibrant essence of the world, the ultimate source of physical movement and biological growth, the light that quickens human thought, the good that men unite with momentarily in contemplation, the power that alone can order the whole and give eternal structure to things and processes—such is Aristotle's God. If he is not wholly required by systematic consideration, he is at least one pinnacle toward which the system—on special assumptions—could be directed.

Was Aristotle religious in the devotional sense of the term? No doubt he performed all the rituals. Perhaps he felt a certain awe when he looked at the starry heavens overhead, though a modern reader may sympathize with Theophrastus' complaint (we find it in the surviving fragments of his own *Metaphysics*): Why, if the stars are so divine, can they not do anything more exalted than move in circles? Again, God might serve to embody ideals of the good, but to think of God as loving man would have seemed a trifle bizarre to Aristotle. He says in the *Eudemian Ethics*, "It would be ridiculous if one were to charge God with not returning love in the way he is loved, or for a subject to charge a ruler; for to be loved, not to love, characterizes a ruler—or to love in another way."[45] Not love, nor a personal interest, but order, permanence, dependability, and a model of the good—these were what Aristotle seems to expect from religion. Hence the impersonality of the God did not seem to trouble Aristotle. Later thinkers might wonder whether Aristotle's God has not been completely removed from all connection with the world, whether he would not be in principle incapable of knowing particular facts, or even universal truths that were other than himself. Such a separation would preclude miracles, divine favor directed to specific individuals, or love of men or mankind. But that was not the kind of help Aristotle sought from the divine. If we strictly consider what he says in the corpus, the help he wanted from the concept of God was twofold. In part, he wanted help in solving a few limiting questions at critical points in his philosophy, made critical by the presuppositions in his scientific theory. Perhaps, too, he saw that a more complete structure would emerge in his philosophy, if the ultimate source of movement could be identified with the source of rationality in the psyche of the highest form of life in the scale of living beings.[46] But perhaps more, as we shall see, he wanted the reassurance of regularity in the universe; in reliance upon it there could be knowledge of the essential character of things.

The Eclipse of Some Concepts

No separate treatment of Aristotle's physics and biology has been given in this book; they are close enough to his metaphysics to have been dealt with, at least in respect to their basic ideas, in the context of our exposition of the metaphysical network. Before going on to explore the way our network operates in Aristotle's psychology and theory of knowledge, then, it might be well to mention here what happened to some of the metaphysical concepts, especially since the main scene of their later adventures was in fact the field of physical science. It is well known that by the time of Galileo and Newton the Aristotelian scheme of the world had unraveled and profound changes had taken place. Some of these had been prefigured in other schools of ancient philosophy, such as the atomists'; but the precise mixture of the old and the new is itself a story in the history of science.

The Aristotelian concept of motion was whittled down in several ways. Locomotion, or change of place, emerged as central; its ties with other kinds of change were cut, and it took over the very name *motion*. It lost its dramatic teleological quality of *movement toward*, and became reduced, first to a kind of almost forceful action, then to a succession of positions in space. Matter came to be identified with particles in space, and discontinuity thus replaced continuity; the idea of action at a distance gained respectability, and so dispensed with the need for contact in motion. Space became an absolute emptiness with quantitative properties, instead of a set of relations. Time similarly became an independent and real framework. Potentiality, in many respects the kingpin of the original Aristotelian scheme, evaporated at least in its sense of power. Instead, force emerged as energy transmissible from one thing to another; and efficient cause, the exercise of stimulative power that effects joint action among participating entities, was recast as the prior event that forces a subsequent event. In this new guise, efficient cause took over the causal scene. Final causes and the apparatus of teleology were banished from science altogether, and formal cause became the equivalent of scientific "law."

As it evolved, the new scheme cast itself gradually in the character of the machine (becoming "mechanistic"), just as the old one had modeled itself on the concepts of craft. As for the cosmos itself, there was nothing now to prevent its being thought of as infinite, spreading out in all directions with no intrinsic center. At the dawn of modern science in the seventeenth century, it was still too early in the career of the new model for the indeterminate to take over, for the merely probable to replace the necessary, or even in later extreme forms for the demonic to replace the rational. Machines are even stricter than purposive action, and so the book of nature was written in the language of mathematics, not in terms of the repetitive processes of biology with its numerous "accidents."

The development of this new model was, of course, accompanied by far-reaching changes in psychology and the theory of knowledge. Concepts of mind and body, intellect and experience, changed just as radically as did concepts of space and time and motion. (We shall not be surprised, in going on to examine Aristotle's psychology and theory of knowledge in parts 3 and 4, to find that much of our work consists in restoring the view from his own perspective, clearing away our modern presuppositions.) Let us suggest the direction of the shift. It began with a retreat from soul to mind. Soul, originally believed to be a pervasive phenomenon in nature (Plato had even used it to explain motion), became reduced to mind as its physical jobs were taken over by other agents and only the intellectual jobs (in the broad sense of consciousness) left to it. And so psychology got to be purely "mental." Thus, while the Newtonian world was cosmologically unified—there was no division between the heavens and the sublunar domain, as in the Aristotelian view—it suffered a dramatic metaphysical split within, between the objective natural domain and the subjective mental domain. As the mind, now cut off from the rest of the world, began to worry about the credentials of its knowledge, philosophy embarked on the great epistemological experiment that Aristotle had rejected in favor of metaphysics. In this process, when the philosophical battle of the rationalists and the empiricists had eventually run its course, Aristotle was bundled in with the rationalists and dismissed by empirical philosophers, who claimed science for themselves. The successes of modern physical science have delayed the attempt to understand Aristotle's physics in his own terms. But in psychology and perhaps epistemology a current sense that an impasse has been reached, and the conflicts between different schools, are prompting a fresh look at the history of thought.

Part 3

MAN AND HIS POWERS

A modern, opening Aristotle's book *On the Psyche*, is likely to be misled by a rendering of *psuchē* as *soul*. In subsequent religious history it became identified with a particular conception of a spiritual or nonmaterial entity that has a career independent of the body—so that it is even meaningful for a man to deny that he has a soul. In the ancient Greek usage, however, the soul is what distinguishes the living from the nonliving. To say "I have no soul" is almost like saying "I am dead." Perhaps we can appreciate this more readily by comparison with our use of *mind*; if a man said "I have no mind," we would probably take him to mean that he had feeble intellectual powers. If one wanted to deny that mind was an entity existing independently from the body, one would not say "I have no mind" but rather "My mind is some sort of function of my body." So it was with *soul*. Opposing theories of the nature of soul could thus be stated without discarding the term. In Plato's *Phaedo*, where the case for immortality was being presented, one of the participants could argue that soul is simply the harmonious expression of the elements composing the body; it is compared to the music expressing the constitution and exercise of the lyre. This would not deny the soul, but would predict its instantaneous annihilation with the breakdown of the body. In the Greek, then, *soul* generally indicates the living being with all its functions, while *mind* (*nous*) is reserved for that which thinks or carries out the intellectual functions, itself construable as a function of a soul-endowed organism. In order to minimize confusion, hereafter the English word *psyche*, corresponding to Aristotle's own term *psuchē* (the latter to be used in transliteration), will be employed for the most part both in the title of his treatise and in discussing his theory. We may compare the broad sense of *psyche* stated by the *Oxford English Dictionary* (1933 edition): "life . . . the animating principle in man and other living beings, the source of all vital activities, rational or irrational."

The growth of modern science in the seventeenth century severely restricted the province of soul as an explanatory concept. As matter and motion (no longer in the Aristotelian sense) gained supremacy in physical theory, soul was no longer considered a cause of motion (except in the deistic conception of the divine maker who imparts motion to matter); growth and other biological functions were assigned purely material causes. The modern near-equation of soul and mind is a compromise dictated by Descartes' dualism to stem still further inroads by matter. Galileo had severed the objective qualities inherent in matter from the subjective realm of secondary qualities occurring in the mind, and Cartesian dualism made a philosophy of the sharp distinction between body and mind, thereby creating the "mind–body problem" of subsequent metaphysics and epistemology. With this abandonment of the unity of nature in all its forms, methodological issues became critical, and they persist in the study of man and mind. Some scientists moved directly to organic-physiological inquiry, shunting aside the mental and the introspective, or leaving it hanging as an inefficacious epiphenomenon. Others made a separate science of the mental with its own laws of gravitation (through association) of mental elements. In the twentieth century, behaviorism proposed to study man's behavior in its complexities without looking either to physiology or to introspection. In revolt, a newer phenomenology reasserted the claims of subjectivity to a scientific status as the analysis of the field of direct experience. Among other options there developed a philosophy of mind that cut itself off from empirical psychology and devoted itself to the analysis of mental concepts as revealed in ordinary language.

Amid this conflict of schools it is not surprising that the longing for an integrated approach to man and his powers has made Aristotle's work on the psyche increasingly attractive. Contemporaries may hope that in spite of the early state of Aristotle's scientific materials, a study of his psychological works might suggest ways of reintegrating their dispersive disciplines. Indeed Aristotle's treatment does map out the main lines of what we nowadays call psychology—unless we cast that science itself in one or another of the conflicting schools.[1]

Interestingly enough, Aristotle is faced with a barrage of alternative approaches that somewhat resemble the array of modern schools. He is intent on holding to what is sound in each and synthesizing the various aspects. For example, he points out that the natural philosopher defines *anger* as a surging of the blood and heat about the heart; the dialectician, as a craving for retaliation or something like it. He wants both the material and the formal elements specified as well as the efficient and final components: "To be angry is a certain kind of movement of such and such a body, or part or faculty of it, roused by such a cause, and for such an end."[2] His account embraces the physiological and the qualitative or introspective, and he sees the latter in purposive terms, not merely as epiphenomenal.

As for dogmatic partial theories, Aristotle is quick to draw out any absurd conclusions they entail. Thus those who assert that the psyche occupies spatial magnitude are pressed to specify how the mind would think, and what definition and demonstration would then be like, and whether if the thinking consists in circular movement, mind must think the same object over and over again! To those who completely isolate the psyche and do not give an account of the bodily side and specific bodily relations, Aristotle says they talk "as though it were possible, as in the Pythagorean myths, that any chance psyche could put on any chance body; this is absurd, for each body seems to have its peculiar form and shape."[3] To avoid the mistaken transfer of properties between body and psyche, he suggests greater precision in language. We should not say that the psyche is angry or the psyche thinks, any more than we would say that the psyche builds houses. We should say instead that a man does these things with his psyche[4]—presumably in a way analogous to that in which he hears with his auditory system or kicks with his foot.

It will be helpful to approach the integrative character of Aristotle's psychology through the conceptual network as we have analyzed it. The success of a particular network when applied to a given field depends on three things: the fruitfulness of its concepts, how well they tie in with one another, and how effectively the lessons learned from applying the network in one domain can be transferred to another domain. While the fruitfulness cannot be judged at the outset, the other two points can be readily seen in Aristotle's psychology.

Aristotle uses his metaphysical concepts directly in defining the psyche, and the tie-ins are almost immediate. The psyche is a substance, but a substance is a form and a form is an actuality; a form is the form of a material and an actuality is the realization of a potentiality. The outcome is that the psyche is the realization of the potentialities of a certain kind of body. Thus whatever the detail, a sharp dualism of body and psyche is simply ruled out from the beginning, and whatever problems dualism generates in the later history of epistemology will be found either to have no place in Aristotle or to appear in some other fashion. For Aristotle the body holds the potentiality of the psyche. Whether the path his concepts mark for psychology is a promising one remains to be seen.

That the study of the psyche includes both the material and the formal means that psychology is a complex science. On the material side both physics and physiology are relevant. They enter directly into the psychological works, not simply into separate treatises—say on the physics or the physiology of vision. What is found on the formal side? We may recall that the Aristotelian notion of form began with a structural idea, absorbed final (that is, functional) components, and was eventually assimilated with actuality. Actuality (fulfillment, realization) itself was a very broad notion; there was the complete actuality of an activity, as in seeing or knowing, and the complete actuality of an embodied form, such as the completed statue; and again, there was the incomplete actualization to be found in motion or change, where a potentiality is working its way out in a given direction to an end. Hence it is not surprising that in the detailed treatment of psychological phenomena, Aristotle uses concepts of form and actuality to deal with what we would regard as the structural, the functional, and the behavioral (whether the phenomena are dynamic or static and qualitative). These need not fall apart into different approaches.

Where in all this, however, do we find the phenomenal or phenomenological? When Husserl, for example, attempted to develop a phenomenological analysis of pure experience, he first wanted to "bracket" the rest of the world—the physical and psychological alike. Now this approach is the heir of the familiar separation of a realm of consciousness from all the rest of all that is. The prior question is whether the initial cut should be made in this way, not whether the contents of the phenomenal realm should be ignored. In examining how Aristotle deals with sensation we shall locate the treatment of the phenomenal or phenomenological[5] among the formal, the functional, the actual; at some points we shall have to clear up ambiguities in his formulation, and see in detail how he relates the phenomenal to the physical and physiological. But the important thing is that he has not the slightest temptation to make an independent field of the phenomenal. The reason seems to be that the various functions or activities of the human being—nutrition, motion, sensation, thought—are regarded as being (metaphysically) in the same boat. A man walking and a man seeing or hearing and a man thinking are all to be analyzed in the same sort of way. This is part of a broader outlook in which such varied phenomena as the rolling of a ball, the changing of a color, the growth of a plant, a man growing angry, a shift from ignorance to knowledge, would all be seen as instances of change without any attempt to reduce them to one fundamental type or to institute fundamental cleavages. Aristotle's theory of change, itself in part an application of his categories (quantity, quality, place, substance) as well as of his notions of form and matter, was largely responsible for this nonreductive outlook. When these concepts of the network are applied in psychology the nonreductive outlook is carried as a matter of course into the functions of the psyche and into the objects to which those functions are directed. The qualities in the field of experience will be a natural part of the formal account.

It was mentioned above that Aristotle's treatment of the material—physical and physiological—aspects of psyche is not removed from the remainder of the psychological investigation. This is justified by the close relation of matter and form. He goes even further. Using the transactional formulation that he developed for the joint actualization of the potentialities of agent and patient (see chapter 6, above), he develops a specific schema for the analysis of functions that integrates both the material and the formal. He applies it first to the analysis of nutrition; then the refined schema is used for sensation, and finally for thought. It will be suggested that some of the traditional difficulties in Aristotle's analysis of thought become understandable (not necessarily resolvable) when interpreted in these terms.

Although our attention to Aristotle's presuppositions and underlying framework is upon the way that the concepts of his network are applied toward an understanding of the psyche, we should not overlook the fact that he is arguing for his position or be inattentive to the evidence he offers. After all, it is the specific establishment of ideas and theses in the different special fields that tests the value of the network itself. Again, it is not our intention in part 3 to recommend Aristotle's psychological theory for contemporary psychology. The aim is simply to interpret the direction in which it seemed to be heading and to explore its possibilities without judging it in terms of later frameworks to which it does not belong. If the disparate tendencies in contemporary psychological theory are used as criteria, the network as we have interpreted it from Aristotle's works has considerable promise for psychology, certainly more than it had for physics.

Of the three chapters in this part, chapter 9 will deal with the methodological aspects of psychology; it will present Aristotle's definition of the psyche, his transactional schema, and how he handles the materials of physical science. Chapter 10 deals with sensation and thought, and chapter 11 with movement and emotion.

9

METHODOLOGICAL ASPECTS

OF PSYCHOLOGY

This chapter examines three topics. The first is Aristotle's formal definition of the psyche, which he carries out in terms of his metaphysical concepts but which when unpacked yields a fairly clear conception of his general psychological approach. The second is his transactional schema for analyzing functions of the psyche; this is set against the background of the conflicts in Greek theories of psychology and the opposing principles that had been generated. An important feature of this second topic is the place of the phenomenal in the schema. The third topic is the way that Aristotle handles the physical materials. This will be dealt with by selected illustration.

Definition of the Psyche

Aristotle builds up the technical definition of the psyche step by step. The psyche is a substance in the sense that it is the form (*eidos*) of a natural body that potentially has life.[1] This means simply that a certain kind of body has an organization which renders it capable of the activities that constitute being alive. Since substance has been identified with actuality or fulfillment (*entelecheia*), the psyche can be viewed as the actuality of such a body. Aristotle then distinguishes two senses of *actuality*. The *first actuality* is the level of organization that can issue directly in the activity, that is, the possession of distinctive developed capacities; his favorite analogy is the man who has knowledge (e.g., of a language) even when he is not using it. The *second actuality* is the actual use of capacities. Both are contrasted with learning a language, which is a movement or change culminating in the first actuality. The psyche can now therefore be defined as the first actuality of a natural body that potentially possesses life.[2] He comments that such is any body which is "organic," and that even the parts of plants are rudimentary organs dividing tasks. Consequently a definition common to every psyche would be "the first actuality of an organic natural body."[3]

The immediate consequence of his general definition is to dismiss as unnecessary the question whether psyche and body are one—as unnecessary, he says, as whether the wax and the shape impressed upon it are one, or the matter and that whose matter it is.[4] Among the many senses of unity, as of being, he adds, the basic is actuality; this, of course, is the conclusion that culminated his search for substance.

Aristotle's analogies are always instructive, and none more than those he offers for the psyche. If an ax were a natural body, that is, if it had the power to set itself in movement and arrest its movement, its ability to cut, which makes it an ax, would be its psyche. Similarly, if the eye were an independent organism, its ability to see would be its psyche. *Psyche* thus designates not a thing, but an organization for a pattern of life functions. It cannot be found by dissecting the body, any more than the sharpness of an ax can be found by cutting up the ax. What would be found is a certain character of the material, a relative hardness and an acute angle between the sides. So, too, there are specific bodily bases for life functions. Again, the psyche is never to be found straying away from the body, any more than the sharpness can be disengaged from the ax.

The specification of psyche as an actuality is no mere metaphysical dressing. It determines the way that Aristotle analyzes the many functions of the human being that constitute "being alive." None of these functions is considered the property of an isolated entity. In each case there is, rather, a unique mode of interaction with specific factors in the environment, involving a specific qualitative pattern of the whole (man-in-environment). This unified actuality can be looked at from opposite ends. As in any actualization of the potential there is a unified actuality such that the activity of the agent and the affection of the patient are one, but they differ as the road from Athens to Thebes differs from the road from Thebes to Athens.

The functions dealt with range from nutrition, reproduction, growth, and respiration, through sensation in its various forms, animal movement, imagining, dreaming, and desiring, to rational intellectual activities. They fall into three large groups. Thus Aristotle speaks of the nutritive psyche, the sensitive psyche, and the rational psyche. Plants have the first, animals the first and second, and man all three sets of functions. Interrelations can also be traced among the functions. For example, touch is the sense for food, and therefore pervasive among animals. Furthermore, whatever has sensation has appetition, since sensation involves pleasure and pain, and desire is the appetition for the pleasant.

Aristotle's general definition of psyche was intended to cover all three types of living beings. They are not regarded as three species of one genus, but rather as a developing series, each term of which presupposes the earlier. (His favorite example of this kind of order is the number series.) This conception reflects the obvious fact that plants, animals, and humans do not merely exist separately but that the sorts of things each does (when arranged in that order) include the sorts of things the earlier does. The very attempt to study them together in psychology presupposes the one-world attitude examined earlier, the naturalism that passes readily among the things of nature and discerns their growing complexities and differences without creating unbridgeable chasms. It is in such a light that Aristotle's biology deals with the development of the individual.

We may, at the outset, have some difficulty understanding what is *not* a natural body capable of life. Presumably Aristotle is referring to the elements, which even if they have a source of motion or rest within themselves, or if they are used by psyche,[5] would have to be turned into the specific materials of plants or animals to yield an organic body. In any case the concept of potentiality is to be used for only one step at a time (earth being potentially bronze, and bronze potentially a statue, does not mean earth is potentially a statue). Aristotle's chief interest is in the timing and conditions under which the decisive marks of each kind of psyche enter the scene—nutrition, growth, and reproduction for nutritive psyche, self-movement and sensory powers for animals, and rational powers for humans. As we may expect, there are twilight zones. He raises the question whether psyche is or is not present in the seed and the embryonic formation to begin with, recognizing that in some sense they have life; he answers that semen and fetus possess nutritive psyche potentially but not actually until they begin to draw the nourishment to themselves.[6] And he goes on to elaborate alternative possibilities about where the potentialities for different types of psyche appear, and where their actuality emerges. It would take us too far into technical detail to follow his answers, which depend on his theory of the actual development of the embryo, the emergence of the heart as the first part to be formed,[7] and its relations to sensation.

The Transactional Schema for Analyzing Functions

The special way in which the functions of the psyche are analyzed must of course be seen against the general background provided by the four causes. The material cause specifies the relevant bodily parts and conditions involved and the physical objects and processes of the environment. The formal cause specifies the organization that constitutes an existent structure (e.g., a sense organ) embodying specific capacities. The efficient cause provides the initiating processes, whether in the body or the surroundings or both, that precipitate the actualization of the function. The final cause is not quite as simple. Generally, in the biological operations it is to carry out the functions of the organ in order to maintain life. Occasionally it also applies to the good life beyond mere survival: for example, touch is needed for survival, but sight for living well in addition to apprehending at a distance and so assuring protection,[8] and reproduction is an endeavor to ensure continuity as a second best to immorality.[9] In the case of humans we need not expect more here than the general reference of final cause, since the full picture belongs to the ethical and political works.

The list of functions that Aristotle examines is a full one. *On the Psyche*, which presents the general structure, treats of nutrition, sensation, thought, and initiation of movement, and *On Sense and Sensible Objects* (the first work in the *Parva Naturalia*) supplements the treatment of some of the specific senses; other short treatises deal with such functions as memory, sleep, dreaming, youth and age, and respiration.[10] Aristotle does not always deal with all aspects of the causal inquiry, nor does he always stop to tell us where he is dealing with forms and actualities, where with material and initiating processes, and where with their relations.

We are employing the term *transactional schema* to designate Aristotle's way of picturing how factors he has distinguished work together in the functioning of the psyche, that is, in the human activities of nutrition, sensation, thought, and so on. The development of this schema can best be seen by tracing Aristotle's reaction to the conflicting theories of his day.[11] He calls attention to them, points out the facts that support or impede their acceptance, and uses his own conceptual approach to restructure the questions they ask, attempting a fresh synthesis. For example, he faces over and over again the opposing theoretical slogans that like is affected by like, and like is affected by unlike. These had grown up in many different areas of observation and inquiry. Fire feeds on what is not fire, but what happens when one fire meets another? Does flesh grow by adding to itself, through selective accretion, elements of a similar nature in food; or does it somehow transform something of an opposite nature? When the eye sees, is it because the fire in it is aware of the fiery component in things and the water senses the liquid component, or is the fire aware of the water and the water of the fire? General issues of a more abstract nature arise as these parallel problems line up. Things that are like, it may be argued, lie peaceably side by side, and neither acts or is acted on with respect to the other; opposites set up a tension. Yet how can utterly different things even get together to have an effect on one another?

Aristotle undertakes his general analysis of the problem in his treatise *On Generation and Corruption*.[12] The reason for this apparent conflict, he tells us, is the partial perspective of each school. If like can be affected by like, he says, it can be affected by itself, and so everything will move itself. And if there is complete difference, how can line be affected by whiteness, or whiteness by line? Agent and patient must be alike in falling into the same genus or general class, and differ in being contraries or opposites within the class; and the active assimilates the passive to itself, just as fire heats what is cold. In the case of food, Aristotle argues, controversy arises only because the analysis is insufficiently refined. "Food" is ambiguous; are we referring to the first or the last form of what is added when we eat?[13] The one is undigested, the other digested. In the former case, contrary feeds on contrary; in the latter, like on like. Both views are then right and wrong. Aristotle then maps the fuller structure of the situation. We must not forget that what is fed is the living body. The organization that is the nutritive psyche does the feeding. The food is the means; but involved as means, too, is the heat that does the work of digestion. The final end is reproduction of the species. (Aristotle promises a special treatise on the question of food, but this, if ever written, has not survived.)

Now a modern reader tends to put all this aside as a historically interesting, but philosophically irrelevant, chapter in the growth of knowledge. Perhaps he might remark that it reveals the sense of mystery that may have then attended ordinary everyday phenomena. To brush aside the account, however, is hasty, for it shows how Aristotle applies the concepts of potentiality and actuality, action and passion, in a transactional mode of analysis for functions of the psyche: *a central process of assimilation in which what is potentially like but actually unlike, becomes actually like, the transformation being set off by some already existent actuality.* If this mode seems trivial in the initial problems with respect to which he forges it, it nevertheless grows in significance as it becomes his framework for analyzing first sensation and then thought. In the end, it shapes his philosophical stand on basic epistemological problems.

Aristotle's use of this schema can be seen particularly clearly in his treatment of hearing and seeing. In any situation that will allow sound to happen, there is an ear, as part of the living body, and a physical object that will later be sounding. Between them, there is a physical continuum provided by the air, which serves as a medium that stretches from the object into the ears. This entire physical basis of hearing—the material side and hence the potentiality—is precipitated into actualization by the act of striking an object. Now the interactive process has begun, and we need not follow Aristotle's physical picture in detail. What is significant instead is the unity in the actuality: "The activity [*energeia*] of the sensible object and that of the percipient sense are one and the same, but their being is different. Take for example actual sound and actual hearing: it is possible for one who has hearing not to be hearing, and that which has sound is not always sounding. But when that which is able to hear is actively hearing and that which is able to sound is sounding, then the actual hearing and the actual sounding arise together."[14]

Now there is a possible ambiguity in the phrase "arise together." The Greek is *hama ginetai*, which means literally "come into being together." One translator renders it "are merged together"; another, "occur together," stressing the simultaneity indicated by *hama*. This typifies the problem of translating Aristotle. Is he saying that there is one actuality of sounding-and-hearing, which can be looked at from either end? Or is he saying that there are two concurrent events? Or does he mean both?

Perhaps it is only fair to Aristotle to assume that there is no ambiguity. Physically, events like soundings and hearings are concurrent, but with respect to form or actualization there is but one actuality. The latter would fit our contemporary notion of a phenomenological description. The sound is in one's ears, it is all through the air, and it is over there. It is "coming from" there. No physical description should alter the picture of the actuality as sense experience maps it. Nor should philosophical perplexities of where the sound is "really"—whether it is subjective and only in the mind—be allowed to confuse the issue. Some commentators on Aristotle feel called on here to apologize for his not raising questions of this sort—in short, for not being a Cartesian or a Berkeleian or a Kantian. Perhaps he is not worried by their problems because they do not arise in the transactional schema in which his potentiality–actuality framework structures the problem. (As a matter of fact, this is one of the strongest arguments for his schema in epistemological analysis.) He does stop to point out that sensible qualities are not dependent on being observed: they exist as potentialities in objects.[15]

The treatment of vision is similar. One precondition is the eye, as part of the living body. The other is the surface of the object. The one is potentially seeing, the other potentially colored. In between is a continuous medium. This Aristotle identifies not as air, but as a finer substance shared by air, water, and the eternal fifth substance; he calls it the "diaphanous" or "transparent." In this situation, fire serves to precipitate actualization, just as the striking does in hearing or heat does in digestion. At once the unified actuality is there. The eye is actually seeing, the object is actually colored, the medium is actually transparent. This energetic state of the medium is what Aristotle calls "light." He means this more in the phenomenal sense in which we report that a room was "lit up" than in our physical sense of light as traveling energy. There is, of course, no incompatability in these viewpoints, since in Aristotle's conception the motion would have to be in the vehicle underlying the illumination. He does consider the suggestion that light has a velocity, but rejects it on the ground that we should notice if it were so. It all seems too instantaneous. An illustration on another point (in the *Topics*) is relevant here: Aristotle speaks of a burning coal, a flame, and light, all as different species of fire.[16] These are all qualitatively different actualities of a single underlying process, and it is easy to grasp how he puts them together. He seems almost to be ordering them in degree of purity, and naturally the purest has the most subtle material base.

Had Aristotle believed that light had a finite velocity, would it have made a difference to his interpretation? We know that much later, in the Cartesian era, a belief in the finite velocity of light helped raise the question whether vision is directly of the object or is a later effect within us; in the modern example, the star we now see may already have exploded and disappeared millions of years ago. What then happens to the unified transactional schema of instantaneous actualization? Is such a framework, which avoids epistemological puzzles and allows for the investigation of the physical, the phenomenal, and their correlation, really applicable only to the short-range ordinary life situation of fairly direct confrontation?

Aristotle tackles the velocity problem in *On Sense and Sensible Objects*.[17] He recognizes that sound and smell do travel in a finite time, and Empedocles earlier argued the same for light. Aristotle seems to be wavering between two theories. One proposes a sort of incremental action, the other a holistic action. To describe holistic action, he appeals to the phenomenon of water freezing all at once; but he recognizes that when a large body grows hot or freezes there is a succession in which each part changes because of a change in a contiguous part. It is this model that Aristotle uses for sound: the initial striking of the sounding object affects the air nearby and gives it a certain form, which is transmitted farther on. In short, a large area in which the holistic action of unified *energeia* is not possible is decomposed into successive small areas in which it is possible. What is needed, then, is simply the physical theory of the underlying transmission processes. After all, even in the ordinary hearing and seeing situations, Aristotle recognizes the possibility of other forms of actualization besides the direct-perception situation. They happen precisely because some physical process sets up a fresh basis for subsequent actualization. The sensible form becomes imprinted in the recipient sense like a shape stamped on wax. Since it now exists in the man, he is able to activate it in the faculty of imagination, and in memory and dreams.

Aristotle's schema of interpreting human functions would thus not be incapable of expansion, even though it applied initially to the familiar small and middle-sized situation. It required only a firm hold on the altered material basis, so that any question about the actuality at any point in the temporal process could be resolved by reference to the matter taking form at that point, that is, to the specific potentialities being actualized. But in fact, as Aristotle works his way up the scale of human functions, the specific emphasis on change and process in the materials diminishes, and the phenomenal aspects come to the fore. We see the balance shifting as we move from nutrition up and into the range of sensation. In nutrition the assimilative process involves the destruction of the object. In touch and taste there is direct contact (though Aristotle decides that flesh serves as an attached medium to an inner organ of touch). When we get to vision, Aristotle speaks of sensible form as being received without matter. Here the account of the physical mechanisms shows Aristotle at times undecided. He is operating in a milieu of debate about the mechanisms of vision. He considers whether emanations come from the object to the eye or the reverse, and talks as if the eye actually takes on the color that it is seeing, and sometimes allows that seeing may affect an object through movements set up in the air. In the case of seeing, he definitely comes out for holistic process. He seems to tie his discussion also to the problem of continuity and the way in which a whole can manifest a quality actually while the parts do it only potentially. (This is, of course, his familiar way of tackling Zeno's paradoxes: we cover an actual distance in a finite time but cover its infinity of potentially divisible intervals only potentially.) Ultimately, perhaps, his paradigm for our modern exploding-star example would be the movement of drawing a line. It takes time. The starting is one actuality (corresponding here to the physical actuality of emitting light energy). The movement of drawing the line is an actualizing process. It could be stopped at any point, but it isn't. The end point is a different actuality from the drawing (corresponding here to the instantaneous seeing).

The unified instantaneous actualization of organ, object, and medium is the dominant note in Aristotle's theory of vision. Seeing is actually like using a language, not learning it. Exploration of the precise movements underlying seeing is a question of identifying the material aspects and the way in which the imprinting of form takes place within the perceiver.

Aristotle has a general account of sense organs. They deal each with a specific range of qualities for which they are adapted by their own constitution. If the stimulus is too strong or too weak, they are either injured or not aroused. In the discussion of touch, sense operates as a kind of mean between opposing sensible qualities.[18] Precisely because the senses are a mean of opposites, they are able to be affected by opposite qualities within their range. (If a sense coincided with an extreme it could not be affected by it.)

As we explained earlier, the contemporary notion of the phenomenal or phenomenological fits quite comfortably into the Aristotelian idea of form (functions, actualities), and we have discussed its relation to material processes (physical movements, changes) in those terms. It is usually quite clear where Aristotle is referring to one level or the other. There are, however, cases in which an insufficient distinction produces theoretical puzzles. In the treatment of vision in *On the Psyche* the interest obviously lies in ordinary-life, as it were macroscopic, phenomena. A human being opens his eyes in the daytime and directly he sees colors and shapes; in the dark of the night nothing is seen, then a torch is lit, and there is seeing. The materials or potentialities in both body and environment were ready at hand, all set to go, given the action of the efficient cause. The material basis of the actualities is an unavoidable issue, but it is referred to only insofar as is necessary for that inquiry. Aristotle does not there go into the internal physiology of the eye and the relations to brain or heart, as he does elsewhere; presumably a man wanting to see in the daytime need do no more than open his eyes. It does not follow that eyes can see alone without other internal connections, but simply that everyday actualities can be described without inference to them.

Aristotle does, however, get into theoretical difficulties in trying to adjust his general concepts to his specific description. His theoretical structure holds that motion is located in the object moved, so that, generally speaking, action and passion are located in that which is acted on, the patient. Hence when he has the material process in mind, as in his physiological account of sensation, he concludes that actual sound and actual hearing are located in that which has the power of hearing.[19] On the other hand, he does speak in another context as if the air itself is sounding,[20] and certainly he talks of the actualization of seeing as if it were a joint activity of the human being and the color of the object seen. Thus the ascription of action and passion seems to vary according as one is talking on the level of form and actuality or on the level of material process. Or, more properly, the language of agent and patient belongs to the level of material process, whereas that of potentiality being actualized belongs to the level of form-actuality.

Aristotle gets close to this problem in a number of contexts where he worries whether sensation is a kind of alteration (*alloiōsis*). Sometimes when he speaks of it thus he is giving others' opinion, and sometimes he appears to talk for himself; but when he gets to a fuller treatment of the issue he makes a careful distinction.[21] He adverts to the difference between learning, knowing, and knowing-in-use, and decides that while the transition in learning that ends in knowing is properly alteration in which the subject is changed, that from potential to actual knowledge is not properly alteration—or else, he says, "alteration" is being used in two senses. Similarly *paschein*, "to be acted on" or "to suffer," has different senses when it involves a kind of destruction of something by its opposite and when it involves preservation, a kind of safeguarding of the potentiality in its exercise. Aristotle decides to continue using the terms "to be acted upon" and "altered" because no specialized terms are available. He is not usually so reluctant to develop a technical vocabulary. Most of the time, where he is clearly discussing a process—even, for example, when it is the form of an object being stamped on the sense, or its analogue in the case of thinking[22]—no problem arises. But where the point is to explain the actualization of the sensory power by the sense-object without reference to underlying material processes, Aristotle simply denies that the sense-faculty (*aisthētikon*) suffers or is altered, or says that if it is motion, it is of a different kind: not the actuality of the incomplete but the simple actuality of the complete or perfected.[23]

I think the careful study of these and other passages will show that we have not here a contradiction on Aristotle's part but an insufficiently explicit distinction between an analysis of the actualities (form, phenomenal properties) and of the underlying material properties. I have suggested throughout that in those contexts where it is clearest, we find a definite and sophisticated mode of analysis in which the formal and the material quite satisfactorily provide a framework for the phenomenal and the physical analysis in psychology without introducing arbitrary dichotomies between the objective and the subjective or mind and matter, particularly when set in the transactional schema in which the cooperation of factors is clearly indicated. In the formal account—the description of actualities—there is no inconsistency in considering the man as active, the color as located on the object, the sound as being everywhere in the room or moving from one end to the other. In the material account, there is the difficult scientific job of tracing the underlying movement, agents, patients, and direction of causality. This latter task becomes clearer if we try to make sense of the way that Aristotle grapples with the physical theses of his time.

The Physical Issues

Let us take two examples from what was discussed above: Aristotle's serious reckoning with the notion that the physics of vision must involve an emanation from the eye to the object, and his apparent acceptance of the idea that in the act of vision the eye takes on the color of the object.

The evidence in the corpus on the question of emanation in vision goes both ways; whether this indicates ambivalence or a change of mind at a later period we cannot say. In the *Meteorology* he appears to use a theory of emanation from the eye. He speaks of our vision being reflected, in considering others' explanation of the comet's tail and in his own explanation of other phenomena.[24] He explains a weak-sighted man's seeing an image going before him and facing him by the suggestion that because of the weakness, the man's vision was reflected back to him by the neighboring air acting as a medium, since his vision was not able to thrust it aside.[25] In *On Dreams*, the case of the menstruating woman reddening a mirror by looking at it is in the same theoretical vein: the emanations from the eye are tinged by her state.[26] On the other hand, in *On the Psyche*, in a context where he is considering how a medium is set in motion by a sensible object and transmits effects so long as the medium itself remains one mass, he concludes that instead of saying sight issues from the eye and is reflected, we might better have the air affected by shape and color, "just as if the impression on the wax were extended through to the other side."[27] In *On Sense and Sensible Objects* he objects to Empedocles' view that vision occurs through light issuing from the eye as if from a lantern, since then it would operate in the dark.[28] He opposes the view that an emanation from the eye can reach as far as the stars or coalesce somewhere on the way with the object.[29] In the passage from *On Dreams* referred to above he seems to have reached a synthesis, for there he says that vision is both affected by the air and affects it in turn, though he adds that this is because the eye is a bright object possessing color. Interestingly, in his discussion of distant vision in *Generation of Animals* he works with both theories, trying to show the conditions under which sight will be keenest; for example, on the theory that the clearest vision involves the least diffuse movement from the object to the eye, he concludes that a continuous tube connecting them would promote the best of all.[30]

It is less important to determine what Aristotle actually decided than to appreciate the outlook on body—medium relations that was implicit in his consideration of alternatives. He does not make an absolute distinction between the body and the medium except in cases where a qualitative difference results. For example, to make hearing possible, the air must act as one continuous whole. This happens only under specific conditions.[31] He goes on to say that the body of air in which the sound-producing movement takes place must be continuous all the way to the organ of hearing, and he treats the air in the ear as part of the organ. Similarly touch involves a medium, and the flesh is such a medium; it is not the immediate organ of touch. Other things can extend the medium —for example, a close-fitting fabric (he even imagines the fabric growing on the flesh). Indeed, there may always be a film of air or moisture between the hand and the object.[32] He makes a subtle distinction between seeing and hearing, in which the medium acts on us, and touch, in which we and the medium are affected at once, like a man wounded through his shield; it is not the shield that strikes him but he and the shield that are struck at once.[33] Aristotle seems here to be suggesting that the medium in such cases is more like a part of us. He conjectures that in touch flesh is either the primary organ, comparable to the pupil in sight, or else the organ and the medium combined in one, comparable to the pupil plus the diaphanous medium in sight.[34] This is almost as if we were to define the organ of vision as the eye plus the glasses we wear plus the air medium between them. Along similar lines, in *Movement of Animals* he suggests that a stick one holds becomes a kind of removable member; he even compares the relation of the stick and the elbow (presumably the stick is held firmly with the wrist in a fixed position) to that of the hand and the wrist in their usual relation.[35]

There is a kind of refreshing literalness about all this. When moderns note such phenomena in their scientific and philosophical reflection, they tend to see them as correlating the physical and the mental. For example, it is pointed out that if I hold a stick against the desk, but loosely, I feel the stick, whereas if I hold it tightly I feel the desk. This is interpreted as an instance of two different partition points between myself and the environment, and so as part of the phenomenal body. For Aristotle it is rather an identification of wholes by functional effects.

Perhaps the more direct parallel to the Aristotelian spirit is found in contemporary discussions of the identity and boundaries of the self— why people tend to accept glasses but not hearing aids as part of themselves; why some of our aims and values are constitutive of our selves, and others are readily given up as external; why so many people regard their property as in some sense an extension of self; why some maintain strict boundaries around their selves and others have vague ones; and so on. A theory investing persons and objects and aims with libidinal energy, such as Freud's, would parallel Aristotle's type of discussion in that no *a priori* boundaries of inner and outer are set up; but insofar as issues of causality are raised, Aristotle would be more likely than a psychoanalytic theorist, generally, to rely on physiology—although Freud would have, at the early stage of his libido theory.

Our second example of Aristotle's mode of scientific inquiry into material processes is his view that the eye in some sense (his qualification) takes on the color that it sees.[36] This is partly forced on him by his underlying theoretical assumptions, partly by his need to explain other facts. (In other senses the parallel arises from a normal natural phenomenon; the hand, for instance, becomes warm on touching a warm object.) An important assumption is, as noted earlier, that in action or production the agent assimilates the patient to itself; this is generalized from fire heating and what is cold cooling.[37] For sensation this means that the sense organ is capable of becoming what the object is like,[38] and this develops into the general position that in sensation the form of the sensible object is somehow transferred to or assimilated by the sense. This is a stronger thesis than simply the unified actuality of sense and object in the actual sensing, for it involves the continuance of the impression after the sensing is over. Aristotle compares the assimilated form to the imprint of a signet ring on wax and generalizes it into the principle that the sense receives the form of sensible objects without the matter.[39] Clearly something like this is required in order to provide his theory with some explanation of imagination and memory.

Nevertheless, writers on Aristotle tend to pass over the idea that the eye in some sense takes on the color it sees, as something slightly ridiculous (one thinks of becoming purple or mauve upon looking at those colors)—unless, of course, it is simply a question of the iris reflecting the color. And yet we cannot be objecting to the view that the eye is differentially affected by different colors; the issue is only with the type of effect that is involved. To understand what Aristotle is up to, we have to see his view in the context of *his* theory of colors. It is important to recall that his physical theory involves a basic explanation in terms of hot and cold, and that objects are liquid or solid according as they are moist or dry; the proportions determine precisely what results. When he discusses these operations in *Meteorology* 4 he reminds us that a thing is white, fragrant, resonant, sweet, hot, or cold by being able to act in a given way upon the senses.[40] The basic interaction will be a definite heating or cooling even in sensory experience.

The selection of white to illustrate color here is no accident for Aristotle. White and black are the contraries from which colors are composed, and these in turn are simply reproducing in bodies the conditions that produce light and darkness in air.[41] He goes on directly to explain how the other colors arise by the differential mixture of white and black particles or, according to another theory, by laying one color on another, as painters do, or as the sun, which shows white when directly viewed but shows red through fog and smoke.[42] The colors intermediate between white and black are red, purple, green, and blue, and the rest are combinations of these, making a total of seven colors if we count gray as a kind of black or else classify yellow with white.[43] The pseudo-Aristotelian treatise *On Colors*, though later, continues in the Aristotelian vein. It is equally emphatic in starting from light or fire and dark or black (which it interprets as sheer absence of light or vision) and gathers its evidence about different colors from all sorts of natural processes, from the making of wine and the dyeing of fabrics to the changing colors of plants, types of plumage, effects in cooking, natural coloration under different conditions, and of course direct mixing of colors.

In similar fashion, when Aristotle considers the different colors found in eyes and the physical bases of different performances in vision, he cites as factors the amount of fluid in the eye (comparing the different colors of seawater according to depth) and the effects of light on eyes so constituted.[44] In general his explanations, whether dealing with the eye or with the color of objects, do not involve unitary patches of, say, purple or mauve being transplanted onto the eye. They are not very different in tone from what a modern would say: that the brain in some sense files away the differences in color we experience, through some coding system expressed in terms of the physical basis of sight. The difference lies, of course, in the theory of the basis.

The three topics we have considered in this chapter outline how Aristotle's philosophical method in psychology makes possible an integrated approach to man and his powers. His definition of the psyche, cast in terms of potentiality and actuality, bypasses the dualism of body and mind. It opens the way to a full naturalism in which the continuities and differences of plant, animal, and human can be studied scientifically. That an actuality is a joint or single actualization or fulfillment of agent and patient (of the organism and the environment) makes it possible to see the phenomenal as qualities of the transactional situation rather than as locked away in a private mind. The relation between the phenomenal and the physical or physiological is captured in the Aristotelian relation of form and matter, which ensures a relative and nonreductive character in their distinction.[45] Moreover, that the formal and the functional (final) are assimilated in the Aristotelian network means that the experiential qualities and behavioral phenomena need not be treated discretely. Neither is truncated and both can be seen in a full scope that allows of purposes, planning, and action.

How all this works out with respect to specific functions remains to be seen in the next two chapters. But it is possible that where it is less successful the defects in Aristotle's theories may be those of the state of his scientific knowledge and not of the integrative schema he developed.

10

SENSE AND THOUGHT

Chapter 9 has given a sufficient picture of vision and hearing for our purposes, and some points have already emerged about the basic character of touch. A few remarks here may round out the treatment of the other senses, along with common sense and the imagination. Thereafter—with careful attention to the text, since problems of serious controversy are involved—we examine thought.

The Senses, Common Sense, Imagination

Touch is the fundamental sense, because it is tied in with nutrition as the sense that perceives food; thus its essential objects are the dry or moist and the hot or cold.[1] Other qualities are also discriminated by touch—movement, rest, number, shape, size (rough and smooth are added separately)—in common with some of the other senses.[2] Hunger and thirst are identified in terms of the objects of touch, as desires for dry and hot, and for cold and wet, respectively. That taste is a kind of tangible is clear at least insofar as we cannot taste through any foreign medium, and what we taste has to be in a liquid material.[3] Flavor is a kind of seasoning. Aristotle lists seven basic flavors: sweet, salt, bitter, harsh, pungent, astringent, and acid.[4] Smells have some analogous objects, such as the sweet and the bitter, and take their names from flavors because smell is not as highly discriminating in humans as it is in animals; Aristotle seems to think this is indicated by the fact that we do not smell without feeling pleasure or pain.[5] Smell is related to breathing: we can smell only while inhaling. Many other features of taste and smell and current theories of their nature are presented in a longer treatment, in *On Sense and Sensible Objects*.[6]

Book 2 of *Parts of Animals*, after dealing with parts of the body concerned with nutrition, has a long section on parts concerned with sensation.[7] The brain is not the cause of any sensation; that is a mistaken inference from the fact that some of the sense organs are in the head. The true source of sensation is around the heart. Aristotle discusses the reasonable placement of the sense organs, which ones are directly connected to the heart and which indirectly, and surveys them in the spirit of comparative anatomy. He is generally interested in the multiple functions of organs—for example, the elephant's nostrils or man's lips. The lips not only protect the teeth but make speech possible; similarly, the tongue combines the function of taste with that of speech. (There is also a discussion here of the way in which the properties of the tongue are related to types of sounds.)

The problem of the so-called common sense is a complex one.[8] *On the Psyche* refers chiefly to the common sensibles, that is, properties discerned by more than one sense, such as the tangibles listed above—movement, rest, shape, size, number, and so forth. Quite separate but kindred questions are how we know that something is the same object when different sense objects are involved (for instance, that bitter and yellow both belong to the same bile)[9] and how we are aware that we are seeing.[10] Although not without some reservations, Aristotle believes these questions point to a central sensorium.[11] In *On Memory and Recollection* he specifies that time, together with magnitude and motion, is perceived by a "common sense," and he identifies the image or appearance (*phantasma*) in these cases as an affection of this faculty.[12] The knowledge of these things is said to belong to the *primary sense faculty* (*prōton aisthētikon*).

The treatise *On Sleep and Waking* forces a more unified consideration of awareness, for in going to sleep we seem to turn off all sensory equipment (except for dreaming, which is a separate question). Is there a general activity we turn off, or is it simply that a necessary condition common to the various senses taken distributively is removed? Aristotle does not exactly ask the question that way. He notes the fact of exhaustion and concludes that sleep is simply the sensitive part of us being affected—a kind of binding or fettering.[13] Here he comes close to talking in our contemporary language of consciousness in general or awareness in general: there is a certain common power (*koinē dunamis*) that goes along with all the special senses, whereby one sees he sees and is able to judge the difference between the objects of different senses.[14] There are remarks about one unified sense faculty (*aisthēsis*) and one chief or "lordly" sense organ (*kurion aisthētērion*) that has a varying sensory mode for different kinds of sense objects. One suggestion connects this with touch, which is indispensable and prior to the other senses, but in *On Youth and Old Age*, putting aside other functions of the psyche and turning to sensation as the distinctive mark of the animal, Aristotle reaffirms the unity of the common sense organ underlying the separate senses and directs us to the neighborhood of the heart.[15] This is confirmed, as noted earlier, in the biological writings. Thus we are told that the heart is the first of all the parts to be formed, that it has blood at the start, and that all movements of pleasure and pain and in general of sensation begin in the heart and are fulfilled there.[16]

Imagination (*phantasia*) holds an appropriate place between sensation and thought. It is different from both, but it does not arise without perception and without it there would be no judgment.[17] It is an affection that lies in our power, for we can summon up images at will. Unlike our judgments, images will be neither true nor false. When we imagine, we may be like spectators looking at pictures. After patiently exploring a variety of other differences, Aristotle defines imagination as a movement coming from sensation actively at work.[18]

Traditional interpretations of Aristotle's use of *phantasia* have taken it for granted that he means some kind of picture-viewing and have accordingly treated *phantasma* (the noun for the object of imagining) as a sense image. Aristotle's close association of imagination with thought has had its place historically in the psychological controversies over the possibility of imageless thought. Recently, however, a number of Aristotelian scholars have begun to offer a broader interpretation of Aristotle's notion of the imagination itself; perhaps the most illuminating is Nussbaum's study in her edition of Aristotle's *Movement of Animals*.[19] She focuses on the contexts in which Aristotle is explaining action and animal movement, and notes that he relies on *phantasia* throughout these explanations. Thereafter she reexamines the familiar passages on memory and dreams and his controversial remarks on thought. As a result of the whole inquiry, she concludes that *phantasia* has a close association with *phainesthai* (to appear) and that *phantasma* is not necessarily a sense image or reproduction but rather the way something appears to a person in all kinds of situations. Such usage is congruent with Aristotle's talk of the apparent good as contrasted with the real good, and makes sense of some views that he occasionally expresses, such as that sensation (*aisthēsis*) is never wrong though *phantasia* can be. Hence the role of sensation in thought is restricted, and that of *phantasia*, as the way sensation is interpreted, becomes expanded. In effect, Nussbaum's analysis seems to show that *phantasia* served for Aristotle as a construct for the physiological (material) residue of *aisthēsis* in which the form is kept available for thinking; it takes actualized shape as an image only in some cases; it gives cognitive shape to appetite (*orexis*) and so is presupposed in all cases of animal movement. As simply "what appears," the *phantasma* derives its specific meaning from the particular context.

Aristotle's analysis of memory, *On Memory and Recollection*, outlines the elements of the problem in terms that have since become familiar.[20] There are at least three elements: the sensory *phantasma*, the fact that it has a past temporal reference, and the original that it purports to represent. The temporal reference decides its location, for time and change are cognized through the primary sense faculty. (Memory storage would thus be "central," not "peripheral.") The *phantasma* is itself a residue, like the impression stamped by a seal; its lasting or fleeting quality depends on the state of the material on which it is impressed. The crucial question is why we do not apprehend a memory-appearance just as we might apprehend an image, why we refer it to the past. The answer is in terms of the double function that any picture may have—as a painting and as a portrait or likeness (*eikōn*). In the latter sense we think of it as a representation. To think of it that way is already an aid to memory. (We may compare my looking at a painting and being told it is a portrait of someone I know.) Of course we may doubt whether in the past we experienced what it represents, or we may misremember. In the act of remembering we get an awareness that we did have the experience. Of course if we took this awareness again to be an image before us, we would land in an infinite regress. Aristotle does not raise such questions. For him the act of remembering is itself the actualization of memory as a kind of sense faculty. Perhaps it is like the phenomenon of being aware that we see. In any case, when a man remembers he is aware that he is doing so.

To recollect is a more complex matter than simply remembering. It has an inferential character, involving a search for the sort of thing one infers he has experienced before. Of course the search can fail.

Dreams are also works of the imagination. The impressions produced by our senses linger after the senses have ceased to be active. Aristotle gives an almost mechanical picture of this in *On Dreams*, comparing it to the way projectiles continue to move once launched, or the way heat gets passed on in a neighborhood, or the manner in which color examined a long time persists when the gaze is averted. Emotions also play a part in ordering the imagination when our critical controls are relaxed. (By contrast, in ordinary waking life we revise impressions such as that the sun is but a foot across, and correct other sense illusions.) In sleep the small residues of impressions and attendant emotions are not overcome by the active play of sense stimuli. Hence dreams take place. Not all images in sleep are dreams, for one may actually hear sounds. The dream consists of the phantasms that arise from the movement of sense impressions during sleep.

The imagination has other important roles in epistemology and ethics; these will be dealt with later.

Thought

Aristotle's application of his developed schema to thinking is brief and compact. Its potential for controversy, we may add, has been fully actualized in the history of philosophy. He states startling theses: Mind before it thinks is actually nothing real. Mind is separate, pure, and unmixed. What thinks becomes one with the object of thought in the act of thought. Passive mind becomes all things, but active mind makes all things. Later commentators pounced on these passages.[21] Active mind was seen as something common, doing the thinking in all of us. It was identified with God or with a realm of truth or with a part of us that enables us to become one with truth. At the very least it has been seen as the Platonic element surviving in Aristotle. Certainly there is a touch of enthusiasm in Aristotle's account of mind; and we cannot forget that the Aristotelian concept of God is pure thought thinking about itself, pure self-consciousness.

Nevertheless Aristotle's analytic conscience is clearly at work in *On the Psyche*. Everything that he says about mind here is presented as an application of a mode of analysis worked out in relation to lower functions, coupled with obvious phenomena that differentiate mind from sensation. To see this we shall have to follow the text in greater detail.

Chapter 3 of book 3 of *On the Psyche* sets off thinking from sensing. By thinking is meant both abstract and practical thought, *noein* and *phronein*. (The latter is the special term in the *Nicomachean Ethics* for practical judgment.) However, before dealing with thought (*noein*), Aristotle analyzes imagination: "About thinking, since it is different from sensing and is held to be in part imagination and in part judgment, let us first talk of imagination and then of judgment."[22] Although the analysis of imagination intervenes, it is clearly on his agenda to determine in what respect imagination may play a constitutive role in thinking.

Chapter 4 turns directly to thinking (*noein*). We must examine both what differentiates it and how it arises on a given occasion[23]—that is, its formal and efficient causes. "If thinking is like sensing," he suggests, "it would lie in the psyche's being acted on [*paschein*] by the object of thought [*noēton*] or something like that." This was of course the way he began the inquiry into sensation. We have to recall the troubles he had there about the meaning of "being acted on." He had distinguished two usages; one referred to alteration, and the other to movement from potentiality to actuality without alteration or change. He had decided to continue using the language of action and passion although he recognized it meant something different in the two cases. (Our proposal was to apply the literal meaning—the first one—to the level of physical process and the other to the level of actualities or functions.) Aristotle is definitely concerned here with the second meaning. The thinking part of the psyche does not undergo alteration, but rather a transition from potentiality to actuality: "It must then be impassive [*apathēs*], but capable of receiving the form, and be potentially such as the object, without being the object; mind must be related to the thinkable as the sensitive [*aisthētikon*] is to the sensible [*aisthēta*]."[24]

Up to this point the focus has been on the similarity of thought and sensation, but now a difference emerges. We can think of anything, but sensing is limited by the range the specific sense can deal with. Aristotle had recognized this early, and also that though we can think on our own initiative, sensation requires the presence of the sensible object.[25] The only other thing we need now recall is his theory of the sense organ as a mean: the sense organ, as a particular material organization, limits the range of its objects. By contrast, I can *think* of a heat so great that I could not stand sensing it; also, I can think of a color and a heat and a sound and a smell, though each of these requires its special organ to sense.

These are only a few phenomena, but they have striking consequences in the context of the general theoretical structure elicited from the analysis of sensation. Directly after asserting that the mind is to the object of thought as the sensitive part of the psyche is to the sensible object, Aristotle concludes that the mind is unmixed, since it thinks all things. Anything mixed with it would limit it, just as a sense organ in virtue of its particular composition is limited to a specific range of qualities that it can perceive. From this it follows that mind (that is, the part of the psyche that thinks) can have no other nature than this—its capacity for actual thought. Thus the part of the psyche that we call mind (*nous*) "is actually none of the things that are [*outhen estin energeiai*] before it thinks."[26]

The translations of this line sometimes have a strikingly mystical character. The Oxford translator, J. A. Smith, says that the mind "is, before it thinks, not actually any real thing," and the Loeb translator, W. S. Hett, puts it that mind "has no actual existence until it thinks." R. D. Hicks, in his comprehensive edition, *Aristotle, De Anima*, says that the intellect "is nothing at all actually before it thinks." All this sounds Megarian, rather than Aristotelian. After all, the mind is a potentiality, and for Aristotle potentiality is real enough; recall how he thundered against those who would deny that. Perhaps we would get closer to his meaning if we took the sentence more literally, even distributively: that mind is actually no thing of the things that are before thinking. D. W. Hamlyn translates it in this way, as "is actually none of existing things before it thinks."[27] This would mean that if we surveyed the things that are, we could not point to anything and say "That's the mind" as we could say of the eye "That's what does the seeing." Let us try the following analogy. Suppose I said of a cruel man that he is capable of hurting others. Where would I locate this capacity? I could not put it in his fist, for he might be cruel by kicking or tripping. I could not put it in his leg, because he might be cruel with his tongue. It would not be mysterious if I said that the man's cruelty is actually nothing before he hurts others; it would not mean that his cruelty is inexplicable, just that it has no one definite base.

The absence of a specific base for thinking in the body means that certain kinds or qualities of behavior cannot be set in a one-to-one relation with a physical or physiological property, since there may be a variety of conditions under which they occur. It does not of course entail that there may not be prior evidence in the behavior of the individual or other members of the species from which we can predict activity of the mind or the likely emergence of cruelty. Questions of evidence for judgments of potentiality or for dispositional properties are a separate question.

Let us return to the text. Aristotle goes on to approve the remark that the psyche is the place of forms; however, with respect to its thinking capacity, the forms occupy it not actually but only potentially.[28] The forms are of course the objects of thought, and so their occupying the place in the act of thinking is precisely parallel to the imprinting of the sense in sensing or, on the level of actualities, the single actuality of the agent and patient in the joint fulfillment of their potentialities. Aristotle does now cite a further fact that differentiates the passivity of the sensing and thinking faculties: strong stimulation incapacitates the senses immediately afterward, but strong thinking improves the mind. (Elsewhere it is argued that old age dulls the senses but not the mind.) The explanation given, however, introduces what is to be a persistent problem in this whole analysis: he says that the sense faculty is dependent on the body (literally, "not without a body") but the mind is separable (chōristos). The precise sense of separability is what is yet to be determined. One cannot ignore that Aristotle does have some kind of notion of the separateness of mind. In Generation of Animals, where Aristotle continues his portrayal of the development of the powers of the psyche we indicated above, he says that "mind [nous] alone enters additionally from outside [thurathen] and alone is divine; for bodily actuality [energeia] has nothing in common with the mind's actuality."[29] Just above that, he has pointed out that where bodily activity is required there is no possibility of outside entry; for example, walking must wait for the development of feet.

Now this passage about the mind's emergence in the development of the individual tells us no more than the argument in On the Psyche does; indeed the latter is more explicit in stressing the absence of a determinate base for thinking. If we speculate for a moment, it is clear that a range of interpretations are possible. One extreme would be a materialist view that Aristotle is simply trying to cope with lack of knowledge about the brain and its specific functions in relation to thinking. The other extreme would be a theological view that he is here driving in the first wedge of a theory that at least part of the psyche is immortal. Our present task is to follow the text strictly and exercise restraint, and so we wait for Aristotle to tell us what sort of separability is being advanced for mind in the psychological theory.

We have not long to wait. The point about the difference between the passivity of sense and that of mind, and the explanatory remarks about separateness, constitute only a brief digression in Aristotle's consideration of the mind as a place of forms. We are then told about the occupation of the mind by the forms, when a learned man (*epistēmōn*) has acquired knowledge.[30] The mark of this is that the man can now actualize his power on his own initiative (*di' hautou*). In short, we might take literally the notion that he has a mind stocked with ideas. The mind is still a potentiality (while the man is not thinking the ideas), but not like it was before he learned those ideas or discovered them. At this point the text adds, "And the mind is then able to think itself [*de hauton . . . noein*]."[31] This seems quite out of place here. It could be a casual aside; it reminds us of Aristotle's concept of God as thought thinking itself. And of course the phenomenon of thinking of thought is mentioned later; but nothing is done with it here. Perhaps our simplest choice would be to adopt a conjecture (Bywater's) about the text, that instead of *de hauton* (the conjunctive particle *de* means "but" or "moreover," and *hauton* is the object of the verb—to think *itself*), we should read *di' hautou* ("through himself," "on his own initiative"), which would simply repeat the mark of incorporation of the forms given a few lines earlier in the text. Textual problems of this sort add a constant uncertainty to difficult passages in Aristotle.

We are barely half a dozen lines from where Aristotle introduced the notion of separability, and so it is not unreasonable to see what comes next as expounding its meaning. Aristotle distinguishes between the thing and its essence in the case of physical objects—such as water and the essence of water—and resorts to his favorite example of the snub nose. Now it is by sense that we judge whether the water is warm or cold or discern the sensible properties of the snub nose. But the essence of water or flesh, or concavity of the nose, is judged either by a separate (*chōristōi*) faculty or by the same faculty in some different mode. He adds, "And in general as things are separable [*chōrista*] from their matter, so are the corresponding faculties of mind."[32] We may recall that the separation of mathematical ideas from the matter of things is only relative, consisting in abstraction. It looks as if Aristotle is suggesting here a similar relation of mind to sense. This would be congruent with his treatment of the separability of objects of mathematics from the physical objects, as in the relation of *concave* to *snub*, as well as with his theory of induction, in which the general idea emerges out of a lineup of particular experiences (see chapter 12, below).

The remainder of chapter 4 contains a number of interesting points. It raises the problem how the mind, if simple and unmixed, will think, if to think is in some sense to be acted upon; and secondly, it asks whether the mind can itself be an object of thought. Aristotle appears to be worried that since action and passion require something in common, we will begin to look for something common to mind and its objects. The situation is rather, he tells us, like a writing tablet on which nothing has been written although the letters are potentially there. Further, mind itself is thinkable, just as other objects of thought. In the case of things without matter, that which thinks and that which is being thought are identical. (Aristotle asks here the further question why mind is not always thinking.) In the case of things that have matter, the object of thought is potentially present.

The question why the mind is not always thinking is a serious one. If the mind is one with the object of thought, in the case of abstract objects thought should be going on all the time. This in effect brings us back to the initial demand that we investigate both what differentiates thought from sensing and how it arises on a given occasion.

These are the questions. The answers have, of course, yet to be considered. Solutions begin to be proposed in chapter 5. This is the center of traditional controversy, and so requires special attention. What are the theoretical concepts that Aristotle is bringing to bear at this point? There is the whole structure of potentiality and actuality he worked out in dealing with sensation, now to be applied in light of the special phenomena of thought he has already considered. There is also the structure of causal inquiry, whose application to sense and thought has not yet been completed. The discussion of the mind's becoming one with its objects, in the previous chapter, has taken care of the formal cause. The formal cause of thinking has already been established as the forms of things. At the beginning of chapter 5 Aristotle clearly turns our attention to the material cause and the efficient cause: "Since just as in the whole of nature there is something that is matter for each class of things (and this is potentially all those things) and something else that is their cause and agent [poiētikon] by virtue of making all things (just as art stands to matter), it is necessary that these differences be present in the psyche also." We may note that all he has told us, speaking of causes *in general*, is that everything has matter and an efficient cause. To be the matter of things or to make things conveys nothing more than being the material or the efficient cause. (The general sense here fits in with Aristotle's frequent example that parents provide the material and efficient causes for the child; for a particular child, for Kallias, we must trace the causes to his particular parents.)

It is also significant that Aristotle is going to look for these differences *in the psyche* (although it might mean simply *in the case of* the psyche). In the case of sense, a search for the material and efficient causes would carry us out beyond the body: for material, to the object perceived and the medium; for the efficient cause, to an action, like the striking of bells or the lighting of torches. But in the case of thinking, the object—the form—is already in the soul, brought in through the sensible form in which it is embedded: we have already met the learned man who has his stock of ideas within him and can start thinking on his own initiative. Hence the whole scene of action is already within the psyche. If thinking is to be analyzed as sensing was, then any parallels to sense organ, medium, and object have to be found within it. They will not be found in material terms, for the mind has been assigned no determinate material base. Object is already in the sense-embedded forms. Material medium is not necessary. What is left? Only a material cause as a surrogate for the organ, and an efficient cause as an activating reality corresponding to light in seeing.

Now what precisely does Aristotle go on to tell us in the next sentence of chapter 5? On the one hand there is mind that satisfies the condition of becoming all things, and on the other hand, mind that makes all things. These have come to be called passive mind and active mind (or active reason) in the controversies through the ages (although in fact Aristotle does not literally use the term *nous poiētikos*). There is little problem about passive mind in general; it is the material cause of thought, the mind that Aristotle discussed in chapter 4, which has no antecedent nature prior to the actual thinking and so becoming one with the object of thought. This oneness was suggested earlier as the culmination of the changing meanings of assimilation in the actualities that constituted the activity of the psyche. For food it meant digesting the food to make it like the body, that is, turning it into flesh. For sensation it meant the single or unified actuality in which the potentialities of the organ and the object and the medium were achieved or realized. For thought, since there is no determinate antecedent material base, it can only mean identity. As we saw, the mind is actually no thing of the things that are before thinking takes place.

What of active mind? Aristotle explains it in the same sentence: the active mind makes all things, "much as light . . . in some way makes potential into actual colors." Aristotle is drawing the parallel to vision quite literally, and here he is looking for the efficient cause of thought, just as in the previous sentence he had cited art (*technē*) as the efficient cause of something that is made. The strictest parallel would have been not to light but to fire, to lighting the torch, since he had earlier described light as the actualization of the medium. But in this analysis there is no material medium involved. Hence the theoretical structure here can be developed only as a description on the level of actuality.

Only after his concept of mind has been developed in this causal inquiry does Aristotle call mind separable and unaffected and unmixed since it is essentially actual, for that which acts (*to poioun*) is always superior to that which is acted on (*tou paschontos*), and the originative source is superior to the matter. He contrasts actual knowledge (which is identical with its object) with potential knowledge: the latter is prior in time in the individual's knowing but not in general. Mind (presumably he is referring to active mind) does not sometimes think and sometimes not. When isolated, it is only what it is (that is, its essence is identical with it), and this alone is immortal and everlasting. Apparently alluding to the fact that we are usually unaware of the constantly active thought of active mind, Aristotle adds the curious remark that "we do not remember because it is unaffected but passive mind is perishable." This statement has invited varying interpretations. It could be seen as an oblique suggestion that *what* we have forgotten is immortality, which would make us suspect that he is referring to Plato's theory of reincarnation of the soul. Taken literally, as explaining why we do not remember, it seems to assign active reason a place in the processes of memory. Seen as a contrast of passive mind with active mind, its minimal meaning would be that the individual's thinking may have problems in "turning on" from the side of passive mind to let in the influence of active mind. In any case, the presupposition throughout, stated immediately thereafter, is that without active mind no thinking is possible.

Aside from the honorific tone toward active mind in this last section, the actual development of Aristotle's theory of thinking is derived by rather strict moves from his previous analysis of functions. In many respects his concept of mind serves in his psychology as a construct, that is, as a term designating a hypothesized entity not directly discerned; in the present case it is introduced into the system by the strict manipulation of schematic rules and in such a way as to preserve readily observable phenomena. He can thus proceed to speak of mind knowing itself, just as a physicist who has deduced a new particle with strange properties he does not understand can nonetheless talk about its behavior. That mind is such a construct would explain why it is capable of such different subsequent interpretations: active mind as God or eternal Platonic ideas, or a system of truth thinking in us (William James said at one point that when we come to scientific truth it would be better not to say "I think" but "it thinks in me"), and so on. Naturalistic versions are equally possible. Perhaps mind as pure potentiality could be identified with the tremendous plasticity of the human animal or the human brain—a kind of undifferentiated basic matter—or else with the early stages of the infant. The growth of experience and the establishment of language and reactive habits would parallel the embedding of ideas within the mind, and the passage from passive to active mind would be descriptive of thought in action, drawing on its established inner resources. Aristotle's remarks about what happens when a man becomes learned, or stocked with ideas he can put to use on his own initiative, would then have to be probed in greater detail. We would have to scour the corpus in different directions, drawing on the theories of qualitative change and its analysis in the physical writings, dispositions and states in the *Categories* and states of character in the ethical writings, and social habits and social inertia in the political works, even going to the biology to consider the action of rennet in "setting," and consulting the chemistry for the causes of the solidification of liquids. It is possible that such investigations could suggest the beginnings of a more determinate base for mind in the framework of Aristotle's theory than is permitted from his conclusion that mind is nothing before it thinks.[33]

Chapter 5 still leaves unanswered why we do not think constantly. Presumably it was intended to expose the efficient cause of thinking in general, not to explain why a particular man on a particular occasion thinks. The latter question is implicitly dealt with in chapter 7, where Aristotle reverts to the individual and relations to sensation. There he recapitulates the way in which the sense object actualizes what is capable of sensing. Now for the thinking psyche, appearances (*phantasmata*) serve as sensations.[34] The thinking takes place with affirmation or denial, and the counterpart for practical thought is pursuit or avoidance. It is in this context that Aristotle says that the psyche never thinks without an appearance; he compares this to the physical process by which the air transmits to the eye, and the eye further on within. This answers our question about the initiation of thought: it is roused by a sensory and imaginative base, which in turn is a response to the movements about us. The thinking thus roused is—to use a modern metaphor—a kind of tuning in to the active mind and so a sharing in the actual thought or actual truth or actual reality that is going on. Whatever the interpretation given to Aristotle's notion of active mind as everlasting actual thought, it is clearly not something personal of which we are expected to be constantly aware, since it was not temporally prior in the individual's knowledge. Functionally, then, active mind is like the truth or reality that is logically prior, but temporally posterior, in the process of the individual's coming to know it. What governs the comings and goings of actual thought in the individual, then, is the stimulation of imagination, and this stimulation is a function of all the happenings within and without that govern and give some order to that faculty. Hence thought can be intermittent.

It is interesting that the much-discussed issue whether Aristotle believed thinking requires imagination is raised in the context of the efficient cause of thinking. It thus leaves unanswered, at least here, whether the process of thinking still requires the appearances after it is initiated.

In chapter 7 he has in mind chiefly the interpretation of sense experience and deliberation that projects its aim imaginatively. He grants the abstract character of mathematical notions, but whether these would nonetheless require visual "diagrams" is presumably a separate issue. At a later point he asserts that appearances are important for learning and necessary even for theoretical thinking.[35] But they are not to be equated with thought.

Chapter 8 sums up the conclusions about sensation and thought together. It stresses again the unity with objects in both sense and thought; the reference in both cases is of course to the forms, since the objects literally (for example, a stone sensed or thought about) are not incorporated. In *Parts of Animals* he calls the hand an instrument (*organon*) that uses many instruments.[36] Here he calls the mind the form of forms and sense the form of sensible things. Presumably this means that the sense, as embodying the sensible form, enables us to handle the objects it represents. So too, the mind, itself a form (whether as becoming one with the forms or simply as an actuality), enables us to handle the forms of things. Interestingly, it is in this summary chapter that Aristotle insists there is nothing outside and separate in existence from sensible magnitudes, that is, no free-floating Platonic forms or mathematical objects; for the objects of thought reside in the sensible forms. The next chapter goes on to the work of the psyche in initiating movement.

We have dwelt at length on the analysis of chapters 4 and 5 because of their importance to the traditional controversies and to the wider questions whether Aristotle is pointing in a religious direction or a Platonic (whether inherited or revised) or a naturalistic one. It might be worth adding to this roster the Hegelian interpretation. One could elaborate the view that actual thought is the higher actualization of the forms, so that the forms become in effect the potentiality of thought, and the intellectual character of the total reality becomes its essence. Indeed, the incorporation of sensible form within the individual and the intelligible form in the development of individual consciousness could be given an Hegelian twist by seeing the constitutive role of "objective mind" (culture and institutions) as internalized in the individual. But our concern in this work is not the subsequent career of Aristotelian thought.

We are not, however, done with thinking. For on Aristotle's own theory the analysis of an activity requires an analysis of both the faculty of the agent and the object of the activity. In *On the Psyche* he deals with a rather scattered batch of intellectual activities: thought, understanding, judgment, practical thought, and so on.[37] The more systematic ordering of these, and more importantly, the object of thought—the character of knowledge, both scientific and ordinary belief—will be examined in Part 4.

I I

MOVEMENT AND EMOTION

The way movement gets started in animals and humans bulks large in the last part of *On the Psyche*. Important contributions to its understanding are also to be found in *Movement of Animals*. These discussions correspond to accounts in modern psychology of the mechanisms that energize conduct or, as in faculty psychology, of the will as initiating action. To focus on this theme will prepare us for considering whether Aristotle has a concept of will at all (for example, in relation to the ethical writings) and how he handles the roles for which that concept has been traditionally cast.

By contrast, the emotions are only lightly touched on in the psychological writings, although they play a considerable part in other places. Yet it is appropriate to begin an account of them in the present context. The remainder of the present chapter will accordingly deal with the initiation of movement and the emotions, in order to show how Aristotle's psychology handled them before they were turned into separate faculties of willing and feeling.

Initiation of Movement

Aristotle's first assumption is that all movement in humans and animals is *purposive*, that is, *for the sake of* something. Negatively this is expressed as a sort of inertia: "No animal moves that does not seek or avoid something, except by compulsion"; or more positively, "movement is characteristic of one who is either avoiding or pursuing something."[1] One might draw a parallel to Aristotle's theory of physical movement in the inorganic domain: an element stays in its place once there, and moves to it when not there, unless there is hindrance or compulsion. He has no law of inertia for something moving. However, his description of humans contains enough purposes to keep people on the move fairly constantly. This is the domain of *praxis* and *poiēsis*, doing (or living) and making. Once movement is purposive, and has its source within the animal in this way, it is no longer compulsion. (In the ethics he goes on to characterize *voluntary* action.)

The next step in his account is to locate the cause of human movement among the different sensory or cognitive-intellectual functions. He does this by examining each and offering counterinstances to its power to affect movement by itself. The purely intellectual part of the psyche, for instance, does not deal with pursuit and avoidance. Even when we think of something as fearful or pleasant we can do it without bidding ourselves be afraid or pleased. Again, even when thought actually bids us act, desire (in the man who lacks self-control) may send the man in an opposite direction. A parallel argument tells against desire, for the self-controlled man may act against the promptings of his appetite.[2] Therefore it must be that mind (if we assume imagination to be an intellectual process) together with appetite produces movement. (It is *practical* mind that he is talking about here, the kind that calculates for an end.) Yet since imagination when it starts movement never does so without appetite, the general conclusion appears to be in favor of appetite.[3] There is a textual problem here: one proposed reading would have "object of appetite" (*orekton*) rather than "faculty of appetite" (*orektikon*), and this would void the issue, since the object stimulates both the desire and the imagination. However, this really does not matter; Aristotle is about to undercut the whole conflict between reason and appetite. He does this in two ways.

The first is by showing that the conflict of reason and appetite actually involves the conflict of two appetites: desire for what is yielded by a reckoning of the future (which is reason's way) and desire for what is pleasing at the moment.[4] This is fatal to any attempt to set reason and appetite as such against each other.[5] As a matter of fact Aristotle had earlier attacked the classification of the soul into calculative, emotional, and desiderative parts, arguing that divisions could be endless and made in different ways; this triple division could not easily find a place for either the nutritive or the imaginative.[6]

The second way is typically Aristotelian; he breaks up the issue and reformulates it.[7] Movement involves an originator of motion, a means by which motion is produced, and a thing moved. The originating cause is of two sorts, one unmoved, the other both moving (as agent) and moved. The former is the practical good, the good in the sphere of action. In the ethical writings Aristotle identifies this as the good or the apparent good, and we shall see shortly that it is the object of desire or appetite. (He points out rather proudly that this same manner of having motion initiated is found in the Unmoved Mover moving the heavens and in the individual animal pursuing the good.)[8] The mover that both is moved and moves is appetite, and the thing moved is the animal. The instrument by which appetite causes movement is a physical matter, and will be dealt with immediately below. In any case the conflict of thought and appetite disappears, because while the capacity for movement depends on a capacity for appetite, appetite itself involves imagination, which is either intellectual or sensory.[9] (The underlying assumption is that imagination is some kind of thinking process.)

The instrument by which appetite effects movement is discussed in detail in *On the Movement of Animals*. Once appetite has been pinned down as the source of movement, we need only to trace the inner processes and to follow the movement outward. Taken as a whole, it is almost as if the journey were being traced from stimulus through inner central point to motor response. The discussion covers the way joints operate in the body and what goes on in the heart. The former requires that there be a point or part at rest so that another part can move. (Similarly, there has to be some part at rest in the environment to support the animal's motion.) The initiation of motion is compared with the way marionettes move as a result of small movements, for example, when strings are released, or the way a small movement of a boat's rudder causes considerable swing of the boat as a whole.[10] So too, alterations due to heat or cold in the neighborhood of the heart, even imperceptible ones, cause blushing or trembling of the body. The alterations near the heart are caused by imagination and sensation and thought; since the primary organ for these is in the center of the body, this is what is affected and what sets movement going.[11] In this process, the subtle, inborn *pneuma* plays a part in the neighborhood of the heart.[12] It need only be added that sometimes the movements do not correspond to the thoughts, depending on the disposition of the matter that is affected.[13]

Finally, Aristotle gives us a full set of concepts for dealing with movement as action; these are used or arise while he is searching out the causes that get movement going. The concepts of appetite, desire, emotion, and wish are not systematized, but appetite emerges as the fundamental term. The Greek term *orexis*, like the English *appetite* (from the Latin equivalent), is literally *reaching toward* and is used for a longing or yearning after something.[14] Both stress the inner-person or inner-body character of the happening. For the standard behavioral manifestation, Aristotle uses the notions of *pursuing*, or seeking after, and *avoiding*, or fleeing from.

A most interesting point in the discussion is his attempt to set up a relation between affirming or denying in intellectual matters and pursuit or avoidance in practical matters. In some respects this reminds us of the argument in *Metaphysics* 4 whereby a man's doing one thing rather than another is evidence that he is not denying the law of noncontradiction.[15] Further, pursuit and avoidance are translated directly into judging that one course is better than another. Thus we have here a three-cornered intimacy between affirming or denying, pursuing or avoiding, and judging better or not better. Aristotle states the roots of these relationships in sensation, and the centrality of pleasure and pain: "Sensation, then, is like simply saying or thinking; and when the sensible thing is pleasant or painful, the psyche pursues or avoids it, like affirming or denying. In fact to be pleased or pained is to function with a sensitive mean toward the good or bad as such. And this is what avoidance and appetite are when actual, nor are the capacities of appetite and avoidance different from one another, nor from the sensitive power, though their being is different. Now for the thinking psyche appearances serve as direct sensations; when it affirms or denies them to be good or bad, it avoids or pursues."[16]

Something like this unity is asserted in contemporary psychoanalytic theory for a child's swallowing or spitting out something. There is no difference at that stage between being pleased or pained, judging good or bad, and swallowing or spitting out. Of course in due time, and especially as self is differentiated from object, there will be three differentiated systems with complex relations. There will be divergences: what pleases may not be good and what pains not evil; there will be gaps between judgment and action, and there will be identifications of the self that function as a seedbed for moral feelings. Then it is the discrepancies that will require explanation, not the congruences. In the ethical writings, Aristotle treats the problem of continence and incontinence in precisely the same way: what happens when the judgment of good and the direction of appetite are in conflict?

We may note that Aristotle's account of the three-cornered relation is extended from sense and appearance to appearance and thought.[17] Thinking deals with the forms in appearances, and its difference from sense is that it calculates and deliberates about the future in relation to the present. When thinking finally declares what is pleasant or painful, then there is pursuit or avoidance. This holds generally for action (*praxis*). Where action is not at issue and the thinking is simply a matter of determining the true or false, the situation is the same as with judging between good or evil; the difference, however, is that the one holds simply, the other with respect to a particular person. So far, then, the differences between theoretical and practical thinking are that the latter concerns action, the former not, and that the latter concerns an individual, the former not. We learn in other contexts that there are other differences: theoretical statements in purest form are concerned with universal relations that cannot be otherwise; practical statements, with the realm of what can be otherwise and thus invites individual action. But both theoretical and practical reason are intellectual; Aristotle is not saying that thought directed to action is itself a form of action. Practical mind (*nous praktikos*) reckons with an end in view and differs from the theoretical in the end it pursues.[18] Appetite itself aims at an end, and that end is the starting point for practical thought. The last step of practical thought is the beginning (*archē*) of action.

Reflecting about animals whose only perception is touch, Aristotle decides that all animals have imagination in the form of sense but that deliberative imagination exists only in those capable of reasoning; for, he adds, to decide between alternatives calls for calculation by a simple standard: one pursues the greater good.[19] This involves an ability to combine several appearances into one. Without this we have merely conflicts of appetite. At this point he offers a syllogistic-sounding statement: "Since one judgment or statement is universal and the other singular (for the one says that it is fitting for this kind of person to do that kind of act, the other that this present act is that kind and I am this kind of person), it is this latter belief, not the universal, that directly causes movement. Or both, but the one is more at rest, the other not."[20] In this case at least, the suggestion that we have here a syllogism is misleading. For one thing, Aristotle draws no conclusion but conjectures which belief (*doxa*) causes movement. He first suggests that it is the belief about the singular features. Then he decides that if both the universal and the singular beliefs are causal, the universal would be like the Unmoved Mover, and the singular would presumably be both moved and moving. After all, the context of the example is the attempt to find out how much the initiation of movement depends on the thinking part of the psyche. Since this is the only passage in *On the Psyche* of this sort, we may conclude that Aristotle's interest, here at least, is in the psychology of initiating movement, not in any logic of practical reasoning.

This point is of considerable importance, for there have been many claims in twentieth-century Aristotelian scholarship that Aristotle is here engaged in fashioning a theory of practical reasoning with a practical syllogism to parallel the theoretical syllogism of the *Prior Analytics*. The sources in the corpus for such a view, apart from this passage, lie in *On the Movement of Animals* and the discussion of internal conflict in the ethics. Hence every passage that may throw light on the question must be considered as we go along, although the summing up has to wait until all the evidence is in.

We turn therefore to chapter 7 of *On the Movement of Animals*. The context again here, as well as in the treatise as a whole, is the causal explanation of the initiation of action, and the causal role of thought. The chapter starts with the query why someone's thinking sometimes results in action and sometimes not. It does, however, look to the inferential links of beliefs, but only as an explanatory issue. Aristotle draws the comparison to theoretical inference—I take this to mean that from some combinations of premises we draw a conclusion, from some not. He points to the distinction between the ends of the theoretical and the practical. In the former the end is speculation, "for when you have thought the two premises, you think the conclusion and conclude it." But in the latter, "the conclusion drawn from the two premises is the action."[21] His examples cut corners: You think every man ought to walk and you're a man; immediately you walk. The action follows, if there is no hindrance. Or you draw the conclusion "A cloak ought to be made." Then he says that that conclusion is action, and traces the thinking from the end desired through the necessary steps to the last step, which one does immediately. He adds, "That then the action is the conclusion is clear."[22] This need not mean that there is no conclusion except the action. It can be the statement of the *identity* of the conclusion of thought and the action done, just as we saw in *On the Psyche* the identification of the judgment of good or bad and the act of pursuit or avoidance. In fact Aristotle goes on in a causal mode to explain that obvious premises such as "I am a man" are dropped where no calculation is required, and that perception or imagination or thought can thus yield an immediate action; the carrying out of desire takes the place of inquiry or thought. We may conclude that in the passages from *On the Movement of Animals* as well, Aristotle is not concerned with articulating a practical syllogism—nor even what is closer to the examples, a practical *enthymeme*—but trying to study how beliefs can issue in action and how even partial thought can produce results.

Perhaps a word should be added on the role of pleasure and the concept of good in relation to affirmation and denial and pursuit and avoidance. Pleasure is closely tied to sensation: that which has sensation has pleasure and pain, and desire is an appetite for what is pleasant.[23] Pleasure is invariably tied with some sensation, such as smell.[24] Again, what is painful or pleasant may be associated with some degree of chilling or heating.[25] But the most important function of pleasure and pain seems to be to prompt the conceptual judgment of good and bad and the practical action of pursuit or avoidance. Aristotle points out that "the apparent good can take the place of the good, and so can the pleasant, for it is an apparent good."[26] This means, in effect, that the prompting of pleasure is at the same time the hypothesis that we are dealing with a good. Except insofar as an apparent good invites criticism as being possibly illusory, action follows the apparent good. The concept of the good itself seems unavoidable; all action is, in Spinoza's later words, done *sub specie boni*, "under the appearance of the good." The very first sentence of the *Nicomachean Ethics* asserts that the good is the aim of all pursuits and enterprises. This is no doubt why in the psychological writings Aristotle does not find it necessary to expound the relations of pleasure to the good, or of pleasantness or goodness to pursuit and avoidance. Perhaps also it is because he is working on the wider comparative scene of animals as well as man. Or perhaps he is following his belief as expressed in the biological works, that nature, like the artist, first sketches in the genus and then draws the species in detail. The particular theory of moral development and conceptual development and internal divergences is discussed in the ethics.

Theory of the Emotions

Aristotle thinks that all the affections (*pathē*) of the psyche—spirit, gentleness, pity, confidence, joy, loving and hating, for example—are probably associated with the body; no external explanation of our emotional reactions is adequate.[27] Sometimes when there are violent and striking occurrences we feel no excitement or fear; sometimes we are moved by small and obscure causes, and the body is excited and in the same condition as when it is angry; sometimes without anything terrible happening we have the feelings of being frightened. Emotions have a material and a formal side and their definitions should express both. Thus, as we noted earlier, he defines being angry as "a certain movement of a body of a given kind or a part or power of it, produced by such-and-such a cause for such-and-such an end."[28] This is, of course, a schema for a definition rather than the definition itself. It is at this point that he distinguishes the way the physicist (*phusikos*) and the dialectician (*dialektikos*) would define anger—the former as a boiling of the blood or heat around the heart, the latter as a desire for retaliation or the like. The one deals with the matter, the other with the form and formula of the essence. Aristotle compares this with the definition of a house as on the one hand a shelter to protect us from harm by wind and rain and heat, and on the other as stones and bricks and timber. The definition should include both; in fact it should account for all the four causes. In the light of our discussion of Aristotle's method in psychology (in chapter 9 above), it is clear that his definition of anger in this manner would open the way to studies of the physiology of anger, the phenomenology of anger, the causes of the occurrence of anger, the functions of anger in a person's life, the moral assessment of anger, the problems of self-control with respect to anger, and so on.

Aristotle's treatment of the emotions is thus markedly comprehensive, making room for the physiological, the behavioral, the introspective, the phenomenological (delineating the object intended by the feeling or emotion), and the dynamic or functional (emotion as purposive). Aristotle wants to deal with all of these in their interrelations. This is not the kind of interest in interrelations that first separates sharply and then seeks correlations, as in psychophysical research into the physical conditions of introspectively identified feelings. It is rather a readiness to follow all of them at any point where they seem relevant to what is going on. Even more, it is the pursuit of an ideal of a full understanding and a full explanation.

We would be attaching too much here to the brief remarks in *On the Psyche* if they simply proclaimed a way of analyzing the emotions that Aristotle never used. Where in the corpus do we find it applied? One notable case is book 2 of the *Rhetoric*, where Aristotle uses what might be called a "field" approach, studying each emotion in detail with respect to the disposition and conditions that give rise to it, the objects to which it is directed, and the typical grounds on which it is felt. (The general purpose there is to give an understanding of the emotions in order to enhance skill in persuasion.) Another is in the *Poetics*, where Aristotle probes the audience's affective reactions to a tragedy. A third, and broader—and most clearly purposive in detail, not only in general—is the ethical writings. There the specific emotional roots of many of the virtues are analyzed, as well as the way the emotions can be blended to produce different kinds of virtues and vices, and different types of even one virtue. And of course, the ethics also contain a detailed analysis of pleasure. We shall examine these major contexts in later chapters.

The one aspect of emotion that is not developed in detail anywhere is the physical or physiological. There are occasional references to the persistence of an emotion when its initial causes are gone, with an attempted physical explanation,[29] or to the way that fear or love can conjure up an image to distort perception,[30] or to the relation on many occasions of temperament and physical constitution.

Although the *Problems* is not Aristotle's own work (though some of the questions probably came from him), it is clearly in his tradition. The author's interest in the emotions and their physical grounding is fairly evident. For example, book 27 asks questions about fear and courage, beginning with why the frightened tremble (is it because they are chilled?),[31] and why they are sometimes thirsty; whether in anger the heart is affected but in fear the bowels; what difference there is in the heartbeat in fear and anger; and so on. Again, as in a nervous actor, is there really thirst, or a dryness due to the draining of blood, so that paleness results?[32] A behavioral bit of evidence is added: the frightened do not drink in large quantity. Even book 30, on thought, intelligence, and wisdom, has many questions about emotional and character effects—for example, the effects of wine on different temperaments. Book 32 considers why the tips of the ears grow red when men are ashamed but their eyes redden when they are angry.[33] The question is raised whether shame might be a chilling in the eyes as an accompaniment of fear, so that the heat leaving the eyes drains easily to the ears, while in anger the heat rises and appears in the eyes because they are light-colored.

In general, it is clear that many of the questions we would raise as psychological are raised by Aristotle in other contexts. For example, we often go to psychological writings to get an answer to questions about *human nature*: Is man inherently aggressive or inherently social? Is the child an inherent egoist to be socialized, or is he inherently affiliative, drawing his egoism from social institutions? But Aristotle's thesis that man is a social animal is found in the *Politics*. The status of egoism emerges in his discussion of self-love in the books of the *Nicomachean Ethics* that deal with friendship. *On the Psyche* deals specifically with the several general functions of living in men and animals; it concentrates on the formal cause. Many of the special problems fall into areas particularly concerned with the final cause: how man lives and can achieve the good. In this respect problems of human nature are in large part normative, and Aristotle deals with them in that context.

Part 4

THE THEORY OF KNOWING:

MIND AT WORK

INTRODUCTION

If we take Aristotle's work as a whole, we find a remarkable array of problems that now go by the names of logic, method, theory of meaning, process of inquiry, philosophy of science, and so on—all of which can be embraced in a single concept of the theory of knowledge or, to give it the more active Aristotelian sense, a theory of knowing. He does not, as we shall see, divide and formulate the questions in the same way as moderns do, but he touches on all of them, systematizes some, and gives a rounded picture of how the field holds together.

On such questions, the modern world since the seventeenth century has gone through a struggle between Rationalism and Empiricism. Rationalism is usually seen as employing a deductive model of the Euclidean type. Empiricism is associated with a theory of induction based on facts and experience, but there have been diverse analyses of induction (and later of probability) and also of fact and experience. Eventually philosophers of science came to think of a hypothetico-deductive-experimental system in which there were rational components in the use of mathematics and logic and empirical components in the entry of observation and both in the progressive mutual correction of theory and experiment. Historians of science began to suggest that this was what had always been, and that Rationalism and Empiricism had been ideological superstructures, or at best that Rationalism marked the imposition of the mathematical model on science, and Empiricism the revolt against it. (Perhaps Francis Bacon had anticipated the outcome of this three-century debate in the philosophy of science and was not merely venturing a metaphor when he said that experimenters, like the ant, only collect and use, and reasoners, like spiders, spin webs out of their own substance, but the bee both gathers materials and transforms them by a power of its own.)[1] In the twentieth century some have even suspected that the conventional picture of continuity in the growth of science showed too smooth a curve and that sociological categories of the rise and fall of paradigms and revolutions could fit the history of science as well.

One of the consequences of this historical reassessment has been to relax the pressure to classify Aristotle as either a rationalist or an empiricist. Historically he has been seen in different ways. In the thirteenth century he was the great scientist opposing the Platonizing mystics. Later on he was given a position as the forerunner of the rationalists, largely perhaps because the *Posterior Analytics* insisted on necessary basic premises. That picture is complicated by the way in which the *Posterior Analytics* has often been singled out as the central account of his theory of knowledge, putting into the shadow the rest of his works, whether logical or rhetorical or physical or humanistic, in which his methods are operative. It is in fact worthwhile to ask how far Aristotle's method of working in the various fields does conform to his picture of knowledge in the *Posterior Analytics*. In any case, we are now free to look for his theory of knowing in the wider range of the mind at work in the various disciplines in which he operates.

Another consequence of the revised outlook has been to invite a search for the empirical in the rationalist philosophies and the rational in the empirical philosophies. (This may be called "looking under the carpet" in terms of the task, or "reality will out" in terms of the outcome.) Thus from this viewpoint, even Plato, the supreme antiempiricist, the supreme derogator of the senses, is reporting lessons of experience in much of the *Republic*. But Plato sees experience differently, not as a voucher for his conclusions, but as a ladder by which to climb to the vision of the truth. In short, induction is made a two-phase affair, the first stage relegating the sensory to the causal process of getting into position, the second consisting in an epistemological act. We shall have to ask whether there is a similar structure in Aristotle's theory of induction (*epagōgē*).

Finally, once we are free from rigid interpretations of Aristotle's theory of knowledge, what relations can we see between that theory and the conceptual network as we developed it earlier? That the same concepts are operative here is clear enough. The outcome of knowledge is cast in terms of essences and the essential, and is thus centrally directed to form. We find that every specific inquiry has its four causes: materials, a form, initiation, and a goal. The central ideas of the network as developed in the psychology and the metaphysics can be seen to furnish a basic unity to the theory of knowledge because they provide the understanding of knowing itself. Knowing is an actualization of human potentialities. As an actuality it is form. The structure of knowledge gives us the form in which the potential knowledge of all things that we come to know becomes actual knowledge when we do know. The various processes of knowledge explored in the chapters that follow exhibit the different human abilities or powers whose exercise plays a part in the pattern of knowing.

Chapter 12 looks at reasoning and other capacities of knowing and shows what structures they are related to. Chapter 13 deals with demonstration, explanation, verification—in short, how a fact is established or understood. Chapter 14 turns to logical–linguistic issues of meaning, definition, and classification. These last involve serious recent questions of interpretation. Chapter 15 deals with epistemological and metaphysical issues of truth, reality, and essentialism. One major topic that keeps reappearing in these chapters is definition. Because in Aristotle's view definition is a way of explaining, our treatment of definition begins in chapter 13. The other functions of definition in the logical apparatus are discussed in chapter 14, and definition as giving essence is of course important in chapter 15.

12

REASONING AND THE

ANALYSIS OF KNOWING

Knowing, for Aristotle as for Plato, may be studied in two ways. The first is through the varied human capacities whose exercise constitutes knowing; some of these were mentioned in dealing with the psychology of thinking, but a more systematic outline is now needed. The second is through the type of order involved, since a capacity fastens upon some feature of the world in cooperation with which it comes to fulfillment in its exercise. Aristotle does not quite divide his many accounts neatly into the two, and they spill over in a variety of ways. For example, once he has developed a science of reasoning, he makes distinctions on the basis of the kinds of premises utilized; and again, his treatment of induction is central enough to come up independently. Accordingly, our account in this chapter will be organized as follows: (1) reasoning; (2) kinds of premises and the *endoxa*; (3) types of order; (4) faculties of knowing; (5) intuitive induction (*epagōgē*). We begin with reasoning simply because the founding of logic was Aristotle's great original contribution.

Reasoning

There is, in the first place, the theory of syllogism. This is meant to be a general theory of deduction, that is, of valid forms according to which conclusions follow necessarily from premises. Hence syllogism covers a great part of what we mean by "reasoning." The theory of syllogism is presupposed by every type of inquiry. By defining a premise as an affirmative or negative statement of something about something, Aristotle's primary account of deduction is cast in terms of statements (propositions) in subject-predicate form. Universal propositions apply to all (or none) of a subject; particular propositions may apply only partially. He does not deal in this context with singular terms that designate individuals, except in invoking examples. As he explains, existing entities may be individuals or highest universals (the categories), or in between.[1] In properly formulated statements in which a predicate is attributed to a subject, individuals can hold only a subject position. "Socrates is white" properly predicates a quality of Socrates, but "That white thing is Socrates" is only predication in an accidental sense, for Socrates is not an attribute of a thing. Nor do we say "every Socrates," as we say "every man."[2] Similarly, highest universals properly have only a predicate position; they constitute an upper limit, and so are predicable of other things (as in the statement "Color is a quality"), but other things are not predicable of them. It is with the intermediate class that arguments and inquiries are chiefly concerned. We can say both "Man is an animal" and "Animals are capable of motion," putting "animal" in a predicate position in the one statement, and in a subject position in the other.

The example so frequently given as typical of a syllogism, "All men are mortal; Socrates is a man; therefore Socrates is mortal," does not get to the heart of Aristotle's treatment, for his formal discussion employs variables throughout. For example, the central type is given as "If A is predicated of all B, and B of all C, A must necessarily be predicated of all C." In this example, B is the *middle term*, a notion that plays an important part in his theory of science as well as in his logic. Different *figures* of the syllogism are distinguished by the relations of the middle term to the extreme terms. The one given above is the first figure; in the second, the middle is predicated of each of the extreme terms; in the third, the extremes are predicated of the middle. The bulk of Aristotle's treatment concerns the establishment of valid forms in the different figures; it also seeks to show how the validity of the forms in the other figures can be established as a logical consequence of the validity of forms in the first figure. (Some of these proofs are done by a *reductio ad absurdum*.)

Aristotle's systematization of this area of what is commonly called the "categorical syllogism" is very successful. It is this part of his logic that entitles him to the position of founder of systematic formal logic. There is discussion today, in the light of modern developments and distinctions, about how Aristotle's contribution is best to be construed. Many technical issues arise that cannot be pursued here: Is he really giving us just the beginning (for three terms) of a calculus of classes, leading on into set theory? Does the syllogism exhibit the structure of inference, or give us logical theorems in a partly systematized domain, or present something different from either? What precisely is he doing (in modern terms) in reducing the other figures to the first figure? Has he successfully steered his way between talking about terms (which in contemporary usage would require putting quotes around the word) and talking in a material way about the objects to which the terms refer? Sometimes modern inquiry seems to start with a provincial bias, as if the questions ultimately concern how far Aristotle got on the road to *us*. But fortunately in many cases it turns into a genuine search for possibly quite different paths that Aristotle might have been trying.[3]

It should be remembered that Aristotle was also struggling with problems that are not even today resolved in a wholly satisfactory manner.

This is particularly true of his attempts at what is called modal logic—arguments employing concepts of *possibility* and *necessity*. Thus Aristotle distinguishes "A is necessarily B" and "A is possibly B" from the simple assertion "A is B."[4] A good part of the *Prior Analytics* is taken up with technical operations to distinguish valid forms that will yield conclusions employing the modal concepts. This part of his formal logic is less successful than his treatment of the simple categorical syllogism. This is to be regretted, for the concept of possibility enters into his idea of the potential. And some of his most dubious arguments in physical fields use this notion to establish necessary truths about physical processes.

Aristotle sees his syllogistic logic as the structure of deduction in any inquiry. In this sense it is preliminary to science rather than science itself. Any mode of arguing that purports to be valid is an approximation to it, and careful analysis will show what presuppositions are required to bring it up to syllogistic standards. At the very end of the *Prior Analytics* there is a brief discussion of a few such modes. For example, we find an illustration of how induction, if taken as a mode of reasoning,[5] would be seen as approximation to deductive form. Suppose one goes from the observation that certain animal forms (man, horse, mule, etc.) are long-lived and are also bileless, to the conclusion that all bileless creatures are long-lived. This is strictly legitimate only provided that the bileless creatures are a definite class coinciding with man, horse, mule, etc. In that case, "Man, horse, mule, etc., are bileless" can be converted to yield "All bileless creatures are man, horse, mule, etc." The whole argument can now be seen as a first-figure syllogism saying that from "Man, horse, mule, etc., are long-lived" and "All bileless creatures are man, horse, mule, etc.," it follows that "All bileless creatures are long-lived."

Contemporary philosophers tend to make a sharper distinction between deduction and induction. They agree on the analysis of deduction, which is in spirit like Aristotle's treatment of syllogism, but incomparably more developed in extent and refinement. They tend to disagree among themselves whether inductive reasoning consists in enumeration going from the frequency with which an item occurs to an assignment of the probability of its occurrence in subsequent long-range predictions, or whether it is a pattern of alternatives fighting it out in attempted predictions to leave one less knocked out than the others, or whether it is even the more complicated pattern that is often called the hypothetico-deductive-experimental method. Against these technical alternatives the Aristotelian view, which is still not without contemporary force, holds that there is no point in multiplying types of logical reasoning, that all reasoning is deductive. All other differences pertain only to the kinds of premises or the presuppositions about kinds of order in the specific field of inquiry; or again, they lie in the exercise of some different faculty of mind or sensation, since after all reasoning is only one among several faculties.

Before moving on from reasoning in general we should note the account of the internal structure of the sentence that furnishes the premises of reasoning. As mentioned above, it is of the subject-predicate form; that is, it involves the joining of two terms. The account is developed in a quite commonsensical way in *On Interpretation*. We have affections in the psyche; these are sense impressions, images or appearances, and thoughts. Spoken words are symbols of these affections; different languages vary in their symbols (terms) for the same objects. Single terms need not be true or false, since one term alone asserts nothing. Assertion requires a combination of terms: it is sentences, affirming or denying something, that are true or false. The universal, as what is naturally predicable of a number of things, is contrasted with the individual, which is not.[6] An illustration of the latter is Kallias, a singular term. This is a contrast in terms, not in statements. A universal statement is said to predicate something of the whole range of the subject, whereas a particular ("in part") statement predicates it of an indefinite part.[7]

On Interpretation also goes into the fundamental relations of statements with respect to truth and falsity. Contradiction is a central notion; of contradictory statements one must be true and the other false. Contrary statements (such as "All pleasures are good" and "No pleasures are good") cannot both be true, but can both be false. The most difficult treatment of relations is concerned with modal statements.[8]

Another study of the internal structure of subject-predicate statements, which pursues a quite different line of inquiry, is found in the fourth and fifth chapters of *Topics* 1. This is generally referred to as Aristotle's account of the *predicables*. One way of understanding it would be as an investigation of the types of relation that the predicate can have to the subject, that is, of what kind of thing is being asserted about the subject by the predicate. (This could also be understood as an analysis of the various meanings *is* could have when we say "S is P.") Aristotle actually poses the problem as an inquiry into what the statement tells us about the subject, and he ends up with four possibilities: it reveals a *property*, the *definition*, the *genus*, or an *accident*.[9] The way he reaches this conclusion is interesting. He starts with a broad notion of property, but then limits it to cover properties that fall outside the essence, since the properties within the essence are contained in the definition. He thinks that the *differentia*, as what differentiates the subject from the genus, should be classed with the genus, because it is generic in character. In the end the differentia is of course included in the definition. Some post-Aristotelian lists of predicables do include it separately.

A traditional example will clarify these distinctions. Suppose the definition of "man" is rational animal. Then to say that a man is a rational animal is to give the definition, and to say that a man is an animal is to give the genus; to say that a man is rational is to give the differentia. To say that a man is capable of laughter (on the assumption that this is peculiar to man) is to state a property. Finally, to say that man may be long-lived is to state an accident. Similarly, the definition of a triangle is a plane figure (genus), bounded by three straight lines (differentia). A property is that the sum of its angles equals two right angles. Its size is an accident.

Aristotle's formal accounts are as follows.[10] A definition is a formula that signifies the essence. A property of something does not signify the essence, but does belong to that entity alone and is convertible with it. For instance, a man is capable of learning grammar, and what is capable of that learning is a man. (He did not foresee our modern investigation of primate "linguistics.") A genus is what is predicated of many things that differ in form or kind (*eidos*), in response to the question What is it? The genus of man and ox would thus be *animal*. An accident is what is not one of the other predicables but still belongs to a thing—for instance, a sitting position.

The account of the predicables actually furnishes a great part of the structure of the *Topics* as a whole. The examination of accidental relations looms large in book 2 and figures to some extent in book 3. Rules and arguments about genus and species constitute book 4, various kinds of properties and rules for the assignment of properties come in book 5, and definition takes up books 6 and 7. It would seem that the general question of identifying the essential and its components as distinct from the accidental constitutes the key theme of Aristotle's earlier philosophical inquiry.

If we now go back to the suggestion that reasoning is deductive and that other proposed differences in reasoning are to be seen as differences in the kinds of premises, in the types of order dealt with, or in the different faculties of mind exercised, then we have three different paths of inquiry leading off in different directions, with only partially overlapping results. While the second is ontological, the first and third are epistemological and psychological.

Kinds of Premises and the *Endoxa*

In the first chapter of the *Topics* different kinds of reasoning are identified in terms of premises. Demonstration (*apodeixis*) reasons from premises that are true and primary, or else derived originally from such. Dialectical reasoning (*dialektikos sullogismos*) reasons from generally accepted opinions (*endoxa*).[11] Contentious reasoning (*eristikos sullogismos*) reasons from what appear to be *endoxa* but are not really such. Beyond these are misreasonings (*paralogismoi*), which start from the premises belonging to a special field but get off on the wrong footing —for example, when a person mistakenly draws a geometric diagram in a way that is not allowable, and reasons from that. Clearly the distinctions here are geared to suggest the weight that different kinds of arguments can have and to show how to detect fallacies among them. As a type of analysis it is not directed toward revealing the real, but is more in the spirit of the *Prior Analytics* when it examines what can be inferred from false premises and how we may happen to get a true conclusion in certain cases.[12]

Plato had offered a much more comprehensive view of dialectic. For him, it was a method of working up to an ultimate or unified knowledge by a critique of the principles of special fields. Aristotle's criticism of any unified account of *being* (or the good) that might serve as the generic object for ultimate knowledge cut him off from such a grandiose conception. He is overmodest when he describes his own conception of dialectic as reasoning from what are (in effect) second-class starting points in contrast with the primary premises of demonstration. In his actual procedures it is possible to find a larger role for his notion. For example, Leszl suggests that dialectic establishes common rules that cross fields, whereas science uses rules restricted to its own genus.[13] Hence though dialectic cannot exhibit the nature of anything, it can exhibit a certain logical correctness for its results. An interesting consequence is that the more general rules established by dialectic have almost the same metaphysical status as the principle of noncontradiction, though they are less sweeping. Again, it is not altogether implausible to assign to dialectic some of the functions of the process by which principles and definitions are arrived at. At a minimum, it constitutes a method of inquiry whose critical nature shares the general character of Socratic and Platonic dialectic in examining beliefs and opinions, although the way of doing it has changed.

The *endoxa*, or generally accepted opinions, are appropriately discussed by LeBlond under the heading "the matter of dialectic."[14] But *endoxa* are not merely the starting points for dialectical reasoning; they also serve as standard starting points in the search for principles and elements to enter into definitions. They thus play the important role of data for philosophical analysis: they have to be sifted, reconciled, in part rejected, reinterpreted, extended, integrated. Hence our understanding of Aristotle's method depends on how the *endoxa* themselves are seen. Look at them as what men *say*, and Aristotle becomes a linguistic philosopher. Look at them as the *facts*, and Aristotle becomes a philosophical scientist.

Look at them as men's *ideas* (as containing categories imposed by the knower), and Aristotle becomes a kind of Kantian. Doubtless there are other ways of seeing them as well. The outcome depends in part on how the *endoxa* are related to the "phenomena."[15] The issue is not unlike the modern disputes in varieties of philosophical realism and idealism about whether the data of knowledge are "hard" or "soft" or whether there is a determinate "given." In recent studies, there has been a tendency unduly to limit the issue to the linguistic versus the empirical.

Actually, of course, there is no need to force a straitjacket on the *endoxa*. They can take all kinds of shapes depending on the material they are dealing with, their level of generality and theoretical development, and so on. Even what people say can itself have different roles, as evidence sometimes of factual beliefs, sometimes of linguistic usage, sometimes of habits of thought, sometimes of theories about nature or human beings. On some occasions the *endoxa* are close to the phenomena; on others they are remote and on a theoretical level, particularly where Aristotle is dealing with highly general issues—for example, where the *endoxa* are the theories of Democritus and Heraclitus. Thus the *endoxa* in the biological works and in the *Meteorology* are usually on a less theoretical plane than in the *Physics*.

Types of Order

With respect to types of order, Aristotle's basic distinction is between the fixed or *what cannot be otherwise*, and the *changeable*; the former is subject only to contemplation, the latter in part admits of control and so of deliberation. Aristotle's concept of "scientific knowledge" is geared to what cannot be otherwise. In modern times we are inclined to apply the term more broadly to the results of the sciences—strings of formulae, properties of individual stars and animal species, historical information about past geological changes, and so on. For Aristotle, scientific knowledge must be causal, and in his sense this means knowledge that the fact could not be other than it is.[16]

From this standpoint it is easy to see why he does not think that sensation by itself can give us knowledge (even though it is the basis of all knowledge). It is not that sensation gives an unreliable account of what is present; that is a modern worry. Aristotle is ready to accept it as reliable enough but regards it as too restricted, since it tells us only about the particular that is here and now, and who knows what happens once it is out of range? He explains his view in a quite understandable way in the *Nicomachean Ethics*: "We all assume that what we know cannot be otherwise; in the case of things that can be otherwise, when they go beyond our view we cannot tell whether they exist or not. Therefore the object of scientific knowledge is of necessity. Therefore it is eternal; for things that are of necessity in an unqualified sense are all eternal; and eternal things are ungenerated and indestructible."[17]

Note how this fuses questions of language, of method, and of being, by suggesting that they reach the same result. We do think of knowledge as what must be; it would sound strange to say "I know this is so, but in fact it is not so," a bit less so but still strange to say "I believe this is so, but it is not so," and quite reasonable to say "I believed it so, but it is not so." Again, the search in science is for laws, hence for universal statements. Where we are dealing with perishable things, Aristotle says, no attribute can be demonstrated or known by strictly scientific knowledge.[18] By "perishable things" he clearly means particulars; presumably science could demonstrate that a certain disease has a crippling effect, but not that individual A must be crippled from it, since perception is required to grasp that individual A has the disease. The proof of his being crippled thus will contain a reference to a perishable subject (A) *that happens to have* the attribute (the disease). Presumably when he is out of sight we would not know whether he is still ill. Perishability in this respect holds also for existents that in Aristotle's view are everlasting. The sun is everlasting, but its position, now here, now there, is a sensory matter, and we cannot know what accidental properties continue in it when it sets.[19] Scientific knowledge in the strict sense is then of universals only. From this Aristotle passes readily to require a *necessary* object of scientific knowledge, that is, being which is ungenerated and imperishable. Scientific knowledge therefore is causal-explanatory, necessary, universal knowledge and is concerned with what is eternal and unchanging.

The difficult and key concept in this bundle is, of course, necessity. (It is considered in detail in appendix C, which supplements chapter 15.) As for the actualities that fit the description of what scientific knowledge apprehends, we have already seen in our inventory of substances that at least the Unmoved Mover and the everlasting motion of the heavens are to be characterized in this way. Below that lies the domain of the changeable and the accidental. There the essential properties of things, the inherent unchanging order, can only be grasped in a knowledge of forms or laws; other faculties will grasp the changing and what happens to be the case, for there is no science of the accidental.

Faculties of Knowing

Aristotle distinguishes five human faculties or capacities concerned with knowledge. (Interestingly, the best list is found not in the scientific writings but in the ethical account of intellectual virtues.)[20] They are scientific knowledge (*epistēmē*), art or skill (*technē*), prudence or practical wisdom (*phronēsis*), intelligence or intuitive reason (*nous*), and wisdom (*sophia*). We have already studied, in the psychological theory, the powers that provide the raw materials for these faculties: sensation, imagination, memory, and recollection. Their importance is not to be underestimated, though they are not given a collective place among the five major intellectual faculties. It should be clear by this time that Aristotle is thoroughly appreciative of the role of sensation in knowledge. That he at times stresses the limitations of sensation is due to the restrictions he places on knowledge rather than any disparagement of the contributions of sense experience. In all epistemological consideration of Aristotle's views it is essential to remember that he regards the universal as being *in* the particular. To come to know is not a process of getting away from the particulars to the home of the universals, as it was for Plato, any more than substance is to be understood apart from the individual, rather than as the individual in its essential action. As a consequence, Aristotle has the task of showing how the mind moves from its base of sensory materials to the exercise of intuitive reason—what he calls induction (*epagōgē*). But first let us look at the big five.

In line with the psychology, his first step in examining any capacity or faculty is to determine its object. In the case of scientific knowledge this has already been done; the quotation from the *Nicomachean Ethics* that we saw just above states that the object of scientific knowledge is what cannot be otherwise. Aristotle goes on there to tie knowledge to teaching, so that its character must be understood in terms of the whole human situation, in both the way knowledge is built and the way it is communicated. He refers us to the point he had made in the *Posterior Analytics* (in its very first statement) that all instruction starts from previous knowledge: if it is by deduction, it assumes premises; if it is by induction, it has the particulars. Scientific knowledge is thus the demonstrative faculty (*hexis apodeiktikē*), that is, the stable power of demonstrating by deducing from known first principles; a person knows when he has the belief or conviction arrived at in this way.

Unlike scientific knowledge, both art and practical wisdom have as their corresponding object what can be otherwise. Theirs is the broad domain of both making (*poiēsis*) and doing or acting (*praxis*), and both involve reason (*logos*). They differ in that art is concerned with making and practical wisdom with doing. Art or skill is then an intellectual or rational state that reasons truly and is concerned with making. Its efficient cause lies in the maker, not in the thing made, and to pursue an art (*technazein*) is to study (*theōrein*) how something that may or may not exist can come into being. Clearly then, art involves a reflective or theoretical component. Practical wisdom or prudence is characterized as the ability to deliberate well about the good; it aims thus at the truth about what is good or bad for man. We shall examine it in detail in chapter 16, in relation to its place in ethics.

Intelligence or intuitive reason is the faculty of grasping the first principles with which scientific knowledge operates. Aristotle arrives at this conclusion by elimination: there must be some way of correctly apprehending what is undemonstrated but presupposed in demonstration. Intuitive reason will be seen at work shortly when we look at *epagōgē*, the leading-up-to process generally called *induction*, not so much in the sense examined earlier, as a type of argument, but as a power of growing insight that enables *nous* to function.

Finally, wisdom, the height of intellectual activities, embraces both scientific knowledge and intuitive reason, directed to the highest objects. This notion had an important role in generating the metaphysical quest for substance.

Though Aristotle here selects the big five from the domain of intellectual powers, there are throughout his works numerous other terms for broad abilities or special intellectual virtues. Among these are understanding, a kind of thinking through or discursive thought; opinion, a root idea in the common beliefs or *endoxa* with which an inquiry starts; and belief, a parallel to the whole domain of knowledge. Other terms are judgment, quickness of wit, and cleverness.[21] Judgment often has a broader scope; the latter two represent facilities in special contexts.

Intuitive Induction

To explore the remaining topic, intuitive induction (*epagōgē*), we have to go back to the psychological roots, to Aristotle's account of acquaintance with particulars and what emerges from sense experience. Thinking requires a sensible form as a basis; there is no doubt that we start with sensation. The *Posterior Analytics* says that loss of any one of the senses entails the loss of a corresponding portion of knowledge, and that sense perception grasps the particulars.[22] On the other hand, Aristotle's treatment of sensations is not that of isolable self-sufficient building blocks for the construction of knowledge in the empiricist fashion that Locke and Hume conceived them. Aristotle does not, in short, equate experience with having sense perceptions: "By nature animals are born having sensation, and from sensation memory arises in some, though not in others."[23] Animals other than man live by appearances, and memories, but in humans several memories of the same thing produce the effect of a single experience. Out of experience come science and art. For that matter, even sensation is sometimes recognized to be of a particular that has a certain character, a "this-such," rather than of a bare particular without special character, a "this-something."[24] There is thus a whole spectrum of psychological phenomena, with a corresponding range of human functions that stretch from initial sensing to the emergence of knowledge. To explore these is the task of psychology, and Aristotle attempts it in his accounts of sensation, common sense, memory, and recollection. But if we look at the last step, where out of all these raw materials the universal and the essence emerge, we find two topics that play a significant role. One is the logical analysis of definition, which is the resultant formulation of the essence; this will be dealt with later. The other is the psychological-epistemological account of intuitive induction.

Intuitive induction is a process in which the mind goes beyond sense perception and memory to stabilize and strengthen the universal in its entirety. Aristotle compares it to the halting of a retreat in battle, when one man makes a stand, then another, and so on until the original formation is recovered. When a particular makes a stand in the soul, the universal is at once present too, since in perception we grasp the universal in the individual. And the process repeats itself on successive levels, until the highest genera are grasped.[25]

Many contexts reveal how carefully Aristotle has explored this process; it is not a simple appeal to a simple faculty in which the already apprehended particulars are lined up, to see what sort of a character they exhibit. The particulars themselves have to be discerned first in a somewhat similar process. In this earlier stage, we begin with a confused mass and then grasp a universal feature, then try it out until we get a clearer view of the particular: the child calls every man father and every woman mother till he distinguishes the individuals.[26] (This passage has sometimes been thought to conflict with the account that says induction proceeds from particulars to universals, but it is clearly complementary if taken as referring to an earlier part of the process.) When we have particulars with given identifications, the ways in which they are further associated is in turn dependent on the universals we go to, a choice that takes place on the basis of likeness or similarity.[27]

That the mind may take surprising directions in the discernment of similarities can be seen from some of the questions raised in the *Problems* —for example, why contact spreads some diseases but does not spread health.[28] Aristotle remarks (in the *Topics*) that it is easy to say that something holds for all cases *of this kind*. But, he adds, "it is one of the most difficult things to define which of the things before us are of such a kind and what sort are not"; people are often misled and take for like what is unlike, and conversely.[29] (He believes, of course, in real likenesses, not just in similarity determined on pragmatic criteria.) He even suggests inventing names for likeness classes, to get them well entrenched in the mind. Much of the discussion of these questions is geared to rhetorical and dialectical purposes. For example, it is good tactics, if we have good material, to make our respondent admit beforehand that whatever holds for one of several similars holds for the rest. There is also the problem of the stubborn opponent who accepts the particulars but refuses to accept the universal.[30] Reasonably, he should have a specific objection or offer a counterargument. Otherwise his reaction is sheer peevishness.

Clearly Aristotle raises many of the points that later were to go into the Humean and post-Humean arguments about the validity of induction. (He even speaks of induction as going from the known to the unknown as well as from particulars to universals.)[31] There are other points in his philosophy of science from which a theory of induction could well have blossomed. For example, he makes a constant association, in speaking of the natural, between what happens universally and what happens *for the most part*. The *Politics* even has an occasional statistical reference. On the other hand, a science of the accidental is firmly denied: if there is a high frequency of similar occurrences, they cease to be accidental and probably represent the natural. Inquiry should presumably, therefore, go after what is essential, not tarry to count proportions. The best we are offered, in one passage of *Parts of Animals*, is a biological correlate for induction: the throbbing of the heart is peculiar to man because he is the only animal that has hope and expectation of the future![32]

The role for intuitive induction is therefore geared to providing universal ideas and primary universal truths. If, however, it is not a mode of reasoning but an intuitive process, a modern would be likely to dismiss it as a purely psychological process of either abstraction or else invention or "getting bright ideas." No one would deny that there is a phenomenon of human *insight*. Book 1 of the *Posterior Analytics* ends on the theme of "quick wit" as a faculty of hitting instantly on the relevant middle term.[33] Why should not induction and intuitive reason be treated in a parallel way? Several scattered contexts show how intelligence operates upon geometric diagrams to elicit in an instantaneous illumination the universal embodied therein.[34] It is this one-answer emphasis that the modern would query. Why not intelligence or intuitive insight as a fertile vision of *possibilities*—and the more the merrier? The fertile mind sees many alternative answers, not just one. Experience and experiment are required to decide which is correct, if the problem is a factual or physical one.

Perhaps Aristotle is considering the ideal case in which all the data are furnished and insight grasps the one and only solution as the one and only answer satisfying *all* the data. If so, can we assume that all the data will ever be in? Has Aristotle concentrated on the finished form of finished knowledge rather than the process of getting it?

The answer to such questions depends ultimately on a more fundamental decision as to what is going on in intuitive induction itself. Plato had made induction a two-phase affair, sharply separating the psychological-causal process in which the mind was stirred by empirical materials (which was like climbing a ladder to get into position) and the epistemological act of seeing or beholding the universal directly, which was no longer dependent on the empirical materials. Aristotle's intuitive induction does seem to have two phases; abstractly they are pictured as the lineup of particulars and the discernment of the universal. But their relation is more like that of matter and form; for the universal is present at every point in the processes of intuitive induction, both in the formation of particulars in our knowledge and in the manipulation of particulars to achieve generality. The formal phase, by itself, is simply a kind of intuitive reason that grasps the universal (concept or principle). In this respect it does not differ from the intuitive reason (*nous*) presented among the five capacities of knowledge, except that *nous* is usually expounded in terms of grasping ultimate first principles, not run-of-the-mill universals.

To regard the object of intuitive induction—the concepts or principles grasped—as truths beheld (Aristotle's view), or as insightful possibilities or possible worlds (a modern alternative suggestion) are only two philosophical interpretations. The history of philosophy offers others, if we continue to keep our eye on the actual process of intuitive induction itself, particularly on what happens in us in the later stage *when the principle emerges in relation to the earlier stage in which there was a preparation of some sort for its emergence.* This is the process that the different analyses all seek to interpret and to which their accounts of the object are correspondingly conformed. The Aristotelian conception has behind it a theory of the activity of thinking and of the mind's becoming one with the object of thought. The modern possible-world theorist seems to presuppose the activity of a free or creative imagination and often cites as his example the scientist who speculates with alternative hypotheses and theoretical models, a view profoundly affected by the sharp separation of the ideas of existence and possibility. Other philosophies have given a voluntaristic turn to the process, whereby intuitive induction works up to an act of will in which usages are *stipulated*, so that our concepts and principles are *stipulations* and *rules*; they are not truths, but rather prescriptions. The last moment's alleged act of insight is, from this standpoint, more properly understood as a locking into place of our commitments. Others, however, place the element of intention much earlier in the process, maintaining that we have built up intentions in our experience and that the process is directed toward analyzing them. Hence while it is true that the results concern our meanings rather than the structure of the world, and in this sense are analytic truths, they constitute a discovery of *conformity to our intentions*. These samples should suffice to show that the theory of intuitive induction deeply reflects the theory of mind and its psychological and metaphysical bases. It cannot be settled on lesser terms.

If we look solely for a phenomenological description of the activity, a variety of interesting accounts can be found. Some see the mind as active: we postulate, stipulate, make commitments, practically fashion categories for a universal structure. In others we are almost passive: we behold or even conform to the shape of what is there. Sometimes our minds even seem to be taken over from outside; we referred earlier to James's remark that to describe the perception of truth it would be better not to say "I think" but "It thinks in me." Amid such variety, perhaps Aristotle's expression that the mind becomes one with the truth in the act of knowing, that it merges with truth, is no more bizarre a phenomenal description than our saying that we recognize or grasp or postulate the truth, or our reliance on any other similar metaphors that might almost come from interpersonal relations if not Freudian psychology.

The significant point about Aristotle's approach is that he does not make a sharp distinction between psychology and epistemology in his analysis of induction. He would not have thought it a virtue to do so, but surely not because he had not advanced far enough to separate the problems. If Aristotle's account of induction is unsatisfactory, it may be because his psychology is inadequate or his metaphysics is inadequate and not because his epistemology is a function of his psychology. It is perhaps Aristotle's psychological theory of thinking that has given intuitive induction its dogmatic form. If the mind, as we have seen, becomes one with its object, then in ultimate insights what the mind grasps is the elementary truth. His occasional remarks on truth bear this out. While in part he adopts a correspondence view, that terms are joined in the mind in the way they are joined in reality, he believes that when the mind is dealing with a single basic unit, the truth is immediately grasped.[35]

Aristotle is more conscious than some modern epistemologists have been of the psychological roots of a theory of knowledge. Perhaps it is the psychology of perception and thought that changed in the shift to modern empiricism. Perhaps some important modern controversies over epistemological questions reflect different presuppositions about sensory and intellectual processes. If so, the study of their interrelations in Aristotle could help the development of contemporary self-consciousness in these philosophical issues. At the very least, his psychological theory of the assimilation of the mind to its object made it unnecessary for him to pursue the question why one primary premise should be accepted rather than an alternative. It also put the stamp of reality upon the entities that were thus actualized in thought. In this respect it imposed the structure of a particular mold of thought on the structure of the world. This is only at the end of the analysis, in its extrasystemic aspects. Aristotle tackles a rich variety of the problems of knowledge with that subtlety that has made his works, even where they may be altogether astray, a source of inspiration for subsequent philosophy.

We are not yet done with *epagōgē*. After a clearer account of demonstration (*apodeixis*) in the next chapter, we shall look at recent reconstructions of *epagōgē* that go beyond traditional rationalistic accounts of Aristotle's methodology and suggest new interpretations of the basic ideas.

13

DEMONSTRATION, EXPLANATION,

AND VERIFICATION

In the previous chapter we dealt (generally) with processes and capacities and their correlates, that are involved in knowing. We now move a step ahead toward the more formal scientific products: demonstrations and explanatory definitions, the major topics of the *Posterior Analytics*. It has usually been taken for granted that this treatise presents Aristotle's conception of the finished form of a science. But there is more at work here than the interests of a philosopher of science. An educational motif enters with the very first words: all teaching and learning that involves the use of reason proceeds from preexistent knowledge. (Distinctions are then made between knowledge of fact, of the meaning of a term, and so on.) Not only in Aristotle's usage and discussions, but even in our own philosophical use of such terms as *explanation* and *demonstration*, the educational flavor is almost uneliminable.

The present chapter turns to the kinds of problems that concern a modern philosophy of science. What does Aristotle's discussion of demonstration tell us about the internal character of a scientific system, or his account of definition and essence about his theory of explanation? Do we find in his scientific investigations or in his reflections about science anything like our own analyses of verification (or something that plays a comparable role)? We begin by examining his treatment of demonstration and then go on to consider the related topics of explanation and verification.

Demonstration

Much of what *Posterior Analytics* I says about demonstration is an analysis of the components and internal relations of a system. There are initial (primitive) terms and primitive statements (basic truths). Some of the latter give the meaning of the terms; some state truths involving those terms. These primary premises must be "true, primary, immediately better known than, prior to, and causal of the conclusion."[1] (A modern at once begins to wonder how many of these criteria are being developed for operations within the system and how many are taken to hold without qualification; for example, are the axioms absolutely true, or simply held true, for developing that system? That, however, is a question for the moderns at a later point in the history of mathematics and logic; Aristotle does not ask it, nor perhaps can he be expected to.) The logic employed within the system is syllogistic. Primary premises are unavoidable if our conclusions are to yield scientific knowledge. The only alternatives are endless regress and circular reasoning. Endless regress will not give us necessity, and circular argument is vicious.[2]

The desirable type of scientific statement is carefully analyzed. Three important terms are distinguished: what is predicated *of all*, what pertains *as such* (*per se*), and what is *universal*.[3] Something is predicated of all of something else when it holds for every instance of that second thing and at every time, as *animal* is predicated of *man*, or *containing a point* of *line*. One thing belongs *per se* to another if it is part of its essence, as *line* is part of the account of what a triangle is; or again, as the attribute *curved*, while it itself belongs to *line*, has *line* as part of its own account. To belong as such is of course distinguished from belonging by accident (as *cultured* or *white* may apply to *animal*). *Per se* is also used of substances, which do not belong to anything else in that they cannot be predicated strictly of anything else, and also of events or connections that happen in virtue of a thing's own nature. What is asserted *per se* of anything belongs to it necessarily. The third term, *universal*, has a special and far from casual meaning. A universal attribute not only has to be predicated of all and belong *per se* in the senses already given, but must be related to the subject primarily, not indirectly. Thus a figure may have angles whose sum is equal to two right angles, but not because it is a figure; it has this property because it is a triangle. The same may be said about an isosceles triangle: its angles have that sum because it is a triangle, not because it is isosceles. This appears to be offering under a special concept of the universal (sometimes translated as the "commensurate universal") the logical ideal of the necessary and sufficient conditions for the application of a term. This is, of course, no simple linguistic matter. In mathematics it presupposes successful analysis and established knowledge of relations between terms or entities, and in science it presupposes discovery of what the conditions in fact are.

Types of basic truths are also distinguished. One type is definitions. Another is common truths that span several domains and have to be interpreted within each; for example, "Take equals from equals, and equals remain" is used by the geometer only for magnitudes, by the arithmetician only for numbers. Another type is statements about existence; these may be proved in the case of defined terms (such as that there are triangles), but only assumed for basic terms (such as points). Again, there are logical laws, such as that of noncontradiction, whose different modes of use are carefully distinguished. Specific logical forms are related to their scientific uses. Thus, within the same form the syllogism that yields the fact is distinguished from the one that yields the reasoned fact, because the latter's middle term is the proximate cause. The contrasting examples are "All planets are nontwinklers; all nontwinklers are near: therefore all planets are near" and "All planets are near; all near are nontwinklers: therefore all planets do not twinkle." In the latter syllogism, the middle term specifies the cause of the fact stated in the conclusion: being near determines nontwinkling, but nontwinkling does not cause being near. (Later usage sometimes distinguished here the *causa essendi*, or cause of its being so, from the *causa cognoscendi*, or cause of our knowing it to be so.) Again, the first figure of the syllogism is scientifically fundamental. It is the only one that can yield a conclusion that is affirmative and universal, and thus it is the one through which we can pursue the essence.

Posterior Analytics 1 can be seen as the first great treatise on the logical structure of system and intrasystemic problems. The kind of knowledge sought might be expressed as "systematic theoretical knowledge." A modern might readily accept the account of demonstration for pure mathematics, or for the mathematical form of a physical system when it is fully developed. Primary truths would then correspond to analytic propositions, either in the sense of logical tautologies or stipulated definitions or sets of postulates implicitly defining their constituent terms, or (in physics) to the theoretical concepts thus systematically defined. Aristotle intends more than this. He has thrown all universals, physical as well as logical, into the same broad hopper, and in some sense expects the primitive truths to express material knowledge of the world. His theory of primary premises is thus extrasystemic.

The explanation of Aristotle's procedure here should also be clear from the account of the basic conceptual network that we have developed. Where the primary premises are statements of essence for physical entities (in the full scope, including biological, psychological, and other entities), we have material truths. These would not be sufficient for predicting all behavior in sublunar domains; we would at best know, for example, what the acorn would grow into, *if* there were no accident of rotting or being eaten by pigs, or the like. Only in astronomy, because the heavenly bodies are simple and uniform and there is no accident there, could we predict accurately from knowledge; but even in this case, our vision is in the sublunar domain, and appearances might be due in part to accidental happenings in the intervening atmosphere. (Aristotle's *Meteorology* has many such explanations of phenomena in the upper sublunar regions.) Apart from the universal knowledge that follows from essence, then, we are in the realm of *opinion*. Reasoning about it would still be syllogistic, but in cases where it starts from premises that are generally accepted and not primary, the reasoning would be, in Aristotle's sense, *dialectical*. But where we would divide the body of knowledge into (a) mathematical and logical, (b) scientific, and (c) ordinary information, Aristotle draws the line in the middle of our (b), putting what is universal and essential in with (a), and the rest with (c). We ourselves have a rather conglomerate group in (b), but we can sort it into theoretical statements, empirical statements of frequency or probability, existential statements, and so on, in rather refined detail. Our sharp separation of (a) and (b) has the advantage of making clear that all matter-of-fact knowledge is empirically supported. Aristotle's fusion of (a) with part of (b) rests on his belief in essences. It can prove useful only insofar as he can successfully show how essence is determined.

We should not leave Aristotle's account of demonstration without noting the drift of recent scholarship on the problem of Aristotle's rationalism. It was mentioned in the introduction to part 4 that the pressure to type Aristotle's philosophy of science has abated. There is accordingly a greater latitude in interpretation, but the drift is consistently in one direction, away from the hard-line view that primary premises are declared true by a separate intuitive faculty in a separate intuitive act. How has this been done in the face of Aristotle's account of demonstration as proceeding from primary premises?

The first step was to compare his practice with his general pronouncements, his digging and construction in various fields with his finished product on display in the *Posterior Analytics*. The comparison might suggest a conflict between the tentative and the perfect or, even more radically, an inner conflict in Aristotle himself. Le Blond's book on logic and method in Aristotle (published in 1939) is a good starting point. Among the several problems he examines, the tone of his conclusions is similar. In analyzing intuitive induction he first finds the consistent sensory theme: nothing in Aristotle's description of the formation of universals in *epagōgē* obliges us to leave the domain of sensation—nothing, that is, until intellectual intuition (*nous*) comes on the scene. Le Blond eventually concludes that there is a conflict between the theoretician and the practitioner and that the *Analytics* "prepare us to appreciate the diversity of inspiration, or even the opposition of spirit that exists between the works of science and the theoretical works of logic."[4] He finds that Aristotle has not reconciled science and dialectics, nor decisively determined whether research into scientific work, especially the establishment of principles, falls outside or within science itself.[5] At almost every point Le Blond's conclusion is the same; he credits the illuminating complexity of Aristotle's analysis and yet finds essential conflicts.

A quite different and more radical approach was to make a frontal attack on the rationalistic facade of the *Posterior Analytics* itself. In an influential paper that appeared in 1969, Barnes recast the concept of demonstration. The educational motif, he contends, is not simply in the background for Aristotle, but almost central to the meaning of demonstration itself; the concept of *epagōgē* is also closely connected with teaching, and the theory of demonstration should be regarded as formalizing didactic conversation, just as the syllogism in general formalizes conversational argument in general. Barnes thus believes that Aristotle is not telling the scientist how to carry on research but is rather giving pedagogic advice on how an achieved body of knowledge is to be presented and taught.[6] This is not, of course, incompatible with the notion that the way a science is to be taught also follows the lines found in the structure of its results. It does, however, shift the emphasis. I am reminded of the story Bertrand Russell tells in his autobiography, of the way he first learned geometry. He saw his elder brother studying it and asked to be taught. Agreeing, his brother began by asking him to grant the postulates. This Russell flatly refused, and accordingly his brother would not go on. Russell immediately granted the postulates. He adds that this was the best reason he ever found for granting them. Necessity in pedagogy is far from the necessity of rationalism.

With the door open, demonstration became a candidate for further reinterpretation. Not it alone, for the effects on one central concept in the methodological subnetwork could not fail to find reverberations on others. If *apodeixis* is altered, *nous* and *epagōgē* cannot stand still. Let us take three further examples of papers from the recent past that move Aristotle away from the rationalistic center. One steers him back to empirical ground, a second moves in an Hegelian direction, and a third completely abandons any relation of *epagōgē* to the determination of truth.

Lesher (1973) examines the role of *nous* in the *Posterior Analytics*. He finds it has a variety of uses in the earlier literature and that Aristotle uses it broadly, not merely for the faculty that grasps first principles but also for the insight that grasps any universal principle. He denies that Aristotle's *nous* is an *a priori* or nonempirical acquisition of knowledge about the world by an isolated intuition. In effect, this likewise denies the separation of the two phases of *epagōgē*. Indeed, Lesher argues that *nous* and *epagōgē* are one single activity of grasping a universal principle described in two ways, the former by an epistemological characterization, the latter by a methodological one. Accordingly the account of *nous* that Aristotle embodies in his analysis of *epagōgē* is not in conflict with his empiricism but a consequence of it. It is consonant with Aristotle's general attitude to the role of experience in science, mathematics, and ethics, in all of which there are only differences of degree in the way the principles arise out of experience.[7]

Kosman (1973) reanalyzes the several concepts in the light of an altered understanding of demonstration. He identifies *epistēmē* (knowledge) in its broadest sense with the explanatory art; *apodeixis* (demonstration) is best understood as (roughly) explanation—proof is not its focal sense. If poiētic *epistēmē* is knowing how to make, and practical *epistēmē*, how to act, then apodeictic *epistēmē* is knowing how to show. It is "discursive disclosure," and the man of understanding is the one who is able to explain.[8] This reinterpretation has a reconstructive effect on *nous* and *epagōgē*. *Nous* does not give us simply the truth of the premises, but the grasp that they are the principles for a given body of phenomena: "*Nous* is not the process by which we come to know the *archai* [principles], but the state we are in when we have, by whatever means, come to know them."[9] The process itself is *epagōgē*, and it turns out not to be different from demonstration itself: it is the insight that sees natures in particulars. It is related to demonstration as teaching is to learning. They are one and the same act, but their being is different; that is, they are different descriptions of the act. Somehow in all this, understanding has absorbed the concepts of the methodological subnetwork into a vision of the coherence of the whole.

By contrast, Engberg-Pedersen (1979) is blunt in his approach to *epagōgē*. He relies on the *Topics*, which describes it simply as "the march [*ephodos*] from particular to universal."[10] *Nous* in this march is not a state of mind that consists in true knowledge, nor is it a capacity to guarantee the truth on the basis of inspection of particular cases. It is a generalizing capacity going beyond what is grasped in sense perception, whether the universal so grasped is true or false. As for *epagōgē*, it is "a simple notion that never betrays its connection with the dialectical situation, where its aim is to generate acceptance, and no more, of a universal proposition. It does not touch on the complicated question as to the certainty of that proposition. But as far as it goes, it has the advantage of being clear and having a point."[11]

Where do we now stand? All three studies agree that the old conception of *nous* as what intuits the truth of isolated principles in the rationalist view of self-evident axioms is an inadequate interpretation. They differ over the relative importance of truth in the process. Engberg-Pedersen simply drops the truth-claim and routes the process to dialectic, which is more concerned with consolidating belief. Lesher appears to rely on empirical processes. Kosman makes the task in some ways more difficult; truth is indeed recognized as pertinent to the grasp of principles in Aristotle's theory, but it is a truth of coherence with what is known of the phenomena. Presumably if we had a relation of commensurate universality between the principles and the phenomena such that not only did the principles yield the phenomena, but the phenomena, the principles, everything would be logically settled by our having in each case the one and only explanatory principles. But this last is not the state of knowledge nor likely to be. This question cannot be ignored by attending only to the knowing state, whatever the means of coming to knowledge. Aristotle is committed in *Posterior Analytics* 2 to showing how the definition that gives the truth is attained. Of course the exhibition of definition, we shall see, comes in the process of demonstration, and perhaps Aristotle should be accepting a modern coherence theory of truth. But does he?

If Barnes is correct in his view that Aristotle first developed the notion of an axiomatized deductive system,[12] then the *Posterior Analytics* marked a significant discovery. It is hard in that case to minimize Aristotle's demand for the truth of the first principles, particularly when we recall that he was rejecting the Platonic conception of a general dialectical science that would claim to work up to an ultimate explanatory insight, and substituting for this the organized and systematized sciences. The contemporary reevaluation of the concepts that Aristotle employed in explicating the establishment of the principles has bent back the stick and restored the explanatory relation of the principles to the demonstrated consequences that are the bulk of scientific knowledge. This has served to point out in the corpus the many detailed processes of gaining knowledge and formulating ideas that bear some resemblance to the standard procedures of standard scientific thought. But to see Aristotle's philosophy of science wholly in that light would make of him almost a modern theorist of science who reckons principles by their scientific consequences. It is well to recall the radical intellectual changes that intervened before such approaches won contemporary acceptance: the development of probability and probabilism; revolutions in mathematics and logic; a new instrumentalist attitude to concepts and principles, which relieved them of a direct realism (itself dependent upon the Darwinian revolution); and many more.

I have suggested in the discussion of *epagōgē* in the previous chapter that Aristotle's psychological analysis of thinking provides the key to our understanding why he could claim the truth of first principles even though his treatment of the processes by which we achieve them could have tentative and exploratory, if not precisely experimental, elements. It unifies his divergent tendencies and explains his readiness to accept so many of his results as completed. The inner conflict that contemporary studies may find is likely to be our conflict once we have abandoned his psychology of thought.

Explanation

Book 2 of the *Posterior Analytics* is cast in the context of the process of inquiry. Here we may expect an account of the nature of explanation in its logical aspects, not simply as a theory of the four causes. Aristotle begins with the kind of questions men ask, whose answers constitute our knowledge. He lists four: (1) the *that*, for instance, whether the moon suffers eclipse or not; whether the earth moves or not; (2) the *on-account-of-what*, that is, the reason for its happening; (3) *if-it-is*, for instance, whether a centaur or a god exists; and (4) *what-it-is*— what a god is; what man is.[13] Both the statement of a reason (2) and the statement of the nature of a thing (4) are really concerned with the same inquiry. The one asks what is the cause of an eclipse (of the moon), the other what an eclipse is. The latter answers, "The moon's deprivation of light through obstruction by the earth"; the former answers, "Because the sun's light fails owing to the obstruction of the earth." So both the discovery of a causal reason and the statement of the essence or nature are interpreted as identifying a middle term. All search for an explanation is conceived as a search for a middle term. For example, we find out that *man* is joined with *mortal* because *man* is joined with *animal* and *animal* is joined with *mortal*: it is in virtue of man's animal nature that he perishes. Thus the notion of a middle term plays the role in Aristotle's language of science that the notion of a theoretical explanation plays in ours. (Of course, as we have seen, not every middle term qualifies; there are additional qualifications.) To give a theoretical explanation of a conjunction of properties is to specify another entity or set of entities and the rules of their relation to one another and to the original terms, such that the conjunction is deducible from these.

Aristotle not only identifies (2) and (4) as asking what the middle term is, but he takes (1) and (3) to be asking *whether there is a middle*. This is an obscure and varyingly interpreted point. We must remember, however, that (1) probably does not refer to whether there is now a darkening of the moon, which would be a matter of sense perception, but to whether the concept of the eclipse is applicable to the darkening. Similarly, in (3), to ask if a centaur exists is to ask whether the concept has any application, that is, whether there is a middle term that specifies some centaurial properties which, in turn, are predicable of something that exists. (To take a rather specious argument from an early dialogue: Gods are prayed to, and it would be senseless to pray to what does not exist; therefore gods exist.) Perhaps the clearest case would be the example *triangle* that Aristotle throws in. To ask whether there are triangles is to ask if we can prove in the system of geometry that a triangle can be constructed, given three straight lines; again, to ask whether triangles have an angle sum of two right angles is to ask whether this is deducible in the system. But such an example almost seems to beg the issue; it is taken from a demonstrative system, and any question concerning a proposition in the system could be construed as a question about provability or a request for proof. On the other hand, it is the best example, precisely because Aristotle is concerned with questions whose answers yield knowledge, and this means interpreting inquiry as the search for middle terms (theoretical explanations), leading back ultimately to statements of essence and primary assumptions of existence.[14]

The relations between these various questions foreshadow Aristotle's treatment of definition. Definition is basically a statement of essential nature. If the term defined is a derived term, like *triangle*, then demonstration helps exhibit its essential nature readily. If it is a basic term, then its definitory assertions will be primary assumptions. They cannot be demonstrated in the system, for they would then be logical consequences and so not primary premises. But in the process of inquiry essential nature may be exhibited by the use of demonstrative syllogism. Thus when we have found the middle term and so have a theoretical explanation of the eclipse, we have an account of the essential nature of the eclipse. This seems to suggest that in building up a system, the discovery of the basic premises that will do the best job in explaining the properties is at the same time the exhibition—not the demonstration—of the essential nature. We see this in Aristotle's mode of establishing his own definition of *psyche* in *On the Psyche*. To know what a thing is helps us understand the causes of its attributes, and conversely, to know the attributes helps us know the essence.[15] For when we can explain most of the presented phenomena, we are in the best position to give an account of the essence: "The starting point of every demonstration is the what-it-is, so that those definitions that do not lead us to know the attributes, not even to conjecture about them readily, are clearly offered for argument's sake and are all futile." Clearly, then, the kind of definition intended is one that incorporates the theoretical results of the inquiry and is fit consequently to take its place among the primary truths as an account of essence.

Because the notion of existence has been discussed here in the context of explanation, its systematic relations have been stressed. To prevent misunderstanding, it is necessary to add some remarks to show how far Aristotle exhibits a clear idea of its ordinary use and even deals with it in a refined way.[16] He not only talks of centaurs not existing and assumes that there are units and proves that there are triangles (whatever the precise meanings assigned to these), but he also recognizes at various points that some words signify things that are and others, such as *goat-stag*, obviously signify what does not exist.

Again, he is certainly aware of some of the refined logical consequences of existence and nonexistence. For example, if Socrates is not, both the assertions that Socrates is well and that Socrates is ill are false.[17] We are not allowed to go from "Homer is a poet" to "Homer is," for the "is" is predicated accidentally of Homer (as a poet) and cannot be asserted unqualifiedly.[18] This is set in a general discussion of the combination of terms—why, for example, we can go from man as being animal and two-footed to his being a two-footed animal, but not from his being good and a cobbler to his being a good cobbler. The primary interest is in the difference between essential and incidental relations. Again, there are numerous contexts in which the question is raised whether something exists. For example, a definition can be tested by seeing whether the term to be defined exists when what it is defined in terms of does not; thus a definition of *white* as color mixed with fire is rejected.[19] Again, properties of nonexistent things can be differentiated: we do not assign motion to nonexistent things, but we can say they are desirable or conceivable.[20]

How, then, does Aristotle's notion of existence differ from ours? Perhaps it is less a notion of "pure" existence, more a matter of contextual relations. Whereas we would first separate off all the descriptive components and then make the judgment of existence into a kind of conferring or stamping of actuality,[21] Aristotle answers the question whether something exists by pointing out attachments to already known parts of the world. It is almost a kind of coherence theory of existence. (It presupposes, of course, the ability to point out and identify individuals, and involves perception, as we have seen earlier, in the treatment of the individual and in the psychology.) We might have anticipated that Aristotle's notion of existence would go somewhat in this direction from his refusal to have a unitary genus of being; and similarly, our unitary abstract concept of existence is the natural correlate of our abstract concept of possible worlds, for a possible world absorbs into itself the full descriptive content of a world, and nothing descriptive falls outside of it.[22]

Verification

At times Aristotle's explanatory expectations are quite modest. In the midst of a discussion of comets in the *Meteorology* he comments that in the case of things that are inaccessible to sensation we think we have explained reasonably enough if we have worked up to what is possible.[23] For the most part he is engaged in explaining rather than verifying. He starts an inquiry with a rich gathering of the descriptive material, as in the *Historia Animalium* or in his collection of the constitutions of a great many states (now all lost, save that of Athens). These materials may include many low-level generalizations, and once in a while those may be uncertain. Under these conditions there is a shift from an explanatory mood (What will best explain these phenomena?) to a verificatory mood (If this is true, what follows that we can look for?).

We may ask three questions about Aristotle's grasp of the problems of verification. First, does he recognize adequately the logical principles of hypothetical reasoning and the logical relation of consequent to antecedent? Second, does he reckon sufficiently with alternative hypotheses that yield different observational results? And third, does he appreciate the possibilities of testing predicted consequences and of experimentation?

Hypothetical reasoning is not only used in all sorts of contexts, but some formal rules of valid hypothetical argument are recognized: that from "If A, then B" it follows "If not B, then not A," and that from the first together with A we get the result B.[24] There is explicit assertion of the need for testing beliefs by their consequences in relation to phenomena of a field—especially when Aristotle is criticizing others.[25] One should not, we are told, believe in science as if one were defending a thesis in debate. Just as in production knowledge is tested by the products, so in physics one goes to the phenomena in sense perception. Even where the subject is not science but debate, instructions are to look for conditions and consequences, and in order to establish something, show that the conditions exist, and for refuting it show that the consequences are false.[26] Similar points are made in detail for refuting and establishing definitions.[27]

There is ample practical illustration in the scientific writings, especially the *Meteorology* and the biology, of alternative hypotheses' yielding different observational results. In formal statements we must not expect Aristotle to express this in terms of our language of hypothesis and confirmatory and disconfirmatory instances. His treatment of such materials falls in the domain of dialectic and rhetoric. The definition of a dialectical premise (that is, an answer to the question which of two contradictory statements is to be accepted), as distinct from a demonstrative one,[28] is parallel to our general notion of a hypothesis. Taking a proposition and asking whether it or its contradictory is true amounts to asking whether it is true or false. But instead of saying, Suppose it is true, what follows? it says, It is true; what establishes it? The tentative element thus comes in the relation of the evidence to the proposition. In the last sections of *Prior Analytics* 2, where this is discussed, the introductory remark indicates a turn to dialectic and rhetoric.[29] After induction,[30] which featured in our analysis of reasoning above, the discussion focuses on different modes of relating the evidence and the hypothesis, and different strengths, and how they stack up in comparison to stricter syllogisms. In some types of cases labels are provided. *Paradeigma*, for example, is the kind of argument we get when we go from the hypothesis to be established to a coordinate instance by invoking a generalization for both, when the coordinate instance is known; it is a part–part relation under a whole. Suppose we want to show that war against Thebes is bad. We appeal to the general statement that war against neighbors is bad. We offer evidence for this by the example that war by Thebes against Phocis is bad. The latter supports the generalization, which supports the deduction to our hypothesis. In the *Rhetoric*, where some of this material from the *Prior Analytics* is summarized, a distinction is drawn between *sēmeion*, "sign" in the general sense, and *tekmērion*, the kind of sign that is a necessary mark.[31] For example, to say that a man is ill because he has a fever or that a woman has had a child because she has milk is a necessary sign, the mark being sufficient evidence. But to say that a man has a fever because he breathes hard is insufficient; a man can breathe hard without a fever. Attention to the underlying body of knowledge or established assumptions in these different cases is directed more toward building up an inventory of reliable signs than to assigning probability values on general mathematical scales. At most we are being trained what to look for in a given context.

The bare formal principles of refutation and acceptance are recognized in many places. For example, the universal can be overthrown by the particular and the particular by the universal; but universal propositions cannot be established by particular ones, although particulars can by universals.[32] Of course, the farther a thesis is removed from the ground level of phenomena, the more its refutation turns out to involve an appeal not merely to observation but also to compatibility with other parts of the science already regarded as established.

The third topic—testing, prediction, and experimentation—is not formulated explicitly in these terms, although much testing is in effect done by asking whether given explanations hold for antecedently gathered observations. It has often been pointed out that Aristotle's empirical science rests on a descriptive basis rather than an experimental one. His work in biology and meteorology was largely concerned with the earlier descriptive levels in which phenomena had to be identified, described through selective features, and arranged in groups and classes. This applies to processes and changes as well as to things and animals. Such tasks were far more difficult than we are likely to appreciate today, since our inheritance already takes for granted a sophisticated classification; the varieties of interpretation found in the corpus about relatively rudimentary phenomena make this quite evident.

Furthermore, most of the sciences Aristotle dealt with, geometry and arithmetic, astronomy and meteorology, even biology (though there is evidence of dissections), lay outside the range of experimentation. Instead, we find reference to familiar phenomena to suggest explanations. He occasionally mentions tests such as blowing up a bladder to see how it behaves in air or in water;[33] he cites an experiment he performed to show that salt water evaporates to yield fresh water and the latter does not condense into sea water again.[34] He certainly was aware of the results of mixing colors. It should be added that he is cautious methodologically in dealing with dissections and the examination of animals.[35] None of this of course amounts to experiment in the systematic sense that modern physical science has made familiar. Aristotle relied rather on the results of nature's "experiments"—in comparative biology and embryology, in history, in the diversity of physical phenomena. What he wanted was more observations to test the theories. As he says after a long account of the generation of bees, "The facts have not been sufficiently ascertained; and if at any time they are ascertained, then we must believe the senses more than the theories—and the theories if they show results in agreement with the observations."[36]

Verification is also an appropriate context for considering how Aristotle builds up support for those wider principles that play an almost structural role in his physical theory. We have met a number of them already: for example, that all forces are exerted through contact and not at a distance, that the actual is prior to the potential, that substantival change is instantaneous, and so on. Some seem to have a large empirical component, some seem to be definitional, and some to be almost wholly conventional. Some end up as theoretical laws, others as methodological principles. In any case we are concerned not with the fundamental principles about causes, matter and form, and so on, but the more intermediate type that appear to have both empirical components and regulative functions. Aristotle recognized that principles are very powerful in human life and knowledge: a small change shakes the foundations and multiplies itself many thousandfold as we go along.[37] For example, if we were to assume that there is a minimal magnitude, it would rock the foundations of mathematics.

In today's perspective, there would appear to be no basic conflict between the empirical and the regulative aspects of general scientific principles. This has been made clear in the history of such important examples as the principles of conservation. The belief in the conservation of mechanical energy was held for isolated systems under conditions that could only be approximated or perhaps only assumed ideally. It was postulated that the kinetic energy that was lost took some undetected form; the suggestion was made by Leibniz and Lavoisier that it was imparted to the atoms. In the nineteenth century the discovery that mechanical energy could be transformed into heat energy seemed to provide an empirical vindication for a broadened conservation principle. Other forms of energy—electric, chemical, and light, for instance—enlarged the roster. If we carry through a logical reconstruction of the process, we see that at each point where the experimental evidence is inadequate, the scientist is faced with two options: abandon the principle, or ascribe the deficiencies to some undetected form of energy (apart from known limitations of conditions of the experiment). In choosing the second, one is hoping for further empirical support in the discovery of the new form, but meanwhile using the principle as regulative. In similar processes in the investigation of subatomic energies, hidden forms and fresh particles are postulated and even named in anticipation, and efforts are redoubled to find them. Principles serve regulatively—between empirical successes. Principles of this sort thus have a complex role that includes empirical generalization, regulative functioning, and even conceptual construction, and can end by becoming constitutive in the prevailing framework of scientific thought.

Let us take two illustrations from Aristotle: first, the contact principle, which we have already looked at; and second, his methodological non-reductionism, which has rather interesting consequences for the place of novelty in his system. The first is on a comparatively low level of generality, the second is quite high.

The contact principle gathered its strength by dealing with the role of touch in action and passion and by explaining the role of action and passion in growth, alteration, coming-to-be, and sensation. It made inroads into the theory of locomotion because it obviously applied to the ordinary exertion of force in pushing, pulling, and so on. Hence it became incorporated as a general principle in the concept of motion, inasmuch as motion was seen as a kind of carrying from place to place. This compelled a special contact interpretation of those phenomena that might have seemed to be counterinstances—projectiles, and also the magnet. The motion of projectiles was explained by the complex thesis that setting the projectile in motion also imparts the power of moving (that is, of moving something else) to the air; the deceleration of the projectile was explained by the waning of that secondary contact power. The magnet's power to make metal attracted to it a magnet in turn, seemed obvious confirmation of the transfer of power, quite enough for adopting the assumption that the power operated on the intervening air. When the problem of a film of water between objects in water and a film of air between objects in air was raised, the film itself furnished the contact and transferred the action or passion. For higher psychological processes one could always assume a still finer, fluid *pneuma* rather than accept discontinuities. As for the familiar phenomena of falling bodies, however, the concept of natural motion obviated any search for contact forces. The theory of natural motion in turn helped render unacceptable the notion of a vacuum. Natural motion itself is the fulfillment of a potentiality, so that it makes no more sense to ask why fire moves upward and earth downward, says Aristotle, than why the curable as such moves toward health, and not toward whiteness.[38]

The contact principle becomes thus thoroughly stable in the system of knowledge. It is buttressed by the conception of potentiality and the abhorrence of the indeterminate and the infinite. In the argument about vacuum Aristotle asks why a thing set in motion in a vacuum should stop here rather than there. He adds that "a thing will either be at rest or must be moved *ad infinitum* unless something more powerful gets in its way."[39] This he finds absurd, rejecting thereby a first approximation to Newton's law of inertia. It is not that the idea of inertia is absurd; in fact the circular movement of the heavens is of such a kind, except that it is conceived as complete actuality rather than in an "inertial" way. To apply the idea to linear movement would have overthrown the principle of natural motion, as well as opened the way to an indefinite or infinite linear motion and so upset the finite world picture.

Though Aristotle was bound to reject this near glimpse of Newton's first law of motion, the really fundamental divergence in their thought can be recognized in Newton's second law of motion. It ties the notion of force to acceleration, whereas the Aristotelian scheme ties whatever notion of force it has to motion. In short, for Aristotle the natural state of fulfillment (except for the circular motion of the heavens) is one of rest, not motion. There can, of course, be unnatural rest when a force exactly counters the natural impulse, as when a projectile slowly comes to rest in its upward motion in the air before falling down. But this is the exception.

It may be added that Newton's third law of motion, that action and reaction are equal and contrary, is approximated by Aristotle in *On the Movement of Animals* when he speculates about the force exerted by Atlas to hold the earth, and under what conditions the equilibrium would be upset.[40] Fortunately his argument implies that the earth cannot be dislodged.

Such comparisons show us how difficult it is to separate the philosophical background, itself incorporating scientific beliefs, from the system of science which generates principles that in turn maintain that system of science. The philosophical concepts may yield eventually in the face of accumulating evidence, but usually this requires a changed philosophical conception embodied in the systematization of that evidence.

Our second illustration, the principle of nonreductionism, is not stated by Aristotle so much as constantly used by him in his battle against the reductionist tendencies of Empedocles and the atomists. It operates alongside his naturalism, noted in chapter 3, which recognizes the continuities in the single order of nature and creates no impassable theoretical barriers. There is no contradiction in these coexisting principles: the seed grows into the animal with the same metaphysical simplicity as the bronze becomes the statue of Apollo. Yet the animal is no mere earth, nor Apollo mere bronze.

Take Aristotle's example of blushing, in the *Categories*.[41] He notes that when men are ashamed they turn red, and when alarmed they turn pale. But this is episodic; a man might equally well be regularly ruddy as a consequence of the same bodily conditions' being permanently in his makeup. Having said this, Aristotle raises no questions about the subjectivity of the component of shame as opposed to the objectivity of the bodily conditions, or about the debatable status of the ruddiness (sensation or objective quality?). Of course shame is not equated with the physical conditions, for emotions have *further* qualitative (including final-functional) elements. The general attitude to qualities is simply that the qualitative appears under the appropriate specific conditions in the world. Presumably nature behaves in sunsets like men turning red, though only a pseudo-Homer would sing of the sun's blushing every evening for the misdeeds of the day.

Aristotle's classification of change embodies his nonreductive principles quite clearly. The integrity of qualitative change or alteration is maintained, rather than quality reduced to its physical causal conditions. Thus it is wrong to define pain as "a separation of conjoined parts accompanied by violence," for this is to speak as if the inanimate parts had pain;[42] presumably pain has the whole animate being as its subject. (His treatment of anger, examined above in the psychology, is a fuller exploration of these relations.) There is no denying the physical aspects of change or the occurrence of motion wherever any changes take place, whatever their level. But each is what it is, and qualitative change is not simply a mechanical transformation.

Equally, however, Aristotle defends substantival change against reduction to qualitative change.[43] Alteration is qualified coming-into-being, but becoming or generation is unqualified or simple coming-into-being. In alteration a perceptible substratum or subject remains the same throughout, but in substantival change the thing as a whole changes, whatever the "microscopic" transformations underlying it.

Substantival change and its startling properties have been examined at several points earlier. It is instantaneous and not of temporal duration. It is the substance that has changed, though matter from other things or from the previous subject has been used. It presupposes the other kinds of change but, so to speak, supervenes on them. Passing-away is similar in type, involving the generation of something else. These features are similar to what a modern emergentist would expect when something new emerges. But the emergentist principle is concerned with the novel as it appears in the evolutionary process. Aristotle is stressing the element of sudden novelty that recurs throughout the processes of nature.

It is not surprising, therefore, to find Aristotle particularly interested in the striking phenomena of critical points in the midst of natural processes. The freezing of a whole body of water impresses him, and he uses this, as we noted, almost as a model for explaining what happens when fire lights up a medium.[44] He is interested in the phenomenon of curdling in milk, is aware that milk is curdled by fig juice and rennet, and attributes the phenomenon to the action of heat.[45] In describing the roles of male and female in procreation he has the male provide the form and the female the matter, drawing a comparison to the fig juice or rennet that coagulates the milk.[46] Setting and solidification require precise and appropriate proportions of elements: if too hot, the fluid is dried up; if not hot enough, it will not set.[47] We seem to have here almost a root metaphor, which colors not only specific doctrines such as that of the *mean* in Aristotle's ethics (see chapter 16 below), but his general approach; for the process in which matter as potentiality takes on form as actuality is itself seen as a kind of setting.

In general, then, the methodological use of nonreductionism has empirical, logical, and metaphysical aspects. Sometimes, as when Aristotle insists that there is no process of beginning or ending in movement, that at any moment a thing is either moving or is not moving, he seems to be applying the law of noncontradiction. Our discussion of that law showed that he also assigned it an ontological role. Again, though he is insistent that whatever change is happening (whether qualitative, substantival, or by growth), there is always some associated change of place (clearly an empirical matter), this is not to be regarded as a reduction on methodological, logical, and metaphysical grounds. It also means that he defends the integrity of each level, particularly where a more complex one such as qualitative alteration emerges from, say, quantitative or growth changes. In general, each fresh level in the process of generation is new with respect to other levels. But as suggested above, the form of the new has appeared in the past. Aristotle thus maintains a very delicate balance between the novel and the tried-and-true eternal. His nonreductionism is firm, and it establishes the integrity of the novel, but the novel thus established cannot stray too far from established order.

I4

MEANING, DEFINITION,

AND CLASSIFICATION

Definition as examined so far has been associated with explanation. It presents ideas that have been clarified and are the formal outcome of inquiry. When Aristotle is engaged in processes of inquiry, however, many less formal modes of specifying meaning are evident, some of which he refers to but does not bother to systematize.

Our interest in seeing what Aristotle has done in this field is sharpened by parallels in the twentieth-century theory of definition. A demand that definition aim at the necessary and sufficient conditions for the use of a term or even, in an older tradition, at furnishing a "real" or "essential" account of the nature of the thing defined, dominated the logic texts as late as the fourth decade of the twentieth century. Even when the advent of symbolic logic caused revisions in the texts, the emphasis on mathematics preserved the reference to necessary and sufficient conditions. But the philosophy of science brought attention to the actual processes of scientific inquiry and the varied way ideas were clarified in different stages of their use in different sciences, biological and psychological as well as physical. Humanistic disciplines added significantly different lessons from rhetoric and processes of communication, and artistic and literary performance, which raised questions about the meaning of meaning and the character of symbols. Meaning was related to the realm of using symbols or symbolic acts, and language came to be understood as a human institution continuous in its voicing and gesture with the physical occurrences of sound and movement. Logical refinement distinguished areas of the study of symbols: syntax, the rules governing the relation of symbols; semantics, the relation of symbols to object; and pragmatics, the relation of symbols to user and recipient. (Semantic analyses in particular led directly into metaphysical questions, just as Aristotle's study of different psychic acts, such as sensing and thinking, had pointed to different forms of being, the particular and the universal.) The rapidly growing field of linguistics, furthered in the twentieth century both by audio devices and by anthropological study of preliterate languages, as well as by fresh models (of grammar, for instance), seemed for a time to dominate the inquiry into symbols. Finally, the psychologists and the physiologists, together with the technologists, in their new efforts to solve the practical problems of impaired hearing and vision, began to unearth some of the more minute mechanisms that disturb the normal development of sensory awareness and linguistic ability.

Of course Aristotle does not furnish us with the integrated model we need to span such varied studies, but his own integrative approach was able to carry him into an appreciation of the whole field of symbolization and its problems once he got beyond the formal account of definition. He raises many of the questions a modern might expect, though some are not carried far: what organs enter into language; at what precise points signifying arises; how psychological processes are related to elementary syntactic structure; how similarities spread among words, and how they can be controlled (the problem of ambiguity); as well as the nature and types of meaning, problems of reference, varieties of definitional processes, and grouping and classification. And he approaches these questions through somewhat the same variety of interests that we do. Some questions are raised in the biological studies. Others derive from rhetorical studies where the aim is to improve methods of persuasion, others from legal argumentation and the problem of logical fallacies, including those that stem from ambiguity. A compact survey of some linguistic points is placed near the end of the *Poetics* simply because a dramatist should know about such things.

The role that the problem of ambiguity plays in philosophy deserves special attention. It is almost coextensive with the theory of how we get our ideas clear. A great part of the analytic method in the Platonic dialogues, as well as in the Aristotelian resolution of paradoxes, consists in distinguishing meanings so as to dissolve a problem. Obviously then, something more must be going on than simply that one word or expression is being used mistakenly twice where two different words should be used. To talk of ambiguity is (for the most part) to use a linguistic formulation. To talk of ideas not being clear is to use a conceptual or ideational formulation. If we want to talk of the objects that the terms refer to or that the ideas are about, we do not speak of ambiguity but may appropriately say that the field of which we are aware is vague; this is an ontological formulation. As we have seen (chapters 7 and 8), such questions as whether *being* was a generic term or an analogical term were not linguistic solely, but metaphysical ones, and had important philosophy-shaking if not world-shaking consequences.

To present so broad an array of topics as are embraced in this chapter can at best be a survey. This is regrettable, but anything less would be one-sided; a selective treatment of Aristotle's view of meaning is likely to lead to a one-sided interpretation of his philosophical method. Our glimpse of this vast field and some of its implications is organized as follows: (1) sound, voice and symbol; (2) ambiguity and types of meaning; (3) definitional processes; and (4) classification.

Sound, Voice, and Symbol

Aristotle distinguishes voice from sound, and speech from voice. Voice is sound that signifies or has meaning, and speech is the kind of linguistic occurrence that we are familiar with in human beings; he takes it to be peculiar to man.

Sound arises in the use of the apparatus of breathing and the manipulation of lips, teeth, tongue, and uvula, backed by the structure of larynx and windpipe. The ear is the receiving mechanism. Different sounds are related to the tongue and the closing of the lips, and even to the sharpness of the front teeth.[1] In *Historia Animalium*, when Aristotle systematically discusses voice among animals, he is dealing with material causes and so distinguishes voice, sound, and speech by the organs involved: the lungs and pharynx are necessary for voice, the tongue for speech; vowel sounds are produced by the voice and the larynx, and consonants by the tongue and the lips.[2] Out of these speech is composed. Aristotle compares the sounds made by other animals that lack speech organs, analyzing the buzzing of bees and the whizzing of scallops, the hissing of serpents, and so on. Dolphins moan and squeak, they have lungs and windpipe, but no lips; frogs croak as they do because of the peculiar formation of their tongue. He notes the cry of the male to the female animal at breeding time and the challenging cries of birds before a fight. Although speech is peculiar to man, there are speech-like occurrences among some animals.[3] Whereas voice, distinguished chiefly by its pitch, does not differ among a given type of animal, articulation does sometimes differ according to locality; some partridges cackle, others make a shrill noise. Young birds sing differently if reared away from the nest and exposed to other birds' singing; nightingales even appear to teach songs.

The physical conditions of sounding involve firm cohesion of air, a movement set up by striking, and a role for air in the ear.[4] Flutes and lyres thus sound, but voice is attributed to them only metaphorically; for voice is now defined as the impact of air that is breathed upon the windpipe under the agency of the psyche in those parts.[5] This revised definition in the psychological context has been extended from the material cause to embrace efficient cause. The definition that follows gives the formal cause: voice is a sound that signifies something.[6] It is not like a cough. A sound may of course reveal something (Aristotle is not always consistent in separating sound and voice), and in this sense animals communicate; but this is not speech, in which there is use of conventional *symbols*.

Speech and symbols bring us to the familiar domain of linguistics. Aristotle develops the linguistic units together with the psychological basis of their syntactic form. The basic linguistic units are words, or as he calls them, names; they are symbols of affections in the psyche (sense impressions, images, or thoughts). Written marks are symbols of spoken words. Parts of a name need not have meaning by themselves. Sentences join words and consist primarily of nouns and verbs. The Greek term for *name* (*onoma*) is also used for *noun*. Basically, *name* is a functional word, signifying the thought held up in contemplation; the verb is what we are told about it. A noun or verb by itself is like a thought (Aristotle gives *the man or the white* as an illustration), and a verb too is a *name*, "for the speaker stops his thought and the hearer pauses."[7] The central syntactic form, subject and predicate, thus expresses the rudimentary psychological process of isolating something in thought and then attributing some isolated idea to it. The rest of the account of syntax—legitimate kinds of sentences, forms of contrariety, and so on—is found in the logical works and the theory of categories (notably among the hints about how not to confuse them in application), and in the account of transformation rules in the theory of validity.

Aristotle's treatment of semantics—at least in his way of handling the topic—may be identified largely with the problems of meaning to be dealt with in the next section of this chapter. Perhaps even more broadly we are led into his whole metaphysics, because given his general mode of analyzing a function by studying its objects, the analysis of signifying (or meaning) directs us to the analysis of things signified. Hence the previous investigations of the categories, universals, genera, species, individuals, matter and form, actualities and potentialities, and the rest, are immediately relevant. This might not be a bad preparation for understanding what has happened at times in contemporary philosophy, when metaphysics, dismissed as "bad grammar" by logical positivism, reentered the fray through the controversies over what good grammar (or good syntax or a proper semantic analysis) would be like.

There are also dispersed contexts in the corpus from which useful Aristotelian notions on semantics may be drawn. For example, the compact treatment of some linguistic matters in the *Poetics* indicates the role that nonsignifying sounds (prepositions, for instance) may play in signifying sentences or in combining signifying sounds.[8] There Aristotle also discusses indirect modes of reference, such as metaphors or the use of genus (for poetic reasons) to refer to what is really a species. The logical and metaphysical writings develop a rich language for pointing and classifying: this, this-something, this-such, such.[9] Terms for space and time are refined in the physical writings. Again, there is an occasional remark (for example, on the difference between saying that pleasure is good and that it is *the* good) that shows a clear sense of *definite description*.[10]

As for pragmatics, though he was aware of the formal differences between different kinds of sentences, Aristotle tended to look beyond to the functional differences. He refers to the distinctions between a command, a prayer, a statement, a threat, a question, an answer, and so forth; and he says that Protagoras criticized Homer's opening the *Iliad* with an imperative ("Sing of the wrath, O Goddess . . .") when a prayer was intended.[11] In general, the *Rhetoric* is concerned with the language of persuasion, the *Topics* with language for argumentation, and the *Poetics* with language and emotional effect. These are all attempts to work out modes of achieving success in the purposive use of language. Aristotle was also, of course, interested in understanding the failures, and warning against fallacies and traps, and even—if we may judge from the *Problems* (a later and non-Aristotelian collection in the Aristotelian spirit)—in raising issues about very specific obstacles to speech. Why, for example, does drunkenness affect speech?[12] Is it because the tongue is surrounded by a quantity of liquid, or because the mind suffers in sympathy with the body? What do fear and anxiety do to the heart and so to the tongue?[13] What are the different effects of weeping and laughter on the tone of voice?[14] And what of stammering and lisping?[15]

This first section has stressed the scope and multidimensional, but unified, character of the approach to problems of language and meaning. It does not state Aristotle's actual conclusions so much as map the avenues of his exploration, although often he had not gone far. But some of the systems he turned to, such as the metaphysics and the logic, were of course fully grown, and the point here is the relevance of their connection.

Ambiguity and Types of Meaning

The very first sentences in the whole corpus concern the difference between *things that are called homonymous* and *things that are called synonymous*.[16] They are homonymous (same-named) when they have only a name in common and the definitions corresponding to the name are different; in the case of the synonymous (together-named, as it were), not only the name but the definition is the same. For example, an animal is called *zōion*, and so is a picture; under this term, then, a man and a picture would be homonymous, but a man and an ox, both being animals, would be synonymous. (Aristotle also introduces here the term *paronymous*, for things that take their name from a difference in the ending of a word, such as *grammarian* from *grammar*, or *brave* from *bravery*.)

Clearly Aristotle is looking at what we would call a difference between equivocal and univocal *terms*. But he is doing so from the other end of the term—thing relation. For him, it is the things that take on the names (or are associated with them, for of course there is already some classification in any individuation), and the latter fit closely or loosely almost as if they were clothes shaped better or worse for the job of clarifying. (It should be added that he is not always steady in this usage and occasionally slips into calling terms themselves homonymous.) In most of the logical works, especially the *Topics* and *Sophistical Refutations*, as well as in the *Rhetoric*, the underlying aim in discerning the fit of the clothes is to achieve this clarity and so not be deceived into accepting a fallacious argument. But in the physical and metaphysical works to distinguish different meanings of the same word may resolve a most delicate scientific and philosophical issue.

In metaphysics, especially, we may suggest that what is taken to be homonymous in terms will depend largely on one's theory of the real, as well as on one's notion of similarity. For example, man and ox can be synonymously called *animal* if one believes in real types (genus or species). A nominalist, who peoples the world only with individuals and takes all types to be loose likenesses, might argue there is homonomy even in calling John and Henry *man*. A theory of shades of ambiguity or looseness of language or the fit of language and things (or language and thoughts) is just one route along which a metaphysics is developed. This does not of course mean that the language determines the metaphysics, or conversely, in a given case. In Aristotle they develop hand in hand or by continual interaction; the factual assumptions sharpen the language and the sharpened language refines discernment of fact.

Let us now examine and briefly illustrate the types of ambiguity and, correspondingly, the types of meaning arising from them. Aristotle detects quite a range, between the sheerly homonymous at one end and the sheerly synonymous at the other, but I make no attempt to order them in a linear way.

(1) Straight or sheer homonymy will be our simple ambiguity, to be unmasked or disposed of. Some instances are obvious: both a stupid fellow and lump of earth are called a clod; both a man and a stick may be called crooked. But when Aristotle devotes a few chapters in the *Topics* to ambiguity, it is toward more than to pointing out such facts.[17] He wants to give us procedures for establishing the ambiguity in possibly doubtful cases. Suppose I said that *crooked* meant the same for man and stick, that is, simply a distortion. You could appeal to opposites and see if they differ: the opposite of *crooked* for the man is *honest*, but for the stick, *straight*. Aristotle's illustration is *sharp* for a note and for a tool: for the one the opposite is *flat*, for the other, *dull*. Or again, *loving* as a state of mind has a contrary, *hating*, whereas *loving* as a bodily act has none. Similarly, *not to see* may mean to be blind or not to exercise sight.

And so on. There are many other devices. One is to examine the genus; for example, the Greek word *onos* is used for an animal (donkey) and for a machine (windlass), and so we have different genera. Another is to use an adjective with different nouns: combine *clear* with *body* and *note* and when the translations are performed, into "a body having such and such a color" and "a note that is easily heard," then remove the nouns and you are left with different accounts.

In a more complex case where much is at stake (Aristotle wants to show that a circular motion and a rectilinear motion are quite different), it is argued that *quick* in their cases does not mean the same.[18] A proof is offered: if one is quicker than the other, there must be some portion of the time in which the distance traversed in part of the arc would equal a distance traversed in the straight line, which would make arc and line commensurable. Hence their velocities cannot be compared. It is just like asking which is sharpest—a pencil, some wine, or a musical note. *Quick* is as equivocal for the one case as *sharp* is for the other. It is suggested that *much* is equivocal in the same way in *much water* and *much air*, and that this is even true for *double*. In the end locomotion is taken to be a genus, not a species. (Circular and linear movement are thus two distinct species of locomotion.) In a different scientific context it is pointed out that we cannot argue from some animals' being keen-sighted and others not that the same causes are at work; *keen* may mean able to see from a distance and it may also mean able to distinguish accurately objects that are seen, and these faculties are distinct.[19] It would be like looking for the same causes for keen hearing and keen smell. Clearly, then, though Aristotle's conceptual tools are sharpened for rhetoric in the *Topics*, they stand ready for scientific use. What Aristotle achieved in this last example by pointing out the ambiguity of a term might have been reached through a material investigation by a fuller initial analysis of the phenomena of vision and their components.

(2) Amphiboly is the kind of ambiguity that arises in a sentence owing to syntactic unclarity. Our stock examples are the devious ambiguities of the Delphic oracle, as in "You, I declare, a great empire will conquer," in which "you" may be subject or object of "will conquer," with devastatingly different results, Aristotle distinguishes different kinds of these ambiguities; one, for example, involves combination, such as "A man can walk though sitting," which might be taken not as a then-unactualized ability, but as doing opposites at the same time; another involves division, such as "5 is 2 and 3," which could be construed to mean that 5 is both even and odd!

(3) Aristotle frequently considers terms that are the same only *by analogy*; in some of these cases the usage is *metaphorical* (etymologically, a metaphor is literally a *transference*). Look back to our example of the crooked man and the crooked stick above. Granted that *crooked* does not mean the same in both cases, one might claim that the usage in the case of the stick was primary and in that of the man metaphorical. Metaphor is "the application of a name belonging to something else, transferring either from genus to species or species to genus or species to species, or transferring on grounds of analogy."[20] Analogy involves four terms so related that as the second is to the first, the fourth is to the third. To use the fourth for the second is then metaphorical. He illustrates: as old age is to life, so evening is to day. Hence we could metaphorically call old age the evening of life, or we could similarly call the evening the old age of the day. Now in the case of the same word used in both cases, *crooked* of man and stick, we could say that it is metaphorical only in the case of man because we have a primary or original or literal use for stick. Hence the metaphorical usage, or the analogical usage, applies to the derived case.

Further complications are possible. Suppose a phenomenological psychologist argued that both *crooked man* and *crooked stick* were to be taken literally, since we could discern a single quality of distortion in both, the same essence in two subject matters. This amounts to a claim (which we need not evaluate here) on material or scientific grounds for a tighter unity to the meaning of *crooked*. It becomes then a literal common property having its own essential character (in the secondary sense that properties have essences as answers to What is it?), and the different usages are its direct illustration. There could then be a science of *distortion* that would systematize the theory common to bending sticks and cultivating dishonesty. Now this is precisely the problem Aristotle faced with terms like *being, one,* and *good*. He saw Plato as having maintained the tight and specific unity of a form of the good, of being, of the one. Aristotle's own theory of the categories as the highest genera did not allow such unity. What kind of unity, then, do such notions have? It thus becomes important on metaphysical grounds to distinguish the finer shades in the types of ambiguity and the types of meaning.

These reflections foreshadow complex ideas of meaning. For the moment we are dealing with simple analogies and metaphors. For example, to call temperance a harmony is metaphorical, since properly the genus of harmony is sounds, not character.[21] Again, Aristotle suspects that Empedocles generalized love and hate from human affairs into physical principles of attraction and repulsion.[22] Aristotle never simply dismisses analogy; sometimes, particularly in the biological works, he uses it to probe structural similarities. For example, the sting of the insect is compared to the trunk of an elephant, or the scales of the fish to the feathers of the bird; indeed, analogical properties take their place alongside the generic and specific.[23] Analogy is an important source for generating important philosophical concepts. One of the significant uses of analogy is the application of an abstract concept in different fields:[24] equal numbers and equal lengths, for instance, do not share the same sense of *equal*.

(4) One quite different class of ambiguity is the use of a term for a thing and for a likeness or a representation of it. If we call a metal saw and a wooden saw both saws, we have a case of homonymy, just as when we use the same word for an eye that can see and one that cannot, or for a dead man (or a stone figure of a man) and a living man.[25] The difference here lies in the likeness's inability to perform essential functions.

(5) Thus far we have been dealing with minimal types, ambiguities to be exposed or understood so as to avoid confusion. Perhaps with analogy we have already moved up the scale; it is a useful tool for discerning similarities and differences. The complex kinds of ambiguity we are now to examine go further. They yield multiple senses of a word, each with its own established usage. Each usage is legitimate; or if there remains a single sense, uniform in the abstract, it takes on different senses in standard applications. In either case, when clarified, the distinction becomes a permanent part of the apparatus of our understanding.

The problem in all these cases is less to avoid ambiguity than to standardize the different meanings and see the relations between their objects. When Aristotle tells us that a word "is said in many ways," this linguistic formulation is not incompatible with a basically ontological orientation to homonymy and synonymy.[26]

In this and the next few cases we are dealing with a selection from the many illustrations he has given of the complex kinds of ambiguity. He does not go in for systematic classification of types of meaning, even in *Metaphysics* 5, where he is constantly pointing out what kind of unity is to be found in the variety of uses. The simplest kind of terms of many senses found both in *Metaphysics* 5 and throughout the corpus is the standardizing of independent and coordinate uses of a given term. For example, the four *causes* are four coordinate types of factors in explanation. Three senses are found for the term *world* or *universe*: one is the outermost circumference of the world, another the heavens, including the sun and some of the stars, the third is the totality.[27] There are eight senses in which one thing may be said to be *in* another.[28] Discussing the several senses of *prior*, he differentiates the initiating cause into the agent and the instrument, adapting and refining his terminology to match the complexity of the organic processes described.[29] *Ruling* has different senses according as it is the rule of a master over a slave, of a father over a child, or of a ruler over a fellow citizen.[30]

(6) As distinct from coordinate senses, there are often cases where the various senses are related in some special way. In *Metaphysics* 5 there is often the *priority of one use.* Thus quality is said to be primarily the differentia of the essence;[31] and the primary sense of *potentiality* is a principle of producing change.[32] In some cases, essential senses are differentiated from accidental ones. One sense of *necessary* is said to be the one with respect to which the others are in some way used.[33] One sense of *nature* is not only primary or first but the strict or proper sense.[34] There does not appear to be one feature that makes a sense primary.[35]

Certainly the phenomenon is common enough in many of our dictionary definitions: for example, the English verb *order* (like Greek *tassō*) conveys the ideas of arranging, systematizing, commanding. *To arrange* might be thought the primary sense; *to systematize* could be seen as a generalization from it, and *to command* as a particular concretization. This suggests that where there is a primary sense, the several other senses may move out from it, so to speak, in different directions and by different processes. The modes of shifting may themselves be of interest.

(7) If we accept that the primary meaning may have other items added to it, we can envision a number of different possibilities, and each may be reckoned a distinct type. First, the addition may be supplied by the subject matter to which the concept is applied. Thus *beginning* or *principle* (*archē*) has the root idea "starting point," and where there are different standardized processes, what is considered the *archē* will hold this position with reference to that process. Hence for demonstration the starting point is known universal premises; for learning, particulars; for deliberation, ends; for political life, rulers.

(8) Second, the additions may themselves come in a systematically ordered way. Thus the term *psyche* is used, as we have seen, in a different sense to cover plant, animal, and human life. It signifies a developing series in which each successor includes the predecessor (or its central properties), not a genus with three coordinate species. Interestingly, though Aristotle criticizes a common meaning someone had assigned to *life* as not fitting all types, he admits that one might try to work out a general definition in pursuit of synonymy rather than homonymy.[36] An interesting case resembling a developing series is the scale of unity he develops in *Metaphysics* 5: analogically one, generically one, specifically one, and numerically one.[37] Here "analogically one" is presumably used in a weak sense.

(9) Thirdly, the primary sense may refer to a fully developed form, and the other senses refer to approximations to it, or partial fulfillments, or less successful fulfillments, or deteriorations from it after fulfillment. Thus we shall see that when Aristotle deals with rationality in the ethics and politics, it has a different sense for slaves, children, women, and men: the slave can obey but lacks the deliberative part of reason; the female has it but in a nondecisive way, the child only in an undeveloped form.[38] In the development of virtue, the completely virtuous man is to be distinguished from the man who resists strong temptation and is self-controlled; if they were both called good men it would be in different senses, the one as internally integrated, the other as having fallen short in the process of internal integration. At the other end of the scale, the deterioration of a good society would produce types that might still be best for it under the conditions of its existence. Goodness here would be as many-sensed as health for a young person and an aged person.

(10) We have a complex form of meaning in connection with which Aristotle frequently uses the term *relational* or *referential* (*pros hen*, literally "with relation to one"). Owen has applied to it the label *focal meaning*.[39] An account of this type is found in the *Eudemian Ethics*, where three kinds of friendship are distinguished, and yet they are not so termed with respect to one thing (*kath' hen*), or as species of one genus, nor yet is the term used altogether homonymously.[40] This seems to place the type of multiple senses or of ambiguity somewhere in the intermediate range. All the senses are used with reference to one (*pros mian*) that is primary, just as the term *medical* is used for a psyche and a body and an instrument and a task, but each if analyzed is seen to refer to the one primary sense. Thus a medical instrument is what a medical man would use, and so for the rest.

Focal meaning is simply another case of the variety of complex senses, but it seems to have a unity because the term *pros hen* so often appears with it! Yet after all, the term *pros ti*, "with respect to something," is Aristotle's general term for the category of relation; we should not therefore expect too much uniformity in focal meaning, since there may be many kinds of relations involved.[41] In the *Nicomachean Ethics*, after he has attacked the notion of a single (Platonic) Idea of the Good, Aristotle argues that the many goods (honor, wisdom, pleasure, and so forth) are quite distinct. In what sense, then, are different things called good, since they do not seem to have the same name by chance?[42] Perhaps, he says, they are so called because they are derived from one good (*aph' henos*) or because they contribute to one good (*pros hen*); or perhaps by analogy— as sight is good in the body, so intelligence is good in the psyche, and so on in different contexts. In the case of *being*, it is quite clear that if *being* is taken to have focal meaning, the *one* referred to will be substance, and the relation of the others to it would stem from the spread of the categories. Focal meaning may well seem to involve a relation that can be as weak as a set of the metaphors variously derived from different features of the same model instance, or as strong as diverse means contributing to one end. It can even approach the fairly weak type of paronymy in which the things are named derivatively from the original term by terminal or inflective changes, as Aristotle shows in his analysis of *healthily*, which he says has three meanings because *healthy* can refer to producing health or preserving health or denoting health.[43]

All these forms of ambiguity or multiplicity of sense that we have been considering can only be identified in specific instances by tracing the details of usage. Once this is done, we can decide whether the case in hand reveals an ambiguity likely to generate a fallacy in argument or instead serves to establish a systematically varying set of usages.

These types of meaning that we have distinguished must suffice here. Doubtless others could be discovered. The ones given are numerous and varied enough to show that Aristotle was interested in detailed distinctions and detailed functioning; he wanted the results to serve as tools for solving philosophical problems. He does not systematize them, although he has labels for bringing them to mind. Thus he can refer in some cases to unity of "common reference" and in others to unity of "serial succession,"[44] and he frequently appeals to analogy or cites a common property. Of course from a scientific point of view what he wants is the meanings that give us genus and species, that furnish insight into substance. That is the goal, the end that is wisdom.

The significant philosophical question is, of course, what each type of meaning can accomplish. Here again it is hard to choose among the major ones. For example, analogy is used to generate the form–matter mode of analysis. It stands out particularly in the definition of matter, which Aristotle explains in the first place as generalizing the relation that bronze has to the statue, flesh and bones to the man, notes to the music, and so on. The unity of meaning that rests in the ordered series is used for explaining both the number system and the unity of the psyche; in the latter case, there are extremely important consequences that would not have followed if the unity of different forms of life had been seen as simply adding different properties at each step. Referential or focal meaning is used to justify a single science of being as being, even though being is not a genus. Even the kinship of meaning that approximations and deteriorations have to the ideal type furnishes Aristotle with a distinctive methodology in his ethics and politics. In general, then, we may conclude that Aristotle's interest in his types of meaning is twofold: beyond the logical interest in greater clarity, there is a functional interest in the advance of the disciplines in which these instruments are to be employed. Since we show most of the instruments in use in various parts of this book, we may here digress on the question of focal meaning, because it has been the subject of recent inquiry and is involved with the discussion we began of the science of being-as-being.

Aristotle never gives up his view that being is not a genus, and that the analogous or focal character of being lies in the relationships of the categories. Yet he ends up with a science of being-as-being. In his account of the way Aristotle came to attend to focal meaning, Owen has stressed the contrast between the *Eudemian Ethics*, which says that there is no one science of being or of the good,[45] and *Metaphysics* 4, which develops a general science of being-as-being. This latter context strikingly introduces the general science with the combined examples of health and the medical and goes on to explain why that science is possible.[46] First Aristotle states the focal character of the various senses of *being*. *Healthy*, he explains, relates to one thing (health, *hugieia*) and one definite nature (*mian tina phusin*), and not homonymously. (There is almost the same phrasing we noted above: *healthy* relates to health as preserving it or producing it or indicating it or as receptive of it;[47] the example *medical* (*iatrikē*) is a weaker echo of the passage we cited earlier from the *Eudemian Ethics*, and it has parallels elsewhere.) So too in *being* there is always the reference to one principle (*archē*). Some things are said to *be* because they are substances, others because they are modifications (*pathē*) of substance, others because they are a road (*hodos*) to substance, or destructions of or generations of substance, and so on. Aristotle is skimming through the categories and the kinds of change attuned to the categories. Then comes the critical statement: "Therefore, just as there is one science of all matters of health, so in the case of other things. For it is a job for one science to study not only cases where things are called according to one common notion [*kath' hen*], but also cases where things are called in relation to one nature [*pros mian phusin*]; for the latter too in a certain way are called according to a common notion [*kath' hen*]. Clearly, then, it is a job for one science to study things that are insofar as they are."[48] This points to the study of what is primary, what is substance.

Owen thus constructs a scenario in which Aristotle, having on his hands the tool of focal meaning, only came to realize at a later date that this made possible a general science of being-as-being.[49] The passage of *Metaphysics* 4 just examined could, however, be seen as a venture in a quite different direction. The question whether there is a general science of being depends upon what a science is taken to be, as well as whether there is a mode of meaning for *being* that gives it a sufficient unity. There were serious questions puzzling Aristotle as to what constituted a science.

We examine the evidence for his answer in appendix B and suggest an alternative scenario, in which over time Aristotle's scientific work matured, took different forms, and outgrew the narrower view that a science must be confined to a single genus. He realized that there were different kinds of sciences with different types of unity. Meanwhile his understanding of the variety of forms of meaning had comparably matured, not only through the study of logical argument but through the utilization of the different forms in different kinds of disciplines. There remained only to select the form of meaning appropriate to the broader study of logical and methodological principles whose character as a possible science had long troubled him. Focal meaning provided the answer, and so he summoned it with the already standardized examples of health and the medical.

In any case, when Aristotle does go into being-as-being, if we look not at his excitement over the possibility of one general science but at the content of that science once it is admitted, we find little changed in his ideas. He wants to set wisdom over and above the special sciences; from the beginning of *Metaphysics* 1 he had seen it as the study of substance. His science embraces the laws of logic and the presuppositions of communication and the structures to be found in this world with all the pluralistic variety that he had always found in things that are and in meanings of *one*. Once he tracks down substance and identifies form and matter with actuality and potentiality, he is on a new road along which he hastens to steer his special sciences. When the science of being has been built up he is less interested in what kind of language is used concerning homonymy and synonymy and (presumably) intermediate forms. Having outlined the alternatives, including focal meaning and the medical example, he says, "However, it makes no difference which way one chooses to say these things; but this point is clear, that primarily and simply, definition and essence are of substance."[50]

Definitional Processes

Our contemporary accounts of meaning and definition are more comprehensive than traditional ones. They include not only formal definitions that come at the end of inquiry and embody its results, but also different ways of specifying meaning in the process of inquiry: stipulations and their revision, use of operations in order to apply ideas, use of paradigms and approximations to them, modes of testing tentative definitions for their utility, informal explication of terms in ordinary language and ordinary contexts, and so on. This broader scope has come from both the interest in ordinary language and the technical concern of the philosophy of science with processes of inquiry. Let us see how far Aristotle's analyses and actual procedures present such definitional processes.

Nominal or purely conventional definition is recognized as "an account of what the name signifies or an equivalent denomination; for instance, it will explain what *triangle* signifies."[51] It is difficult to grasp in this way the definition of what we do not know to exist. Aristotle regards nominal definition as fairly trivial. One cannot get far by just giving a name to some collection of words; one could even regard the *Iliad* as a definition in that sense.[52] His point is that while such a nominal definition *signifies*, it does not tell us either that the thing signified exists or what its essence is. We could just as well have a definition of something nonexistent, like a goat-stag.[53] His view that a term having no existence can have no essential nature (and hence no essential definition) makes sense in his system; for the nature of something is expressed in the way that thing behaves universally or for the most part, and what does not exist cannot determine such behavior. Nevertheless he is quite ready to make up a term to equate with existing terms in order to show some inadequately understood relation. For example, he remarks in the *Politics* that there is no name to cover serving on a jury and being a member of the assembly.[54] Since citizenship is identified by the right to participate in such offices, he decides to call it simply *office* (*archē*); he is then able from this nominal equation to define a citizen as someone who participates in office.

A great deal of commonsense operationalism can be seen in his practical indices for applying concepts. Sometimes a whole network of relations is involved. For example, the tests for *light* and *heavy* are respectively what moves upward and toward the extremity and what moves downward and toward the center.[55] This presupposes one world, and one heaven over our heads, and also the notion that the center is where earth moves to when it falls without hindrance. The account of *above, below, front, back, right,* and *left* is associated with simple tests: the front of an animal is where sense perception takes place; the head is where food is ingested (in man it coincides with the real *up*; in plants the root is the head); the right is where movement originates (a rather obscure test, but he defends it).[56] Aristotle is, of course, looking for operations that cover animals generally, not only humans. Usually operations are supplied with their associated theoretical assumptions. When time is measured by change, the absolute standard becomes the motion of the heavens, on the assumption that it is regular; if there were more heavens than one, there would be many times at the same time.[57] Again, in inquiring whether the term *hot* has several senses, he looks for the effects that a hotter object has on the less hot.[58] He explores transmission effects, whether melting takes place, the rate of warming and cooling, and the violence of sensation that results. These will not always yield the same results, and since there is no correlation of test results it is necessary to specify context and respect.

A kind of operationalism also permeates book 3 of the *Topics*, where the marks are given by which something can be judged better than something else (a rather miscellaneous set of criteria), and emerges in some parts of the *Rhetoric* where comparable ways of judging good or better are listed.[59] In the latter, however, an ingenious procedure is at work. A variety of competing theories of the good are turned into complementary criteria for what is good in different specific contexts where each is best applicable: what people praise, seek, or wish for; what is desirable for its own sake; what people would choose if they had understanding and practical wisdom; happiness and what yields happiness; what reason prescribes; and so on.

Finally, there is the standard kind of complex operation that consists in specifying a kind of person whose judgment will be the test—like the modern qualified observer in science or the trained informant in social-science survey or anthropological fieldwork, or the native speaker who responds to give the linguist original data. In the ethics, Aristotle uses the prudent man, the man of practical wisdom (*phronimos*), whose desires and choices help determine the real good or the exact right, just as the healthy man is a gauge of the difference between a sick man's fever and the actual state of heat in the room.

Aristotle's treatment of the process of establishing a definition, the process whose end product is the real definition that states the essence, is carried out in books 6 and 7 of the *Topics*. Here are found the rules of definition that used to be duly reported in our logic texts: the general point that the kind of definition sought is by genus and differentia; that the definition must not be obscure or figurative; that it must not be too broad or too narrow; and so on. The wealth of illustration and subtle points is vast and no attempt will be made here even to outline it. The effort that it takes to frame good definitions—it is not simply a matter of immediately grasping intuitive first principles, as in *Posterior Analytics* 2 (though even there the treatment of induction showed there was more behind the scenes)—can be seen in the comparison Aristotle draws at the end of his treatment of definition in the *Topics*: "Furthermore, as in assemblies they are accustomed to introduce a law and, if the newly introduced one is better, to abrogate the old one, so too one ought to act in the case of definitions, and oneself bring forward another definition; for if it appears better and makes clearer what is being defined, obviously the definition already laid down will have been abrogated, since there is not more than one definition of the same thing."[60] It is no wonder that

Aristotle believes it is more difficult to construct than to destroy a definition.[61] This account should of course be correlated with his actual procedure in exploring alternative theories and reaching a definition in his own scientific works (see, for example, the definition of *psyche* in *On the Psyche*).

Concerning the metaphysical issues in definition we need add little here. It is already clear that there is no definition of the individual, although the account (*logos*) that is contained in a definition is universal and presents the form, and so may be given of the individual.[62] Central, of course, is the question discussed at length in the treatment of substance, namely, wherein lies the unity of the parts in a definition. Aristotle's answer for definitions in the primary sense is his solution of the problem of substance.

Classification

There are two approaches to classification, in contemporary and in ancient philosophy alike. One stresses the formal development of a matrix for classifying, with a full (both exclusive and exhaustive) set of compartments. (The logic of classes, with 2^n compartments, where n is the number of terms and each term either applies or does not apply, is the simplest case.) The other, by contrast, is inductive in style: starting in the midst of a mass of material and many features, one builds up tentative types and revises them by the results that come from using them. There is, of course, no inherent incompatibility between the two; modern theory is especially adept at clarifying their relation. For example, after a tentative classification is developed inductively, a matrix for the marks used can be worked out if they are not unmanageably large (and this is relative to the state of computerization), so that there can be research on the compartments neglected in the purely inductive approach.

Both of these procedures are to be found in Aristotle's work, though the formal one is in a rudimentary state. He is also conscious of the basic presupposition of any attempt at classification: that the term either apply or not apply to a given instance. This is stated in his law of the excluded middle, though it does not prevent him from recognizing areas of vagueness. Again, the kind of classification he wants, one that yields genera and species as real structures, requires that we be able to distinguish sameness, not merely likeness or similarity. Some followers of Antisthenes had claimed we could only say that silver was like tin but could not say what silver is; Aristotle comments that this would make definition ultimately impossible.[63] The topics of definition and classification are of course intimately related, since a successful classification depends on discovering the correct defining marks for the class term. Some relevant questions, like the method of dichotomous division, are discussed with respect to both definition and classification.

The formal approach considered is the method of division, especially dichotomous.[64] It is found earlier (for example, in Plato's *Sophist*), and became known in later logic texts as "Porphyry's tree." It is chiefly oriented toward tracking down one species through specifying successive bases of division and discarding the direction that does not lead to its desired result. Thus, in a stock illustration of the tree, substance divides into corporeal and incorporeal; body is corporeal substance. Body divides into animate and inanimate; a living thing is an animate body. And so on through sensible and rational till we end with man. Aristotle's logical objections are that at each stage the choice between alternatives is based not on proof but on assumption, that it is also assumed the division is complete, and that what is true of man is assumed to indicate the essential nature. He does not wholly condemn such division, and for the purposes of definition finds it a useful aid, just as induction is. It can help us check whether we have omitted something. His objections to dichotomous division for biological classification are that it may lead us astray and put unnecessary constraints on us. For example, it wants a single differentia, whereas major group divisions, such as bird from fish, require many differentiating marks. Further, it tends to break up natural groups, like birds, with dichotomies like land animal–water animal.

Basically, what Aristotle wants at the outset is a rich domain of descriptive data that includes all sorts of similarities and differences. As Peck has stressed, it is this that the *Historia Animalium* provides, rather than an attempt at taxonomy.[65] Similarly we know of the 158 constitutions that Aristotle and his assistants described (the *Constitution of Athens* is our surviving example), which provided the basis for the classifications and generalizations of the *Politics*.

This insistence on a base of data does not mean that Aristotle opposed the formal approach when it was possible. He uses it most obviously in his theory of the natural elements, making a matrix out of the selected qualities (hot, cold, moist, dry), eliminating inconsistent classes (hot–cold, moist–dry), and combining the rest into the four possibilities that then are shown to satisfy the phenomena. In a similar way, Aristotle works out an initial classification of the forms of government by asking on the one hand whether or not they aim at the common welfare, and on the other whether the rule is in the hands of one, a few, or many.[66] This matrix yields six types: monarchy, aristocracy, and polity (aiming at the common welfare) and their corrupt forms, tyranny, oligarchy, and extreme democracy. It is only a surface classification, to get things started; a deeper one that reckons with the causes of things would have to refine the criteria, if not actually change them. In a comparison of the biological and the political classification he explains how the biologist would first have to know the properties necessarily belonging to every animal (such as indispensable organs).[67] Then, given a finite number of such marks and the variations they admit of, he could work out the combinations of possible species. This holds for forms of governments too, as states are composed of different classes (food-producers, mechanics, traders), which are the parts. Aristotle proceeded accordingly with political phenomena, but the biology proved less amenable to such a prior matrix.

Even within the political analysis Aristotle refines his terms for understanding the classification. Essentially, for oligarchy and democracy the criterion of number (the *few* and the *many*) is replaced by that of wealth and poverty, so that oligarchy is taken to be the rule of the rich and democracy that of the poor. Classification theory thus may start with initial distinguishing marks, but has to lead on to exploration of the underlying causes of the phenomena, and so to a possible readjustment of the marks in terms of the appropriate elements that play a causal role.

The same kind of internal process seems to be going on in the biological writings. There is a background low-level classification in terms of familiar named kinds—man, elephant, snake, beaver, hawk, owl, and so on. There are studies of differences in broad terms that differentiate blooded and bloodless, viviparous and oviparous, land and water and air animals. The main groups of animals are listed as birds, fishes, cetacea (sea mammals), shellfish, softshelled animals (crayfish, for instance), soft types like cuttlefish, and insects; beyond these main groups the remaining animals seem to fall into no large groups (man is a kind belonging to no more general type).[68] All this already presupposes some analysis of the parts of the body, which is carried out more fully in *Parts of Animals*, and involves a classification into uniform parts (flesh, bone, hair, sinew, etc.; blood, marrow, fat, semen, etc.) and nonuniform parts or organs (head, mouth, liver, heart, etc.). A causal theory had been begun at the end of book 4 of the *Meteorology*, at least for the uniform parts, in terms of the effect of heat and cold in solidification, softness, hardness, fragmentability, and the like.[69] For the organs, in *Parts of Animals*, it is associated with a study of functions, much in the spirit in which the various functions are examined in the psychological works. This involves and makes possible a comparative study of what kind of parts in what animals perform what functions and how. Out of this are established the differences between species characteristics, genus characteristics, and analogous characteristics. Occasionally, Aristotle also invokes the idea that nature, working like an artist, draws the general (generic) sketch first and then fills in the detail.[70] The study of reproduction puts the detail in a developmental setting for each animal type.

The final scheme of classification for the animal world as a whole, refining the earlier classifications and unifying the comparative results, is based on the degree of perfection of the animal as reflected in the degree of perfection reached by the offspring at birth or upon leaving the parent.[71] This yields (I follow Peck's analysis) the classification as follows: *vivipara*, those that bear progeny similar to the parents (for example, man, land and sea mammals); *ovovivipara*, which bear a complete young animal that is preceded by a perfect egg within the body (certain kinds of fish and vipers); *ovipara*, which produce a perfect egg, that is, one that does not increase in size after deposition (birds, horny-scaled animals, serpents other than the viper); another type of *ovipara* whose eggs complete their growth after being laid (scaly fish, crustacea); and *larvipara*, those that produce a larva, which according to Aristotle must develop into a kind of egg before the young can emerge (locusts, spiders, ants, wasps). Below these are the insects, like fleas, lice, and flies, that are spontaneously generated from putrefying matter. Testacea (snails, for instance) seem to be on a still lower level. The difference between all these types is explained in terms of the proportions and features of the hot, the cold, the solid, and the fluid. In cases where classes overlap, Aristotle resorts to other kinds of differentia with which he has dealt.[72]

Aristotle's sophisticated sense of what goes into classification is sometimes expressed in criticizing others' views even where he does not himself carry through a classification. For example, as we noted in *On the Psyche*, he criticizes the oversimplified division of parts of the psyche into calculative, emotional, and desiderative, or the even more simplified partition into rational and irrational.[73] In one sense divisions can be made *ad infinitum*. Certainly the rich material of psychic functions simply cannot be distributed into these few compartments. Where, for instance, would the sensitive part go, or the imaginative? The appetitive would have to be divided up among all three parts.

A quite different area, well worth studying from the point of view of Aristotle's classifications, is *Meteorology* 4. Here he starts from known effects of heating and cooling and aims to classify the various species of processes they effect. Thus heat causes concoction, whose species are ripening, boiling, and roasting; cold produces inconcoction, whose species are unripeness, scalding, and scorching (as we might say "frostbite" or "refrigerator burn"). He recognizes that these terms are only approximate and do not cover all the phenomena.[74] Hence he goes on to examine them in detail, from hardening, softening, drying, solidifying, and liquefying, on down to squeezability and viscosity. In general, what he is doing here is sorting qualitative processes, guided by a theory of causation. The relations are, of course, much less tight than the classification of change into the four types determined by four selected categories (substance, quantity, quality, place); in that case the chief burden, not wholly successful, lay in showing that the other categories could not properly yield a form of change.

In general, Aristotle's practice in classification is consonant with his theoretical consideration of its nature. If anything, his practice shows more clearly the interplay of formal and material approaches, and the relativity of results to the state of the field and the extent of background knowledge.

15

TRUTH, REALITY, AND

ESSENTIALISM

The analysis of knowing naturally ends with the analysis of truth. Since the analysis of truth for Aristotle involves relating our knowing to the real, or what is, some further remarks on his conception of the real are required—not a retelling of the whole story of *being*, but an examination of how it operates in the processes of knowing. Finally, we face the heated question of the sense in which Aristotle is an "essentialist" —long a term of praise, long thereafter a term of reproach, and now apparently in a pendular swing towards being praiseworthy again. How far is essentialism a technical doctrine, how far a faith about the nature of the world, how far a postulate? These are the problems of this chapter.

Truth

The discussion of truth is found in logical, epistemological, metaphysical, and psychological contexts. On the whole, a fairly coherent account emerges. The topic arises in examining the inner structure of the sentence. Words are construed as symbols for affections and impressions of the psyche.[1] Though languages differ, the affections symbolized are the same for all, and the things (*pragmata*) of which these are likenesses are also the same. The question of truth or falsity arises not when we entertain a single thought but when thoughts are combined or separated. Aristotle thus holds what is roughly a correspondence theory in which the words symbolize the thoughts and complex thoughts correspond to things. The word *things* in this sense, *pragmata*, means literally *that which has been done*, and therefore covers our *facts* and *states of affairs* or actual *goings-on*. The combination or separation (on the logical level, affirmation or negation) is usually carried out by the addition of a verbal expression (this should be construed broadly, since *is healthy* is given as an instance), which conveys a present tense. Past and future expressions (*was healthy* or *recovered* or *will be healthy* or *will recover*) are set off not as verbs but inflections. The significance of a time reference in predication will be considered shortly.

True characterizes intuition (*nous*), knowledge (*epistēmē*), and belief or opinion (*doxa*) as well as the discourse that results from these, that is, what is reached by inference.[2] In short, it is our *thinkings* in their various forms that are true. Opinion, of course, unlike knowledge, can be false. The object of true and false opinions is the same—that is, the facts. This dispenses with problems that led, in the later history of logic, to many a tortured attempt to stock the world with false facts, true facts, and impossible facts to boot. A false opinion is more like one that has missed the mark than it is a representation of a possible but nonexistent world; how it has missed would seem to be a psychological question. The object of knowledge can also be the object of true opinion, the latter grasping only that an attribute holds but not its derivation from the essence. It follows that one cannot be knowing and believing the same thing at the same time. Truth and falsity that stem from inference raise simply such logical questions as what combinations of true and false premises will yield.[3]

Immediate graspings by intuition and by sense have both proved to be controversial issues in epistemology. Aristotle considers them in their psychological relations. We have already discussed his views on the intuition of essential truth, their congruence with his theory that the mind becomes one with the object of thought in the act of thought, and the extent to which the intuitive status of basic truths of essential nature was an inner requirement of his view of demonstration. Geometrical constructions by diagrams seem to provide moments of immediate insight. The act of dividing, for example, is an actualization in thought, and it reveals relations quite directly—for example, that the angle sum of a triangle is equal to two right angles, or that the angle in a semicircle is always a right angle.[4]

The immediacy of grasping truth in sensation is complex. Perception at best is limited to the here and now, even if it is of a this-such and not merely of a this-something.[5] Generalization for all cases cannot be carried through on the basis of sensation alone unless by an inductive stirring of insight; but sometimes a further or deeper seeing is precisely the occasion for inductive intuition.[6] Nor can we generalize over time for the singular object, since once it is out of the reach of perception changes may take place. What then can we say that is definite of the here and now? There can be existences such as dreams that create the impression of what they are not; emotions and imagination may affect our interpretation of what is before us; we have perceptual illusions, such as the double vision we can cause by pressing the finger below the eye.[7] The sober conclusion is modestly stated, that sensation of the objects proper to that sense is true *or has the least amount of falsehood*.[8] Next in reliability comes the interpreted sensation—not, for instance, that an object is white but whether the white object is one thing or another. Third comes perception of common attributes, such as motion and size.[9]

And of course possible error is greater when we go beyond the here and now, when we say not that Cleon is white but that he was or will be white.[10]

The implications of Aristotle's account of the *now* in *Physics* 4 seem to carry the analysis deeper for the here-and-now sensation (red-here-now). If the out-of-range future and past introduce possibilities of error, how long is the actual now, which divides the future from the past? Aristotle wonders in what way nows are the same. He considers whether the now is a kind of substratum, like the body substratum that remains the same despite changes in, say, Corsicus;[11] it sounds almost as if the now is a constant through which events are streaming. The now is different in that different points can divide its continuous line. But the span of the now seems to depend on our distinguishing two different points as a before and after, as well as an intermediate distinct from them.[12] When an interval escapes our notice, the interval does not seem to be time; this is not simply a "subjective" matter, since it depends on whether there has been motion.[13] It would seem then that there can be longer and shorter nows. If so, red-here-now is already an interpretation of the persistence of the quality over the span. Aristotle might have thought the sensory phenomenon sufficient evidence of the stability.

He does not correlate his discussion of time and the now with his epistemological view. Yet the discussion of stability over time plays a prominent role in his probing for the metaphysical presuppositions of his concept of truth. In *Metaphysics* 4, where this takes place, he is concerned with the Heraclitean view of existence as pure flux, and the Protagorean view of sensation as being simply what it appears to be, and the impact of both on judgments of truth.

Against Protagoras, Aristotle firmly insists that thought goes beyond sensation.[14] We have norms of health and ability and wakefulness in terms of which we judge what is true. Sensation never reports opposites about the same thing at the same time, even though it may report that things are different at different times. For insight into the future we rely on experts rather than laymen. Against Heraclitus, he declares that the logical and epistemological consequences of complete flux are horrendous: if contradictory predicates are asserted of some thing, then anything follows, even opposites,[15] and all statements would be true and all false. From this discussion there emerges the view we have already met, but can now see as a presupposition of truth: things that are (*ta onta*) shape up in a definite way, they have a definite nature; judgments are truer according as they are closer to that nature.[16]

The character of truth is thus secondary to and dependent on the character of the real. This is most clearly seen in the brief discussion of truth as one of the senses of being itself. *Metaphysics* 6 distinguishes being as (in effect) essential–accidental, being as truth–falsity, and being as potential–actual. Being as truth and falsity is secondary, since the false and true are not in things (*pragmata*) but in thought.[17] After going on to discuss the primary senses of being, Aristotle comes back to the secondary and recapitulates the correspondence theory of thought and being.[18] But this simple correspondence does not mean truth is easily grasped. At the beginning of *Metaphysics* 2 the study of truth is said to be difficult in that no one person can attain it adequately; but it is also easy in the sense that every thinker contributes a bit.[19] Aristotle throughout the corpus clearly regards progress toward knowledge as possible.

The Reality That Truth Faces

The relation of truth to reality does not of course settle the question of what aspects of reality it is most closely tied to. The usual interpretation is that it concerns the universal atemporal necessary aspects that Plato had proposed in his theory of forms and that Aristotle, while denying the transcendent forms, found to be a real structure in the things of this world. The premises of demonstrative knowledge are primary and necessary, and while we have yet to examine the notion of necessity, it is easy to fall into the traditional contrast between the present-sensory and the eternal-necessary-intellectual. Hintikka has strongly challenged this type of view by amassing evidence from the corpus for an interpretation of eternity as everlastingness and of necessity as simply the assertion that something has always and will always act in a given way.[20] (See appendix C for a technical discussion of necessity as well as criticism of some of Hintikka's further theses.)

Hintikka points out that Aristotle uses temporally indefinite sentences such as "Socrates is walking" where the present-tense reference of the verb makes the sentence true at some times, false at others.[21] He does not use tenseless presents in which a specific value of t is incorporated into the content of the sentence. He seems on occasion to regard any formula as an expression for application and even suggests that every account (proposition, formula, definition) is false when misapplied: the account of a circle is false, for example, when applied to a triangle.[22] If this is the way Aristotle uses *true* and *false*, then we miss his meaning by thinking of them as characterizing timeless propositions rather than sentence-forms that contain a time-variable and are given a reference by the present utterance. In line with this, Hintikka takes necessary statements to be asserting temporal invariance: what is now, always was, and always will be.[23]

Hintikka's view—which he believes also holds for Plato's equation of the sensory with the changing—radically restructures the traditional understanding of both Plato's and Aristotle's attitude to the sensory. They identified the sensory with the changing material process; hence Plato spoke of it as what is and is not. The sensory was not exactly an inferior brand of the real; it simply furnished only a limited present and could not guarantee what would happen in the next temporal interval. The fallibility of sensation is a common theme in both ancient and modern philosophy, but it has a different focus in each. Modern philosophy with its dualism of mind and body often raises the question whether sense experience corresponds to the qualities of the real world, so that the fallibility of present sensory experience would depend on whether or not it is truly representative. Aristotle does not question that. He relies on the psychology of sensation and the physics of sense production to certify their product. He is concerned rather about the extremely limited character of possible extrapolation from the given moment. No matter how large the slice of the world we view at any moment, there would be no guarantee that the reality seen would not undergo change in an adjoining time interval. Ultimately, then, our knowledge depends on the degree of stability in the world. We may recall Aristotle's diagnosis of Plato's belief in forms: Plato was convinced of Heraclitus' view that the material world grasped in sensation was always changing; he concluded that this could yield no knowledge, and so turned to the eternal. Aristotle has a less pessimistic view of stability in the world. But in his formulation at least, he has as high an ideal for what knowledge consists in. Modern philosophers of science often reduce their expectations for knowledge to progressive accumulation based on a relatively stable (not eternally fixed) reality.

Certainly there is ample evidence that Aristotle leans heavily on a belief in the stability of things which makes knowledge and truth possible. For example, at the very end of *Metaphysics* 4, having battled against Heraclitus and Protagoras on behalf of the laws of noncontradiction and excluded middle, he concludes that if all things are at rest, the same things will always be true, and the same always false; but clearly there is change—the speaker himself once did not exist and will go from the scene.[24] If all things are in motion, nothing will be true, and so everything will be false. But whether stability is all there is to the face of reality that makes knowledge and truth possible depends in turn on whether stability is all there is to necessity, or whether unpacking necessity reveals some additional ontological entities.

Aristotle's notion of the necessary (*anankaion*) is complex. It is the crossroads of many ideas from different contexts. One is the practical context of what one could not do without—the requisites for survival. Another is the necessities for a good life. Then there is the idea of compulsion. Add to that mathematical demonstration. There is also the basic idea of the unavoidable, in the sense of what cannot be otherwise.[25] Again, there is the major search for the essential as against the accidental, as well as the logical distinction of the necessary as compared with the possible and the merely categorical. The idea among all these that emerges as fundamental or most general is *that which cannot be otherwise* (literally, what does not allow of being situated differently, *to mē endechomenon allōs echein*). This would make *allowable* or *possible* an even more basic notion. Its more immediate effect is to broaden the scope of the ontologically necessary. It need no longer be limited to the universal, as it seemed to be when the necessary was identified with primary truths. What cannot be otherwise covers the whole of the past; Aristotle points out that even God, as the poet says, cannot change the past.[26] Moreover, the present event is also seen as necessary. Thus in the argument about the sea battle tomorrow Aristotle says, "What is, necessarily is, when it is; and what is not, necessarily is not, when it is not."[27] If something is actually happening, even though potentially it could have been different it is too late now for it to be otherwise.

Potentiality is a feature in Aristotle's conception of the world insofar as the world has matter. While there are certain absolutely dependable processes in the movement of the heavens, below that the greater part of what happens will not be necessary till it actually happens. Possibilities may be narrowed down and probabilities increased, but interfering factors are still not out of question. His outlook is thus temporal, and the indeterminate element due to alternate potentialities is taken seriously. This perspective underlies his refusal to grant that of the two sentences "There will be a sea battle tomorrow" and "There will not be a sea battle tomorrow" one or the other is now true and the other is now false.[28] (His argument is examined in appendix C.)

It follows that the reality that truth faces is many-sided. It lies not only in the universal features that stability supports, and the particular and incidental with which sensory observation is correlated, but also embraces the large measure of the potential that we learn of in coherent experience, the alternate capabilities and readiness of things. Whether unpacking the notion of necessity yields still more in the theory of essence is the problem of essentialism.

Essentialism

What has been called Aristotle's essentialism—it is not his own label—may be roughly described as the belief that there are correct classifications of existents that do not simply or solely reflect human purposes or convenience but reveal real properties of those existents, necessarily belonging to them; we are thereby able to state necessary truths about them. Such an essentialism clearly has, in Aristotle's work, a metaphysical aspect, a theological aspect, and a logical aspect. Need the first mean more than the modern view that there are definite scientific laws to be discovered, which are increasingly approximated as science advances? Certainly the second does not mean that God made the world and imposed on it a fixed path for each particular kind of thing in line with a general plan, for Aristotle thinks that the world has always existed and that the accidental occurs where the careers of different kinds of things cross. Was the third some highly theoretical claim, analogous to what some modern logicians argue, that the things we say of the world, especially in science, cannot adequately be analyzed in a logic that dispenses with classes or with modal terms? Let us look at each aspect briefly.

Aristotle was clearly a metaphysical realist in a double sense. He believed that there were scientific concepts whose sharp distinctions had clear application, and that there were definite natures (laws) to be discovered for the kinds of things in this world. Generally speaking, metaphysical realism assumes (in modern times) that when a scientific order is disrupted, an order will be found on a more profound level. Aristotle's confidence that there are natures in things is of the same sort. His working attitudes are consonant with his confidence. Thus although he is ready enough to revise classifications, when he has one going he is not stopped by the threat of vagueness or the appearance of twilight zones. For example, when in the *Parts of Animals* he comes to discuss sponges, he says that they are in all respects like plants and live only while they grow on something.[29] He is prompted to comment on nature's continuous gradation from lifeless things to animals, but does not abandon the distinction between living and lifeless. Rather he tries to specify precisely where and under what conditions there is life, and where not. In the case of "monstrosities," he recognizes that they cross the natural orders but explains this by nature's mistakes in the sublunar and less perfect part of the world.

The theological aspect of Aristotle's essentialism is evident in that to some degree the necessity found in nature is given a religious meaning. But this very meaning also has a scientific function. It comes in at the limits of science to tie up the unifying scheme. The Unmoved Mover is the ultimate source of movement. In the biological works, reproduction has as its final overall cause the desire for the eternal, which can only take the form of perpetuating the species.[30] Aristotle even invokes the Unmoved Mover at the beginning of *On the Movement of Animals*, as the paradigm for animal motion. In the physical writings the approaches to necessity and the divine ensure that the world is eternal and movement endless. The heavens come as close to the eternal as possible in that they go continually around, and the stars are always actual in their motions.[31] Further, the structures we grasp in our thought have at least the pure actuality that constitutes our thinking. There is thus a pervasive theological dimension to the order of the Aristotelian world, though it is quite different from the transcendent all-embracing teleology of Western religions. The divine component functions for scientific purposes, to solve and tie up the theoretical needs of the different fields and to assure them of a dependable order. In this respect, it functions as an ally of the metaphysical realism, much as presuppositions of an eternal order did in later philosophy, only to be succeeded by secular presuppositions of the uniformity of nature or principles of limited variety, which make induction more dependable. Aristotle sometimes himself relies directly on the stability of existence in time.

Aristotle's system is not formally well enough advanced to face the technical question of an independent and irreducible modal logic. Certainly he tries to work out the syllogisms with premises of the form "A is necessarily B" separately from those with "A is B." But as appendix C suggests, since the proper premise of the latter sort is an essential one, the difference between the modal and the categorical is minimized. Nevertheless, this assimilates the demonstrative to the modal syllogism just as much as the modal to the categorical. In short, once again Aristotle is doing a different job, guided by concerns different from ours. If the question is whether to label him a logical essentialist, it almost answers itself, for his work is where the search for essence begins.

Part 5

THE THEORY OF PRACTICE

INTRODUCTION

We turn from the theory of knowing to the theory of practice. Since practice is doing, which contains its own end, as distinguished from production in which the end lies in a product beyond the doing or acting, we expect the theory of practice to locate the final cause of human action in the picture of the action itself. This means exhibiting the structure of the life that is desirable for human beings: the kind of character to be developed in individuals within the community, as well as the kind of institutions that are best for the organized community under ideal conditions or second best under the usual conditions of conflict. This analysis is carried out with a manifest continuity between the ethical and political writings. They are not distinguished by a gap, as in much of modern philosophy, between the autonomous inner individual and the outer social person. These are later distinctions tied to later metaphysical systems and later epistemologies. Even more striking, there is no sharp line between ethics and politics that matches our distinction between individual and society.[1]

It does not follow, however, that Aristotle's *Nicomachean Ethics* is not a work in ethics—unless "ethics" is restricted to a narrow sense. The *Nicomachean Ethics*, by almost any reasonable sense of ethics, can be regarded as the first large-scale book in ethical theory in the Western tradition.[2] It is still, perhaps, the best textbook for presenting the full range of problems, though not the full range of answers. It integrates the ethics within a whole philosophical outlook; it has a sense of the dependence of ethical conclusions on the deeper understanding of the human being. At the same time we can detect localisms that come from the particular values of Aristotle's age and personal milieu.

So steeped is our contemporary ethical theory in individualistic—usually Kantian—formulations of its problems that we shall constantly have to remind ourselves that Aristotle was not answering those questions.[3] Half our job will be to make sure that we are asking Aristotle's questions and seeking his own answers to them. For the moment it is enough to recognize that ethics in the Aristotelian tradition is not a separate province in which a freely willing moral agent struggles within himself in a fretful effort to do his duty or conform to a universally binding moral law or even calculate profit and loss. It is a sober reckoning, within communal life, of policy in the whole domain of practice: goals of life and the types of character they call for both in personal development and in institutional relations, modes of decision and guidance of conduct, problems of internal conflict, and ultimate reflections on well-being. It is not surprising, then, that the *Nicomachean Ethics* is sometimes approached as a treatise on education, nor that it moves, almost without break, into the *Politics*.

The *Politics* presents few problems to the modern reader. The chief one is the relation of normative and scientific components. There is a traditional myth that the ancients confounded these until Hobbes and Machiavelli came along and introduced a value-free political science. This itself reflects the twentieth-century demand for the separation of fact and value, which is itself grinding to a halt as new conceptions of "policy science" and complex changes in decision theory try to compensate for the inadequacies of the separation itself. Whatever the case in general, the historical picture is certainly suspect. The changes from Aristotle to Hobbes, for example, are not from values to value neutrality, but from ancient teleology to a revolt against that teleology, from one conception of rationality to another, and (most important for politics) from a goal of achieving the good life to one of achieving the minimal conditions necessary for the good life. Thus Hobbes is ready to expect nothing more from the state than peace and security, and leaves the rest to the individual; Aristotle wants communal organization for the good life. This is a difference in values, not between value and value-free theory. We should not forget also that there had intervened the religious conception of the Fall, of man's life in sin and incapability of achieving the good in this life; a hopeful attitude to achievement by secular organization was less likely. In any case, we shall see that Aristotle distinguishes descriptive and policy judgments sufficiently even to meet positivistic scientific requirements.

We may expect to find that Aristotle makes use of the key ideas we examined in our general conceptual network, for developing both his ethical and his political theory. Potentiality and actuality appear as human nature expressed in stable forms of associated life and secure institutions, matter and form as human beings governing their desires by rational directives. The relation of this rationality to the desires involves all the problems that entered into the psychology in Aristotle's attack on the Platonic concept of human nature and its outcome in government by a self-perpetuating elite. On the other hand, we will certainly find that Aristotle, like Plato, rates education highly and sees ethics as a kind of growing consciousness of the good.

What concepts does Aristotle use to carry out the actual job of morality, and how do they help the individual guide his conduct? How do they constitute a subsidiary network? Taken as a whole, is the effect to cultivate critical attitudes in morality, or traditional ones; self-oriented, or cooperative, institutional attitudes; a concern with social justice, or with private interest? Similarly, in the community, does the ethical theory have a social potential, inclining one way or another in the economic and political conflicts of the time—toward the rich or the poor, the oligarchic or the democratic? Or is Aristotle's theory geared, as Plato's was, to transcending class conflict, but in a different way?

Chapter 16 will study in detail the ethical network that lies just below the surface in the *Nicomachean Ethics*—its concepts, their associated content (psychological, social, and moral), and their mode of operation. Chapter 17 takes up three important topics set aside for special exploration: justice, internal conflict, and friendship. Chapter 18 deals with central social and political concepts of the *Politics*.

16

THE NETWORK OF ETHICAL CONCEPTS

Aristotle begins with the good as the object of all human striving. The good is identified with happiness, and the question then becomes What is happiness? To answer this Aristotle turns to the notion of the function or activity of man. This is taken to express the nature of the psyche, which is equated with the activity of the psyche in accordance with its appropriate virtue or excellence. Virtue in turn is analyzed as a state of character concerned with choice of the mean in domains of action and feeling. The mean is determined by a rational principle, and that is explicated as the principle that a man of practical wisdom would use. So we have gone from the good all the way through intermediate concepts to the man of practical wisdom. This pattern acts as a kind of shuttle for the man who wants guidance in living. He is looking for the good, and is sent along from office to office, as it were, hoping for an answer. At some points the man of practical wisdom is even identified as the one who chooses what is *really* good as distinct from what only *appears* to be good. If so, the circle is complete, and our patient inquirer will find himself back in the office from which he set out!

This kind of circularity is obviously a familiar phenomenon in an abstract set of related concepts. It could be avoided by reducing them all to a single undefined concept (or a selected two or three), heading toward a formalized system; or they could be cut loose to operate on their own in an informalist way, related to one another only as the contexts of their use intersect. But Aristotle does neither. He does precisely what he did with his general metaphysical concepts. The concepts are related abstractly or conceptually, but in this case each has a particular field to which it is connected. The field may be psychological or biological or moral or social or linguistic or a combination, as we shall see, and the gains and lessons from each tie-in are passed along the network to clarify the remaining concepts. In sum, Aristotle has a subnetwork of ethically relevant concepts tied to human existence, its tasks and its problems, and these concepts operate to deal with those tasks and problems. We shall take up each of the concepts in turn, seeing how it is fashioned and what went into its construction, what its fastening points are, and how the network operates, and what it accomplishes.

Before we begin this analysis, it is worth noting that the development of the abstract concepts gives Aristotle's ethical theory a comparative breadth that many a subsequent theory has lacked. Some, like the diverse forms of pleasure theory, have focused primarily on the end or good; some, like Stoicism, primarily on virtue; some, like the Kantian, on an interpretation of rational principle; some, like the British moral-sentiment theorists of the eighteenth century, have seemed to pin everything on the critical sensitive approbation of an ideal spectator, a more passive version of a man of practical wisdom; and so on in numerous specializations. By relating the concepts, Aristotle holds together all phases of human regulative processes. For men do guide themselves by ends, they do grow into relatively stable characters, they do formulate principles of judgment and reckon by them, and they do invoke outstanding models and draw distinctions between adequate and inadequate judgment. Even apart from the content we shall find in his conception of morality, and the specific valuations that become embedded in his theoretical notions, Aristotle has a realistic grip on the fullness of human moral processes.

It is probably this integrative character in his ethical theory that most attracts the moral philosopher today, beset as he is by the conflict of schools. Aristotle's is not the only way to achieve integration, but it is the best historical way to become conscious of the need for an integrative approach. Yet how difficult this is can be seen from the interpretation of Aristotle's ethics itself. Every once in a while someone makes the passionate discovery that Aristotle "really" falls into this, that, or the other modern ethical school. It is easy enough to see how it is to be done. Stress the role of happiness together with the critique of pleasure and mute the rest, and he becomes a utilitarian in the style of J. S. Mill, with a reasonably liberal definition of happiness and all else following from it. Stress the flow of the concepts into the man of practical wisdom as a culminating point and reduce the rest to preparing for that man's act of insight in the particular situation, and Aristotle becomes a rational intuitionist. Underscore the prominence of virtue with all else leading up to it or flowing from it, and stress the themes that point to the unity of the virtues from which a concept of the self might be built, and Aristotle is laying the groundwork for a future absolute idealism. Or stay close to the detailed depiction of the virtues, and Aristotle is the founder of a phenomenology of ethics. If we were compelled to enter this competition in search of the "real" Aristotle of the ethics, we might propose as the candidate the philosopher who was able to show all these faces in a work that held them all together. How he does this remains now to be explored.

As to the sources in the corpus, there are three specifically ethical works: the *Nicomachean Ethics*, the *Eudemian Ethics*, and the *Magna Moralia*. In recent times scholars have generally considered *Nicomachean Ethics* Aristotle's most mature treatment and the *Eudemian Ethics* an earlier work, where occasionally connections are tighter and there are variant emphases. The *Magna Moralia* was long considered a later Peripatetic summary, but its status as an Aristotelian work is debated with fresh vigor today. The question of the relation between the *Nicomachean Ethics* and *Eudemian Ethics* has been reopened by Kenny's advocacy of the latter as the mature Aristotelian position.[1] In addition, substantial summaries in the special context of the *Rhetoric* give different and interesting slants on ethical problems. There are also numerous insights in passages scattered throughout the corpus, often in the *Topics*. The treatment of the concepts in this chapter corresponds on the whole to the order of the *Nicomachean Ethics*, except that discussions of pleasure and happiness, which come later in the book, will be considered earlier, and justice will be isolated from the virtues and treated in chapter 17.

The Good

Several themes run through the treatment of the good, and certain problems dominate the discussions. Teleological presuppositions permeate the concept. The good, Aristotle begins, has correctly been declared to be that at which all things aim.[2] There is thus a fixed character to all striving. But this constrains the variety and plurality of human goals less than it appears. It simply imposes a purposive structure on ethics in conformity with his analysis of the human psyche. Furthermore, his opposition to the indeterminate and the infinite (which we discussed in chapter 6) is evidently presupposed when he rejects a flux in human striving such that every end is a means to something else without stop. He also explicitly rejects belief in a transcendent Good; it is the human good in action with which ethics deals. Occasionally, too, the question arises whether the good is something common, in the sense of being shared, or something individual. Such issues will be developed gradually as the different concepts bring different phases to light.

A purposive structure in human action could well have been taken for granted by Aristotle in the light of his whole teleological philosophy. It is interesting to sample the kind of evidence and argument he invokes specifically regarding ends and having ends. There is the assurance that there are ends, for example, in *Parts of Animals*: "Whenever there is plainly some end to which a motion tends when nothing stands in the way, we always say that this is for the sake of that."[3] There is a procedural argument for the ultimacy of ends, comparing them to postulates in theoretic sciences;[4] here it is said that ends are not proper subjects for deliberation, a question that involves Aristotle's special meaning of *deliberation* (to be considered later). In addition there are normative arguments, about the desirability of having ends: for example, "It is a mark of much folly not to have one's life regulated with regard to some end."[5]

There is also the assumption that we do not choose everything for the sake of something else, "for in that way the process would go on to infinity, so that our desire would be empty and vain."[6]

The argument against a transcendent good follows readily from his metaphysical views. Aristotle rejects the unified notion of good that this would require just as he rejected a unified notion of being (see chapter 7) and dismissed a Platonic Idea of Being. In any case, what stands out are the richly varied fields in which goodness is assessed. *Good* has different senses in different categories: in quality it refers to justice, in quantity to moderation, in time to opportunity, and so on.[7] Even within one category the differences are great: opportunity and moderation with respect to food are a medical matter; with respect to warfare they are a question of military strategy. It is not true that all things aim at some one good; rather each kind of thing seeks its particular good, as the eye seeks sight and the body health.[8] Our concern in ethics is the human good in action.

The human nature that Aristotle appeals to in discussing the human good for man is, of course, that of the species man, not of the individual as individual. We have seen in discussing the individual (in chapter 8) how carefully balanced is the treatment of the relations of individual and species. Yet ethics adds serious further issues. It is easy to say that man has a common human purpose, but this is ambiguous. Does it mean that men everywhere have the same purposes, whether or not they know of one another and have any relationship; or that they have shared purposes, purposes in common? The answer depends on the content assigned to the purposes, not on the mere fact of having purposes. In Aristotle's ethics there is no doubt that for the most part some form of life in common constitutes the human good, and that the individual has to find his place within that scheme.[9] The scheme is supposed to take care of the needs of individuals. The individual does not start with a set of his own demands and bargain with others to agree on a morality that will serve his antecedent purposes. This does not mean that we may not have a conception of what is good for us; that would be in the secondary sense in which we may ask whether an admittedly good food or an admittedly good athletic exercise is good for us—almost whether we are in good enough shape for it. As Aristotle puts it, we pray for the good, but we ought to pray that what is good in general be good for us.[10] (At several points, in both morals and politics, humans have to compromise on second bests because of their own inabilities or conditions.)

Nevertheless, the individual's claim for some sort of primacy is not wholly neglected in the ethics. We shall see it coming to the fore in that he is the bearer of pleasure and happiness, that he is the center of his own consciousness, that he enters into relations of justice and friendship and is faced with problems of self-aggrandizement and self-love, and perhaps ultimately that the good of contemplation seems to be a lone activity. On the other hand, though the individual's moral place must always be found within the communal context, never as a prior or antecedent unit outside it, there is no transcending group consciousness, and the equation of communal well-being with happiness points the quality of group life directly to individual well-being.

The teleological structure inherent in Aristotle's conception of the good has been the source of several serious problems and puzzles that ought to be anticipated here. One is that if teleology describes a *motivational* structure—that is, if we do everything else in order to achieve the ultimate end—it is inconsistent to hold later on that we do virtuous acts for their own sake. (This contradiction would disappear if teleology were a justificatory structure; for example, we could say we engage in right actions because they are moral and it turns out on deeper analysis that they further group cohesion, which justifies them.) Second, Aristotle's discussion of deliberation is usually taken to be employing a means–end model in which we deliberate only about the means and ask how far they will yield the end of happiness; this, it is alleged, does not fit his picture of virtue. Third, there seems to be some uncertainty as to whether there is one ultimate end or several ends in some hierarchical arrangement. Since Aristotle clearly thinks in terms of one end, it may be regarded as in some sense *inclusive*, that is, as a harmonious organization of major desires or objectives, or else it may be regarded as *dominant*, that is, as a strong dominating interest that prevails over competing interests (as at times Aristotle seems to talk about theoretic contemplation).[11] The discussion of this third issue has tended to fuse the analysis of the good with that of happiness. In one sense this is justified by Aristotle's assertion that happiness is the aim of the political art and that most people agree it is the highest of the goods that action can achieve.[12] It is worthwhile, however, to pursue independently the investigation of *good*, *better*, and the like apart from *happiness* and then to see how they are related. (The problems raised about the teleological structure will be in part clarified and in part resolved later.)

Once we get beyond the teleological foundations, our discussion of the theory of the good leads us in several directions. Four of these may be briefly elaborated: (1) anchoring the concept to human strivings, (2) analyzing the inner structure of the concept, (3) specifying modes of determining comparative goodness, and (4) determining properties of the good by reference to its extension, things that are good.

(1) The good is anchored in human strivings by the initial characterization that the good is what all things aim at, that is, the purposive structure. Accordingly, the nature of goodness can be clarified by a fuller

understanding of the basic human apparatus of appetite and its forms—desire, wish, impulse, and the rest, and their interrelations—as dealt with in the psychological writings. We shall see how Aristotle summarizes this in the ethical context when he gets to *choice*. Of course, looking back down the ages of ethical theorizing, it is clear how different psychologies of appetite led to different paths for moral philosophy.

(2) Refined studies of the inner "logic" of the concept of good are largely a recent pursuit encouraged by conceptual analysis and linguistic analysis. For example, various types of good (intrinsic, extrinsic, instrumental, contributory, and so on) or different senses of *good* are distinguished, as well as the kinds of entities to which goodness can apply (things in the world, feelings, experiences, and so on) and the formation rules for sentences in which *good* is a predicate. We do not expect Aristotle to organize a study along contemporary lines, but we can gather distinctions he makes at various points that furnish materials for such study. The modern distinction between intrinsic and instrumental good, for example, is paralleled by Aristotle's distinction between what is pursued and welcomed for itself and what only produces or safeguards these and is called good on that account.[13] Sometimes Aristotle uses the language "pursued for its own sake" and "pursued for the sake of something else"; but we have here no mere dichotomy of ends and means, for there are intervening forms and shades of differentiation that appear in the classification and in judgments of comparative value. Some goods (happiness, for instance) are prized or honored; some (like virtue) are praised; some (like authority, strength, and beauty) are potentialities, since they can be used in a good or bad way; and some (like exercise) are productive or preservative of some other good.[14] Along different lines we find distinctions between a good everywhere and altogether worth choosing and one worth choosing only under special conditions, and between complete good and partial good.

As to kinds of subjects *good* can apply to, Aristotle's concern is chiefly whether actualities or potentialities are primary. This is particularly relevant to the goodness of the virtues or in general to habits and states of character. The answer, as we might expect from the metaphysical treatment of the priority of activity over potentiality, takes the primary sense of *good* to apply to actualities; it is the exercise of virtue, the virtuous act, not the mere being virtuous (for we can be virtuous while we sleep), which is central.

(3) The treatment of comparative goodness raises questions about both the meaning of *better* and *best* and the criteria to be employed in judging value. There is, surprisingly, little on this in the *Nicomachean Ethics*, but

considerable help can be found in the *Topics* and *Rhetoric*. The view of comparative value that emerges is quite unlike the familiar modern one, standardized largely in utilitarian terms, in which goods can be ordered in a linear quantitative way according as they possess more or less of a given property, as in a pleasure–pain calculus. Aristotle's approach is instead constructional in character, in a kind of craft model: a job is being done or an enterprise engaged in, and the best is equivalent to the good, which is equivalent to the complete or perfect, that is, the finished job. Thus in the first book of the *Nicomachean Ethics* the search for the highest good, the best (*ariston*), is not distinguished from the search for *the* good, which is complete and self-sufficient, with no part lacking.

The examination of the criteria of preference belongs more to argument, and so it is given a book (the third) in the *Topics*. The criteria themselves are piecemeal and dependent on context. In effect, they are indices for particular situations. The concern is not with widely divergent goods such as happiness or wealth, for there we have no problem, but with closely related goods in which we have difficulty deciding which is more worthy of choice.[15] Among the criteria invoked are the more durable, what a wise man would choose, what the expert would choose, what would be chosen for its own sake rather than for something else, what is more highly honored, the means to a broader goal, and so on. The *Rhetoric* considers comparative value—the greater good and the more expedient—because it is a common point in dispute.[16] Here, although it starts out with quantitative language, the actual discussion ranges over different contexts and gives contextual answers: for example, the scarcer is more valuable from one point of view, the more abundant, from another; what characterizes better men; what is more pleasurable, what we desire more; what our enemies recognize as more valuable; what is praised more. In the ethical treatises, there are also occasional small "scales": for example, the range *prized, praised, potential, instrumental* (indicated earlier as a classification of goods) clearly constitutes a value order. And as we shall see in the *Politics*, different constitutions can be ordered in value terms. On occasion quite striking indices are suggested: for example, whether we would choose to relive a period of life (Aristotle thinks no sensible person would want to be a child again), or for what one would choose to come into existence rather than not.[17]

(4) The last of the four directions from which the theory of the good may be considered here carries us to the extension or denotation of *good*, the kinds of things found or taken to be good. It is to be expected that these will govern to some extent the general properties assigned to the good. Take, for example, the temporal property of duration: can the

good be found in a short stretch of time? Can a person live a good life in twenty-four hours? Obviously it will depend on what one takes to be the content of the good. Aristotle discusses this temporal issue directly by reference to happiness and decides that happiness requires an all-life scope. Rather quaintly, he wonders whether even the fate of a man's descendants and works, after his death, does not affect his happiness. Not too much, he decides, and we get the feeling that he is concerned not with an onlooking immortal soul but with an overall judgment of happiness: could we call a life happy that rested on foundations of sand, although they did not crumble until after death?

Similarly, if we ask where the good is to be located, answers would depend on the kind of actualities or activities involved in the conception of happiness. Here we shall have to probe the delicate balance between the individual and the social.

Aristotle's analysis of the good, then, is anchored in biology and psychology and supported by his metaphysical conclusions and the way he partitions the field of human activity and experience, his rough systematization of preferential choices, and his view of the major directions of their purposive striving. His conclusions here are applied in the rest of the network. Their influence can be felt in all the analyses, from defining virtue to characterizing the man of practical wisdom.

Happiness and Pleasure

The term used for happiness, *eudaimonia*, means faring well, prospering, flourishing. It thus denotes a quality of living (*eu zēn*, to live well) rather than a feeling assimilated to a pleasure-pain complex. (In this sense, a man cannot really be judged happy until the configuration of his life is discerned.) Moreover, though happiness is the highest good, it still has to be decided what constitutes happiness.[18] In part, Aristotle answers this by articulating some of the properties of the good: its pursuit for its own sake, its being prized rather than praised, its complete and self-sufficient character. In part, he lines up in an inductive way the several major candidates for the position of happiness that are to be found in people's pursuits. These turn out to be the competing goals and kinds of lives that Plato had presented in the *Republic* as issuing from the different parts of the psyche: wisdom and the theoretic life, honor and the political life, and pleasure and the life of riches and material comforts. In the *Rhetoric* Aristotle gives a comprehensive statement that happiness is living well with virtue, or self-sufficiency of life, or the pleasantest life with security, or abundance of possessions and slaves with the power to protect and use them—in short, all the kinds of lives and almost as you like it.[19] He goes on to give an inventory of the components of happiness, covering family, external goods, internal goods, social standing, and so on in detail. The *Nicomachean Ethics* takes the practical general stand that happiness requires external goods; indeed we shall see that some of the virtues cannot be practiced without them.

In one sense, the greater part of the *Nicomachean Ethics* is an extended investigation of happiness, for the investigation passes along from concept to concept. Our concern here is with the independent anchorings of the concept of happiness. Beyond surveying the general properties and the content of happiness, as mentioned above, Aristotle undertakes a selective evaluation of the different ways of life, which culminates in the last part of book 10 in the exaltation of the life of contemplation, and the analyses (in books 7 and especially 10) of pleasure.

The ultimate reckoning with happiness pulls in two directions, considering both the individual theoretic life and the social practical life. In either case, whether in the exercise of reason or the practice of moral virtue, happiness lies in a life of activity, and of activities that are desirable for their own sake. It lies not in amusement, or in relaxation, which have their own instrumental roles, but in organized active expression of our powers. Aristotle's tracing of these powers culminates in praise of the contemplative life. In the end, as the *Eudemian Ethics* puts it, to live is to perceive and to know; social life (to live together) is to perceive together and to know together.[20] No social consciousness apart from individual consciousness is intended: if absolute knowledge were indifferent to who knew it, then another person might be knowing it instead of oneself. That is like another person's living instead of oneself. The *Nicomachean Ethics* finds Aristotle more entranced by what happens to the individual in the act of contemplation and by the intrinsic values of the theoretic activity of reason involved. Contemplation combines worth, intrinsic end, heightened pleasure, self-sufficiency, leisureliness, and unweariedness—all the attributes of the complete or supreme end. It is the divine in man. Yet we must not avoid it as unbecoming to mortals, but "must, so far as possible, make ourselves immortal, and do everything we can to live according to the highest thing in us; for even if it be small in bulk, much more does it excel all things in power and worth."[21]

Having reached this culmination, having identified our ultimate individual aspiration with the contemplation of the eternal, Aristotle characteristically puts it on a pedestal beyond the reach of most men, and beyond more than occasional reach even for those who are capable of it. He moves down to reconcile us to the life of practical wisdom, and soon, in the last chapter of the *Nicomachean Ethics*, we are on our way to the

Politics; for man is a social animal, and so by far the greater part of the ethical and political writing deals with social practice.

Aristotle's theory of pleasure is subtle; its sophistication is not always appreciated, because it stands under the shadow of Plato's great achievements in depth psychology. Contemporary philosophy, however, has witnessed a growing interest in both the concept of pleasure and Aristotle's treatment of it.[22] Plato had probed deeply, examining the pleasures of men not merely by introspection, but in terms of a dynamic theory of the human makeup, so that each pleasure was related to the part of the psyche and the inner dynamic components that it expressed. Yet Plato tended to scorn the bodily pleasures and regarded most pleasures as simply indicating a release of tension. Much of Aristotle's discussion of pleasure is a skirmish with Plato and his followers, as well as a defense of pleasure against attacks by contemporaries of other schools. He insists that it has the earmarks of the good, that just because some pleasures are evil it does not follow some may not be good, even the greatest good. Pleasure as such does not interfere with our nobler activities; rather the activities issuing in one kind of pleasure conflict with those issuing in another. But when he gets down to fundamentals we realize that he is not advocating pleasure as an end but setting it in a more intelligible perspective. He has learned depth psychology from Plato, but he has basic criticisms of Plato's specific theory of pleasure and has worked out a remarkable alternative.

Pleasure and pain in Aristotle's accounts have several roles. The broadest, as we have seen in considering the initiation of movement, is to serve as the affective side along the behaviors of pursuit and avoidance and the cognitions of good and bad.[23] In his account of affections or emotions— he lists desire and joy as well as fear and hatred and envy and pity—he includes "in general those that are accompanied by pleasure or pain."[24] Thus the broad use of the terms covers emotion as well as purposive action. On the other hand, the substantive use of *pleasures* is usually with respect to bodily feelings and satisfactions (food, sex, smells, tastes); indeed, one of the specific virtues, temperance or self-control, is concerned with pleasures of taste and touch. Pleasure in a more general but still quite specific sense is seen as the motivation in one type of friendship. Aristotle seems to see no problem in moving from broader to more specific and localized uses for the concept. Pleasure is associated with activity, and activities may be described in general terms or in specific localized terms. The differences are in the activities; the affective aspect of pleasure or pain accompanies them and takes general qualitative form or general mood form or specific localized form in correspondence with the activity. (The activity itself may be describable in behavioral or in phenomenal language or both.) Perhaps one reason why Aristotle discerns no problem in these varied cases of pleasure and pain is that he assumes a general physiological account to cover them all, related to the operation of heat in the neighborhood of the heart.

The questions that most concern Aristotle about pleasure are two. First, with what processes in the psyche is it to be associated? Second, what precisely does pleasure consist in, and what is its function? The answers to these questions combine into a fairly systematic theory.

On the first question Aristotle is clearly joining issue with Plato. Plato had often treated pleasure as the concomitant of release of tension; thus bodily pleasures occur in the round of depletion and repletion. When one is healthy there is no particular pleasure in health, but when one is sick there is pleasure in the recovery. Hence Plato sees pleasure chiefly as a process of restoration to a normal state. Perfect beings, then, such as the gods, would feel no pleasure. Plato's full analysis is of course much more complicated,[25] but it is this basic model that Aristotle challenges. Aristotle shares Plato's view that pleasure is to be understood by reference to deeper psychological processes, but he differs on what is going on. When a person is recovering his health, the pleasure comes from the activity of the healthy parts that are engaged in the restoration,[26] not from the removal of illness in the unhealthy parts. Similarly, it is the functioning of our sense organs in a healthy state that explains our pleasures of sense. Pleasure is defined as an unimpeded activity of the natural state; indeed, a god would enjoy continuous pleasure.[27] Thus pleasure as such is not to be evaluated, but rather the different actions with which pleasure is associated.

This difference with Plato is not small. It affects both principle and practice. Aristotle focuses on the operations of the organism as a system, rather than on the areas of disturbance, and this involves a different approach to the treatment of disturbance as well as to the sources of value in the organism. Perhaps the medical strain in Aristotle gives him the deeper insight. It is not enough to say that tension is being reduced; we have to know what activities in the system brought it down; those activities are the source of the pleasure. A modern example of different attitudes in psychiatry may show this point strikingly. If neurosis is regarded as a disturbance, it is a failure to achieve a mature adjustment to life's situations—a formation to be gotten rid of. On the other hand, if it issues from the basic system at work to achieve its goals, it almost deserves respect as a hard-won compromise under shocks and trying conditions in which a person nevertheless manages to achieve some degree of stability; the therapeutic situation, if therapy is possible, would be to move to a better formation without disrupting the positive elements. Finally, as to the sources of value in the organism, the one approach looks to lacks and needs, the other to realization of powers.

When Aristotle comes to inquire what precisely pleasure consists in, he answers that it is an actuality (*energeia*), not a movement or a process (*kinēsis*). This is argued in terms of the contrast already established. Pleasure is whole or complete at any moment. It has none of the temporal properties of a process; you cannot, for example, be pleased quickly as you can walk quickly.[28] That pleasure is an actuality or activity does not mean that it occurs by itself. If one were asked what he is going to do for the next ten minutes he could not answer that he is going to be pleased. He would have to engage in some activity, and the pleasure would perfect the activity, supervening, says Aristotle, like the bloom of youth at its height.[29] There is no difficulty in the concept that an activity supervenes on or comes on top of another and is inseparable from it. Aristotle points out that the pleasures are so close to the activities that some would take them to be identical.[30] He rejects this, pointing out that pleasure is not to be identified with a thought or sensation. Now thought and sensation are themselves in some sense supervening actualities. Perhaps, we may note, thought is the clearest case, since any actuality or activity can be thought about; but still the thought is not identical with the actuality that is thought about, although the *energeia* of the mind and its object of thought is one. Thus there seems little doubt that Aristotle gives pleasure the status of a real occurrence or actuality even though it derives its character from the activity on which it supervenes.[31]

So far, then, the answer to what precisely pleasure is would seem to be that it is an *energeia* that supervenes on an activity and completes or perfects it. It looks as if we are now being given the last of the four causes —the final cause—of pleasure. The previous discussions have given the other causes. That pleasure supervenes on activities means that activities are the material cause of pleasure. The dispute with Plato about the source of pleasure—whether it comes from release of tension—can be seen as concerned in part with efficient cause. That pleasure is an *energeia* gives us its formal cause; so does the earlier definition (offered to refute the Platonic theory) that pleasure is an unimpeded activity of the natural state. If completing an activity or perfecting it be taken as the final cause, then it must be, in the light of the importance Aristotle assigns to final cause in scientific explanation, a significant part of the theory of pleasure.

The significance of the functional question with respect to pleasure was clearly understood in later theories. For example, Augustine, whose psychology is markedly different from Aristotle's insofar as he accentuates the will, took the occurrence of pleasure in an act to be an act of will indicating consent; this gives a voluntaristic core to pleasure rather than simply an affective one. Later more instrumental psychologies understood pleasure as a temptation to continue or repeat the act; this invitational function in due course acquired an evolutionary gloss (for example, in Spencer), to the effect that on the whole, natural selection associated pleasure with what promoted survival of the organism.

Aristotle recognizes not only the general function of pleasure, but specific ones as well. In special contexts he is ready to use the occurrence of pleasure as a mark of the completed or matured phenomenon; thus he takes the pleasure in doing virtuous acts to be a sign that the virtue is fully established, whereas the mere act itself is consistent with inner struggle. For pleasure in general, if we pursue the comparison that pleasure supervenes on the activity like the bloom on youth, its occurrence in an activity signifies the good condition of the organ, and even suggests a heightened consciousness and almost a decorative beauty. It is a perfecting or completing role, consonant with both the definition that the best or the good is the complete and the view that the highest good has no element of the instrumental about it.[32] Aristotle would have rejected the idea that a still higher good would have some self-sufficient value *plus* massive instrumentality for other goods—as if, for example, happiness were justified also by keeping a person healthier and extending his life. Ultimately, then, his theory of pleasure, with respect to the final cause, is theory-laden, but the theory with which it is laden is not wholly one of psychology or of evolution but in part at least a theory of the ultimate good. Pleasure is not the ultimate good, but it is the stamp of completeness or perfection that is a structural quality of the realization of the good.

Man's Function

When Aristotle wants a clearer account of happiness, he proposes to investigate man's function. He plunges lightly into this enterprise, saying that if the carpenter and the shoemaker have a function (*ergon*), why should not man as such?[33] Of course this rapid transition simply shows the depth of his teleological presuppositions; the conceptual apparatus of the natural is fully entrenched. As we would expect from his metaphysics, he would never step out of the teleological framework far enough to consider either an evolutionary shift of human nature that would entail a changing good, or an existentialist denial of human nature that would leave to the individual the creation of a good by choice at every moment of his existence. Nor would we find a Nietzschean sense of man's nature as something to be transcended by an effort toward future development. Aristotle remains throughout bound to an ethics of definite or fixed human nature, that is, to an ethics resting on a psychological theory that man has a certain definite makeup that determines his good. That is why it matters what he takes man's nature to be.

The importance of a theory of human nature in ethics is that it sets constraints and limits to both what is possible and what is desired, and ultimately to what is regarded as good. When a particular theory furnishes a basic plan for man, its selection of function determines the preferred path of life. If that function is narrowly defined, it assigns a dominant task; if broader, it gives a more inclusive role. If all the component functions fit readily together, a smooth and unified life process results; if they are discrepant, there will be inner conflict. Aristotle's most mature picture of human nature is of course located in his psychological writings. It is there too that he has a sweeping critique of attempts to present "parts of the psyche."[34] He asks how many there are and says that in a sense they appear to be endless. This is meant to criticize what he regards as arbitrary divisions. Some thinkers divide the psyche into calculative, spirited, and desiderative faculties. (This looks like Plato's tripartite division in the *Republic*.) Some divide it into rational and irrational parts. (This looks like the division that Aristotle himself uses in *Nicomachean Ethics* 1.13.) Aristotle nevertheless criticizes both of these notions on the ground that there are other parts that do not fall readily into such classifications; for example, they omit the imaginative and unduly subdivide the appetitive. We would do well to remember this mature criticism, for the rational–irrational division supports many of his own particular conclusions.

What are we to make then of the divisions he uses in his ethics? Take the rational–irrational scheme just mentioned. He finds the irrational itself to be double, one part vegetative, but the other part amenable to and capable of obeying the rational. The latter conclusion prompts Aristotle to make a distinction between moral virtues and intellectual virtues, which becomes basic to his ethical theory and raises serious problems for the analysis of practical wisdom. Perhaps the rational–irrational dichotomy is an earlier one, or perhaps he is relying on a popular distinction; he remarks hypothetically that if it is correct to take appetite as rational, then the rational part is divided in two, one part rational in the proper sense, the other in the sense of obeying as a child obeys its father. Thus obedience is located either within the rational or within the irrational or both. One suggestion might be that he has in mind different instances that later appear in the *Politics*: the child has one kind of rationality, genuine but immature, the slave another, lower and capable only of following! If so, then the classification of the parts here is largely guided, as Plato's was in the *Republic*, by social class distinctions imposed on psychological functions.[35]

Apart from these structural features, Aristotle does not here give us any specific properties of the irrational element. In general, in his ethical writings, man's nature, even on the appetitive side, is not treated as irrational, but more as the raw material with which man is to deal and out of which, in craftsman's style, he is to fashion his life. This more neutral picture of the human raw material contrasts strongly with Plato's view (in the *Republic*) that the third part of the psyche is a dragon of appetite that is demanding, capricious, unable to endure tension, and greedy and aggrandizing in its acquisitiveness, aggressiveness, and sexuality. Again, there is no condemnation of human nature in Aristotle, as in later Christian attitudes that sex is inherently evil, or in some subsequent evolutionary attitudes that aggression is something serviceable in the distinct past but now a hindrance to cooperative living. Yet Aristotle's picture of man's nature is not unselective. He emphasizes the rational as the unique element in man (man is defined as a rational animal), the nutritive psyche being shared with plants and the sensitive psyche with animals, and he recognizes the basic sociability and occasionally the sympathy of human beings. These are the major general features in his view of human nature.

The crucial points of ethical influence that arise from Aristotle's conception of human nature thus rest upon what is to be his specific interpretation of rationality, together with sociability and specific human drives and emotions. We shall meet and explore these in detail later on in discussions of the relation of intellectual and moral virtues; the analyses of internal conflict; the theory of friendship; the relations of master and slave, man and woman, parent and child; and so on. Immediately relevant here in our development of the ethical network is the way the notion of a function enables Aristotle to get to the notion of virtue. This is done very simply. There corresponds to every function or task an *excellence* or *virtue* that enables the craftsman to accomplish it well. A defect or vice ensures it will be done badly. If man is to carry out his human function he has to have or build up virtues as stable ways of performance. Hence it is not surprising that Aristotle, who appealed to the notion of function to clarify that of happiness, concludes: "Why then should we not say that he is happy who is active in accordance with complete virtue and is sufficiently furnished with external goods, not for a chance time but for a complete life?"[36] And with minor qualifications he settles on this.

Virtue and Moral Development

Aristotle's formal definition of virtue is "a state of character involving a capacity of choice consisting in a mean relative to us, which is determined by reason, that is, as the man of practical wisdom would determine it."[37] This definition contains almost all the rest of the concepts in the network. Let us first consider virtue and the moral development in which it arises, and then step by step move through the rest. We have three important questions to answer. What is a state of character? How is it developed? Why is there so fundamental a division between moral and intellectual virtues, that is, between excellences of character and excellences of intellect?

In deciding that states of character, or habits, are the genus of virtue, Aristotle rejects two other possibilities. Virtues are not simply emotions such as desire, anger, fear, and confidence. Nor are they capacities that render us capable of the emotions. In short, native endowments are rejected in favor of dispositions that can be learned or cultivated by habituation. The emotions are part of the raw material to be fashioned into virtues. Often associated with emotions in the consideration of virtues are actions, either social activities such as giving and taking or individual activities such as eating. Virtue is thus a regulative form in which emotions and actions are patterned. Perhaps a virtue may be regarded as a first entelechy, like a language that has been learned or a skill that is mastered. Under appropriate circumstances virtues issue directly into conduct. There are definite conditions for virtuous action: the agent must act from knowledge, he must choose the acts for their own sake, and the acts must issue from a firm and unchangeable character.[38]

A clear mark that the virtue has been achieved is that doing the acts is pleasant.[39] This is qualified for certain cases, such as the courageous man who faces wounds or death, especially if he is a good man and knows the worth of the life he stands to lose; but the virtuous man prefers the noble, and the pleasure comes only in attaining that end. Pleasure becomes a property of virtuous action and men become literally lovers of justice, lovers of the noble, and lovers of virtue.[40]

In addition to serving as indicators of mature development, pleasure and pain have another specific role in relation to virtue. In the *Nicomachean Ethics* particular pleasures and pains are treated as the matter of some of the virtues (such as temperance and intemperance, which are concerned with gastronomic and sexual pleasures), and in some they offer the easiest mark for determining the *too much* and the *too little* in the reaction (as a jealous man is overpained by another's good fortune). The *Eudemian Ethics* uses a simpler schema that glosses over these fine shades. Its formal definition of virtue specifies pleasures and pains as the subject matter for choice of the mean.[41] Virtue is a kind of tranquillity in regard to pleasures and pains.[42]

That the virtues and vices are learned by doing the kind of acts involved until the state of character is fashioned, is only part of the story of moral development. Aristotle seems to have a fairly coherent wider picture even though he does not spell it out systematically. The earlier books of the *Nicomachean Ethics* use the concept of the noble (*kalon*) or fine or beautiful rather than the good (*agathon*) when talking of what motivates virtue in the process of development. Doing the virtuous act for its own sake is doing it because it is a fine thing to do. For example, the brave man faces dangers as he ought and as reason dictates "for the sake of the noble; for this is the end of virtue."[43] Now the idea of the noble is explained as "that which, being worthy of choice for its own sake, is at the same time worthy of praise."[44] In short, to be praiseworthy is the differentia of the noble among goods. This is confirmed in a discussion of the virtue of nobility (*kalokagathia*).[45] This Greek term combines the words for nobility and goodness. The "fine and good" were the "gentlemen," and the term was also at times employed in politics to mean the aristocratic party. Aristotle now separates the compound term into its parts. The good and the noble are different in fact as well as in name: all goods have ends that are desirable for their own sake; of these, the noble are those praiseworthy as existent for their own sake.[46] The latter is illustrated by the virtues, the former by health. There thus arises a comparable terminological distinction for the good man which is useful in contexts of virtue. Instead of *agathos* we find *spoudaios*, which may be translated as "moral" or "earnest" or "serious."

The way Aristotle uses the concepts of the noble and the moral man throws light on his view of moral development. The young respond to the praise of their elders and gradually adopt models of the fine thing to do. As they cultivate the virtues and as guidance by the noble becomes their stable end, they become moral persons. When their minds mature and they come to see the wider relations of these character traits and lines of action—at least the more sensitive and philosophical do so—then they develop a rational conception of the good to replace the felt intimations of nobility. At that point rationality and practical wisdom come to the fore, and the intellectual virtues are presumably matured.

In his statement that the genus of virtue is states of character or habits, and also in his picture of development in virtue, Aristotle talks as if there could be different virtues existing separately, so that one could be courageous but intemperate or illiberal. Such a view, if he had continued to hold it (in fact it is only provisional), would have parted company with the Socratic conception that all virtue is one. Historically, there have been important advocates on the side of the unity of virtue. They see all life as a continuous enterprise of struggle, so that there are no safe and detachable victories, no achieved havens of stabilized separate virtues. Augustine looks on human life that way, and so in effect does Kant, who says that virtue is always at the starting point and reduces the dynamic of virtue to conscientiousness. If we do not construe these merely as different basic value patterns for human life, then the issue may be largely psychological, concerned with what habits are like, whether behavioral configurations are trustworthy bases for understanding future behavior, and so on. For example, a behavioristic psychology with a belief in the conditioning of separate items of response could think of separate states of character. A psychoanalytic psychology might find different inner meanings associated with the same apparent behavior and so seek its patterns not in habits but in dynamic depth configurations. There have been changes in psychological fashions as well as accumulations of knowledge in these areas. Perhaps today's search would trace patterns of personality in relation to cultural goals rather than in terms of sheer habituation.

Questions of greater complexity arise about the apparently obvious distinction Aristotle makes between intellectual and moral virtues. On the face of it such a distinction seems to be required. The *Eudemian Ethics* comments on the view that to know what virtue is makes one virtuous, just as learning geometry and architecture makes one a geometer and an architect.[47] That will do for theoretical sciences, where the end is contemplation, but the productive sciences aim to secure health or social order and therefore have to look not merely to the nature of virtue but to the sources from which it arises. Underlying the separation of the two classes of virtues is thus the sharp separation of contemplation from doing or making. The matured ability to acquire knowledge in different modes is removed from practice, and practice is left to operate with an oversimplified notion of habituation that is guided from outside, not by the consolidation of the learning involved in its own operations. The cost of this separation is seen in the difficulties that beset the concept of practical wisdom when the theoretical is used for the guidance of practice.

There seems to be a strong social component in the theoretical separation of the intellectual and the practical. In Plato's tripartite psychology reason (the human in us) is pure and independent; appetite is an utterly irrational dragon; spirit (the lion) is capable of following reason's direction. Thus the administrative class (the lion), taking its indoctrination from the guardian class (reason), becomes imbued or dyed with the rational pattern. Although Aristotle came to criticize Plato's classification, nevertheless in the *Nicomachean Ethics* the division of the rational and the irrational parts of the psyche is maintained. And the latter part is in turn divided into the wholly irrational and a part amenable to rational control. He allows that this part may instead be a lower division within the rational. It is precisely with respect to the division of the two kinds of rationality that he institutes the division of virtues into the intellectual and moral.[48] This same division in rationality appears in the *Politics* in the contrast between free men on the one hand and women, children, and slaves on the other. The social picture thus parallels the philosophical analysis. Only in some modern epistemologies and philosophies of science has a conception of reason emerged in which it is not a sovereign source of authority but a quality of systematically funded experience. On such a theory, learning is permeated with insight and intelligence, so that habit as a psychological concept loses its sheer dull inertia and is capable of having almost an inner critical spirit. Although relative distinctions between the intellectual and practical components may continue to be made in terms of specific features in some contexts, the implications for ethical and social theory are surely considerably altered.

The Mean

Since virtue is defined as a state of character concerned with choice and lying in the mean, the concept of choice still has to be treated to round out the genus. But Aristotle goes on next to the mean, which is the differentia. The mean is a proper, just-right point between excess and defect. It is not an arithmetical mean but a mean relative to the individual. If ten pounds is too much for a person to eat and two pounds too little, it does not follow that a trainer will recommend six for a particular athlete. It depends on the person and the purpose. Aristotle compares the mean rather to the idea of proportion in art.

Actually, Aristotle is here drawing on an idea of the mean that has manifold roots in the Greek tradition. It can be found in religion and science, as well as art. Homer refers to the gods' envy when a man tries to be more than human; *hubris* is a violent self-assertiveness motivated by the pride that invariably leads to a fall. There was a general cultural stress on moderation, on avoiding excess—the Apollonian outlook noted earlier. In medicine there arose conceptions that the harmony of the elements in the body, a kind of balanced unity of opposing tendencies, is a mark of health. In music and the arts the concept of harmony was similarly developed.

Scholars have sometimes sought very specific sources for Aristotle's idea of the mean.[49] But in its broadest outline, the idea of the just-right, as opposed to the too-much and too-little, seems to be an integral element in all craftsmanship. Moreover, the model of the crafts is, as we have seen, frequently invoked in the biological works themselves, for nature is understood to work like an artist. What significance then should be attached to the fact that concepts of blending and proportion, which have a distinct currency in medical and biological explanation, are also in the background of ethical usage in discussing the mean? It may be simply that the general concepts of craft construction, not the specific properties of different senses of mixing and different types of proportion, are relevant for the general theory of the mean. Specific properties may pertain only when special modifications of the general schema—that is, special models—are applied in different fields in different ways. For example, the process resulting in the mean is different when a single act or quality is involved (as in giving not too much but not too little) from what it is when two components (for instance, fear and confidence), each of which has its own scale, are to be blended, or when two processes each require a mean before they interact (for instance, in sensation; the sense organ is a mean, and the stimulus must be moderate to yield the resultant proportion that supports the sense quality—almost a mean of means). The general Aristotelian view of the relation of the sciences, each on its separate track, would suggest examining how the mean is interpreted within each field.

For both ethical and political purposes, the concept of the mean takes two different forms. In one the extremes are rejected alternatives and have no place in the finished product, which might be the just-right amount of food, the just-right amount in giving, the correct size for a building board, or the right length for the arm in a statue of Apollo. In the other there remains a tension of the extremes; they are operative in the finished product, balanced so that the mean that is expressed lies in between. This is well illustrated in the *Politics*, where governmental mechanisms are devised to balance the oligarchic and democratic demands that continue to exert their pressures within the state. (It also has its place in the arts, both in the balance of forces in architecture and in the many aspects of the balance of tension in the visual and auditory as well as dramatic arts.) These two kinds of mean are not necessarily in conflict. The first characterizes the perfectly virtuous man who not only exhibits the mean in his acts but has internalized or incorporated the mean into his character, so that it holds of his feelings. (The evidence of this is that he finds pleasure in doing virtuous acts.) The mean as a differentia of virtue is thus the form of a state of character in the virtuous man.[50] The second kind characterizes the approximations to the perfectly virtuous man; in them, because it is a matter of balance between opposing forces, there may be inner conflict rather than assured stability.

Let us illustrate the way Aristotle applies his concept of the mean to the analysis of specific virtues. Courage is concerned with fear and confidence, temperance with certain pleasures, liberality with giving and taking as socially unavoidable practices, and so on. In each case Aristotle identifies extremes that in habitual expression would be vices. Always fearful, never confident betokens timidity; always confident, never fearful, rashness. Excessive pursuit of certain pleasures is self-indulgence; deficient interest in them is insensibility. Always giving, never taking is prodigality; always taking, never giving is miserliness. The mean lies in each case somewhere in the middle. Courage is a state of character that has worked fear and confidence into a stable fusion such that a man knows when to be fearful and when to be confident with respect to a huge diversity of situations, persons, relations, motives, and reasons. Aristotle illustrates these but makes no attempt to reduce them to a general formula, relying instead on sensitive experience to stabilize a rational attitude. So too in temperance: it lies not in dogged abstinence nor in perpetual indulgence, but in moderation. (Neither drunkenness nor abstinence; the Greeks mixed water with their wine!) Liberality characterizes the man who gives and takes appropriately, depending on all the circumstances. It is not easy to find the mean: "Any one can get angry, and easily, and give and spend money; but to do this to the right person, to the right extent, at the right time, with the right purpose, and in the right manner, is not something that anybody can do, nor is it easy; that is why good conduct is both rare and praiseworthy and noble."[51] It is equally hard to be truly vicious, though easy to do acts that a vicious man would perform. Most men fall in between. Aristotle is often highly practical in his suggestions; he recommends, for instance, that we find the vice we are most prone to, and pull for the opposite extreme, hoping to land at the virtuous act. (The compromises that are found when there are inner conflicts will be examined in relation to continence and incontinence, in chapter 17.)

The virtues analyzed in detail and commended are varied. Some have a perennial role in human life. A special emphasis marks off a particular historical cluster of virtues with a special tone of its own. Chief among these is the virtue of pride. The proud (literally, "great-souled") man has a just estimate of his great worth; he is open in his loves and hates; he is not given to admiration, since to him nothing is great; he has a slow step, a deep voice, a level utterance, for he takes few things seriously. The full chapter on this subject has to be read to appreciate its quality. Clearly Aristotle shows an undue admiration for the upper-middle-class gentleman of his day, unless (as Joachim suggests in his commentary) he is being humorous here.[52] Few have adopted the latter interpretation, for to grant Aristotle such a sense of humor would certainly cause revolutionary repercussions in Aristotelian studies. In any case, the contrast between pride as here set forth and Christian humility is as great as that of both with Benthamite calculating prudence.

Choice and the Voluntary

Aristotle's account of choice and the voluntary presents three related matters. The first is a general background in which, more by use than explication, his general philosophical concepts of beginning or source (*archē*) and the concepts associated with it are applied to the initiation of human action. The second concerns the criteria for identifying responsibility and assigning praise and blame. The third is the character of choice as a species of voluntary action, set off from kindred psychological phenomena such as wish and related to deliberation.

(1) The theoretical background has to be examined with special caution because both translators and commentators often have in mind our later problem of free will. Translation and comment may be cast in this vein, and when problems arise Aristotle is accused of not having yet achieved a full understanding of our problem. He is, in short, seen as making a good start, but not going far enough. But it is sheer philosophical ethnocentrism to assume that the historical development of our problem of free will constituted theoretical progress. It may very well be that by regarding will as a unitary faculty rather than as a complex phenomenon we obscure the actual process and generate pseudo-problems. The reaction of contemporary linguistic philosophers like John L. Austin, who eschewed free will and investigated concretely what kinds of "excuses" were intelligible, looks rather like a return to the Aristotelian track.[53]

What, then, lies in the background? Aristotle says of a certain action that in its actual occurrence the person does it voluntarily, "for the origin of the movements of the parts of the body in these actions is in him, and where the origin is in him, to do or not to do is dependent upon him."[54] The phrase "upon him" carries the full weight of such translations as "is dependent upon him" or "is in his power." Both it and the phrase "origin within him" are regularly invoked to explain the basis of responsibility. The notion of origin here is not simply temporal. Aristotle does associate it with cause; for example, acts are compulsory or forced when "the cause is in things outside and the one who does it contributes nothing."[55] The cause in these contexts is clearly the efficient cause; there is an explicit comparison of begetting actions to begetting children.[56]

What is taken for granted, almost relegated to asides, in the *Nicomachean Ethics*, is explicitly unfolded in a chapter of the *Eudemian Ethics*.[57] All substances are by nature first principles of a sort in that they generate things of the same sort, as men generate men and plants generate plants. Man alone among animals is the source of certain kinds of actions. Principles in the strict sense are those that are a source of motion, especially when the results follow necessarily. Principles in mathematics are so called by analogy in the sense that if we changed them, the consequences would change; for instance, if the angle sum of a triangle were not two right angles, the angle sum of a quadrilateral would be different. Now suppose there were no other cause of the triangle's having that particular property: the triangle would then be a kind of source and cause of what followed.[58] Though men are the source of their own actions, opposite actions are possible. In short, it would seem, men are the source of their actions in the same way that axioms are the source of theorems, but since we are in the domain of what can be otherwise, any one of our alternative actions is possible.

Conceivably, we might object that it has been shown only that a man is the source of A-or-B's taking place, not of A's taking place or B's taking place, which requires further determination. But Aristotle is being fairly cautious. He is saying that in the case of actions whose source lies within a man, it depends on the man whether they come to be or not. Since those actions involve virtue and vice, a decision is required. That is why Aristotle goes on to examine the voluntary and actions according to choice. In short, the theoretical background has shown what to look for in subsequent inquiries. The answers will have to come from those inquiries themselves.

The theoretical background is, of course, not unfamiliar. It is the conceptual apparatus he used in his physics and psychology. The motion even of a material like earth can follow from its nature or from outside forces. Suppose we have an earthen object dislodged from a tree by the wind. Its falling down is explicable by its nature as *archē*; that it did not fall down before was caused by the tree; that it fell at that moment was caused by the wind. Aristotle's concepts of origin and cause employed in the theoretical background of action are no more pointed to the human being than this. The vital content for moral judgments has to come from the further inquiry in application.

If the background in the theory of human actions employs the same concepts as in the theory of physical motions, we have to recall a significant thesis in Aristotle's view of motion. There was, we saw, no beginning of motion: an object is either moving or it is not. To look for the causes of its motion is either a search for its nature, to explain the kind of motion it engages in when unhindered, or a search for happenings that serve as efficient causes. So in the case of the initiation of action there cannot be first of all deliberation, followed by an act of willing that is the beginning of the action, followed in turn by a period in which the action takes place. There has to be a division in time, such that at every moment thereafter, no matter how close to the division, the action is taking place, and at every moment before, no matter how close, the action is not taking place. In widely varied contexts, Aristotle takes for granted the unity of choice with action. In the *Topics*, in a chance illustration, the object of pursuit is equated with the object of choice, and in the *Rhetoric*, on the question whether a man did something, it is said that if a man was able to do something and wished it, he did it; also if he wished to do it and was in a state of anger; or was able and desired to do it; and so on.[59]

(2) Aristotle starts his discussion of responsibility by considering the genus of choice, which is the voluntary. It is approached through its opposite, the involuntary. Acts done under compulsion or through ignorance are generally taken to be involuntary. In the case of compulsion the extremes are clear enough. Where there is physical coercion, the act is involuntary; if the act is desired and chosen, it is voluntary. What of yielding unwillingly to threats? Such acts are a mixed type; to do that kind of act in general might be involuntary, but under the particular conditions it is consented to and so inclines to the voluntary. There are, however, extreme coercive pressures no one could resist; but again, there are also some cases in which the act is so dreadful that one ought rather die than yield. Enticements do not constitute compulsion; Aristotle refuses to regard the enticements of pleasure as coercive.

Ignorance as a ground for exculpation is analyzed in some detail. Some types of ignorance obviously excuse, but only if a person regrets the act. (Perhaps Aristotle has in mind that the absence of regret would leave it uncertain whether the person would have refrained from the act if he had been informed.) If the ignorance is a consequence of a person's own acts (for example, drinking too much or neglecting to inform himself), it does not wholly excuse him. Aristotle goes on to examine half a dozen different things a person may be ignorant about that would help excuse an act: not knowing that something was supposed to be kept secret, mistaking a friend for an enemy, and so on.

On the whole, he deals with current practice and usage much as a legal theorist might stipulate a set of heterogeneous conditions that would invalidate a contract. Such a procedure codifies people's intuitions and practices; the list can be increased or altered in explicit reaction to new cases, or definite purposive inclusions or exclusions can be made for some type of social goal. Perhaps such an interpretation of the voluntary and involuntary could survive on its own. Aristotle, however, has tied it to the idea of the agent's begetting the action—that is, that the origin is within him—so that a fuller exploration must lead to a consideration of choice. The analysis of choice will tell what is going on *in* the agent. Aristotle does not say it will give the whole story, since choice is a subtype of voluntary action. Sudden actions without choice can also be voluntary; so may children's actions. Choice is central to deliberate action and so to moral virtue and vice.

Aristotle's conclusions about the grounds of responsibility are not wholly definite at the limits. He is realistic in his recognition that a person can be responsible for what he becomes and that merely wishing cannot turn back the clock.[60] In the end, against those who favor a general disavowal of responsibility, he rests on a tactical victory by pointing out that if we cannot be blamed for evil deeds because they are in some sense caused, then we have to forego being praised for our good deeds, and this, he assumes, is enough to silence the opposition. Really, of course, it only raises the further question of evaluating praise and blame as human procedures; but Aristotle never questions these.

(3) Choice (*proairesis*, sometimes also translated as "selection" or "preference" or even "decision") is pinned down by contrasting it with desire, passion, and wish, as well as in part with opinion. Desire is too broad; animals have it. Passion is quite unlike choosing, because it lacks deliberation. Wish can be directed to what is known to be impossible (for example, one may wish to be immortal or to be king of all mankind),[61] but no one can choose what he knows to be impossible. Opinion, again, is too wide, for we can have opinions about what is eternal; in addition, opinions are true or false, but choices are good or bad. Of these candidates, opinion comes from the intellectual camp, though it is not the salient intellectual feature; choice proceeds with reason and thinking through, or understanding. The other three candidates, even wish, are all classified as forms of appetite in the discussion of the general initiation of motion.[62] In some sense, choice must then be a combination or fusion of intellectual and appetitive processes.

The differentia that Aristotle offers for choice within the genus of voluntary action is *that there has been prior deliberation.*[63] By this initial definition, choice is thus deliberation that ends in action. A final definition must await the analysis of deliberation.

Deliberation is about things that can be otherwise, about things that can come to be through our action and are attainable by action. This excludes nature and chance as well as necessity. We do not deliberate about what we know completely and can predict wholly—that is, what must be—but about things that do not always produce the same results. Moreover, we do not deliberate about ends; these are the objects of wish. A doctor does not deliberate about whether to cure his patient, or an orator about whether to convince his audience and so on. Accepting the end, they consider how and through what ways it will come to be.[64] If there are many possible ways, they ask which serves the end most easily and best. If there is only one way of reaching the end, deliberation inquires how to achieve it, then seeks the steps to that interim goal, and so on till it works down to the first cause in our power, which is the last in the order of discovery. Aristotle compares this to the method of analyzing in geometry, where the last step in the search is the first in what comes to be, unless some impossibility is discovered. So too in action, for example, "if it requires money and it is not possible to provide it. But if it appears possible, they [the people deliberating] begin to act."[65]

This account faces us with several important problems: (1) Is Aristotle really imposing a rigid means–end model on all deliberation, forced perhaps to do so by his original assumption of a teleology of an ultimate end in human motivation? (b) Do we never really deliberate about ends? (c) To face at last the question raised at the outset of this chapter, is there an inconsistency between Aristotle's teleology and his assertion that we choose virtuous acts for their own sake? (d) What is the relation between deliberation and choice, and how does the resulting picture of choice compare with the traditional conception of the will? In other words, does Aristotle have a concept of the will, is he on the road to one, or is he heading in another direction?

(a) Aristotle says we do not deliberate about ends (*peri tōn telōn*) but about, literally, the things in relation to ends (*peri tōn pros ta telē*). This is usually translated as "the means," and *pros* is taken in a directional sense: the things *toward* the ends. This translation is unduly constricted; for *pros ti* is also Aristotle's technical term for the category of relation, so that *pros ta telē* can be more generally construed as referring to all the things *in* (relevant) *relation to* the ends.[66] This broader interpretation is supported by Aristotle's list of the kinds of questions pursued in deliberation (including what tools to use and how to use them)[67] and, with respect to the virtues, in determining the mean (the right time, place, person, manner, and so on). Often what is at issue is not the means, but the form in which the end will find particular expression, and that form— virtuous conduct, for instance—is itself pursued for its own sake. Hence while the hierarchical means–end relations are perhaps the clearest case of deliberation, they are only a part of it.

(b) In modern times Aristotle's conception of choice has been much criticized for not admitting deliberation about ends, since it is felt that most serious ethical questions are those of competing ends. If, however, his teleology is taken as providing an ultimate inclusive end of happiness, there remains much to deliberate about, particularly which among many admittedly good ends should be pursued here and now in these conditions. What Aristotle seems to have most in mind when he says we do not deliberate about ends—to judge from contexts and examples—is a parallel with the first principles of a science, which are not questioned in the pursuit of the science, and also with the aims of an enterprise or a profession, which are not questioned in the practice of the profession (the doctor does not ask whether to heal, or the rhetorician whether to persuade). Usually many subordinate ends come between those that do not admit of deliberation and the means or other referential questions that are obviously open to deliberation. Aristotle's own questions about the respective merits of different kinds of life (whether the political or the theoretical life in the ethics, or the Spartan and the Athenian and similar patterns more specifically compared in the *Politics*) are in one sense deliberation about different ends rather than different means.

Here again, as in the discussion of means above, we are faced with the tyranny of the means–end model in modern philosophical thought. It has permeated ethical theory, and so it is not surprising that it has permeated Aristotelian scholarship and even Aristotelian translations. It is correlated with a sharp fact–value distinction in which the end containing the value is separated from the factual means, and each is to be studied separately. Such ethical theories as hedonism, in which all value is concentrated in pleasure as separated from the activity that the pleasure accompanies, prepared the way for these tendencies, and the attempt to have a calculus of pleasure by itself intensified them. Against this movement, the philosophical idealists of the nineteenth and early twentieth centuries developed organic categories of system and analyzed the way a system is expressed in the part–whole relations of things and beings. Some neo-Hegelians, such as Bradley and Bosanquet in England, were much influenced by Aristotle and brought out that side of his ethical framework. In that case one end may be seen as a constitutive part of a wider end, contributing to it neither as an antecedent means nor as a purely instrumental concomitant. Two or more ends with different degrees of independence may contribute to one another within the wider system of which they are constitutive parts.

Aristotle did concern himself (in *Metaphysics* 5) with the analysis of such concepts as whole, part, complete, and the like, and he applied them in detail to biology and in some measure to politics. There is now a growing interest in studying the way in which they enter more intimately into his ethical theory and how they may free its interpretation from the tyranny of the means–end model. Certainly one of the immediate consequences has been to recognize that Aristotle's dictum that there is no deliberation about ends allows a great deal of room for wide reflection about ends. There might even seem to be room all the way to the top, given the wide-open meaning of happiness. In this sense deliberation would be limited only by the conditions that are set for happiness: that it be the ultimate object of striving, complete, self-sufficient, expressing determinate purpose, and the like—indeed the same Apollonian features we noted in chapter 7 in considering Aristotle's attempt to grapple with the infinite and the indeterminate. Whether these almost formal features can be themselves the subject of deliberation is another matter. Aristotle would seem to regard them as inherent in the character of human purposive action. Modern ethical theory could readily see them as constituting a selected goal-pattern to which there are conceivable psychological–

cultural alternatives, and so demanding comparative evaluation. But this would bring us far from the ends of ordinary action.[68]

(c) Most of the difficulties raised at the outset about a possible inconsistency between Aristotle's teleology and his theory of virtue have been dissolved in the light of recent criticism. The teleology of happiness can be regarded as inclusive and thus liberalized; the means–end model has lost its monopoly, and so virtue does not have to be a means. However, the question should be faced directly whether there is an inconsistency in virtuous acts' being done for their own sake, that is, as ends. It should be clear by this time that there is none. They express a pattern of character that supports or tends to yield a mode of life that is happiness. They are not a means to happiness, they are expressions that are happiness. Perhaps they may seem garbed as a means when they call for repression of desire or when they call for sacrifice. Should someone really feel strongly that way, then (as we shall see) perhaps it is not a case of virtue, but of self-control, insofar as he is overcoming temptation to act otherwise. For the typical case, virtuous action is action in which the agent finds pleasure; that is the mark of achieved virtue.

If there is no conflict between doing a virtuous act for its own sake and desiring happiness, there is no conflict between a general purposive motivational structure and the particular form of life in which that structure finds expression. Only in constricted forms of teleology and in constricted forms of expression does such a conflict emerge. Only then has the theoretical question arisen whether Aristotle ought to have abandoned his basic teleology and become some kind of rationalistic intuitionist of a later sort.

(d) Finally, there remains the relation between deliberation and choice, as well as the difference between Aristotle's concept of choice and later conceptions of the will. The object of deliberation and that of choice are the same, "except that what is chosen is already determined; for what is decided from deliberation is what is chosen. For a man who is seeking how he shall act stops when he has carried back the origin of action to himself and to the leading part of himself, for this is the part that chooses."[69] Choice is "the deliberative appetite of things that depend on us [bouleutikē orexis tōn eph' hēmin]; for judging from having deliberated we reach out in accordance with our deliberation."[70]

This account does not seem to make a separate act out of choosing. The term *choice* is almost a term of success or of achievement. We do not first complete deliberation and then engage in an act of choice. The deliberation all along seems to be a shaping up of choice, and when the deliberation is successfully completed the choice has been made and action is on. Choice is thus a name for the fusion of appetite and thought in a situation where appetite has projected an end in its form of wishing something possible and provides the motive power throughout (for thought alone moves nothing in Aristotle's view); thought permeates the whole process and gives shape to appetite. The relation of the two components seems almost to be that of matter and form.

Can choice as so conceived be regarded as an efficient cause in the Aristotelian scheme? It obviously can if no mysterious separate step of willing is inserted in a knife-edge cut between deliberative appetite or appetitive thought that precedes action and action itself. We may take literally Aristotle's analogy that choice begets action as the parent begets the child. There is no separate "begetting" after the sexual mating of male and female; if the intercourse is not followed by offspring, it is like deliberation that reached an unsuccessful outcome. The last step in the coalescing of sperm and ovum and the first step in the existence of offspring are one and the same. Just as here the scientific inquiry can give a fuller picture in terms of which the dividing line of "begetting" can be drawn, so in human action the psychology of the fusion of thought and appetite can give us a fuller picture in terms of which the line between choice and action can be drawn. In both cases there need be no doubt about efficient causation.

Aristotle's concept of choice would appear thus not to be the unitary concept of will as in Augustine and the voluntaristic tradition, nor even to be heading in that direction.[71] The concept of action issuing from choice no doubt requires fuller development and has had it in the history of ethics. It is to be looked for among those philosophers who have geared their concepts of freedom to psychological analyses of the processes involved in choosing, rather than to "free will."

Rational Principle and the Ought

Logos, whether construed as reason, rational principle, formula, or proposition, has a vast task in discerning the mean. The list of "rights" or "oughts" in every context—with respect to time, place, circumstances, persons, sources, manner, and so on—alone shows the far-flung front on which it operates. The variety of aspects where a middle is to be located adds to the work. For example, the virtue of liberality involves not only giving in a proper way, but getting from the right sources. In the *Eudemian Ethics* the profiteer (literally, the one who makes shameful gain) is listed among those who exhibit the corresponding vices.[72] Thus judgments about liberality might in effect evaluate the economic operations of a society. Was Nicias, who is agreed to be an honorable gentleman,[73] really illiberal because his wealth rested on hiring out slaves for work in the silver mines of Laurium? Would Aristotle's opposition to making money out of usury condemn as illiberal even the lavish and graceful spending of the bourgeoisie? The decision lies with the meaning of "determined by rational principle (or reason)" in the judgment of the mean.

We must accordingly consider three main issues. (1) We must decide what we are to understand by *rational principle* in Aristotle's use of the term, or how we are to go about understanding it. (2) Since that term completes the complex of virtue–mean–reason (except for the man of practical wisdom), we must see how the complex is anchored in the whole field of the virtues themselves, at least to note what lessons the virtues might contribute to ethical understanding. (3) We must pinpoint the Aristotelian conception of *ought* or *right* and face the difficult question whether it is anything like our own concept of moral obligation.

(1) A simple way to interpret *rational principle* is to see it as referring to the use of reason. This is too general, because for Aristotle reason covers a multitude of faculties. At the outset of book 6 of the *Nicomachean Ethics*, which deals with the intellectual virtues, Aristotle sets out to explain the rational principle involved in the mean. He assumes that the part of the human being that has reason divides into two: one is the epistemic capacity or faculty; the other is the logistic power or calculative faculty, so called because calculation is the same as deliberation.[74] One part thus is addressed to the eternal, the other to the changing or what can be otherwise.

From this it follows that whatever else the rational principle may be, it is not to be construed in Kantian fashion as furnishing moral rules for some other faculty to apply.[75] No doubt reason always involves some element of generality. The kind of generality here at issue was indicated by Aristotle in his previous analysis of deliberation: "Deliberation concerns things that happen for the most part, but are unclear as to how they will turn out; and in matters where the issue is indeterminate, and we call upon fellow counsellors in important matters, mistrusting ourselves as not sufficiently able to decide."[76] The calculative faculty in moral deliberation and in determining the mean thus engages in reckoning and weighing and discriminating in relation to particulars, rather than in universalizing or generalizing. Now if we look for an account of this kind of rationality in Aristotle, we discover very much what we saw in the treatment of induction: an account of how a rational being develops and stabilizes habits in experience so as to have the precise fund of universals in the psyche, and the appropriate intellectual virtues and sense of relevance and insight in application, to determine the just-right. This would send us along the ethical network to the man of practical wisdom. Before we move on, let us see what can be gathered from the experience of rationality in its applications, and particularly in the anchoring of the virtues.

It was noted above, in considering the meaning of the mean, that some attempts have been made to narrow its sense to a notion of proportion, and comparable suggestions have been made for *logos*.[77] The conclusion proposed above was that in the light of Aristotle's general recognition that broad philosophical terms are used by analogy in different fields, we should regard the mean in the definition of virtue as offering a *schema* rather than a specific model or formula. Applying this policy here, "determined by a rational principle" would mean simply "determined by the calculative faculty." It would remain open to try out in different specific contexts of different virtues in different fields whatever models might be proposed from other areas, whether physiological or psychological, musical or mathematical. These should no longer be seen as proposed meanings of *logos* but as concretizations that may fit and clarify a particular area (for example, the great complexities of seeing justice as a mean). This enterprise cannot, of course, be dealt with here. It not only indicates a problem of research in Aristotle; it suggests for ethics generally the task of trying out useful models from other fields on the different materials of morality without imposing them dogmatically on the whole moral domain.

Finally, there is Aristotle's occasional use of the phrase *orthos logos* (right reason or rational principle). For example, in his summary just before discussing the particular virtues, Aristotle speaks of the virtues' leading us to actions as the right reason enjoins.[78] If we take this to be "the right rule" (the right formula), we are back to a more specific sense; if we take it as right reason in general, we may engender subtle disputes over whether there can really be a "wrong reason." On the whole, in the way it is used in the book, there seems little difference in Aristotle's usage between *reason* and *right reason*, although there could of course be mistakes in reckoning, that is, in the exercise of the calculative faculty, and there is a genuine question (to be considered later) whether the vicious man is following a wrong rationality of his own or has abandoned rationality completely. In general, the right rule can be identified with what conforms to practical reason.[79]

(2) Let us note briefly how extensively the whole complex of virtue–mean–reason is anchored in the actual virtues that constitute a large part of the moral pattern of a society. This bulks larger than in many other ethical theories where more is invested in codes of moral rules. In this respect Aristotle's ethics is predominantly an ethics of virtue, in spite of being set in a goal-framework. The description of the particular virtues constitutes a quarter of the *Nicomachean Ethics*, if we consider justice

under the rubric of virtue in his analysis. This is the moral virtues alone, not the intellectual virtues. Now so vast a domain embodies within itself the collective funded reactions and appreciations of character and personality in a culture. It is the patterned direction of praise and blame addressed to persons, refined in reflection and introspection. In modern ethics, which has been more oriented to right and obligation than to virtue, the corresponding domain would be intuitions about what is right or wrong in particular situations (as well as counterintuitions). Virtue, then, provides an extensive domain of moral data, not in the sense of unchallengeable truths, but precisely in the Aristotelian sense of the *endoxa*, the common beliefs that serve as raw material for moral reflection. In virtue, they include both the reactions of sensibility and the different extensions, generalizations, delimitations, and interpretations of them, both customary evaluations and sensitive critical reevaluations. Clearly as human experience grows and is refined in such a domain, the lessons for the concept of virtue and the subformulae for reckoning or calculating will be handed on in the selection of authoritative figures or moral models in the man of practical wisdom. Aristotle, of course, does not have this in mind. He is, rather, concerned with establishing a fixed framework of virtue. But in historical perspective this growth of experience is clearly one of the places where localisms and provincialisms and cultural specializations are most easily discerned. Detailed study of the Aristotelian virtues is not only fruitful in this respect, but would be fruitful also for distilling perennial elements and discovering broad alternative possibilities in the human repertoire.[80]

(3) Our final problem is the nature of the *oughts* that appear in the description of the mean in the particular virtues. Here the individual, facing a decision, has to determine what the mean, the just-right, is with respect to a whole string of factors—time, place, persons, circumstances, manner—in the act that he is contemplating. Thus to exhibit courage he has to measure out the proper degrees of fear and confidence; to exhibit liberality, the proper amount of giving and taking; and so on for the rest of the relevant virtues in the situation. Translators vary in the language they employ for the parameters here. Some say "at the right time, on the right occasion, toward the right people, for the right purpose, in the right manner," while others (probably more often) say "when he ought, in the way he ought, toward those he ought," and so on. Either way of translating is likely to convey modern meanings of right and wrong, duty and obligation, and so to be regarded as expressing Aristotle's theory of that part of ethics which in contemporary moral philosophy falls under the heading of the ought. (A similar historical problem arose above in our discussion of the will.) Since Aristotle's treatment here does not satisfy

contemporary analyses of *ought* (for example, the universalism so often proclaimed as the core of our notion of "I ought"), he is often criticized for not having worked out an adequate theory of obligation. It is rarely considered that he may be moving in a different direction.

The question whether ancient morality and modern morality are on a single line of development is no new one. It was much debated in the early part of our century and has become thoroughly interwoven with such controversial issues as the existence of a single absolute or correct morality to which all moralities and all moral theories at all times are partial approximations, a possibly discoverable development in human history such that the later represents a higher stage, and the validity of the modern pattern of a universalistic morality with its ideas of duty and conscience. It is worth examining an illustration of this controversy to see how it impinges on actual interpretation of the Aristotelian text, and to raise the question how our problem of the meaning of *ought* in Aristotle is best to be dealt with.

Gauthier's *La Morale d'Aristote* has it that in Aristotle's morality there is a *duty to be happy*; admittedly the expression is not found in Aristotle, but it translates his thought well.[81] Further, since in our usage right is the correlative of duty, Gauthier has Aristotle committed to a right to be happy. Aristotle is thus brought quite directly within our own moral framework. In discussing the virtues, Gauthier's translation for what the English renders with a string of "oughts" is "ce qu'on doit," "quand on le doit," and so forth, and he apparently sees no problem in having what we ought to do prescribed by "la règle morale."[82] The issue comes to a head after a brief discussion of the noble (*kalon*). Gauthier explains that the primary moral use of *ought* in relation to the mean is "in the conformity of the action to the rational rule that is its measure and that makes it a *duty* to us."[83] (Duty has here become a working concept in the explication of Aristotle, not just an interpreter's conceptual device or comparison.) At this point Gauthier dismisses Brochard's view that there is no idea of duty in Aristotle's morality. He offers a statistical refutation with respect to the term for *ought*, the Greek word *dein*, which is used in the strings of oughts or rights in connection with the mean. He says that in the *Nicomachean Ethics* alone, apart from its use a hundred times in a nonmoral sense, it occurs about 170 times in an incontestably moral sense. He proceeds to refer to some of them, but they are of course the ones in the accounts of the virtues or comparable ones that initiate the original inquiry. To show further that Aristotle has a fairly clear idea of duty, Gauthier points to Aristotle's identification of what one ought to do with what the right rule orders. Thus he thinks that Aristotle conceived the right rule (*orthos logos*) in some contexts not merely as providing the measure but as going beyond, expressing *imperative* and *law*.[84]

Gauthier has carried Aristotle pretty far into the modern pattern, with duty and right, imperative and moral law. He cannot of course bring him all the way, for the concepts of sin and conscience so fundamental to the modern sense of duty are lacking. Aristotle's humanistic disregard of sin comes from pushing to the extreme an ethics of wisdom that concentrates on the means before action in optimistic expectation of what can be achieved.

Brochard, whom Gauthier so brusquely dismissed in a sentence, was the serious proponent of a diametrically opposing thesis. His "La morale ancienne et la morale moderne" insists that the idea of duty or obligation is completely absent from ancient morality, and that there is no word to express it.[85] Similarly, he argues that "moral law," "unwritten law," and any Greek term that is so rendered means merely "custom."[86] He finds Greek morality less imperative than optative, reliant on models and ideals rather than on commands. Modern ideas of duty and moral law arise from the Judeo-Christian religious tradition and are reflected in the Kantian ethics; notions of sin and conscience are thus shaped by a belief in the evil character of the natural world. The ancient conception of the pursuit of happiness as the human end had no room for such notions. (Even Plato, Brochard argues, the one definite believer in immortality, does not put his religious view into his ethical theory, but adds it as a further inducement to virtue after his ethics is fully presented in humanistic terms.) Brochard does not want Aristotle to be modernized; he wants him to be understood as he was. It is interesting to note further that Brochard does not think the two systems will mix. He objects to modern attempts at moral eclecticism, on the principle that it is better to give to the Church what is the Church's, and to Aristotle what is Aristotle's.[87] Lest one think he has no preference, his concluding view is that just as Aristotle's *Organon* laid the theoretical foundations of immutable logic, so his *Nicomachean Ethics* laid the theoretical foundations of eternal morality.[88]

Clearly, then, behind these opposing views there is a conflict between religious morality and secular humanistic morality, with Aristotle as the prize. This general intellectual battle has been going on since the French Revolution. It is hard on the innocent student of classical philosophy, when he approaches the texts of Aristotle in the late twentieth century, to become embroiled in the intellectual aftereffects of almost two centuries of turmoil. How is he going to decide, when he reads *hōs dei*, whether it means "as duty [or the moral law] decrees" or something quite different? Can he just take it in his stride with "as he ought" and let it go at that without asking what "ought" meant for Aristotle?

The lexical question ought to be isolated and treated in its own terms, although this is not always possible. The conceptual question should be handled frankly in line with an awareness about how concepts in ethics are to be handled, so that if such ideas change there can be a reconsideration of the results previously secured. Gauthier assumed that there was a single correct theory of morals. That was probably why he so readily inserted the language of duty into Aristotle's ethics and followed up with interpretations of the evidence that allowed the rest of his terminology. Brochard was adopting initially the assumption that was becoming more acceptable, that there were cultural differences of possibly ultimate kinds. The theory of ethical analysis has advanced considerably beyond these limits and no longer operates in terms of fixed isolated concepts. No matter what the differences in schools, there is now recognition of conceptual uses or functions—the possibility of different functions for the "same" concept in different contexts, and the possibility that the same function may be carried out under different concepts. There is also recognition of the complexity underlying the apparent simplicity in a concept, and thus of the need for analytic unpacking. In comparing ancient and modern uses, it is quite possible that even the "same" components may be scattered in different conceptual bundles.

As for the lexical question, the Greek word employed in the string of oughts is, as noted earlier, *dei* (the impersonal third person of the verb *deō*). Its root sense is most probably lack or need or require. Hence the list of oughts is really a list of what is in different respects needed or required or appropriate or proper or fitting.

As for the conceptual question, we may start by listing some of the functions that our modern concept of *ought* has been found to serve and then go on to see whether and where such functions are dealt with by Aristotle. Apart from the means–end relation of the hypothetical imperative ("If you want this, you ought to do that"), which is often a nonmoral usage, one can distinguish at least three functions in our modern *ought*. (1) It expresses acceptance of a legislative *universal*: to say "I ought to do this" is to entail "Anyone in such-and-such a situation ought to do such-and-such an act." (2) It is judgmental, or *decisional*, for the particular situation; there may be several applicable rules of right or *prima facie* duties, but the expression "I ought" sums up the result of a reflective reckoning. (3) It is *prescriptive* in commanding or ordering. Now every morality will need some generality, some particular deciding, and some authoritative prescribing. There are different kinds of generality (Aristotle denied, as we saw, a rigid eternal unvarying universal for morality in the domain where things can be otherwise), different concepts for judgmental decision (honorable, noble, useful, profitable, or expedient), and different kinds of authority (autocratic, parental, consensual-democratic). As different patterns of these are internalized, we develop different forms of sensibility, of which our traditional conscience with its strictly dichotomous notion of right-or-wrong and its stress on guilt is only one pattern. And—what is immediately relevant here—the different functions need not all be packed in one concept or one linguistic bundle, as they tend to be in our concept of *ought*.

What we find in Aristotle is that the three functions are handled separately. The second of the functions, the judgmental or decisional application for particular situations, is the one that is carried by *dei*. It does no generalizing and states no universal laws. To discern the mean is indeed to discern what ought to be done in the particular situation, but it is not our kind of ought; it has rather a conceptual quality of fittingness, and it is what fits the particular situation. For the other functions we have to look in different conceptual and linguistic directions.

The nearest thing to generality in ethics is to be found in the treatment of justice. Aristotle distinguishes two forms of political justice, one of which is natural, the other conventional.[89] In the general types of naturally just relations we might have expected to find universal moral rules universally applicable; but Aristotle does not develop this aspect to any great extent.[90]

Finally, the prescriptive or commanding function takes two distinct forms. One is the authoritative character ascribed to the rational part of man; to have a judgment made by reason involves an embedded order or command. In this mode the use of the rational principle in the analysis of the mean ties a prescriptive element to the decisional. The second form lies in the suffix *-ton* and *-teon*, as in *epaineton* (to be praised) or *haireton* (to be chosen) or *timēteon* (to be honored). The *-ton* ending conveys the object of the act, and so usually the capacity for being acted upon, for instance, being praised or chosen; this slips readily in many contexts into the value quality of expressions like "praiseworthy," with a general prescriptive tone. The *-teon* ending carries a future reference and so seems in its use to be more clearly prescriptive. It is interesting to note that at one point in the *Magna Moralia* the distinction is utilized for a philosophical purpose: in the context of what is loved or wished for, *-ton* is said to indicate what is simply to be loved or lovable, *-teon* what is so for a particular individual.[91] While this probably does not capture Aristotle's general usage, it does show a sensitivity to the task of differentiating linguistic expressions for different shades of ethical function.

In general, then, Aristotle's notion of *ought* as it appears in the accounts of the mean is that of doing what is *fitting* in the full complexity of the situation, with a sensitive rational view of all the relevant factors. It is not an arbitrary relativism, since he assumes that every situation has its correct answer. It is not a universal rule or legislative one; it has a tinge of generality suggested by the rational element, but that rationality is rather one of reckoning than of legislating. It has a certain authoritative component but it is less sheer command than the assent that reason wins or the respect that is willingly given to a role model. Phenomenologically, it is quite different from the modern notion of obligation that was born of a religious conscience in a legalistic moral framework. From the point of view of the comparative study of moral systems, it carries out some of the major functions that a concept of obligation is entrusted with, while others are shipped elsewhere in the moral structure.[92]

Practical Wisdom

Practical wisdom as an intellectual virtue is treated in book 6 of the *Nicomachean Ethics*, among the faculties of mind that we examined all together in our discussion of logic and science. The notion is a kind of copestone in the ethical theory; comparable conceptions are found in some modern ethical theories that go so far as to equate the meaning of an ethical statement with the reaction of an "ideal observer" to the proposed conduct. This is one of the points at which the conceptual network of Aristotle's ethics can readily be anchored—if one could find a way to select the man of practical wisdom. Then we could observe and generalize his behavior and try to feel about things the way he does, in the hope of being able to make specific judgments as he would make them. This is in fact the procedure Aristotle describes in the young and immature who are guided by feelings of nobility.

Obviously the task of identification is not so simple. In an authoritarian society, children might come to regard their parents in this way, and monarchs have certainly wished their subjects so to look upon them. We cannot, however, dispense with a theoretical understanding of what makes a man of practical wisdom. Even if every time we met one we saw a halo around his head, or felt a very unique identifiable internal glow, we would want to know why he grew the halo or how he produced the glow. What otherwise would we do with the claim that X had a halo but that we were too wicked to see it? Modern uses of the concept of an ideal observer usually begin by specifying him as impartial and disinterested and thoroughly informed on the facts, but are drawn on and on until they either articulate a large part of morality explicitly or else do it implicitly in an account of how that observer is to be brought up.[93]

Aristotle's analysis begins with the distinction we have noted between the epistemic faculty of the human intellect, concerned with what cannot be otherwise and knowing the truth, and the logistic or calculative faculty, concerned with what can be otherwise and guiding action. Calculation is the same as deliberation. We considered the virtues and abilities that involve the epistemic faculty when we dealt with Aristotle's theory of knowledge. Here discussion will be limited to *practical wisdom*, which is the virtue of the calculative faculty.

Aristotle's treatment of practical wisdom proceeds in two different directions. In one he distinguishes it from other intellectual capacities by its connection with moral virtue. In the other he distinguishes it from moral virtue by pointing to its intellectual character. But then he has the job of showing how it ties in with moral virtue. In this he is somewhat hampered by the sharp separation he had originally made between intellectual and moral virtue. Only near the end (in chapter 13) does he embark on a reconsideration that (if it had been carried through) would have shown so intimate a relation between intellect and habit as to justify abandoning a sharp distinction between the two types of virtue.

Two preliminary comments are relevant. One concerns Aristotle's method of defining a complex idea by its final or perfect form. The other brings us to the point raised earlier about misunderstandings that may arise from reliance on a means–end model.

Both for understanding practical wisdom and for formulating the issues later in dealing with continence and incontinence, it is important to realize how Aristotle analyzes a concept that refers to a developmental process. He does it by working with the completed state or condition *on the assumption that the development has been successful*. This is the same as describing the human being by the properties to be found in the mature and normal adult. What happens when the development is over but not successful can then be considered. It is not just that a given component is missing or has emerged differently; the other parts may also be functioning differently as a result of its absence or deviation. It is not an analysis into mechanical parts each of which is satisfactory but which do not mesh properly with one another. Each of the parts may be different because the development went astray.

The relation of practical wisdom and moral virtue is likely to be misunderstood if it is approached with an insistence solely on the means–end model—for example, with the interpretation that practical wisdom furnishes the means and moral virtue furnishes the end. Some of Aristotle's formulations, we shall see, do sound like that. But it was suggested earlier that in the analysis of deliberation the term translated "means," *ta pros ta telē*, should be construed more broadly as things related to the end; in fact the clear example of means at that point was the special case in which there was only one way to reach the end.

Both of these points are reinforced immediately after the epistemic is divided from the calculative reason. At the beginning of chapter 2 he notes that the virtue of a state of character or faculty (*hexis*) is related to its own special work. He reverts to his psychological theory and points out three elements in the psyche that control action and truth: sensation, intellect, and appetite. Dismissing sensation as not originating action, he is left with intellect and appetite, the two elements in his definition of choice. He goes on: "Since moral virtue is a state of character involving choice, and choice is deliberative appetite, the rational principle must on this account be true and the desire right, if the choice is good [spoudaia], and the principle must affirm and the appetite pursue the same things."[94] This, in short, is the ideal case of complete and mature development. The speculative intellect is concerned only with truth and falsity, but of course it is not concerned with action (praxis) or production (poiēsis). Truth is the aim of every part of the intellect, but for the practical intellect it is truth in agreement with right appetite. It is significant that he speaks here of the practical intellect's referring to praxis, not poiēsis. He continues with points that are familiar, but their resumption here is significant: choice involves both appetite and that reason which is for the sake of something; motion cannot be initiated by thought by itself, but only by thought that is for the sake of something and deals with action; production or making also is for the sake of something; in praxis, however, what is done is an end, since doing well is an end and this is what the appetite aims at.[95] His reversible formulation of choice as appetitive thought or thoughtful appetite shows the extent of their unity.

Aristotle has thus labored mightily to explicate the mature type of moral choice. He has at the same time focused on the difference between action or conduct, which has its end within itself, and production, whose end lies beyond itself. In virtuous action, it will be recalled, the agent does the noble thing for its own sake. The traditional means—end sequence of production is quite simple compared to the complex things relating to the end that practical wisdom has to discern in pinpointing the mean in its numerous contextual relations. In dealing with art (technē) in chapter 4 of book 6 Aristotle continues to insist that the rational character of praxis is different from that of poiēsis.

In chapter 5 Aristotle at last attempts a definition of practical wisdom (phronēsis). He is here engaged in studying intellectual powers and virtues, so of course the definition is directed toward setting practical wisdom off from the others: it is "a truthful state embodying reason, concerned with action about what is good and bad for man."[96] A significant difference from art is that voluntary error in art is preferable to involuntary, but in practical wisdom it is worse. Practical wisdom is imbued with moral virtue or right appetite, whereas art is more like a "neutral" skill.

Practical wisdom weaves its way through the discussion of the other intellectual states. Its status is below wisdom (sophia); the latter is directed toward universal truths, and practical wisdom deals only with particular applications to human affairs. Indeed experience with particulars is more important for it than general formulations without application. Practical wisdom and political judgment are akin in this respect; you do not expect the young, without experience, to have either of those, though they can be good mathematicians.

The character of the intellectual processes in practical wisdom emerges from comparison with other intellectual states and skills. Extremely important is the comparison with intuitive reason (*nous*). Practical wisdom, too, deals with an ultimate (*eschaton*)—not like the ultimate simple concepts that *nous* grasps, but rather like the ultimate for sensation. Here too it is not like the kind of perception the special senses have, but rather like that whereby we perceive in mathematics that the ultimate figure is a triangle. This is a difficult passage, varyingly interpreted.[97] Traditional interpretations tend to take *ultimate* to refer to a particular, so that we would have here some kind of immediate intellectual intuition of the particular akin to the sensory grasp of a perceptual quality. Since we are dealing with the man of practical wisdom as he determines what is to be done—the culmination of the conceptual analysis of the network— this interpretation in terms of a quasi-perceptual intuition may mislead modern readers into thinking that Aristotle resorts to some kind of ethical intuitionism. Of course some philosophical schools would be insulated against this, since their analysis of sensation precludes intuitionism; Hegelian idealism, for example, insists there is already a large measure of interpretation, never just brute datum, in sensation as such. Accordingly, any particular that practical wisdom perceives is already an interpreted particular, not just an intuition of rightness as such—even if it is rightness that is being "sensed."[98]

In any case, the prior question is the interpretation of the text here. Recent study has undercut the traditional interpretation. While experience is, of course, concerned with particular situations and involves insight into their character or form or type, the ultimate (*eschaton*) that is the object of insight in this context is not the particular as such but the *last step* in the process of deliberation. As John Cooper states it in his examination of the textual evidence, "Aristotle has in mind here a geometer analyzing a process of construction, and the perception in question seems to be that by which he recognizes that the particular problem he is working on has been solved, once he has found a figure, a triangle, that he already knows how to construct, from which he can, by following the steps of the analysis in reverse, produce the desired figure. So the corresponding perception in the case of deliberation would be the agent's recognition that he has found something he can employ to attain his end without further calculation."[99] This use of insight, experience, particulars, and analysis is quite consonant with Aristotle's whole methodology.

Some intellectual processes and skills fit almost too neatly within practical wisdom. For example, in chapter 9, *deliberative excellence* turns out to be a kind of correctness. But a man who has no self-control or exhibits vice rather than virtue may correctly achieve something evil after deliberating. Hence Aristotle defines deliberative excellence as hitting the mark that is good. Yet this might be done by accident. So the final definition is "a correctness with respect to what conduces to the end, of which practical wisdom is a true understanding."[100] Once again, the definition is in terms of the ideal mature situation. (A simple parallel is the refusal sometimes found in modern ethical literature to define "good as a means" as purely "useful to the end in view," and the insistence on defining it as "useful means for a good end.")

In the comparison with understanding, which also deals with things about which we deliberate, practical wisdom is authoritative, whereas understanding is merely judgmental. This looks like the prescriptive element, noted earlier, that is added to the recognition of what is fitting by the judgment emanating from reason.[101]

Once the review of intellectual capacities is over, the analysis of practical wisdom is aimed toward moral virtue. In chapter 12 Aristotle raises the interesting question of what use practical wisdom can be. Since it studies what is just and fine and good for a man, are not these precisely what a good man will do as a matter of course?[102] If the virtues are states of character, knowing them will not add to our capacity for acting according to them, any more than a study of medicine makes us more vigorous. Even if the study of virtue helps make us virtuous, it is not necessary once we are virtuous. We do not learn medicine just because we want to be healthy.

Of course Aristotle answers that both wisdom and practical wisdom as virtues of the intellect are desirable in themselves apart from consequences. Still, practical wisdom has a practical function. It joins with moral virtue in the complete performance of man's work (*ergon*). Then comes a sentence that has generated enormous controversy: "For virtue makes the mark [*skopos*, object sighted] right, and practical wisdom provides the things related to that."[103] If we take this as referring to setting up the end as a target and devising means, then the nature of practical wisdom is reduced to mere means, virtue to dealing with the end; and all the problems of the contemporary means—end and fact—value dichotomy are saddled on Aristotle.

If, however, we recall that practical wisdom is concretizing the actions that are done for their own sake, then there is no fresh partition here involved, but simply a reference to the familiar role of appetite and reason in choice. In the structure of a situation of choice there is wish for the end, and wish is a form of appetite. There is the motor power of desire throughout, which is again appetite. Intellect gives a specific character to the end: one does not just wish, but wishes for something. It turns appetitive force into specific desire, and it sets the direction toward particular action in appropriate time, place, person, manner, and so on. All this is deliberated on so as to yield *praxis*, which is action done for its own sake. Will it really be possible to partition this whole complex unity into a separate end from one source and a separate means from another? For that matter, virtue does not, in the critical passage cited, even literally set up the end, but makes the mark right! That is, moral virtue ensures that whatever mark the person aims at will be a good one. Indeed, Aristotle goes on to spell all this out, explaining that it is possible to do the acts that a virtuous man would do but without the inner character that virtue demands. There is a faculty of cleverness, he says, that can work out for us how to hit a mark. Here he begins to think in terms of a good or supreme good that is presupposed in reasoning on practical matters. And he reasserts the unity of practical wisdom and the grasp of the good. One cannot be a man of practical wisdom without being good.[104] The word for "good" here is *agathon*, not just *spoudaion* (moral). The full maturity of thought is required. Cleverness alone for any end will not do.

In the concluding reconsideration in chapter 13 Aristotle makes the same division for moral virtue that he has made all along for intellectual aspects. Excellence in deliberation is not practical wisdom; neither is cleverness by itself; but both have a relation to practical wisdom. So too natural virtue has a relation to complete virtue.[105] Aristotle is simply reaffirming that practical wisdom is the culmination of a development on both sides of choice. The natural tendencies to do the right thing are the raw material out of which the finished product of character, the truly good, takes shape. The intelligence that operates if the development is not consummated is different from the intelligence in the mature product. In the light of this lesson, the conception of virtue is itself clarified: "For not only is the state of character that is according to the right principle virtue, but that which shares in the right principle. And the right principle about such things is practical wisdom."[106] In this distinction between "according to" and "shares in" (*kata ton orthon logon* and *meta tou orthou logou*), Aristotle is contrasting moral virtue in which the habit of good action is established and moral virtue in which the rational element is alive at every point. He is not just talking of natural virtue in the first place, nor of a person who understands fully how he came to have the habits he does, in the second place.

Aristotle is so concerned with showing the complete unity in the good man that he faces here a problem he has barely touched hitherto: whether a person can have some of the virtues and not others. He says it is possible if we are dealing with natural virtue, but not with practical wisdom. If one has practical wisdom, one has all the virtues. In the *Magna Moralia* the same issue is raised practically as the conflict of virtues in a situation in which both cannot be exercised (for example, shall one act bravely or justly?).[107] The answer is the same: there may be a conflict on the impulsive level, but not if there is deliberate choice with rational solution. Practical wisdom involves the working together of all the virtues under its own guidance. In the end it is clear that practical wisdom is not an isolated virtue, but the whole virtuous man, well-developed and intellectually equipped, functioning in relation to particular situations.

Aristotle has worked practical wisdom into an ideal of the culmination of moral development in which not only the separation of the moral virtues from the intellectual is overcome, but the sharp separation of the virtues from one another is weakened. Though he does not go back to refashion his earlier treatment of moral virtue and perhaps does not realize how far he has abandoned the presuppositions of the early view of rationality, he nevertheless fully employs his advances in analysis when he comes to study continence and incontinence, the imperfect character patterns in which the development of virtue has not been achieved.

The Real Good and the Apparent Good

The last concept in the network that operates in Aristotle's moral philosophy as we have analyzed it is a distinction between the real and the apparent good. It is not discussed in any one part of the book, as the others are, but it shows up in different contexts to solve difficulties. It keeps open the possibility that a person may have made a mistake in judging the good. Controversies have erupted throughout the history of philosophy about the dangers of arguing from the desired to the desirable, from what one wants and can do to do what is worth doing. The distinction between the apparent and the real good is one way of engendering inquiry about the morality of one's desires and tendencies. Of course it is not the only way. A man might more readily ask in the Aristotelian framework whether what he proposed to do is what a man of practical wisdom would advise. Then if we asked why the verdict of practical wisdom is superior and authoritative, the answer would be, as already seen, that it applies the knowledge of the good to the particular situation.

The notion of a *man of practical wisdom* is anchored to figures accepted as authoritative or as guiding models of leadership. In the long run, however, human beings outgrow particular models and realize what features in different models give them their strength. There is today a whole theory of authority figures and why we use them, as well as of the ethics of advice, that goes far beyond the Aristotelian picture and can enrich it. But even in the terms that Aristotle presents, much can be learned from considering the way the man of practical wisdom would justify his own judgment. He would not say, "It is my intuition and I am a man of practical wisdom." He would be led back to a discussion of the good in that situation, the factors of choice, the interplay of the appetitive and the intellectual, and the reason why some lines that seemed to lead to the good would not really do so. The return, with all that has been gained in the process, would redound to the clarification of the good.

At one point in the *Topics* Aristotle raises the question of where the qualification *apparent* (*phainomenon*) should be used.[108] Should we say, for example, that wish is for the good and desire is an appetite for the pleasant, or should we speak of the apparent good and the apparent pleasant? People do not realize that the object may not be good or pleasant; the qualification would thus seem necessary. But if one allows this, strange consequences follow. Aristotle traces them in terms of the belief in Platonic Ideas: there would have to be an Idea of the apparent good. Perhaps the point can be made without that reference: a person who says that he wants this orange, wants the orange and not the apparent orange, even if it turns out that he was mistaken in his perception and there was no orange before him. *Apparent* has to do with what went wrong in the process of looking or the process of desiring. It does not refer to a different object substituted for the real object. In another context Aristotle makes a suggestion about what can go wrong in identifying the object of desire.[109] The particular thing desired can have many relations: it may be desired as an end (health, for instance) or as a means (if it is the medicine that is desired), or as an accidental circumstance. The illustration given for the last of these is the man who desires wine not because it is wine but because it is sweet; his essential desire is for the sweet, and that for the wine is only accidental. The distinction between the accidental and the essential here could explain why men go astray in describing the object of desire. A desire for something under a given description may be misdirected: when the individual wants wine and rejects dry wine, his essential desire is for sweetness.

The contrast of the real and the apparent with respect to the factors of choice could go in two directions. Opinion or belief, the intellectual factor, can be true or false, as compared to knowledge, which is of what is the case (see chapter 12 above). As to the appetitive factor, Aristotle raises the question about wish.[110] Some hold that wish is of the good, others that it is of the apparent good. If we use the first formulation, we have to say that when a man made a mistake about the end, the object of his wish was not wished for. Those who take the second formulation imply that there is no natural object of wish or a natural good. Both views are unacceptable, so Aristotle settles it with a distinction: simply and in truth, the object of wish is the good; but for each individual the object of wish is what appears good to him. Yet if he is a good man (*spoudaios*), the object of his wish is in fact the true good.

Here two different questions cross, and their overlapping may produce a confusion. The real and the apparent is one matter; the general and the particular is another. Thus we may raise the question whether long-distance running is really good for man, or only apparently good because it is classified with exercise, which we know to be good. Suppose the answer is that it is really good. We could now ask the second question: whether, even if it really is good for man, it is good for John (who happens to have a bad heart); the answer is no, and it is really not good for John. But the question is crossed by John, if he assumes that because it is really good for man it is really good for him. Aristotle at times speaks as if the real good were what appears so to the man in normal condition and the apparent good were what the man in deviant condition perceives. But this is only because the question is about the normal reaction. For example, is sugar sweet? Don't ask the man who is ill, just as you would not ask the man with a fever whether the room is hot. But even the normal appearance may be known to be deceptive when we have fuller knowledge (the apparent size of the sun, for instance, is just a foot across).[111] Where relevant, Aristotle definitely distinguishes general–individual and real–apparent from one another. For example, he asks whether men love the good or what is good for themselves, which may sometimes differ.[112] He decides that while what is good without qualification is the object of love, for each man what is good for him is the object of love. And then he moves on to the separate question of each man loving what appears good for him rather than what is good for him.

Where the context is clear enough to avoid misunderstanding, a number of criteria are employed by Aristotle. For example, he may be establishing norms for goodness and pleasantness, not denying that the appearance appears. Thus he invokes the contrast of the healthy body and the sick body,[113] the uncorrupted and the corrupted taste (he is vehement about the pleasanter wine not being that pleasant to a man who has been drinking hard and even has put sharp vinegar into his wine), the adult and the child, the wise man and the foolish man. And once in a while. the appeal is to what is natural or not natural.[114]

The distinction of the apparent and the real is thus anchored in specific contexts embodying knowledge of stages in a developmental process, or of the conditions of the normal as against the deviant, or the operation of an already articulated standard. It offers no independent input into the moral operations, but helps route the judgmental process of reason and practical wisdom back to the established knowledge of the good.

The attempt in this chapter has been to show how a network analysis brings out the fuller structure of Aristotle's ethics, the relation of the concepts he employs (those that operate in the background as well as those in the foreground), their material relations and the presuppositions concerning their habitual contexts, and the lines that connect them to the rest of Aristotle's philosophical outlook. In these respects it has been claimed that a network analysis is more successful in giving a comprehensive understanding of the ethical theory of a philosopher than either treating it formally on the basis of a selected one or two primitive concepts to which the rest are reduced or taking an informalist approach in which the relation of the contexts would tend to be lost.

It is tempting to say that Aristotle's ethics submits to a network analysis because he does his ethics that way, just as he has nature analyzed teleologically because nature works like the artist. We have resisted that temptation and treated the mode of analysis throughout as our way of analyzing his works. Still, his ethics is more readily analyzable in this way than, for example, Kant's ethics would be or hedonistic ethics, both of which focus on one central concept. The challenge for a network mode of analysis would be to show that when carried out in detail in those cases too it will bring a deeper understanding of the specific historical moral philosophies. This is what is being suggested with the Aristotelian investigation as a case study.

Normative consequences also follow for ethical construction from consciously using a network analysis of ethical concepts and their anchoring. Some were suggested in the criticisms of the static character of Aristotle's structure. With a modern emphasis on the growth of knowledge, refinement at any point in the structure can be passed along to other points, so that an ethical network can become an increasingly powerful and more systematized way for dealing with moral problems. Thus recognition of the merits of the Aristotelian structure does not of course mean setting it up as a final model for moral philosophy, even in its theoretical aspects. There can and have been other theoretical experiments equally broad in scope. For example, Dewey's attempt to slice the field in three parts—the good, tied to the appetitive; the right, tied to mutual claims in the social group; and virtue, tied to interpersonal appreciation and sympathies— was another proposal based on both analytic and historical grounds. And modern value theory constituted a fresh experiment, which has, however, been developed with insufficient sharpness to structure the field.[115] Aristotle's still remains the most integrative of the approaches that have been tried.

17

JUSTICE, INTERNAL CONFLICT,

AND FRIENDSHIP

This chapter examines the three large topics of the *Nicomachean Ethics* not discussed in the previous chapter. Justice is one of the virtues, and its treatment occupies the whole of book 5. Internal conflict, the topic of book 7, goes to the heart of the imperfect forms of virtue, following on the exalted picture of practical wisdom. Friendship constitutes almost a separate treatise, occupying the whole of books 8 and 9. The three topics have little in common save that they are parts of Aristotelian ethical theory, but on the contemporary scene they have been woven together as the core of ethics. Justice occupies a central place in Kantian and post-Kantian ethics, either directly or in the form of the right in contrast to the good. Internal conflict, the struggle of principle with temptation, becomes the hallmark of the moral situation, for the completely virtuous man no longer defines the moral agent. Finally, duties of self to others becomes the form in which the large classifications of ethical problems are cast, with the struggle of egoism and altruism at the center. The three become interwoven inasmuch as justice furnishes the principles and the conflict is whether to obey them or gratify the self, usually to the detriment of others. It is salutary to examine these themes before they attained their present dominance. The study of Aristotle gives us a fresh insight into the shape they can have a under a different conceptual structure.

Justice

In modern ethics justice is usually discussed as a moral principle of right and wrong, or of social organization. For Aristotle it is chiefly a moral virtue. Yet these are connected, because principles may be relevant in some of the fields in which the just man exhibits his justice. If, for example, he distributes something, there may be principles that determine whether he has made a virtuous choice. So too for domestic justice in the attitudes of the father and for political justice in the judgments of the ruler. On the whole, however, as we have seen, the interpretation of virtue as a mean does not readily yield a formulation of rules and principles, but rather judgments of practical wisdom in particular complex situations. There is one formulation of a wholesale sort (in the *Eudemian Ethics*) where, in a list of mean-regarding virtues alongside of extreme-regarding vices, justice is said to be a mean between the extremes of pursuit of profit from any source and loss (in the sense of neglect or waste).[1] Aristotle is seldom interested in settling the problem wholesale. He tries at length to see how the different forms of justice may be construed as patterns of the mean, but these investigations are of marginal interest for our present purposes.

Aristotle distinguishes a general concept of justice from justice as a special concept. The first parallels Plato's use in the *Republic*, when he asked, "What is justice?"—which means in effect "What is right and wrong? How should we organize our lives?" In this sense, it is simply complete virtue in interpersonal and social relations. The law attempts to capture this social morality when it prescribes the conduct of a brave man, a temperate man, a gentle man: to carry out one's military duties, not to commit adultery, not to assault others, and so on. Here the law defines only part of justice, the rest being "unwritten."[2] In this sense, to be unjust is simply to go contrary to law. Behind this, of course, lies the concept of the good at which the law aims, since the law aims at "either the common interest of all or the interest of a ruling class determined by excellence or in some other similar way; thus, in one sense, we call just the things that produce and preserve happiness, and its components, for the political community."[3]

Aristotle's major concern, however, is with justice as a special or particular virtue, that is, justice as a kind of fairness or equality. It takes two chief forms. Distributive justice (*to en tais dianomais*) is manifested in the allocation of goods; corrective (or remedial) justice (*to diorthōtikon*), in restoring a loss that has been unfairly produced or has created an inequality. The discussion of these two, though brief and compact, shapes extremely important ethical concepts.[4]

Distributive justice calls attention to the fact that every society must have some principles of the distribution of gains and losses, or goods and burdens. Aristotle speaks of this in regard to "distributions of honor or money or the other things that are to be divided among those who have a share in the constitution."[5] Even this limited reference has the virtue of suggesting a whole-society approach that makes it possible to trace distribution through many different forms. Thus in modern society we can get an integrated view of the division of benefits and burdens as it is routed through taxes, wages, division of profit, social security, regulation of interest rates, and so on, and we can raise the general question of how to articulate general standards of fair distribution. Similarly, within the schema of a general formula of proportionate distribution according to merit, Aristotle compares the results under different constitutions that offer varying interpretations of merit: a democracy thinks all freemen equally deserving and goes in for equal distribution; an oligarchy takes wealth to be the mark of merit and apportions more to the wealthy (to him who hath shall be given) or in some cases uses noble birth as a criterion; and aristocracy equates merit with the possession of virtue or excellence.[6]

Corrective justice operates largely with respect to private transactions and spans the domain of fraud, injury, and what we would regard as criminal wrongs, with an eye toward restitution. In the simplest cases, it means taking away from the violator and restoring to the aggrieved party. It extends to cover cases of A's wounding B by considering that A has in a sense "gained." It also covers involuntary injuries, what our legal system would regard as actions in tort. A modern inquiry in the same spirit would go even further, seeking patterns in the way burdens are borne in cases of accidental harm—for example, in the growth of workmen's compensation and other protective devices against unforeseen injuries or illnesses that are no man's fault. Thus the whole of our modern insurance system could be viewed in the same light as a principle of corrective justice.

In both these cases, Aristotle's approach succeeds in doing what the modern separation of ethics and politics so often ignores: finding the moral issues at the root of social institutions. Indeed, he goes on to consider the element of justice in "reciprocity," with special reference to exchange. He stresses the need for reliable expectation of exchange and the role of money both as an embodiment of demand and as ensuring the commensurability of utterly different commodities, but he offers no theory of exchange value. Interestingly, retribution is included under reciprocity (in *Magna Moralia*), with consideration of how it takes proportionately different form when the guilty party is a slave and when he is a free man. Thus exchange would appear to take its character from the specific associational context; there is no general treatment of it.[7]

There are two further conceptual points in the treatment of justice that are worth noting, apart from other reasons because they were destined for great careers in legal theory. One is a brief attempt, in dealing with political justice, to set off that part which is natural from that which is conventional. Aristotle holds, as we saw in chapter 5, not merely that universal rules such as those against murder and adultery are natural, but that we can tell which principles, though changeable, are natural or inherent. These are contrasted with edicts, such as those enjoining a commemoration for a local hero. The attempt to apply the theory of nature to political justice adds little new; indeed it rather strains the general theory. Later on, when conceptions of natural law developed in a legislative spirit under the Stoic and Christian ideas of a ruling divinity, this was the only place in Aristotle's ethics where a tenuous foothold might be sought. And since attempts to revive natural law in jurisprudence, morals, and theology are perennial, the Aristotelian doctrine of nature and natural political justice is likely to be repeatedly invoked.

The second point is of a quite different sort. It is the construction of a concept of equity to compensate for the inherent weakness of strict law: "All law is universal, but about some things it is not possible to speak correctly in universal terms."[8] Accordingly Aristotle suggests that problem cases be decided by projecting the idea of what the legislator would say, were he present, in light of the purposes for which he was originally legislating. He is not rejecting the universal or making a sharp contrast as if to say that the letter killeth but the spirit maketh quick; rather he is correcting the universal when it goes astray. There is no appeal, moreover, to a special faculty of the particular; nor should this be likened to the function of the chancellor in the history of English law, who embodies in his departures from common-law rules the conscience of the king. Any such dichotomies taken seriously might threaten reason. Aristotle makes his point quite simply with a comparison: "For a thing that is indefinite, the rule too is indefinite, like the leaden rule used in making the Lesbian molding; the ruling adapts itself to the shape of the stone and does not remain fixed, and so too the decree is adapted to the state of things."[9] Aristotle's succinct analysis of equity thus includes a view of the complex indefiniteness of human situations; the limits of law, whose inability to encompass all possibilities is not to be held against it (there is no resort to a situation ethics or an idea of complete discretion); the anticipated necessity for correction in some cases; and the underlying purpose of the law as the basis for correction. This analysis has remained a clear basic formulation in the long history of equity theory in jurisprudence. It also contributes insights to kindred problems that surface whenever legal systems attempt to do justice to both the desire for security through general laws and the effort to cope with the particular and the novel—for example, in broad issues of rule versus discretion in legal theory, or in specific institutions such as administrative law that appear to fall between the courts and the executive power.

Internal Conflict and the Imperfect Forms in Moral Development

The placement of the topic of internal conflict is significant. The previous book ends with practical wisdom as the culmination of the virtues. We have noted the practice—in both Plato and Aristotle—of first stating the ideal and then giving the approximations from the second best to the utter failures. Plato's *Republic* was an outstanding example: first the theory of the ideal state, and then (though after a long digression) the deteriorations of the ideal all the way down to tyranny. There is, however, this difference: Plato was giving the deteriorations after the achievement of the ideal; Aristotle is depicting approximations and failures in the stages of moving *toward* the ideal. Accordingly, the theory of internal conflict, which turns out to be very complicated, has to be read in light of the full theory of virtue (as the ideal) and takes for granted its full background, that is, Aristotle's account of the initiation of movement (see chapter 11 above), and of choice, moral development, and practical wisdom (see chapter 16).

Aristotle narrows his field of inquiry somewhat schematically. There are three characters to be avoided: vice, incontinence, and brutishness. Their opposites are virtue, continence, and superhuman virtue. Superhuman virtue is rare and so it is not discussed. Brutishness, too, is rarely found and sometimes seems to come from some disease or deformity; some illustrations are given but the theoretical issues of its causes and nature are not elaborated. Virtue and vice have of course been amply treated. There remains then, says Aristotle, incontinence and softness (and effeminacy), as well as continence and endurance. This group is not identified with vice and virtue, but it is not a different order (another genus). Continence (*enkrateia*) and incontinence (*akrasia*) and the theoretical problems that have been raised about them constitute the chief content of the discussion.[10] It is precisely these that focus on the phenomenon of inner conflict.

I shall continue to use the terms *continence* and *incontinence* largely because they seem to be close to the literal meaning and the phenomena. The root idea is that of control, and the contrast of being controlled (in the sense of self-mastery) and uncontrolled stays close to the picture that emerges of some inner conflict whose exact nature has to be ascertained. The common translation of *akrasia* as "weakness of will" seems to make a commitment in advance to a particular interpretation.

From common beliefs about these character formations a value scale and an initial characterization emerge.[11] The value order would seem to be (leaving out extremes) virtue, continence, incontinence, vice. Praise shifts to blame at the midpoint. The characterization of continence and incontinence is in terms of whether the person abides by calculation or abandons it in his action: the incontinent man does what he knows to be bad through passion; the continent man, knowing that his desires are bad, does not follow them on account of reason.

Recalling that practical wisdom involves both true reckoning and right desires, we can list eight logical possibilities concerning knowing the good (G) or not (−G), desiring the good (D) or not (−D), and acting according to the good (A) or not (−A). The negative of knowing the good has to be taken as a false reckoning; we are dealing only in cases where there is thinking or calculation, not expression of passion without thought. The negative of desiring the good means desiring the opposite of the good, not having no desires. Combining G, D, and A and the negative sign as indicated, we get eight cases, each of which we may briefly examine. Our list oversimplifies in at least one significant respect: it does not show separately the rational desire that accompanies the presence of G, an important feature in the two cases of G−D since it means the presence of a conflict of desires. This can be taken care of in examining the dynamics of each case where it is relevant. (It is also important to note at the outset that the data in the list comes from either observation or report about the three items. The list separates these from either causal explanation or interpretation, or possibly ontological theory about their significance.)

(1) GDA obviously fits virtue, as represented in the account of practical wisdom.

(2) GD−A would seem to be ruled out as a possibility. This is only because the causal picture underlying choice assured us that knowing the good *and* desiring it are sufficient conditions for doing it (if nothing interferes). Since our list is constructed in terms of the picture of possible phenomena, all we could suggest is that if such a possibility were actual in a given instance, it would not be a matter of choice but some external accident or involuntary movement.

(3) G−DA fits the picture of continence: the action conforms with the knowledge rather than the opposite desire. No analysis of why this happens, such as how the desires become repressed or whether they do, is here involved. The rational desire accompanying the recognition of G together with that cognition is seen to prevail over the dissident desire.

(4) −GDA is the strange case in which the person is wrong about the good, has the desire for what is actually good, and acts according to the desire. It looks like incontinence since action follows desire against calculation; but since it is not action against knowledge of the good, it only resembles incontinence. Aristotle raises the question whether if there is a mistake in the calculative reasoning plus a correct desire, we may not have a good incontinence that follows the desire.[12]

(5) G−D−A is the straight case of incontinence: the person knows the good, desires the bad, and acts according to his desires. The rational desire accompanying the recognition of G together with that cognition does not prevail over the dissident desire.

(6) −GD−A is a strange case comparable to −GDA: the person has a wrong reckoning, the right desire, but sticks in action to the reckoning. It then resembles, but is not, continence. Aristotle says that the continent man must have strong evil desires.[13] In some respects it is like the account of endurance, if we think of it as withstanding the pain of frustrated desire.

(7) −G−DA, like GD−A, is either ruled out as a possibility or is the accidental good fortune of doing what is right contrary to one's thought and desire.

(8) −G−D−A is the clear case of vice: wrong principle, wrong desire, wrong action.[14]

What is going on in these various phenomena, especially in continence and incontinence? If desire is strong or weak, are we to change the classification? (For example, if a man has weak desires, is it really a matter of continence if action overrides them?) If the calculative reason works with generalities and particulars, what parts of this knowledge are at the center of the scene and at what point? If the standard cases of incontinence are the outcome of choice, what happens at the last moment, and how is it different from what went on in the deliberative process before? If there is an internal conflict in the deliberative process, what are the parties to the conflict? Can there be a burst of passion that determines choice, or does that mean simply that choice is suspended and action determined without choice? These are the kinds of questions that come in at critical points in the unfolding of the argument. It is a pity that Aristotle did not go at them directly, instead of crossing the question with Socrates' view that no one acts contrary to his knowledge of the good, which implied that there could be no such thing as incontinence.[15] Aristotle does not brush Socrates aside, as he brushed aside in physics the view that motion is impossible. And he does not formulate his own question as to how incontinence is possible.[16] Rather he canvasses the types of knowing— whether the problem will be solved if the incontinent man acts contrary only to opinion, or perhaps to practical wisdom. The latter is of course long ago ruled out, and the substitution of opinion for knowledge is of little use; Aristotle notes later that people may hold their opinions as stubbornly as if they were knowledge.[17]

To pursue in depth the problem of incontinence requires that we explore within incontinent men what kind of knowing is involved and how it may become inoperative at the critical point where delibera-tion culminates in choice. Aristotle explores (1) having as opposed to using knowledge, (2) partial knowledge, which lacks an important link, (3) interrupted knowledge, and (4) shift in focus or selective attention in knowledge. These need not be pitted against one another as different explanations; they may all help our understanding or even cover different kinds of cases of incontinence.

(1) There is the familiar distinction between having knowledge and not using it on the one hand, and actually using it on the other. It would not be surprising if a person acted against his knowledge if he were not actually thinking it.[18] Aristotle does not give an illustration here, but suppose that in a critical situation someone shouted directions to me in a foreign language I could understand but was not expecting to hear. I might through a delayed response take a wrong turn in action with harmful consequences. I would then be acting contrary to a knowledge I had but did not use.

(2) The knowledge that is involved in choice—the operation of the calculative reason—is manifold. Its concern is action, and it tells us what is fitting, having an eye on the object of wish and the multiple relations in which wish is to find expression in action that is to be done for its own sake as noble. Some of this knowledge is general, some particular; some is of the facts of the situation, some is of the goodness of the object of wish and the fittingness of the particular act to be done. All this, I take it is the background here. A person's actual knowledge in such a situation of choice might turn out to be partial: for example, he might know a uni-versal premise or premises and their relevance to himself, but not neces-sarily a particular.[19] He might have actual knowledge that dry food is good for every man and that he is a man, and even that certain foods are dry, but not know or actualize the knowledge that the particular food before him is of that kind. Here the bits of knowledge are partly of fact, partly of relevance, partly of goodness; but altogether they are not enough.

(3) What Aristotle next suggests may be called interrupted knowl-edge. He points to the sense in which a person's knowledge may not be available when he is asleep or drunk or out of his senses, and sug-gests that passions (anger, sexual desire, and so on), which affect the body, have the same effect. (Even the utterance of the words of knowl-edge is no proof that such people have the knowledge itself on hand.) Clearly we must say the incontinent are like those people.[20]

(4) So far, the suggestions have included a metaphysical conceptual distinction, the ordinary experience of partial knowledge, and familiar phenomena of the extreme emotions. In turning to the fourth point Aristotle moves into the scientific consideration of what we might call depth processes: "Again, one might also look at the cause scientifically [*phusikōs*] in the following way."[21] This remark is important because the passage that follows is often invoked as evidence that he is constructing a theory of the "practical syllogism" (see chapter 11 above). The remark strengthens the view suggested in that previous discussion, that Aristotle is here concerned with the psychology of the initiation of action, not the logic of practical reason. It is the causal role of thought in choice—not the logic of thought—that is at issue. On one side there are general opinions, on the other opinions about particulars determined by sensation. When a single opinion arises out of them, the psyche must then affirm the conclusion, and in matters of action, immediately act. The immediacy of the action is often treated, in attempts to force a practical syllogism on Aristotle, as if the two premises yielded an action of themselves. One may more plausibly see the immediacy as simply in line with his account that when the deliberation is ended the choice (which involves appetition fused with thought) is already made.

Aristotle's example here is a simplified one: if everything sweet should be tasted, and that is sweet, "it is necessary for one who is able and not hindered at the same time to act accordingly."[22] Next he goes on to a conflict, not a direct contradiction but two general premises leading in different directions. Suppose there is a universal that forbids tasting and also a universal that everything sweet is pleasant. (We may interpret both of these as having some reference to the good, with whatever rational desire is attendant upon it, the first through dental and dietetic information, the second through the character of pleasure as setting up an apparent good.) And there is also the particular belief, actually present, that this is sweet, and desire for the sweet happens to be present. (There is nothing wrong with desire being present since all choice involves desire, but the assumption must be that here the desire for health is the appropriate one, the desire for sweetness the wrong one.) Then, while the forbidding opinion bids avoidance, the desire leads you to attend to the particular belief that this is sweet, for it can move each of the bodily parts. For a moment it looks as if Aristotle is giving a victory to desire in a straight confrontation with opinion. This is misleading. The result is indeed incontinence in the example he offers, judged in terms of the forbidding opinion as the good and the desire as appetite. But the desire in pushing the one particular before us would seem to leave its favored universal unchallenged in the field at the last moment, and it is this opinion that everything sweet is pleasant that fuses into the pattern that initiates action. If on the one hand we are tempted to say that in incontinence intellect plays a rationalizing rather than a reasoning role, it is at least significant that desire has to take on a rational garb to move a human being in choice.

One is tempted to amplify this in terms of the difference between incontinence (G−D−A) and vice (−G−D−A). If at the last moment, when a choice is about to be incontinent, the incontinent man musters a principle congenial to his desires and action, then the pattern shifts from the impending G−D−A to −G−D−A, which is the character formation of vice. It would follow that every case of incontinence is a slide into the state which, if it became a permanent formation, would be vice. It is reckoned incontinence because G rather than −G was present throughout the deliberation and only was lost under desire or passion at the end. This has the interesting consequence that an *incontinent choice* cannot literally take place.[23]

The analysis has remained throughout at the scientific level. Aristotle even adds that if we want to know how the incontinent man recovers we should go to physiology, that it is the same sort of explanation as one would give for rousing from drunkenness and sleep.[24]

Now that the analysis is complete, Aristotle concedes that there was something to Socrates' view that knowledge of the good could not be overwhelmed. The incontinent man had to replace it by false "knowledge" to make action contrary to the good possible. This is a graceful gesture on Aristotle's part. Socrates had talked about knowledge of the good without any qualifications; Aristotle replaced this with a scientific analysis of the complex relations of different kinds and roles of knowledge in choice and action.

Since this context is the last serious one in which the question of the practical syllogism appears, what our earlier consideration of the initiation of motion began may now be appropriately completed. The conclusion to which the examination of passages in On the Psyche and On the Movement of Animals pointed can be summed up briefly. Most of the texts invoked turn out to deal with psychological causation or explanation rather than logical form. Most of the passages, with one or two exceptions, are third-person investigations of the conditions under which movement gets under way. The unity of thought and action is found in the pleasure−pain, pursuit−avoidance, and good−bad character of movement, and it is elaborated in the analysis of choice. There are, of course, analogies drawn occasionally between theoretic affirmation and practical appetition, and opinions and beliefs have a causal role that becomes important in practical wisdom. But the search for a logic of action parallel to a logic of belief is not to be extracted from these passages. In this sense, one might almost speak of the myth of the practical syllogism in recent Aristotelian studies. Unfortunately, it has affected translations occasionally, so that an element of self-validation grows with the myth.[25]

Returning to the text, Aristotle tries next to delimit the raw materials of continence and incontinence. Primarily they are the same emotions and actions that underlie temperance and intemperance: the bodily pleasures of food and sex. When we say people are incontinent with respect to anger or honor or gain, we qualify our statement by making explicit reference to the content, showing thereby that we are using incontinence in an analogical way. Another mark of this is that we speak of people as soft when they are incontinent with respect to food and sex, but not with respect to anger.[26] The line is sharply drawn between the virtue and vice of temperance and intemperance on the one hand, and continence and incontinence with respect to the same materials. The intemperate choose, but the incontinent do not choose.[27] Although this last is said casually, it is important to compare it with his previous account of incontinence; it confirms our analysis that while in continence there is choice throughout, in incontinence it practically vanishes at the last moment. Incontinence would seem to be a type of initiation of action in which there was deliberation but no choice.

Softness and endurance, though included in the initial list of character formations, are not treated extensively. They are simply assigned as the correlates of incontinence and continence when the content is pain rather than pleasure.[28] Incontinence is differentiated as impetuousness and weakness; the weak deliberate but do not stick to their results, the impetuous follow passion but do not deliberate. Here Aristotle seems to be moving to extend the concept into the domain of the voluntary that lies outside of choice. He thinks it is possible to resist attacks of passion by foreseeing them. He also elaborates subtypes of incontinence in comparison with the vice of intemperance and evaluates the different kinds. Thus new types appear in the interstices of different questions; for example, unlike the continent man, who is firm against desire but is ready to be persuaded, the obstinate man holds onto his convictions whether right or wrong, is not amenable to reason, and is often led by pleasure.[29]

Aristotle's concluding social comparison is interesting. The incontinent man is like a state that votes all the fitting decrees and has good laws, but never keeps them; the bad man is like a state that keeps to its laws, though the laws are bad.[30]

The extended concern with continence and incontinence is quite understandable. These, not complete virtue and vice, are the character formations of most men. Continence is a second best to virtue in the domain of moral character; it is, like polity in the *Politics*, a realistic compromise where aristocracy is not feasible. The inner structure of continence exhibits a mean that is not a finished just-right pursued without conflict, but a balance of opposing forces maintained sufficiently to follow the good. In spite of their prevalence, however, continence and incontinence are not given in Aristotle's ethical theory the central position they have come to occupy in modern moral philosophy, in which the moral predicament is often defined in a Kantian vein as one in which the agent struggles to obey the moral law in the face of temptation. (In Kant's ethics, the nearest thing to Aristotelian virtue is the "holy will" acting morally without temptation.) For Aristotle ethical theory remains essentially the theory of virtue and the good, of the directions in which man's nature is striving. Not until vast changes had taken place in the view of man's nature and his predicament did it become customary to give the moral struggle of continence and incontinence the center of the theoretical stage. In the contemporary world, with the further psychological study of inner conflict, the question has again arisen whether the Aristotelian analysis should not be regarded as the more appropriate, and the conflicts themselves be understood in terms of more basic strivings and aspirations entangled under difficult conditions.

Friendship

Aristotle's account of friendship, although fully one-fifth of the *Nicomachean Ethics*, tends to be overlooked in the press of other theoretical problems presented in the work. Nevertheless, friendship has an appropriate niche in the scheme of the ethical and political writings. It concerns the interpersonal dimension that lies between the individual orientation and the group or social. Let us first see how far the analysis of this dimension has been developed before the explicit discussion of friendship.

In the earlier part of the *Nicomachean Ethics*, happiness was looked at from the individual's point of view, though comprehensively from the perspective of a whole life. In the treatment of virtue and moral development an element of the impersonal entered in the concept of the noble (*kalon*), which was the mark of the good. If this was the surrogate for praise from the father figure, it still stood out impersonally in the individual's consciousness. As compared to pleasure, which was the index of achieved virtue, it carried the individual a step out from his own personal feeling. Yet there was little in the analysis of virtue that referred directly to the needs and feelings of *the other person*. Choice and the processes of appetite and reason were once again treated as intraindividual.

Of the specific virtues, justice reached out most directly to others. There is a fine point of balance involved. Treated primarily as a virtue rather than as a mutual relation or a mutual obligation, justice in its particular sense is oriented to the person who is making the distribution or doing the correcting. It is almost as if the question were what makes a just judge or a just executive rather than what formulae of distribution or of restitution meet the needs of the community or what evils are wrought on the other person by the injustice. Yet in the brief discussion of justice as a general concept Aristotle is well aware of the difference. General justice is defined as perfect virtue, not simply, but in relation to others.[31] Many people can practice virtue in their own affairs but fail in relation with others and in association. Because of its relation to another and to society justice is thought to be *another's good*, for it does what is advantageous to another.[32] Admittedly, the best man is one who practices virtue toward others—a difficult task. The conclusion is that though virtue and justice-in-general are the same, the latter is cast in terms of interpersonal relations, the former simply as a state of character.

The treatment of practical wisdom is oriented toward the individual. One passage says that practical wisdom is particularly thought to be the kind concerned with oneself, the individual.[33] This should not be misunderstood: the context is the comparison of political wisdom and practical wisdom. They are the same state, that is, practical wisdom, applied in different fields. With respect to the city (*polis*) the controlling kind is legislative wisdom, while its application to particulars is called political wisdom. Similarly in dealing with a man's own affairs we can distinguish the practical wisdoms of household management, legislation, and politics. The practical wisdom concerned with the self—knowing what is good for oneself—is one of the many practical wisdoms: it is just a linguistic matter that the generic name is used for this species; it is not an assertion that egoistic concern is the essence of all the species.

The orientation in dealing with continence and incontinence is even more strongly intraindividual; for that is the stage on which the inner conflict takes place.

When at last the topic of friendship is broached, it turns explicitly to the interpersonal aspect that has not been a theoretical concern hitherto. Whether the previous individualistic emphasis carries with it a moral individualism remains to be seen. A modern reader must also make allowances for the use of the term *friendship* (*philia*) and recognize that it is a broad concept that can cover any association that has any kind of value; this is made immediately clear by its use to cover business relations. The corresponding verb (*phileō*) can cover anything from love to fondness, diluted almost to interest. The word for the feeling of friendship (*philēsis*) has a similar range.

A second and equally important caution for a modern is to remember that friendship is always personal or interpersonal. The concept of the social in modern thought has been oriented predominantly to the group and its group characteristics. It was quite a wrench in recent social thought to recover the concept of the *interpersonal* as distinct and located between the individual and the social; its reemphasis in quite different philosophies (for example, George Herbert Mead's *Mind, Self and Society* or Martin Buber's *I and Thou*) makes an interesting chapter in the history of ideas. In political philosophy the interpersonal is found in an emphasis on the small-scale community of face-to-face relations and not the broad organized state, where thinking is in terms of a common welfare. Practical politics has always, of course, known the difference between pursuing the common welfare and rewarding one's friends (the morality propounded by Polemarchus in the first book of Plato's *Republic*). In the ancient Greek city-state the latter policy held a quite respectable position.

Aristotle starts with a packed presentation of the phenomena, their embedded values, current beliefs, and initial problems. Friends are most necessary: "No one would choose to live without friends, even having all the other good things."[34] Men live in a network of interpersonal relationships; friends are a good thing for rich and poor, young and old and middle-aged. There is a natural grounding of affection in parent-child relations, in members of a single species. It spreads to chance human encounter, is a bond in the society, and becomes (in the face of faction or class conflict) the positive social aim in state action. Indeed, where men are friends, they do not need justice. Aristotle adds that friendship is not only necessary but noble. In short, throughout, its values are both instrumental and intrinsic and scarcely need to be neatly parceled. So important a phenomenon requires investigation: what are its bases and relation to character and emotions, its types, its possibilities?

Since friendship involves love, Aristotle looks to the object of love. There are three types: the good, the pleasant, and the useful. The last is instrumental, productive either of what is good or what is pleasant. Here the possible reemergence of an individualistic orientation is indicated. Do men love the good or what is good for them? These sometimes diverge both for the good and the pleasant; the answer is that a person loves what is good for him. This is the context, noted earlier, in which the further question was raised of a person's loving the apparent good; but this does not affect the current argument.

Friendship as a phenomenon excludes love of inanimate things, in which there can be no return of affection. Further, in friendship it is thought one ought to wish the friend good for his own sake. If this feeling is not reciprocated, we are said to have goodwill; this we can even exercise towards someone we have never met, and who has never met us. The summary definition includes goodwill toward one another, the wish for each other's good, and mutual consciousness of this, on one of the three grounds (good, pleasant, useful) initially distinguished.[35]

Three kinds of friendship are distinguished by their object of love: friendships of utility, of pleasure, and of the good. Utility characterizes business associations, pleasure the more carefree associations, the good a common pursuit of ideal interests. This classification of types, together with their emotional bases, provides the structure for the rest of the inquiry.

Aristotle considers friendship from so many different perspectives that no brief outline can be adequate. There are pure types, in which the same base is found in each party; mixed types in which (for example) one party finds pleasure in the other but the second only utility in the first; and also combined types, in which the same two parties both share the same goal and in addition have different goals. Indeed, the friendship of good men would also involve their taking pleasure in their association; Aristotle remarks that one could not stand even the Absolute Good if it proved painful.[36] He considers questions of permanence and change, and the obligations that may alter as the bases of the friendship disappear; and he even reflects on problems of morality and sentiment in the ending of friendships. There are reflections on capacity for friendship at different ages, on the extent to which dispersion of friendship is possible. Friendships of utility can be numerous, but friendships of the good can only be few, because they require the kind of mutual acquaintance that can only come in living together or sharing a common life. Bad men can have friendship based on utility and pleasure; only good men can be friends on the basis of what they are.

Friendship is traced in different role relations: ruler–ruled, master–slave, parent–child, husband–wife, that of kindred fellow citizens, of comrades. (Some of these questions we shall discuss in the next chapter, in relation to the *Politics*.) Contrary to modern expectations, there is no systematic discussion of marital relations or of sexual relations. There is an interesting remark on love, which is seen as a sort of excess of feeling, naturally directed toward one person. (The term used for *love* here, *eraō*, conveys the sense of passionate desire, and the context is Aristotle's comment that it is not possible to be a friend in the complete sense of friendship to many.)

On the question of moral principles in friendship relations, Aristotle seems most concerned with issues of what one owes to the other or which rules which or what typically one gives to the other. Such questions seem more to characterize the two lower grades. They are seen as questions of justice, differing in different relationships; yet equality in justice differs from equality in friendship.[37] In the former proportionate equality prevails over quantitative equality; in the latter, however, the reverse appears true. The friendship will not last if the disparity in proportion becomes too great. In business relations, differences of perspective often render the decision of obligations difficult; for example, the giver and the receiver often place quite different values on the object given or service performed, and this raises the interesting question how the value should be decided.[38] As we may expect, Aristotle's answer is contextual: in a friendship of virtue, return should be proportionate to the intention of the benefactor; in business friendships there should, if possible, be agreement in advance, or if not, reliance on the evaluation of the recipient— but at the value he put on his "purchase" before he received it!

The affective side of friendship is handled sensitively. Goodwill is distinguished from friendly feeling by the absence of intensity and desire; it can, however, be the beginning of friendship, just as the pleasure of the eye can be the beginning of love. Concord is the feeling aspect of a situation in which citizens agree about policy and carry it out. A particularly interesting question is why benefactors love the recipients more than the reverse.[39] The hardboiled view is that the benefactor is taking care of his investment to ensure a return, while the recipient would like the "debt" to vanish. There is a deeper explanation, more plausible because often the matter of possible return is not involved: the benefactor's feeling is allied to that of the artist in creating his work, or the parent in loving the child. Among other reasons given is that loving is an active feeling, while being loved is passive, and here too the benefactor falls on the active side.

Extremely subtle inquiry into shades of feeling enters into such topics as a friend's feeling for a friend as another self or (a problem discussed at length) whether a person ought to love himself. This last brings us back to the initial question of the moral balance between self and other. There have been relevant comments on this at various points. For example, in deciding that a friend wishes his friend the greatest goods, but not such as will make a god of him (which would presumably carry him out of reach), Aristotle adds the afterthought, "But perhaps not all of these; for it is for himself most of all that each man wishes what is good."[40] We noted above Aristotle's belief that the individual loves primarily what is good for himself. And he keeps in mind "good for oneself" as a separate index of a completely good friend, together with the indices *good* and *pleasant*.[41]

Two chapters deal directly with self-love. The earlier (9.4) suggests a psychological thesis, the second (9.8) propounds a moral thesis. The psychological thesis is that friendliness toward others is derived from friendliness toward oneself. We are familiar in contemporary depth psychology with theses that a person cannot really love others unless he loves himself or respect others unless he respects himself. These often stress that the child's first relations are to others, so that the causal direction is the opposite of the one Aristotle suggests. This is a separate issue, and it is of course possible that there is a continual interactive process in development so that neither causal direction alone would suffice. Aristotle prefaces his hypothesis by showing a parallel in the features of friendship to others and to oneself. Each of the following (here stated only for "friend . . . friend") holds whether we say "friend . . . friend" or "person . . . (him)self": (1) A friend does good or apparent good to his friend for the friend's sake. (2) He wishes his friend's existence and preservation, for his friend's sake. (3) A friend lives with his friend. (4) A friend desires the same things as his friend. (5) A friend shares his friend's joys and sorrows. Interestingly, in (2) and (5) a mother is given as an illustration—almost as though the indices were being tried out on the mother–child relation. The structure is applied to the individual–self relation not for any individual but for the good man and his self-feelings, the good man being the recognized standard.

In the case of the bad man the fit is not achieved. Bad men neglect their own interests (1); because of their crimes they run away from themselves and even commit suicide (2); they try to forget by being with others rather than with themselves (3); they are in internal conflict and so have no stable wishes (4); their conflict drags them in different directions, so they do not share their joys and sorrows with themselves (5). Most men insofar as they have some self-regard can fit the pattern of friendliness to themselves.

The minimal implication of the psychological thesis seems to be that there is a moral development of the self in which the basis of self-love and love of others becomes possible if there is sufficient unity of the self. The crucial point for the moral thesis is that where the unity is not achieved there will be an ambiguity in the notion of the self, so that we have to ask what the individual who loves himself is in fact loving. Self-love gets a bad name because the ordinary kind of self-love gives oneself preference in acquisitive pleasures or status or bodily pleasures.[42] If self-love meant competition in virtue and nobility, one would approve of it! The answer to the question whether a man should love himself is simply that a good man should and a wicked man should not.[43] Aristotle has thus at least avoided *some* of the questions that beset our modern problems of egoism and altruism, for he does not have to give a single answer to the question. He is not committed to the idea of a fixed nature behind the character that each person develops. Nor is he committed to classifying virtues as self- or other-regarding, nor to seeing every act in one or the other light. He is thus able to say that the answer depends on the *kind* of self.

This does not, however, dispose of the whole issue. The question is not merely whether a man should love himself but whether he should love himself most or someone else.[44] Here the issue is more complex. Part of the way to an answer can be traveled by arguing that for good men the question does not arise until some extreme situation. Before that the governing object is impersonal. In the young person's development of virtue it is the noble. In the mature life of good men it is the good. For there is a scale of selfhood that seems to vary inversely as the ladder of friendship. Men are most apart in relations of utility; they are most united in pursuit of the good. Perfect friendship is between good men alike in virtue. Such friendships are permanent, though they are infrequent because good men are rare. When they occur, the effect is that each loves the good in the other and in himself because they both love the good. The phenomenon is familiar in modern discourse of ideals. The ideal takes hold of the parties, the self becomes identified with it, and the distinction of persons moves into the background. For many kinds of cases the question of who ought to bear the burdens or make the sacrifices would then be answered by asking whose doing this would most advance the achievement or progress of that ideal.

Aristotle does not follow this path, though it was open to him by his description of the good and of human thought. Instead he remains conscious throughout that two good men are different persons. As we saw earlier in discussing happiness, even in the transport of contemplation it makes a difference whether I am doing the contemplating or someone else. So too in the present context, if one should love most one's best friend, that best friend may turn out to be oneself.[45] This is presented as only one side of a debate. Yet he has previously argued for the unique quality of being oneself: no one would choose all good things on the condition of becoming somebody else, "but only by being whatever it is that he is."[46] Aristotle appears to identify this with the individual's consciousness.

Yet he wavers. Although he asserts that "reason [*nous*] always chooses what is best for itself, and the good man obeys reason,"[47] the question still remains what reason will choose and how to interpret the choice. It is admitted that the good man does many things for the sake of his friends and his country and if necessary will die for them. Aristotle interprets this as securing the noble for oneself, choosing a short glorious period instead of a long mild one, or a year of noble life instead of many ordinary ones. He is thus returning it to a personal calculation. In arguing shortly after about even the good man's need for friends, he makes it clear that life itself is pleasing and good, that life is defined by the capacity for consciousness (sensation and thought), and that self-consciousness enhances the goodness of living.[48] A supremely happy man will find his self-conscious existence desirable, and his friend's "almost equally desirable to him." Living together means an extension of consciousness to the shared life.

Clearly what Aristotle ends up with is not a calculation of my good versus another's good, but rather a deliberation of what in human character and institutions will yield a governing concept of the good life and happiness as the quality of a good life. The individual orientation remains ultimate in one major sense; the impersonal element of a good that wins assent without a reckoning of the self enters only at points. Ethics in its history has witnessed different theoretical experiments, both the extreme of individual calculation and that of transcendent goods without return to a justification in individual consciousness. Neither has been a happy experiment. But in the long run, if the Aristotelian insistence on a psychological basis for moral concepts is taken as fundamental, we cannot get an answer until we know more than we do as yet about the psychology of the impersonal and the ideal in human life, and the full range of factors that enter into choice.

The books on friendship furnish a rich picture of the interpersonal. But the full context of the types of relations is to be found in their institutional setting. Hence we move naturally into the *Politics*.

SOCIAL AND POLITICAL CONCEPTS

The *Politics* continues the search for the understanding of the good life begun in the ethical writings. Man is a social animal, and the governing framework of his good life is therefore to be found in the institutions that make up communal organizations. The *Politics* shows how it is possible to combine scientific description and generalization with the specification of norms and programs toward their achievement. Assumptions about human nature and human values are explicit and thus open to criticism. Since the good was initially defined as what man aims at, the normative is now not invoked from outside but systematically grounded in the assumed needs, goal-seekings, and possible outcomes of human social living. Political theory is concerned with finding ways in which human nature can find fullest expression, the social relations and institutional forms that are desirable, under what conditions they are achievable, and how in less favorable conditions some approximation to the good may be achieved. Aristotle's integration of ethical and social, of norm and fact, is thus not a failure to discover the modern distinction between fact and value but the implicit rejection of a sharp dichotomy in light of an assumed continuity of man and nature and an underlying teleology.

He works with a very rich background. The *Politics* reflects conclusions from a study of the history and development of 158 actual constitutions. Of these, the one surviving document is the *Athenian Constitution*. There is also constant reference to proposals and utopias, and to other experiments that were actually tried. Moreover he is attentive to alternative conceptions of the good embodied in different modes of life. Thus there is an evaluation of Spartan life, with its dominant pursuit of war and empire, from its own point of view (for example, he considers what effect Spartan institutions concerning the role of women had on Spartan military power) as well as from the standpoint of life's goals. Similarly, he looks into what an oligarchic society requires to maintain stability, and comments on the weakness of oligarchy in its inner operations and the pettiness of its life goals. He even asks what a tyrant should or should not do to maintain power. He ponders the causal conditions under which these different policies and programs are adopted, and where something less than the ideal is the only thing feasible, and how much weight should be given to the fact that a given form exists, in deciding whether to change or not. In short, he is quite explicit in distinguishing the ideal as he sees it, the approximations possible under different conditions, the comparative value of different schemes, the gains and losses in specific changes—and all in a comprehensive theory both of the good on the one hand, and of factual and causal conditions on the other. It is detailed explicitness about norms, rather than abandonment of norms, that is his strategy.

This, however, makes it especially important, in evaluating Aristotle's views, to remember the philosophical framework he is applying and the factual assumptions and value components already built into it. The *Politics* also illustrates how effectively these operate to foreclose alternatives and to add weight to one alternative as compared to another. We shall see this in a number of detailed cases, so perhaps one general illustration will suffice here. We saw earlier that his approach to change, while developmental, was not evolutionary. He vindicated the reality of change; he construed it in a developmental way so that all natural change was a maturation in which a preassigned form emerged. There was nothing there of the evolutionary concept of emergence, in which forms that have never existed before come into being. If this muted further speculation about alternatives in biology, its immediate effect would not be disastrous: why conjecture about possible species when there are so many actual ones to examine? On the other hand, to have construed mutations as monstrosities, as the result of accident with no regular status in the order of things, might inhibit studies of transition processes. In any case, in developing a theory of human affairs, a lack of openness has a momentous practical impact. Aristotle studies history to discern natural culminations. He limits reflection to the comparison of types that have had some stable appearance: "Almost everything has been discovered already, but some of the things discovered have not been coordinated, and some, though known, are not used."[1] He is scarcely ready to speculate about, much less to advocate, novel possibilites that involve wholesale transformation of human institutions. In short, in social philosophy the tie to existence becomes a tie to the past and the present—even if its aim is the discernment of the best in the past. Aristotle is no revolutionary, either in the modern sense of aiming at a wholly new mode of life for mankind, or in the sense in which Plato, looking intently on the ideal, could yet be ruthless about bringing existence into line.

The themes treated in the *Politics* are varied. We find at least the following: a theory of community and social relations, the projection of an ideal order, a classification and evaluation of social forms and constitutions, an analysis of primary social ills and a program for dealing with them, some rudimentary formulation of economic concepts, some treatment of legal concepts, and a well-outlined theory of education. This is the order—only in part Aristotle's—in which we shall deal with them.

Community and Social Relations

The concept of the *polis*, the city-state, is not restricted to political organization, in the sense that the term *state* has come to be used in modern times. It designates the organized community, and it denotes specifically the city-states of the Greek type: not-too-large organized communities that had often emerged from a fusion of villages or the expansion of one of them with sufficient power to effect the consolidation. Aristotle sees the city-state as the resultant form of a natural development—from the family to the village as a kind of extended family, to the *polis* as an association of families operating for the sake of the good life. Here the individual finds fullest expression, for a man is naturally a political (of the *polis*) or social animal. He is also by nature a pairing creature even more than a political or social creature, since the household is earlier and more necessary than the city.[2] We noted the account of interpersonal relations in the *Ethics*, carried out under the rubric of friendship, with its gradations of utility, pleasure, and common pursuit of the good. The *polis*, with its focus on the community, is the social analogue of the highest form of friendship in the domain of the political. Aristotle is, of course, aware of existent societies that differ in quantity or quality from the natural outcome he describes. There are the larger human aggregations, such as Babylon, but these are unnatural products. They are either communities piled on one another, or else large metropolitan areas in which the lone individual has no communal life. Even the apparent *polis* may sink into some lower form and be a *polis* only in name. When it does not pursue the good life for its members, it becomes merely an alliance and differs from alliances in which members live at a distance only in that its participants live close by.[3] In short, the utility relation has been substituted for what later writers called the moral bond; Aristotle thinks both oligarchy and democracy have done this by their concentration on property as the goal of association.

Use of the concept of the natural in this context thus fuses the central components we have seen earlier. The *polis* is natural in the genetic sense of "growing up," as contrasted with the Sophists' idea that it is conventional or contractual in origin. It is natural in expressing the needs of the individual on a high plane, not just some instrumentalities. It is rational in that it incorporates the aim of the good for man.

We must bear this explicit normative element in mind when we hear the usual complaint that Aristotle was turning his back on what Alexander was doing, and glorifying the *polis* while the *cosmopolis* was being forged. Aristotle's belief that the small community was the vital center of individual good life was not incompatible with an appreciation of wider relations and organization. He even expresses a wish for Greek political unity.[4] The context gives this special significance, since it is in the midst of an explanation of the natural superiority of the Greeks, who are said to possess spirit together with skill and intelligence and thus constitute a mean between the people of the rest of Europe, who have the former with less of the latter, and the people of Asia, who have the latter but less of the former. Aristotle might have accepted Greek empire, not expanded unity. We noted in chapter 2 Plutarch's report that Aristotle advised Alexander to treat the Greeks as friends and relatives and deal with the barbarians as beasts or plants—and that Alexander rejected the advice. This and other fragmentary sources have seemed to support a view that Alexander envisaged the unity of mankind, perhaps anticipating the Stoic universalism that was believed to have followed upon the broadening of empire. Recent critical historical probing has, however, considerably weakened that interpretation, suggesting rather that Alexander was responding to immediate problems and that the economic and social basis of the Greek world gave little ground as well as little scope for such projections.[5]

Whatever holds for Alexander, the evidence of Aristotle's devotion to the small-community life is clear enough. Nor should we too readily sweep aside his judgment; in different form it is still a most pressing problem in growing urban centers. His principle of size for the units is that the *polis* be no greater than would allow political participation and enable citizens to know one another's character.[6] He even worries about the large multitude's being able to hear orders from the herald—a problem contemporary radio and television communication could solve for him.

What Aristotle has done is to pose the problem of community life and to offer some criteria for adequate solution. Historical experience has both shown the complexity of the problem and added to its scope. The contemporary world faces the reckoning of local, national, and global organization, with issues of loyalty and participation on a scale that the ancients, of course, could not have dreamed of.

The treatment of specific social relations includes master–slave, husband–wife and parent–child, and ruler–ruled. These are not of one type. In distinguishing them, Aristotle is unlike later political theorists who saw everything in terms of power and domination; they ignore the fact that relations differ in role and function, as well as in the nature of the participants.

His treatment of slavery sounds harshest to modern ears. It was a dominant social institution of the time, but there must have been some challenge to it, for he says, "According to others, it is contrary to nature to be a master, for by convention one man is a slave while another is free, there is no difference between them by nature, and therefore it is unjust, for it is a matter of force."[7] Aristotle sets about defending the natural character of slavery, invoking a number of considerations. Economically, work has to get done; it will not do itself. Even if it did, slaves would still be needed as instruments in living—what we would call service, as distinct from production. The *Ethics* had referred to a slave as a living tool; no friendship could exist between a man and his slave any more than between a craftsman and his tools; but since the slave is a man, there could be a friendly concern for him.[8] The *Politics* adds the biological argument that nature intended some men to be slaves; these are persons for whom slavery is the better and just condition, and if they look like freemen occasionally, it is because nature's intention is not always realized. If we could see the difference that is really there, exhibited in bodily form, we would all agree who ought to be the slaves. The theoretical underpinning, chiefly psychological, is that the soul contains a rational ruling part and an irrational part that is ruled. The slave lacks the deliberative part altogether, the female has it but not in an authoritative way, and the child has it in an undeveloped form. Thus the master must order and the slave obey. Aristotle goes so far as to say that hunting may properly be practiced not only against wild animals but against men whom nature intended for slavery but who refuse to be slaves.[9] The most he will concede is that war results in the enslavement of some people, especially Greeks, who should not really be slaves.

His attitude toward women is comparable. The general Athenian attitude toward women had been to keep them in the home, uneducated and dependent. Even Pericles in his famous funeral oration, after extolling the liberty and democracy of Athens, turns to the women, condoles with them on the loss of their husbands, children, and brothers, and reminds them that "among us that woman is thought best who is least talked of, whether for good or ill." Spartan women had greater freedom, and Plato's *Republic* proposed equality for women on the theory that abilities were distributed on an individual, not a sexual basis. Aristophanes had jibed in his comedies against proposals for emancipation of women. Aristotle finds theoretical grounds in nature for maintaining their subordinate position. In his biological writings he regards the female as an incomplete male. The male is a male in virtue of a particular ability: he has the heat that can concoct basic nourishment into semen, which then can act on the material provided by the female so as to set it and give it form. The female is a female in virtue of a particular inability: she cannot achieve what the male does.[10] It is not surprising that he finds an indecisiveness in the female mentality—though not denying deliberative power to her, as he did to the slave—that makes the husband's stamp of authority necessary. And so a man's rule over his wife is like the statesman's over fellow citizens, whereas he rules his children as a monarch does his subjects.[11] The *Rhetoric* simply mentions among the indices of the noble that "the virtues and activities of naturally worthier people are nobler—for example, those of a man [more so] than those of a woman."[12]

Children are regarded as undeveloped adults. Nature here sets the lines of authority by clear marks, and youth accepts this authority especially because it knows it will inherit it.[13] On the whole, there is little treatment of children in the *Politics* apart from questions of education.

The relation of ruler and ruled obviously takes on a different shape according to the type of constitution. This opens the whole broad topic of the ideal order and the classification and evaluation of constitutions. The scope is even broader in the *Politics* because the topic is not reduced to cover only one kind or one aspect of relationship. Relations are discussed not only from the point of view of the ruler who seeks to impose and maintain his power but also from the point of view of the ruled, and in light of the multiple goals of political life. The analysis begins in a formal way, raising questions of political structure, then explores social and economic contexts, and in the end reformulates more comprehensive concepts in terms of which normative judgments can be made. Thus the inquiry about rulers and subjects leads off (book 3) by seeking a definition of citizenship and asking whether the good citizen is identical with the good man. The definition of the citizen as one who shares in deliberative or judicial office marks out the potential ruling body.[14] On the second question the conclusion is typically Aristotelian: in some societies the good man and the good citizen coincide, in some they do not. In the ideal state they should coincide; but even here, not all citizens would be good men, only those having the appropriate virtues that render them capable of controlling public affairs. He has doubts about the situation in many states where mechanics and laborers are citizens; his own belief is that the best state will exclude them from citizenship.[15] The issue is thus clearly who should rule. The treatment of the formal questions in concrete social materials quickly moves over into the systematic study that calls for both projecting an ideal and investigating the range of existing types.

It is not surprising that the account of citizenship should have focused directly on active participation in ruling. It reflects the situation in the city-state, preeminently in Athens, in which actual citizenship involved direct voting in the assembly that made policy, service on the executive council that was selected by lot, and taking part in large juries, also selected by lot, whose votes determined the legal decision and often through it numerous political issues. It was not thus the passive citizenship of the modern world, exercised chiefly in periodic voting for political leaders and within a limited set of rights and obligations. For Aristotle, the ideal case would be one in which capable citizens rule and are ruled in turn.

But he has his own idea of who the capable are—a crucial variable that can even under exceptional circumstances make room for monarchy.

Projection of an Ideal Order

The question of an ideal order occurs in two different ways. One (book 2) is through the critique of ideal societies, primarily Plato's. The other (books 7 and 8, in the traditional order; strong arguments based on internal clues would put them after book 3) begins the construction of an ideal society, embracing everything from theoretical consideration of the highest good and selection of site to determination of population and principles of education. There is ample indication of political structure, but the account breaks off without a full treatment.

This second, positive account of the ideal society exhibits a clear conception of basic values in social life. The good life is a life of action, in the technical sense that activity contains its goal within it. Its joy is found in living, not in constantly preparing for life or sharpening instrumentalities. It values leisure over business, peace over war, virtue or excellence over wealth. In political principles it is devoted to equality, the proportionate equality that distributes according to merit, not arithmetic or numerical equality. All in all, the ideal is an aristocratic society that feels itself morally justified.

It is often pointed out that in Greek the positive term *scholē* means leisure; business is *ascholia*, the absence of leisure. Leisure is necessary for a man who is to devote himself properly to his pursuits as a citizen, to the criticism and judgment it entails. To lead a life of leisure and peace is a definite ability not to be taken for granted but requiring education.[16] Aristotle criticizes the Greek states of his day for developing character directed to utility and to war. He is especially blunt in condemning the Spartan way of life precisely because it is so often invoked as a model. Even in their own terms, he says, the Spartans have followed the wrong path; their empire is gone, and they are not happy. Their lawgiver was not a good one: "It is indeed ridiculous: they abided by his laws and never were hindered in carrying them out, and yet they have lost the noble life."[17] Different virtues are required in business and in leisure. The former demands courage and endurance, the latter wisdom; both need temperance and justice, but more particularly the times of peace and leisure.

The priority of virtue over wealth is not, of course, intended as a recommendation of poverty. The good life cannot be achieved without external goods, of which wealth is an important one. It plays some part in several of the central virtues—for instance, the liberality of the proud man. But here it has a clearly instrumental role. The conflict with virtue comes when riches usurp the role of end and become the criterion of excellence. We shall see shortly the role of wealth in oligarchy, and its effect on character; also how the economic theory limits the role of money.

The emphasis on leisure also leads to an aristocratic disdain for labor and the life of the craftsman: "A particular work or art or science must be considered vulgar if it makes the body or soul or mind of free men useless for the employments and actions of virtue. Thus we call vulgar all such arts as put the body in a worse condition, and also the occupations that work for wages; for they make the mind preoccupied and degraded."[18] Mechanics are not allowed to be citizens in the best society. The ideal society also excludes shopkeepers and farmers from its citizenry; they do not have the leisure needed for development of virtue and for political activities.[19] Accordingly, the farmers would be slaves or barbarian serfs. The land is owned by the class that bears arms and shares in the government.

The view that aristocracy operates on a principle of proportionate equality seems a strange formulation in a society that is as class-divided as Aristotle's ideal. It shows clearly how self-justified the aristocratic outlook felt itself. This apportionment according to virtue or merit is constantly contrasted with the oligarchic apportionment according to wealth. Nevertheless, Aristotle does not really expect that in most societies conditions will be favorable for his ideal. Thus his practical program is about second bests worked out from a comparison and evaluation of existing constitutions and societies.

Classification and Evaluation of Social Forms and Constitutions

Aristotle uses two bases for his classification. One is the distinction between constitutions directed to the common interest and those directed to the interest of the ruling party; since the good life is the underlying aim of the *polis*, these are respectively the "genuine" and the "perverted." Number—the rule of the one, the few, the many—provides the second basis. The genuine forms are kingship, aristocracy, and polity. (Polity is rule by numerous substantial citizens.) Their respective perverted forms are tyranny, oligarchy, and democracy. The number basis continues to be used but it proves inadequate in the light of underlying realities. Thus he concludes: "The real basis of difference between oligarchy and democracy is poverty and riches. It follows necessarily that wherever men rule on account of their wealth, whether they are few or many, we have an oligarchy; and wherever the poor rule, we have a democracy."[20] The difference in number, though accidental, fits because the rich are usually few and the poor many.

The distinction of subtypes (five of kingship, five of democracy, four of oligarchy) uses a variety of criteria: the concentration of powers in certain forms of kingship and oligarchy; formal features, such as hereditary descent; difference in socioeconomic bases, such as agricultural predominance in some democracies; the extent of participation in democracies; and so forth. Alongside the treatment of oligarchy and democracy there is a direct classification based upon economic factors. For example, subtypes of oligarchy are reclassified according to the extent of distribution of property in the community, from a majority possessing a moderate amount to the large concentration of wealth in a few.[21] Clearly this is a complex task, but one quite in accord with the theory of science. Political features are first classified by the configurations in which they have appeared, as phenomena in the society's rules and actual procedures. Then there is a search for underlying social and economic causes. Then comes a revision of classifications and definitions in terms of criteria drawn from the account of causes. The final step is to show that the revised classifications actually explain the political phenomena. Take, for instance, the shift between the initial and the revised discussion of types of democracy. The earlier account points to two types of cases where the law is sovereign, as contrasted with those in which the people, not the law, is final sovereign.[22] The final account explains this feature of legalism by the fact that a farming class and a class possessed of moderate means are in control: "They are able to live by their work but cannot be at leisure, so they set up the law as supreme and hold only necessary meetings of the assembly."[23]

Aristotle has, in fact, a quite rich analysis of social classes. The basic concentration on the conflict of rich and poor as a principle of explanation in politics is, of course, not new with him. It stands out in Thucydides' history of the late fifth century and in Plato's analysis of the evil state of society. What is new, and what characterizes Aristotle's treatment of the topic, is detailed refinement and attempts to trace detailed explanatory relations, and even beyond these, the use of the explanatory relations to carry out evaluations and propose policy. Democratic and oligarchic constitutions vary because both the people (dēmos) and the class called the "notables" can vary. The people may be made up of different groups: farmers, artisans and craftsmen, marketpeople, maritime workers (the navy, merchant shipping, the ferries, the fisheries), unskilled laborers, and those not of free birth. The notables are differentiated among themselves by wealth, birth, merit, culture, and the like.[24] Different kinds of peoples and different kinds of notables will naturally have different kinds of interests. It is the composition of the classes, not the fact of being wealthy or poor alone, that is significant.

Even so, the contrast of rich and poor does have a very special character. Other bases of differentiation may be crossed by given individuals—the same persons can be soldiers and farmers and craftsmen—but "it is impossible for the same persons to be both rich and poor."[25] That one group is small and the other large gives them a further appearance of opposites. The *Rhetoric* outlines the character of the rich.[26] They are arrogant and think they possess all good things. They are luxurious and swaggering and think they are worthy to rule. Their attitude is reinforced by those who come to them in need. The *Politics* generally contrasts the arrogance of the rich and the desperation of the poor.

In actual explanation, the class analysis is fused with a variety of other factors, ecological, social, and psychological. For example, a strong form of oligarchy is possible where territory is suitable for the use of cavalry, since only rich men can afford to breed and keep horses. A weaker form of oligarchy is likely where there is heavy infantry, and democracy where there are light-armed troops and a navy.[27] In analyzing the occurrence of revolutions, personal reactions such as outrage at a tyrant's behavior are given their place as precipitating factors within a picture of more pervasive causes such as the sense of inequality.

The evaluation of constitutional forms has several different strata. Sometimes a form is evaluated in terms of its own goals and the effectiveness or inadequacy of its rules and procedures. Different types of constitutions may suit different types of societies depending upon their situation, facilities and resources, distribution of abilities, and so forth. Constitutional changes should grow out of a system that already exists,[28] and there is no imposing one ideal for all.

The criterion of stability naturally plays a great part in this assessment. Revolutions are studied both to discover their origins under different constitutional forms and to determine how each form can best avoid them. The greatest source of dissent is found to be a sense of inequality. Aristotle's spirit in this detailed investigation achieves a kind of scientific detachment, so that he is almost in the position of giving the tyrant advice on how to maintain himself—until the conclusion, when he points out that though a tyrant cannot be good, he may at least be only half-bad. This is the closest he comes to an apology for playing the neutral social scientist whose research could be put to work for antisocial purposes.

The overall evaluation of constitutional forms is carried out in terms of the projected ideal and its constituent goals and principles. Aristotle's evaluative attitudes emerge best with respect to specific forms. Of these, his attitude toward democracy is most important in light of the conflicts of his day. At many points Aristotle defends democracy against too sweeping or too glib attacks on the part of the rival claimants—wealth, birth, and goodness. The mass of men collectively are richer than the rich, stronger than the strong, and even better than the good; even in goodness it may be possible for all to be good collectively, without each being good individually.[29] Democracy is a safer form than oligarchy, less disturbed by sedition and dissension, and there are no serious internal dissensions dividing democratic parties.[30]

On the whole, Aristotle seems to have a sober respect for the many. (In Plato's *Republic*, it will be recalled, the masses were represented symbolically as a dragon, the many-headed hydra of appetite or desire, utterly capricious and lacking an internal principle of control.) But at some points the *Politics* makes disparaging references to the masses or to human nature. Wickedness is actually the source of the evils that Plato had attributed to private property.[31] Men are endlessly grasping: there once was a time when two obols was sufficient allowance for theatre seats, but men got used to it and always want more. Indeed, they "always need more until they get to infinity; for the nature of desire is infinite; and the mass of men live for the satisfaction of desire."[32] Restraint is necessary because if men have the power of acting at will, they have no defense against "the evil present in all of men."[33] Further afield, the *Rhetoric* says that "most men are a worse lot, and the slaves of gain and cowards in time of danger."[34] That Aristotle's outlook is generally aristocratic is obvious from many contexts; *On Prophecy in Sleep* even says that it is absurd to suppose that God would send prophecies not to the best men but to any chance person.[35] The ethical works take a more neutral attitude, seeing human nature as raw material to be fashioned insofar as possible in practice and education. All in all, inherent wickedness has very little part in Aristotle's explanations; the view that it is difficult to become good and that some men have inherent advantages plays a large role. Certainly the *Politics* is more friendly to democracy than to oligarchy. The practice found in some oligarchies of swearing an oath to do harm to the people is condemned.[36] A general rule for coping with revolution is that "we should not have faith in arguments put together to trick the masses; for they are confuted by actual experience."[37] This is congruent with the view that the people, when they put their minds together, may have a sound critical sense.

Aristotle often strikes the theme of extremism. The principles of democracy are sovereignty of the majority and liberty of individuals. Democracy identifies justice with equality and equality with popular sovereignty and so ushers in the view that liberty is doing what one likes; democratic rejection of property qualification and the use of the lot in selecting officials are related to these principles.[38] In an extreme democracy the people become autocratic; rule by decree replaces rule of law; demagogues cleave the state in two and wage war against the rich.[39] "What if the poor, on the ground of their being a majority, divide up the possessions of the wealthy—is this not unjust? No, it may be said, it has been decreed by the sovereign in just form. Then what should we call the extreme of injustice?"[40]

This crucial ending is a perennial historical theme. In the seventeenth-century Puritan debates, Ireton, representing Cromwell, objects to the Leveller view that every man should have a vote just because he has one life to live: what would prevent the impoverished from taking away private property? In the nineteenth century Herbert Spencer practically regards taxation as robbery. In many cities of the Greek world the demands of the democrats for redistribution of land and cancelation of debts grew loud and strong. Both Philip and Alexander, when their dominant position in Greece was recognized by deputies of the various cities meeting at Corinth, supported the guarantee that every city discourage confiscation, redivision of land, and abolition of debts.

Aristotle is clearly not prepared to abolish private property. But he is not prepared to give a free hand to the vice of the extremes, whether of wealth or of poverty. His normative judgment parallels that of the man of practical wisdom analyzing the concrete situation to discern the mean.

Analysis of Primary Social Ills and a Program for Dealing with Them

Aristotle's diagnosis of social ills has already been presented: the root of the troubles is the war of rich and poor, of the arrogance and despair that breeds revolution and instability. His criticisms of oligarchy reinforce it. So central is this picture that he is not really concerned with instituting the projected ideal state. The focus is on oligarchy and democracy and on finding a realistic path between their extremes. His practical proposal is polity, construed as a mean between the other two constitutional types. Since he would not abolish riches or eliminate poverty, he realizes that the forces they represent continue to operate in the society. Polity balances the two so that neither overweights political action. The effect is to place power in the middle class that forms the mean. Its moderate outlook makes it amenable to rationality, whereas the extremes tend to violence or crime. The mean knows both to command and to obey; the extremes know only one or the other.[41] Like Plato, Aristotle assumes that there is a rational solution to problems of class conflict. Polity works best where there is a large middle class, but even so, it is the practicable best for most states. In fact the general security of democracies comes from such a middle class; when this is absent, insecurity results.

Balancing the extremes with respect to rules and procedures has all the complexity of finding the mean. Various kinds of mixtures are distinguished.[42] For example, it may prove useful to seek a midpoint, as when a moderate property qualification is set for attending the assembly, where oligarchy wants a high one and democracy none at all; or different elements may be combined, as when voting, but not property qualification, is used in appointing magistrates—here the democrats surrender the system of choice by lot, the oligarchs the property limitation. Ingenious techniques are developed—for example, a composite decision index including both numbers and property.[43] In spirit this is like some modern attempts by believers in world government to work out a voting system whereby both the population and the industrial power of a country would have weight in its vote; and for that matter, it is not unlike J. S. Mill's attempt to increase the weight of the intellectual classes by proposing plural votes for college graduates. In the light of such procedures, it is not surprising that both oligarchy and democracy may be tolerable forms of government if not pushed to extremes.[44] The mixtures must, however, be real mixtures, not illusory benefits that fool the people while the rich encroach upon them.[45]

It is curious that in looking back on Athenian history Aristotle makes a hero of polity out of Theramenes. Theramenes, as we know from Aristophanes' caricature, had been called the "buskin," the reference being to an actor's shoe that could fit either foot. He turned up now on one side, now on the other in the hectic politics of the last two decades of the fifth century B.C. and was finally put to death by the Thirty Tyrants.[46] But Aristotle was not concerned only with the past. It is not unlikely that his influence with Antipater helped mold the latter's policy; certainly what Antipater forced on Athens when he had put down the rebellion after Alexander's death—a property qualification for citizenship whose effect was to exclude more than half the number of citizens—was an application of the Aristotelian conception.

Economic Concepts

Strictly speaking, Aristotle does not fashion economic concepts, for his discussion of what we would call economic ideas—production, distribution, and exchange—comes in ethical contexts (as we noted in considering reciprocity in relation to justice) or in considering household management, the art of acquisition, and property forms, the last especially in the criticism of Plato's proposals of community in property in his *Republic*.[47]

Aristotle does hint at the role of different modes of production in supporting different institutions of social life. For example, in considering slavery, he invokes what we might call an automation myth: conditions in which slavery would not be required, a situation in which a shuttle would weave of itself and a plectrum do its own harp-playing.[48] Even here slaves would be required, as they are really instruments for life's activities. Contemporary economists sometimes, in describing the growth of automation and the long-range drop in percentage of population employed in agriculture and in industrial production, look to service industries to take up the slack. Equally, economic statisticians have sometimes popularized the growth of technical services and powers available to the modern housewife by translating them into an equivalent number of ancient slaves, so that on this front too human slavery is diminishing. Aristotle has not, however, a theory of economic progress. He realizes the importance of economic bases to life but does not, like Marx, assert the primacy of productive processes, or the development of the mode of production to a point where exploitation will be unnecessary.

Aristotle takes for granted the point of view of a society of agricultural estates. He is set against any disruptive tendencies whose outcome intensifies accumulation and oligarchy. This outlook is clearly reflected in his treatment of exchange, both in relation to the theory of justice (noted above in chapter 17) and in considering the art of acquisition in the *Politics*. We saw that he traces in an indirect way the growth of money as a device to facilitate exchange but offers no account of the manner in which exchange value is determined in complex trade relations. The use of money to produce more money—the practice of usury—is roundly condemned as unnatural.[49] The context is the way in which the household secures its materials for livelihood. Setting aside exchange and trade, ways of life are distinguished as the pastoral, the farming, the freebooting, the fishing, and the life of the chase.[50] What is natural about them apparently is that they go directly for the products. Freebooting seems a strange thing to regard as a natural way of life, but hunting down slaves is admitted as an acceptable kind of hunting. Even trade for the purpose of getting specific products for use is natural: a state should engage in export and import to secure what it needs, but it should not act as a merchant for others.[51] The condemnation of usury is then not an isolated phenomenon. Usury is simply the most extreme and conspicuous instance of a tendency to turn everything into a source of monetary profit—an unlimited process, as contrasted with the limited ends of household acquisition. This distortion issues from men's anxiety about livelihood, rather than their concern about well-being. It clearly exalts means over proper ends, substituting an endless acquisitive process that perverts human living. The concept of the natural here conveys both the aristocratic contempt for commercial values and the philosophical insistence on a concept of the good life.

On the question of property, defense of private ownership emerges strongly in the critique of Plato's proposals. It is central to the fear of democratic extremism. The grounds against Plato's "communism" are diverse: it will discourage labor and interest, foster controversy, remove responsibility, deprive men of the opportunity to exercise liberality, and so on. But private property is not equated with absence of public control. There are other possibilities than complete private ownership and use: private ownership of land with common property in the produce, common ownership with division of produce for private use, and also common ownership with common use.[52] Aristotle seems to allow considerable social demands on private property with respect to the use of the products. In the ideal state land is owned by the class that bears arms and shares in government.[53] It is farmed by slaves or serfs. Part of the territory is public, part private. The public section will be used in part to support a system of common eating-tables, a device that ensures subsistence to all citizens.

Legal Concepts

A number of legal concepts have already been considered in relation to justice, in the *Ethics*. These included principles of distributive and corrective justice, natural law as against positive enactment, and the idea of equity. The *Politics* adds some central discussion on the concept of laws.

The most important is the evaluation of the concept of rule of law. This occurs in the consideration of kingship and takes the form of the query Is it more expedient to be ruled by the one best man, or by the best laws?[54] The defenders of one-man rule say that laws are only secondhand general rules to help figure out in the absence of the ruler what he would have done. If you have the ruler, why bother with the laws? The other side argues that law is without passion, whereas individuals unavoidably have such bias. Not merely men's appetites affect the holders of office, but even spirit or ambition in the best of men.[55] In short, law is a necessary bulwark against weakness and human bias. The favorite Platonic comparison with medicine, with the doctor as living knowledge—the query here is Would you rather be cured by the doctor or the medical textbook?—is not helpful for politics. If patients were afraid of their doctors' conspiring with their enemies to destroy them, they would prefer the book. Law and politics are a matter of friends and enemies. Even in medicine the freedom of the doctor has to be limited: for example, there is the Egyptian rule that a doctor departs from standard treatment in the first four days of an illness at his own risk; only thereafter, if the treatment has not been effective, may he alter it.[56] This is not, of course, to advocate legal rigidity. Individual discretion is necessary, but only when the law has failed, as in the need for equity. But these are the residual cases, not the usual ones. In general, too, acceptance of a rule of law provides the most viable outlook, for men develop antiautocratic attitudes. It also avoids extreme democracy that is liable to substitute momentary will for rule of law. Moreover, laws should not be too readily changed, since there is some loss in tampering with established habits; and habit is the source of strength in securing obedience.[57]

Aristotle also discusses deliberative, executive, and judicial powers, although we must be careful not to see him as advocating a "separation of powers." His approach is comparative, surveying the complex variety of forms found in different constitutions and attempting to systematize possibilities.

In historical perspective, Aristotle stands out as a staunch defender of rule of law whether in a kingly or a democratic context. We shall see more of his attitudes in relation to training in the law, in the *Rhetoric*.

Theory of Education

Of course, a great part of the *Ethics* is concerned with education in the sense of the moral development of young people and the kinds of character (virtues) that are desirable. Emphasis there was on practice under guidance; this would fashion the dispositions, and intellectual flowering would produce the sensitively cultivated perception in men of practical wisdom.

Explicit principles of education, and some of its content, are worked out in the projected ideal state in the *Politics*. The account is unfortunately incomplete and breaks off in the midst of a discussion of music. Like Plato, Aristotle is convinced of the educative role of laws and institutions, and he grounds educational theory in the analysis of human psychology and the human good. Peace and leisure are superior to war and instrumental activity. Thus the goal of education emerges primarily as training for character, citizenship, and cultural activity. Education for character is necessary because even though human beings start with some natural endowment, they have to form habits. Citizenship training is determined by the particular character of the society: the education is for the growing citizens, and in their constitution they are to rule and be ruled in turn. Cultural activity is geared to develop especially the rationality of men, in which a critical judgment is pivotal. The emphasis on leisure turns education firmly toward the "liberal arts" rather than utility. Similarly, the virtues stressed are the ones particularly relevant to peace and leisure: wisdom, justice, and temperance. Bodily training is given early, and emphasis falls on regulation of appetite; both of these are not ends in themselves but are encouraged for the sake of the psyche, that is, for the kind of life made possible. There is also some regulation of games and of influences operative on children; for example, indecent language is proscribed, and attendance at comedies deferred. In spirit, Aristotle hews to his philosophy of maturation: one tries to follow nature's program and make up for her deficiencies.[58]

In light of the state's objectives, education is not a private matter; it is to be publicly provided. It includes, of course, reading, writing, physical training, and music, in the wide Greek sense of culture. Crafts are not neglected, but a fine balance is insisted on: they should not be carried to the point of making a man unfit for the good life or turning him to specialized utility. The good life of leisure is not meant to be play. Play is intended to provide relaxation from work or exertion; it has this limited application. The object in teaching drawing is not to save people from buying the wrong articles, but rather "to make them observant of bodily beauty. To look everywhere for the useful is least becoming to high-minded and free men."[59] Similarly, sports should aim at "the noble heart, not the ferocious temper."

Perhaps the best illustration of Aristotle's spirit here is found in the more detailed discussion of music, in the narrower sense, with which the book ends. There are three possible goals in teaching music: character formation, amusement, and cultivation of the mind. Music can serve all these roles and should. The reason for teaching performance is that without it, critical judgment is impossible. This emphasis on critical power as an aim in education is not found solely in relation to the arts. The opening sentences of *Parts of Animals* distinguish the knowledge of the expert and the knowledge of the educated person in relation to science in the same way. The mark of the educated person is precisely the ability to judge correctly what has been well presented and what not. In music, then, we should stress performance enough to achieve the critical purpose, not to the extent that professional expertise or a mechanical habit results. Thus the youth will come to enjoy beautiful melodies and rhythms and not merely have an uneducated, animal-like response.[60] It is not unfitting, unfinished though the *Politics* is, that it end on a note in which the aristocratic bias breaks into the more universally human value of an intrinsic joy in reflective appreciation.

Part 6

THE THEORY OF PRODUCTION

INTRODUCTION

Accounts of Aristotle's philosophy generally conclude with the art of persuasion and the art of poetry and drama, that is, with the *Rhetoric* and the *Poetics*. These are his major works on *production*, the third in the trinity *theōria*, *praxis* and *poiēsis*—contemplation, action, and production or making. From the human point of view the object of contemplation is beyond deliberation, for we can change nothing of it but simply come to understand it. Action concerns our activity as living beings—that kind of acting in which there is no product aimed at beyond the activity itself. *Poiēsis* is quite explicitly productive; an art is concerned with fashioning a specific product. Nevertheless, in all three cases, Aristotle is concerned with sciences, or bodies of knowledge and experience. The *Ethics* and *Politics* are, in a broad sense, theoretical studies relevant to the organization of living. So too the works on *poiēsis* are theoretical studies or sciences relevant to production. This is the sense in which, for example, medicine is a theoretical study, and there is a theory of therapy as well as a theory of physiology. As Aristotle says in the *Rhetoric*, "No art looks to the particular, for example, medicine [not] to what is healthy for Socrates or Callias, but [rather] what is healthy for such a person or such persons (for this is a matter that is within the art, whereas the particular is infinite and not an object of science)."[1] Of course, he is careful here too, as he was in the *Ethics*, to insist that one should not model these sciences on the mathematical or the more rigorously physical sciences.

Art as a human capacity (*technē*) belongs among the intellectual virtues.[2] It is a rational state. It is concerned with production or making, not action. Moreover, where we have an art, it reasons truly. Though all art is concerned with something's coming into being (*genesis*), this is differentiated from the coming-into-being that is by necessity or natural. The latter has its source of change (*archē*) in the thing made, whereas in art the source is in the maker. Thus art can at last be defined as a certain state, concerned with making, that reasons truly, dealing with what can be otherwise.

Although the *Rhetoric* and the *Poetics* are the two treatises devoted wholly to studies of production, there are other bits in other works that deal with materials in a similar fashion. We have already noted the treatment of music in the *Politics*, incidental to questions of education. There is a poiētic strain in the *Topics*, which at points bears a strong resemblance to the *Rhetoric*. Aristotle himself assigns multiple uses to the *Topics*: mental training, conversation, and the exercise of philosophical method.[3] As a matter of fact, there is a poiētic strain in the *Ethics* and *Politics* as well, especially when we think of educators as *producing* certain types of character in the youth, or again, of the legislator as fashioning a certain type of constitution. Even in the biological writings, we see that when nature is particularly craftsmanlike, the species in their continuity seem to be poiētic products. Perhaps the continuities between the three types of science would have been more evident to Aristotle if he had not believed in the unchangeability of the heavens and held to an aristocratic attitude on the superiority of action which, having its goal within itself, produces nothing beyond itself. Indeed, it is interesting historically to observe that in later Puritan theology the continuity becomes complete where not only is the eternity of the world rejected but its creation looked at from the point of view of God as creator. Thus William Ames, a seventeenth-century Puritan philosopher (whose influence was decisive in Massachusetts), working in the spirit of Ramus, rejects the sharp distinction between a science that contemplates and an art that produces; what is science to us is really art to God, and scientific discovery is a way of finding God's purposes in His production. Instead of metaphysics, then, we have a discipline of *technologia*. Such a shift is doubtless congenial to a twentieth-century technology that has begun to trespass on nature's productions, astronomical as well as biological.

There is a short section in the *Politics* dealing with city planning, in the context of the ideal state, which illustrates well the basic method in poiētic studies.[4] It renders explicit the goals that determine the means in light of given conditions, with due regard to alternative goals that men have aimed at, and finally, with an eye to the impact on human character. The site for the city is selected with a view to centrality and relation to the sea. The slope is chosen in terms of a theory of which winds are most healthful. Due attention is paid to water supply and the separation of drinking water from water for other purposes. The utility of citadels depends on the kind of constitution: for example, citadels are suited to oligarchies and monarchies, a level plain to democracies. Whether to have regular streets or an irregular housing arrangement is weighed in terms of military impact in case of the entry of a foreign garrison; the solution is to confine regularity to some parts of the town. City walls are approved as security measures; the idea that they strengthen cowardice in the inhabitants is rejected. Common eating quarters, temples, and market arrangements are made to reflect the values in the already determined institutions. For example, the public square intended for leisure and recreation is kept quite separate from the market square and its buying and selling; and the public square is to be on higher ground. All this is not, of course, an extended treatise on city construction. If it were, we should expect many a digression—such as, after deciding on walls, an excursus on masonry and styles of construction. In fact, if it were an entirely separate treatise we might well find, in the midst of the treatment of the citadel problem, a summary of the major features of oligarchy and democracy! In short, the study of *poiēsis* for Aristotle must never be without its scientific and ethical foundations.

Aristotle's approach to production has the philosophical thoroughness that could yield an integrated analysis of technology, including both the organization of craft and the ethics of profession. Why is it not applied more broadly? Why, for example, though healing is so frequent an illustration in metaphysics and ethics and in law and politics, is there no work on the art of medicine—in spite of Aristotle's probable training in the field? It is clear enough from occasional references (for example in the *Meteorology*) that he is aware of technological processes, but he produced no work on any such field. When he gets close to any applied field it is only from the point of view of the people who will have to administer and govern such an area. As we saw in the discussion of music, Aristotle wanted education to give enough competence to sharpen powers of judgment, appreciation, and criticism, not to make one a performer. So too with production: one should know enough about it to be able to govern the producers—those mechanics and tillers of the fields and slaves—as well as to make proper use of or appreciate the product, but not to engage in such production oneself. The only production permissible for the citizens of the preferred society would be works of administration and culture.[5]

Ironically, however low its social position, production has its theoretical revenge: its categories dominate Aristotelian metaphysics. As we have seen, the craft model, entrenched in the basic concepts of the conceptual network, wins in the court of the theoretical what it could not hold in the court of the practical. Tension among basic structural concepts is not, however, to be taken lightly. There is a sense in which such ultimate structural concepts of a system reflect not only basic metaphysical assumptions but also basic values and social attitudes. When Cartesian dualism came to dominate modern thought, the Aristotelian trichotomy of *theōria*, *praxis*, and *poiēsis* eventually was succeeded by the familiar dichotomy of theory and practice, the one in the domain of mind, the other in the realm of matter and motion. Theory maintained its elite status in both schemes. In fact to the present day, even among materialists who believe that all is body, there lingers a status dichotomy between "brain" and "brawn," so that skilled labor of the hand occupies a lower step than professions of the mind, even though equal intelligence may be involved.

On the other hand naturalistic philosophies, stimulated by the growth of evolutionary theory, have attempted in different ways to overcome

Cartesian dualism and in comparable fashion to bring together theory and practice. For example, in its program of naturalizing the intellect, pragmatism interpreted intellectual principles as rules of action. In the contemporary world there have also been attempts to develop a concept of *praxis* that would include intellectual activity as an integrated expression of human living rather than as a special energy, and in which many technologies could also be satisfying expressive activity not justified solely by their external end products. From such pragmatic and naturalistic standpoints, the Aristotelian trichotomy would be seen as a relative classification of activities based on selected features rather than as a recognition of essentially different types of separate activities. This analysis might also readily spill over into a critique of Aristotle's treatment of *kinēsis* and *energeia*, at least to the extent that instead of being labeled as one or the other, every activity might be seen to share aspects of both. This would rule out both the pure *energeia* that is the Unmoved Mover and the pure *theōria* that Aristotle envisages. The objection to these might be put in language parallel to Kant's critique of metaphysics: that concepts meaningful in the analysis of experience are being turned into separate realities.

The consequences for ethics and politics are obvious. The theoretical is not separated from the practical and productive but permeates all human life and indeed all that is. (This in turn would blunt the sharp distinction between the domain of necessity—what cannot be otherwise—and what can be otherwise, and much in the metaphysics might, though not necessarily, begin to unravel.) The productive classes are not kept out of the citizenry as a group inferior to those who use their products in a life of self-justifying activity. To work out the positive character of an integrated *praxis* and a democratic ideal requires the same power and scope as Aristotle put into his analyses. Many changes would have to be made in empirical assumptions and in social values; some would have to be conceptual and structural as well.

19

RHETORIC

The *Rhetoric* is sometimes regarded as tedious, and so it is in some of its detail. To approach it properly we have to keep an eye on its structure and the basic problems to which it is addressed. We have to take the point of view of the educator. The book is presenting in outline a curriculum for teaching people interested in the uses of rhetoric. Rhetoric served in ancient Greece primarily as an instrument in political and legal activity, and (as we have seen) there were controversies about how it should be taught. The comparable issues in our own day are such questions as are raised by legal training—for example, whether law schools should include a basic education in social and psychological science as well as in legal case materials and legal techniques; or comparably, whether schools of education should stress method or content. Seen in this light, the *Rhetoric* not only becomes immediately significant, but can make a contribution to our modes of thought and evaluation. It had, of course, the same significance for Aristotle himself, for early in his career (see chapter 2 above) he had taught rhetoric, presumably along such lines, in opposition to the school of Isocrates.

Aristotle starts by criticizing the usual teaching of rhetoric not only for its narrowness but also for the ethical effect of this narrowness. The usual manuals are so empty of substantial materials, he says, that if they were kept strictly to the issue in a case, there would be nothing left for the rhetorician to say. They deal mostly with arousing irrelevant emotion, and to do this to judges is like distorting the rule one is going to use in measurement.[1] Aristotle is calling for a comprehensive treatment of the subject with first things first. We shall see later how he goes about dealing with tricks of the trade and emotional appeals.

Rhetoric is defined formally as "the faculty of observing in each case the possible means of persuasion."[2] Persuading is a three-term transactional relation—someone persuades somebody about something—and so attention is called to the three factors that may prove effective: the character of the speaker, the frame of mind into which the hearer is put, and the demonstrative or apparently demonstrative force of the speech itself. All three are pointed toward the hearer. Aristotle never loses sight, in a poiētic endeavor, of the effect that is the product, or of the immediate vehicle of the production; confidence in the speaker must come through the speech itself, not through a preconceived idea of the speaker's character.

There are three kinds of hearers, and it is the role of the hearer that determines the type of rhetoric. He may be one who has to make a decision; this may be a decision either about the future, as in deliberation of the assembly, or about the past, as in the judgments of the lawcourts. Or he may be an observer, usually of a present state of affairs. The three processes corresponding to these tasks are the *deliberative*, which exhorts or dissuades with respect to future action; the *forensic*, which accuses or defends about the past; and the *epideictic*, which assesses by praising or blaming. This does not merely divide the field for convenience, but fixes the contexts by different concepts appropriate to each: deliberative rhetoric is concerned with the expedient (advantageous) or harmful; forensic, with the just or unjust; epideictic, with the honorable or disgraceful. Context thus determines the type of activity, and the type of activity has specific correlative concepts. The concepts mark out different areas, whatever their relations, on which the rhetorician must be prepared. In addition, of course, the would-be orator must have the general tools, now applied to his special areas, which have been dealt with in the *Topics* —such as an understanding of possibility and impossibility in dealing with alternative paths, or methods of comparing the greater and the less to determine what is more expedient or more honorable.

The student of rhetoric is therefore to be given a short course on materials drawn from ethics, politics, and logic, in a way relevant to the argument. Deliberative rhetoric, the use of rhetoric in political persuasion, comes first. The would-be orator must know what he is going to talk about. There is a fascinating episode in Xenophon's *Memorabilia* in which Socrates meets Glaucon, Plato's brother, who is thinking of going into politics. Socrates assumes an air of great seriousness and says something like "That's fine, our city needs good statesmen. I'm glad you're seriously interested. You must be putting your mind to the questions involved. Now take defense: how many troops do we have for such-and-such a purpose?" And so on for field after field. In each area Glaucon proves utterly ignorant. Socrates conveys the lesson that political persuasion needs a bedrock of knowledge—and Xenophon notes that Glaucon never went into politics. So too Aristotle here lists ways and means, war and peace, imports and exports, and legislation as areas of knowledge required for political oratory and goes through topics in economics, military history, geography, food supply, and so on. Especially with respect to legislation, the would-be deliberative orator must be well grounded in political science. It sounds almost as if Aristotle is recommending that he take a course in Aristotle's *Politics*.

Science alone will not do. If you are exhorting to action, you must know what people are aiming at. Well, we know that that is happiness; so the student of deliberative oratory needs a short course in ethics.

There is a packed quality to this short course. Components of happiness are itemized from noble birth and numerous friends down to reputation and luck. Then each is expanded and commented on. Nothing is left out, neither goods of body and mind, nor tokens of honor such as public burial. An anthropological approach is operative here, telling us what people prize, not necessarily what the philosopher approves. Such a comment as "and among the barbarians, obeisances and giving place"[3] is a clue to what is going on.

A mere list of goods, however, is not enough. The student must have at least a smattering of theory; his oratory is to be about what is expedient, so he must know the marks of the good. What follows is a most enlightening assemblage of the various accounts of the good that appear in different parts of the ethical writings. This is no place for pitting them one against another to ask which gives the most systematic analysis; instead, they are just piled up as indices: what is desirable for its own sake, what is the aim of all things that possess sensation and reason, what makes a man independent, what yields pleasure, and so on. If we are in doubt in a particular case, there are more specific indices provided: what has cost much in money and labor, what is praised, what even enemies praise, what is deliberately chosen, and so forth.

After the good comes the better, since the deliberative orator will be making preferential recommendations. It was noted above in discussing the better (chapter 16) that this section of the *Rhetoric* and the third book of the *Topics*, and not the strictly ethical writings, are the places where comparative value is discussed at length. The procedure is to furnish various indices for application in different contexts, rather than to provide any general principles submitting to quantitative measurement, as in the felicific calculus of the later Utilitarians. The indices are quite varied. Something may be preferred for being scarcer, or more abundant, longer in duration, easier to attain, or harder; perhaps it is praised more, or is inherently (rather than instrumentally) desired, or is preferred for itself rather than for the sake of public opinion—the list goes on for page after page. The final remarks stress the importance of knowing the different customs, interests, and institutions of different constitutions—democracy, oligarchy, and the rest—for principles of valuation differ in these, and the weight of authority is cast in different directions.

Epideictic oratory comes next. The concepts now central are virtue and vice, the noble and the disgraceful, as objects of praise and blame. As we may expect, there are indices of virtue and vice, lists of virtues, and a general characterization of nobility. Victory, honor, what we are remembered for after death, what helps others rather than oneself—all find their place, along with a note that the Lacedaemonians believe long hair is a mark of nobility, being a gentleman's style because the performance of a servile task is difficult for one with long hair.

Finally, there is forensic oratory. Here we receive the brief course on law and justice. Injustice is defined as voluntarily causing injury contrary to law, and Aristotle sets himself no less a task than to outline the motives that lead men to act unjustly, the state of mind of such actors, and the kinds of persons who are wronged, and their condition. Human action is attributed to seven causes: chance, nature, compulsion, habit, reason, anger, and desire. Their analysis involves pleasure and pain, the varieties of desire, revenge and resentment, and so on. Describing the state of mind of wrongdoers involves questions of ability and opportunity and probabilities of discovery and punishment. The salient characteristics of victims that invite their victimization are then tabulated, from carelessness to unaggressiveness and a readiness to forgive. Among other topics treated is comparative injustice, that is, what makes the wrong greater or less. The course on law is rounded out with a survey of how to argue to best advantage on questions of the letter and spirit of the law, witnesses, the existence of contracts, the use of torture (a permissible Greek procedure under definite conditions), and the use of oaths.

This packed treatment of the several ethical concepts in the *Rhetoric* lights up an important lesson for ethical theory, one that the close juxtaposition of the concepts in relation to different tasks suggests more readily than the extensive and spread-out treatment of the ethical writings. The three great competing conceptual structures of the history of ethical theory—the good and the teleology of goals, the right (or just) and the legalistic model, and virtue, which gives prominence to the development of the self in present action—are here put in a functional relation to different human tasks relating to planning for the future, criticizing the past, and appreciating the fuller meaning of the present. Later ethical theory (Utilitarian, Kantian, Intuitionist) lost its grip on a coherent balance of the three contexts and turned them into alternative and competing types of theory. Perhaps this story is not unrelated to the different kinds of metaphysical outlooks that emerged and to shifts in the field of practical social problems. Aristotle's theoretical balance was certainly helped by the comprehensiveness of his approach, by attentiveness to context, and by the close relation of the ethical to the social and institutional.

Book 1 having dealt with the knowledge required to make the speech itself sound and persuasive, book 2 turns to the character that the speaker should convey—what in current terms would be called the "image" that he should project—and the disposition to be produced in the hearer. All this requires another short course: a basic grounding in the psychology of emotion and character.

The approach employed is what might be called a field theory of the emotions. Each one is mapped in detail with respect to the disposition giving rise to it, the kind of people toward whom it is directed, and the typical grounds on which it is felt. The account treats of anger and its opposite, gentleness or mildness, love and hate, fear and confidence, shame, kindness or goodwill, pity, indignation, envy, and emulation. One has to read these sections to realize the rich detail and the fine shades of distinction. We are not merely told, for instance, that one man slights another, but that disdain is to be distinguished from spite and both from insult. The whole passage is an excellent supplement to the treatment of feelings as the raw material of virtues in the *Ethics*. So is the section on character, with its picture of youth and age and the prime of life, of the effects on character of wealth and power. We can see the training that lies behind Theophrastus' *Characters*: the sharp insight into human weakness, and the selection of incident to display the exact fine shade of human reaction.

The remainder of book 2 gives the promised short course on applied logic. The materials are taken from the more general *Topics*: how to estimate what is possible and impossible or what is likely or improbable, how to use examples and where to place them for greater effect, the role of maxims, fallacies to be avoided, and so on.

Book 3 deals with style and mode of presentation. Before we turn to this, we should note the explicit attitude adopted toward tricks and adventitious elements, the deliberate playing on belief and emotion, which at the beginning of the work others had been criticized for making central techniques. A moral purpose is set forth in the thesis that the true and the just are naturally superior; if they do not prevail, something has gone wrong with their communication. Hence the art of communication needs attention.[4] Again, some people are not capable of being persuaded by sheer knowledge; this seems to be the view taken of the multitude. The orator has to be able to prove opposites—not in order to persuade people to do what is wrong, but to be able to counter others' use of false arguments. If harm can be done with such skills, so too harm can be done with strength, or wealth, but we do not avoid these as a consequence. With such a statement of principles, there is no reason to misunderstand Aristotle's intent when he later elaborates arguments to suit opposite positions: If the written law is counter to your case, appeal to general law and equity; but if it is in your favor, what's the point in having laws if they are not followed?[5] If you have no witnesses, appeal to the probabilities, saying that witnesses can lie, probabilities don't; if you have witnesses, argue that witnesses can be cross-examined, probabilities can't.[6] Similarly, we are shown how to enhance the credit of, and how to discredit, evidence given under torture.[7] More devious, however, is such advice as that the speaker should guess what his hearers' preconceived opinions are and then enunciate some general maxim that fits in with them.[8] One is not quite sure whether we are being told to use maxims because they give a moral atmosphere to the speech, or because good maxims are influential for good as well as for making the speaker's character impressive.

The moral attitude is continued in the discussion of tricks of style or presentation. They are quite defensible in one basic sense: we cannot persuade by fact and demonstration alone if audiences themselves are corrupt or deficient.[9] Stylistic devices are thus really necessary counter-influences in a good cause. Style is also necessary because it affects clarity. Still, the prior reason is the stronger; no one teaches geometry with stylistic persuasion. The account goes on to deal with poetic language and ordinary language, how to use metaphors, why "rosy-fingered dawn" is preferable to "purple-fingered dawn" and still more to "red-fingered," what is wrong with using epithets "not as a seasoning but as a regular dish," when to use a name and when a description; the difference between unpleasant, endless discourse and pleasant, moderate-sized periods that can be readily grasped, neither too short so that the hearer stumbles nor too long so that he flounders; when to resort to antitheses, what kind of jokes to use, and a great deal more. Of course, among these are the tricks again. There is the overworked phrase "Everybody knows," which shames the hearer into agreeing lest he be proved ignorant. There are the names that honor and the names that abuse; just as pirates call themselves purveyors, so when your client has commited a crime, you may simply say he has made a mistake. And there are times when it is appropriate to tell the audience that you are going to tell them something important. (A sophist like Prodicus would throw in a bit of his fifty-drachma lecture whenever his audience began to nod.) Some tricks are most unfair—for example, to praise a number of things in the opponent, just to condemn the one thing that most concerns the case. The *Topics* touches many similar questions and techniques: Bring an objection against yourself, so that you will give the impression of fairness.[10] Don't put the conclusion in the form of a question answerable yes or no, since your opponent will just shake his head and thus make your reasoning appear a failure.[11]

In general, much of the *Rhetoric* is a compendium of other works of Aristotle. But it is not repetition. We can see in his compact summaries here a real effort to orient his materials toward the liberal education of the professional political and legal man. It is an interesting reflection that often in exploring this reorientation we become aware of fresh shades of meaning in the materials themselves.

20

POETICS

The *Poetics* has a long history of service in western civilization as a foundation for aesthetic theory and craftsmanship. It has inspired both heavy and sparkling treatises in German and British aesthetics, given rise to rules for the unities of drama that for a period governed classic French theater with an iron hand, and even been invoked in contemporary writing on the American cinema. How does it fit into the scheme of Aristotle's works?

It was scarcely novel to investigate philosophical problems of art. Plato had already treated of beauty, music, theater, imitation, poetry, and their effects on men's emotions. Aristotle disagreed with some of Plato's theses, and in due course he came around to dealing systematically with the subject. Nor is it surprising that a work on culture should find its place alongside a work on rhetoric. As suggested in the introduction to part 6, the fields in which the poiētic investigations fall are distinctly those that are important for the education of a citizen who is to be a person of influence and critical understanding. The criteria we noted in the discussion of music hold for the study of the arts: to know enough of construction and performance to have sound critical judgment as well as critical appreciation. That drama in particular was influential in the life of the society, playing on ideas and emotional moods of the public and offering a critique of political and moral trends, is clear enough. A comedy like Aristophanes' *Frogs* is a revealing example. It was produced at a critical point in the Peloponnesian War. Aristophanes indicts the new-fangled morality and calls for a return to the old moral order. Euripides and Aeschylus respectively are his standard-bearers for the competing moralities. When the god Dionysus goes to Hades to bring back Euripides and thus restore Athens, there ensues a mock battle in which the two tragedians lampoon each other's art and then step to the scales to see whose lines will be the weightier. Aeschylus wins in a last-minute reversal and is taken back to Athens instead, while the chorus sings of its new hopes for the reform of the city. Aristophanes not merely conveys his own message, but shows us through his caricature of the tragedians how tragedy itself affected social and moral attitudes. Such important material is a natural topic for Aristotle's writing and lecturing. If he had lived in seventeenth-century England he would surely have written on the proper construction of sermons; if he were in twentieth-century America, he would doubtless include chapters on the cinema and television—news-papers would have been discussed in the *Rhetoric*.

The *Poetics* apparently had a wider scope than is found in its fragmen-tary remains. What we have is mostly about tragedy, quite systematically presented, and a bit about epic poetry. The book starts with a declaration that it will treat of *poiētikē* itself—let us call it "poetic art"—and its various forms. The general mark of the poetic arts is imitation (*mimēsis*), and epic poetry and tragedy, comedy, dithyrambic poetry, and for the most part the music of the flute and the lyre, and dance as well, are forms of imitation, differing in their medium, their objects, and their manner. As a group they are contrasted with such arts as use color and shape; they work through rhythm, language, and harmony. The objects of imi-tation are actions, involving characters.

Underlying the whole treatment there is quite clearly the framework of the four causes. To forestall some difficulties, we begin our discussion with the materials of poetic art. After this we go on to the concept of *mimēsis*, which presents the central element in the formal cause and includes also some aspects of efficient cause. We then consider the nature of tragedy, in Aristotle's full account of its parts, which furnishes the remainder of the formal cause and the final cause; and the construction of tragedy, which presents some of the consequences of the analysis.

Materials of Poetic Art

What are the materials of the field on which Aristotle draws? Of his writings on *praxis*, on doing or living as against *poiēsis*, the materials of ethics included the whole realm of human interrelations and actions on the one hand, and their modes of organization on the other. This is quite a contrasting combination. The field of ethics was initially less structured than that of politics, and it was focused on virtues, that is, patterns of character fashioned from emotions and actions and issuing in turn in actions. In politics, there was a more obviously structured ma-terial in the constitutions, or forms of government. On the ethical side Aristotle had a broad acquaintance with human action, but in the field of politics he consulted the specific history of the formation and shape of numerous constitutions. The field for the poetic arts offers in some sense a combination of the types of resources of both ethics and politics. The poetic arts produce works of art, which are there in relative isolation, complete as it were in themselves, to be heard, read, watched. Clearly Aristotle has in mind, and uses in his work, the whole range of Greek tragedies and epics and comedies, at least through the fifth century, with which he shows complete familiarity. But in characterizing the genus as imitation he has added the raw materials of ethics, since actions (*praxeis*) are the objects of imitation and they involve character (*ēthē*), which in turn also involves feeling or emotions (*pathē*). It is thus not too much to expect that he will draw on his ethics in such questions as the general aim of life (happiness), the standard for character (*kalon*, the noble or fine, with its shades of the attractive and the beautiful), and the various ways that pleasures of specific sorts function as justifying ends. These relations between the poetic and the ethical will be genuine ones, not mere parallels. Making can never be self-sufficient ethically, since it involves generating a product, and so it is what we *do* with the product that counts. Of course the act of making can have its own pleasures just as the performance of virtuous acts can, and the observation of the art in the making or in its product also yields it distinctive pleasures. The *Poetics* speaks of the *proper* pleasure of tragedy.[1] Of course underlying having these pleasures is our psychological makeup, and it is the task of the inquiry to see what is involved. Thus the whole of the psychology and the ethics as well lie at the base of the inquiry into the poetic arts. We can no more expect them to be ignored here than the physical theory of the elements would be ignored in the biological inquiries. Any attempt to see the *Poetics* as a purely separate inquiry cut off from the whole philosophical system—prompted perhaps by modern notions of the autonomy of fine art—is likely to be self-frustrating.

The Concept of *Mimēsis*

Returning to the generic activity, we have now to ask what Aristotle means by imitation, by regarding the arts as forms of *mimēsis*. To the modern reader this term is likely to suggest photographic realism, except that photography as an art has taught us how important the selective element can be. Imitation is natural to man from childhood. This is the way we learn, and we delight in representations even of painful scenes or objects. At bottom it is because we find pleasure in learning, in meaningful recognition. If we do not know the object, we take pleasure in the execution or the color.[2] Thus several pleasures are already distinguished, the basic pleasure in learning and also derivative pleasures in imitation, in beholding imitation, in specific recognition, or in a more reflective form of grasping meaning, in admiring execution. There are also the pleasures that arise from the specific medium, such as color, and from the sense of harmony and rhythm that is natural to us. This is not an itemization of pleasures; the effect is rather to suggest a confluence of tendencies that are worked into art.

The concept of *mimēsis* is not a narrow one. For one thing, the poet may imitate not only things as they were or are, or things as they are said or thought to be, but even things as they ought to be.[3] Again, the complex character of *mimēsis* is shown by the treatment of music as in a sense the most mimetic of the arts.[4] The *Politics*, where the context of the discussion is education, does not classify music under a single aim but rather touches on functions of amusement and relaxation, entertainment, and (that most complicated of issues among commentators) *catharsis* of the emotions. Music shapes our feelings into correspondence with the feelings it represents. Its representation is direct: when it conveys anger and mildness and the rest, it embodies within itself actual imitations of character. Visual arts operate more indirectly; painting, for example, relies on indication through form and colors. One is reminded of Schopenhauer's later distinction, that all the arts but music lead us to ideas, whereas music works directly on the will. How music does what it does in the soul, Aristotle says, is a field well explored by philosophical musicians of his day. There are different kinds of melodies—expressing character, stimulating to action, engendering "enthusiasm" and bringing it to a climax—and they can be used for the different aims of music. Its educational effect on character can be secured by judicious selection of melodies; for we know from the *Ethics* that character is formed through practice and the way feeling is expressed. On the cathartic or purging effect of music the *Politics* says:

> Any affection that occurs strongly in some souls is present in all, but with difference of degree—such as pity and fear, and also religious excitement [*enthousiasmos*]; for some people are possessed by this form of emotion, and under the influence of sacred music we see them, when they use strains that violently excite the soul, become calm and composed as if they had been medically treated and taken a purge; the same affection then must come also to the compassionate and the fearful and those generally who are moved to the extent that it affects each one of such people, and in all there must come a sort of purgation and a feeling of relief; and similarly also the purgative melodies bring a harmless joy to people.[5]

It looks as if we are here catching a basic inference. The catharsis that occurs when religious enthusiasm is worked to a pitch by a special type of music is simply an extreme case of a process that occurs in all of us, in the milder as well as the excitable. Because of the reference to pity and fear, which play a central part in the analysis of tragedy, we shall have to ask whether this passage in the *Politics* does not provide the key to understanding the analysis of catharsis in tragedy. For the present our concern is still to understand *mimēsis*.

Bernard Bosanquet warns us not to interpret what Aristotle says about the imitative character of music as the refinement of imitation into the aesthetic idea of symbolism.[6] Certainly for Aristotle *mimēsis* is not freed from its physical relation to what it is representing. In many respects this is like his treatment of imagination as a movement produced by sensation actively operating.[7] That is, imagination preserves the likeness, and in some of its functions selects and spins out but does not cut its roots or become wholly creative. By this point, however, we would have passed from imagination to thought, which is also involved in art. But even thought, as we have seen, is not prone to go off into purely creative formation of ideal alternative possibilities. Mathematics studies the properties of forms abstractable from matter; its business is not to fashion models or ideal symbolic systems.

Further, what of the character of imitation in light of Aristotle's general metaphysical view that nature works like the artist? The converse is that the artist works like nature, but does it consciously. As we explained in the Introduction to this part, the difference between what happens in art and what happens in natural growth (*genesis*) is that the source of motion in the latter lies in what is acted on, wheras in art it lies in what does the acting. Aristotle's favorite paradigm for what nature is like is the doctor curing himself, that is, natural process made self-conscious. Hence we can infer that not only are the poetic arts imitative, but even the technical crafts imitate natural processes. If the other favorite illustration of Aristotle's—the builder—does not seem to fit the picture, or if he follows nature's ways only in the several parts of his work and has no natural houses to imitate, we should not forget Aristotle's remark that if nature were to grow a house it would do so in the way the builder builds it. Hence there is no metaphysical objection to regarding the arts as imitative.

Before going on to examine Aristotle's treatment of tragedy, let us take stock for a moment, in terms of the theory of the causes; the treatment in the early chapters of the *Poetics* is too packed for us to see how systematic the account has really been.

The attention to what the arts imitate—character, emotions, and actions—has given us the matter, or material cause, of the arts, matching the materials of ethics and politics.

Specifying the generic property of the arts as imitation has given the central part of the formal cause. The different kinds of arts and the bases on which they are differentiated—for example, by medium or vehicle, by manner of presentation—constitute the remainder of the formal cause. This would also include other properties that turn up on the way, such as that a work of art is complete, that it has magnitude, and the like.

The several natural tendencies cited in *Poetics* 4 as the sources of the poetic arts (imitation, learning, our pleasure in imitation and harmony and rhythm, our pleasure in noting technical accomplishment) provide the efficient causes in the individual both for creation and appreciation of art. But next in the same chapter is another aspect of efficient causation we have not yet noted, which is of historical interest: the development and differentiation of poetry. Tragedy in particular, having gone through many transformations, reached its natural form and stopped[8]—much as, we may suppose, the individual stops growing when he reaches adult form. The account is quite parallel in type to that of the emergence of the state (*polis*) in the *Politics*. The significant point is, of course, that in these cases we are dealing not with individuals, but with cultural and social forms. Aristotle is thus, by a natural transference from his biological accounts of development, begetting the historical discipline of studying social and cultural evolution. In his view, the social and cultural development of a form stops when it reaches its inherent maturity; in later, Hegelian histories, the focus turns to the unfolding of social and cultural patterns as part of the evolutionary history of mankind. For Aristotle this maturation of poetic type seems to function as the historical efficient cause alongside the efficient cause in the individual's nature.

For the final cause, we have to look to the definition of tragedy itself.

The Nature of Tragedy

The formal definition of tragedy, at the beginning of chapter 6, makes the following points: (1) that tragedy is imitation, (2) that it imitates action, (3) that the action is serious, complete, and has magnitude, (4) that it is in language, embellished with each of the artistic forms, in separate parts, (5) that it is in the form of action, not narrative, and (6) that it uses pity and fear to carry through a catharsis of the emotions.

In his commentary on the *Poetics*, Else points out that all the parts of the definition except the last have been prepared for in the previous chapters.[9] If, however, our causal analysis above is correct, this should not be a ground for surprise or suspicion. The final cause, which Aristotle generally regards as his distinctive contribution, stages its entry dramatically when everything else is ready. Take, for example, the definition of motion in the *Physics*. Book 1 gives the principles of change, both formal and material; book 2, with its discussion of nature, includes the efficient cause of change, both natural and accidental. Book 3, in its first two chapters, carries through the definition of motion with its finalistic character of a potentiality in the process of realization. In the definition of tragedy it is the sudden appearance of the term *catharsis*, together with the fact that it does not appear again (except once where it is used in the limited sense of a purificatory rite in a particular play),[10] that has fueled controversy about the nature of catharsis over the centuries.

Only a few comments are required on the preceding items in the definition. The centrality of action emerges as an important philosophical point, and plot as concerned with the organization of action in the drama is given primacy over character.[11] This expresses directly the ethical view that the end of life is a kind of living and acting, not being of a certain sort; doing makes up happiness, not being of a certain character. It embodies also the metaphysical view that actuality is prior to potentiality. In describing the action as serious Aristotle employs the term *spoudaios*, which was used for *moral* or *good* in the ethical writings in contexts of virtuous conduct. Tragedy thus deals with serious and moral (in the broad sense) actions, not trifling ones. As for the artistic forms and separate parts, the embellishment lies in rhythm, harmony, and song, and some parts of the tragedy operate through verse alone, other parts through song. The six parts of a tragedy distinguished are, in the order of importance assigned to them, plot, character, thought, diction, song, and spectacle.[12] This constitutes the structure of the treatment, and the parts are dealt with almost in the spirit in which the biological works deal with the organs or parts of animals in their interrelated functioning with respect to the organism as a whole. This makes it important to look at the last item in the definition and see what the tragedy as a whole is up to.

In one sense, of course, the final cause of tragedy is to give the audience who hears or reads it a certain pleasure. But this is scarcely more enlightening than it was in the ethics to say that the aim of life was happiness. One wants to know what kind of pleasure it is and with what activities it is associated. Clearly, the tragic pleasure is associated with the production of a certain pattern of pity and fear. The usual interpretation of catharsis keeps its eye on the audience. This is very much like the procedure in the *Rhetoric*, where the aim is not merely to produce a speech but to have a persuasive effect on the hearers. The *Rhetoric* introduces topics and judges treatment of technical points in the construction of a speech ultimately by what that effect will be. So too the *Poetics* uses the extent to which different procedures contribute to successful catharsis as a crucial test for evaluating plot and character. This concentration on the interactive relation of artist, work, and spectator makes the theory of what happens to the spectator (or reader) the essential point for understanding the analysis of tragedy, even though the presentation is formally ordered and reaches this point in its own unhurried time.

We do not go to tragedies expressly to experience catharsis, but when we go to the theater for enjoyment, the enjoyment will not come unless the cathartic experience takes place, and this does not take place unless the play is well constructed to produce this effect. There has been serious controversy over what catharsis is really meant to be. In the *Politics* passage there is reference to a clearer treatment in the *Poetics*, but the latter gives so brief a mention that scholars have been tempted to infer a lost fuller account. The theories of catharsis vary from the simplest observational to the most complicated theoretical. There is the behavioral view that all you have to do is watch an audience, and you will see them grow tense and then weep, and they would tell you, if you asked them after the show, that they enjoyed it. Medical interpretations take *catharsis* to be a metaphor from purging undesirable bodily humors. Some interpretations take the basic model to be religious purification. Psychoanalytically inspired interpretations emphasize that irrational emotions are brought to the surface by identification with one or another dramatic figure and vicariously expressed rather than repressed. There are ethical interpretations that stress not the removal of emotions but their purification, so that rational forms would survive with irrational components eliminated or with a harmonious balance of the emotions achieved as a mean, the excess being drained off. There need not be a conflict among some of these. Aristotle's use of the term is general enough, the evidence limited enough. Whatever the process, the outcome is clear: there must be some pleasure in the result; it must leave the spectator in a more rational state, not without emotion but with emotion somehow clarified, and with a greater general insight into life's problems—one might say a moral insight, if "moral" be used in the broad Aristotelian way.

There is, however, a further problem worth raising that seems to have been largely subordinated in the traditional disputes about catharsis. The question is why fear and pity are regarded as the basic emotions on which tragedy operates. After all, the *Rhetoric* and the *Ethics* deal with a fairly large repertory of feelings and emotions. Why should not tragedy intensify love or hate, anger or indignation? When Euripides showed the Athenians the unjust absurdity of their treatment of women and foreigners, can he not be seen as intensifying shame? And there are the emotions of religious ecstasy referred to in the *Politics* passage, in which the orgiastic quality predominates rather than fear. Of course, many emotions can enter in relation to the content. Modern aesthetic discussions readily reject a primary role for some: a drama would be propagandistic if it roused to action, erotic if it roused desire, didactic if it satisfied curiosity—but such is not "art." Aristotle, however, does not have this kind of puristic conception of art. Perhaps it is simply that other emotions are variable in audiences at tragedy, while their tenseness and sympathetic response are generic. Or perhaps the answer lies in the especial stress in Athenian tragedy on the horrendous themes of the ancient myths; by concluding that tragedy reached its natural fulfillment in the Athenian theater,[13] Aristotle may be accepting the typical content. Perhaps also he is simply formulating assumptions in prior treatments of tragedy. Certainly Plato, in his attack on tragedy in book 10 of the *Republic*, points specifically to the fear it rouses and to the relaxation of emotional control as each man weeps in response to the poet's presentations.

More likely, the answer is to be sought in the nature of the central emotions themselves. Their depiction in the *Rhetoric* suggests some clues to their position. Fear is defined as "a pain or troubled feeling due to the appearance [*phantasia*] of a destructive or painful evil that is imminent."[14] In the midst of this account Aristotle gives advice to the orator that might even be transferable to the tragedian: "Whenever it is advisable that the audience feel afraid, it is necessary to make them think that they are likely to suffer. For others greater than they have suffered, and their equals should be shown suffering or having suffered, and at the hands of those from whom they did not think it would happen, and in a form and at a time when they did not think it would happen."[15] Fear is thus the correlative of suffering, and since tragedy involves a portrayal of suffering, there will always be in a successful tragedy the generic reaction of some element of fear. Pity is "a kind of pain due to the appearance of a destructive or painful evil that happens to a person who does not deserve it; an evil that one might expect oneself to suffer, or one of his friends, and this when it seems near."[16] The evil must be at a moderate distance. If it is too near, men may become panic-striken; if too far, there will be no pity. Pity seems to be the concomitant in an adult audience with some experience of life, of beholding suffering at a sufficient distance. It is precisely such distance that the known fact of *mimēsis* creates and presents. (Aristotle does not go into the psychology of identification here or in the *Poetics*, but we have seen enough in his discussion of the relation of self and other in dealing with friendship to realize that he has his eye on the phenomena, whatever the explanation, and so can presuppose them in other inquiries.) Fear and what appears to be its consequent pity are thus the general emotions of the tragic presentation when it is successful.

The distinctive impact of Aristotle's treatment of catharsis is that it constitutes a justification of tragedy. Plato's attack had rested on a different psychological basis with a different ethical import. For Plato, tragedy, by heightening emotion, was adding to the power of the lowest (appetitive) part of the soul. It was weakening defenses, where morality called for constant vigilant repression. Aristotle's more realistic psychology of the normal emotions suggests the way emotional expression clarifies feeling and fortifies rational insight.

The interpretation of catharsis presented here is in line with the dominant contemporary interpretations, as well as with what we would expect from the other works and from Aristotle's general philosophical approach applied to the problems of the *Poetics*. We should, however, note a seriously different approach to catharsis offered by Else, cited above.[17] Else denies that catharsis is directed to the audience; the audience merely judges that a catharsis or purification has taken place and that a given dramatic figure may be pitied. Thus the catharsis does not take place *in* the audience; it is rather a process in the structure of the plot in which a calamitous act of a polluting sort is purged or purified by the character's discovery of the nature of his act and his remorse or consequent plight. In developing this thesis, Else appeals to Aristotle's use of the term *pathos* for the destructive or painful action, like death or wounding, that takes place in a tragedy,[18] and counts pathos as part of the plot along with reversal and discovery (the change of fortune and the recognition of what one has done or who someone really is). Now *pathos* is the normal word also for feeling or emotion, both in the ethics and in some parts of the *Poetics*. The crucial point is that *pathēmata*, which is an equivalent of the plural of *pathos*, is used in the formal definition of tragedy (given above) in relation to *katharsis*. Thus Else claims that in this context the *katharsis* of the *pathēmata* means the purification of the calamitous acts and not the catharsis of the emotions. We cannot of course enter here into the lengthy disputes about the interpretation of the passage.[19] On the whole, Else's thesis seems to rest on isolating the *Poetics* from the interpretation of the *Politics* and the *Rhetoric* for the understanding of catharsis. We should not be daunted by Aristotle's remark in the *Politics* that he is using the term *katharsis* without qualification (*haplōs*) and will talk about it more clearly in the works on poetics.[20] Indeed it suggests that the meaning he gives to it without analysis in the *Politics* is the one he is going to explain in the *Poetics*. Lane Cooper points out that if the phenomenon of catharsis is clear enough, the *Poetics* is in fact explaining it by showing the conditions under which it takes place.[21] Even, however, if the term had not occurred in the *Poetics*, the issues about the way pity and fear operate would themselves have posed the questions we have raised.

The Construction of The Tragedy

How intimately Aristotle's account of the psychological function of tragedy enters into his recommendations on the construction of the drama can be seen most directly in his derivation of the appropriate character for the hero. If we are to identify with a person, that is, to feel fear and pity, then he has to be sufficiently like us, and his suffering has to be undeserved. If he is very good we will simply be outraged, and if he is very evil we will feel that it served him right. Our best choice is neither: "There remains the intermediate kind of person, a man not outstanding in virtue and justice, nor falling into misfortune through evil and wickedness, but by some error [or flaw: *hamartia*]."[22] Later theorists eventually magnified *hamartia* into the "tragic flaw." Characters may of course have flaws not amounting to vice: Oedipus is stubborn, Agamemnon is proud. The vicissitudes of this concept at the hands of interpreters have been striking. For a long time it was thought of as a moral defect. Then scholars agreed that it meant an error of judgment resting on some factual ignorance. Now a "mean" is emerging, that the term has a range of application extending from ignorance of fact at one end to moral defect at the other. *Hamartia* must thus be interpreted in each case according to the situation.[23] Aristotle also adds to his delineation of the hero's character that the person involved be one of renown and prosperity. This is probably the same point as that quoted above from the *Rhetoric*: fear is inspired more readily by our seeing that even the more fortunate are afflicted.

This reversal of fortune, from good fortune to disaster, is taken to be integral to the best plot. In fact the general outline of plot structure is derived according to the same criteria as character: what will best produce the psychological effect desired in a good tragedy.

In the actual order of the *Poetics*, the section on tragedy, after its formal definition and the distinction of the six parts, goes on to discuss each part. Plot is primary; it is "the soul of tragedy."[24] Details of the organization of plot range from the kind of unity required to such important devices as discovery, in which the errors that precipitated the fall are cleared up. Of the other elements, character ranks as second in importance. Thought ranks third; this refers to ideational content and its appropriateness—what is possible and pertinent in different circumstances. Diction is fourth. Melody or song is regarded as a major embellishment. As for spectacle, a play can produce its effect on reading. Performance is extra and has its own emotional effect.

Concluding Remarks

We have limited our chief consideration to tragedy, which constitutes the bulk of the *Poetics*. There are also interesting suggestions about narrative as contrasted with dramatic poetry, about the differences between history and narrative poetry, about epic poetry, and about comedy. One finds many a dictum that has since become a classic subject for philosophical elaboration—for example, that poetry is more philosophical than history, for it tends to express the universal, and history merely expresses the particular.[25] An occasional definition stimulates fine phenomenological probing; the ludicrous in comedy, for instance, is treated as a division of the ugly.[26] But it is the full treatment of tragedy that gives the book its special significance. As a case study it also provides the best basis for inferring Aristotle's general aesthetic theory.

We have come today to expect of a philosophy of art at least four things: some analysis of the nature of the creative process, some analysis of the nature of appreciation, some standards for evaluation of art works, and some relation of art as a field to the remainder of life, its goals, and its processes. Of these, Aristotle's analysis of the creative process and of appreciation are now clear at least in outline. His standards of evaluation tend to be closely tied to the ends that emerge in the analysis of creation and appreciation. Certainly he is ready to point to what he regards as great art (the *Oedipus Rex* is his prime example), but even more, there is a constant proliferation of criteria close to every issue discussed, whether it be the tightness of a plot, the reality and consistency of character, or the reinforcement of plot effect by spectacle effect. Finally, his moral and social judgments about art and its relation to the rest of human life are presupposed throughout. There is no theory of fine art that has as its end beauty for beauty's sake; but there is no countertheory of beauty for the sake of something else. Rather there are multiple aims for the human activities that become self-conscious about their techniques, and there are functions that develop the character of man and give joy in their performance and beholding. The good has been identified broadly as human happiness, and good character as the virtues that express and fulfill and apply men's search for happiness. Under such a broad formulation, the appeal to goodness, whether in character or in the intimate identification of spectator and dramatic figure, represents no narrow moralism or parochial harness for the artist. Aristotle's moral and social judgment in art therefore requires for its understanding a full relation to his whole philosophical outlook. Of course, a detailed examination of the *Poetics* would also be required to itemize the specific ways in which specific values of time and place and class and temperament enter into specific pronouncements about specific techniques.

If this calls for a union of the broadest theory and the most minute detail, it is not out of step with Aristotle's own spirit. One can only marvel at the energy with which, when most of his discussion is over and he comes to diction, he launches on nothing less than a short course in linguistics. He tells us the parts of speech, touches the rudiments of phonetics, works up to the structure of metaphor, and so on, even recommending what kinds of words to use in what kinds of poetry.

In theorizing on the arts, in fact in all his work, Arsitotle is conscious of the importance of initial ideas and formulations, the difficulty of getting started, and the need for research and development of knowledge on which action may rest. He is equally conscious of the importance of teaching how to think and do, not just handing on products, however good. He says this explicitly at the end of *On Sophistical Refutations*, in criticism of the rhetoricians: "They assumed they could train by imparting not an art but the products of an art, just as if one who said he would impart knowledge for preventing pain in the feet would then not teach the cobbler's art nor the means of providing such things, but would offer many kinds of shoes of all sorts; for he has helped with respect to the need but he has not imparted an art."[27] He then points out that in his work on rhetoric at least there was an accumulation of past materials, but in his research on reasoning he had to start from scratch. With a mixture of modesty and self-satisfaction he concludes in words that might be applied on the historical scene to all his philosophical endeavors: "If then it seems to you after consideration that, given the original state of the materials, our inquiry is in a satisfactory condition, compared with the other modes of treatment that have been traditionally developed, there remains but for all of you or those who have studied with us, to pardon the shortcomings of our inquiry and to give many thanks for the discoveries."

Part 7

EPILOGUE

2 I

PREDICAMENTS OF

ARISTOTELIAN SCHOLARSHIP

The purpose of this epilogue is to share with the reader some of the concerns, problems, and misgivings that arose during the writing of this book. It is natural to do so at the conclusion since I have tried all along to suggest the processes as well as the outcome of Aristotelian scholarship, and to show how complex they are, how questions of text and language and intepretation and history and social context and philosophical outlook intermingle in reaching decisions. (Where the prevailing views of scholars were reported the reader was not left without some glimpse of how they went about their business.) I want now to comment on five topics that are unfinished business—though for various reasons. They are textual and historical issues about the texts; the relation of Aristotle's ideas to his predecessors', particularly Plato's; the relation of the ideas to the history of Greek science and the crafts; their relation to social and economic institutions and historical context; and the impact of philosophical differences on interpreting Aristotle. Some are unfinished business because they raise problems about the security of interpretation; some because they are questions on which a great deal more could be said than was said (either because of the character of the book or as a matter of policy that should be explained); and some because they represent areas of research insufficiently cultivated. My purposes are roughly twofold: to assure that interpretation of Aristotle is not threatened by a basic skepticism on textual, historical, or philosophical grounds and to suggest some avenues of research that have been insufficiently tapped and that may yield fruitful results.

Textual Problems

We met three kinds of textual problems: (1) Occasionally there were alternative readings and proposed emendations, the residual problems of the long process by which the texts were stabilized. (2) There were not infrequent differences of linguistic interpretation concerning the meaning of a passage. (3) There were questions concerning the order of composition of some of the works and the genuineness of others.

How do these three problems now affect the reliability of Aristotelian interpretation?

(1) The vast work of classical scholars in providing an adequate text was briefly noted in the Introduction. This is a wholly separate study—a model of devoted professional scholarship—which is not here under review. At best we looked at a few examples of passages in which textual variations made a difference in interpretation. For the most part it is now possible to take such textual variations in one's philosophical stride, because on the whole interpretation in terms of other passages and the developed system of ideas prevents a changed reading from constituting a decisive crash argument concerning a philosophical point. It would be a very rash philosopher who would rest a whole thesis solely on embroidering a dubious passage. On the other hand, fresh evidence might settle some philosophical dispute—for example, if we were sometime to find a manuscript that quoted *On the Psyche* and gave a variant concerning active and passive reason. Yet even if the whole of the fifth chapter of book 3 were dropped out, many of the conflicting interpretations of the precise nature of thought in Aristotle would still arise. The future work of classical scholars remains a possible constraint rather than a decisive determinant for Aristotelian interpretation.

(2) A somewhat similar conclusion seems indicated for linguistic problems concerning the meaning of a text passage. These were not dealt with save in a few examples, the most striking of which was Else's thesis about catharsis in the *Poetics*. Linguistic interpretations certainly can prescribe limits, but within those limits they cannot rule out shades of meaning that are proposed in the light of philosophical ideas made clear in other contexts. This is particularly so where Aristotle seems to be developing his own technical usage. Usually the clarification is an interactive or cooperative one in which linguistic considerations serve as partial evidence. Moreover, the relations are not themselves all of one type. For example, the meaning of *essence* (*to ti ēn einai*) is probably determinable from context and usage with roughly the same result irrespective of varied linguistic interpretations of the phrase, but its shades of meaning are certainly affected substantially by the linguistic interpretation selected. On the other hand, the fresh hypothesis offered about the analysis of *ought* in Aristotle's ethics was markedly helped by linguistic considerations about *dei* and *-ton*, though it might have been suggested in any case on the basis of comparative studies in ethical theory. In some sense, then, ideational items in interpretation are not without dependence (though not in a simply one-to-one relation) on the long-range products

of linguistic research. The guiding rule here was to exercise caution in relating philosophical meaning and linguistic argument, but to note possible doors that the latter might open. Not all references to linguistic questions, however, were specifically of a linguistic nature. For example, the question of the broader or narrower meaning of *pros ta telē*, raised in the ethics, was less a linguistic issue than one of overcoming a narrowing philosophical model (the means–end model) imposed in translation with harmful effects on interpretation.

(3) The question of the temporal order of Aristotle's writings, and the kindred question of the genuineness of certain of the works, is more internal to Aristotelian philosophical scholarship. Take the latter first. The philosophical impact of a disputed work depends on what it says. Thus book 4 of the *Meteorology* fits in so neatly with the rest of the corpus in its mode of analysis and its materials that it amplifies rather than alters interpretations. The *Magna Moralia* on the other hand might affect specific issues of ethical theory and raise questions of a shift at different stages in Aristotle's development. *Meteorology* 4 was for a time rejected but seems now firmly established. On the Aristotelian authorship of *Magna Moralia* there have been startling changes of view; an onlooker might almost say that the pendulum swings wildly. The important thing is therefore the kind of use made of disputed works in interpreting Aristotle's views. Now there would be no hesitation in an evidential use of the content of *Meteorology* 4, but I used the *Magna Moralia* only for illustrative items. Even the definitely post-Aristotelian writings can be consulted for the atmosphere of ideas and the way things were carried on, or for suggestive items. Such use was made, in a few places, of the *Problems* and *On Colors*.

The question of the order of Aristotle's works (including strata within individual works) and what should be done with the reconstructed early dialogues is perhaps more pressing. If the detailed use of hypotheses in this area is avoided, as was our decision, one runs the risk of bypassing significant leads in interpreting the philosophy. On the other hand, to use them is to risk carrying one's whole product out onto a shaky limb.[1] The fact is that the study of the order, in spite of all the intensive effort devoted to it and even though it has produced some stable points, has for the most part piled conjecture on plausibility. It is not unknown for a great scholar to say a question has been settled to his satisfaction by the work of so-and-so, only to find that definitive solution questioned in a decisive swing of opinion soon after. What is one to do in this dilemma? We could speculate on alternatives, writing "non-Euclidean" Aristotles. Perhaps a simpler path is to limit oneself to the philosophical presuppositions of the different hypotheses about order and to the points in the corpus on which they appeal for evidence. This is logically prior to the dispute and usually lies back of it.

An example we encountered may be pursued to make this procedure clear. The order of the several writings on psychology is an important matter, especially if we are to decide whether Aristotle went by stages from a Platonic belief in a separate immortal soul to the almost naturalistic functional view of the psyche we find in *On the Psyche* 2. (The mere question whether he held at the start to the view of a separate soul requires only the authenticity of one of the early popular works in which such an item appears, provided we are sure that fragment is Aristotle's view and not someone else's up for consideration.) Nuyens proposed a theory of stages and Ross to some extent supported it. But Block, in an incisive fresh look at the internal evidence, made a strong case for an opposing thesis that placed *On the Psyche* earlier than the *Parva Naturalia*.[2] Now, as Block argues, underlying the one view is the assumption that the two doctrines—the treatment of the psyche as the form or actualization of the organic body, and the use of the heart as the *archē* for psychological phenomena—are distinct and even incompatible; underlying his own view is the assumption that they are quite compatible. This philosophical question is clearly prior to the whole dispute and could properly be considered without entering into the dispute about the order of the works. In fact, in chapter 9 we found it necessary to work out carefully the relation of the phenomenal and the physical and to look at the evidence in the corpus bearing on that relation. Of course if the problem of order were decisively settled *independently*, it might have some bearing on the use of the evidence in the philosophical interpretation. But such issues are rarely so independent. This example may stand as a paradigm of the policy that was adopted: not to attempt a review of disputes about order (except for an occasional reference where relevant) but to deal with some of their implicit philosophical presuppositions. On the general theories of order and development, Jaeger's work of course opened up an era of research and controversy, and Düring has, if not closed it, at least stabilized many of the problems by delineating alternative approaches.[3] Refinement and further development remain for the future, and we cannot overlook the possibility that eventually established results could seriously affect the philosophical interpretation. Meanwhile the present state of the corpus and its internal examination deserve philosophical priority. Whether it keeps that, however, depends on the results of the philosophical scrutiny or, in short, on whether a case has been made for a coherent inner philosophy that is possibly freer than we have thought of the puzzles that are likely to make the order issues crucial.

Relation to Predecessors, Particularly Plato

The view just considered will help explain what was the hardest decision to make: not to pursue constantly the vexing questions of Aristotle's relations to Plato, both in general and on specific items. This is, of course, a fascinating and important area of its own, with all sorts of problems, not the least of which is the correctness of Aristotle's expressed interpretation of Platonic ideas.[4] To make some reference to Platonic sources is, of course, unavoidable. Sometimes the relation is clear, and Plato's view is what Aristotle is using or fighting against—for example, in the analysis of pleasure. On many a tangled issue it is enough merely to grasp what Aristotle says is the Platonic issue he is discussing; whether it is a correct report is an external problem, for correct or incorrect it is what Aristotle addresses. Specific studies of the relation of Aristotle's writings on physics or politics to specific Platonic dialogues are of course extremely valuable. But to make the relation to Plato the framework for the exposition of Aristotle's philosophy can build-in one or another of conflicting theories of their relation, which will influence what parts of the corpus we attend to and even the selection of evidence. On occasion such a governing scheme will even—if we may allow a slight caricature—base its exposition on the formula *Plato plus misunderstanding or confusion equals Aristotle!*

It is important to clarify the significance of our decision to focus primarily on the corpus and put Platonic relations aside as a separate inquiry. The one thing it definitely is not is an attempt to turn back the clock to the situation before Jaeger and simply assume a unified Aristotelian philosophy in the corpus. The work that has been done on the development of Aristotle and on Platonic relations is not lost by our procedure, for it has itself usually fastened attention on neglected aspects of the corpus and probed their significance. We can now look at these phases in Aristotle irrespective of how we got to them and at passages that have been unearthed in the corpus and in the earlier dialogues, so that we have a richer Aristotle to inquire into even apart from Platonic relations.

Again, we must recognize that sometimes the back-to-Aristotle movement is a reaction against the distracting effect of the search for sources. For example, Aubenque strikes a partially responsive chord when he says that reaction against the exegetical tradition and the desire to put Aristotle back in his historical context and to increase the inquiry into source and development has only ended in stressing the marginal texts and neglecting the essential text. (He is talking of *phronēsis*.) He regards the fundamental task as that of interpretation, for the interpretation is what sends us to one or another source.[5]

From time to time the slogan is revived that we must carry out the exegesis of the works of Aristotle through the works of Aristotle. But when Düring raises this issue by asking whether it is possible,[6] he has already settled in his own mind an account of the relations between Plato and Aristotle and concluded that Aristotle had a fairly constant outlook of his own from the beginning, whether he used Plato's language or developed his own. We do not assume this conclusion, nor do we assume a general theory of the autonomy of a philosopher's work. Of course there is the simple courtesy of finding out a philosopher's ideas before one starts deriving them, but it is quite possible that some of them may not be clear until we see how they are derived. That remains a question open to investigation, not requiring a uniform answer for all parts of Aristotle's corpus. If Plato's philosophy were itself crystal clear to begin with and if the relations to Aristotle were independently and definitely established, the situation might be different. As things stand, it is possible that independent study of Aristotle at the present stage might change the terms of the study of the relationship—once again, depending on how stable or reliable the result of the Aristotelian study itself is.

Our policy with respect to Platonic (and earlier philosophical) relations thus rests on a complex decision about the present state of the field. Controversies about Plato and about Platonic-Aristotelian relations make judgments speculative, and there is no longer the first wholehearted acceptance of Jaeger's scheme or any other. Again, even a successful exhibition of specific relations does seem to have a distracting effect. For example, to become interested in the religious as against the scientific origins of the concept of nature, or even in the conflict of nature and convention in Greek thought, defers systematic examination of how that concept *operates* in Aristotle's thought, apart from the question of how he defines it. (That is why we reversed the emphasis, concentrating on the operational analysis and relegating the rest to notes.) Again, to discover that fundamental Platonic dialectical puzzles gave shape to Aristotle's formulation of physical questions, while very important, seems often to end investigation of the *Physics* and overshadow the fact that Aristotle was dealing with scientific issues and producing a physical theory that in the long run had to be rejected by Galileo. It embodied different physical principles, and it is the job of the philosophical analyst of Aristotle's ideas to find out how they got there, to what observations and theories and commitments they are related. In short, the Platonic relation has carried Aristotelian study in recent times to the logical-metaphysical pole; it needs to be bent back to the scientific pole. This requires a careful study within the corpus to see how the metaphysical ideas were related to the ideas in the scientific works.

It may very well be that some of the Aristotelian ideas cannot be thoroughly cleared up without their Platonic antecedents. Perhaps the initial distinction in the *Categories* between *being predicable of a subject* and *inhering in a subject* makes better sense if tied to the controversies about the Platonic Forms. Without that it may be seen simply as a difference between the essential and the accidental in the relation of predicate to subject. But there are other very important questions in which we clearly become more and more entangled as we seek light in Aristotle's relations to Plato, much as the subject matter draws us on because of its interest. Attempts to settle Aristotle's theory of human nature by reference to its derivation from changes in Plato's psychology were, we suggested, of this sort.

Aristotle was distinctively a scientist and his ideas have to be dealt with from the point of view of their role and possible impact in a scientific setting. Even when he is dealing with dialectic, with logic, and with rhetoric, it is always possible that questions stemming from his science and how it is to be carried on enter into his consideration. Somehow the way in which he is related to Plato rarely brings this into focus.

There is another matter of a quite different sort. Plato has a hold on the philosophical emotions that probably no other philosopher has ever had. People are Platonists for temperamental reasons, for religious reasons, for humanistic reasons, for political and moral reasons. Even dispassionate scholars may want to rescue Plato from his earliest serious critic. Reverence for Plato often gets in the way of understanding Aristotle. (So perhaps does reverence for Aristotle.) The remedy here is first to focus on Aristotle directly, and second, to see his study where possible (as I have tried to illustrate it) in the comparison of different philosophies.

The impact of these several themes explains the decision not to give a central place to Platonic relations in the expositional structure. It is not set forth as a permanent principle, but as a desirable policy for the present in light of the present state of the field. It is in effect a pause that enables us to return to a focus on Aristotle and the corpus to see, with some clearing of the decks, whether a plausible unity in the philosophy is discoverable, and what kind, in terms of the problems that Aristotle himself sets forth and the relations of the fields that he himself investigates.

Relation to Science and the Crafts

Philosophical interpretation of Aristotle has long taken for granted that some ideas are to be understood in relation to mathematical beliefs, theories, and procedures. For example, the influence of the phenomenon of incommensurables is profound in many parts of the philosophy, and the relation of diagrams and proof is not without place in the epistemology. No philosophical objection arises to the notion of such relations, no matter how they are construed in detail—as analogy, partial evidence, suggestive model, field of marked application, or whatever—and it is agreed that intensive investigation into the history of Greek mathematics will bring fresh light to the interpretation of Aristotle.

The same open entry has long been allowed for medicine. It is clear that some of the important philosophical concepts, such as *dunamis*, had definite medical usage and that others, such as *phusis*, may have serious medical support in the picture of health and disease and recovery. At the very least, striking phenomena captured in medical concepts and developed in medical theorizing could be paradigmatic for branches of philosophy. For example, harmony, interpreted in medical theory as an appropriate balance of the elements preserving health, was apparently conflated with the notion of harmony in music to yield an intellectual support for the Aristotelian idea of the mean, in the ethics. (Whether we speak here of a "seed-bed" or of "forging" ideas is a still further problem in the models of "intellectual production.")

Such examples do not come from medicine operating as a craft but from medicine as an attempt to understand and theorize about the processes of the human body as part of nature. In this respect it is no different from any of the other sciences, and if it can be the source of philosophical ideas, so possibly can the other sciences. Perhaps this kind of influence is overlooked because it is not recognized that the way in which philosophical generalization is effected is often the same as the way in which scientific generalization is effected in the study of the natural phenomena. For example, in the *Meteorology* interpretations of unreachable phenomena in the heavens are made in terms of familiar terrestrial reactions, and in the writings on physics and biology, biological processes are interpreted by comparison to physical ones, and conversely. The action of heat in general, and fire specifically, is a widespread instance, and it passes into philosophical generalization when it becomes clear that it is a likely model for metaphysical propositions about the active and the passive. Hence all this is not simply a case of using some phenomena that science scrutinizes to suggest only other *scientific* generalizations. Accordingly, the continuity and influence between the scientific materials and the philosophical ideas was stressed here (for example, in chapter 13 in examining the rise of some philosophical principles, and in chapters 9 and 10 in noting the relation of the controversies about the physiology of perception to the philosophical principles for interpreting the epistemological relations of the knower and the known). We might even be tempted to construct a notion of the *distinctive scientific base* for philosophical ideas, in the sense that the understanding of different philosophical networks in widely varying philosophies might have to be referred to the process of generalizing from different scientific areas and scientific theories.

Turning now to the crafts—the other aspect of medical operations—there is no antecedent reason why they should not, like the scientific knowledge of natural processes, have an influence in generating or developing philosophical ideas. Aristotle certainly treated the analysis of craft and nature in the same breath, so to speak, for nature works like the artist and the artist imitates nature. So if we follow Aristotle's advice, we shall look carefully for the role of the crafts in general and the specific crafts in particular upon the interpretation of Aristotle himself. Thus we would expect any results of current and future research into Greek crafts to give us fresh light. At present there is some use of such material for specific passages. For example, Lee adds to his translation of the *Meteorology* an extended and interesting note on ancient ironmaking, to explain a particular passage.[7] Aristotle's concern here is a specific difference in the behaviors of earth—water compounds in which earth predominates, according to the different ways in which they have solidified. A careful search through Aristotle with the problem of craft relations, in mind may very well show higher-order generalizations, and contemporary researches into ancient metallurgy as well as discoveries about ancient instrumentation may turn out to assist interpretation. In addition to the influence of specific craft processes, we have seen that the model of craftsmanship generates or supports some of Aristotle's basic philosophical concepts.

Why has scholarship so readily accepted mathematical influence, but moved so slowly to the systematic exploration of the influence of the sciences and even more slowly to that of the crafts? Perhaps there were ideological factors involved. The influence of mathematics on philosophy seems to be that of ideas on ideas, and that is quite acceptable. But the influence of craft processes may be thought to be the subtle influence of behavior surreptitiously molding ideas without the active consent of the thinker. Thus when a Veblen or a Dewey explores the difference between a hunting and a craft society and finds the one giving large place in its attitudes and ideas to luck and chance and the will of supernatural beings, and the other to orderly processes of cause and effect, philosophers sometimes feel outraged, for it suggests a technological theory of determinants for intellectual production. When Farrington advanced the thesis that the Milesian philosophers drew the positive content of their philosophical ideas from the techniques of their age, it similarly provoked heated controversy, and even more so when he traced political influences in philosophical ideas.[8] This seemed to be arguing the Marxian thesis that intellectual production reflects modes of material production and the relations in which that production is organized and the struggles that ensue over these institutions.

It is to be hoped that such defensive reactions in scholarly research are now over. No thesis of absolute philosophical autonomy of ideas is needed to maintain the integrity of scholarship, any more than the moral ideal of the integrity of the individual need belie the facts of birth and growth or the influence of human institutions on aspirations and attitudes. Indeed, once we get beyond theoretical dogmatisms, we can see that fresh hypotheses are opened up that may be extremely fruitful; but we shall not know how fruitful in a particular field like Aristotelian scholarship until they are intensively and systematically pursued. Equally important is the philosophical analysis of the idea of influence or determination. This determination is not all of one piece, and specific exploration of Aristotelian contexts can help refine it—differentiating, for example, as suggested above, the cases of analogy, partial evidence, suggestive model, field of marked application, and no doubt many other subtle modes of influence. General determinisms about intellectual production are a quite distinct matter. The role of the crafts, like that of science, in Aristotelian philosophical ideas is a field for much-needed serious systematic research.

Relations to Social and Economic Institutions and Historical Context

In general, the point just made for the sciences and crafts holds equally for the influence of social, economic, and historical relations as well—that is, for the influence of social processes, practices, and institutions. Why should they not also suggest models, influence attitudes in analysis, and even provide explicit hypotheses?

The case of religion is instructive. Its influence in philosophy is recognized because it has so large an ideational development, which in theology is directly philosophical. There is no hesitation therefore in noting religious influences such as that of Orphic beliefs on Plato or traditional Greek views of the properties of the divine on Aristotle's conception of the Unmoved Mover as eternal. But there has been little attempt to explore the influences upon a philosophy that institutional aspects of religion may have, such as the ritual and ceremonial with their attendant emotions, organizational structure, and social attitudes. These may have operated in the background to furnish vital models, for example, for such philosophical concepts as participation, guilt and responsibility, political organization, individual autonomy, or interpersonal relations. And since this aspect of religion is usually related to the broader cultural pattern, to discover its influence in the development of the philosophy may also open the way to a view of influences from other cultural forms and social institutions.

Certainly complex relations of philosophical conception and social relations are evident in the Platonic and Aristotelian ideas of human nature—routed directly, that is, not through religion. Plato had no difficulty, in the *Republic*, finding clues in the class structure of the society for the internal structure of the psyche and its parts; his equating appetite and the masses, reason and the rulers, and the properties of each, is read off largely from the social model. Now what is the place of slavery as an institution in influencing the theory of human nature? If we assume no prior sweeping thesis and examine it in Plato and Aristotle separately— again, not assuming it to be the same unless we find it so—we have a legitimate and possibly illuminating inquiry. Note, however, that it cannot be carried out fully without exploring the actual character of Greek slavery itself in that period. The essence of slavery will not do; we have to know how slaves were in fact regarded, what differences there were in their use in the household, in administration, in agriculture, in mining, and which dominated in Greek consciousness, how helots were distinguished from slaves, and how far if at all the idea that slavery was not natural issued in any programs of liberation. We have referred earlier to M. I. Finley's exploration of such questions; the textual analysis for Plato has been carried out in Vlastos's paper "Slavery in Plato's Thought."[9] In the long run, to give the full picture for Aristotle, one needs a comparable textual study correlated with the socioinstitutional study, and with the sophisticated analysis of influence suggested above.

Aristotle himself points the way to the influence of social materials on specific philosophical ideas in that he deals concretely in the *Politics* with the constitutional forms he studies and the economic and social conditions in terms of which he refashions his classification of constitutions. This explicitness has its limits where his own values operate in limiting the data and scope of an inquiry. Here the evidence for the limitation, and in part for the presence and operation of the values, has to come from the comparison of what Aristotle deals with in the text and what was going on in the society. An excellent example is his treatment of money; as Finley has shown, it is geared only to exchange among producers and reflects nothing of the actual relations of traders.[10] This evidence can go along with Aristotle's treatment of usury, and his expressed general attitudes to trade in other contexts, to support our understanding of his aversion to the traders and their mode of life. This in turn can serve as a key to understanding his general social outlook and so increase our sensitivity to its possible influence in other specific contexts. In similar fashion, in relation to specific historical conflicts, Aristotle's discussion of revolutions is enough to open the doors. His own place in relation to Macedonia and Athens is of course a tempting point of speculation, as we have seen.[11] And his treatment of specific historical events is essential if we are to have an adequate understanding of his philosophy of history.[12] The same kind of exploration is required in many other areas—for example, in the relation of Aristotle's legal ideas to specific Athenian legal procedures, and of educational ideas to modes of Greek education.[13] Scholars may have different hopes about how far the results will carry us, but the job is worth doing more intensively and with refined concepts of influence.

Philosophical Differences and the Interpretation of Aristotle

We have dealt with many aspects of the role of philosophical differences in interpreting Aristotle, but two may be considered particularly at this point. The more obvious is whether the interpreter is finding an Aristotle that meshes with his own philosophical outlook. The other is how the setting of philosophical problems in contemporary terms may influence our reading of Aristotle. The relation between them is simply that the setting of philosophical problems itself reflects a philosophical outlook whose influence, because it is often more pervasive in a given period, may escape notice. We are used to philosophical answers that reflect school differences, but we do not always expect philosophical questions to do the same.

A constant effort has been made here to keep open the possibility that Aristotle was working in a different direction from the modern one rather than taking first steps in our direction. It should not be inferred, however, that the attempt to use the best contemporary analyses is therefore out of place, or that comparisons, both of similarity and difference, with later doctrines will not be enlightening. An approach from the contemporary formulation may sometimes break through the rather encrusted modes of classical scholarship with startling effect and bring a fresh and subtle attentiveness to Aristotelian materials—even where the object is only to find Aristotelian clues for solving modern problems. This can be seen both in contemporary formalistic and in informal ordinary language approaches. The refinement of contemporary logical questions and distinctions was brought to bear on the reconsideration of the *Prior Analytics*, while the ordinary language philosophers found congenial the rich materials of the *Topics* and reawakened interest in its logical as distinct from its rhetorical character. There are, however, dangers to be guarded against in both approaches. Some limits to the formalistic treatment in relation to the formal logic are suggested in appendix C. And the informalists often generalize their linguistic approach and forget that many of the questions in Aristotle have to be treated as scientific as well as linguistic issues and related to the results of the sciences as he saw them. On the whole, the gains in our time have been perhaps greater than the losses. There is no royal road to interpretation; all paths have to be tried out and can be judged by their fruits.

On the question of fashioning an Aristotle congenial to particular philosophical outlooks there is of course no need for deep probing. The battle over Platonizing Aristotle is not only a modern one; it goes back almost to the early schools. There is also the neo-Platonizing of Aristotle, the Christianizing of Aristotle (for example, in the struggle with Arabic interpretations in medieval times and with secular interpretations today), and later on the Kantianizing of Aristotle, the Hegelianizing of Aristotle, the naturalizing of Aristotle, the pragmatizing of Aristotle, and so on. Perhaps even the ordinary classical treatment of Aristotle appears neutral by being eclectic, or by using the philosophical terms current in the age and so presupposing the deeper, more common philosophical background of that time. Sometimes, however, an outlook may set up Aristotle as the archenemy; some existentialists may tend to see him as the philosopher of essence as against existence. It would indeed be a useful philosophical enterprise to trace the different outlooks implicit in the different books on Aristotle in contemporary times, not excluding the present work.

Nevertheless, the crucial question is not the philosophy with which the interpretation of Aristotle is approached, but *how that philosophy is used*. If it is used to bring out the new and unnoticed aspects, then it is all to the good, whether the writer is conscious of his perspective or not. For example, suppose the interpreter is an emergent evolutionist, and so stresses by contrast that Aristotle has an unchanging world with a constancy of forms. If he stops there, his own approach is oversimplified. But if he also asks himself where questions of novelty and emergence (which the interpreter takes to be central) break through in Aristotle, he will focus in a new way on the theory of substantival change and the fundamental role of the accidental. (He has, in any case, to be principled in his appeal to the corpus and not simply selective of what supports his view alone.) At the other extreme, the aim simply to convert Aristotle to a philosophical faith is clearly philosophical abuse. On the whole, the tradition of Aristotelian scholarship is too rich and too experienced to need a homily on this point.

No despairing thesis of historical relativity need be the outcome of these reflections. What is needed is both self-consciousness about the possible influence of one's perspective and, even more, a sense of *comparative* philosophy that will seek the lessons of different outlooks in their impact on the investigation without commitment to the outlook itself. When these are coupled with respect for the corpus itself and attentiveness to its evidence (including the varieties of interpretation of the evidence), progress becomes and remains possible. Perhaps then one approaches the ideal of a readiness to learn from Aristotle rather than to teach him what he has said.

In the long run, a richer interpretation of Aristotle's philosophy will reflect advance in all the areas of work we have mentioned and no doubt in others. But insofar as they explore *relations* of the Aristotelian ideas to sources, philosophical and scientific precursors, Greek institutions and practices, and the rest (not excluding his successors and the demands raised by contemporary problems), it seems essential—at least in our present period—that there be initially a firm focus on the ideas themselves. Only in this way will there be something definite for the relations to attach to, even if in the long run the ideas come to be seen in a changed light through some of the discoveries in pursuing the relations. This accounts for, and I hope it helps justify, the constant and sometimes dogged focus of the book on the corpus.

APPENDIXES

NOTES

BIBLIOGRAPHY

INDEX

APPENDIX A.

THE WORKS AND THEIR CONTENTS

What have the twentieth-century scholars, after all the sifting, more or less agreed upon as authentically Aristotelian, plus or minus a dissenting opinion here and there?

The standard edition has first a batch of logical works, commonly referred to as the *Organon* because they came to be perceived as an instrument for thought or inquiry. These start with the *Categories*, chiefly a brief analysis of a set of notions for classifying terms in discourse, or correspondingly for pigeonholing items in carrying out an inventory of what the world contains. Such broad concepts as substance, quantity, quality, relation, place, and time are here introduced. There follows *On Interpretation*, which tells how nouns and verbs are woven into sentences, what kinds these are and how related—for example, what *contradiction* means—and has some reflections on truth and falsity, possibility and necessity. Then comes the *Prior Analytics*, the famous treatment of syllogistic reasoning that marks the beginning of systematic formal logic in the Western world. The *Posterior Analytics* analyzes the nature of theoretical science, which Aristotle regards as knowledge in the strict sense. It corresponds roughly in theme to what we would today call "philosophy of science." The *Topics* deals with modes of arguing in dialectical discussion, more fragmentary or piecemeal in approach. It includes many syntactic and semantic problems, with a strong admixture of rhetorical advice. Perhaps because it seems to be dealing with logical applications and is full of practical examples, its theoretical riches may be overlooked. Finally, *On Sophistical Refutations* is a discussion of fallacies, with illustrations; emphasis is on uncovering and avoiding them.

A large part of the Aristotelian corpus consists of writings on natural science and analyses of its pertinent concepts, from physics and astronomy to biology and psychology. The *Physics* is largely concerned with basic concepts: change, motion, nature, chance, infinity, place and vacuum, time, continuity, and types of movement and their relations. It ends up with a theory of the eternity of motion and of an Unmoved Mover as a cause of motion. *On the Heavens* examines the basic elements of which the world is composed, distinguishes the composition of the heavens and the sublunar regions, and studies the typical properties and motions of the various elements. *On Generation and Corruption* (also translated as *On Coming-to-be and Passing-away*) seems rather like our introductory qualitative chemistry. It considers qualitative alteration, modes of combination, transformation in substance, growth and decay, and the derivation of the four sublunar elements themselves from more basic qualitative concepts. The *Meteorology* for the most part considers phenomena in the sublunar regions—for example, comets, rain and snow, winds and rivers, earthquakes, thunder and lightning, rainbows, and so on. In its last (fourth) book there is a discussion of basic interactive processes—everything from boiling and ripening to solidifying and melting, with suggestions on the constitution of the uniform materials that make up the animal body.

A modern classification of the sciences would generally move next to biology and then to psychology. The corpus as edited does the reverse, in line with Aristotle's view that psychology maps the functions of living beings. Let us for the present pursue the modern path. On this basis we would go next to his *Historia Animalium* (more nearly his "investigations" into animals), which collects all sorts of facts about animals as a kind of preliminary casebook. He touches comparatively on different kinds of animals and on the parts of the body and physical functions and processes (the miscellany includes generation, the nesting habits of birds, the psychology of different animals, chewing the cud, limbs and their movements, and problems of heredity). Then there comes the *Parts of Animals*, which gives an organized exploratory inventory of the constitution of an animal—parts common to all animals, such as bone, flesh, blood, etc., as well as all specialized organs. In spirit it is at times like a modern account of the percentage of carbon, phosphorus, water, etc., in the body; for the rest, it is comparative anatomy with an eye to comparative physiology. There is a famous first section on method in the study of life. A little treatise, the *Progression of Animals*, goes into the parts necessary for all the various types of movement in different animals. It includes, for example, the swimming of fish, the flying of insects, the bending of limbs, and the undulating of snakes.

On the Psyche gives his overall view of the nature of functions in living things. It goes from a general theory of the nature of living and functioning to specific discussions of nutrition, sensation, thought, and initiation of action. The numerous other works treating of functions are mostly in the form of brief, compact studies. They are causal-explanatory studies that bring in whatever is required of environment or the world at large to analyze and explain the functioning. The *Movement of Animals* is a kind of companion piece to the *Progression of Animals*. There is a group of little works on natural functions, usually known by the collective Latin title, *Parva Naturalia*, which starts with *On Sense and Sensible Objects*. This supplements some of the treatment of sensation in *On the Psyche* and adds some general considerations. It is followed by the extremely interesting *On Memory and Recollection*, then *On Sleep and Waking*,

On Dreams, *On Prophecy in Sleep*, *On Length and Shortness of Life*, *On Youth and Old Age*, *On Life and Death*, and *On Respiration*. Finally, there is the full-length work the *Generation of Animals*, with both descriptive accounts and theoretical treatment of sex differentiation, generation and its mechanisms in different forms of animal life, embryology, secondary characteristics, and much else. Obviously missing in this whole biological–psychological complex is an authentic work on plants. Aristotle appears to have written one, and we do have a text, though not thought to be his, in a thirteenth-century Latin form, itself taken to be a translation from the Arabic, which in turn was translated from an original Greek version. We do have a fuller work on plants by his disciple, Theophrastus.

Philosophical preferences might have assigned the *Metaphysics* to different positions in the corpus, but in the accepted collection it stands as a kind of climax, following the knowledge about the world and man. Actually, the term was coined by an ancient editor and means literally the works that come after the physical writings. The *Metaphysics* is a heterogeneous work about whose structure and inner unity, or lack of it, there has been much controversy. Its fourteen books cover topics such as the nature of being or substance, matter and form, potentiality and actuality, God and nature, causality, and the interpretation of mathematics. One can only add "and so on." Its fifth book looks like a philosophical handbook, giving a brief exposition of many of Aristotle's technical concepts.

Beyond the *Metaphysics* lie the social and humanistic works. First come the ethical and political writings, conceived as a unity by Aristotle. The major work on ethics is the *Nicomachean Ethics*. There is also the *Eudemian Ethics*, which overlaps in part with the *Nicomachean Ethics* and is generally believed to be an earlier work, though this has once again been questioned. The third ethical work, the *Magna Moralia*, is often taken to be post-Aristotelian, but at present the scholarly swing appears to be toward reascribing it to Aristotle. The *Nicomachean Ethics* deals with the human good, moral character (including both moral and intellectual virtues), responsibility, justice, the nature of moral self-control, moral aspects of human associations, and pleasure and happiness. The *Politics* is a reflective treatment of the state, in the wider sense of a community within which social life is organized. It considers such central issues as the nature of the state, slavery and property, proposed ideal organizations of society, citizenship, types of political organization (especially oligarchy and democracy), revolution and the maintenance of stability, and Aristotle's own ideal society. It is incomplete. The *Politics* embodies the lessons of a major research project by Aristotle and his colleagues, which surveyed the constitutions of 158 states in their historical development. These are lost, except the *Athenian Constitution*, which was discovered in part in 1880 and almost in full in 1890, in Egyptian papyri. (In a fuller version, the front side of the sheets has expense accounts of a farm bailiff in an Egyptian town for the years 78–79 A.D.)

Finally, there are Aristotle's two works on the arts, in which he takes accumulated methods and materials and develops them into a systematic study. The *Rhetoric*, concerned with persuasion and its means, compresses into a short course its presuppositions (psychological, logical, ethical), its methods, and its stylistic techniques. The *Poetics* chiefly treats of tragedy, its elements, and how they can be related to produce the desired effect on the audience.

Our list has not included a large number of works that modern scholarship has authoritatively ruled out as spurious. These include another work on rhetoric, an economic treatise, and hosts of lesser works on everything from colors and reported marvels to lists of problems that require research. Perhaps some among these we could wish Aristotle had written; some we are glad he did not write. And there are still others that are wholly missing, with only the titles to tantalize us. Some of these— e.g., on growth and food, and on dissections—Aristotle mentions himself; others occur in ancient lists or in fragments quoted in later Greek and Latin writings. Some of the works that give us these clues are themselves of interest because they probably come from the later Aristotelian school and show us its philosophical and scientific concerns. Perhaps the most interesting from the standpoint of philosophical history would be missing dialogues and more popular works that Aristotle is said to have written in his earlier years. There are quotations and references sufficient to give us at least a scant idea of *Eudemus, or On the Soul*, of *Gryllus, or On Rhetoric*, of the *Protrepticus*, which is an exhortation to philosophize, and of *On Philosophy*, which appears to have been regarded as a major early public statement of Aristotelian philosophical views.

WHAT IS A SCIENCE?

We suggested that the question of what constitutes a science is a vital link in understanding why Aristotle first denied there could be a science of being and finally established such a science. His grounds for the first are clear: a science is associated with a genus, and being is not a genus. But eventually he reached the point where he says explicitly that he has now solved the problem as to "how there will be one science of many things which are different in genus."[1] Of course the problem of metaphysics was not the only source of Aristotle's interest in determining what constitutes a science. He was delimiting fields, founding sciences, giving them shape, relating them to one another, deciding which were subordinate to which, resisting tendencies to reduce some to others, and establishing principles for what he was doing as well as arguing against others who reached different decisions. It is worth tracing the outline of his questioning until he reached his answer and then comparing it with his practice.

He began by confronting inherited views of the Platonists. At least as he states them they are of two sorts. One is the claim that there is a single science of all being; the other is that sciences are concerned with forms. The objection to the first is to a Platonic assumption of a Form of Being. Among the arguments on this, in *Metaphysics* I, there is the quaint elaboration of the consequences for science if there is a single science of all that is.[2] When a man begins to learn geometry, he can know other things but does not know geometrical things. So if there were one science of everything (presumably like Plato's dialectic), a man would start learning it while ignorant of everything; but learning proceeds from the known. (We rather expect Aristotle to go on to explain some fallacy involved, but he does not.) We need not pursue this, since after all, Aristotle rejects a Form of Being or even that Being is a single genus, and we have noted the logical grounds for his view.

The view that sciences are concerned with forms depends upon what forms are taken to be. Not everything has a form; Aristotle indicates that questions were raised in the Platonic view as to what sort of things do have forms—for example, artifacts like a house or a ring are said not to.[3] Even more, one of the tests for whether something has a form was that there was a science of it.[4] In that case, Aristotle goes on to argue, there will be forms not only of substances, but of what are not substances, which would contradict the tying of sciences to forms. The implication seems to be that the relation of what a form is to what a science is has not been adequately resolved. It is possible, however, that a philosopher more sympathetic to Platonism than Aristotle might give the notion of form a more basic interpretation. He might, for example, believe that Plato hoped geometry would have its assumptions "destroyed" in a dialectical analysis. It would then be reduced to arithmetic, so that he would deny there were geometric forms and see such alleged forms as simply consequent attributes of the arithmetical. Such interpretations, however, cannot be used to explicate Aristotle's development of the question of what a science is, for we are limited to how Aristotle saw the theory of forms, whether he was correct or not. And he felt that it gave no clear, much less, reliable answers. In fact he felt surer of what are to be considered sciences than what would be forms.

At the same time that he is worried about such matters, Aristotle finds on his hands batches of metaphysical materials that ought to belong to some science or other and wonders where they should go. Thus in *Metaphysics* 3, where he is outlining questions to be dealt with, he wants to know whether the axioms of demonstration (such as the law of non-contradiction) belong to one science or several,[5] and whether the study of substance falls into the same science as that of logical principles. He does not see why these logical principles, which are used in all sciences, should particularly belong with a science of substances, and even wonders whether we need a science of the logical principles since we already have them. And he adds, "If there is a demonstrative science of them, it will require some underlying genus"—with some axiom and some derived principles. This would mean one genus of demonstrable things.[6]

The central tendency to associate a science with a genus and to see as the task of the science to demonstrate the attributes that are found in the genus is spelled out in the *Posterior Analytics*: "A science is one science if it deals with one genus."[7] Sciences differ when their principles do not come from a common science or from one another. The principles of each science must be peculiar to the science,[8] except in subordinate sciences such as harmonics, whose theorems may be proved by arithmetic, or optics and mechanics, whose theorems are proved by geometry.[9] Common principles, such as "when equals are taken from equals, the remainders are equal" are interpreted as analogical, since they are not used in the same way in each science, but with respect to, for instance, magnitudes in geometry and numbers in arithmetic.[10] In either of these cases, no assumption is made about the other in the actual work of each science.

Aristotle's application of his view in biology is quite consonant with this analysis. The science he presents is of the genus *animal*, not a separate science for each of the species. Similarly, plants constitute the subject of a science. In his psychological science there is some hesitation, presumably because the different forms of psyche (nutritive, sensory, intellectual) constitute a developing series, so that it is not wholly clear what sort of unity is involved. Aristotle allows a common definition to fit them all, just as a definition of *rectilinear figure* would fit different-sided figures, while describing no particular one; the general definition may get us started, but the most proper account of psyche would go into each of the several functions.[11]

This may sound as if psyche were a universal, having no generic character. But the notion of genus is broad enough and for that matter loose enough—to cover complex combinations and to fit extremely varied contexts. For example, in *plane figures* it is *plane* that is the genus because it underlies the differentiae (almost in the sense that matter does);[12] and plane geometry is a science within the mathematical group of sciences. The notion of genus can be used on higher and higher levels, as is evident from the fact that the categories are themselves called genera of things that are. It can equally well be used on a comparatively low level; for example, where the species is a quality such as white, the genus is a quality such as color.[13] And there can be a science of color in the Aristotelian sense, as seen in the pseudo-Aristotelian treatise *On Colors*. Or perhaps, more properly, this would be part of the broader science of sense and sensible objects, fitting into the group of psychological sciences. Finally, an extremely broad use of genus is conveyed in his argument that *object of conjecture* (something thinkable, believable) cannot be a species of being since it is wider than being—for both that which is and that which is not can be objects of thought—while a genus should be wider than the species.[14]

The general conclusion would seem to be that genus is becoming an elastic notion, indeed, almost context-relative. In the entry on *one* in *Metaphysics* 5 Aristotle seems to suggest that what is generically one may even include cases of things that are analogically one.[15] Several factors seem to contribute to the stretching of the notion of genus. It allows of secondary uses, just as definition allows of secondary uses for qualities as compared to definition of substances. Another is the relative use of genus and species in almost any context, for what may be loosely the broader and narrower terms in defining. More decisive, we suggest, were problems of practice in Aristotle's own concern with the sciences.

Aristotle's resolution of his problem—how there can be a single science whose object crosses many genera—rests ultimately on his view of what a science is. This can be seen if we examine the two chief contexts in which he reaches his conclusion—*Metaphysics* 4.2 and 11.3. (Let us refer to them for brevity as Gamma and Kappa respectively, the Greek names for the books.) Gamma is the chapter that argues for a science of being-as-being. Kappa, usually dismissed as a secondary summary of

Gamma, nevertheless has independent examples and suggestions. Treating the two together gives a clearer picture of the place of reference to the sciences in the argument for a science of being-as-being.

Both begin with a reference to health, Kappa briefly, Gamma more amply. This is the staple illustration of focal meaning. The point is, from our present concern about a single science reaching into many genera, that a single science of health can deal with food, exercise, gymnasia, and hosts of other classes of things because in different ways they are related to health as expressing, servicing, preserving, achieving it; and the term *healthy* as used in these various contexts is analyzable ultimately *by reference to* a healthy person. This is then the central model of unity by some primary reference, that was described as focal or referential meaning. Aristotle's formulation in Gamma is: "For not only in the case of things that are named according to one common notion [*kath' hen*] is the investigation the job of one science, but also in the case of things named in relation to one common nature [*pros mian phusin*]."[16]

Both chapters, however, go on to provide other scientific examples that point to other complex kinds of meaning. Kappa turns to an analysis of geometry.[17] The mathematician abstracts from an analysis of what is sensible, such as heavy or light, hard and its opposite, hot and cold, and leaves only quantity and continuity (in one, two, or three dimensions), and examines properties such as relative position, commensurability, and ratios. Yet we take these different studies to constitute one science and call it geometry. (Here, however this may fit with other contexts, Aristotle seems to be taking the geometry of line, plane, and solid as different fields, whether as coordinate or each adding something to the other, and the result as the complex object of one science.) Physics is unified by the idea of being in motion. (This might well have added to the argument, for the types of motion cut across four categories and so four genera.) So it is in the case of being: its many attributes are studied in respect to one common idea and fall under one science. Then Aristotle states the conclusion quoted earlier, that he has solved the problem of "how there will be one science of many things which are different in genus."

Gamma adds: "For each class of things, as there is one perception [*aisthēsis*], there is one science."[18] Grammar as the investigation of articulate sounds is offered as an illustration. (The unity here seems to lie in a sensory-intellectual apprehension corresponding to sound and signification.) Finally, comparing philosophy and mathematics, Aristotle suggests that mathematics too has a primary science and a secondary science and others in successive order (*ephexēs*) within it.[19]

In an apparent aside later in Gamma, he says that terms belong to one science if they have the same nature or have reference to a common nature; otherwise they belong to different sciences.[20] We may conclude from our evidence that *reference* to a common nature cannot be limited to one type of referential unity, that it covers a variety of complex meaning. In discussions about the possibility of a science of being-as-being, focal unity was probably uppermost in his mind because the structure of that emerging science had the focal type, with substance central and every other idea referring to it. But the types of meaning we explored in chapter 14 show a variety of complex kinds, several of which proved useful in the development of different sciences. Physics was a science of motion in the sense of independent coordinate kinds. Psychology was a science of psyche, defined as a developing series each form of which included the prior form—the type Aristotle labelled successive order (*ephexēs*). Some of his descriptions of geometry sound like the kind of complex meaning in which there is a primary sense and other parts added onto it. The several examples given in Gamma and Kappa other than the focal seem to be of these various kinds.

Our scenario for Aristotle's confrontation with a science of being-as-being in terms of the character of a science is briefly as follows. At the outset, having gotten rid of (what he took to be) Plato's association of science with forms, he assigned a genus as the object of a science. Since being was not a genus, and different things-that-are have their being only by analogy, there is no one science of being. From the beginning Aristotle was aware of more unified kinds of meaning, but they did not lead him to accept a wider unified type of science that crossed the lines of genera. What apparently was required to have this impact was Aristotle's own scientific experience, together with his development of a logic that would allow of many kinds of complex meaning. His theory of meaning was not a separate affair. It grew, as his own analyses and examples throughout show, in close relation to his work in various fields—logical, rhetorical, scientific—and there was an interaction between his theory of meaning, as it furnished conceptual instruments, and his scientific and practical work. The rigid theory that limited a science to a genus was modified by the contours of Aristotle's own sciences and by the elasticity of the notion of genus at his own hands. At that point the kinds of complex meaning became firm enough to usher in a science of being-as-being and to appear, even if cursorily, in the arguments for it. There is enough, however, to show that the whole development, and not any one crash argument, is what carried through the process. It was not a return to Platonism nor a change in philosophical direction. It was a genuine broadening, through logical, scientific, and practical advances, of what science could be like and the diversity of its unities.

In the end too, Aristotle has a general classification of kinds of sciences, in his threefold scheme of the theoretical, practical, and "poiētic" or technological, resting on contemplation (*theōria*), acting or doing (*praxis*), and making (*poiēsis*). In *Metaphysics* 6, where Aristotle makes this distinction, he speaks of every intellectual activity (*dianoia*) being either practical or poiētic or theoretic.[21] This should warn us that he is talking of sciences, not of science versus action and production. The poiētic science, for example, is as much as science as we would regard engineering or medicine to be. The three constitute, in a sense, something like a developing series. The outcome of theoretical science is knowledge; practical science guides life and conduct; poiētic science is geared to producing something beyond the activity involved (such as a house or health). The practical must not be confused with our *practice*, which may cover both practical and poiētic.

With respect to the object, the theoretical is marked off from the rest: it aims at apprehending what cannot be otherwise. Thus physics and biology and any science looking for the essence of entities in a field are theoretic.[22] On the other hand, from the point of view of method, since biology approaches its inquiries by looking for final causes, it differs from the method of the other theoretical sciences, for they demonstrate from what *is*, whereas it demonstrates from *what is to be*.[23]

Aristotle also calls attention to an interesting difference in these types of science, if we look to the source of movement in each.[24] In the poiētic or productive, the source is in the producer, and in practical science, it is in the agent. But in the theoretic sciences the source is in the objects: the objects of natural science have in themselves a source of motion. He is not talking of the object of knowledge as primary and determining our knowledge. If the question were one of motivation, he could go back to the opening sentence of the *Metaphysics*—that all men naturally desire to know—as the source of the theoretic.

. Finally, types of activity correspond to types of object. Contemplating (*theōria*) has knowledge as its end. Acting or doing (*praxis*) contains its own end too, for it is in effect living for its own sake. Making (*poiēsis*) is instrumental and is done for the sake of a product. Aristotle's value ranking is in the order given. We make things in order to use them in living. But contemplation is in his view the highest end.

In the rest of the corpus, the ethical and political writings are centrally about *praxis*, the *Rhetoric* and the *Poetics* about *poiēsis*. But there is much concerning constructing or making in the others. And, of course, much of the theoretic in all.

APPENDIX C.

NECESSITY AND DETERMINISM

The intention here is to gather some of the threads in Aristotle's analysis of the complex notion of necessity and examine its implications for his view of determinism and process in the world. We have seen that there is not a fully worked out conception of necessity and that what enters into it ranges from invariance over time (Hintikka's thesis) at one end to pure divine actuality at the other extreme. Aristotle's treatment of the incidental, of chance, of the sea battle tomorrow, and of the reality of the potential with its alternative possibilities, makes it clear that he leaves only a little place for absolute predictions of what will be. But precisely what that amounts to in more technical terms needs examination. And at least a look is required into the logical writings to see how far notions of necessity and possibility are formalized.

The Senses of the Necessary and Its Types

The concept of the necessary has many roots. It ties in with the four causes, yielding final (hypothetical) and material (efficient) necessity and thus forging a link to the biological and physical sciences. The formal cause is tied to the notion of essence, as against accident, and so to the mathematical and demonstrative sciences. The logical works attempt to capture the interrelation of both groups in a general concept of necessity that brings complex relations to possibility and potentiality. These ideas in turn enter into a quasi-theological concept of endless motion and divine actuality. Because of its different shapes, a fruitful approach to necessity is to locate its sources and then see how the products grow together.

THE ACCOUNT OF THE NECESSARY
(TO ANANKAION) IN METAPHYSICS 5.5

As suggested in chapter 8, note 9, *Metaphysics* 5 serves as a collection of raw materials for the analysis of major metaphysical concepts. Thus its chapter on the necessary gathers the kinds of things or complex factors that are called necessary from what appear to be different contexts of ordinary life, ethics, purposive action, logic, and (in a brief reference) theology. The underlying sense of necessity is elicited by the middle of the presentation and is used from there on.

In a practical context, that without which life is impossible is called necessary (food is necessary). Similarly for the good: that without which the good is impossible is necessary; that is, it is required for achieving what we need or want. Again, in purposive action we meet necessity in the form of the compulsory: force (*bia*) hinders or prevents impulse and choice. The primary sense from which all others are somehow derived is recognized as that which cannot be otherwise (literally, that which does not allow of being situated differently, *to mē endechomenon allōs echein*). The logical context follows: demonstration is called necessary because if something has been demonstrated absolutely it cannot be otherwise; the absoluteness of the necessity is ascribed to the primary premises of the demonstration, not simply to deduction. Finally it is concluded that the primary and chief case of the necessary is where we have what is simple, for the simple or unitary does not allow of a plurality of conditions; if there are eternal and immutable things, there is nothing in them that is compulsory or contrary to their natures.

The commonsense notion of what cannot be otherwise will have to bear the major burden of the Aristotelian notion of necessity and will lead in startling directions.

HYPOTHETICAL NECESSITY AND SIMPLE NECESSITY

Aristotle distinguishes what is hypothetically necessary and what is simply (*haplōs*) necessary.[1] The former embodies the teleological or craft model to be used in physical and biological explanation: processes can be explained as necessary to the end result to be achieved. Simple necessity, on the other hand, occurs when the sequence is determined by what precedes it. Aristotle seems to cover here both the mathematical processes in which the premises determine the conclusion and the efficient causality of material processes.

In the biological investigations, he is forced to refine the distinction under the almost literal pressure of the phenomena. The chief method in biology is teleological, referring the developments that take place to the results and functions to be attained.[2] Some explanations, however, are in material–efficient terms. As we have seen, an instance of the former mode would be the way we explain our having eyes; of the latter, the way we explain their being blue.[3] There are also intervening cases in which the material and the final coincide. For example, man's hair is materially necessitated by the fluid character of the brain and the outgrowth that occurs where there is a large amount of fluid and hot substance; but it also serves the purpose of protecting the brain from excessive cold and heat, especially since the brain needs protection, being the largest and most fluid of all animal brains.[4] The heart and liver appear to be teleologically necessary, but the spleen is regarded as a necessary concomitant incidental to other parts or processes; it is compared to residues in the stomach and bladder.[5] But a use is apparently found for it by the body. Thus we have several cases: the teleologically determined, the materially determined, the cases where they coincide, cases where the material has its own consequences which are, however, utilized by the teleological organization, and cases where the material goes its own way without relevance to the rest.

A SPECIAL CASE OF SIMPLE NECESSITY

There is one more type of simple or absolute necessity that appears in the physical writings and yet is more akin to the hypothetical or teleological than to the material–mechanical. Its character can be approached in the following way. Nature deals with change, and a change is a process of reaching an end state. Where there is no guarantee that the end state will be reached, the end functions hypothetically to impart necessity to the process: if an animal is to have sight, eyes must be developed in the generation of the animal. But suppose we have a guarantee that the end *is* to be achieved. Then the hypothetical step becomes categorically necessary. Here we could argue from the presence of foundations that a house will be built—not because necessary conditions have become sufficient, but because it is guaranteed that the end is to be achieved. Something like this seems involved in Aristotle's complex argument to show that absolute necessity cannot be established in a "linear" way.[6] Of course this kind of thing does not happen when the potential is being actualized, but only in pure activity (*energeia*) or what flows from it. If there are everlasting activities—and Aristotle often puts this hypothetically—then their end is fully embodied in their activity and they thus exhibit absolute necessity that is teleologically and not mechanically determined. This, of course, is what he assigns eventually to the Unmoved Mover and its derivative actualities, the circular movement of the heavens and the sublunar essences of things. The example actually given is the solstices: it is impossible they should be unable to occur.[7]

THE NECESSITY FURNISHED BY ESSENCE

The kind of necessity furnished by essence varies with the contexts. Since an account of the essence of something gives primary premises, deductions from it to properties of the thing will be giving what follows necessarily in the mathematical sense; and also, if we know that this is the essence of a domain of existence, it is an absolute sense (barring nature's mistakes below the moon). When Aristotle asks whether it is necessary that the solstices come to be and not possible that they should not admit of recurrence,[8] he is talking of simple or absolute necessity. The necessity of the solstices is derivable from the necessary revolution of the sun, which is derivable from the necessary revolution of the upper heavens.[9] What is meant therefore by saying that statements about the natural world are necessary is that a system of essences applies to that world.

WAYS OF DISTINGUISHING THE ESSENTIAL

To establish ways of distinguishing the essential from the nonessential or accidental is the great motif of the whole earlier part of the corpus, until emphasis is transferred to the construction of the world in terms of the potential and the actual. The effort permeates Aristotle's logic and his physical and biological science.

In the logic, the very early distinction between being said (or predicated) of a subject and being present in a subject,[10] whatever else may be involved in its obscurities, is certainly an attempt to set off what is essential. Aristotle offers as a test for predication that what is said of the predicate will also be said of the original subject. Thus if Socrates is a man and man is an animal, then Socrates is an animal. Presumably if white (which is present in Socrates) is a color, we cannot conclude that Socrates is a color. Again, in discussing universality in the *Prior Analytics*, Aristotle is careful to distinguish essential statements such as "All men are rational" from accidental ones that just might happen now to be true, such as "All animals in motion are men."[11] The same search goes on today to identify precisely what makes a universal statement "law-like" (nomological). In matters of definition Aristotle takes it for granted that the same thing has only *one* definition and one essence.[12]

In the writings on physics the nature of a thing is expressed in what it does universally or for the most part. When Aristotle defines universality, he says not merely that a universal holds of all instances but that it does so *per se* (*kath' hauto*) and *qua* itself (*hēi auto*)—in short, essentially—and adds that universal attributes (that is, universal in his definition) clearly inhere necessarily.[13] In the biological researches, the explicit teleological method marks the essence as its goal. The existence of stable species is taken for granted.

We have already seen in the metaphysical writings the importance to Aristotle of rejecting the Heraclitean flux as disruptive of essence. Stabilities in all fields, but with an occasional invocation of the divine and the eternal, assure the perpetuation of the necessary order.

What Determinism Is and In What Sense
Aristotle Is Concerned about It

The order that a system of essences maintains is not, however, deterministic in our sense. It yields hypothetical necessity, and only where the heavens and their consequences are concerned does it yield simple necessity. Where potentiality looms large, there is much that is accidental. This naturally raises, for us, the question whether events are completely determined, and we want to know whether Aristotle had an answer to that question. There are a few passages and contexts where it seems to arise, and others where we would expect it to arise but surprisingly it does not. For example, we would think of chance as the denial of causality. But when Aristotle discusses chance he is more interested in whether it is itself a cause and decides it is an incidental cause of a certain sort.[14] In *Metaphysics* 6.3, where he gets close to discussing directly whether we can declare a future event as settled on the basis of present evidence, he insists on a persistent contingency: this man will die of violence if he goes out, and he will go out if he gets thirsty, and he will be thirsty if he happens to be eating pungent food. But even if he eats the food now, it does not get rid of chance—perhaps (we may add) he is being poisoned before he is able to go out to satisfy his thirst. It is of necessity that a man will die sometime, but chance how or when he dies.

Discussing Aristotle's account of accident, in chapter 7, we noted Sambursky's belief that the Stoics first developed a scientific idea of determinism as distinguished from a general idea of causality. We suggested that Aristotle had some of the elements Sambursky lists, but not all, and in any case not sufficiently focused to make the idea central. We should not in the first place expect Aristotle to discuss whether there are or are not causes, since the analysis into the four causes constitutes his mode of explanation, but rather that he would ask whether causes in a particular case are determinate or indeterminate. In particular causal investigations he allows a place for the accidental as a type of cause, even in explaining the past, and so *a fortiori* in predicting the future. His explanation of particular events in these terms resembles more what a historian does who engages in specific inquiries in an open context, than what a physicist does in dealing with relatively isolated systems governed by specific laws. Although he has a conception of the world as a finite system, he does not see it as a totality determining the future completely on the basis of a known past. His own pattern of determination is chiefly the hypothetical necessity of the system of essences or final causes, particularly as seen in biology, which enables us to say of a thing that if no accident occurs this is the form the thing will take in its maturity and these will be its capacities. That was the kind of determination Aristotle thought the evidence supported.

The Sea Battle Tomorrow

The chief, though rather oblique way in which the question whether a future event is necessary arises for Aristotle is through the logical route of trying to decide whether sentences about the future can be said to be true or false now.[15] Sentences about what is or has been are necessarily either true or false, but he denies that this is so for asserting two opposite singular statements with a future predicate—for example, "A sea battle will take place tomorrow" and "A sea battle will not take place tomorrow." He carefully lines up the correspondence of statement and fact, of the epistemological and the ontological: "If it is true to say that something is white or that it is not white, it is necessary that it be white or not white, and if it is white or not white, it is true to say or deny this"; and similarly with respect to falsity.[16] If the same holds for future statements, it would seem that there will be no chance but only necessity, for the present assertions of what will or will not be are now true or false, and of the opposites one must be true, one false. Aristotle spells this out in greater detail. He looks back to the past from the present and in effect shows the present as the future of some past at which time the statements about the then future, now present, could have been made. He rejects the attempt to get out of the dilemma by regarding neither of the opposing future statements as true; the sea battle could not be in the position tomorrow of neither happening nor not happening.

Having posed the problem, Aristotle declares the consequences unacceptable. If everything is necessary in this way, if whatever is to happen is necessary, then there is no room for deliberation, everything is necessary ten thousand years ahead, and everything is or comes to be of necessity. But experience goes counter to this. We see that our deliberations and actions make a difference. We recognize opposite possibilities: this coat may be cut up, or it may not be cut up but wear out first. (In short, judgments of potentiality lose their meaning, and we are back to the Megarian view that there are only actualities.)

Aristotle does not offer a case against determinism in a full argument. He does not raise the question whether in deliberation our turnings are themselves necessary antecedently. The accidental is too well entrenched in his conceptual network. To eliminate it would destroy the distinction between essence and accident and so make no sense of science and its search for law as well as of our way of looking at change and development. All he tries to do here is to see where the argument got off the track. In doing this he shows in part how he regards the relations of present and future.

He locates the derailment: "It is clear then that not everything is or happens from necessity, but some things as chance has it, and of the affirmation and the negation *neither is true rather than the other*."[17] In short, he has to make some distinction or somehow reconstruct the formulation so that the opposing sentences about the sea battle tomorrow will not be regarded as forcing the present truth of one, whichever it be.

There is heated controversy over what Aristotle is actually doing in the remainder of the chapter. A few points seem clear. He does take a temporal stance, for he says, "What is, necessarily is, when it is; and what is not, necessarily is not, when it is not." He denies that this entails saying of what is, that it necessarily is simply or unconditionally.[18]

Since he maintains that epistemological questions of truth and falsity are derivative and ontological questions of what is and what is not are primary, let us set aside the epistemological attempt to understand what is going on, and look at the ontological side first. Aristotle's world is one in which there are absolutely dependable processes (in the heavens) and a domain of variably changing processes below that. Potentiality is a definite characteristic of most of the world; hence the greater part of what happens will not be necessary until it actually happens. Possibilities may be narrowed down and probabilities may increase for a given happening, but there is a real becoming in time, and up to the moment of happening there could be interfering forces. In such a world we can quite understand the view that what is necessarily is, when it is—because the possibilities are now closed. Similarly for the past. Aristotle reminds us that we do not deliberate about the past and even God cannot change the past.[19] Now the term that Aristotle uses for *necessary*, alongside of *anankē*, is *what is incapable of being otherwise*, the sense regarded as basic in the account of necessity in *Metaphysics* 5. That present and past happenings are necessary when they occur (and the past after it occurs) seems quite in line with common sense. That future events are not yet necessary follows in the same vein, except of course for the future that expresses simple or absolute necessity such as the revolution of the heavens and the solstices. The *Rhetoric* includes, among the objects we do not deliberate about, what cannot be otherwise in the future.[20]

On the epistemological side, judging the truth and falsity of sentences has to be brought in line with this picture of the world. For statements of the present and past there is no problem; Aristotle dismisses them at the beginning of the chapter. There already are definite realities to correspond to. The statement that there will be a sea battle tomorrow has nothing yet to correspond to.[21] Hence both the affirmation and the denial about the future event will be held up, pending the formation of the reality. To assign them a present truth value (even though uncertain which) is already to presuppose a reality for them to correspond to. This does not mean that Aristotle has proved a case against determinism; he has simply shown that the assignment of truth values here is automatically presupposing a certain kind of world that is not the kind of world picture he has established..

Of course there remains the job of restructuring the logical language of possibility and necessity to fit his world. What does he mean by denying that what is, necessarily is, simply or unconditionally? It might mean that without a time reference there is no general assumption of necessity when we say something is the case, because it might be taken to cover the future. Hintikka adopts an extensional interpretation of "simply": to deny that what is simply is necessary might mean that there may be temporal values for which it does not hold.[22] In any case, Aristotle does include almost immediately thereafter the logical lesson that the disjunction as a whole may be necessary without entailing that one or the other of the disjuncts is necessary. Thus it is necessary that there will be a sea battle tomorrow or there will not be one. But it is not the case that either necessarily there will be a sea battle tomorrow or necessarily there will not be one.

Of course one could go on to offer Aristotle suggestions on how he might argue here in terms of what he says elsewhere. For example, he could use a formulation parallel to what we saw above he says of "Socrates is well" and "Socrates is ill." If there is no Socrates, then both are false. So too if we said "What will be tomorrow is a sea battle" and "What will be tomorrow is not a sea battle," both are false because there is now no such thing as what will be tomorrow. Another possibility is suggested by On Generation and Corruption 2.11, in which the discussion of whether there is anything that will necessarily exist in the future raises some of our present issues. Aristotle draws a distinction between saying "this will be" (estai) and "this is about to be" (mellei). He takes the first to entail that it is true, whereas the second does not rule out the event's not happening; for example, a man might not go for a walk though he is now about to go.[23] Aristotle has specifically in mind the domain of the uncertain with respect to the future. If we developed this distinction as a linguistic recommendation, we would not say "this will be" (estai) except in contexts of assurance, because we know there is absolute necessity in the order of nature, such as (on Aristotle's view) the future revolution of the heavens. In the domain where potentiality and possibility apply we would use the other term (mellei), indicating probabilities and possibilities. Still another possibility would be to reject completely the use of true and false for future events, just as Aristotle denies that at a single moment there can be motion or rest.[24] If one spoke of motion at an instant it could only mean that on both sides of that instant, no matter how small one defined the time interval for which that instant was a terminus, there would be motion during that interval. So too, perhaps, to say there will be a sea battle tomorrow might have to be translated into statements about the converging effect of determinants over time intervals.

Of our various suggestions, Aristotle would allow only those that would preserve a meaning for a statement about a future event's happening being true or false. He is not interested in assigning it an indeterminate truth value any more than a double-false value, because given the correspondence of the ultimate fact to the present disjunctive statement, we would be predicting an indeterminate fact or two opposite states of affairs neither of which were occurring. It is quite another matter to say now that one or the other state of affairs will take place but the causal processes or the accidental processes or the other kinds of processes that are operative have not yet worked their way to a finish.

Even these brief examples show that the reconstruction on the epistemological side could go in different directions perhaps depending on the type of logical system developed. Of course Aristotle developed his own way of dealing with modal terms, particularly in the *Prior Analytics* where modal syllogisms are discussed, but also in *On Interpretation* 12 and 13. How do we find him expounding the notion of necessity there?

Necessity and Possibility in the Logical Works

If the primary sense of necessity is *what cannot be otherwise*, then its meaning would seem to depend on *cannot*, thus on what is *not possible*, and hence on *possibility*. This is a complex and even ambiguous notion. In contemporary thought we find such distinctions as *logically possible*, that is, without inconsistency; *scientifically possible*, that is, not contradicting any known scientific law; and *technically possible*, that is, able to be constructed whether it has been or not. Aristotle moves along quite different lines. The basic term in the complex expression *cannot be otherwise* is *endechomenon* (allowing of, permitting, receptive of). It seems to be the most general term in his family of concepts here, since he occasionally gives *dunaton*, the other term he uses for *possible*, as one of its senses.[25] *Dunaton* is readily translated into *possible*; it is the term associated with *dunamis*, potentiality. Even here Aristotle is careful to make fine distinctions.[26] A potentiality usually is capable of alternative realizations: this coat may be cut or remain uncut; a man who is capable of walking is also capable of not walking. Not every potentiality is like that. So-called nonrational potentialities have only one direction of realization; for example, fire can only heat. Finally, Aristotle points out, we often say that someone is capable of walking when he actually walks; in short, the actual is also reckoned possible or else it would not be happening.

Endechomenon exhibits the same problem in relation to the necessary. In the passage referred to above, Aristotle includes the necessary, together with *dunaton*, under that which is allowable (*endechomenon*).[27] In this sense if something must be, it certainly can be. Yet we have to be careful with our usage, for if we do not make appropriate distinctions we will land in a contradiction: the necessary is possible; the possible can not be; therefore the necessary can not be.

In a later chapter of the *Prior Analytics* Aristotle offers a more general explication of the *allowable*: we use that term for something when "it not being necessary, but assumed to be true, there is no impossibility [*adunaton*] on its account."[28] This gets closer to our wider sense of logical possibility. Here he seems content in concluding that "the allowable is not necessary and what is not necessary is allowable." He goes on to distinguish two senses of *allowable* that arise in applying it to the physical world. One is what happens generally though not necessarily, such as a man's becoming gray-haired. This, we saw earlier, was one of the marks of the natural. The other is the indeterminate (*aoriston*), which is simply the potentiality for alternatives , such as walking or not walking, or a chance earthquake while walking, none of which is more natural than its opposite.

Hintikka, in line with his extensional interpretation of necessity noted above, that something is necessary means it always was and always will be so, interprets the sense of *possibility* we are considering as equivalent to saying that what is possible has happened or will happen at some time.[29] He invokes as an explanatory assumption on Aristotle's part the "principle of plenitude," namely that every possibility will in due time be realized, as contrasted with the modern notion of worlds that are only logically possible. He recognizes that this needs clarification and greater specification. Obviously the coat that gets burned never will be cut, though until it was burned it had the potentiality of being cut. The principle of plenitude therefore needs more precise formulation to apply to Aristotle's problem. It would at least have to refer to *kinds*, not individuals. But in that case it would seem to make a great deal of difference at what level of generality it applied. If coats are cuttable because cloth is cuttable, and this is so because certain kinds of solids are separable under certain conditions, all that would be needed to realize the relevant potentiality would be one bit of such matter separated into two parts.

Perhaps the strongest Aristotelian formulation supporting the plenitude interpretation is *On the Heavens* 1.12, where Aristotle is trying to prove that the world is everlasting. He distinguishes the impossible from the false but will not allow us to say that a thing might have a given potentiality forever without ever realizing it. In *Metaphysics* 9.4, he states this as follows: "It is not allowable that it is true to say 'this is possible, but it will not be.'"[30] In both contexts he uses the same procedure, arguing that a contradiction follows: what is potential can conceivably occur; imagine it occurring; but we have also said that it will not occur; therefore imagining it to happen contradicts our assuming it will not happen. In the passage from the *Metaphysics* Aristotle gives the example of saying we can do an impossible task but never will. Let us take instead a speculative physical example. Suppose someone held that we could shoot an arrow out beyond the finite world, and Aristotle were to argue that any arrow shot up with whatever force would be coerced into circular orbit in the heavens. If his theory of the heavens were regarded as *knowledge*, would there be any sense in saying that we *could* shoot the arrow beyond the world but never will? A similar mode of argument occurs in *On the Movement of Animals* when he speculates on the force that might be used to dislodge the earth (in the Atlas fable) and decides there is no such possibility.[31]

We do not therefore have to assume a principle of plenitude to take care of this Aristotelian argument. The guaranteed knowledge that something is ruled out is as much a ground for denying a potentiality as the guaranteed motion of the heavens is for assuming that time is potentially infinite. The principle of plenitude may be an additional interpretation, but it would have to be established separately as an Aristotelian belief.

Much of the complexity in the concept of necessity thus stems from its relation to what is allowable (*endechomenon*) and what is possible (*dunaton*). But even in its other root, necessity as *anankaion* or, in the logical context of what follows necessarily or out of necessity, *ex anankaiou*, there are many difficulties. These can be seen, for example, in questions that arise about the forms of syllogism that Aristotle accepts and rejects in which the concept of necessity appears.[32] Thus there has been controversy as to why he accepts (1) *If* all B is necessarily A, *and* all C is B, *then* all C is necessarily A, but rejects (2) *If* all B is A, *and* all C is necessarily B, *then* all C is necessarily A. Some argue that both arguments are invalid on the ground that a necessary conclusion requires necessary premises. Aristotle seems to think that to bring something as a special case under a necessary connection allows one to assert a necessary connection but that this is not permissible where the major premise may state a possibly contingent relation even if the minor premise is necessary. (He illustrates the unacceptability of the latter with "*If* all animals are in motion, *and* all men are necessarily animals, *then* all men are necessarily in motion," where presumably the first statement just happens to be the case at a given time and the necessity in the conclusion is unjustified.)

Modern logicians have made attempts to formalize Aristotle's modal logic to take account of the forms that he certifies.[33] Others suggest that such a formalization may not be feasible. Perhaps Aristotle's concept of necessity combines too many different aspects to be formally manipulated. Or the problem may lie in a difference in interest, namely that modern formalization has a greater concern for generality, so that it removes complexities from the basic formal ideas and leaves the complexities to be dealt with in processing materials that are to make use of the system, while Aristotle retains them in the original ideas of the system. Certainly he himself calls attention to two factors that we can readily see as serious obstacles to the kind of formalization moderns have sought.

One concerns the types of premises that yield necessary conclusions. In the *Posterior Analytics*, Aristotle insisted that premises of a demonstration be necessary first principles, as well as universal, and that they deal with and yield connections that are eternal (*aïdion*).[34] In short, the premises in demonstration state essential connections. But syllogistic premises that are universal in form will not all be of this sort. They may be accidental universals, or state consequences for our processes of learning, so that the premises give us the *causa cognoscendi* for the conclusion rather than the *causa essendi*. The *Prior Analytics* classifies premises in a simple formulation: "Every premise is either of inhering [a predicate in a subject] or inhering from necessity or allowing to inhere."[35] These simple differences—A is B, A is necessarily B, A may be B—are usually referred to in formidable translation as assertoric, apodeictic, and problematic. Now the mere appearance of a universal premise cannot by its form indicate whether it is essential or accidental. So we have to go beyond bare form. For example, in syllogism 1 above, if for "All C is B" we had "All men are animals," that would be an essential assertion and thus as good as a necessary premise. Aristotle warns us to be careful in selecting premises, to distinguish the accidental and the rest, in effect along the lines of the predicables, primarily aiming at getting essential statements.[36]

The second complicating factor comes from the meaning of *inhere* (*huparchein*). This term is the standard one in the *Prior Analytics* for the relation of the predicate term to the subject: the predicate *inheres* in the subject or *applies* to it. Now *inheres* has as many senses as *to be*; Aristotle states this even more explicitly: "That this inheres in [or applies to] that and this is true of that must be taken in as many senses as the categories are distinguished."[37] Presumably if we spelled out the mode of application we might avoid invalid inference. For example, "B is a quality of A and C is a genus of B" would not yield a conclusion relating C to A, though we might have thought so if the statement were simply "B applies to A and C applies to B." (Recall the example given above in differentiating *present in* from *predicable of*: Socrates is white; white is a color; therefore Socrates is a color.) Aristotle does not work out a separate logic for each category, but he is constantly attentive at least to the broad difference between accidental and substantival inherence. In our modern mechanized version of the syllogism, the purely formal is made uniform by separating subject and predicate by means of a copula, treating the terms as classes in extension, and regarding the copula as stating inclusion or exclusion of classes. This makes the logical machine more general, and as a machine more powerful. The specific questions that concerned Aristotle here, those that would require going into the content of the premises, become matters of "processing" the ordinary language sentences to fit them to the machine. This was indeed a formidable step in building formal systems. But it should not obscure insight into what Aristotle was doing.

A broad view of necessity is required if we are to be true to the state of Aristotle's work. It is neither completely systematized on the one hand nor reduced to one of the themes on the other hand. Attempts to make a system of his modal logic thus far seem to use him primarily as a jumping-off point for something more formal than his work will bear. On the other hand, Hintikka's view that necessity is simply invariance over time and that this is the content of Aristotle's statements about the eternal and the imperishable, insightful as it is with respect to the temporal element in the logic of sentences, is overreductive for the analysis of necessity. Though Aristotle does say that "what is from necessity also at the same time is always,"[38] such an equation ("at the same time" is *hama*, whose broad meaning would not solve the question) need not be identity of meaning; it could be copresence or invariance, each side having surplus meaning.

The alternative is not to reduce necessity to invariance but to see it as a complex of several strands, whose problems arise in the convergence of the strands and the attempt to fuse them. The history of thought confirms the particular richness of the concept; it embraces invariant relation, historical invariance and continuity, a natural order, logical connection, causal force, and the consolidation of properties in concept formation, as well as divine power that prescribes or maintains the universe. Aristotle's necessity does not have all these components, but it does include invariance (both as recurrence and historical continuity), logical connection, and the conceptual form grasped in induction and embodied in definition; its religious background stems from the old idea of Necessity (*anankē*), which allotted the destinies and limits of the gods and humans. More fundamental still there is his belief in a world that always was and always will be, with stable ways.

NOTES

Part 1

CHAPTER 1

1. See Grayeff 1974, who maintains that the works are reports of lectures given and that they were kept in the library of the head of the school, used for subsequent courses and added to, and so passed on for generations—and that they suffered some of the vicissitudes of the legends (see especially his ch. 4): "It appears, therefore, that Andronicus's edition of the Corpus reflects the teaching, not only of Aristotle, but of two or three generations of Peripatetic philosophers. Nevertheless, Andronicus published his edition as the sole work of Aristotle" (p. 82). Grayeff argues that Andronicus tried to expunge non-Aristotelian elements. In part 2 of his book, Grayeff looks at several of the books of the *Metaphysics* in this light and attempts to analyze them as different batches of "courses" on different topics.

2. Decision on this question rests on a complex interrelation of different lines of inquiry: the ancient lists of Aristotle's works as reported in various sources, which have to be dated and interpreted; the quotations and fragments of other ancient writers with definite or possible reference to individual works or views; and the works of Aristotle's successors in the school and their attention or lack of attention to his technical writings. For a study of the lists see Moraux 1951 (especially his conclusions, ch. 7). See also Moraux 1973, pp. 3–31. Lynch 1972, especially pp. 146–49, examines the problem in the special context of inquiry into the reasons for the decline of the Aristotelian school between the time of Theophrastus and that of Andronicus. He suggests that the failure of Aristotle's school to make use of his esoteric writings in their subsequent work could come from other reasons than not having them. McKeon 1979 points out the way in which changes in the conception of philosophy reflect changes in the modes in which it is pursued and suggests that the treatment of Aristotle's philosophy in subsequent schools shows this. Thus, although McKeon regards it as unlikely that there was no copy of Aristotle's works in the Alexandrian library, it remains that Aristotle's influence in the Hellenistic period did not depend on consulting his works. The history of the Lyceum is rather one of science and the development and use of scientific methods.

3. See Cameron 1969 for a restudy of the evidence. Justinian's edict simply prohibited pagans from teaching. Apparently it was not strictly enforced and did not affect the Alexandrian school. The group in the Athenian Academy went to Persia but returned to Athens after a short stay. Cameron emphasizes the fact that Simplicius wrote his commentaries on Aristotle after his return. He suggests that the Academy was vulnerable because its Neoplatonic views were being directed against the Christian beliefs.

4. See Kristeller 1961, ch. 2.

5. Joachim 1922, p. v.

6. For a discussion of the problem of different modes of analysis and their impact in school conflicts, see Edel 1979, especially "Modes of Analysis: A Philosophic Overview."

7. McKeon 1976, p. 2, has suggested that "changing interpretations of Aristotle are among the significant characteristics by which successive ages in the West may be interpreted."

CHAPTER 2

1. Bury 1924, p. 834.
2. *Pol.* 1340b26–29.

3. *Pol.* 1339a1 ff.
4. *Rhet.* 2.12.
5. *Part. An.* 686b10 f.
6. *Eud. Eth.* 1214b30 f., 1224a28 f., 1215b22 f.
7. *Nic. Eth.* 1161b18 ff., 1162a4 f.
8. Historical judgments vary with the times and the swings from an emphasis on discontinuity and contrast to one on continuity and development. There is no general way of deciding antecedently where these shifts will embody greater accumulation of and insight into historical evidence. The sharp contrast between the Hellenic age (classical Greece at its height until the death of Alexander in 323 B.C.) and the Hellenistic age (from the death of Alexander to the battle of Actium in 31 B.C.) is largely an evaluative expression of admiration for Greek accomplishments of the fifth and fourth centuries and is influenced by conceptions of a silver age following a golden age, or decadence as a sequel to unusual vitality. It has taken major efforts to secure a just appreciation of the later period as one of great intellectual progress and accomplishment in science and philosophy alike, and as building on rather than falling away from the previous successes. For a general view of the Hellenistic period in this light, see Long 1974, ch. 1. For a reevaluation of the scientific contributions of Stoicism, see Sambursky 1959. For analysis of some continuities between Aristotelian and Stoic thought, see Long 1968; between Aristotelian and Epicurean, see Furley 1967, especially Study II.
9. For the interpretation of slavery in ancient Greece, see M. I. Finley 1968 and 1973, ch. 3.
10. *Meta.* 1078b12 ff.
11. For problems about the character of the Academy, see the discussion of the Lyceum in n. 30 below.
12. Diogenes Laertius 1959, vol. 1, 381. This remark occurs in his "Life of Xenocrates."
13. For an account of Isocrates' educational approach in its relation to the Platonic, see Jaeger 1944, vol. 3, chs. 2 and 6. For an evaluation of Isocrates and his tradition, see M. I. Finley, "The Heritage of Isocrates," in Finley 1975, pp. 193–214. The subsequent stories are presented and assessed in Düring 1957, pp. 299–314.
14. For this quotation from Quintilian, see *The Works of Aristotle*, Oxford translations, vol. 12, p. 3.
15. Jaeger 1962.
16. *The Works of Aristotle*, Oxford translations, vol. 12, p. 41 (*Protrepticus* 8).
17. See Solmsen 1960; Owen 1961.
18. De Vogel 1960.
19. *Nic. Eth.* 1096a11–17.
20. Düring 1957, p. 276. This comprehensive scholarly work goes perhaps furthest in its critical rejection of many of the stories that are usually associated with Aristotle, by finding the sources to be unreliable.
21. *Pol.* 1334b29–1335a35.
22. *Pol.* 1260a12 ff.
23. *Eud. Eth.* 1242a32, 1238b25.
24. *Nic. Eth.* 1162a24 ff.
25. *Pol.* 1335b13 ff.
26. Düring 1957, pp. 264–67.
27. Taylor 1955, p. 12.
28. Diogenes Laertius 1959, vol. 1, 459.
29. For this quotation from Plutarch, see *The Works of Aristotle*, Oxford translations, vol. 12, p. 67. This contrast of Aristotle and Alexander is discussed in chapter 18 below. It is the subject of extended controversy.
30. Düring 1957, p. 346 (cf. p. 260), in part challenges the correctness of this picture. He suggests Aristotle simply frequented the Lyceum and philosophized there, keeping his library at home. Düring believes Theophrastus set up the permanent school later on. Aristotle would thus be the founder only of the Peripatetic philosophy. Lynch's subsequent reanalysis (1972, chs. 1 and 2) clarifies the picture by setting it in the general development of Athenian education, as well as comparing the Academy and Lyceum to other schools and

investigating in more detail the physical setting and its customary uses. The picture that emerges is briefly as follows. The chief centers of educational activity in Athens were the three gymnasia—the Academy, Lyceum, and Cynosarges. Initial training in music (including literature), gymnastics, and reading and writing was carried on in these public places in group lessons, as a private enterprise with teachers paid by parents. Any further education was acquired by association, not formal training. The emerging needs of Athenian democracy, noted above in considering rhetoric, were met in a new way by the lectures of visiting sophists. Socrates reacted against the sophists, favoring education by association rather than formal institutions, but he shared with them making advanced education a conscious intellectual pursuit. The more formal education caught on, whether labeled sophistic or rhetorical or philosophical; the transition from individual lecture to school institution lay not in location, but in the increased regularity and permanence over generations, and in cooperation. The gymnasia remained the operative centers and were constantly frequented by all sorts of teachers who set themselves up on an individual, temporary or regular basis and charged for their lectures. Isocrates, however, who taught rhetoric in a private building, perhaps his home, was a school fixture for his lifetime of activity. Antisthenes, one of the older Socratics, possibly was the earliest to set up on a regular basis. Plato started operating in the Academy in about 387, on his return from Syracuse. Lynch 1972, pp. 54–63, building largely on Cherniss's (1945) analysis, dispels any tendencies to think of Plato's Academy in terms of a modern college or even in terms of the fixed state educational program Plato works out in the *Republic*. Plato's school was completely organized, with advanced members and younger students; it was a cooperative enterprise under his intellectual leadership, not a fixed curriculum. Apparently fees were not charged; anyone could attend, but he did have to be able to support himself. Plato bought an estate near the Academy and thus gave the school in part a private location. The Peripatetic school, when Aristotle founded it, though a different kind of school educationally, had organizational similarities to the Academy. It had the same openness; it gained continuity over generations by the selection of a permanent "scholarch" to head the school. An important distinguishing factor in the career of the school was its relation to Macedonia. Plato's Academy was well grounded in Athenian citizenship. Aristotle's Lyceum went up and down with the degree of Macedonian control over Athens. Aristotle himself could not provide a permanent private base for the school, because a noncitizen could not buy land. Theophrastus was able to do so; he was also a noncitizen but was given special state permission—an exceptional honorific procedure—when a member of the school, Demetrius of Phalerum, was ruler of Athens under the protection of Macedonia (Lynch 1972, pp. 98–105). The whole picture thus makes clear that Aristotle was the founder of a functioning Peripatetic school, not merely of the Peripatetic philosophy.

31. *Rhet.* 2.14.
32. Düring 1957, p. 199.
33. Jaeger 1962, p. 321.
34. *Rhet.* 2.13.
35. *Rhet.* 1398b27–29.
36. *Nic. Eth.* 1.11.
37. The history of the Peripatetic school after Aristotle and Theophrastus raises many problems. On the one hand there is a philosophical decline; on the other there is marked scientific progress. For a collection of the fragments of the successors in the school, see Wehrli 1944–59. For Wehrli's explanatory hypothesis about the decline see his vol. 10, pp. 93–128 ("Rückblick: Der Peripatos in vorchristlicher Zeit"). See also Lynch's criticism (1972, pp. 145 ff.) of Wehrli's thesis, and his own analysis of relevant factors (ch. 5). Lynch stresses institutional factors such as the Macedonian dependence and the effect of the wars, the loss of Aristotle's library, and the fragmentation of the school, as well as the situational fact of the Lyceum being outside the walls of Athens and thus open to partial destruction in the warfare. As to the common notion that the schools were closed by Justinian in 529 A.D. (see chapter 1, n. 3, above), Lynch argues that the Peripatetic school had long ceased to exist by that time. He suggests (pp. 206–7) that when Sulla removed the library of Aristotle and Theophrastus to Rome, the institution that Aristotle had founded in Athens ceased (after 86 B.C.) to make any contribution to the history of Greek philosophy. Of course the renewed

Aristotelianism set in motion by Andronicus' edition opened up a new chapter unconnected with the parent institution.

38. Taylor 1955, pp. 11–12.
39. Diogenes Laertius 1959, vol. 1, 460.
40. *Rhet.* 1389b11 f.; cf. *Eud. Eth.* 1234a4–23.
41. *Rhet.* 1419b5 f.
42. Reported in Plutarch; cf. Düring 1957, pp. 351–52.
43. *Pol.* 1315b8 f.
44. E.g. *Nic. Eth.* 1131a25 ff.
45. *Rhet.* 2.4, 6.
46. *Pol.* 1314a2 f.
47. *Pol.* 1332a8–10.

CHAPTER 3

1. *On Dreams* 459b27 ff.
2. *On Prophecy in Sleep* 1.
3. The complex problems on this point are dealt with in chapter 7 below. There are important differences of direction between Socrates and Aristotle here. In one sense, Socrates is trying to rouse the mind of the hearer through the material into a flight to ideas, whereas Aristotle is using the ordinary material to keep the flight responsible. Socratic method has long challenged philosophers who attempt to locate its effect and its logic as well as its charm; see Nelson 1949; Vlastos 1956, introduction; and Edel 1963, ch. 4.
4. *Top.* 105a3 ff.
5. *Gen. Corr.* 325a19–23.
6. *Part. An.* 646a25–29.
7. See, for example, *Gen. Corr.* 325a13–19 (the passage just preceding the one in n. 5 above). Aristotle reports the argument—from initial general assumptions—of those who reach such conclusions as that motion does not exist. He says they go further and disregard observation as necessary to following *logos*. Their beliefs seem to follow in terms of the *logoi*, but to believe them in view of the *pragmata* is near madness.
8. It is important at the outset to contrast this interpretation of Aristotle, which sees the linguistic as furnishing partial evidence, with some current interpretations that draw sharp distinctions between the linguistic and the empirical. The latter want to decide precisely where Aristotle is engaging in a linguistic inquiry (and so "doing philosophy"), and where an empirical inquiry (and so "doing science"). This attitude is a familiar one in contemporary linguistic analysis, which has made serious contributions to Aristotelian studies by sharpening our linguistic sensitivity and occasionally by furnishing modern linguistic tools, but at some points it creates obstacles by applying its own doctrines of language rather than looking through Aristotle's eyes at how he saw language. Some of the issues involved will be discussed later in this book, but one fundamental point should be noted in a kind of preview. This is that Aristotle looks at words from the point of view of things, not things from the point of view of words. At the beginning of the *Categories*, when he defines *homonymy* and *synonymy*, he says that *things* are homonymous if they share the same name but the name has a different definition in the two cases, and synonymous if they share the same name and its definition is in both cases the same. (If this sounds outrageous to modern ears, please remember Aristotle was there first—we are the ones who *re*defined it.) We are more linguistically oriented when we start with *words* and call the words equivocal or univocal, and speak of the words as synonymous. Ackrill 1963, p. 71, in his comment on the same passage in the *Categories*, explains this whole point clearly and adds, "It is encumbent on the translator not to conceal this, and, in particular, not to give a misleadingly linguistic appearance to Aristotle's statements by gratuitously supplying inverted commas in all the places where *we* might feel that it is linguistic expressions that are under discussion." We shall have occasion to come back to this important topic in several different contexts later on.

The significance of this fundamental point is that Aristotle does not have to segregate language in general from things in general as a sharply distinct order. Of course there are the different inquiries mentioned—one *logikos*, a dialectical inquiry, and one *physikos*, a scientific inquiry—but we would be hard put to construe the first as pure language and the second as pure observation. There is for Aristotle, then, no general or metaphysical question of the correspondence of language and reality, or whether the structure of language mirrors the structure of reality, such as modern philosophers like to raise about language and about Aristotle. (There are notions of correspondence in his theory of truth, but that is another matter.) It is doubtless a perfectly reasonable question to raise on some presuppositions, but not on Aristotle's.

Some illustrations of the effect of these modern approaches on interpretations of Aristotle will be found later when we compare different modern philosophical viewpoints on specific passages and issues in the corpus.

9. *Meteor.* 347a11f., 380b28ff.

10. *Soph. Ref.* 166b16 f.

11. *Gen. Corr.* 321a29–b2, 322a31 f.

12. *Meta.* 7, 1030a27 ff. "How the facts actually stand" translates *to pōs echei.* The "fact," in this context, turns out to be a reiteration, no matter which way we choose to speak, that in a primary sense definition and essence belong to substance. "How things stand" has here, then, more of the character of an established principle from which usage must not detract.

13. *Meta.* 8, 1045a20 ff.

14. *Heav.* 268a16 ff.

15. *Gen. An.* 742a19 ff.

16. *Psych.* 415b20 f.

Part 2

INTRODUCTION

1. Though developed and energetically pursued in idealist philosophy (especially the neo-Hegelian) with a coherence theory of truth, it has also emerged in pragmatic and neopragmatic philosophies, and is not uncongenial to naturalistic and even positivist outlooks. Differences lie, of course, in the principles posited for relating the concepts and in the interpretations of the schemes. That an activist spirit of conceptual construction is pervasive admits in itself the possibility of different interpretations—e.g., for the positivist, largely conventional; for the idealist, a response to the larger whole; for the naturalist, a response to realistic constraints. The way Aristotle interprets his concepts, their relations, and their associated principles has therefore to be sought from the detail of his treatment. It is not predetermined by our thinking of a conceptual network.

CHAPTER 4

1. *Rhet.* 1358a36–59a6.

2. What if, in this case, a future-oriented philosopher were to argue that judgments about the past, and even the observer's appreciation, were all indirect ways of persuading about or guiding the future? The three contexts would now (if this were granted) be integrated into one context by the single task, and the three concepts would thus have to be focused into one primary concept of the expedient. (Hedonistic utilitarianism did precisely this.)

3. *Phys.* 194b9 f.

4. *Meta.* 1044b8 ff.

5. The Greek term is a little less dramatic than the terms of Latin derivation: "subject" is literally what is thrown or hurled under, "substratum" what is spread under, and both have in their Latin source military overtones of subjection. It is also interesting to note that etymologies are sometimes exploited in later philosophy. For example, "object," as what is thrown across one's path and so obstructs beyond one's control, has sometimes been

invoked to distinguish the "objective" from the "subjective." But of course etymologically the subject is equally compelled.

6. *Gen. Corr.* 320a2 ff.

7. *Gen. Corr.* 329a24 ff.

8. *Meta.* 1015a7 ff.

9. Aristotle's conception of "prime matter" has been an especially controversial issue, particularly where it was treated as a separate doctrine from his general theory of matter. Scholastic usage distinguished between secondary matter (the enformed matter, such as bronze and stone, which served in the relative sense for statues and buildings) and primary matter (the formless ultimate matter known by analogy from which all physical things are constituted). Historically there has often been a tendency to regard the former as an empirical conception, the latter as a philosophical conception. As we have expounded the Aristotelian view, the drawing apart of the two aspects is unnecessary, and so the controversy whether Aristotle did or did not believe in prime matter rests on obscure foundations. It is unnecessary because: (1) The description of prime matter in the controversy usually drops the Aristotelian qualification that matter in the strict sense does not exist without properties or by itself. It is only in abstraction that it is so considered. Aristotle talks about lots of things in abstraction—for example, lines and planes and their properties in geometry—without assuming they exist by themselves. They are nonetheless real features of the world in his philosophy. The properties are forgotten when we talk of prime matter as a philosophical concept, because they cannot be specified by philosophy; they are furnished by the physical theory of the time. (2) If it is thought that the notion of basic matter is an intellectual construction while that of relative or enformed matter deals with an observable, this is not strictly correct. The difference is one of degree, as we saw in discussing the origin of the conceptions. The persistence in change, that is, the assumed continuity of a subject changing, is an interpretation of experience, expressed in discourse. There is more of extrapolation in the case of basic matter, but there can be confirmation in further experience as we see what happens in the substantival changes around us. On both grounds (1) and (2) there is no reason to distinguish a separate problem of prime matter from the general discussion of matter including its basic forms. This conclusion cannot be taken, in the traditional controversies, to mean that Aristotle did not have a concept of prime matter, nor that he did. It denies the formulations in terms of which those controversies have generally taken place.

For a recent attack on the concept of prime matter, see Charlton 1970, Appendix, "Did Aristotle Believe in Prime Matter?" Charlton reanalyzes passages alleged to support it and suggests how, from Plato's doctrine of the receptacle in the *Timaeus* on, the traditional acceptance of the view became hardened. For a critique of Charlton's account, suggesting that some of the Aristotelian passages have been misinterpreted and that in others the interpretation leads to serious difficulties, see Robinson 1974. Robinson not only defends the dominant view that Aristotle holds to prime matter, but takes the notion of prime matter to entail that some aspect of what underlies must remain.

In many respects, prime matter acts as a kind of Rorschach to bring out the philosophical attitude of philosophical writers on Aristotle. Zeller 1897, p. 354, takes matter never to present itself to us without form, yet includes the first purely formless matter at the foundation of all things. Ross 1959, p. 165, takes Aristotle's followers to have "rightly regarded it as one of the most important implications of his system," though it nowhere exist apart and is only an element in individual things. Mure 1964, p. 71, takes it to be a "purely logical *terminus a quo* of process, a moment distinguishable but not separable in any concrete of matter and form." Randall 1960, pp. 212–16, points out that generally Aristotle uses "first matter" for either the proximate material or else for an ultimate material or element like water; anything more fundamental really expresses an interest in transformations and something like a conservation principle. Santayana 1957, p. 240, in his "Secret of Aristotle," has Avicenna recount the revelation that the only proper cause in the world is "the radical instability in existence by which everything is compelled to produce something else without respite." To understand Aristotelian matter is thus to learn the basic philosophical secret.

The equation of ultimate matter with pure potentiality, which would follow from the equation of matter and potentiality (which we shall see in a later chapter) gives matter the dynamic character that may pallitate a bit the sense of its uselessness often stressed by opponents in the controversies over prime matter (together with its mysteriousness). There is another important point to be considered, however, if we think of the concept not in terms of ancient science, where Aristotle speaks as if he had a finished system of physics, but in terms of modern science, in which the physical theory furnishes the ultimate picture of the properties of matter (from molecules to atoms to protons and electrons to hosts of subtler particles and even to the constructs of one day that become the discovered entities of the next day). Now if we focus on the fact that basic matter never exists without some properties and that physical theory tells us what these properties are, what underlies substantival change and remains as basic matter or as pure potentiality is rich with the possibilities of subsequent discovery and description of properties. It is not a mysterious indeterminate nor a static emptiness. It suggests that from a modern point of view Aristotle did well not to shear off the idea of a basic matter and equate it with the elements on the one hand nor cut it loose into an indeterminate existing by itself on the other hand. It is easier to see these virtues through a contemporary pragmatic or functional notion of meaning that asks for the consequences of the conception in a developing science rather than a finished science. (This does not of course say that Aristotle held such a view, though his use of final cause, we shall see, has its functional aspects.)

It is worth noting also that a comparison of theories of indescribable or indeterminate matter in the history of philosophy shows that usually they paved the way for an idealistic or a subjectivistic philosophy. To get rid of matter is to leave everything to soul or spirit or mind—whether in Platonic fashion, or in theological arguments of the need for a divine start for inert matter, or in Berkeleyan arguments that a Lockean something-I-know-not-what is unintelligible and therefore matter does not exist, or in a Hegelian treatment of matter as simply the extreme self-alienation of spirit. Aristotle's sober concept of matter was spared the pain of turning into its opposite.

10. E.g., *Meta.* 1002a4–18; cf. *Heav.* I.1.

11. *Meta.* 1029a23 f.

12. *Categ.* 2a11 f.

13. *Meta.* 1029a26 ff.

14. For opposing treatments of the passage compare Charlton 1970, pp. 136–38, who takes this to be a line of thought Aristotle rejects, and Owens 1965, who takes Aristotle to be definitely expounding here a theory of primary matter as indeterminate. Interestingly, Owens is not concerned with rescuing Aristotle's consistency but wants to draw a philosophical lesson. If indeterminate matter cannot be assigned to any categorial determination positive or negative but may yet somehow be conceived and set up as a subject for predication and understood through analogy, then the door is open to an understanding that is *positive*, although not *determinate*. Such a mode of arguing points to a distinct level of explanation in natural philosophy. (Owens, of course, assumes that Aristotle's argument as he interprets it holds up.)

15. For suggestions on why Aristotle's concept was not geared for this task, see McMullin 1965a, pp. 19 ff. (in McMullin's introduction). See also McMullin 1965c, pp. 25–45.

16. The impact of different philosophical schools on Aristotelian studies at such points is an extremely important question. It is worth illustrating at length here. But to avoid misunderstanding an initial comment is necessary. Every school in virtue of its special emphases develops special insights and usually grows special forms of blindness. Both have to be pointed out. Sometimes they are a function of individual interpreters, sometimes invariant for the school. Again, certain schools tend to dominate the field at certain times in certain areas. The scholastic interpretations of Aristotle had their recognized period of dominance; today there are varying internal tendencies. In the later nineteenth and early twentieth century the Hegelian approach loomed over Aristotelian interpretation. In the mid-twentieth century in English-speaking countries ordinary language analysis dominated Aristotelian studies and probably still does, but recently it has widened the range of its perspectives. Phenomenological interpretations have spread considerably since mid-century, as have naturalistic interpretations.

As a specific illustration of differences in approach, let us take the interpretations of

Aristotle's inquiry in fashioning such concepts as matter and cause in the *Physics*. For example, Charlton, in his translation of books 1 and 2 of the *Physics* (1970) says in the Introduction: "It is important to recognize (as W. Wieland has shown at length) that the distinction between underlying thing and form is not a presupposition of the whole discussion, but a conclusion to which Aristotle argues, and argues, moreover, not from metaphysical principles but from linguistic considerations, by considering how we ordinarily talk" (p. xv). (It is also clear that Charlton does not believe Aristotle is carrying on an empirical investigation here.) Wieland 1962, who is invoked in this passage, has as a major aim to see what the theme of language that has entered so pervasively in various schools of contemporary philosophy can contribute to classical philosophy (Foreword, p. 7). His general point with respect to Aristotle's principles of matter, form, and privation (pp. 110–40) is that they are derived from the formal structure of our ordinary discourse about change and coming-into-being; we check which constructions we will allow in discourse and which we consider illegitimate. In this way we decide that there has to be something that undergoes the change and remains in the result, which is our substratum or subject, and similarly—to take Aristotle's example—that a man who becomes musical must have been unmusical beforehand; otherwise he would have been musical all along.

Straightforward and sensible as this sounds, is this what Aristotle's principle of change represents? Is the stability that the concept of matter as substratum gives to change in the things we talk about really nothing but the stable structure of our speech? (Cf. Wieland, p. 129.) It is interesting to note that other scholars find other Aristotelian answers equally "obvious." For example, Düring 1964, p. 86, has Aristotle doing a metaphysical job modeled on the sort of thing Plato was doing in the *Timaeus* (e.g., 52d) but going in his own direction, using a biological analogy, fashioning a concept of form that would tie in with his teleology and a concept of matter that stems from an analogy with the crafts (this last point Theophrastus confirms).

We have thus a linguistic interpretation and a metaphysical interpretation with underlying analogical models. But what about empirically oriented interpretations, whether starting with a direct experiential base or working toward broad principles of a scientific sort? Owens 1969 is equally affirmative: "Even a perfunctory acquaintance with the first two books of Aristotle's *Physics* will indicate clearly enough that his argument for an ultimate material principle is based on the generation of natural bodies" (p. 193). He adds that the argument is summed up in an analogy with artifacts and the reasoning starts from "the observable change wrought in bronze or wood by art and craftsmanship." The reasoning is extended to anything that has such a status prior to receiving a designated form, and the conclusion establishes a substrate by analogy. In the light of this approach Owens picks up the passages that point to the observational base—for example, in the very heart of *Physics* 1.7 there are references (beginning at 190a34) to what is found from which something comes into being, such as the seed in generation (Aristotle goes on to the sculptor working and to housebuilding). Owens says that "the overall procedure of *Physics* 1, therefore, shows clearly enough that Aristotle establishes a general notion of change from an investigation of its observable instances" (p. 198). (He then goes on to the one case where it is not directly observable.)

Again, Happ 1971, a voluminous study focusing on the Aristotelian concept of matter, takes issue with Wieland (pp. 290–91). For one thing, Happ keeps his eye on different parts of the corpus and correlates them. For example, he finds no difference between matter as substratum and matter as one of the four causes (the material cause to be examined in our next chapter). Again, referring to criticisms by a reviewer of Wieland (Ernst Tugendhat in *Gnomon* 1963: 543–55) Happ argues that Aristotle often begins with an analysis of speech and ends up with a structure of existence so that the speech is corrected by the facts. An important case for the present context is *On Generation and Corruption* 318a27–319a22, where Aristotle uses the concept of matter as a substratum and its related concepts not only to maintain the distinction between qualitative change on the one hand and coming-to-be and passing-away on the other, but to exhibit the thesis that the coming-to-be of one thing is the passing-away of another and vice versa. This is a kind of empirically grounded conservation principle; there has to be investigation into the sources of what appeared and the consequents of what disappeared. The principle in the long run depends on the success or failure of such investigations. (We shall consider this type of principle in Aristotle's science in chapter 13 below.) The controversies, even in modern philosophy of science, over the empirical versus conventional status of conservation principles (whether of matter or energy) have shown at least that views of physical statements as simply either empirical or linguistic are unduly constraining. (For an attempt to make finer differentiations in the chapters of *Physics* 1, see McMullin 1965, pp. 173–212.)

We might add that even in the midst of the linguistic analysis Aristotle is taking for granted *ordinary experience* as well as *ordinary language*. We not only say that an unmusical man has become musical and an ignorant man learned but we have known people who could not play an instrument and later surprised us, or who could not speak a foreign language and later on were fluent in it. (Happ cites *Phys.* 188b8–11 as a reference to experience.)

The outcome of such a critique is that to be fruitful linguistic analysis has to be integrated with the empirical, the phenomenal, the purposive, the metaphysical, and any other phases that may be relevant to a particular context. One cannot tell in advance where it should be separately pursued and to what extent, but it cannot be set up as a wholly distinct method of philosophy set off from "doing science." For Aristotle at least, it is part of a comprehensive inquiry, not a separate department with autonomous results.

When linguistic analysis isolates itself from the empirical, it often misses insights that its sensitivity to language might have yielded. For example, the notion of the out-of-which, one of the sources, as we saw, of the concept of matter, is examined in a careful study by Barrington Jones (1974). In spite of valuable probing into the question of what "underlies" a substantival change (pp. 482 ff.), his focus is only on individual terms, thus underplaying the functions performed. The interplay of different terms doing similar or complementary jobs is consequently ignored. For example, one might have expected the analysis of *out of* in the material sense to be coupled with that of *element* and *part*, while in the context of genesis or process *out of* might have been studied in comparison with the *efficient cause* or *whence* as well as with *prior* (in order to pinpoint the line between stimulating or initiating and being a material source). The separation of the linguistic use from the physical account (which Aristotle, taken as a whole, does not do) here robs the analysis of relevant material, since the factual content of a physical theory often shows how a term can be refined. It is not surprising then that Jones's conclusion is limited to the view that *out of* or *from* is used in a purely chronological sense (p. 493). His insistence (pp. 476–78) that in *Physics* 1.7 Aristotle is engaged in a linguistic investigation and not in an empirical investigation impoverishes the analysis.

The second concept—Aristotle's theory of the four causes—raises similar problems, but the way in which it is treated points to other issues in Aristotelian interpretation and it is worth looking at more briefly. (The specific content of Aristotle's theory of causes as a theory of explanation is not involved in this note and will be discussed in chapter 5.) Charlton 1970, p. 99, quotes Ross 1936, p. 37: "We do not know how Aristotle arrived at the doctrine of the four causes: where we find the doctrine in him, we find it not argued for but presented as self-evident." Charlton goes on shortly thereafter to say that "it is obvious (cf. Wieland, p. 262) that the doctrine with which we are presented here is the immediate result of a survey of how we ordinarily speak." He cites four passages: about what is called a cause, about a question and answer ending up with a cause, a reference to the ways the term is used, and "the causes mentioned." This is sparse fare for a concept that is pervasive and active throughout the whole Aristotelian corpus.

We turn accordingly to Wieland 1962, p. 262. He gets to the problem in the context of teleology and he notes the lack of a foundation for the theory of causes. At this point he quotes Ross. That quotation seems to serve him—and it looks as if Charlton gets the same mileage out of it—to make a mystery out of Aristotle's theory of causes so that any hypothesis of its origin will be welcome. Wieland wastes no time in enunciating the thesis noted above. The formal unity of the causal idea lies in the unity of the linguistic term *why?* (*dia ti*).

Perhaps it is time to turn to Ross and ask why the origin of the theory of causes should be regarded as so inexplicable. The answer is that when we read the Ross quotation in context it is not so regarded. Ross adds immediately a plausible conjecture that both Wieland and

Charlton leave out: "He may have reached it by direct reflection on instances of natural process and of artistic production." And he proceeds to the assistance of Aristotle's predecessors, following Aristotle's own account in *Metaphysics* 1 of how the early history of Greek philosophy shows the material cause, Empedocles and Anaxagoras implicitly recognized the efficient cause, Plato the formal cause (in the theory of Ideas), and Aristotle himself the final cause. (In this progression theories of science mixed with theories of mathematics and logic. At one point, 984a16 ff., Aristotle says that the facts themselves, *auto to pragma*, led investigators on to discover further types). Presumably the only reason Ross did not invoke *Metaphysics* 1 in the first place was because it refers to the *Physics* as having already expounded the four causes. But this need not mean that the historical material later embodied in *Metaphysics* 1 had not operated previously in Aristotle's thought.

Charlton has a reference to *Metaphysics* 1 (983b5–6, 988b18) on the question whether there are any other kinds of causes (p. 99) but does not refer to the prior history of philosophy as a source of the Aristotelian theory of causes—a source in which scientific, linguistic, and theoretical considerations were mingled and which Aristotle unified in his conceptual reconstruction. It cannot be the dating question as such that determines this neglect, since Charlton takes books 1 and 2 of the *Physics*, in spite of early origin, to have been kept up to date and used for lectures to the end of Aristotle's career (p. xiii). I suspect that the operative cause of the neglect is the sharp distinction between linguistic analysis as alone "doing philosophy" and anything else as irrelevant, whether science or history, and hence not a proper source for a philosophical concept like cause.

17. *Gen. Corr.* 2.2, 3.

18. *Gen. Corr.* 331b25 f.

19. *Meteor.* 383b20–27. Cf. *Gen. An.* 735b13 ff. and *On Plants* 823a31–b18; in the latter Aristotle also discusses why leaves and some stones float.

20. *Gen. Corr.* 329b30 ff.

21. *Meteor.* 340b6 ff., 370b13 ff.

22. For a study of Aristotle's treatment of this notion, see Peck 1953, appendix B. See also Solmsen 1957, and Solmsen 1961 (particularly pp. 169–78 dealing with Aristotle); and Nussbaum 1978, interpretive essay 3.

23. *Meta.* 1010a12 ff. The serious Heracliteans with whom Aristotle is reckoning are perhaps best represented in the flux theorists of Plato's *Theaetetus*.

24. Whether the Greeks had an idea of progress has been the subject of considerable controversy. Many criticisms have been raised of the traditional view that progress is a modern notion. For example, John H. Finley, in his *Thucydides* (1942) grants that decline from a happier past and cyclical rise and decline were more common views in antiquity. "But that Athenians generally should have believed in progress through the great creative period of the mid-fifth century is both natural in itself and well attested by our sources" (p. 82). He appeals to the optimistic faith in man's developing powers accompanying the rise of democracy, Aeschylus' *Prometheus* and *Eumenides*, Sophocles' ode of the triumph of man in *Antigone*, the *Sisyphus* of Critias, and Pericles' speech on Athenian achievements. But he grants that Thucydides states that his own work will be of value to future generations because history repeats itself. Similarly, Dodds 1957 takes Protagoras to have had an optimistic view of improvement by modernizing Nomos, and takes it to express a reaction to the swift growth of material prosperity after the Persian Wars and the flowering of spirit. "For that generation, the Golden Age was no lost paradise of the dim past, as Hesiod had believed; for them it lay not behind but ahead, and not so very far ahead either" (p. 183). But, he adds, this faith in the inevitability of progress was soon disappointed by events.

The most formidable defense of an idea of progress in classical times is in Edelstein 1967. He gathers comprehensively the hints of an open world, the suggestions of development, and the bursts of confidence, beginning with Xenophanes' dictum that "The gods did not reveal to men all things from the beginning, but men through their own search find in the course of time that which is better" (p. 3). His strongest presentation comes from the expressions of faith in the growth of knowledge, and his argument seems also to be guided by the conviction that where improvement is made progressivism is indicated. Even Aristotle's confidence that men can accumulate scientific knowledge is grist to his mill, and Hellenistic scientific progress seems to strengthen this position.

Such a controversy rests in part on its conceptual foundations. Edelstein uses as his definition of a belief in progress the assumption of improvement in the past, the present, and the future (p. xxix). He puts aside as irrelevant whether this improvement comes from nature or man, what standard of improvement is used (whether material, moral, intellectual, greatest happiness), or any other philosophical considerations. Nevertheless, from a historical point of view (which he takes his to be) the different shades of assigned meaning and the fuller historical context should surely be important. It matters a great deal whether accounts of early improvement are simply showing how man got to his present position (how he managed to survive or the discovery of the crafts) without anticipating endless advance, whether the belief in a growth of knowledge includes a belief in growing application or only a deeper contemplative satisfaction; whether the idea of improvement is taken to depend on divine or human effort; whether it is enclosed within a cyclical theory so that over and over again men will start from scratch; and whether the idea occurs in a few scattered individuals or saturates the cultural atmosphere. The modern idea of progress has increasingly leaned on the idea of increased human control, on learning leading to technical improvement, and on a strong sense of practical possibilities.

In this sense I find more convincing for the ancient world the judgment offered by M. I. Finley as a result of his many-pronged studies of technology and economy as well as ideology, and his cautious restraint in applying to the ancient world concepts that have their distinctive color in relation to modern conditions. For his basic estimate of technical innovation and economic progress in the ancient world, see M. I. Finley 1973. His basic criticism of Edelstein's position (M. I. Finley 1974, pp. 46–47, esp. n. 76) is that the argument is vitiated by neglect of the fundamental distinction between material and cultural progress. Much of the description of progress is an account of the prehistory of the *polis* and its necessary conditions as the "natural" form of social organization. He finds in the literature that progress in some cultural spheres such as mathematics and astronomy can take place, that there can be "improvements in ethical, social and political behavior (more often than not put in terms of a return to older virtues)," that men can gain a better understanding of life and society. "But none of that adds up to the idea of progress which, in my judgment, has been the background of all modern economic analyses at least since the late eighteenth century" (p. 47).

The case for an unbridgeable gap between ancient and modern is summarized in his study "Utopianism Ancient and Modern" (M. I. Finley, 1975, pp. 190 ff.). The differences lie in (1) "the fact that it was not possible by any means to bring about an equitable society in antiquity, given the poor resources, the low level of technology, the absence of growth possibilities (other than conquest) in the economy, and the absence of the very idea of progress"; (2) the acceptance of human inequality and domination as natural and immutable; and (3) the smallness of scale in ancient organization compared to the vast character of the modern. The modern idea of progress is thus tied to a view that problems are technically solvable, that a just society implies equality and freedom, and that large-scale organization is possible.

Clearly the controversy over the existence of a belief in progress in ancient times involves at bottom a decision on how the very concept of progress is to be understood and the desirable policy in interpreting and refining such concepts. The search for hints and possibilities in the literature, though an important contribution to the overall problem, does not resolve this question.

25. The Greek terms for the specific forms of change are *auxēsis* (growth), *phthisis* (diminution), *alloiōsis* (alteration), *phora* (locomotion), *genesis* (generation), and *phthora* (corruption).

26. *Gen. Corr.* 319b14 ff.

27. *Meta.* 5.27.

28. E.g., *Heav.* 280b8 f.

29. *Gen. Corr.* 320a19 ff.

CHAPTER 5

1. The Greek terms for the causes are *to ex hou*, the out-of-which, for the material cause; *to ti ēn einai*, literally the-what-it-was-to-be, for essence, the formal cause, a technical term of obscure origin to be discussed in detail in chapter 7; *to hothen*, the whence, for efficient cause; and *to hou heneka*, the for-the-sake-of-which, the final cause.

2. This is not a simple transfer of heat for Aristotle, but the stimulation by the outside source of a capacity within the body. See Balme 1972, p. 92; he illustrates: "If my hand becomes sunburnt, the alteration is provoked by sunshine but caused by something in my body." The efficient and formal cause would be one, since the form would include the patterned capacities of the body. (How the interaction in which sense-qualities occur is to be seen as a unified one is discussed in the treatment of sensation in part 3 below.) Clearly Aristotle's notion of efficient cause is a complex one, not to be equated simply, as it often is, with our later notion of the "pushing" cause. Its function varies from being a stimulator, to providing the initial material of being, to shaping, to being an agent, according to different examples.

Rosenfield 1971, p. 59, attempting more systematically to differentiate the Aristotelian causal model from the later one, includes the following among the Aristotelian postulates concerning the nature of change: (1) Perfective impulses inhere in individual objects. (2) Change depends upon the interaction of an agent possessing the generically proper acting impulses and an object-to-be-changed possessing the generically proper acquiescent impulses. (3) Change involves not a transfer of energy, but a realignment of the generically related impulses between agent and object. The absence of a concept of a uniform energy that is transferred would seem central here; efficient causation is thus more like providing the right stimulus to get appropriate cooperation.

3. *Part. An.* 1.1.

4. Plato, *Timaeus* 70d.

5. *Part. An.* 2.7.

6. Ross 1961, p. 54, interprets this in the more limited sense that no creature finds itself in a position that calls for a certain faculty without nature's having supplied the faculty.

7. *Phys.* 199b10 f.

8. *Part. An.* 687a10–12.

9. *Heav.* 310b3 ff.

10. *Phys.* 215a19 ff.

11. This means that teleological explanation has universal scope. Aristotle does say at times that some phenomena are to be understood in terms of the material cause—as in the standard example that our eyes are a teleological product but that the blue of one's eyes is due to the specific physical operations—but this should not be generalized into a doctrine of two independent modes of causation. For a careful analysis of this issue, see Balme 1972, pp. 76–84, in which it is argued that for Aristotle all natural movements are either directly or ultimately teleological. Clearly, Aristotle's remarks are to be taken in relation to his theory of the causes, necessity and accident, his general theory of potentiality, and his teleological view of motion as such. (See below, particularly chapter 6, on potentiality, and the appendix C, which supplements chapter 15, on necessity.) They are not isolated remarks that use an independent self-explanatory notion of matter and finality. In short, a piecemeal analysis without an overview of the operation of the network as a whole is likely to be misleading. Preus 1975, p. 187, goes so far as to conclude that Aristotle does not have a concept of mechanical necessity in the modern sense of the word.

Balme's argument, pp. 79 ff., is directed in part against Charlton's interpretation (1970, pp. 115 ff.), which states that Aristotle asserts a distinct absolute material necessity. Charlton's interpretation is associated with an underlying general assumption that the scope of Aristotle's teleology is not universal but confined to living things: "[Aristotle] proposes teleological explanations only in cases where it seems correct to speak of some form of life" (p. xvii). The use of teleology with respect to the stars is explained on the supposition that they were regarded as somehow alive. But Charlton ignores the theory of natural movement of the elements in making this claim and neglects to consider that the concept of locomotion is itself inherently teleological on Aristotle's analysis. There are several points at which his attempt to sharpen the dichotomy between the teleological explanation of the living and the mechanical explanation of the purely material yields forced interpretations. For example, he takes book 1 of the *Physics* to be more about the philosophy of physics and book 2 more about the philosophy of biological science (p. xiii). We find it more plausible that book 1 is working out the terms to enter into a definition of motion, that book 2 establishes the teleological perspective to be incorporated into it, and that the early chapters of book 3 go on to give the actual definition of motion in the terms developed in books 1 and 2. Again, Charlton's discussion of natural things' having an internal source of motion or change (pp. 88 ff., particularly 89) is directed at the lack of an internal source of change in artifacts rather than at the source of change in the natural elements out of which artifacts are made. When we are told (p. 93) what Aristotle "would have wished to say," it turns out to be the standard dichotomy of the mechanical and the intentional as stressed in contemporary theory of action. The behavior–action distinction that is so fundamental in ordinary language analysis cuts the phenomena along quite different lines from Aristotle's. Aristotle's "action" theory is concerned with the difference between action and passion, not action and behavior; and in the case of the animate–inanimate distinction it is concerned with the difference between "rational" potentialities that admit of alternative actualizations and "nonrational" potencies that admit of only one type of actualization.

12. For a clear example of this kind of teleology, see Spinoza's attack on final causes in the appendix to book 1 of his *Ethics*. Spinoza criticized those who argue that when a tile falls from a roof onto the head of a man and kills him, God must have intended it. He brands taking refuge in the will of God as an asylum of ignorance. Often a monistic teleology is prepared to overlook a wide area of unimportant happenings in order to concentrate on the design in crucial occurences. For the extent to which teleological explanations of this sort have penetrated all fields of human life, see the comprehensive study of field after field in Andrew D. White's *A History of the Warfare of Science with Theology in Christendom* (1955; originally published 1895).

13. For this aspect of Aristotle's cosmological picture, see our discussion of essentialism in chapter 15. Dante's world in the *Divine Comedy* is the medieval analogue, in a Christian teleology, to Aristotle's cosmological picture. Hell is at the center of the earth, and Heaven in the outer spheres, with God at the outermost limit.

14. Apart from the general admiration for the ways of nature and her economy, cited earlier, there are several passages that require interpretation. One is *Part. An.* 696b26 ff., in which Aristotle refers to fish that have their mouths underneath and says nature appears to have done this to give other animals a chance to escape while those fish turn over on their backs, which is the way they eat. Peck 1955, p. 4, points out that Aristotle qualifies this by saying it serves a useful end by preventing gluttony for the fish themselves, so that an internal teleology is part of the explanation. Indeed, we may add that a consequence of physical structure is also relevant—the snout is round and small, so that it cannot have too great an opening! Balme 1972, p. 96, takes the illustration in a weakened sense, as if it were giving a necessary condition: that the smaller fish exist implies that the larger fish cannot take them too easily.

A second passage is in *Pol.* 1256b16–23, where Aristotle says explicitly that plants exist for the sake of animals and animals for the good of men. He goes on, however, directly to the conclusion that the art of war is an art of acquisition, hunting being part of it, and that it can properly be used against animals and those people who are naturally designed for subjection but refuse to yield to it. This argumentative context in the touchy problem of slavery may be responsible for looser popular conceptions of nature's intentions.

A third passage (*Phys.* 198b18 ff.) raises the question whether Aristotle regarded rain as being for the sake of the growth of the crops. It has been disputed whether Aristotle is here conceding an explanation of rain that would have it happen of necessity as cold condenses vapor, or whether this is a supposed view he is expounding preparatory to denying it when the same explanation is offered for the growth of the teeth. He does go on to identify the natural with the usual here: rain in one season is natural, in another a matter of chance. Since his interest at this point is to distinguish what is natural from what is chance, it would seem to carry no different account of rain than would be given, say, of the presence or absence of food in the environment of a given species. (In the conjectural account he points out that if the rain spoiled the grain on the threshing-floor, it would not be happening *in order to* spoil it.)

Other passages that might be cited are not likely to establish more than a general idea of an ordered world, which Aristotle assimilates to a good world and a naturally operating world. The effective teleology of his scientific work is a pluralistic internal one. Balme's discussion (1972, pp. 93–98) is useful on the whole question of explaining the appearance in these passages of an "extra factor" in Aristotle's teleology.

15. *Meteor.* 353b1 ff.

16. Contemporary philosophy of science has made it clear that a teleological approach in the sense of a functional one need not be in conflict with causal explanation (as Aristotle also realized), and that often it represents instead a difference of interest in the kinds of problems raised and connections traced in a given subject matter. Contemporary notions of "regulatory systems" and "teleological mechanisms" in cybernetic accounts embody comparable ideas. See the collection *Purpose in Nature* (Canfield 1966), which contains papers by Braithwaite, Hempel, Nagel, Scheffler, and Richard Taylor, and one by Rosenblueth, Wiener, and Bigelow. For an attempt to refine the concept of teleology in the light of contemporary biology, see Mayr 1976. See also Nagel 1977.

17. For the view assigning metaphors to the prehistory of science, see Topitsch 1954. For the opposite extreme, see Pepper 1942.

18. In the fragments of his early work the *Protrepticus* (fragment 13 in the Oxford translations, vol. 12), Aristotle says that we derived from nature our best instruments in the mechanical arts, such as the rule and the plummet and the lathe (some take this as the compass instead), which were suggested by the surface of water and the rays of light. In the same way, we modeled our airplanes initially on birds. To this way of thinking, our architecture seeks out in trees and rocks and caves nature's secrets for holding up structures—which casts a new light (when we reverse direction of nature and art) on Aristotle's remark quoted in chapter 3, that if nature grew a house it would do it in the way we build it. Presumably this is because we build it in the way we suspect nature would plan it to make a firm structure.

19. *Part. An.* 1.1.

20. For an interesting survey of concepts of craft in Greek views of nature, see Solmsen 1963; he draws the evidence from the earlier myths and literary materials as well as from philosophers, and weighs the Aristotelian concepts with judicial subtlety.

21. *Meta.* 1023b26 f.; 1021b12 f. The Greek terms are *holon* and *teleion*, respectively.

22. There is a rich literature that deals with the interpretation of the concept of *phusis* from different perspectives which have sometimes seemed to involve conflicting hypotheses about the origins of Greek philosophy, but which can certainly be regarded as mutually supplementary. For example, Burnet 1957 (first published 1892) stresses the scientific character of the early Greek philosophical quest for the nature of things as an expression of curiosity with an audacity almost amounting to *hubris*, that is, as a new way of looking at the world. Cornford 1957 (written 1912) brings out the religious sources of the search for the *phusis* of things, seeing its kinship with primitive beliefs in a dynamic power (much like the primitive concept of mana), and traces the growth of the scientific and the mystical tradition within philosophy itself. Mansion 1946 gives a useful review of different interpretations of *phusis* (pp. 59–65) and discusses Plato's and Aristotle's conceptions of nature at length (ch. 4). See also Düring 1960 for an interpretation of Aristotle's view of *phusis* as inferred from a fragment of his early *Protrepticus*; Düring believes this view remained fairly constant.

23. *Progression of Animals* 704b17 f.

24. E.g., *Republic* 353a10 f.

25. *Mov. An.* 699b16.

26. In fact, Aristotle initiates the discussion of chance and the spontaneous because they are reckoned as causes, not as the denial of causes (*Phys.* 196a31 f.). For a fuller discussion of "determinism" and Aristotle's view of contingency, see the appendix C, which supplements chapter 15, on necessity.

Aristotle's denial of a science of accidental properties is clearly stated in *Metaphysics* 6.2.

The Greek terms are: *tuchē* (chance), *automaton* (the spontaneous), and *to kata sum-bebēkos* (the incidental or coincidental).

27. *Nic. Eth.* 1134b31 ff.
28. *Phys.* 230a18–b27.
29. *Gen. An.* 767b8 ff.
30. *Gen. An.* 770b15 ff.
31. *Phys.* 254b14 ff.
32. *Phys.* 7.1, 2; 8.4.
33. *Phys.* 255a5–10, 28–30.
34. *Heav.* 301a4 ff.
35. *Gen. An.* 715b12–16.
36. In the long-overdue contemporary turn to an intensive study of Aristotle's biology, one of the significant questions that has arisen is the interplay of his general philosophical ideas and his specific biological inquiries, particularly how his notion of essences interacts with that of fixed species and any biological data that might provoke evolutionary ideas. The general question is discussed in a full-length study of Aristotle by Marjorie Grene (1963). She is concerned with what role Aristotle's "deep and inspired biological interest may have had in shaping his philosophical beliefs" (p. 34). For example, in interpreting Aristotle's logic and metaphysics, she notes the importance of his attentiveness to individual specimens, and in examining his physics she underscores its biological slant. But she does not appear to allow sufficiently for reciprocal influences. See, for example, her comment (p. 255) on Hantz's view that the concept of the four causes is derived from biological experience; she takes it rather to be applied to the biology after development in the physics. We have seen in this chapter that it is difficult to determine whether an organic model stemming from the biology or a craft model embodied in a teleological philosophy takes priority as the root metaphor of Aristotle's thought, largely because the craft model also played a part in the biology itself.

On the question of evolution and fixed species, Grene finds no compromise: "Aristotle's biology, and the philosophy founded on it, are radically non-evolutionary and anti-evolutionary. Our vision of species as a concretion of history, our belief that kinds are only snail-slow rhythms in a world forever in change, would be for Aristotle a betrayal of the very spirit of knowledge, of mind and of the real" (p. 137).

In spite of this, does Aristotle recognize biological data that could open the door to an evolutionary interpretation? Balme 1972, p. 97, decides that "there is room to doubt whether Aristotle in fact believed that species do not change." He cites *Gen. An.* 746a30, where Aristotle recognizes that mating among animals of different species can produce offspring that are fertile. Mules are the exception, and Aristotle insists on a specific explanation for this, not general theories. Unfortunately he then becomes interested in the problem of infertility in individuals and does not come back to the significance of the creation of new species. Balme also calls attention to the overlapping of generic classifications and to "twilight zones" that suggest a continuity. There is in addition Aristotle's interest in the progressive deterioration of offspring (*Gen. An.* 4.3), from resembling a female instead of a male, to actually being a female, to resembling remoter ancestors, to having species properties or even just generic ones (that is, being animal-like). We may note that in 4.4 Aristotle goes on to examine monstrosities. What seems to me to explain his equanimity in considering such possibilities is precisely the view I have quoted (from 1.1; 715b12–16) that suggests some limit to such processes, preserved in nature. I take it that Aristotle is here relying on an observed stability of the species which implies that the deformations described in 4.3 and the monstrosities in 4.4 will not go too far astray. (Some of them, like the resemblance problem, will not matter very much, and the occurrence of females is, Aristotle recognizes, required!) Perhaps Balme's sober conclusion seems most reasonable: "There is nothing in Aristotle's theory to prevent an 'evolution of species,' i.e. a continuous modification of the kinds being transmitted. But he had no evidence of evolution, having no palaeontology, and therefore had no occasion to consider such a theory, of which there was no proponent in ancient philosophy" (pp. 97–98).

Clark's chapter "The Biological Continuum" (1975, pp. 28–47) adds to the array of materials that may be invoked to soften the antagonism between Aristotle's fixity of species and possible evolutionary interpretations. His attempt to elicit from what he calls these oddities a speculative "devolutionary transformism" for Aristotle, in which animals and plants are literally (or mythically?) seen as deformations of perfect man, nature's pinnacle, is another matter. Clark seems to me to make a somewhat hurried transition from a possible logical order (based on devices of comparison) to a genetic order.

CHAPTER 6

1. *Phys.* 233a24 ff.
2. *Phys.* 239b30 ff.; cf. 234a31 ff.
3. Book 10. There is also a briefer account in 5.6.
4. *Meta.* 1052a34 ff. The Greek term for "one" is *hen.*
5. The corresponding Greek terms are *tauto* (identity), *homoion* (similarity), *ison* (equality), *plēthos* (plurality), *heteron* (otherness), *anomoion* (dissimilarity), and *anison* (inequality).
6. *Meta.* 1052b1 ff.
7. *Meta.* 5.6, 1016a1 ff.
8. *Phys.* 219a10 ff.
9. E.g., *Phys.* 6.1.
10. *Phys.* 5.3. The Greek terms are *hama* (together), *haptesthai* (touching), *metaxu* (between), *ephexēs* (in succession), *echomenon* (contiguous), and *suneches* (continuous).
11. *Gen. Corr.* 1.6.
12. *Gen. Corr.* 327a3 ff.
13. *Phys.* 7.2.
14. E.g., *Heav.* 301b23–30; *On Dreams* 459a28 ff.
15. *Phys.* 266b28–67a20.
16. *Meta.* 9.3.
17. *Phys.* 3.1.
18. Descartes, *The Principles of Philosophy*, part 2, xxiv. In rule 12 of his *Rules for the Direction of the Mind* Descartes ridicules Aristotle's definition of motion. He says that although motion is a fact with which everyone is familiar, Aristotle's definition is so complex as to be unintelligible. It became clear by our time that Descartes' own concept of action in his own definition is not without complexities, though more deeply buried. Philosophers should be wary of throwing the first stone, especially at other philosophers.
19. *Heav.* 310b16 ff., 311a4.
20. *Meta.* 1044b29–45a6.
21. *Meta.* 1047a30 ff.
22. *Phys.* 202b13 f. Aristotle illustrates the same idea earlier in the chapter with the example of a steep uphill slope and a downhill slope (202a20 f.): they are one but have a different *logos.* Teaching and learning are similar; their actualization is identical, but teaching is not learning (202b17 ff.). He generalizes this for action and passion (*poiēsis* and *pathēsis*): a favorite way of expressing the difference is to say that though they are the same, their being (*einai*) is different. The important point is that though we have a single happening—the motion (202b22)—the difference of directional description may carry different properties.
23. *Phys.* 201b8 ff.
24. For Aristotle's adoption of a unified transactional approach, see *Physics* 3.3. It is integral to his analysis of potentiality and central to his physics and psychology. For an analysis of 3.3 see Edel 1969. For application to psychology, see chapter 9 below.

Ackrill 1965 points out serious difficulties about the distinction between *energeia* and *kinēsis.* They are serious enough to suggest that the difference may not be found in a clear set of defining marks alone, but requires reference to a set of functions and relations to other concepts and jobs to be done in different areas of inquiry, such as setting off the practical from the productive sciences (see the introductions to parts 5 and 6) and distinguishing the phenomenal field from the field of material conditions of perception (see chapter 9). (The distinction may also be building on a distinction in the categories in which *kinēsis* would be associated with *poiēsis* and *pathēsis*, while *energeia* would build on *echein* and *keisthai*; this is a speculative suggestion mentioned in chapter 7.)

25. *Interp.* 9. The sea battle tomorrow has been the subject of endless controversy in Aristotelian studies and in the development of modal logics. For its analysis in relation to the possible attitude of Aristotle on determinism, see appendix C, a supplement to chapter 15, in which Aristotle's concept of necessity is considered.

26. *Heav.* 1.12.

27. *Meta.* 1034b4–7; cf. *Gen. An.* 762a35–b12: "Those natural objects that are produced, like artificial objects, spontaneously, are those whose matter can also initiate for itself that motion which the seed initiates." The phenomenon of friction, in which heat is produced by motion (e.g., *Meta.* 1032b25 f.: the doctor produces heat in the patient by friction), might seem to be a counterinstance. Certainly Aristotle invokes it as the fundamental process of the heating effect of the sun's movement, whereby the fiery layer of air below is ignited (Meteor. 341a12–23; cf. *Heav.* 289a19–35). But when we think of such processes as motion causing fire, that is, as fire coming to be from what is not fire, we are reckoning without Aristotle's theory of fire. The motion simply helps actualize the potentiality in the air that blazes up. Fire (*pur*) is an excess of heat and a sort of boiling (*Meteor.* 340b23). Flame (*phlox*) arises from the constant changing of moist and dry (355a9 f.). We may recall that the initial analysis of fire was the hot dry. Accordingly the change in the balance of moist and dry due to the neighboring motion can produce the surge of fire. Even fire spreading by, as it were, feeding on timber, would admit of a similar explanation. It is less fire making fire than fire stimulating the fiery potentialities of what is about to burn—like a kind of flammable material that often needs only a little motion to make it burst into flame (smoke, for example)—for flame is the boiling up of a dry current of air (*Meteor.* 341b21 ff.). In this way, with the assistance of his theory of the elements and the concept of potentiality, Aristotle can take friction in his stride and maintain the priority of the actual. A slight departure is to be found, perhaps, in Aristotle's remark that cold may cause warmth by turning away and withdrawing (*Phys.* 251a31 f.).

28. *Gen. An.* 734b21 f.

29. *Gen. Corr.* 321b10–22a4.

30. *Meta.* 1072a8 f., b10 ff.

CHAPTER 7

1. For an interesting analysis of Aristotle's thought as a stage of development out of systematic paradoxes, see Miller 1969. Miller distinguishes the logical, epistemic, and óntic forms taken by the paradoxes that center around sameness and difference, identity and change, truth and error, as a framework for presenting Aristotle's solutions.

2. This is the point at which the temptation to lose oneself in Plato becomes almost irresistible. Many works on Aristotle really turn out to be works on how Plato fashioned the problems that Aristotle tackled, in which discussion of Aristotle is almost reduced to a footnote. For comment on this problem, see the Epilogue.

3. For example, in *Phys.* 1.2–4.

4. E.g., *Top.* 127a26–38; cf. 122b18–24.

5. For a particularly clear statement of this point, see *Eud. Eth.* 1217b27–1218a1. The context is an attack on Plato's form of the Good, and Aristotle preserves a strict parallel between the denial of a single science of Being and that of a single science of the Good. "Being-qua-being," which he eventually allows to be the study of a science (in *Metaphysics* 4), is literally "That which is, insofar as (or in the respect in which) it is" (*to on hēi on*).

6. This whole passage (6.1, 1026a23–33) occasioned much controversy, particularly the possible contradiction that a completely transcendent divine being together with a natural world would negate the universal character of the science of being-as-being. See comments on the passage in Ross 1953, vol. 1, p. 356; Kirwan 1971, p. 188; and the treatment of several different phases of the problem in Leszl 1975.

7. *Meta.* 1051a34 ff., 1069b27 ff., 1089a26 ff., and especially 5.7. The last is the fullest account of being, and here accidental being is contrasted with essential being, whose senses are given by the categories.

8. "Philosophy has become mathematics for present thinkers" (*Meta.* 992a32 f.). The reference is generally taken to be to Speusippus, with whom Aristotle seriously differed.

9. Samburski 1959, ch. 3, esp. pp. 49–57.

10. *Part. An.* 640a33 f. See the careful construction of the concept in Buchanan 1962, ch. 4.

11. Ross 1959, p. 27; Tredennick 1935, vol. 2, p. 112, note b.

12. For this thesis, see Trendelenburg 1846. His own summary of this position is in part 2, "Die Kategorienlehre in der Geschichte der Philosophie," pp. 209–16. Ross 1953, vol. 1, p. lxxxiii, comments on this view: "Trendelenburg thought that the doctrine was based entirely on grammatical considerations; Bonitz had little difficulty, however, in showing that this is an exaggerated view, that Aristotle draws distinctions where grammar draws none and ignores some which grammar does draw." (The reference is to H. Bonitz, *Über die Kategorien des Aristoteles*, Vienna, 1853.) Cf. also Zeller 1897, pp. 280–81.

13. Ross 1959, pp. 27–28, says: "Aristotle's object seems to have been to clear up the question [certain difficulties about predication] by distinguishing the main types of meaning of the words and phrases that can be combined to make a sentence. And in doing this he arrived at the earliest known classification of the main types of entity involved in the structure of reality." On the other hand Kapp 1942, p. 23, suggests, relying on the *Topics*, that "the doctrine of the categories was originally a doctrine of sentence-predicates and was only later transformed by Aristotle himself into a scheme for pigeon-holing whatever carries a single word as its name." (Cf. his pp. 37–42.) This contrast carries Kapp throughout the book into the interesting distinction between what we may briefly epitomize as an isolating logic and a logic developed in relation to communication. Kapp's interpretation verges on defining the categories as different senses of *is*. The possibility that the copula in the proposition varies according to the categories, and the effect this would have on the validity of the syllogism, is noted in our appendix C, which supplements chapter 15.

14. Brentano 1975, pp. 49–148, gives a good survey of this conflict of opinion.

15. Ackrill 1963, p. 79. Certainly many of the terms come from questions—What is it? What sort? Where? It is possible, however, to interpret some as indefinite adverbs, which can designate answers to questions.

16. Moravcsik 1967, p. 144.

17. An interpretation of this sort is outlined in Edel 1975.

18. *Top.* 120b36 ff.

19. E.g., *Phys.* 5.2.

20. *Meta.* 1020a33.

21. This would explain in part why there is no very tight inner system among the categories. Both Kant and Mill objected to the lack of system and the apparently haphazard selection of items. See Brentano 1975 for an attempted systematization in terms of a tree with successive differentiae. Leszl 1975, pp. 366–75, objects to the criticisms on the ground that they usually expect a deductive relation within the categories. He pursues the search for a loose system by listing the properties that hold for categories (e.g., the capability of assuming opposites, of being equal or unequal, etc.) and determining by the extent of conformity of the different categories which are dependent on others. Edel 1975, pp. 59–60, suggests that the order of the categories goes (after substance as what "really" is) from those that have the closest relation to the eternal to those that have more to do with change. Clark 1975, p. 82 n. 3, takes the order to be one noun, two adjectives, three adverbs, four verbs.

The thesis here proposed about the relation of the categories to the rest of the Aristotelian conceptual network would militate against the common practice of isolating the little treatise, the *Categories*, as an early work. Its differences from later works on points of doctrine are probably no greater than those among the later works themselves.

22. For the outline of evidence on state and situation, see Edel 1975, pp. 54–58. It is also interesting to note that the Stoics included state (in their terms, *to pōs echon*, or "being in a condition") as one of their four categories, to which they added a "highest notion" of the

indefinite something (*to ti*); the other three were substratum, quality, and relation (Mates 1961, p. 18).

23. That quality does not easily assimilate the categories it subsumes is suggested by the various reservations Aristotle has to make about what is not within its scope. For example, *Phys.* 7.3 constitutes almost a secession for shapes and intellectual states of the psyche. For an analysis of this chapter, see Verbeke 1971. See also our discussion, in chapter 9, of some of the restrictions Aristotle imposes on what may be regarded as qualitative change in his psychological analysis.

24. Trendelenburg 1846, p. 256, reports the following as Campanella's substitutes: *substantia, quantitas, forma* or *figura, vis* or *facultas, operatio* or *actus, actio, passio, similitudo, dissimilitudo, circumstantia.* Edel 1975, p. 59, refers to an eighteenth-century text by Brattle in which the latter proposes instead of Aristotle's categories those of matter, measure, rest, motion, position, figure, and mind. Such proposals—especially as notions of force and mind come in—suggest that the categorial list is selecting the notions basic to the science and metaphysical outlook of the period. There is no reason to ignore similar bases in Aristotle's own list. The clearest case of this sort is to be found in the Port-Royal Logic (Arnauld 1964), which first appeared in 1662. Its chapter on the ten aristotelian categories (pp. 42–45), which simply condemns them as arbitrary and founded on imagination, substitutes a set based on the new Cartesian philosophy: mind, body, largeness or smallness of each part of matter, relative position of portions of matter, shape of parts of matter, motion of parts of matter, and repose or lesser motion of parts of matter.

25. Rosenfield 1971, pp. 50 ff. His entire treatment of the Aristotelian model in comparison to the Newtonian is illuminating.

26. Compare, for example, the way Zeller and Mure look at it. Zeller 1897, p. 274, points out that in light of Aristotle's realism the categories can be neither "merely subjective forms of thought" nor merely concerned with logical relations. He says, p. 278, that "the purpose of 'categories' is not to describe things by their actual qualities, nor yet to set forth the general conceptions which are needful for this purpose. They are confined to pointing out the different sides which may be kept in view in any such description. In Aristotle's intention, they are meant to give us, not real conceptions, but only the framework into which all real conceptions are to be set." In a note commenting on others' views, he even states that "the categories are *not themselves* directly taken as predicates, but only as designating the *place* of certain predicates in the scale," and goes on to distinguish "real and definite facts," "abstract metaphysical expressions," what is "given in experience," and "real concepts."

Mure 1964, p. 183, says: "The categories are the highest universals of a pluralist system, and the universals of a pluralist system are inevitably empirical. They tend to become mere abstract common characters which classify externally. Universal and particular make claims that pluralism cannot reconcile." Aristotle is criticized for refraining from the final step of recognizing that all judgment has ultimately a single subject, reality as a whole.

Zeller's interpretation has a Kantian direction: the categories ultimately reflect neither subjectivism nor realism but somehow express a way of ordering experience. Mure's is explicitly neo-Hegelian. Contemporary linguistically oriented analysis is beginning to treat the categories as a classification of "criteria of existence." Naturalistic and scientific interpretations are either overtly realistic or largely functional. Theological interpretations steer toward substance. And so on.

27. For studies of Aristotle's theory of the infinite or some of its special problems, see Edel 1934; Hintikka 1973, ch. 6.

28. *Phys.* 207b10–15; cf. 223a22 ff.

29. *Phys.* 3.7, 207b27–34. For a discussion of this difficult passage, see Hintikka 1973, pp. 118–21. The issue is whether Aristotle is only objecting to an actual infinite line (which his account would rule out) or whether he is going further and prescribing a procedure for reducing any figure that would, even in thought, exceed the limits of the universe; and if the latter, whether this would have interfered with some geometrical proofs in Euclid.

30. E.g., *Heav.* 1.5–7.

31. The Greek terms are *chōra* (room), *diastēma* (interval), *kenon* (empty), *to mē on* (what-is-not), and *topos* (place).

32. *Phys.* 212a20.

33. For a study of mathematical questions in the Aristotelian works, see T. L. Heath 1949. For Aristotle's criticism of Plato's view of mathematics, as well as a characterization of Aristotle's approach, see Annas 1976. Some of the issues concerning the relation of mathematics and existence are discussed below in chapter 13, nn. 9, 10.

34. *Phys.* 193b34 f.

35. *Meta.* 1005b18 ff.

36. *Meta.* 1007b26 ff.

CHAPTER 8

1. *Meta.* 1003b16 ff.

2. *Meta.* 1028b2 ff.

3. One way of relating them is that argued for in Leszl 1975—that being-as-being is a *neutral* science of ontology, and substance (in different ways in which it is interpreted) is the answer to one topic in the field. Clearly other topics include the laws of logic, unity and related ideas of equality, potentiality and actuality, and so on.

4. A variety of interpretations of the expression is succinctly given in Kirwan 1971, pp. 77–78. Kirwan himself inclines to the adverbial interpretation, pointing out that, for example, to say a doctor has visited some patient *qua* patient tells us not about the nature of the patient but the visit: "Probably we should conclude that to say that metaphysics studies that which is *qua* thing-that-is is not to say anything about the nature of the things studied by metaphysics, but about the nature of the study."

5. For the first, see Owens 1951, pp. 295 ff. For the second, see Randall 1960, pp. 109 f. The third is the explicit thesis of Leszl 1975. Leszl couples a Kantian and a linguistic approach, and suggests that Aristotle's ontology furnishes a clarification of conceptual and linguistic structures. Note his argument (pp. 161–62) that to study being-as-being need not be an abstractive undertaking; he compares studying man as man with studying man as solid—the latter deliberately abstracts, the former aims at an integrated account. For a survey of some further interpretations see Reale 1980, ch. 3.

6. *Meta.* 1003b19–22. For a discussion of the conflicting interpretations of this passage, as well as what the science covers, see Leszl 1975, pp. 236–52.

7. *Meta.* 1003b6 ff.

8. Leszl 1975 gives an explicitly Kantian interpretation along these lines. He works carefully to select in Aristotle's metaphysical writings what can or cannot satisfy the criteria, what is centrally satsifactory, what is only peripherally so (for example, general properties like motion in the *Physics*), and what is excluded. Leszl calls this science of being-as-being "ontology," a term that is intended to be strict and exclude other heterogeneous materials found in the broader notion of metaphysics.

9. For a summary of fairly recent beliefs about the *Metaphysics*, see Ross 1953, vol. 1, pp. xiii–xxxiii. Cf. Jaeger 1962, chs. 7 and 8.

As an example of the complexity of decision involved, consider speculatively the issues concerning *Metaphysics* 5 (book Delta), the so-called philosophical lexicon. Ross says (p. xiii): "Not only are Books *a*, *Δ*, and *K* [2, 5, 11] manifest intrusions, but even the other books lack the continuity of thought that one expects in a single work." And again, "*Δ* is evidently out of place where it is, and as evidently it is a genuine Aristotelian work" (p. xxxii). Now even if it is a separate Aristotelian work, why should its insertion by Aristotle or an editor be a reason for thrusting it aside as intrusive? Many a book—even a good book—is compiled out of writing from different strata of the philosopher's thought, if there is a unified conception at work. What is the character of Delta and can we envision a ground plan of the *Metaphysics* in which it is rightfully where it belongs?

The impression of intrusiveness may be intensified by a tendency to see book 5 only as a lexicon. But Aristotle approaches language, as has been indicated (in chapter 3 above; see also its n. 7), not as a separate domain, but as the way things are talked about. In this sense the lexicon is not a dictionary where words are explicated, but an exhibition of how different things get called by the same name, and where the similarities lie and how connections are discerned. Aristotle is an incorrigible ontologist in this respect; it is clearest, as we shall see later, in his discussion of homonymy and synonymy. As already noted, he calls two *things* synonymous if they have the same name and the definition of the name applies to both; we think of synonymy as the equivalence of two linguistic *expressions*. In his translation of book 5, Kirwan (1971) calls explicit attention to the difference. He departs from the usual translations "*beginning* means," "*cause* means," and so forth, and says instead, "We call an origin . . ." and "We call a cause . . ."; and in the notes (p. 123, on 1012b34) he conscientiously remarks that "Origin is called . . ." would be the literal translation. He states his point plainly on p. 79: "In many occurrences elsewhere of the common phrase 'is called in many ways' the context makes it clear that things, not words, are the subject."

It follows from such considerations that book 5 is not just a lexicon but a metaphysical treatise. It shows the structural relations that different things or situations can have, that lie beyond the essential ones of genus and species—relations by analogy, common reference, and so on, which will be explored in chapter 14 below.

The selection of material in book 5 can also be shown to consist of metaphysical concepts used in explanation and in structural analysis in either a substantive or an operational way. We can do this by checking off the concepts listed in book 5 as we come across them in passages that set out the science of being-as-being, and in addition by keeping count of what Aristotle explicitly mentions as the content of that science. In the first manner, for example, if we scan the fewer than twenty lines of the opening chapter of book 4, which introduces the science of being-as-being, we find *being, in virtue of, part, principle, cause, nature, necessary, elements,* and *accident*. (*Principle, cause,* and *element*—the first three items in book 5—are often found together; see for example, "principles and elements and causes of mathematics," 1025b5 f.) In the course of 4.2, in which Aristotle justifies the single science of being-as-being and describes its content, we can tally up *one* (as well as *being*), *same* (and *other*), *opposites,* and *substance* (1003b30–1004a6); *privation* (1004a28); *prior* and *posterior, genus* (and *species*), and *whole* and *part* (1005a17 f.). This already gives us seventeen of the thirty items in book 5. Now in discussing the partitions of being we said that the forms of being included the categories, potentiality and actuality, and the true and the false. We can thus check off *potentiality* and *false* on our list from book 5. The categories give us (besides *substance*) *quantity, quality,* and *relative*; if we include subcategorial divisions of quality—*affection* and *disposition,* and *having* and *to have* (as kindred to the category of state)—there remain only four to be accounted for: *complete, limit, to be out of* (i.e., *from*) *something,* and *mutilated. Complete* and *limit* should not surprise us, for they are notions that play a part in the understanding and goodness of form (there is a relation of limit and essence referred to in 1022a9); what is surprising rather is that form (*eidos*) itself does not appear. *To be out of something* covers at least matter (1023a26), though it also seems to cover efficient cause and temporal relations. Given the absence of *matter* from the list in book 5, such a surrogate is understandable. Finally there remains only *mutilated.* Kirwan 1971, p. 177, finds its inclusion a mystery. But it comes right after *part* and *whole,* and its concern with rendering precise what parts have to be altered to change the essence of a thing taps a deep metaphysical problem; it seems quite justified.

These considerations suggest that book 5 is a metaphysical collection, with partial organization, of concepts found in substantive or operational aspects of metaphysical inquiry. Judged from its omissions (e.g., matter, form, actuality) and from the treatment of some of its concepts (e.g., under *privation,* no mention of its being a principle of change, as it is in *Physics* 1), it belongs to an early phase of Aristotle's thought, and its miscellaneous character is that of a collection of data. In many respects it resembles what Aristotle is usually believed to have done in the *Historia Animalium* in comparison with *Parts of Animals* and the *Generation of Animals.* We would not go too far astray if we thought of book 5 as a similar collection, this time of metaphysical materials. As such it does not seem out of place after book 4, which has just launched the science of metaphysics and given the broadest example of its inquiry (in the principle of noncontradiction), and before book 6, where we plunge into the central concept of substance.

A sweeping defense of Delta as an appropriate part of the total scheme of the *Metaphysics* and as being in its fitting place is presented by Reale 1980, ch. 8. He also examines the different views of the order of items in Delta and concludes (p. 342) that it is a preliminary classification of terms that later books of the *Metaphysics* examine or make use of. He does not, however, consider the implications of omissions and specific content.

10. How to learn all things in general, not in detail, is also part of a theory of education. Aristotle occasionally indicates the kind of learning he proposes for the nonspecialist; see, for example, *Part. An.* 693a1–11, on biology, and *Pol.* 1341a13–17, on music.

11. *Meta.* 1030a27 f. The facts are "how things stand" (*to pōs echei*). For a comment on the meaning of the contrast here, see above, chapter 3, n. 12.

12. *Meta.* 1030b12 f.

13. *Interp.* 17a12–15.

14. *Interp.* 20b17 ff.

15. *Interp.* 20b31–21a28.

16. *Meta.* 10.9.

17. *Meteor.* 390a12 f.

18. *Meta.* 1045a12–17. "Animal-itself" was a Platonic way of saying "*form* of animal."

19. *Meta.* 1045a23 ff.

20. Balme 1972, p. 74, in commenting on *Parts of Animals*, distinguishes four senses of *eidos*: a *kind*, as distinct from other kinds; the *kind*, as distinct from its numerical instances; *form*, as distinct from matter; and *species*, as distinct from genus. The root meaning is "apparent shape." See also Balme's comment (p. 88) on 640b24–28, where Aristotle uses the terms *schēma*, *idea*, and *morphē* (figure, appearance, and shape) in explaining the *eidos* of a bed. By contrast, the *eidos* of a living thing would have to include much more—its life and ability to function. Clearly Aristotle has the roots of the notion of form well in mind and can arrange them to make a point as needed.

21. For an insightful treatment of the themes that enter into Aristotle's principle of individuation, see A. C. Lloyd (1970). See also Anscombe 1953. Hartman 1977, chs. 1 and 2, offers a very rewarding analysis of the relation between substance, essence, and identity. He is especially helpful on the question of forms of individuals.

22. The term for a this-something is *tode ti*, as contrasted with this-such (*toionde*). The word *hekaston*, "each," occurs typically in logical contexts in *kath'hekaston*, "individually," in opposition to *katholou*, "universal" or "universally." The *idion* is what is private or peculiar to the thing. There is of course also the numerical idea of "one" of a given class or type of thing.

23. *Psych.* 413b15 f.

24. *Meta.* 12.8., 10 (1075b34–1076a5).

25. *Meta.* 1034a5–8, 1058b10 f., 1016b32 f.

26. *Heav.* 278a32 ff.

27. *Heav.* 278a8 ff.

28. *Meta.* 1022a27.

29. *Meta.* 1071a27–29.

30. *Gen. An.* 767b32–68a2.

31. *Meta.* 7.6.

32. *Meta.* 1031a17 f.

33. *Meta.* 1043b2 f.; cf. 1036a16 ff., 1037a7 f.

34. *Part. An.* 655b29 ff.

35. *Heav.* 285a29.

36. *Heav.* 1.12, at 281a28–b25. At 283a25 f. Aristotle says that "it is impossible for something that is destructible never to be destroyed."

37. *Gen. Corr.* 336b31 ff.

38. *Meta.* 1072a26 ff.

39. *Mov. An.* 699a27 ff.

40. *Mov. An.* 700b30.

41. *Nic. Eth.* 1178b10 ff.

42. *Nic. Eth.* 1178b20 ff.; *Meta.* 12 reaches the same conclusion.

43. *Meta.* 1072b29.

44. *Meta.* 1074b22–26, 33–35.

45. *Eud. Eth.* 1238b27 ff.

46. The role of the Unmoved Mover in putting together the cosmology, the biology, and the psychology, is pointed out by Farrington 1969, pp. 84–85.

Part 3

INTRODUCTION

1. A good illustration of the continuing difficulties that come from viewing Aristotle's psychology in the light of conflicting modern schools is seen in Hamlyn 1974. He begins in his Introduction (p. ix) with the following:

> Aristotle's *De Anima* is often referred to as Aristotle's psychology. This is not a very accurate description of it, as there is comparatively little psychology in it in the modern sense of the word. There is a certain amount of physiology and in many sections the emphasis is definitely biological, involving, as elsewhere in Aristotle, considerable emphasis on teleology. But the great bulk of the discussion is concerned with "philosophy of mind." That is to say that Aristotle is concerned to elucidate the nature and role of the concepts necessary for an understanding of the mind.

Note how completely this operates within the confines of a single contemporary analytic philosophical school and imposes it on Aristotle and the rest of contemporary philosophy as well. There is no suggestion that others may in fact regard physiological psychology as part of psychology, or psychological theory as equally a part of psychology. In these cases there need be no great gulf between the clarification of psychological concepts and the "doing of psychology." It is also not clear why what Aristotle is doing should not be reckoned in terms of his own context, where the emphasis on teleology is related to psychology because the final cause is his prime mode of explanation. Later (p. xiii), Hamlyn writes that

> Aristotle's dealings with the traditional mind–body problem are perfunctory. He assumes in general that his concern is with functions which are those of both body and soul. Indeed this must be so, given his account of the soul as the form of the body. But there is an almost total neglect of any problem arising from psycho-physical dualism and the facts of consciousness. Such problems do not seem to arise for him. The reason appears to be that concepts like that of consciousness do not figure in his conceptual scheme at all; they play no part in his analysis of perception, thought, etc.

Now instead of urging us to see whether Aristotle is pursuing an alternative path that might avoid some of the puzzles that have beset our epistemological inquiries, Hamlyn takes it for granted that Aristotle has simply not hit upon our happy road and looks rather for hints that he was getting there. Again, he complains (p. xiv) that Aristotle has no real discussion of action with its related notion of intention, though he has one of movement and imagination. Here he has failed to see that Aristotle is following a different path that (as we shall see later) bypasses the problems of will and the puzzles of freedom of will.

For an argument that Aristotle is in general pursuing a path of his own, and a brief comparison of his position with that not only of Descartes and others but with the positions some contemporary interpreters have tried to force upon him, see Sorabji 1974a. For an attempt to face directly the question of the relation of consciousness and body in Aristotelian terms, see Kahn 1966, who points out that the antithetical term to *psyche* was likely to be not *body* but *death*.

2. *Psych.* 403a26 f.

3. *Psych.* 407b21 f.

4. *Psych.* 408b13 ff.

5. The terms *phenomenal* and *phenomenological* are being used in their now common, not technical, sense. *Phenomenal* refers to the phenomena in the experiential field, not to a contrast with the real. *Phenomenological* similarly refers to what is often called phenomenological description, not to the more technical aspects of the search for essences in contemporary phenomenological movements. Perhaps the best paradigm of what I have in mind is the way in which the Gestalt psychologists study the phenomena of the visual field. Historians of thought may also be interested in the possible influences of Aristotle on the development of phenomenology through Brentano.

CHAPTER 9

1. *Psych.* 412a20; Aristotle lays the groundwork for this definition in the earlier portion of that chapter (2.1). This, of course, does not mean that the psyche is a *separate* substance from the body in a dualistic sense, in the light of the discussion of *eidos* in chapter 8 above. The point is well discussed technically by Barnes 1972.

2. *Psych.* 412a27 f.

3. *Psych.* 412b5 f.

4. *Psych.* 412b6 ff. A complex and detailed discussion of the relation of form and matter and its reflection in a definition is found in *Meta.* 7.10, a 11. The psyche is one of the prominent examples.

5. Cf. *Part. An.* 652b7 ff. Peck 1953, p. lviii and app. B, section 13, takes the closest relation of psyche to the elements to be to *pneuma*.

6. For the question, see *Gen. An.* 736a30 ff.; for the answer, 736b8 ff.

7. *Part. An.* 666a10 ff.

8. *Psych.* 434b24 ff.

9. *Psych.* 415a29 ff.

10. The question of the order of these writings has been the subject of much recent investigation. Ross 1955 and Nuyens 1948 held to the earlier composition of the *Parva Naturalia*, while Block 1961 initiated a reconsideration that made *On the Psyche* the earlier work. For a further study of Aristotle's changing views, see Lefèvre 1972.

Beliefs about the order of the writings depend to a large extent on analysis of the different stages of Aristotle's thought. It seems clear from fragments of the earlier dialogues (see Jaeger 1962, pp. 40 f., 99 f.) that at the outset Aristotle followed the Platonic view of the separate immortal soul, but at the end, in *On the Psyche*, he decided the psyche is the actualization or "entelechy" of the body. (This latter conclusion is often called "hylomorphism," since it embodies his matter–form analysis.) The question is what, if anything, came in between. Nuyens, and Ross in agreement with him, associate with the biological works and the *Parva Naturalia* a view that the psyche is present in the heart and operates chiefly through the heart, which seems to be a two-substance theory and so distinct from and perhaps incompatible with the latest view. A large part of Block's case lies in reanalyzing the material to show that there was no incompatibility in the conceptions as Aristotle presented them. For further discussion of these issues, see Hardie 1964 and Kahn 1966.

11. See Beare 1906.

12. *Gen. Corr.* 1.7.

13. *Psych.* 416b3 ff.

14. *Psych.* 425b25 ff. I have translated *hama ginetai* in the last sentence as "arise together." Hett (Loeb edition) says "occur together," Hicks 1907 says "occur simultaneously," and J. A. Smith (Oxford translations) says "are merged together."

15. It is interesting to note that Hegel finds the unity of sounding and hearing—that is, the joint activity of the body and the subject—to be indicative of the fact that the distinction of subjective and objective is the reflection of consciousness. Sense perception is the abrogation of this separation. But from this it follows for him that just as form and matter are nothing apart from their actuality as a "this," so subject and object are nothing apart from their actuality in consciousness. (See Weiss 1969, pp. 34–36.) Weiss's study of Hegel's account of Aristotle's philosophy of mind shows how exposition can readily point a direction to the philosophy that is being shaped and yet at the same time light up a potentiality in the material expounded. In this example it does so only by neglecting what Aristotle insists on as the reality of the potential when it is not being actualized. Weiss (p. 55) remarks, however, that Hegel was consciously emphasizing the idealistic tendencies in the belief that the empirical strain in Aristotle had been overemphasized.

16. *Top.* 134b28 ff.

17. *Sens.* 446a20 ff.

18. *Psych.* 424a4 f.

19. E.g., *Psych.* 426a2 ff.

20. *Psych.* 419b22.

21. For others' opinions see, e.g., *Psych.* 410a25 f.: to perceive is to suffer something and to be moved. In one common opinion (see 415b24) sensation was thought to be a kind of alteration. For Aristotle's own view see, e.g., 416b32 f., 417a14–18a6 (a fuller treatment).

22. E.g., *Psych.* 429a13 ff.

23. E.g., *Psych.* 431a5 ff.

24. The comet's tail: *Meteor.* 343a1 ff.; other phenomena, e.g., 372a16 ff., 372b15 ff.

25. *Meteor.* 373b4 ff.

26. *On Dreams* 460a1 ff.

27. *Psych.* 435a9 f.

28. *Sens.* 437b11 ff.

29. *Sens.* 438a25 ff.

30. *Gen. An.* 781a3 ff.

31. *Psych.* 419b35 ff.

32. *Psych.* 423a2 ff., 423a25 ff.

33. *Psych.* 423b12 ff.

34. *Part. An.* 653b24 ff.

35. *Mov. An.* 702a36 ff.

36. *Psych.* 425b22.

37. *Gen. Corr.* 324a10 ff.

38. Cf. *Part. An.* 647a6 ff.

39. *Psych.* 424a17 ff.

40. *Meteor.* 385a2 ff.

41. *Sens.* 439b14 ff.

42. *Sens.* 440a10 ff.

43. *Sens.* 442a20 ff.

44. *Gen. An.* 779b12–81a13.

45. This is the point at which the contemporary theorist of mind–body relations, particularly identity, is likely to feel uncomfortable with Aristotle's nonchalance in treating the material and the formal or the physiological and the phenomenal as relative distinctions within a single thing or process. He may think that Aristotle did not face the question, rather than that he may have formulated it in a different way, and insist that Aristotle ought to show whether he is relying on a logical identity or an empirical correlation and specify what the analysis of his *is* or *same* is to be. Perhaps these issues now loom large because the residue of a mind–body dualism has so separated the phenomenal and the physical in general that a general identification does require a precise sense. Nussbaum 1978, p. 147, makes the interesting point that "the 'is' of a *particular* statement might well be the 'is' of identity—*this* act of perceiving just *is* *this* physiological change—but that no more general identities should be postulated, since a certain function can always potentially be realized in different matter, even if it has not been so far in our experience." She suggests we think of the *is* of realization or constitution in regarding *aisthēsis* (sensings or sensations) as a certain type of qualitative change. This would almost fit *Psych.* 424a25 ff., where Aristotle says that the organ and the potentiality are the same but their being (*einai*) is different, and notes that what is sensed has the property of magnitude whereas the sensing (or its capacity) does not. We may ask, however, why Nussbaum has the identity pointed only one way, namely toward the physiological change. Although that might be relevant for some (e.g., causal) purposes, Aristotle's way of talking about the relation does not do this. (For the associative character of the relation, see Nussbaum, p. 151). Aristotle denies (*Meta.* 1045b16 ff.) that there is a single general relation that can be embraced in a unifying formula between the potential and the actual, or between matter and form, such that we can ask for a cause of their unity; the causes are always specific efficient ones. He adverts readily to the fact that a single happening can be looked at from different directions and have different properties, just as a single road goes up in one direction and down in the other (see above, chapter 6, note 22); certainly for the traveler the difference in properties would have a distinct effect. This is the kind of intellectual apparatus Aristotle seems committed to in dealing with the qualitative and the physiological in sensation—as the same actuality that can be described

from different directions. To be a full-fledged theory it requires considerable extension, which is quite different from pressing on it the form of identification of the phenomenal with the physiological.

CHAPTER 10

1. *Psych.* 414b7 f.
2. *Psych.* 418a14 ff.
3. *Psych.* 422a8 ff.
4. *Sens.* 442a17 f.
5. *Psych.* 421a26 ff., 421a10 ff.
6. *Sens.* 4, 5.
7. *Part. An.* 656a13–661a30.
8. For a study of the common sense, see Hamlyn 1968.
9. *Psych.* 425a31 ff.; cf. *Sens.* 447b21 ff.
10. *Psych.* 425b12 ff.
11. *Psych.* 426b8–27a14; cf. *Sens.* 449a14 ff.
12. *On Memory and Recollection* 450a9 ff.
13. *On Sleep and Waking* 454b10.
14. *On Sleep and Waking* 455a15 ff.
15. *On Youth and Old Age* 467b28; cf. 469a12, where the common sense-organ of all the sense organs is said to lie in the heart.
16. *Part. An.* 666a10 ff.
17. *Psych.* 427b14 f.
18. *Psych.* 429a1 f.
19. Another recent example of the broadening trend is Lykos 1964, who departs from the translation of *phantasia* as "imagination" and uses "presentation," which allows the use of "appearance" for *phantasma*. The relation of judgment and appearing shifts the investigation into areas where image is dispensable. Rees 1971 explores the uses of "imagine" in nonimage contexts, from imagining a thousand-sided figure or supposing a situation to holding a false belief; he decides that Aristotle's usage covers the propositional, with sensation as an essential base. See especially Nussbaum 1978, essay 5, pp. 221–69. See also Schofield 1978.
20. For a full study of Aristotle's theory of memory, see Sorabji 1972.
21. *Psych.* 3.4, 5.
22. *Psych.* 427b27 ff.
23. *Psych.* 429a12 f.
24. *Psych.* 429a15 ff.
25. *Psych.* 417b24 ff.
26. *Psych.* 429a24 f.
27. Hamlyn 1968, p. 57. In commenting on this passage (p. 136) he suggests that the potentiality in question "is one of the whole man and is dependent on the other faculties which do have organs."
28. *Psych.* 429a27 f.
29. *Gen. An.* 736b27 ff.
30. *Psych.* 429b5 ff.
31. *Psych.* 429b9–10.
32. *Psych.* 429b21 ff.
33. Even as it stands, however, the statement that the mind is nothing before it thinks might yield the striking philosophical conclusion that each act of thought is a fresh (creative?) phenomenon, and consequently that thinking is the range of possible novelty in the life of man. It is worth noting in general that Aristotle's philosophy emphasizes the many sources of order and stability, such as the concepts of order and substance, but the sources of possible novelty are more scattered and difficult to pinpoint. Among those we have noted and shall subsequently note are the instantaneous character of substantival

change, the opposition to reductionism, the pervasiveness of accident, and the possibly creative character of mind as Aristotle describes it.

It is essential in treating chapters 4 and 5 of *Psych.* 3 to maintain the distinction between phenomena and interpretation. The mind becoming one with its object, as a purely phenomenological act, is no more bizarre than the mind *grasping* its object or whatever is indicated when we ordinarily say "It dawned on me" or "It struck me that . . . ," or for that matter when we refer to the mind's simply "beholding the truth that. . . ." The point is simply that phenomenologically we experience the mind active and the mind passive, the mind taking hold, the mind invaded and the mind merging, the mind losing its identity in and becoming one with, mind sharing an idea and even becoming one in a common ideal. We come to regard these as metaphors when we begin to treat them as more than phenomenal experience and try to make a metaphysical reality out of them. But they are original experiences. Aristotle is using a selection out of such data and parallel facts from the analysis of sensation to fashion the construct we have considered, which he then interprets in terms of his system.

For comments on and interpretations of active reason, particularly as regarded by the ancient commentators, see Ross 1961, pp. 41–47.

34. *Psych.* 431a14 f.

35. *Psych.* 432a7–14. For the broader interpretation of *phantasma* as *appearance* rather than always as *image*, see the discussion above, and n. 19.

36. *Part. An.* 687a19 f.

37. The Greek terms are *noēsis* (thought), *dianoia* (understanding), *hupolēpsis* (judgment), and *phronēsis* (practical thought).

CHAPTER 11

1. *Psych.* 432b16 f., b28 f. The Greek for "compulsion" is *bia*.

2. *Psych.* 433a7 ff. For the translation of *orexis* as *appetite*, see below, n. 14.

3. *Psych.* 433a20–21.

4. *Psych.* 433b5 ff.

5. Plato does (or appears to do) this in some contexts in the *Republic*. For example, when he is distinguishing three parts of the psyche, he uses the fact of opposite directives at the same time to establish that there are separate parts. The rational and the appetitive are thus distinguished (*Republic* 439a5 ff.) and on the whole found to be enemies both within the individual and on the social scene in the sense that reason together with the third part of the psyche, spirit or mettle—or socially, the rulers together with their auxiliaries or administrative army—have continually to repress the appetites (or the masses). But of course in another sense Plato does talk of reason's having its rational desires, so that the differences would lie in the source of desires.

6. *Psych.* 432a24 ff.

7. *Psych.* 433b13–30.

8. *Mov. An.* 6.

9. *Psych.* 433b28 ff. For a fuller interpretation of imagination, see chapter 10, esp. n. 19, above. Imagination prepares the appetite in the sense of giving it cognitive direction; it is not the consequence of a fully formed appetite. That we are not here dealing with a mind–body dualism is well analyzed by Nussbaum 1978, pp. 149–56.

The fashioning of appetite by cognition leaves open the degree of specificity in the content. Appetite can take shape in general drives or in very specific desires. For an inquiry as to whether Aristotle is committed to a Humean belief in the positing of ends, see Irwin 1975. This question is discussed below (chapter 16) in considering the good.

10. *Mov. An.* 701b2 ff., b26 ff.

11. *Mov. An.* 701b16 ff., 702b20 ff.

12. *Mov. An.* 703a9–19. For an analysis of *pneuma* in its psychological role, see Nussbaum 1978, essay 3. See also chapter 4 above, in the treatment of Aristotle's physical concepts, and chapter 4, n. 22.

13. *Mov. An.* 703b36 ff.

14. *Psych.* 414b2. The Greek terms are *orexis* (appetite), *epithumia* (desire), *thumos* (emotion), and *boulēsis* (wish). There is some variation today in the translation of *orexis*. A growing tendency, appealing to contemporary English usage, favors "desire" instead, treating it as the generic idea, with "appetite" reserved for the animal desires. Against this there are several weighty considerations: (1) Greek *oregō* is etymologically parallel with *appeto* in Latin and *appetite* (or *appetition* or *appetency*) in English. (2) The philosophical tradition from the seventeenth-century foundation works of moral psychology employs *conatus* (endeavor) as a basic term and associates *appetite* with it as the most general psychological term. Spinoza in part 3 of his *Ethics* (note to proposition 9) states the connections with precision: "This endeavor, when referred to the Mind alone, is called *will*, but when referred to the Mind and Body together it is called appetite. . . . Between Appetite and Desire [*cupiditas*] there is no difference, except that Desire is generally referred to men, insofar as they are conscious of this appetite, and may accordingly be defined thus: *Desire is appetite with consciousness thereof*." It is well to recall that Aristotle uses *orexis* for animals as well as humans. (3) If we reserve "appetite" for *orexis*, "desire" can be assigned to *epithumia*. *Orexis* appears to have a greater breadth: Liddell and Scott's *Greek-English Lexicon* (1940 edition) embraces under *orexis* "all kinds of appetency"; *epithumia*, *thumos*, and *boulēsis* are given more specific limits. (Santas 1969, p. 169, follows a still different path, translating *orexis* as "want" and *epithumia* as "desire or appetite.")

15. *Meta.* 1008b14 ff.

16. *Psych.* 431a8–16. I am indebted to Daniel Marino for insightful suggestions in connection with the Freudian parallel that follows, as well as for general discussion of the relation of Aristotle's and Freud's theories of the emotions.

17. *Psych.* 431b2 ff.

18. *Psych.* 433a14 f.

19. *Psych.* 434a5 ff.

20. *Psych.* 434a16 ff.

21. *Mov. An.* 701a11–13. Since the word translated "is" is *ginetai*, one might be tempted to render it as "the conclusion drawn from the two premises *becomes* the action." Forster does so in the Loeb translation. For the argument against this see Nussbaum's commentary on the passage (1978, pp. 342–43). Little would result in any case since the point is recapitulated in lines 22–23, and interpretation is still required. Kenny 1979, pp. 142–43, cuts through the knot in interpreting Aristotle's examples here by saying that "Aristotle is willing to call a decision to act 'an action' " and points out that sometimes Aristotle says the conclusion is the action and sometimes that the two are simultaneous (702a17).

22. *Mov. An.* 701a22 f. Cooper 1975, pp. 56–57, points out that the major premises here express the contents of decisions or occurrent appetites (in this case the *need* for a covering). Thus the agent has already determined to do a certain thing under certain conditions: "The tendency of some interpreters of Aristotle to read into his discussions of practical syllogisms a peculiar, not to say mysterious, kind of thinking, the rules for which require that actions and not propositions be inferred from the given premises, is therefore based on a failure to understand properly the presuppositions under which Aristotle's agents are thought of as acting, even in the case where they actually do go through the steps of the syllogistic argument before they act." Cooper refers to Anscombe's *Intention*, 1957, sections 33–35.

23. *Psych.* 414b4 f.

24. *Psych.* 421a11 f.

25. *Mov. An.* 701b34 f.

26. *Mov. An.* 700b28 ff.

27. *Psych.* 403a16 ff. For the sense in which the phenomenal is associated with the bodily, see chapter 9, n. 45.

28. *Psych.* 403a25 ff.

29. E.g., *On Memory and Recollection* 453a24 ff.

30. *On Dreams* 460b3 ff.

31. *Probl.* 947b12 ff.

32. *Probl.* 948a3 ff.

33. *Probl.* 961a8 f.

Part 4

1. Bacon, *Novum Organum* (1620), book 1, section 95.

CHAPTER 12

1. *Pr. An.* 43a25–43.
2. *Meta.* 1018a3 f.
3. For a good traditional exposition of Aristotle's logic, see Joseph 1916. The revived intensive study of Aristotle's logic in the light of contemporary symbolic logic was stimulated at mid-century by Łukasiewicz's work (1st ed., 1951; 2nd enl. ed., 1957). This was taken up by others (e.g., Patzig 1968). Łukasiewicz held that Aristotle's syllogistic was a codification of certain true universal conditional sentences rather than of valid arguments, that is, that they are of the form "If A belongs to all B, and B belongs to all C, then A belongs to all C" rather than

> "All B is A.
> All C is B.
> Therefore,
> All C is A."

More recently, Corcoran 1974 has pointed out that on such a view Aristotle would not be the founder of logic; he would only have been exploring a limited set of entities and relations. His work would be parallel to that of Euclid or Peano as founders of axiomatic geometry or axiomatic arithmetic, and his universe of discourse would be a class of universals with the primitive relations A, E, I, and O: inclusion, disjointness, partial inclusion, and partial disjointness. The Stoics would then be the real founders of logic. Corcoran asserts that in the *Prior Analytics* Aristotle "was developing the underlying logic for the axiomatically organized sciences that he discusses in the *Posterior Analytics*." Certainly, as *Metaphysics* 4 shows in its treatment of noncontradiction, Aristotle regarded his logic as giving the fundamental laws of reasoning and thought and being. An earlier paper, Corcoran 1973, proposes a mathematical model of Aristotle's syllogistic, analyzing it as a theory of deduction that is "fundamental in the sense that it *presupposes no other logic*, not even propositional logic" (p. 196), against Łukasiewicz's view that Aristotle's theory of syllogistic is an axiomatic science presupposing a theory of deduction of which Aristotle was unaware.

For an example of the tendency to impose on Aristotle our own (often valuable) distinctions, take Łukasiewicz's criticism that Aristotle is inexact when he says that one thing may be predicated of another: "It is not correct to say that a thing may be predicated of another thing. Things cannot be predicated, because a predicate is a part of a proposition and a proposition is a series of spoken or written words having a certain meaning" (1957, p. 6). Patzig 1968, p. 5, comments on this: "That is obvious; however, we are dealing with Aristotle, and in such a case we ought perhaps to try to understand why he uses such peculiar language." Such an attempt should go much further than apology. It should look into Aristotle's whole metaphysical orientation, as contrasted with a contemporary linguistic orientation. (See above, chapter 3, n. 7.) It is also significant that in *Categories* 2 Aristotle introduces the parallel concepts that one thing can be *said of* another and that one thing can *be in* another. For an exposition that these are both to be taken ontologically, see Ackrill 1963, pp. 74–75.

4. *Pr. An.* 25a1 f.
5. *Pr. An.* 68b15–30. More literally, Aristotle says "Induction, that is, the syllogism out of induction. . . ." Tredennick, in the Loeb edition, translates, "Induction, or inductive reasoning," and Jenkinson, in the Oxford translations, "Induction, or rather the syllogism which springs out of induction."

Aristotle does not appear to be speaking of inductive reasoning as a form of induction. Induction is the process (intuitive induction) to be discussed later in this chapter. Reasoning that springs out of induction simply uses the material that comes up in that process and combines it with other knowledge to construct a syllogism (or enthymeme) of standard valid form. If this is not recognized we begin to worry unnecessarily about the different meanings of the term *induction* in Aristotle.

It is only fair to point out that there is disagreement about this interpretation. Hamlyn 1976, p. 169, takes the "or rather" to be equivalent to *that is*, "or at least a specification rather than a qualification. The passage indicates nothing which suggests that Aristotle wants to distinguish between *epagōgē* as a process of discovery and the argument or arguments associated with that." Of course this means nothing once the "or rather" interpretation is discounted. I do not think the case hangs on this passage itself, but on the general interpretation of *epagōgē*. It makes better sense if we do not think of it as sometimes a type of argument that is an imperfect form of deduction and sometimes a way of getting to first principles. Hamlyn's analysis involves to some extent reinterpreting the character of the latter itself as a dialectical argument. Larger questions are therefore involved.

6. *Interp.* 17a39 f. The Greek terms are *katholou* (universal) and *kath' hekaston* (individual).

7. E.g., *Pr. An.* 25a5. "In part" is *merei*.

8. *Interp.* 12, 13.

9. The several Greek terms here involved are: *genos* (genus), *idion* (property), *sumbebēkos* (accident), *diaphora* (differentia), and *horos* (definition). Essence is the familiar *to ti ēn einai*.

10. *Top.* 1.5.

11. *Top.* 100b21–23: "Generally accepted opinions (*endoxa*) are those that are acceptable to all or most or the wise—that is, to all of the wise or to most or the most famous and distinguished of them."

12. *Pr. An.* 2.2–4.

13. Leszl 1975, pp. 92–99. He points to *Rhet.* 1358a10 ff.

14. Le Blond 1939, pp. 9–20. Le Blond is particularly concerned with the element of probability in the *endoxa*, as well as the generality of dialectic. See also the characterization of *endoxa* in Evans 1977, pp. 77–85.

15. A useful study that focuses attention on the notion of *endoxa* in relation to that of *phainomena* is to be found in part 1 of Owen 1961 (conveniently reprinted in Moravcsik 1967; part 2 is concerned with the importance of Plato's *Parmenides* in the formulation of the problems of Aristotle's *Physics*). Owen recognizes that what is "said" with reference to *endoxa* "may be an appeal either to common belief about matters of fact or to established forms of language or to a philosophical thesis claiming the factual virtues of the first and the analytic certainty of the second" (p. 89; p. 174 in Moravcsik). He takes not only the *endoxa* but also the phenomena for the *Physics* to be largely linguistic facts, in the sense of conceptual puzzles, but leaves open the question whether linguistic usage is to be taken as revealing conceptual structure. If the latter is something different, and the *Physics* is taken quite literally to be concerned with theoretical physics and its philosophical analysis, then its conceptual structure may very well be a construction to which language, empirical fact, the growth of knowledge, human purpose, cultural tradition, and other factors, could all contribute in varying proportions. Whether at any given time the linguistic structure is a significant clue to the conceptual structure would itself be an empirical question.

16. *Post. An.* 71b9 ff.

17. *Nic. Eth.* 1139b21 ff. For the fuller explanation why sensation cannot give us knowledge, see *Post. An.* 1.31. Cf. *Top.* 131b19–25.

18. *Post. An.* 1.8. Aristotle usually expresses what is here translated as *attribute* by saying that one thing is *of* another, or that it belongs to the other, or that the second *has* the first.

19. *Top.* 131b19–30.

20. *Nic. Eth.* 6.3.

21. The Greek terms for this family of more special intellectual abilities or virtues or states are *dianoia* (understanding), *doxa* (opinion), *endoxa* (common beliefs), *pistis* (belief), *hupolēpsis* (judgment), *eustochia* (quickness of wit), and *deinotēs* (cleverness).

22. *Post. An.* 1.18.

23. *Meta.* 980a27 ff.

24. E.g., *Post. An.* 87b29 f.

25. The concept of intuitive induction is expounded particularly in *Post. An.* 2.19. Barnes 1975, pp. 248–60, comments at length on that passage. His discussion of the many complexities, and particularly of the way in which Aristotle is not addressing just one question, shows why it is possible to explain or reconcile the rationalistic and empiricist aspects of Aristotle's thought. (Perhaps it is even better seen as undercutting the opposition.) See also Hamlyn 1976 for an interesting presentation of some of the complexities. Hamlyn shows clearly that mere abstraction will not do the job that Aristotle wants done. Our discussion here goes on to suggest it has to be supplemented with Aristotle's analysis of what is involved in the prior grasping of particulars. Thayer 1979, pp. 96–97, takes seriously the metaphor of taking a stand: "Aristotle associates the concept of *epistēmē* with the term *stēnai*, 'coming to a stand.'" Thayer cites *Phys.* 7.3, 247b10–11, and *Psych.* 434a16, as well as the several uses of the idea in *Post. An.* 2.19. On the other hand, Barnes 1975, p. 253, dismisses this idea that the universal comes to rest (stand) in the mind: "'Resting' here amounts to no more than presence (the phrase comes from *Phaedo* 96b)— *Int.* 3, 16b20, and *Phys.* H 3, 274b10, have nothing to do with the case." There seems to be an interesting philosophical difference in approach here which is relevant to interpretation. Barnes is isolating propositional knowledge—that is, the epistemological question—and so turns the discussion to the question of the logic of demonstration (the possibilities of perfect induction), whereas Thayer clearly is looking for Aristotle's metaphysical presuppositions based on his physics and psychology (and Barnes's reference to *Interp.* 3 adds linguistics). The reference to Plato's *Phaedo* actually supports the broader approach. That Socrates rejected these physical inquiries about how knowledge comes from memory and opinion in a state of rest, shows that these inquiries were going on; Aristotle's attention to them as indicated in the citations suggests what we already know, that he does not agree with Socrates here. We shall see below (chapters 13 and 15) that Aristotle was profoundly concerned with processes of stabilization, and there is no reason to put aside his remarks involving them when they occur in epistemological contexts.

26. *Phys.* 1.1.

27. *Top.* 108b9 f.

28. *Prob.* 886b4 f.

29. *Top.* 157a24 ff.

30. *Top.* 8.8.

31. *Top.* 156a5 f.

32. *Part. An.* 669a19 ff.

33. *Post. An.* 1.34.

34. E.g., *Meta.* 9.9.

35. Cf. esp. *Psych.* 3.6.

CHAPTER 13

1. *Post. An.* 71b21 ff.

2. *Post. An.* 1.3.

3. *Post. An.* 1.5. The Greek words are *kata pantos* (of all), *kath' hauto* (*per se*), and *katholou* (universal). Translations of these terms differ. For example, in the Oxford translations Mure uses, respectively, "true in every instance of a subject," "essential," and "commensurate universal."

4. Le Blond 1939. His section "La saisie des principes" appears pp. 126–46. On the sensory, see p. 134; on *nous*, see p. 136; for his conclusion, see p. 146.

5. Le Blond 1939, p. 186.

6. Barnes 1969, pp. 143, 147. Lesher 1973, p. 57, disagrees with Barnes's emphasis and finds an analysis of *nous* will tell against it. Thayer 1979, pp. 97, 102–3, develops the theme of the educational character of demonstration and accepts Barnes's view.

7. Lesher 1973, esp. pp. 58, 64–65.

8. Kosman 1973, pp. 374, 378–80.

9. Kosman 1973, p. 385. See in general the discussion in pp. 383–89.

10. Engberg-Pedersen 1979, p. 304. The reference is to *Topics* 105a13–14.

11. Engberg-Pedersen 1979, p. 318; see also pp. 307–8.

12. Barnes 1969, p. 150. He says that there is no mathematical ancestry for *apodeixis* and little evidence for axiomatization before Euclid (pp. 130–31). See also Scholz 1975.

13. The Greek terms are *to hoti* (the that), *to dioti* (the on-account-of-what), *ei esti* (if-it-is), and *ti esti* (what-it-is).

14. On the matter of the existence of the triangle and more primary units, Barnes 1975, p. 92, questions whether the usual reference to construction, though it fits Euclid's practice, should be attributed to Aristotle. The passages he cites to support his doubt do not seem to me to be convincing. For example, in *On the Heavens* 1.10, 279b32–280a10, Aristotle criticizes those who for purely instructional purposes tell stories of how the world was constructed even though they believe the world is eternal, on the ground that doing so introduces a fresh property, order out of disorder, whereas in geometrical construction the resulting figure does not differ from its constituents. Here at least he does not seem to be denying geometrical construction in the way Plato did by saying there was no room for any idea of constructing as movement in eternal mathematics. Perhaps Aristotle's view that we prove the existence for defined terms and assume it for the undefined can be related in a different way to construction if we think of geometric theorems that *prove* constructions (e.g., bisecting an angle or line, constructing a triangle, drawing through a point a line parallel to a given straight line) as *proofs* that such entities *exist* in the domain. This would fit Aristotle's remark precisely. *Triangle* is defined and its existence proved; the primary unit (whether *line* or *point*) is undefined and its existence assumed or grasped as a primary truth.

Even in the apparently simple cases where the question is whether a centaur or a god exists, a complex analysis may prove warranted. Kahn 1973, p. 305, referring to this passage in Aristotle (89b32), says, "*There is no (god) Zeus* means that all sentences of the form *There is a god Zeus who does such-and-such*—and indeed, all sentences of the form *Zeus is (or does) such-and-such*—are false. To deny the existence of someone or something is to deny its availability as subject for any first-order predication whatsoever." The whole of chapter 6 in his book, dealing with the verb of existence, is relevant to our theme.

A serious (and in some respects more traditional) view of this passage about the distinction between what-it-is and if-it-is as evidence for a basic distinction between the judgment of essence and the judgment of existence is developed in Suzanne Mansion 1976. She begins with the paradox that Aristotle's basic theory of science makes a distinction involving a judgment of existence, though his theory of existence ties it to particulars and his theory of science ties knowledge to universals. She examines attempts to align existence with essence, such as claims that the only reason existence does not fall in essence is because it is common to all things, not being a genus (while essence gives what is distinctive)—not because it is something sheerly outside. She concludes that for Aristotle, the spirit is incapable of attaining a true essence without the knowledge of existence (p. 258). But as she develops this, it takes on a verificatory tone, and we are at last told (p. 261) that the activity of the spirit that constructs objects in assembling concepts is sanctioned by reality, by existence, in Aristotle's view: "Thus, it is true to say that existence is not a mark of essence but that is because it is more than that: it is the condition which gives to what is (*ti estin*) its reality." She disposes of the original paradox that generated her inquiry by pointing out that the particular individual's existence is not needed but just that of the species: for example, a theory of human nature requires the existence of man, not Socrates or Callias.

The tendency to draw existence closer to essence is encouraged by an overemphasis on the mathematical examples. If we attend to biology, and for that matter to the fact that Aristotle's philosophy of science is oriented to the order of learning as much as to the order of being, then his remarks that essence requires existents admit of a simple interpretation. It was suggested earlier that the search for essence could be viewed as the extension of the search for the nature of things. Since the nature of a lion is discovered by seeing how it behaves universally or for the most part, we need specimens not merely to sanction its being but to dissect and learn about it. Perhaps Aristotle should have spelled it out more precisely: that the knowledge of essence presupposes the knowledge of existence, for otherwise one never would have learned the essence. See also Le Blond 1939, pp. 168–84; he considers both synthetic and analytic features of the judgment of existence and finds it a merit of

Aristotle's account to have realized that a purely copulative meaning for *is* is a chimera, and that a reference to existence permeates even abstract affirmation.

There are, of course, many gradations of lessons to be drawn from the names of things and the contexts of their use and the knowledge that goes into selecting and suggesting names. For a study of the nominal definition in Aristotle, see Bolton 1976.

15. *Psych.* 402b16–403a2.

16. For a careful study of *to be* in its existential use in Aristotle, see Owen 1965.

17. *Categ.* 13b14–18.

18. *Interp.* 21a25 ff.

19. *Top.* 149a37 ff.

20. *Meta.* 1047a32 ff.

21. This is most clearly seen in logical usage where the separate existential operator, "There is an *x*," extends over the function "*x* has the property *P*." Similarly, in diagrammatic representation in the logic of classes, circles may be used to represent classes (or compartments of circles), but a separate notation—a star for having members and shading out for not having members—shows existence and nonexistence. Such conventions enshrine the hard-won lesson that existence is not a property, first propounded in the twelfth century by the monk Gaunilo in his attack on Anselm's ontological proof of the existence of God. Anselm tried to show that when the fool says in his heart that there is no God, he logically contradicts himself by implying that a perfect being who therefore possesses the property of existence does not exist. Gaunilo, speaking on behalf of the fool, begins the isolation of the notion of existence as something to be discussed only *after* the description of the entity in question is finished. It was Kant who summed up this development in the assertion that existence is not a predicate. By that time, Leibniz had already developed the idea of logical possibility and Hume had used conceivability of the opposite as the mark of a matter-of-fact empirical assertion.

The great pay-off in this conception of existence came in the development of non-Euclidean geometries. Euclidean geometry ceased to be regarded as intuitively true. Alternative systems could then be compared and the question of which best represented some existent domain (or which could most usefully be employed for an existent domain) became an empirical matter. Empirical science too shifted in focus from what had once been the descriptive-explanatory account of things that are, to elaborating alternative models (possibilities) to be tried out on things that are. All this is now commonplace. The advantages of a conceptual network that separates pure possibility and pure existence are clear enough. There may be hidden problems, such as how one tests for consistency in a model, which may reintroduce a relation of possibility and existence in the very heart of possibility; but these can be carried along with only occasional discomfort.

Aristotle structures things differently. He certainly did not deal with possible worlds in Leibniz's sense, and he had troubles with relating the mathematical and the physical. In the next note there will be some consideration of the ways in which, within his own concept of existence, he tried to gain some of the advantages that our concept has given us.

22. It does not follow of course that Aristotle's concept of existence and ours have to differ on every aspect. For example, both can be used on different levels of abstraction—for individuals and for events, for numbers and for series and for frameworks. Thus in the physical writings Aristotle raises questions about the existence of motion (against Zeno), whether there is an infinite (he distinguishes in which sense), the senses in which place and time exist, whether a vacuum exists (his answer is it does not), whether there are indivisibles, whether there is another world besides this one (there is not), and so on. In most of these he is concerned with clarifying the concept and seeing whether admitting such an existent would be in conflict with his accepted concepts and assumed general knowledge. He does not say of any of these, they could exist or they could not exist, let us therefore look and see whether they exist. In part this is unnecessary because the knowledge against which he lines up the concept (motion, the infinite, etc.) already includes the generalizations from experience. Furthermore, to assert that something exists would be to say that some form was embodied in matter.

In the whole area of transformation where something comes into existence from previously existent materials, there is not much difference in Aristotle's notion of existence and ours. Both are contextual. His exposition of substantival coming-into-being is perhaps more dramatically formulated, since he stresses its instantaneous character. Again, like us, he recognizes in his psychological writings that imagination may produce impressions of what does not exist and that one can also think of what does not exist. But he has some tendency to regard a thing being thought of as a kind of instantiation in thinking, and thinking as an event in the world in which the form is actual. Thus the assertion that something thought of exists would be equivalent to saying that the form was instantiated in some matter outside the matter involved in human imagination and thought.

On the whole, Aristotle seems able to get along without a concept of bare existence like ours. At most points he can raise any question we would want to raise about the existence of specific objects, about the enduring or ephemeral character of different forms of existence, about the dependent properties of existing things, about the emergence and destruction of existents, about the general approach to what is in this world through sensation. It is doubtful that we do much more when we apply the concept of existence in practice or consider how we would decide that something exists. (We have our own troubles philosophically deciding whether to limit *existence* to the physical order and think of *subsistence* or some other special sense of being for mathematical and logical domains.) Aristotle could not have accepted the general concept of existence in any case, because, in its having no descriptive properties, it could only be understood in an analogical way and might have been confused with either basic matter or being.

The notion of pure existence is valuable insofar as it is tied into logical systems for purposes of greater manipulation of symbols. But problems of extrasystemic meaning are likely to arise when the systems are being applied in different subject matters.

The one serious advantage Aristotle seems to lose is a clearer distinction between model and application, or pure mathematics and physics. Yet to some extent he is able to make distinctions that in part achieve some of the results we get. The chief result is that the properties of a model or pure system are not automatically asserted for a domain to which it is applied.

Fine distinctions sometimes help Aristotle keep the mathematical and the physical apart. He does, as we have seen, regard mathematics as the study of some aspect of things, abstracted or isolated for the purpose of investigation. Just as we can study the attributes of an animal in virtue of its being male or female without making these features independent of the animal, so too for lines and planes (*Meta.* 1078a5 ff.). His distinctions sometimes show considerable subtlety. For example, he says (*Phys.* 224a12 ff.) that the number of two groups (say ten dogs and ten sheep) is the same number, but it is not the same decade, since one is of dogs, the other of sheep.

In the analysis of the sciences Aristotle gets a result somewhat similar to the separation of pure and applied systems through insisting that proofs be made within each genus, not by crossing or by a transcending principle (e.g., *Post. An.* 1.7). Thus we are forbidden to prove a geometrical proposition by arithmetic; even though the proofs are similar—suppose they concern the addition of numbers and the addition of lines—terms like *equality*, he often tells us, have a different sense in the different genera. The only exception is proof drawn in a subordinate science (as distinct from a parallel one, in the sense that optics is subordinate to geometry and harmonics to arithmetic). In consequence, Aristotle objects generally to attempting to explain particular phenomena by too abstract and too remote principles; a good detailed example is his rejection of the attempt to explain infertility of mules on abstract grounds of interspecies mating, and his insistence on more detailed grounds involving the specific animals. In making the transition (*Gen. An.* 748a7–16) he actually appeals to the view that a geometrical argument must start from geometrical principles.

The view that each science should explain in its own terms is aided by his theory of the categories, by the multiplicity of senses of *being* and even more of *one*. The last of these compels him to have, as it were, different operations for applying ideas in areas in which *one* has a different meaning. All in all they go some way toward getting the same result that the sharp separation of pure existence from pure possibility and of physics from mathematics have secured for us. If Aristotle were aware of our concepts at this point, he might have multiplied his many instruments for a broader theory of analogy rather than abandoned his treatment of existence for our framework. And his argument would probably be that existence is a multiple problem best handled piecemeal by relating anything whose existence is questioned through contextual processes to some accepted part of the world, that the existence of a world is not at issue. And behind this lies the fact that his framework is intended to face up to a different problem, to explore the difference between essence and accident, not to create a gulf between essence and existence. He would no doubt have claimed that his interest is closer to what scientists are doing in their work.

Yet it is hard to conjecture what he might have done. In the corpus the weakness pointed out earlier—that the results of mathematical properties such as divisibility in geometry are taken for granted for the physical world and made the basis of the attack on atomism—is not overcome. That imaginative insight could envisage far-flung possibilities is not incompatible with this. An example from the post-Aristotelian *Problems* shows this. Why, it is asked (910b23 ff.), do all men, Greek and barbarian, count in tens? The writer immediately shows how a system of fives would work, or a system beyond ten. So far the flight of imagination. But now come the constraints of tradition: the unanimity of counting by tens must mean it is natural. And then comes the list of possible explanations, from ten being the perfect number to men having ten fingers. Finally he notes the exception that was ignored in the theory: the Thracians count in fours; they must be like children who don't remember very far, and anyhow they don't have use for large numbers. Let this stand as a paradigm of the mixture of insight and shrewdness mired in habitual belief, that so often shows up in the corpus.

23. *Meteor.* 344a5 ff.
24. *Pr. An.* 53b12 ff.; cf. *Top.* 124b7 ff.
25. E.g., *Heav.* 306a11–17.
26. *Top.* 111b17–23.
27. *Top.* 7.5.
28. *Pr. An.* 24a22 ff.
29. *Pr. An.* 68b9 ff.
30. *Pr. An.* 2.23.
31. *Rhet.* 1357b1–25.
32. *Pr. An.* 43a10–15.
33. *Heav.* 311b9 ff.
34. *Meteor.* 358b16 ff.
35. E.g., *Hist. An.* 511b14 ff., 513a12 ff.
36. *Gen. An.* 760b30–33.
37. *Heav.* 271b8–13.
38. *Heav.* 310b16–19.
39. *Phys.* 215a20–22.
40. *Mov. An.* 699a33–b4.
41. *Categ.* 9b11–19.
42. *Top.* 145b2 ff.
43. *Gen. Corr.* 1.3, 4.
44. Cf. the discussion of all-at-once phenomena in *Phys.* 253b14–30.
45. *Hist. An.* 522b2 ff. Rennet, he says, is a sort of milk formed in the stomach of young animals that are still being suckled.
46. *Gen. An.* 729a9 ff.; cf. 771b21 ff.
47. *Gen. An.* 767a16 ff.

CHAPTER 14

1. E.g., *Part. An.* 659b13–60b2, 661b12 ff.
2. *Hist. An.* 4.9. The Greek terms are *phōnē* (voice), *psophos* (sound), and *dialektos* (speech).
3. *Hist. An.* 536a32–b23.
4. *Psych.* 2.8.
5. *Psych.* 420b27 f.

6. *Psych.* 420b32 f. The exact words are *sēmantikos tis psophos*; *sēmantikos* is often translated as "means."

7. *Interp.* 16a13 ff., b20 f. The Greek terms are *onoma* (name; noun) and *rhēma* (verb).

8. *Poet.* 19–22.

9. The Greek terms are *tode* (this), *tode ti* (this-something), *toionde* (this-such), and *toiouton* (such).

10. *Pr. An.* 49b10 f.

11. *Poet.* 1456b11 f.

12. *Prob.* 875b26 ff.

13. *Prob.* 902b30–38.

14. *Prob.* 900a20 ff.

15. *Prob.* 902b16–29.

16. *Categ.* 1.

17. *Top.* 1.15–18.

18. *Phys.* 248a18–b19.

19. *Gen. An.* 780b12 ff.

20. *Poet.* 1457b6 ff.

21. *Top.* 123a33 f.

22. *Phys.* 252a25 ff.

23. *Part. An.* 682b32 ff., 644a21 f., 645b26 f. Cf. what he says on different kinds of unity in *Meta.* 1016b32–1017a3.

24. *Post. An.* 76a37–40.

25. *Meteor.* 390a10–14.

26. Chapter 8 above, n. 9.

27. *Heav.* 279b9 ff.

28. *Phys.* 210a14–24.

29. *Gen. An.* 742a19 ff.

30. E.g., *Pol.* 1255b16 ff.

31. *Meta.* 1020b14 f.

32. *Meta.* 1020a4 f.

33. *Meta.* 1015a35 f.

34. *Meta.* 1015a13. "Strict or proper sense" is *kuriōs legomenē*.

35. Aristotle is sensitive also to the processes by which meanings are extended or "carried over" (*metapheretai*, which is kindred to our *metaphor*); for example, some properties are regarded as quantitative because they are properties of what is quantitative (*Meta.* 5, 1020a25–30). Some examples—*cultured* and *white*—are not particularly significant, but others, such as *motion* and *time*, would have important scientific bearings. (Motion is quantitative because the interval covered is quantitative.)

36. *Top.* 148a26–36.

37. *Meta.* 1016b31–17a3.

38. *Pol.* 1260a5–14.

39. Owen 1960; cf. Owen 1968.

40. *Eud. Eth.* 1236a15–25. The masculine, feminine, and neuter of the Greek for *one* are, respectively, *heis*, *mia*, and *hen*.

41. For example, *Meta.* 5, 1022a3, where Aristotle is explaining the primary sense of *perfect*, gives a list ending up with "or are referred in some way or other *to things which are called perfect in the primary sense.*" The italicized part (my italics) begins *pros ta....* This illustrates that the *hen* in *pros hen* is simply rendering more specific the *ti* in the general term for relation (*pros ti*). Instead of "with reference (or relation) to something" focal meaning requires "with reference (or relation) to some one thing." But what that one is or what kind of unity it has is not determined. It could be very tight or very loose.
Fortenbaugh 1975b has examined Aristotle's analysis of friendship in the *Nicomachean Ethics* and found that the concept of focal meaning does not apply. Going back to the passage in the *Eudemian Ethics* where Aristotle enunciated the notion but did not work it out, Fortenbaugh also questions its applicability. In both cases, he finds a complexity where functional ideas enter, and the unity of meaning lies rather in analogy and resemblance.

42. *Nic. Eth.* 1096b25 ff.

43. *Top.* 106b33 ff.

44. E.g., *Meta.* 1005a10–11 (*pros hen . . . tōi ephexēs*). The passage has been questioned but it is usually accepted.

45. *Eud. Eth.* 1217b34 f.

46. *Meta.* 1003a33–b23.

47. In *Top.* 106b33 ff.

48. *Meta.* 1003b11 ff.

49. See Owen 1968, esp. pp. 166 ff., on the relation of Aristotle's science of being-as-being to Plato's science of dialectic and Aristotle's own interpretation of dialectic in the *Topics*.

50. *Meta.* 1030b3 ff. On the interpretation here offered, it is clear that the benefits of the metaphysical science are returned to the fields of special inquiry. A great deal of the controversy about focal meaning in Aristotelian scholarship has hinged on the background problem whether Aristotle is eventually pointing up to Plato and the divine. For example, Owens 1951 relied on the basis of a general science of being in referential (*pros hen*) meaning to apply the same approach to substance. Thus substance itself turns out to have different senses, of which the primary is the divine substance. Thus metaphysics becomes theology. Alarmed by such a direction for the interpretation of Aristotle, Leszl 1970 battles for an interpretation of focal meaning as a type of homonymy rather than as an approach to synonymy. (Cf. also the discussion of "one science of many things" in Leszl 1975, pp. 79–85.) While these questions of the general bent of Aristotle and historical relations to Plato are separately important, I think that in this technical question of the nature of focal meaning the corpus can tell its own technical story in terms of the complexity of ambiguity and multiple uses of terms and in terms of Aristotle's changing notions of what constitutes a science. On the other hand, Evans 1977, pp. 47–49, argues that those passages where Aristotle rejects a science of all being refer to a study of everything about everything, whereas his acceptance of a universal science of being is a study of something about everything. Hence Evans discounts the apparent inconsistencies that suggested a theory of Aristotle's change of position.

51. *Post. An.* 93b29 ff.

52. *Post. An.* 92b26–34; cf. *Meta.* 1030a7 ff.

53. *Post. An.* 92b5 ff.

54. *Pol.* 1275a30 ff.

55. *Heav.* 308a29 ff.

56. *Progression of Animals* 4, 5.

57. *Phys.* 218b3 f.

58. *Part. An.* 648b12–49b8.

59. *Top.* 3 and *Rhet.* 1.5–7, respectively.

60. *Top.* 151b12 ff.

61. *Top.* 154a23 ff.; cf. 155a3 ff.

62. Cf. *Meta.* 1036a5 ff.

63. *Meta.* 1043b23–28; cf. 1024b33 ff.

64. *Meta.* 7.12; *Pr. An.* 1.21; *Post. An.* 2.5, 13; *Part. An.* 1.2, 3.

65. See Peck 1965, introduction to his translation of *Historia Animalium*. For an interesting study of the development of Aristotle's theory of classifying animals, see G. E. R. Lloyd 1961.

66. *Pol.* 3.6–7.

67. *Pol.* 1290b25–39.

68. *Hist. An.* 490b6–19.

69. *Meteor.* 390b2 ff.

70. *Gen. An.* 743g20–25.

71. *Gen. An.* 732a25 ff.; also 754a24f.

72. *Gen. An.* 732b15 ff.

73. *Psych.* 432a24 ff.

74. *Meteor.* 379b12 ff.

CHAPTER 15

1. *Interp.* 16a3 ff.
2. *Post. An.* 88b37 ff.
3. Cf. *Post. An.* 1.16, 17.
4. *Meta.* 1051a21 ff.
5. E.g., *Post. An.* 87b28 ff.
6. E.g., *Post. An.* 88a12 ff.; cf. 90a26 ff.
7. *Meta.* 1024b21 ff., *Psych.* 427b21 ff., *Meta.* 1063a6 ff.
8. *Psych.* 428b18 f. "The least amount of falsehood" is most likely meant in a probability sense. Further on Aristotle speaks of cases in which we are most or especially deceived, again in the sense of our being most likely to be deceived.
9. Cf. *Sens.* 442b8 ff.
10. *Psych.* 430b4 f. For the character of incidental perception, see Cashdollar 1973b.
11. *Phys.* 219b12–33.
12. *Phys.* 219a25 f.
13. *Phys.* 218b28 f., 219a32 f.
14. *Meta.* 1010b1 ff.
15. *Meta.* 1007b19 ff.
16. E.g., *Meta.* 1008b6 f., 1009a1 f.
17. *Meta.* 1027b25 ff.
18. *Meta.* 9.10.
19. *Meta.* 993a29 ff.
20. Hintikka 1973, esp. ch. 4.
21. E.g., *Categ.* 4a17 ff., *Meta.* 1024b20 f.
22. *Meta.* 1024b27 ff.
23. Cf. *Post. An.* 73a28 ff., 75b22–36; *Nic. Eth.* 1139b7–24.
24. *Meta.* 1012b24 ff.
25. All these are found in *Meta.* 5.5.
26. *Nic. Eth.* 1139b8 ff.
27. *Interp.* 19a23 ff.
28. *Interp.* 9.
29. *Part. An.* 681a10 ff.
30. *Gen. An.* 731b20–32a11.
31. *Meta.* 1050b22 f.

Part 5

INTRODUCTION

1. Burnet 1900, p. xxvi, says, "It is quite wrong to say that the Ethics studies the Good for Man from the point of view of the individual, while the Politics deals with the realisation of that good by the agency of the state. The subject of both works is equally 'Politics,' and there is not a single word in either of them or anywhere else which could be interpreted as setting up any such science as *ethikē* in distinction to *politikē*." He points out that to work from premises derived from an examination of human character has no special reference to the individual considered apart from the community.

2. For an interesting presentation of the view that Aristotle does not have an autonomous ethics, see Fisch 1975. Fisch examines both content and linguistic formulations. His conclusion, however, is that ethics had not yet been discovered. This seems to surrender the domain too readily to later ways of conceiving it. It seems quite possible to utilize a broader conception of ethics that would say, even granting Fisch's picture for Aristotle, that under certain presuppositions ethics would not be carried out "autonomously." Whether at present, after we are conscious of different possibilities, we should follow one or another path, becomes a higher-order decision. See also Cashdollar 1973a.

3. This is, of course, not meant to exclude self-conscious attempts to draw Aristotle and

Kant together as an explicit hypothesis. For example, Ando 1958, ch. 3, analyzing the Aristotelian concepts of practice and production, finds them insufficiently clear until he recognizes the objective end in *praxis* to be the moral significance: "Certainly, Aristotle was not yet aware of the clear distinction between value and fact. The reason why he was at a loss to determine and exemplify the concept of practice, was that he did not clearly conceive the objective end in practice to be a moral value" (p. 189). Aristotle thus looks for practice in performance instead. Ando at many points stresses Aristotle's precursory relation to Kant by making detailed comparisons. Eventually he ends with the view that "practice and production are the activities of the irrational part of the soul which is dominated by the rational part. They are irrational on the material side but rational on the formal side" (p. 207). How far this is true for Aristotle or is instead a selective Kantian assimilation would require an independent textual analysis—and perhaps too a projection of how Aristotle might have criticized Kant, not only the reverse!

CHAPTER 16

1. Kenny 1978. For a brief summary of different positions in the controversies as well as ideas about the relations of the three ethical writings, see Hardie 1968, ch. 1. For a fuller discussion of the relation between *NE* and *EE* (let us borrow Kenny's abbreviations for the moment) see Rowe 1971. Much in this relation pivots on how the three books (5, 6, and 7 in *NE*) they have in common should be treated; on the wavering about where to assign these, see Hardie pp. 8–9. Kenny's reopening of the question and his conclusion in favor of *EE* has put the question once more on the agenda of current scholarship. He has explored fresh avenues of style, using quantitative methods, reexamined the manuscript tradition, and reassessed the arguments based on philosophical content. In setting the problem, he has firmly restored the common books to an initially independent status by labeling them *Aristotlelian Ethics* (*AE*), as distinct from *NE* and *EE*, so that stylistic and ideational studies have to be carried on with a three-point reference. The resolution of the problems that Kenny has raised will take a long time because of the complexity of issues, variety of fields of evidence, and especially the impact of differences in philosophical interpretation and evaluation. The following comments and examples will suggest why this is so.

(1) For reliability, statistical style studies of ancient philosophers probably need a wider base of comparison. How much variety is to be found among those writers generally in the kinds of features (particles and connectives, prepositions, adverbs, pronouns, technical terms) in their different works? And how far will differences appear in *known* different times of writing? Kenny's analysis is sophisticated, not cursory, but the background of general comparison seems in too early a stage for drawing decisive conclusions.

(2) The psychology of a writer as he makes later versions of earlier material is too uncertain, even if we hold the purposive context constant. Some tend to expand and refine, some to do rapid summaries. Do we know enough about Aristotle to judge which he does? For example, *NE* 3.1 deals with the voluntary and involuntary largely by specifying marks of the involuntary, but assuming (and alluding to) the general fact that voluntary acts have their source (*archē*) within the person. By contrast, *EE* 2.6 gives a general-theoretical account. But that account does not have greater depth, it is simply elaborated. The account in *NE* could then be earlier, or it could be later and briefly allusory, or it could be a later presentation of the negative approach to the problem through the marks of the involuntary as the more fruitful way, or it could be guided by a different purpose such as to give the genus of virtue. Again, the chapter in *EE* elaborates by drawing the analogy between *archai* as originating movement and as axioms in mathematics; it gives the priority to the domain of change over that of the eternal (the mathematical use is seen as analogical, the other as the strict sense). Which order in Aristotle's thought does this support? Is it a growing naturalism with a receding Platonism, which would make *EE* later, or is it the simple recognition of common usage, conforming to the analysis of *archē* in *Meta.* 5.1, which would put *EE* into the earlier period?

(3) Perhaps the most serious are cases where the general view of Aristotle's ethics comes to bear on the interpretation of specific points used to support dating. Two examples from Kenny's argument can be offered.

One concerns the relation of the good and happiness. Kenny finds a principal difference in structure: *EE* begins with the concept of happiness, whereas *NE* begins with the supreme good as the subject matter of ethics. The former treats goodness in relation to the definition of happiness; the latter treats happiness as an answer to the question of what is good (pp. 200–203). Is the structural position given to the good in *NE* a mark of greater theoretical maturity, or (perhaps) an earlier abstractness before getting down to the tasks of ethics as a practical discipline? If we regard it as a definite reconstruction (cf. Rowe 1971, pp. 26–33), then our conception of ethical theory is likely to determine our judgment of maturity. For example, the reconstruction seems to me to provide a greater theoretical scope and firmer connection of the ethics with the body of Aristotle's philosophical ideas, and so marks an advance in his systematization of ethics. A different conception of the tasks of ethics might lead to a different judgment; Kenny lists some of the features that make *EE* more appealing to an analytical philosopher in the latter half of the twentieth century (p. 4).

The second example concerns the relation of the concepts of good (*agathon*) and noble (*kalon*). *EE* (at 8.3) treats complete virtue under the concept of *kalokagathia*, which embraces both the noble and the good. In Kenny's analysis (pp. 206 ff.), the idea of the good (*agathon*) is almost reduced to a pursuit of goods as instrumental. The pursuit of virtue for its own sake is directed to the noble. If the interpretation of the noble in *NE* that I offer later in chapter 16 is correct, then *NE* differs markedly from *EE*. It contains a view of moral development in which the noble is the surrogate for the good when the child merely responds to praise without a full understanding. (The noble is what is praised, sometimes regarded by Aristotle as one step below what is prized.) Thus *NE* reverses the relation of *kalon* and *agathon* in a way more consonant with Aristotle's general ethical theory. The theory of *EE* may be more tied to earlier practical concerns, particularly if *kalokagathia* retains any political connotations of the aristocratic party for which the term *kaloi kai agathoi* seems to have been employed. (See n. 46, below.)

(4) There is always the problem of specific interpretations that are possibly given undue weight. For example, in a later book (1979) Kenny is rather vehement about Aristotle's using subsequent regret or remorse as a mark of the involuntariness of the original action. He finds the connection puzzling (p. 53) and says, "But it seems clear that a person's subsequent state of mind can have very little to do with whether a particular action is voluntary, involuntary or neither"; and again (p. 169) he says that this view is regarded as "a blot on the book in which it occurs: the *EE* is better off without it." Now it does not seem unreasonable to look among such consequences of action to find even tentative marks of a person's having acted in ignorance: if one is horrified by discovering something in what he has done, the horror may clearly be evidential that he did not intend this, and the lack of horror perhaps less decisive evidence that he may have had some such intention. It does not seem to be different in principle to use subsequent emotional reaction as evidential than to use accompanying pleasure (which Aristotle does) as evidence for a virtuous action done in a virtuous spirit.

In general, Kenny has presented a wide range of material that requires full and detailed consideration, even if in many cases the result may be to show how many presuppositions joined in the inference. The present effect of his thesis can at least be to give *EE* the kind of close attention *NE* has long had.

2. *Nic. Eth.* 1094a2 f.
3. *Part. An.* 641b24 ff.
4. E.g., *Eud. Eth.* 1227a5–9.
5. *Eud. Eth.* 1214b10–12.
6. *Nic. Eth.* 1094a20 f.
7. *Eud. Eth.* 1217b32 ff.
8. *Eud. Eth.* 1218a30.
9. Fisch 1975, p. 39, argues for a stronger interpretation: the teleology Aristotle is discussing at the outset does not concern the individual's single acts and decisions on private

occasions, it concerns practices and professions. With respect to the opening sentence of the book, in which it is said that every art (*technē*), every investigation (*methodos*), and likewise every practice (*praxis*) is thought to aim at some good—and that is why the generalization is offered that the good is what all things aim at—Fisch takes the discourse to concern the arts and crafts practiced in the *polis*. "*Technē, methodos, epistēmē,* and *gnōsis* emphasize their more theoretical aspects; *praxis, proairesis,* and *dynamis* their more practical aspects." He goes on to take the opening sentence as "*Every* art and *every* science, and likewise *every* practice and *every* profession, is taken to aim at some good; so it has been well said that the good is what is aimed at in *all* such cases."

If such an interpretation is taken (at least for chapters 1 and 2) it would obviate some of the problems about teleology, but only until the good is equated with happiness and happiness is seen to be in some sense an individual objective

10. *Nic. Eth.* 1129b4 f.

11. A clear focus on the problem, as well as the introduction of the terms *inclusive* and *dominant* for its discussion, is found in Hardie 1965, conveniently reprinted in Moravcsik 1967, pp. 297–322. See also detailed discussion of the problem and its textual evidence in John Cooper 1975, pp. 89–115. Ackrill 1974 brings out clearly the inclusive character of rationality as well as happiness in Aristotle's theory and explores the ways in which a teleology may be rendered compatible with action for its own sake by thinking in terms of part—whole and comparable relations rather than rigid means–end relations.

12. *Nic. Eth.* 1095a15–18.

13. E.g., *Nic. Eth.* 1096b10 ff.

14. This range is well summarized in *Mag. Mor.* 1.2.

15. *Top.* 1164a4 ff.

16. *Rhet.* 1.7.

17. *Eud. Eth.* 1215b23 f., 1216a11 ff.

18. *Nic. Eth.* 1097b22 f.

19. *Rhet.* 1.5.

20. *Eud. Eth.* 1244b23 ff.

21. *Nic. Eth.* 1177b33ff. This passage is a crucial one in the claim that Aristotle abandons an inclusive view of happiness, in which contemplation is integrated with the practical as a higher value among other values, for contemplation as a dominant end to which all else is to be subservient or instrumental. (See n. 11, above.) We must not, however, make too much of the purely methodological contrast of inclusive and dominant in spite of its utility, for the same kind of concrete conflict can be found whichever path is taken. If an inclusive view of happiness has the problem of integrating varied interests, a life of contemplation would have to integrate the infinity of contemplative material—unless like Aristotle's god it contemplated only one thing, itself. We could see the same problem even if happiness were identified with the possession of power. It could be an inclusive end and have the task of organizing diverse forms of acts of power; or it could make a dominant end of the psychological thrill of being in a position of power, regarding all else as a means. Similarly for pleasure: sometimes pleasure has referred to the variety of human preferences, sometimes to a specific feeling that (in the visions of science fiction) could be stimulated directly by controlling brain pleasure centers. The conclusion would seem to be that the content of the activities, not the methodological contrast, is the important thing to explore.

Most of the time, when Aristotle talks of the intellectual life, it is a concrete mode of life, virtually a vocation, contrasted with the political life or the life of the pursuit of wealth and material comfort. In the part immediately preceding the present passage, the contrast has been with the political life. But immediately after the passage the contrast becomes much sharper; it is contemplation versus *all* the virtues of practical social life. The intellectual life has now become the purely contemplative reason, and the stage has narrowed to a focus on the individual within himself. John Cooper 1975, pp. 168 ff., analyzes this as an identification of the true self with the contemplative intellect and looks to Aristotle's theory of thought in *On the Psyche* to explain the shift. But one might just as well look to the sharp dichotomy of *theōria* and *praxis* that is ingrained in the whole philosophy. At any rate the narrowing of meaning is there, along with a shedding of the calculative reason that plays a critical part in determining the mean and so is integral to virtue. If we take that passage literally, it is not just a variant emphasis in the kind of good that is supreme, nor a remark on the practical problems of how to accomodate a concrete intellectual life in a world of social practice. It is rather a full rejection of Aristotle's own ethics as he has developed it. Aristotle does not in fact take it as seriously as his commentators. He says that contemplative reason is the divine part of us, that it is authoritative and we should live according to it. But this can just as well mean we should let reason permeate our whole life, not that we should abandon everything for contemplation or steer everything to it. He recognizes that pure contemplation is a life for gods, not men. The context of the discussion is the culmination of happiness, and the passage occurs just before he moves on to the *Politics*. It is perhaps like the university president's sigh for the laboratory before he goes on to discuss the organization of faculty committees.

22. Cf. the treatment of pleasure in Ryle 1956, for example, in his essay "Pleasure." For studies of Aristotle's concept of pleasure, see Urmson 1967, Owen 1972, Gosling 1974.

23. Cf. *Psych.* 431a9 ff.; *Sens.* 436a8–11.

24. *Nic. Eth.* 1105b21 ff. The Greek terms are *hēdonē* (pleasure) and *lupē* (pain).

25. Pleasure as release of tension is expounded in *Republic* 583c3–587a1. Plato's fullest treatment of pleasure is in the *Philebus*.

26. E.g., *Nic. Eth.* 1154b17 ff.

27. *Nic. Eth.* 1154b26 ff; see also 1153a14–15.

28. *Nic. Eth.* 1173a34 ff.

29. *Nic. Eth.* 1174b31 ff.

30. *Nic. Eth.* 1175b33.

31. Such considerations based on Aristotle's remarks at this point seem to me decisive against the otherwise attractive view (Gosling 1974, p. 27) that for Aristotle pleasure perfects an activity not as something separate but as humor perfects a joke and validity perfects an argument.

32. Cf. *Nic. Eth.* 1097a28–34.

33. *Nic. Eth.* 1097b22–98a1. Hardie 1968, pp. 23–24, rejects this, largely on the assumption that it would make man an instrument. Even bodily organs are only to be thought of in this way by analogy. A cobbler can have a function and be a means only because a cobbler is an abstraction. On the other hand, Plato falls readily into this kind of language: e.g., *Republic* 1 (352d–354a) speaks of the function (*ergon*) of a horse, of eyes and ears, of pruning-knives, of the soul. In fact both Socrates and Thrasymachus take it for granted that man (the soul) has a function, but differ on what it is.

Clark is a staunch and illuminating defender of Aristotle on this issue (1975, p. 16). He quotes Aristotle himself (*Poet.* 1461a31 f.): when a word seems to imply a contradiction we should consider how many things it could mean in that context. (Aristotle goes on to say that critics jump at conclusions and find fault if a thing is inconsistent with their own fancy.) Clark takes *ergon* to be the particular form of life that "makes sense" of its function. He adds that life is acting and that to inquire into an entity's function is to be concerned with what the entity does, not what is done to it. Eventually (p. 26) he finds *ergon* and *eidos* to be identical in these contexts. We may note also that Aristotle couples *ergon* with *praxis*, so that instead of speaking of *function* we could speak of *work* and *business*—here used in an obvious teleological sense. (*Praxis* is one of the items in the list given in the first sentence of the *Nicomachean Ethics*, of things that aim at some good.)

34. *Psych.* 432a22–b7.

35. Fortenbaugh 1975a proposes a complex scheme in which Aristotle's moral psychology rests on a bipartite view of the psyche developed out of a later bipartite view of Plato's that replaced the tripartite view of the *Republic*. Aristotle's is the rational–irrational scheme, with a well-developed theory of emotion within the irrational part. Fortenbaugh maintains that it is quite distinct from the mature analysis of the psychological writings but provides the basis for the ethical and political works.

I am not sure, in spite of the complexity of the argument and its assemblage of the evidence, that it will hold together. For one thing, it seems to make a virtue of the separation of moral and intellectual that (we shall suggest later in the chapter) Aristotle is beginning to question in his mature treatment of practical wisdom. Second, the assumption that the psychological writings are unrelated in their treatment, rather than complexly interrelated (even though showing some revisions) with the ethical, is forced, as is the view that Aristotle is not criticizing all bipartite divisions in his general critique but only somebody else's. A preferable alternative is that his distinctions at various points are relative to particular—usually political—contexts, as Plato's often are. For example, even a Platonic tripartite psychology would appear as bipartite if one were ignoring the third class and simply discussing the relation of the rulers and the trainees. (In Aristotle's ethics, unlike Plato's *Republic*, we do not start with everybody initially being let into the educational system.) Again, there are too many cross-questions complicating the discussion. For example, which parts of the soul (for Plato) are associated with the body, which with the soul in itself? Did not Plutarch, moreover, follow up with a belief in a second death on the moon, after the first death had shed the appetite of the tripartite soul? In this second death the second part of the soul was shed, and only reason was left. Wilford 1959 argues that for Plato even reason expresses a mode of the soul's operation in the body, no less than the other two parts: "It does not mirror the activity, but only the aims of the soul in her true nature" (p. 58). In short, discursive reason is a consequence of embodied reason: "No doubt Socrates has been disappointed in his hope of practising dialectic in heaven." Wilford's picture of the contemplation of pure soul approximates Aristotle's god.

A further point: Fortenbaugh underestimates the vigor of the tripartite view in Plato's *Republic*. In its combination of the phenomena of honor–shame and ambition, the spirited part taps deep psychological roots, as contemporary psychoanalytic theory has shown. Plato's psychological insight was deep, and we should not believe that he lightly abandoned it. Again, the three types of lives—the intellectual, political, and material-hedonistic—express the tripartite division and are clearly evident in Aristotle. This phase is neglected in the argument.

All this is not an argument against Fortenbaugh, but grounds for suspicion that the theory of the psyche in Plato and Aristotle has complexities—social and theological as well as psychological and biological, contextual as well as textual—that make the answer a much larger and more systematic affair.

36. *Nic. Eth.* 1101a14 ff.

37. *Nic. Eth.* 1106b36 ff. The important Greek terms relevant to this definition and in what follows are *hexis* (state of character or habit), *proairesis* (choice), *mesotēs* (mean), *logos* (reason), *phronimos* (man of practical wisdom), *pathē* (emotions), and *dunameis* (capacities).

There is a variant reading to "as [*hōs*] the man of practical wisdom would determine it," which is "by which [*hōi*] the man. . . ." it is interesting to note that the difference in reading might yield a difference in interpreting social direction. Thus Jaeger (1957, pp. 58–59), who takes Aristotle here to be using a medical model, prefers *hōs* and points out that if the mean is determined by reason *as* the man of practical wisdom would determine it, we are referred to a professional judgment parallel to that of the physician. I take it that to have the mean determined by the principle (which narrows the meaning of *logos*) *by which* the man of practical wisdom would determine it, would narrow the scope of professional authority. It is almost like the rule of men versus the rule of law, debated in the *Politics*. See also n. 93 below.

38. *Nic. Eth.* 1105a31 ff.

39. *Nic. Eth.* 1099a20 f.

40. E.g., *Nic. Eth.* 1099a7–21.

41. *Eud. Eth.* 1227b8 ff.; cf. 1221b23 f.

42. *Eud Eth.* 1222a3 f.

43. *Nic. Eth.* 1115b11 f.; cf. *Mag. Mor.* 1190a28 f., *Eud. Eth.* 1229a4.

44. *Rhet.* 1366a33. An alternative is added: "or which being good, is pleasant because it is good." This preserves the same combined role for the noble; it is something worthwhile that also provokes a positive reaction.

45. *Eud. Eth.* 8.3.

46. *Eud. Eth.* 1248b16 ff. The use of this term has engendered historical controversy that has serious implications for the way moral terms are to be analyzed and how we are to understand the moral language of a given period. In his *Genealogy of Morals*, Nietzsche propounded the thesis that the two pairs "good and bad" and "good and evil" were utterly

distinct, that in origin the first represented a contrast of the aristocrat and the baseborn, while the second was a religious concept with psychological roots in the process by which the helpless mass, unable to express the will to power, turned on itself in blame. MacIntyre 1967, ch. 2, discusses the meaning of *agathos* in Homer as characterizing the role of a nobleman and so as indicative of bravery, skill in war, possession of wealth, and so on. Only when the social order changed did the question arise whether any man can be *agathos*.

Aristotle's use of *kalokagathia* in this passage of the *Eudemian Ethics* presents us with a socioethical knot that is still untied. His separation of the components here seems to put *agathos* a notch below *kalos* in that his illustration of the former is merely health; although he does say it is pursued for its own sake, it is not something to be praised, as justice is. Moreover, he goes on to describe the character that reverses the values and pursues what is noble for the sake of the natural goods. The net effect is that nobility becomes the higher criterion; this is not the case in the *Nicomachean Ethics*, where the good is the ultimate theoretical referent.

The question whether *kalos* carries a social tinge which at this point keeps it in the superior position has serious implications. It used to be assumed that *kaloi kai agathoi* did have this social, aristocratic reference; it was used not merely in the sense "the best people" but in fact for the antidemocratic elite. This view rested on materials in Thucydides, Aristophanes, Plato, Aristotle, and Xenophon. Dover 1974, pp. 41–45, has challenged this interpretation. He concludes (p. 45) that from the point of view of the poor Athenian it was applied to any who had what he himself would have liked to have (wealth, distinguished ancestors, etc.) and who was what he would have liked to be (cultured, educated, etc.). Dover does not then think it denotes a social category, even though rich and noble men might regard only their peers in these terms. On the other hand, de Ste. Croix 1972, pp. 371–76 (an additional note to Appendix 29, in which he analyzes the materials on political outlook in Aristophanes), strongly defends the traditional interpretation. He allows that expressions have a primarily moral connotation in some contexts, but insists on the political in others. He deals with a broad range of evidence (including the orators) and pays attention to changing usage as well. So far, Dover's arguments seem to me to convey simply a sense of caution in interpretation rather than to establish a conclusion. When he calls attention (p. 45) to de Ste. Croix's remark that Aristophanes does not ridicule the wealthy as such and adds "But did anybody?" one is reminded of Plato's picture in *Republic* 8 (556d) of the sturdy poor man next in battle line to the fat rich man who is puffing despairingly—which makes the poor man decide he is the equal of the rich and move to overthrow the oligarchy. Even here we would have to refine the point to see whether it was directed against the aristocrats or the money-loving oligarchy. I rest content in this context with suggesting the stake that the analysis of the ethical terms has in this controversy. Conceivably their relation might add at least tangential evidence on both issues.

47. *Eud. Eth.* 1216b3–25.

48. *Nic. Eth.* 1103a3 ff. The Greek terms here are *dianoētikai* (intellectual) and *ēthikai* (moral).

49. See Tracy 1969.

50. Burnet 1900, p. 71, compares the mean established in the virtuous man to the qualitative change expressed in a chemical formula, for instance the combination of hydrogen and oxygen resulting in water. His point is that it is not merely a quantitative *more* or *less*.

51. *Nic. Eth.* 1109a26 ff.

52. *Nic. Eth.* 4.3; Joachim 1951, p. 125. However, Joachim goes on to say that the principle behind the proud man's claim is that "moral worth has absolute value, and can therefore never be adequately measured by any such valuable things." Cf. also Gauthier 1958, pp. 118–23, where *magnanimité* is treated as a kind of autarchy of spirit that attains through a sense of grandeur and honor a consciousness of being a value worthy of honor and a consciousness of its right.

53. Cf. Austin 1961, pp. 123–52, "A Plea for Excuses". For an example of the view that Aristotle does approach the free will problem obliquely but gets in trouble because he has not gone far enough and has no concept of the will, see Gauthier 1958, pp. 37–45. Gauthier

sees Aristotle's use of *voluntary* (*hekōn*) as capable of expansion into a general idea of consent. He takes voluntary activity, capable of determining itself, to provide the only true foundation for morality. It is worth noting that Gauthier's interpretation of the *Nicomachean Ethics* uses Nuyens's developmental framework for Aristotle's psychology (see above, chapter 9, n. 10). He maintains along the lines worked out in Gauthier and Jolif (1958) that the *Nicomachean Ethics* belongs to the stage in which the psyche is thought to work through a biological instrument which it dominates, and that Aristotle has not yet reached the hylomorphic position of *On the Psyche*. The fate of Gauthier's interpretation is therefore largely bound up with Nuyens' specific schema. In the present book I have accepted the critique of that schema in current studies, following Block's lead as suggested in the note mentioned above.

54. *Nic. Eth.* 1110a15 ff. The relevant Greek terms are *archē* (origin), *en autōi* (in him), and *ep' autōi* (upon him).

55. *Nic. Eth.* 1110b2 f. The relevant Greek terms are *aitia* (cause) and *baia* (forced).

56. *Nic. Eth.* 1113b18 f.

57. *Eud. Eth.* 2.6. The relation of this conception of the origin of action to Aristotle's physical analysis of self-motion is discussed in Furley 1978.

58. It is interesting to note that this passage is invoked in a recent claim that Aristotle was aware of geometrical reflections akin to non-Euclidean geometry before the time of Euclid. See Tóth 1969, pp. 92–93.

59. *Top.* 133a28; *Rhet.* 1392b18–24.

60. *Nic. Eth.* 1114a11–21.

61. Aristotle offers this illustration in *Eud. Eth.* 1225b32 f. The Greek terms relevant in pinpointing choice are *epithumia* (desire), *thumos* (passion), *boulēsis* (wish), *doxa* (opinion), *logos* (reason), *dianoia* (understanding), and *orexis* (appetite).

62. *Mov. An.* 700b17 ff.; cf. *Psych.* 414b2. See above, chapter 11.

63. *Nic. Eth.* 1112a15 f.: *probebouleumenon*, from the verb "to deliberate," with *pro* as prefix.

64. *Nic. Eth.* 1112b15 ff.

65. *Nic. Eth.* 1112b25 ff.

66. For an analysis of Aristotle's conception of choice, examining what appear to be contradictions in the notion of dealing only with means and comparing the accounts in the *Nicomachean Ethics* and *Eudemian Ethics*, see Aubenque 1963, pp. 119–25. For recent analyses directed against the view that choice deals only with means in the narrow sense, see Hardie 1968, pp. 255–57; Ackrill 1974; and John Cooper 1975, pp. 19–22. The chief tendency in this recent literature is to try to liberalize the notion of means in the means–end model. Perhaps it is time to start at the other extreme and recognize that the category affiliation of *pros ti* makes its use much broader; the means–end model is only one special case, and Aristotle very often has other uses in mind. One head-on attack against the usual translations is found in Fortenbaugh 1965. He finds a conjunction of two vocabularies in these Aristotelian contexts; one is a means–end language, the other a syllogistic language; he takes *ta pros ta telos* to be quite parallel to the relation of two extreme terms *pros to meson* (to the middle term) in the syllogistic vocabulary. He seems to press this quite literally in looking for a practical syllogistic structure in deliberation. While the reference to possible alternate structures is helpful in liberating deliberation from enslavement to the means–end model, it would be sad to shackle it immediately to a would-be rescuer. A more likely possibility is to follow the path suggested later in this chapter in the discussion of reason (*logos*): to interpret in terms of a wider schema that would allow a variety of more specific models.

67. *Nic. Eth.* 1112b29 ff.

68. For the liberation from the tyranny of the means–end model, see n. 66 above. Cooper 1975, ch. 1, and Ackrill 1974 are particularly helpful for the analysis of ways in which deliberation can center around ends under the revised conception. For similar concern also with the rule–case model, see Wiggins 1976. For a concern with limits and whether Aristotle is driven to be a Humean in his theory of desire and deliberation, raised in chapter 11, n. 9 above, see Irwin 1975. (His answer seems to be "Not quite; but. . . .")

69. *Nic. Eth.* 1113a4 ff.

70. *Nic. Eth.* 1113a11 ff. "The deliberative appetite of things that depend on us" is *bouleutikē orexis tōn eph' hēmin*.

71. Aubenque 1963, p. 125, makes the point bluntly: to approach the notion of *proairesis* in the perspective of the problem of the "freedom of the will" is to condemn oneself to look in the Aristotelian texts for what is not to be found there and to neglect what is to be found there. What is not to be found there is a doctrine of freedom and responsibility. What is to be found there is a new contribution to an ontology and an anthropology of action. See also Kenny 1979, pp. vii–viii. He takes it for granted that Aristotle had no theory of the will, that "the will is a phenomenon of introspective consciousness." He finds that contemporary attempts to pass by this chapter in the history of philosophy and "build afresh a philosophical theory of the springs of human action" strongly resemble the Aristotelian view. The task of such reconstruction is to relate human action to ability, desire, and belief. He finds that Aristotle furnishes corresponding material on voluntariness, intentionality, and rationality.

72. *Eud. Eth.* 1232a13.

73. *Athenian Constitution* 28, section 5.

74. *Nic. Eth.* 1139a12. The part that has reason is *to logon echon*. The faculty of knowledge is *to epistēmonikon*, the calculative *to logistikon*.

75. Gauthier and Jolif 1958, vol. 1, p. 45, in the definition of virtue, do translate the part dealing with *logos* (coming after "a mean relative to us") as "dont la norme est la règle morale." The attempt to construe *logos* as a moral rule will be considered later in this chapter.

At the other extreme, the attempt to treat *logos* and even *orthos logos* as simply reason within us cannot be wholly ruled out. For example, in the *Eudemian Ethics* (1249b3 ff.) Aristotle says: "Now in what was said earlier, the standard was 'as *logos* directs.' This is as if in matters of diet one were to say 'as medical science and its *logos* directs,' and this though true is not clear." (In the earlier passages there was mention both of *orthos logos* and of *judging rightly*.) In such a passage *logos* in the first use can easily mean reason, and in the second simply the answers that reason gives which may take the form of principles. See below, n. 79, on *orthos logos*.

76. *Nic. Eth.* 1112b8–11.

77. For example, Peck 1953, pp. iv–v, calls attention to a passage (*Gen. An.* 767a14 ff.) in which Aristotle says, "For all things that come into being according to art or nature are in a certain logos [*logōi tini*]"; he translates the latter part as "exists in virtue of some due proportion." Aristotle goes on to say that if the hot is too powerful it dries up the fluid things; if very deficient it fails to make them set; it must have *ton tou mesou logon*, which Peck takes as the mean proportional. Now the definition of virtue uses parallel language: the mean relative to us determined by rational principle (*logōi*).

78. *Nic. Eth.* 1114b29.

79. E.g., *Nic. Eth.* 1144b23 f. The occurrence of the phrase *orthos logos* without explanation may mean either that it is used in a very obvious sense or that it has an already established technical use taken for granted and so needing no explanation. It is therefore a tempting plum for the scholarly palate. In one direction the meaning leans toward the "rational rule" and the moral law, in the other toward simply a "correct account." The obvious move is to track down the historical antecedents of the usage. For a well-documented study, see Dirlmeier 1960. The Platonic origins of the phrase are treated on pp. 298–304: *orthos logos* starts from a "correct account," almost as in "correct belief," but gathers normative force, operating as a kind of true opinion in the soul. For Plato the norm is the Idea; in rejecting the Platonic Idea, Aristotle is left with the norm in us as a kind of calculative discourse of the psyche.

Düring 1957, in his review of Dirlmeier's first edition (1956), criticizes this interpretation of *orthos logos*, seeing it rather as an intellectual qualitative capacity (p. 182). He takes *orthos logos* as synonymous with correct judgment and quotes the comparison to seeing correctly (1143b14). Düring also points out that Dirlmeier's interpretation is affected by his general hypothesis that Aristotle's views developed out of Plato's, whereas Düring assumes the constancy of Aristotle's general position throughout. See Düring 1960 for his own interpretation: Aristotle substituted "nature" for Plato's ideas, and so the search for the natural and the wise man's insight in applying the knowledge of nature's order furnished the normative judgments.

80. Aristotle's full treatment of the various virtues and vices—for which there is no place in the present book—has its own fascination and is well worth detailed study. It has had considerable influence in literature on character study, initially through Theophrastus' *Characters* with its vignettes of types. More importantly, it has inspired the detailed study of the virtues in the history of ethics. For example, in the twentieth century, the most comprehensive treatment of moral values, Hartmann 1932, vol. 2, had its inspiration directly from the *Nicomachean Ethics*, which the translator's preface (vol. 1, p. 11) tells us Hartmann studied in the trenches in World War I; it was the only book he had besides one volume of Nietzsche, and from it arose the chapters of volume 2 on the virtues. Hartmann's approach is phenomenological and tends toward a distillation of essence rather than a presentation of cultural fullness and variety, but it does constitute the most systematic work in the phenomenological approach.

81. Gauthier 1958, p. 48. See also n. 53 above.

82. Gauthier 1958, p. 67.

83. Gauthier 1958, p. 87.

84. Gauthier 1958, p. 88.

85. In Brochard 1926. This essay first appeared in *Revue philosphique* in 1901. Brochard's influence in Aristotelian interpretation is dealt with more amply in Gauthier and Jolif 1958, pp. 565–68.

86. Brochard 1926, pp. 491–92.

87. Brochard 1926, p. 533.

88. Brochard 1926, p. 503.

89. *Nic. Eth.* 5.6.

90. Perhaps this should not surprise us. We expect greater localism in the primitive world and the ancient world. It is only since the eighteenth century that one-world universalisms have become intensified; Kantian morality and philosophy of history give forceful expression to it, as does almost all subsequent moral philosophy reflecting the spread of communications and the growing economic unification of the world. (Aristotle, as we shall see, takes the Greeks-versus-barbarians approach to politics, in contrast to Alexander's broader outlook.) On the other hand, the belief in a common human nature is an old one and usually has normative consequences. Perhaps the balance that Aristotle strikes is a "mean." There is some universalism at the borders of the morality, but it does not penetrate to the core; certainly it will not be allowed into the *meaning* of *ought*.

91. *Mag. Mor.* 1208b37 ff.

92. Implicit in the foregoing remarks on the combination and separation of functions and their relation to concepts is of course a general approach to the comparative study of ethical theories. At this point it seems to be quite in line with Aristotle's own view of the relation of function, context, and concept as illustrated earlier from the *Rhetoric* (at the opening of chapter 4 above). The general lesson for ethical theorizing is that ethical conceptual constructions may take different shapes with respect to the same functions, and that therefore their comparative evaluation is an important task of ethics. This is especially urgent today in light of the large theoretical superstructures that have been built on the allegedly simple concept of obligation. Aristotle's ethics here constitutes an extraordinarily useful case study for comparison.

For studies in the foundations of comparative ethics, see Edel 1963.

93. That the concept of the man of practical wisdom carries a strong authoritarian potential in the Aristotelian ethics is not to be denied. But it would be locked in place only if it turned out to be the primitive concept to which all the others in the network were reduced—not if the gains (and problems) kept being passed on from concept to concept. Aubenque 1968, a study of practical wisdom in Aristotle, raises in an interesting way the roots of the concept of the *phronimos* (the man of practical wisdom) in the aristocratic tradition (p. 63). It also provides a brief indication of the contrasting schools of interpretation of the notion (pp. 27–29), arguing that the controversy whether Aristotle's practical wisdom is intellectualist or empiricist is asking the wrong question. Aubenque's point is that

the *phronimos*, as Aristotle pictures him, combines many of the opposites (for instance, applying the right rule to the contingent particular) but does not have a Platonic science of the good that is teachable knowledge; the central question thus becomes whence he derives his authority (pp. 39–41). Aubenque makes the neat contrast with Aristotle's position in the *Politics* (which we will note in chapter 18): Aristotle wants a government of laws, not, as Plato did, a government of men; but in the *Nicomachean Ethics* men of practical wisdom as the living carriers of the norms constitute the moral authority!

Aubenque also provides an interesting view of the interlocking of interpretation and practical concerns. What, he asks (p. 55), are the examples of men of practical wisdom suggested by different interpreters? Gauthier accepts Aristotle's mentioning Pericles, but wants *phronimos* translated as "sage" and says that in the eyes of all Frenchmen Gandhi more than Einstein or Bergson fits the type. Jaeger goes for "Realpolitik" as Aristotle's approach, for Aristotle had consorted with men like Hermias of Atarneus. Aubenque accordingly wants to know whether our choice for the *phronimos* has to be between Gandhi and Bismarck.

94. *Nic. Eth.* 1139a22 ff.
95. *Nic. Eth.* 1139a31–b4.
96. *Nic. Eth.* 1140b5 f.
97. *Nic. Eth.* 1142a23–30.
98. Joachim, whose idealism emerges strongly in his commentary on the *Nicomachean Ethics* (1951), simply takes the "see" when we say that "we see that 'this has to be done'" as metaphorical (p. 212). It cannot be perception through one of the five senses, nor a common sensible. He adds, "Aristotle compares this kind of immediate apprehension to the seeing that the 'last' thing is a triangle: i.e. (apparently) that in the geometrical problem in question the last step in the geometer's inquiry and the first step in the construction is a triangle." He thus points the meaning toward the process of inquiry and what makes the subsequent choice possible.
99. John Cooper 1975, pp. 39–40. For the full presentation, see pp. 34–41 and the appendix, pp. 183–86. Earlier suggestion of a process interpretation is found in Burnet 1900, p. 273, who however at the same time speaks of the ultimate individual which can be analyzed no further. Gauthier and Jolif 1959, vol. 2, part 2, p. 503, refer to Burnet's interpretation, pointing out that he would like to mean by *to eschaton* the last term of the deliberation, but add that this sense seems here excluded by the context. Stewart 1892, vol. 2, p. 77, had earlier made a clear suggestion in favor of process: "This *eschaton* is a *particular reached at last*, and recognized *as a means now to be taken* for the attainment of the end in view." Cooper's analysis is particularly convincing because he makes an investigation of *eschaton* as a separate problem and broadens the base of the evidence; also because he is careful to see where the individual and where the species is intended; and finally because throughout he keeps the investigation of the textual passages related to the contexts of practical deliberation and choice with which Aristotle is concerned.
100. *Nic. Eth.* 1142b33 f..
101. Some Greek terms of interest in these contexts are *euboulia* (deliberative excellence), *sunesis* (understanding), *epitaktikē* (authoritative), and *kritikē* (judgmental). For a useful analysis of the role of intellect in virtue, that focuses largely on practical wisdom, see Sorabji 1974b.
102. *Nic. Eth.* 1143b22 ff.
103. *Nic. Eth.* 1144a8 f.
104. *Nic. Eth.* 1144a36 f.
105. *Nic. Eth.* 1144b3 f. Cleverness is *deinotēs*; natural virtue, *phusikē aretē*; complete or true virtue, *kuria aretē*; the truly good (mentioned below) *to kuriōs agathon*.
106. *Nic. Eth.* 1144b25 ff.
107. *Mag. Mor.* 1199b36 ff.
108. *Top.* 146b36 ff.
109. *Top.* 111a1 ff.
110. *Nic. Eth.* 3.4.
111. *Psych.* 428b3 f.
112. *Nic. Eth.* 1155b22 ff.

113. *Eud. Eth.* 1235b33–36a7.

114. E.g., *Eud. Eth.* 1237a17 f.; cf. 1248b28 ff.

115. See Dewey 1960. For value theory, seen with freshness as an experiment, see Laird 1929. He writes (p. xix): "It is possible that the current philosophy of value is essentially new; with the wine of adventure in its veins. Value *may* prove to be the key that will eventually release all the human sciences from their present position of pathetic, if dignified, futility." But he adds reservations.

CHAPTER 17

1. *Eud. Eth.* 1221a4, 22 ff. Relevant Greek terms are *kerdos* (profit), *zēmia* (loss), and *dikaion* (just).

2. *Nic. Eth.* 1162b21 ff.

3. *Nic. Eth.* 1129b15–19.

4. Aristotle speaks of justice in distributions (*to en tais dianomais*) and corrective justice (*to diorthōtikon*). These are accordingly not so much different species of justice as justice engaged in two kinds of tasks. For their analysis, see *Nic. Eth.* 5.2 (1130b30)–5.4.

5. *Nic. Eth.* 1130b31 f.

6. *Nic. Eth.* 1131a24 ff. The Greek phrase for "according to merit" is *kat' axian*.

7. The relevant discussion appears at *Nic. Eth.* 1132b31. The reference to *Mag. Mor.* is 1194a29. The Greek term for reciprocity is *to antipeponthos*. For a clarifying examination of the text on reciprocity, see M. I. Finley, 1974, pp. 31 ff.

8. *Nic. Eth.* 1137b14 ff.

9. *Nic. Eth.* 1137b29 ff. r

10. *Nic. Eth.* 1145a15–b2. The Greek terms for the various characters are *kakia* (vice), *akrasia* (incontinence), *thēriotēs* (brutishness), *aretē* (virtue), *enkrateia* (continence), *huper hēmas aretē* (superhuman virtue), *malakia* (softness), *truphē* (effeminacy), and *karteria* (endurance). Aristotle's account of what remains to be discussed begins at *Nic. Eth.* 1145a35 ff.

Of all these (apart from virtue and vice in the earlier books) it is the negative, *akrasia*, that here wins chief attention from Aristotle and in contemporary discussion. For a full discussion of Aristotle's concept in its Socratic and Platonic background, and of the variety of contemporary interpretations, see Walsh 1963.

11. *Nic. Eth.* 1145b8–20.

12. *Nic. Eth.* 1146a16–21; cf. 1146a28 ff.

13. *Nic. Eth.* 1146a9–13.

14. The idea of a "wrong" *logos* carries different connotations according to the meaning of *logos* that is uppermost. If *logos* is a principle or formula, then a wrong *logos* is a false one (as in *Nic. Eth.* 1151a32). On the other hand, in *Mag. Mor.* 1203b28 the *logos* of the vicious man is a consenting party to evildoing. Here *logos* is not a rule but an inner guide, though it is not treated as on a par with the inner guide of the virtuous man. This kind of wrong *logos* is declared to be unhealthy (1203a24 ff.).

15. *Nic. Eth.* 1145b25 ff.

16. *Nic. Eth.* 1145b21 f. has been taken to ask how incontinence is possible. But Hardie 1968, p. 266, has argued convincingly that it should not be construed as asking how a person can be incontinent if he understands rightly, but rather in what sense a person is understanding rightly in being incontinent. (The Greek is *pōs hupolambanōn orthōs akrateuetai tis*.) His chapter 13 gives an excellent study of the variety of interpretations of *akrasia* and reviews the controversies over specific textual passages.

17. *Nic. Eth.* 1146b29 f.

18. *Nic. Eth.* 1146b31–35.

19. *Nic. Eth.* 1146b35–47a10.

20. *Nic. Eth.* 1147a18 ff.

21. *Nic. Eth.* 1147a24 f.

22. *Nic. Eth.* 1147a29 ff.

23. Something like this conclusion seems to me to be reached by another route through

the analysis of choice by Anscombe 1965, pp. 143–50. (The remainder of her paper deals with the practical syllogism.) Anscombe's point is that you have to have a basic goal back of the choice to make a choice. The licentious (vicious) man can choose, if he aims at pleasure. But the incontinent man is in a state of inner conflict and so never really chooses.

24. *Nic. Eth.* 1147b6 ff.

25. The expression "the myth of the practical syllogism" is a strong one, but I have meant it here in the spirit in which Aristotle recommends that the bent stick be bent back in the opposite direction in order to straighten it out. The attempt to exploit the parallelism of the theoretical and the practical has of course a long history with many twists, but its rise in Aristotelian interpretation as a minor industry in the mid-twentieth century (giving rise in turn to a counterindustry of its deflation) is an intellectual phenomenon that needs some explanation. I suspect that the scenario at least in part runs something like this. Problems in ethical theory, in the wake of G. E. Moore's standardization of the "naturalistic fallacy," took the shape of a conflict between a descriptivist, "naturalistic" definition of ethical terms and a more active, "prescriptivist" interpretation. In the latter, ethics began to be construed in a more active first-person decisional practical way rather than from the observer's reporting perspective. By the later 1940s it had occurred to some philosophers that Aristotle's treatment of ethics as *praxis* made him a natural ally, and if he talked of a practical syllogism and even of an action as a conclusion, that would place him squarely alongside the prescriptivists. Anscombe 1958, p. 59, probably expressed the prevalent mood when she said of Aristotle, "It was, I am sure, perfectly clear to him that he had found a completely different form of reasoning from theoretical reasoning, or proof syllogism; but it pleased him to give cases of it which made it as parallel as possible to the theoretical syllogism." Philosophers went in different directions. Some accepted a practical syllogism in principle and moved to prescriptive logics. Some, like Anscombe herself, looked to Aristotle's more general theory of deliberation and the good to find what distinguished his practical from his theoretical reasoning. Cf. Mothersill 1962, who concludes her analysis of Anscombe with the assertion that "the logic of intention is distinctive and not to be confused with the logic of science or with the logic of morals." Others rested content with criticizing Aristotle for the practical syllogism, suggesting that he had not worked it out clearly enough (cf. Milo 1966, pp. 44–57.). In the old tradition the sins of the father were visited on the child; here it appears, the sins of the children are visited on the father.

The enterprise of expanding the practical syllogism did not stay within the confines of one philosophical school. After all, Kant has as good a claim to generate disputes about "practical reason" as Aristotle. Thus Ando 1958, ch. 5, seemed very reasonable in refining the Aristotelian conception by pointing out that most of the examples of the practical syllogism were really the *productive syllogism*, concerned with making or getting products; the practical syllogism would concern itself with doing virtuous acts and would have as a conclusion "what I ought to do" as virtuous conduct.

Comments on passages and occasional articles by classical philosophers on the practical syllogism had appeared from time to time; see, e.g., Allan 1955. By the end of the 1960s it was time to set the record straight with fresh reviews of the Aristotelian text. The reader will find this done with thoroughness by Hardie 1968, ch. 12, John Cooper 1975, ch. 1, secs. 2–4, and Nussbaum 1978, Interpretive Essay 4. The one possibly additional aspect that I have stressed is the *scientific* context in which Aristotle's examples occur—the context in which he is studying how movement gets started in causal terms, how far general or particular opinions or desire play a role, and how the direction of movement becomes diverted. It is, in short, the context of psychological explanation, not logical reasoning. Our very translations sometimes insert the term *premise* when *belief* or *opinion* might be more appropriate.

The breakdown of the practical syllogism has even reached the point of textual reconsideration. Kenny 1979, pp. 111–12, reminds us, following Hardie, that the passage in the *Nicomachean Ethics* that was central in launching the language of "practical syllogism" has been generally misconstrued. The words *hoi gar sullogismoi tōn praktōn archēn echontes eisi* (1144a31 f.) should not be translated as Ross does, "the syllogisms which deal with acts to be done are things which involve a starting-point," but rather as "those syllogisms which contain the starting-point of acts to be done are. . . ." In short, it is not a question here of practical syllogisms as a unit, but of syllogisms that talk about the end or the highest good. For discussion of the passage, including the possibility that *syllogism* here is used in a wider sense of reasoning and that *archēn* here does not necessarily mean a major premise, see Hardie 1968, pp. 249–54. Kenny decides that "in spite of its misleading overtones the expression 'practical syllogism' is now so enshrined in the tradition of Aristotelian commentary that it would be foolish to attempt to substitute a new technical term" (p. 113). Of course one could simply abandon it without a substitution and talk of reflecting or reasoning about ends.

26. *Nic. Eth.* 1148a11 f.

27. *Nic. Eth.* 1148a17 f.

28. *Nic. Eth.* 1150a12–15. The Greek terms that follow are *propeteia* (impetuousness), and *astheneia* (weakness).

29. *Nic. Eth.* 1151b5 ff.

30. *Nic. Eth.* 1152a20 ff.

31. *Nic. Eth.* 1129b26 f.

32. *Nic. Eth.* 1130a3 f. The Greek terms are *koinōnia* (association) and *allotrion agathon* (another's good).

33. *Nic. Eth.* 1141b30 f.

34. *Nic. Eth.* 1155a5 f.

35. *Nic. Eth.* 1156a3 ff. This definition is well formulated and amplified in *Rhet.* 2.4. See also John Cooper 1977a.

36. *Nic. Eth.* 1158a24 f.

37. *Nic. Eth.* 1159b35 ff., 1158b29 ff.

38. *Nic. Eth.* 1164a22 ff.

39. *Nic. Eth.* 1166b32 ff. The relevant Greek terms are *eunoia* (goodwill) and *homonoia* (concord). On benefactors' love, see *Nic. Eth.* 1167b17 ff.

40. *Nic. Eth.* 1159a11 f.; cf. *Eud. Eth.* 1218a30 ff., which states the general point that it is not true that all things that are seek one good; each seeks its own good.

41. *Nic. Eth.* 1158a26.

42. *Nic. Eth.* 1168b12–25.

43. *Nic. Eth.* 1169a11 ff.

44. *Nic. Eth.* 1168a28.

45. *Nic. Eth.* 1168b1 ff.

46. *Nic. Eth.* 1166a19 ff.

47. *Nic. Eth.* 1169a17 ff.

48. *Nic. Eth.* 1170a25–b19. For a detailed analysis of Aristotle's arguments on the value of friendship, see John Cooper 1977b.

CHAPTER 18

1. *Pol.* 1264a3 f.

2. *Nic. Eth.* 1162a17 f. A pairing creature is *sunduastikon*; a political or social one, *politikon*.

3. *Pol.* 1280b22 ff. This contrast underscores the importance of the notion of *koinōnia* (community). M. I. Finley 1974, pp. 31–32, has a relevant comment on this notion, though it is made in the context of interchange of services and the idea of reciprocity. Noting the breadth of the notion, as covering associations from the *polis* to temporary ones even in exchange of goods, he specifies the conditions for genuine *koinōnia*: the members must be freemen, with a common purpose, sharing something (from mere place to the desire for the good life), expressing mutuality (*philia*), and dealing fairly. The parallel to the discussion of friendship is evident. (It also suggests why business associations may, but need not, be cases of friendship.)

4. *Pol.* 1327b31 ff.

5. This shift in view itself constitutes an interesting chapter (with valuable lessons) in historical interpretation. That Alexander identified with an ideal of the unity of mankind is argued at length by Tarn 1948, vol. 2, esp. pp. 399–449 (the basic hypothesis was of course,

advanced much earlier). Tracing the roots of Stoic universalism, he finds that Theophrastus asserts that all men are kin and bound by friendship (*philia*), and he concludes that something happened between Aristotle's time and Theophrastus'—it can only be Alexander. Pulling together and reinterpreting scattered fragments, Tarn decides that Alexander enunciated that God is the common father of mankind, that various races should live in unity, and that various peoples in the empire are to be thought of as partners rather than subjects. He traces a keynote in the conception of *homonoia* (Latin *concordia*), a likeness of mind and sentiment of unity that Isocrates had carried from the unity of the family into an idea of national unity. The core of Tarn's position is thus that Alexander had a vision of brotherhood as well as a policy of fusion for Greeks and Persians.

Evaluation of the fragmentary sources is of course crucial. Ehrenberg 1938 had already arrived at a quite different conclusion (p. 109): it is "a mistake to regard Alexander's object the idea of a cultural unity of empire and world. Unity for him was enclosed in his own person." His practical program, as Ehrenberg sees it, was to create a uniform subjection.

The most systematic attack on Tarn's thesis is to be found in the work of Badian (e.g., 1958, on reexamining the fragments; 1968, on Alexander's actual relations with the Greek cities in Asia Minor). By the early 1970s the revisionist outlook appears to have become standard. For example, Hamilton 1973, p. 163, tells us that "as a politician, too, Alexander was pragmatic. He was not concerned with the 'Brotherhood of Man' or the 'Unity of Mankind.' His 'policy of fusion,' it must be emphasized, was confined to Persians and Macedonians." Badian, however, did not stop at this point but went on to draw the professional historian's lessons about the motives in doing history. He traces (1976) the kinds of ideals that were projected on Alexander, in the context of modern history: "Tarn merely substituted the ideals of his own environment for those of German Kultur as the precise content of the benefit conferred on the conquered" (p. 287). (There was a traditional German near-worship of Alexander.) He points out that though Tarn developed his view in the 1920s and 1930s, its dominance came after he published his two-volume work in 1948, in the atmosphere of the United Nations; "it embodied the proud nostalgia of the British ruling classes, and at the same time appealed to the sentimental international imperialism characteristic of American intellectuals in those days Before the Fall" (p. 290). Badian concludes (p. 300) that it is time to declare a moratorium on comprehensive books and all-embracing theories and to do real work on the sources. I take it that such work will show whether we have ground for larger theorizing again, and whether Badian has himself been overreacting to the reaction or himself expressing "the Fall."

6. *Pol.* 1326b14 ff.

7. *Pol.* 1253b20–23. Slavery in ancient times has proved by no means a simple concept. For a general conceptual and socioeconomic study of its complexities and the dangers of seeing it through modern eyes, see M. I. Finley 1973, ch. 3. Even those who regarded it as conventional rather than natural in ancient times could very well have accepted it as an institution, as they accepted war with its harsh and often unjust fate for the losers. Finley also (1975, pp. 184–85) finds suspect the alleged utopias of antiquity that involve abandoning the institution. Slave revolts, he adds, were generally "neither salvationist nor Utopian. Their aims were to obtain freedom for themselves at the minimum, to turn the social relations upside down at the maximum; to turn themselves into masters and their former masters into slaves, but not to alter the fundamental structure of society."

8. *Nic. Eth.* 1161a32–b8.

9. For the underlying psychology, see *Pol.* 1260a5–14. For hunting the slaves, see *Pol.* 1256b23 ff.

10. *Gen. An.* 766a31 ff.; cf. 739b20 ff.

11. *Pol.* 1259a37 ff.

12. *Rhet.* 1367a16 ff.

13. *Pol.* 1332b35 ff.

14. *Pol.* 1275b18 f.

15. *Pol.* 1278a20 ff.

16. *Pol.* 1333a41 ff.

17. *Pol.* 1333b23 ff.

18. *Pol.* 1337b8–15.

19. *Pol.* 1328b39–29a2.
20. *Pol.* 1279b39–80a3.
21. *Pol.* 1293a12–34.
22. *Pol.* 1291b30–92a37.
23. *Pol.* 1292b27 ff.
24. *Pol.* 1291b17–30. The Greek term for notables, *gnōrimoi*, is sometimes used as an equivalent for the *kaloi kai agathoi*; see chapter 16, n. 46.
25. *Pol.* 1291b7.
26. *Rhet..* 2.16.
27. *Pol.* 1321a5–14.
28. *Pol.* 1289a1 f.
29. *Pol.* 1283a41 ff., 1332a36.
30. *Pol.* 1302a8 ff.
31. *Pol.* 1263b23 f.
32. *Pol.* 1267b2–5.
33. *Pol.* 1318b40 ff.
34. *Rhet.* 1382b4 f.
35. *On Prophecy in Sleep* 462b20 f.
36. *Pol.* 1310a8–12.
37. *Pol.* 1307b40 ff.; cf. 1397a7–13.
38. *Pol.* 1310a30 ff., 1317a40–b38.
39. *Pol.* 1292a6 ff., 1310a4 f.
40. *Pol.* 1281a14–17.
41. *Pol.* 1295b1–21.
42. *Pol.* 1294a30–b40.
43. *Pol.* 1318a21–b5.
44. *Pol.* 1309b31 f.
45. *Pol.* 1297a7–13.
46. *Athenian Constitution* 28, section 5; also 36–37.
47. *Pol.* 1 and 2. There would seem to be two methodological policies involved, pointing in opposite directions. One is to regard Aristotle as having an economic theory, but one that involves the economics of an earlier form of society. This looks for the continuities and studies ideas and institutional traits for what they contribute as precursor forms to later ideas and institutions. The other is to stress the discontinuities, to insist on the profound difference of the phenomena, the ancient economy having no "enormous conglomeration of interdependent markets" (M. I. Finley 1973, p. 34, using Erich Roll's phrase). Finley follows the second policy in his examination of the ancient economy (ch. 1) and in insisting that economic science dates only from the eighteenth century, when conditions had changed. There is something to be said for using both methodological policies alternately, but each at its appropriate time, to correct prevalent one-sided tendencies. Finley's concrete relation of the ideational and the socioeconomic is persuasive as to the needs of current emphasis and critique. The problem arises, of course, in relation to all disciplines and institutional studies, not merely economics, and even in tracing the antecedents of philosophical ideas. Perhaps eventually we will have a fuller evolutionary model that can use the notion of precursor ideas in a responsible way that integrates both continuities and discontinuities. For further suggestions on relations of institution and idea, see the Epilogue.
48. *Pol.* 1253b37 f.
49. *Pol.* 1258a38–b18.
50. *Pol.* 1256b1 ff.
51. *Pol.* 1327a27 f.
52. *Pol.* 1263a3 ff.
53. *Pol.* 1329b36 f.
54. *Pol.* 1286a8 ff.
55. *Pol.* 1287a31 f.
56. *Pol.* 1286a12 ff.
57. *Pol.* 1269a20 f.
58. *Pol.* 1337a1 f.

59. *Pol.* 1338b1 ff.
60. *Pol.* 1341a13–17.

Part 6

INTRODUCTION

1. *Rhet.* 1356b28 ff.
2. *Nic. Eth.* 1140a1–23. The Greek for "rational state" is a state *meta logou*, "with reason."
3. *Top.* 101a27 ff.
4. *Pol.* 1330a34–31b23.
5. Farrington 1944, vol. 1, has called attention to the sharp distinction made early in the history of science between the sciences that dealt with nature and those useful for the administration of men, and the social conditions that gave the latter a privileged place.

CHAPTER 19

1. *Rhet.* 1354a24 f.
2. *Rhet.* 1355b26 f.
3. *Rhet.* 1361a36 f.
4. *Rhet.* 1355a20 ff.
5. *Rhet.* 1375a27 ff.
6. *Rhet.* 1376a17 ff.
7. *Rhet.* 1376b31 ff.
8. *Rhet.* 1395b10 ff.
9. *Rhet.* 1404a5 ff.
10. *Top.* 156b18 ff.
11. *Top.* 158a7 ff.

CHAPTER 20

1. *Poet.* 1453b10 f. "Proper" is *oikeian* (own, distinctive).
2. *Poet.* 1448b4–19.
3. *Poet.* 1460b10 f.
4. Cf. *Pol.* 1340a18 ff.; also the contrast with painting as indirect, 1340a32–39.
5. *Pol.* 1342a4–16.
6. Bosanquet 1904, pp. 60–61.
7. *Psych.* 429a1 ff.
8. *Poet.* 1449a14 f.
9. Else 1957, p. 222 ff.
10. *Poet.* 1455b15.
11. John Jones 1967 makes the primacy of action a ground for revising many of the traditional views about the *Poetics*. Relying heavily on Aristotle's assertion that tragedy is a representation not of men but of action and life (1450a16), he argues that the usual interpretations have shifted the order of importance by focusing on an alleged "tragic hero." This shift involves seeing the action as pointing to the inner man, rather than seeing character, in Aristotle's formulation (1450b8 f.), as what reveals the choices people make and the acts they shun. Jones also emphasizes that Aristotle uses the plural in describing what the dramatic protagonists should be like, as well as the phenomena of reversal of situation, surprise revelation, precipitating flaws, and so on—in effect, treating them all as situational properties of the action—whereas translations sometimes employ the singular (pp. 19–20) and thus spotlight the "hero," which diverts our interpretations in such a way as to impose on ancient tragedy a model of a Hamlet-like figure and its inner vicissitudes.

Jones denies that there are heroes in ancient tragedy or in Aristotle's analysis of it. His whole reformulation (sec. 1), irrespective of the overall value of his position, raises important questions concerning the categories of interpretation and their history, as well as serious issues in the understanding of chapter 6 of the *Poetics*.

12. The Greek terms are *muthos* (plot), *ēthē* (character), *dianoia* (thought), *lexis* (diction), *melopoiia* (song), and *opsis* (spectacle).

13. *Poet.* 1449a14 f.

14. *Rhet.* 1382a21 ff.

15. *Rhet.* 1383a8 ff.

16. *Rhet.* 1385b13 ff.

17. Else 1957, chs. 6, 14, esp. pp. 224–32, 423–50.

18. *Poet.* 1452b10 ff.

19. The line is: *di' eleou kai phobou perainousa tēn tōn toioutōn pathēmatōn katharsin.* The subject is still tragedy, effecting (*perainousa*) through pity (*eleou*) and fear (*phobou*)—some interpret this to mean pitiful and fearful incidents—the catharsis (*katharsin*) of such (*toioutōn*) emotions (*pathēmatōn*) or, according to Else, such painful or fatal acts. Butcher 1951, translating as "through pity and fear effecting the proper purgation of these emotions," points out that the genitive can refer to either what is purged away, or what the catharsis takes effect on—a man, say, or the body, or the emotions. He thinks the second usage is involved here (pp. 254–55). He takes *toioutōn* as "aforesaid." One may wonder whether, even if *pathēmatōn* were taken in Else's sense in this context, the genitive would have to be the objective genitive—the catharsis of the fatal acts—and whether it could not be a subjective genitive, meaning the catharsis that the fatal acts perform through the pity and fear that they arouse. (Compare "the driving of the participants is magnificent" with "the driving of this car is difficult.") I suspect that with the great variety of possibilities the decisive evidence has to come outside this passage.

20. *Pol.* 1341b38–40.

21. Lane Cooper 1927, p. 33.

22. *Poet.* 1453a7 ff.

23. See Stinton 1975. He distinguishes three senses of the term—to miss the mark, to make a factual mistake, to offend morally—and restudies each. There is no incompatibility, for example, in the actions being mistakes and the dispositions moral flaws.

24. *Poet.* 1450a38.

25. *Poet.* 1451b5 ff.

26. *Poet.* 1449a32 f.

27. *Soph. Ref.* 184a2–8.

Epilogue

1. The best example of this in the works we encountered is Gauthier and Jolif 1958, who based their whole treatment of the *Nicomachean Ethics* on a framework of Nuyens's hypothesis of the development of Aristotle's psychology (to be discussed immediately below)—not only their interpretations but their divisions, arrangements, siftings, glosses, and emendations in the text. If the basis is rejected, as seems increasingly likely, what will happen to the superstructure? Or will it be simply the occasion for more scholarly effort to see how far it can stand on its own feet?

2. See above, chapter 9, n. 10.

3. Jaeger 1962; Düring 1966.

4. Cf. Cherniss 1944.

5. Aubenque 1963, p. 26. He adds: "La recherche des sources ne dispense pas de la tâche essentielle, qui reste l'interprétation. Bien plus, c'est l'interprétation, et elle seule, qui permettra de reconnaître les 'sources' comme telles. C'est donc par elle qu'il faudra commencer."

6. Düring 1960, p. 36.

7. Lee 1952, pp. 324–29.

8. Farrington 1944; Farrington 1939.

9. Vlastos 1968; M. I. Finley 1968, and his treatment of slavery in Finley 1973.

10. M. I. Finley 1970, pp. 3–25. Finley's point runs deeper and is directed to the insufficient development of the economic phenomena themselves; see above, chapter 18, n. 47.

11. Chroust 1973, vol. 1, gives a central place to Aristotle's Macedonian relations, interpreting particular events in such a way as to give Aristotle roles varying from unofficial ambassador to roving courier.

12. See, for example, Day and Chambers 1962. This work also considers the operation of Aristotle's general methodological concepts in his historical work. See also Weil 1977.

13. A good illustration of a highly specific relation is the attempt to connect the notion of "topics" in Aristotle with existing procedures of memory training. See Sorabji 1972, ch. 2 ("Mnemonic Techniques").

Appendixes

APPENDIX B

1. *Meta.* 1061b16 f. Since this comes from *Metaphysics* 11 (Kappa), chapter 3, it involves the question of the authenticity of that book of the *Metaphysics*. For a discussion of the question see Ross 1953, pp. xxv–xxvii. Reale 1980, ch. 6, argues that there are no convincing grounds for its rejection. Our passage comes from the earlier part of Kappa, which contains a shorter version of topics from books 3, 4, and 6. (This particular passage obviously is concerned with how a science of being is possible when being is not a genus.) Ross takes the first part of Kappa to be quite Aristotelian in thought and favors the possibility that it is a student's notes. If so, we are indebted to the student's insights.

2. *Meta.* 992b24–93a7.

3. *Meta.* 1080a5 f.

4. *Meta.* 1079a7 f.

5. *Meta.* 996b27 ff.

6. *Meta.* 997a5 f.

7. *Post. An.* 1.28 spells this out explicitly in several ways. Of course in the corpus as a whole there are looser uses of the term *genos* as well. Balme 1972, p. 74, points out that its root meaning is *kinship-group*, that Aristotle uses it at different levels from infima (or lowest) species to major genus, but also for genus as opposed to species when required. In some passages *genos* and *eidos* are interchangeable. The variability that Balme finds gives way to a firmer sense in the *Posterior Analytics* when Aristotle attempts to identify a science. See also Balme 1962 on the question of *genos* and *eidos* in Aristotle's biology. Balme finds the distinction of species and genus quite undeveloped in usage, though more sharply developed thereafter in the logic. Clearly any question we might be tempted to ask about whether a science concerns an *eidos* rather than a *genos* would thus make sense for Aristotle not in terms of species versus genus but only in terms of Platonic form versus genus; and the Aristotelian answer would be clear.

8. *Post. An.* 1.9.

9. Cf. *Post. An.* 1.7.

10. *Post. An.* 76a38 f.

11. *Psych.* 414b19–28, 415a12 f.

12. *Meta.* 5.28, 1024a37 f.

13. *Top.* 121a7 ff.

14. *Top.* 121b1 ff.

15. *Meta.* 5.6. The suggestion is at 1016b35–17a3. Ross 1953, vol. 1, p. 305, suggests of this passage that by mere inadvertence "Aristotle has extended the principle of 'the greater unity implies the less' to a case in which it is hard to attach any definite meaning to it." Perhaps the problems involved in a single definition for the psyche may make such an extension intelligible.

16. *Meta.* 1003b12–14.

17. *Meta.* 1061a28 ff.

18. *Meta.* 1003b19 f.
19. *Meta.* 1004a7 ff.
20. *Meta.* 1004a22–25.
21. *Meta.* 1025b25 ff.
22. *Meta.* 1026a6 ff.
23. *Part. An.* 640a3 ff.
24. *Meta.* 1064a10–16; cf. 1025b18–24.

APPENDIX C

1. *Phys.* 2.9.
2. *Part. An.* 1.1
3. *Gen. An.* 778a32 f., b16–19. This should not, of course, be taken as the contrast of the purposive and mechanical in our modern sense, since for Aristotle the material itself has a nature and is expressing that in its action. The matter–form distinction is relative. For the confusion of Aristotle's distinction with the modern, see above, chapter 5, n. 11.
4. *Part. An.* 658b2 ff.
5. *Part. An.* 670a23 ff.
6. *Gen. Corr.* 337b14–38a3.
7. Balme 1972 takes the position that Aristotle has all natural necessity reducible to hypothetical necessity. His careful analysis (pp. 76–84) is convincing against any sharp distinction of hypothetical and material necessity, but with respect to the special type of simple necessity described for which Aristotle gives the illustration of the solstices (in *Gen. Corr.* 2.11), his argument seems to rest rather on finding Aristotle *mistaken* than on taking it not to be Aristotle's view.
8. *Gen. Corr.* 337b12 f.
9. *Gen. Corr.* 338a17 ff.
10. *Categ.* 2.
11. *Pr. An.* 34b11 f.
12. *Top.* 151b16 f., 141a35 f.
13. *Post. An.* 73b26 ff.
14. *Phys.* 2.4, 5. See above, chapter 5.
15. *Interp.* 9.
16. *Interp.* 18a33–b4.
17. *Interp.* 19a18 ff.
18. The remainder of the chapter is 19a23–b4. The quotation is at 19a23 ff. The sea battle is a fruitful source of commentary and sharpening of ideas in Aristotelian studies. For interesting analyses in different directions, see Anscombe 1967 and Hintikka 1973, ch. 8. Aquinas' discussion (Thomas Aquinas 1962, pp. 101–24) focuses on the primacy of the metaphysical. For attempts at formalization of the different possibilities, see Rescher 1967.
19. *Nic. Eth.* 1139b8 ff.
20. *Rhet.* 1357a4 ff.
21. Ackrill 1963, p. 141, makes this point in one of two interpretations that he examines. His whole discussion of chapter 9 provides a useful commentary.
22. Hintikka 1973, pp. 170–71.
23. *Gen. Corr.* 337b3–8.
24. Hintikka points to the analogy of velocity or motion at an instant, but turns it to the concept of possibility concerning a moment of time; he takes Aristotle to be regarding such statements as primarily statements of frequency (1973, p. 162).
25. E. g., *Pr. An.* 25a37 ff.
26. *Interp.* 22b29–23a23.
27. *Pr. An.* 25a37 ff.
28. *Pr. An.* 1.13.
29. Hintikka 1973, ch. 5.
30. *Meta.* 1047b3 f. This question was raised in chapter 8 above and its n. 6. If Aristotle is worried only about impossibilities' being called possible, then of course the problem is

simple, for to call something impossible (his example is to measure the diagonal of a square) already implies that it is necessarily not possible. Hence a contradiction would be implicit.

31. *Mov. An.* 3.4.
32. *Pr. An.* 1.9.
33. See, for example, Łukasiewicz 1957, chs. 6–8; McCall 1963; Hintikka 1973, ch. 7.
34. *Post. An.* 74b5 f., 75b22 ff.
35. *Pr. An.* 25a1 ff.
36. *Pr. An.* 1.27.
37. *Pr. An.* 48b2 ff., 49a6 ff.
38. *Gen. Corr.* 337b35.

BIBLIOGRAPHY

This listing includes all works referred to in the book, except for casual mention (such as Dante's *Inferno*) or a general reference (such as Thucydides' *History of the Peloponnesian War*). In the case of works of well-known modern philosophers (such as Spinoza or Descartes), where precise chapter and section are given, it has not seemed necessary to cite a specific edition.

Ackrill, J. L. 1963. *Aristotle's Categories and De Interpretatione*. Translation with notes. Oxford: Clarendon Press.
————. 1965. "Aristotle's Distinction between *Energeia* and *Kinēsis*." In *New Essays on Plato and Aristotle*, edited by Renford Bambrough, pp. 121–41. London: Routledge and Kegan Paul; New York: Humanities Press.
————. 1974. "Aristotle on *Eudaimonia*." *Proceedings of the British Academy* 60:3–23.
Allan, D. J. 1955. "The Practical Syllogism." In *Autour d'Aristote: recueil d'études de philosophie ancienne et médiévale offert à Monseigneur A. Mansion*, pp. 325–40. Louvain: Publications Universitaires de Louvain.
Ando, Takatura. 1958. *Aristotle's Theory of Practical Cognition*. Kyoto: n.p.
Annas, Julia. 1976. *Aristotle's Metaphysics: Books M and N*. Translated with introduction and notes. Oxford: Clarendon Press.
Anscombe, G. E. M. 1953. "The Principle of Individuation." In *Berkeley and Modern Problems*, pp. 83–96. Aristotelian Society Supplementary Volumes, 27. London: Harrison and Sons.
————. 1958. *Intention*. Oxford: Basil Blackwell.
————. 1961. "Aristotle and the Sea Battle." In *Aristote et les problèmes de la méthode*, pp. 15–33. Proceedings of the Symposium Aristotelicum, Louvain, 1960. Louvain: Publications Universitaires.
————. 1965. "Thought and Action in Aristotle: What is 'Practical Truth'?" In *New Essays on Plato and Aristotle*, edited by Renford Bambrough, pp. 143–58. London: Routledge and Kegan Paul; New York: Humanities Press.
Arnauld, Antoine. 1964. *The Art of Thinking: Port-Royal Logic*. Translated by James Dickoff. Indianapolis: Bobbs-Merrill. Originally published 1662.
Aubenque, Pierre. 1963. *La prudence chez Aristote*. Paris: Presses Universitaires de France.
Austin, J. L. 1961. *Philosophical Papers*. Oxford: Clarendon Press.
Bacon, Francis. 1620. *Novum Organum*.
Badian, E. 1958. "Alexander the Great and the Unity of Mankind." *Historia* 7:425–44.
————. 1966. "Alexander the Great and the Greeks of Asia." In *Ancient Society and Institutions: Studies Presented to Victor Ehrenberg on His 75th Birthday*, pp. 37–69. Oxford: Basil Blackwell.
————. 1976. "Some Recent Interpretations of Alexander." In *Alexandre le grand: image et réalité*, pp. 279–301. Entretiens sur l'antiquité classique, 22. Geneva: Fondation Hardt.
Balme, D. M. 1962. "*Genos* and *Eidos* in Aristotle's Biology." *Classical Quarterly*, n.s. 12:81–98.
————. 1972. *Aristotle's De Partibus Animalium I and De Generatione Animalium I (with passages from II 1–3)*. Translated with notes. Oxford: Clarendon Press.
Barnes, Jonathan. 1969. "Aristotle's Theory of Demonstration." *Phronesis* 14:123–52.
————. 1972. "Aristotle's Concept of Mind." *Proceedings of the Aristotelian Society*, n.s. 72:101–14.
————. 1975. *Aristotle's Posterior Analytics*. Translated with notes. Oxford: Clarendon Press.

Beare, John I. 1906. *Greek Theories of Elementary Cognition from Alcmaeon to Aristotle.* Oxford: Clarendon Press.

Block, Irving. 1961. "The Order of Aristotle's Psychological Writings." *American Journal of Philology* 82:50–77.

Bolton, Robert. 1976. "Essentialism and Semantic Theory in Aristotle." *Philosophical Review* 85:514–44.

Bosanquet, Bernard. 1904. *History of Aesthetics.* 2nd ed. London: George Allen and Unwin.

Brentano, Franz. 1975. *On the Several Senses of Being in Aristotle.* Edited and translated by Rolf George. Berkeley and Los Angeles: University of California Press.

Brochard, V. 1926. *Études de philosophie ancienne et de philosophie moderne.* New ed. Paris: Librairie Philosophique J. Vrin.

Buchanan, Emerson. 1960. *Aristotle's Theory of Being.* Greek, Roman, and Byzantine Monographs, 2. University, Miss., and Cambridge, Mass.: n.p.

Burnet, John. 1900. *The Ethics of Aristotle.* Edited with an introduction and notes. London: Methuen.

————. 1957. *Early Greek Philosophy.* New York: Meridian Books. Originally published 1892.

Bury, J. B. 1924. *A History of Greece to the Death of Alexander the Great.* London: Macmillan.

Butcher, S. H. 1951. *Aristotle's Theory of Poetry and Fine Art.* 4th ed. New York: Dover.

Cameron, Alan. 1969. "The Last Days of the Academy at Athens." *Proceedings of the Cambridge Philosophical Society* 195, n.s. 15:7–29.

Canfield, John V., ed. 1966. *Purpose in Nature.* Englewood Cliffs, N.J.: Prentice-Hall.

Cashdollar, Stanford. 1973a. "Aristotle's Politics of Morals." *Journal of the History of Philosophy* 11:145–60.

————. 1973b. "Aristotle's Account of Incidental Perception." *Phronesis* 18:156–75.

Charlton, W. 1970. *Aristotle's Physics, Books I and II.* Translated with introduction and notes. Oxford: Clarendon Press.

Cherniss, H. F. 1935. *Aristotle's Criticism of Presocratic Philosophy.* Baltimore: The Johns Hopkins Press.

————. 1944. *Aristotle's Criticism of Plato and the Academy.* Baltimore: The Johns Hopkins Press.

————. 1945. *The Riddle of the Early Academy.* Berkeley and Los Angeles: University of California Press.

Chroust, Anton-Hermann. 1973. *Aristotle: New Light on His Life and on Some of His Lost Works.* London: Routledge and Kegan Paul.

Clark, Stephen R. L. 1975. *Aristotle's Man: Speculations upon Aristotelian Anthropology.* Oxford: Clarendon Press.

Cooper, John M. 1975. *Reason and Human Good in Aristotle.* Cambridge: Harvard University Press.

————. 1977a. "Aristotle on the Forms of Friendship." *Review of Metaphysics* 30:619–48.

————. 1977b. "Friendship and the Good in Aristotle." *Philosophical Review* 86:290–315.

Cooper, Lane. 1927. *The Poetics of Aristotle: Its Meaning and Influence.* New York: Longmans, Green.

Corcoran, John. 1973. "A Mathematical Model of Aristotle's Syllogistic." *Archiv für Geschichte der Philosophie* 55:191–219.

————. 1974. "Aristotelian Syllogisms: Valid Arguments or True Universalized Conditionals?" *Mind* 83:278–81.

Cornford, F. M. 1957. *From Religion to Philosophy.* New York: Harper Torchbooks. Originally written 1912.

Day, James, and Chambers, Mortimer. 1962. *Aristotle's History of Athenian Democracy.* Berkeley and Los Angeles: University of California Press.

Descartes, René. 1644. *The Principles of Philosophy.*

De Ste. Croix, G. E. M. 1972. *The Origins of the Peloponnesian War.* London: Duckworth.

De Vogel, C. J. 1960. "The Legend of the Platonizing Aristotle." In Düring and Owen 1960, pp. 248–56.

Dewey, John. 1960. *Theory of the Moral Life*. With an introduction by Arnold Isenberg. New York: Holt, Rinehart and Winston.

Diogenes Laertius. 1959. *Lives of Eminent Philosophers*, vol. 1. With an English translation by R. D. Hicks. Loeb Classical Library. Cambridge: Harvard University Press.

Dirlmeier, Franz. 1960. *Aristoteles, Nikomachische Ethik*. Translated. 2nd, rev. ed. Berlin: Akademie Verlag.

Dodds, E. R. 1957. *The Greeks and the Irrational*. Boston: Beacon Press.

Dover, K. J. 1974. *Greek Popular Morality in the Time of Plato and Aristotle*. Berkeley and Los Angeles: University of California Press.

Düring, Ingemar. 1957a. *Aristotle in the Ancient Biographical Tradition*. Studia Graeca et Latina Gothoburgensia, 5. Göteborg: n.p.

————. 1957b. Review of the 1st (1956) ed. of Dirlmeier 1960. *Gnomon* 29:178–85.

————. 1960. "Aristotle on Ultimate Principles from 'Nature and Reality.' " In Düring and Owen 1960, pp. 35–55.

————. 1964. "Aristotle and the Heritage from Plato." *Eranos* 62:84–99.

————. 1966. *Aristoteles: Darstellung und Interpretation seines Denkens*. Heidelberg: Carl Winter–Universitätsverlag.

Düring, Ingemar, and Owen, G. E. L., eds. 1960. *Aristotle and Plato in the Mid–Fourth Century*. Proceedings of the Symposium Aristotelicum, Oxford, 1957. Studia Graeca et Latina Gothoburgensia, 11. Göteborg: n.p.

Edel, Abraham. 1934. *Aristotle's Theory of the Infinite*. New York: n.p.

————. 1963. *Method in Ethical Theory*. Indianapolis: Bobbs-Merrill.

————. 1969. " 'Action' and 'Passion': Some Philosophical Reflections on *Physics* III, 3." In *Naturphilosophie bei Aristoteles und Theophrast*, edited by Ingemar Düring, pp. 59–64. Heidelberg: Lothar Stiehm.

————. 1975. "Aristotle's Categories and the Nature of Categorial Theory." *Review of Metaphysics* 29:45–65.

————. 1979. *Analyzing Concepts in Social Science: Science, Ideology and Value*, vol. 1. New Brunswick, N.J.: Transaction Books.

Edelstein, Ludwig. 1967. *The Idea of Progress in Classical Antiquity*. Baltimore: The Johns Hopkins Press.

Ehrenberg, Victor. 1938. *Alexander and the Greeks*. Translated by Ruth Fraenkel von Velsen. Oxford: Basil Blackwell.

Else, Gerald F. 1957. *Aristotle's Poetics: The Argument*. Cambridge: Harvard University Press.

Engberg-Pedersen, T. 1979. "More Aristotelian Epagoge." *Phronesis* 14:301–19.

Evans, J. D. G. 1977. *Aristotle's Concept of Dialectic*. Cambridge: Harvard University Press.

Farrington, Benjamin. 1939. *Science and Politics in the Ancient World*. London: Allen and Unwin.

————. 1944. *Greek Science*, vol. 1: *Thales to Aristotle*. Harmondsworth: Penguin Books.

————. 1969. *Aristotle, Founder of Scientific Philosophy*. New York: Frederick A. Praeger.

Finley, John H. 1942. *Thucydides*. Cambridge: Harvard University Press.

Finley, M. I. 1965. "Technical Innovation and Economic Progress in the Ancient World." *Economic History Review*, ser. 2, 18, no. 1:29–45.

————. 1968. "Was Greek Civilization Based on Slave Labour?" In *Slavery in Classical Antiquity: Views and Controversies*, edited by M. I. Finley, pp. 53–72. Cambridge: Heffer; New York: Barnes and Noble.

————. 1970. "Aristotle and Economic Analysis." *Past and Present*, no. 47 (May):3–25. Reprinted in M. I. Finley 1974.

————. 1973. *The Ancient Economy*. Berkeley and Los Angeles: University of California Press.

————, ed. 1974. *Studies in Ancient Society*. London and Boston: Routledge and Kegan Paul.

———, ed. 1975. *The Use and Abuse of History*. New York: Viking.

Fisch, Max H. 1975. "The Poliscraft, A Dialogue." In *Philosophy and the Civilizing Art: Essays Presented to Herbert W. Schneider on His Eightieth Birthday*, edited by Craig Walton and John P. Anton, pp. 24–48. Athens, Ohio: Ohio University Press.

Fortenbaugh, W. W. 1965. "*Ta pros to telos* and Syllogistic Vocabulary in Aristotle's Ethics." *Phronesis* 10:191–202.

———. 1975a. *Aristotle on Emotion: A Contribution to Philosophical Psychology, Rhetoric, Poetics, Politics and Ethics*. London: Duckworth.

———. 1975b. "Aristotle's Analysis of Friendship: Function and Analogy, Resemblance, and Focal Meaning." *Phronesis* 20:51–62.

Furley, David J. 1967. *Two Studies in the Greek Atomists: Study I, Indivisible Magnitudes; Study II, Aristotle and Epicurus on Voluntary Action*. Princeton: Princeton University Press.

———. 1978. "Self-Movers." In Lloyd and Owen 1978, pp. 165–89.

Gauthier, René-A. 1958. *La morale d'Aristote*. Paris: Presses Universitaires de France.

Gauthier, René-A.; and Jolif, Jean Y. 1958. *L'éthique à Nicomaque*, vol. 1. Introduction, translation, and commentary. Louvain and Paris: Publications Universitaires de Louvain.

———. 1959. *L'éthique à Nicomaque*, vol. 2.

Gosling, J. 1974. "More Aristotelian Pleasures." *Proceedings of the Aristotelian Society*, n.s. 74:15–34.

Grayeff, Felix. 1974. *Aristotle and His School: An Inquiry into the History of the Peripatos with a Commentary on Metaphysics Z, H, Λ, and B*. London: Duckworth.

Grene, Marjorie. 1963. *A Portrait of Aristotle*. Chicago: University of Chicago Press.

Hamilton, J. R. 1973. *Alexander the Great*. London: Hutchinson University Library.

Hamlyn, D. W. 1968a. *Aristotle's De Anima, Books II, III*. Translated with introduction and notes. Oxford: Clarendon Press.

———. 1968b. "Koinē Aisthēsis." *Monist* 52:195–209.

———. 1976. "Aristotelian Epagoge." *Phronesis* 21:167–84.

Happ, Heinz. 1971. *Hylē: Studien zum Aristotelischen Materie-Begriff*. Berlin and New York: Walter de Gruyter.

Hardie, W. F. R. 1964. "Aristotle's Treatment of the Relation between the Soul and the Body." *Philosophical Quarterly* 14:53–72.

———. 1965. "The Final Good in Aristotle's Ethics." *Philosophy* 40:277–95.

———. 1968. *Aristotle's Ethical Theory*. Oxford: Clarendon Press.

Hartman, Edwin. 1977. *Substance, Body, and Soul: Aristotelian Investigations*. Princeton: Princeton University Press.

Hartmann, Nicolai. 1932. *Ethics*, vol. 2: *Moral Values*. Translated by Stanton Coit. New York: Macmillan. Originally published 1926, in Germany.

Heath, T. L. 1949. *Mathematics in Aristotle*. Oxford: Clarendon Press.

Hicks, R. D. 1907. *Aristotle, De Anima*. Cambridge: Cambridge University Press.

Hintikka, Jakko. 1973. *Time and Necessity: Studies in Aristotle's Theory of Modality*. Oxford: Clarendon Press.

Irwin, T. H. 1975. "Aristotle on Reason, Desire, and Virtue." *Journal of Philosophy* 72:567–78.

Jaeger, Werner. 1943. *Paideia: The Ideals of Greek Culture*. Translated by Gilbert Highet. Vol. 2: *In Search of the Divine Centre*. New York: Oxford University Press.

———. 1944. *Paideia*, vol. 3: *The Conflict of Cultural Ideas in the Age of Plato*.

———. 1945. *Paideia*, vol. 1: *Archaic Greece: The Mind of Athens*.

———. 1957. "Aristotle's Use of Medicine as a Model of Method in His Ethics." *Journal of Hellenic Studies* 77:54–61.

———. 1962. *Aristotle: Fundamentals of the History of His Development*. 2nd ed., paperbound. Translated by Richard Robinson. London: Oxford University Press. Originally published 1923, in Germany; 2nd ed. first published 1948.

Joachim, Harold H. 1922. *Aristotle's On Coming-to-be and Passing-away*. A revised text with introduction and commentary. Oxford: Clarendon Press.

_____. 1951. *Aristotle, The Nicomachean Ethics*. Oxford: Clarendon Press.
Jones, Barrington. 1974. "Aristotle's Introduction of Matter." *Philosophical Review* 83:474–500.
Jones, John. 1967. *On Aristotle and Greek Tragedy*. London: Chatto and Windus.
Joseph, H. W. B. 1916. *An Introduction to Logic*. 2nd ed., rev. Oxford: Clarendon Press.
Kahn, Charles H. 1966. "Sensation and Consciousness in Aristotle's Psychology." *Archiv für Geschichte der Philosophie* 48:43–81.
_____. 1973. *The Verb 'Be' in Ancient Greek*. Part 6 of *The Verb 'Be' and Its Synonyms: Philosophical and Grammatical Studies*, edited by John W. M. Verhaar. Foundations of Language, Supplementary Series, 16. Dordrecht, The Netherlands; and Boston: D. Reidel.
Kapp, Ernst. 1942. *Greek Foundations of Traditional Logic*. New York: Columbia University Press.
Kenny, Anthony. 1978. *The Aristotelian Ethics: A Study of the Relationship between the Eudemian and Nicomachean Ethics of Aristotle*. Oxford: Clarendon Press.
_____. 1979. *Aristotle's Theory of the Will*. New Haven: Yale University Press.
Kirwan, Christopher. 1971. *Aristotle's Metaphysics, Books Γ, Δ, E*. Translated with notes. Oxford: Clarendon Press.
Kosman, L. A. 1973. "Understanding, Explanation, and Insight in the *Posterior Analytics*." In *Exegesis and Argument: Studies in Greek Philosophy Presented to Gregory Vlastos*, edited by E. N. Lee, A. P. D. Mourelatos, and R. M. Rorty, pp. 374–92. Assen, The Netherlands: Van Gorcum.
Kristeller, P. O. 1961. *Renaissance Thought: The Classic, Scholastic, and Humanist Strains*. New York: Harper Torchbooks.
Laird, John. 1929. *The Idea of Value*. Cambridge: Cambridge University Press.
Le Blond, J. M. 1939. *Logique et méthode chez Aristote: étude sur las recherche des principes dans la physique Aristotélicienne*. Paris: Librairie Philosophique J. Vrin.
Lee, H. D. P. 1952. *Aristotle, Meterologica*. Loeb Classical Library. Cambridge: Harvard University Press.
Lefèvre, Charles. 1972. *Sur l'évolution d'Aristote en psychologie*. Louvain: Éditions de l'Institut Supérieur de Philosophie.
Lesher, James H. 1973. "The Meaning of *Nous* in the Posterior Analytics." *Phronesis* 18:44–68.
Leszl, Walter. 1970. *Logic and Metaphysics in Aristotle: Aristotle's Treatment of Types of Equivocity and Its Relevance to His Metaphysical Theories*. Padua: Editrice Antenore.
_____. 1975. *Aristotle's Conception of Ontology*. Padua: Editrice Antenore.
Lloyd, A. C. 1970. "Aristotle's Principle of Individuation." *Mind* 79:519–29.
Lloyd, G. E. R. 1961. "The Development of Aristotle's Theory of the Classification of Animals." *Phronesis* 6:59–81.
Lloyd, G. E. R., and Owen, G. E. L., eds. 1978. *Aristotle on Mind and the Senses*. Proceedings of the Seventh Symposium Aristotelicum. Cambridge: Cambridge University Press.
Long, A. A. 1968. "Aristotle's Legacy to Stoic Ethics." *Bulletin of the London University Institute of Classical Studies* 15:72–85.
_____. 1974. *Hellenistic Philosophy: Stoics, Epicureans, Sceptics*. London: Duckworth.
Łukasiewicz, Jan. 1957. *Aristotle's Syllogistic, from the Standpoint of Modern Formal Logic*. 2nd ed. Oxford: Clarendon Press.
Lykos, K. 1964. "Aristotle and Plato on 'Appearing.'" *Mind* 73:496–514.
Lynch, John Patrick. 1972. *Aristotle's School: A Study of a Greek Educational Institution*. Berkeley, Los Angeles, and London: University of California Press.
McCall, Storrs. 1963. *Aristotle's Modal Syllogisms*. Amsterdam: North Holland Publishing Co.
MacIntyre, Alasdair. 1967. *A Short History of Ethics*. London: Routledge and Kegan Paul.
McKeon, Richard. 1976. "Person and Community, Individual and Society, Reformation and Revolution." Presented at the International Society for Metaphysics' Conference on Man and Society, New York, October 6–7.

————. 1979. "The Hellenistic and Roman Foundations of the Tradition of Aristotle in the West." *Review of Metaphysics* 32:677–715.

McMullin, Ernan. 1965a. "From Matter to Mass." In *Boston Studies in the Philosophy of Science*, edited by Robert S. Cohen and Marx W. Wartofsky, vol. 2, pp. 25–45. New York: Humanities Press.

————. 1965b. "Matter and Principle." In McMullin 1965c, pp. 173–212.

————, ed. 1965c. *The Concept of Matter in Greek and Medieval Philosophy*. Notre Dame, Ind.: University of Notre Dame Press.

Mansion, Augustin. 1946. *Introduction à la physique Aristotélicienne*. 2nd ed., rev. and aug. Louvain: Éditions de l'Institut Supérieur de Philosophie; Paris: Librairie Philosophique J. Vrin.

Mansion, Suzanne. 1976. *Le jugement d'existence chez Aristote*. Louvain: Éditions de l'Institut Supérieur de Philosophie; Paris: Desclée de Brouwer.

Mates, Benson. 1961. *Stoic Logic*. Berkeley and Los Angeles: University of California Press.

Mayr, Ernest. 1976. "Teleological and Teleonomic: A New Analysis." In his *Evolution and the Diversity of Life: Selected Essays*, pp. 383–404. Cambridge: The Belknap Press of Harvard University.

Miller, Alfred Eric. 1969. *Physis and Physics: Aristotle's Descriptive Phenomenology of Nature as the Metaphysical Foundation and Critique of Modern Science*. Hamburg: n.p.

Milo, Ronald D. 1966. *Aristotle on Practical Knowledge and Weakness of Will*. The Hague and Paris: Mouton.

Moraux, Paul. 1951. *Les listes anciennes des ouvrages d'Aristote*. Louvain: Éditions Universitaires de Louvain.

————. 1973. *Der Aristotelismus bei den Griechen: von Andronikos bis Alexander von Aphrodisias*, vol. 1: *Die Renaissance des Aristotelismus im 1 Jh. v. Chr.* Berlin and New York: Walter de Gruyter.

Moravcsik, J. M. E. 1967a. "Aristotle's Theory of Categories." In Moravcsik 1967b, pp. 125–45.

————, ed. 1967b. *Aristotle: A Collection of Critical Essays*. Garden City, N.Y.: Doubleday Anchor Books.

Mothersill, Mary. 1962. "Anscombe's Account of the Practical Syllogism." *Philosophical Review* 71:448–61.

Mure, G. R. G. 1964. *Aristotle*. New York: Oxford University Press. Originally published 1932.

Nagel, Ernest. 1977. "Teleology Revisited: The Dewey Lectures 1977." *Journal of Philosophy* 74:261–301.

Nelson, Leonard. 1949. "The Socratic Method." In his *Socratic Method and Critical Philosophy*, chapter 1. Translated by Thomas K. Brown, III. New Haven: Yale University Press.

Nussbaum, Martha Craven. 1978. *Aristotle's De Motu Animalium*. Text with translation, commentary, and interpretive essays. Princeton: Princeton University Press.

Nuyens, François. 1948. *L'évolution de la psychologie d'Aristote*. Louvain: Éditions de l'Institut Supérieur de Philosophie; Paris: Librairie Philosophique J. Vrin.

Owen, G. E. L. 1960. "Logic and Metaphysics in Some Earlier Works of Aristotle." In Düring and Owen 1960, pp. 163–90.

————. 1961. "*Tithenai ta Phainomena*." In *Aristote et les problèmes de la méthode*, pp. 83–103. Proceedings of the Symposium Aristotelicum, Louvain, 1960. Louvain: Publications Universitaires. Reprinted in Moravcsik 1967c.

————. 1965. "Aristotle on the Snares of Ontology." In *New Essays on Plato and Aristotle*, edited by Renford Bambrough, pp. 69–95. London: Routledge and Kegan Paul; New York: Humanities Press.

————. 1968. "The Platonism of Aristotle." In *Studies in the Philosophy of Thought and Action*, edited by P. F. Strawson, pp. 147–74. London: Oxford University Press.

————. 1972. "Aristotelian Pleasures." *Proceedings of the Aristotelian Society*, n.s. 72:135–52.

Owens, Joseph. 1951. *The Doctrine of Being in the Aristotelian Metaphysics: A Study in the Greek Background of Mediaeval Thought*. Toronto: Pontifical Institute of Mediaeval Studies. 2nd, rev. ed. 1963.
———. 1965. "Matter and Predication in Aristotle." In McMullin 1965c, pp. 79–93.
———. 1969. "The Aristotelian Argument for the Material Principle of Bodies." In *Naturphilosophie bei Aristoteles und Theophrast*, edited by Ingemar Düring, pp. 193–209. Heidelberg: Lothar Stiehm.
Patzig, Günther. 1968. *Aristotle's Theory of the Syllogism: A Logico-Philosophical Study of Book A of the Prior Analytics*. Translated from the German by Jonathan Barnes. Dordrecht, The Netherlands: D. Reidel; New York: Humanities Press.
Peck, A. L. 1953. *Aristotle, Generation of Animals*. With an English translation. Rev. ed. Loeb Classical Library. Cambridge. Harvard University Press.
———. 1955. *Aristotle, Parts of Animals*. With an English translation. Loeb Classical Library. Cambridge: Harvard University Press.
———. 1965. *Aristotle, Historia Animalium*. With an English translation. Loeb Classical Library. Cambridge: Harvard University Press.
Pepper, Stephen. 1942. *World Hypotheses*. Berkeley and Los Angeles: University of California Press.
Preus, Anthony. 1975. *Science and Philosophy in Aristotle's Biological Works*. Hildesheim and New York: Georg Olms.
Randall, John Herman, Jr. 1960. *Aristotle*. New York: Columbia University Press.
Reale, Giovanni. 1980. *The Concept of First Philosophy and the Unity of the Metaphysics of Aristotle*. Edited and translated by John R. Catan; authorized translation from the 3rd Italian ed. (1967). Albany: State University of New York Press.
Rees, D. A. 1971. "Aristotle's Treatment of *phantasia*." In *Essays in Ancient Greek Philosophy*, edited by John P. Anton and George L. Kustas, pp. 491–504. Albany: State University of New York Press.
Rescher, Nicholas. 1967. "Truth and Necessity in Temporal Perspective." In *The Philosophy of Time*, edited by Richard M. Gale, pp. 183–200. Garden City, N.Y.: Doubleday Anchor Books.
Robinson, H. M. 1974. "Prime Matter in Aristotle." *Phronesis* 19:168–88.
Rosenfield, Lawrence William. 1971. *Aristotle and Information Theory: A Comparison of the Influence of Causal Assumptions on Two Theories of Communication*. The Hague and Paris: Mouton.
Ross, W. D. 1936. *Aristotle's Physics*. A revised text with introduction and commentary. Oxford: Clarendon Press.
———. 1953. *Aristotle's Metaphysics*. A revised text with introduction and commentary, from sheets of the 1st ed. (1924), with corrections. Oxford: Clarendon Press.
———. 1955. *Aristotle, Parva Naturalia*. A revised text with introduction and commentary. Oxford: Clarendon Press.
———. 1959. *Aristotle: A Complete Exposition of His Works and Thought*. Cleveland, Ohio: Meridian Books.
———. 1961. *Aristotle, De Anima*. Oxford: Clarendon Press.
Rowe, J. C. 1971. *The Eudemian and Nicomachean Ethics: A Study in the Development of Aristotle's Thought*. *Proceedings of the Cambridge Philological Society*, supplement 3. Cambridge: Cambridge Philological Society.
Ryle, Gilbert. 1956. *Dilemmas*. Cambridge: Cambridge University Press.
Sambursky, S. 1959. *Physics of the Stoics*. Westport, Conn.: Greenwood Press.
Santas, Gerasimos. 1969. "Aristotle on Practical Inference, the Explanation of Action, and Akrasia." *Phronesis* 14:162–89.
Santayana, George. 1957. "The Secret of Aristotle." In his *Dialogues in Limbo*, chapter 13. Ann Arbor: University of Michigan Press.
Schofield, Malcolm. 1978. "Aristotle on the Imagination." In Lloyd and Owen 1978, pp. 99–140.
Scholz, H. 1975. "The Ancient Axiomatic Theory." In *Articles on Aristotle*, edited by Jonathan Barnes, Malcolm Schofield, and Richard Sorabji, vol. 1, pp. 50–64. London: Duckworth.

Solmsen, Friedrich. 1957. "The Vital Heat, the Inborn Pneuma, and the Aether (*De gen. an.* II, 3, 736b30–737a1)." *Journal of Hellenic Studies* 77 (part 1):119–23.

———. 1960. *Aristotle's System of the Physical World: A Comparison with His Predecessors*. Ithaca: Cornell University Press.

———. 1961. "Greek Philosophy and the Discovery of the Nerves." *Museum Helveticum* 18:150–97.

———. 1963. "Nature as Craftsman in Greek Thought." *Journal of the History of Ideas* 24:473–96.

Sorabji, Richard. 1972. *Aristotle on Memory*. Providence: Brown University Press.

———. 1974a. "Body and Soul in Aristotle." *Philosophy* 49:63–89.

———. 1974b. "Aristotle on the Role of Intellect in Virtue." *Proceedings of the Aristotelian Society*, n.s. 74:107–29.

Spinoza, Benedict. 1903. *The Chief Works of Benedict Spinoza*, vol. 2: *Ethics*. Translated from the Latin by R. H. M. Elwes. Rev. ed. London: George Bell and Sons.

Stewart, J. A. 1892. *Notes on the Nicomachean Ethics*. Oxford: Clarendon Press.

Stinton, T. C. W. 1975. "Hamartia in Aristotle and Greek Tragedy." *Classical Quarterly*, n.s. 25:221–54.

Tarn, W. W. 1948. *Alexander the Great*, vol. 2: *Sources and Studies*. Cambridge: Cambridge University Press.

Taylor, A. E. 1955. *Aristotle*. New York: Dover.

Thayer, H. S. 1979. "Aristotle on the Meaning of Science." *Philosophical Inquiry* 1, no. 2:87–104.

Thomas Aquinas. 1962. *Aristotle: On Interpretation*. Commentary by St. Thomas and Cajetan. Translated from the Latin by Jean T. Oesterle. Milwaukee, Wis.: Marquette University Press.

Topitsch, Ernst. 1954. "Society, Technology, and Philosophical Reasoning." *Philosophy of Science* 21:275–96.

Tóth, Imre. 1969. "Non-Euclidean Geometry before Euclid." *Scientific American* 221, no. 5 (Nov.):87–98.

Tracy, Theodore. 1969. *Physiological Theory and the Doctrine of the Mean in Plato and Aristotle*. Chicago: Loyola University Press.

Tredennick, Hugh. 1933. *Aristotle, the Metaphysics*, vol. 1. With an English translation. Loeb Classical Library. New York: G. P. Putnam's Sons.

———. 1935. *Aristotle, Metaphysics*, vol. 2. Cambridge: Harvard University Press.

Trendelenburg, [Friedrich] Adolf. 1846. *Historische Beiträge zur Philosophie*, vol. 1: *Geschichte der Kategorienlehre*. Berlin: Verlag von G. Bethge. Reprint ed. Hildesheim: Georg Olms, 1963.

Urmson, J. O. 1967. "Aristotle on Pleasure." In Moravcsik 1967c, pp. 323–33.

Verbeke, G. 1971. "The Aristotelian Doctrine of Qualitative Change in *Physics* VII, 3." In *Essays in Ancient Greek Philosophy*, edited by John Anton and George L. Kustas, pp. 546–65. Albany: State University of New York Press.

Vlastos, Gregory. 1956. *Plato's Protagoras*. New York: Liberal Arts Press.

———. 1968. "Slavery in Plato's Thought." In *Slavery in Classical Antiquity: Views and Controversies*, edited by M. I. Finley, pp. 133–49.

Walsh, James Jerome. 1963. *Aristotle's Conception of Moral Weakness*. New York and London: Columbia University Press.

Wehrli, Fritz. 1944–1959. *Die Schule des Aristoteles: Texte und Kommentar*. 10 vols. Basel and Stuttgart: Benno Schwabe.

Weil, Raymond. 1977. "Aristotle's View of History." Translated from the French by Jennifer and Jonathan Barnes. In *Articles on Aristotle*, edited by Jonathan Barnes, Malcolm Schofield, and Richard Sorabji, vol. 2, pp. 202–17. London: Duckworth.

Weiss, Frederick Gustav. 1969. *Hegel's Critique of Aristotle's Philosophy of Mind*. The Hague: Martinis Nijhoff.

White, Andrew D. 1955. *A History of the Warfare of Science with Theology in Christendom*. New York: George Braziller. Originally published 1895.

Wieland, Wolfgang. 1962. *Die aristotelische Physik: Untersuchungen über die*

Grundlegung der Naturwissenschaft und die sprachlichen Bedinungen der Prinzipien-forschung bei Aristoteles. Göttingen: Vandenhoeck and Ruprecht.

Wiggins, David. 1976. "Deliberation and Practical Reason." *Proceedings of the Aristotelian Society*, n.s. 76:29–51.

Wilford, F. A. 1959. "The Status of Reason in Plato's Psychology." *Phronesis* 4:54–58.

Zeller, Eduard. 1897. *Aristotle and the Earlier Peripatetics*, vol. 1. Translated from Zeller's "Philosophy of the Greeks" by B. F. C. Costelloe and J. H. Muirhead. London, New York, and Bombay: Longmans, Green.

INDEX

Abelard, Peter, 7
Accidental, 92; in predicables, 189–90; no science of, 197
Ackrill, John, 98, 406 (n. 8), 418 (n. 24), 420 (n. 15), 431 (n. 3), 443 (n. 11), 459 (n. 21)
Action and passion, 37, 81, 418 (nn. 22, 24); unity of, 84–85; in transactional analysis, 148
Actuality: distinguished from potentiality, 84–85; complete and incomplete, 84–85; prior to potentiality, 86; and substance, 128; and form, 123; first and second, 144; in defining psyche, 144–45
Aeschylus, 347, 421 (n. 24)
agathos, 442(n. 1), 446 (n. 46)
Air: as element, 52
akrasia: defined, 302. *See* Incontinence
Alexander, the Great, 25, 26, 319–20, 328–29, 404 (n. 29), 405 (n. 8), 449 (n. 90); his destruction of Thebes, 18; taught by Aristotle, 25; and unity of mankind, 453–54 (n. 5)
Alexander of Aphrodisias, 6
Allan, D. J., 452 (n. 25)
Alteration. *See* Quality; Change
Ambiguity, 219; and types of meaning, 222–31; coordinate senses, 226–27; primary senses, 227; primary meanings plus additions, 227; developmental forms, 228; focal meaning, 228–29, 439(n. 50), serial succession, 229
Ames, William, 338
Amphiboly, 224
Analogy, 225–26
Analytic element: in Aristotle's thought, 30
Anaxagoras, 19, 109
Ando, Takatura, 441 (n. 3), 452 (n. 25)
Andronicus, 6, 403 (n. 1)
Annas, Julia, 422 (n. 33)
Anscombe, G. E. M., 424 (n. 21), 430 (n. 22), 452 (nn. 23, 25), 459 (n. 18)
Anselm, 435 (n. 21)
Antipater, 26, 28, 329
Antisthenes, 234, 405 (n. 30)
apodeixis. See Demonstration

Apparent good, 294–96; and real good, 295–96
Appetite, 173–74; conflict with reason, 173; as preferred translation for *orexis*, 430 (n. 14)
Aquinas. *See* Thomas Aquinas
Arabic commentaries, 7
archē: and the meaning of "principle," 33–34
Archimedes, 53
Aristophanes, 347, 446 (n. 46)
Aristotelian scholarship: issues in, 363; textual problems, 363–66; relation to predecessors, 367–69; to science and crafts, 369–72; to socioeconomic and historical, 372–74; to philosophical differences, 374–76
Arnauld, Antoine, 421 (n. 24)
Aubenque, Pierre, 367, 447 (n. 66), 448 (n. 71), 449–50 (n. 93), 457 (n. 5)
Austin, J. L., 273 446 (n. 53)
Averroës, 7
Avicenna, 7, 408 (n. 9)

Bacon, Francis, 183, 431 (n. 1)
Badian, E., 454 (n. 5)
Balme, D. M., 414 (n. 2), 414–15 (n. 11), 415–16 (n. 14), 417 (n. 36), 424 (n. 20), 458 (n. 7), 459 (n. 7)
Barnes, Jonathan, 205, 207, 426 (n. 1), 433 (nn. 6, 25), 434 (nn. 12, 14)
Being, 37, 436 (n. 22); its puzzles, 89–91; not a genus, 91; how partitioned, 91–94
Being-as-being, 91, 111; interpretations of, 113–17
Beare, J. I., 426 (n. 11)
Bekker edition of Aristotle's works, 5
Bentham, Jeremy, 272
Bergson, Henri, 450 (n. 93)
Berkeley, George, 409 (n. 9)
Better, 257–58
Bismarck, O. E. L., 450 (n. 93)
Block, Irving, 366, 426 (n. 10)
Body, 37, 49; natural body, 146
Boethius, 7